Web-Based Education: Learning from Experience

Anil K. Aggarwal
University of Baltimore, USA

 **Information Science Publishing**

Hershey • London • Melbourne • Singapore • Beijing

Acquisition Editor:	Mehdi Khosrow-Pour
Senior Managing Editor:	Jan Travers
Managing Editor:	Amanda Appicello
Development Editor:	Michele Rossi
Copy Editor:	Lori Eby
Typesetter:	Amanda Appicello
Cover Design:	Jason LaMontagne
Printed at:	Sheridan Books, Inc.

Published in the United States of America by
  Information Science Publishing (an imprint of Idea Group Inc.)
  701 E. Chocolate Avenue
  Hershey PA 17033
  Tel: 717-533-8845
  Fax: 717-533-8661
  E-mail: cust@idea-group.com
  Web site: http://www.idea-group.com

and in the United Kingdom by
  Information Science Publishing (an imprint of Idea Group Inc.)
  3 Henrietta Street
  Covent Garden
  London WC2E 8LU
  Tel: 44 20 7240 0856
  Fax: 44 20 7379 3313
  Web site: http://www.eurospan.co.uk

Library of Congress Cataloging-in-Publication Data

Web-based education : learning from experience / [edited by] Anil
Aggarwal.
     p. cm.
Includes bibliographical references and index.
  ISBN 1-59140-102-X (hard cover) -- ISBN 1-59140-110-0 (ebook)
 1. Education--Computer network resources. 2. Internet in education.
3. World Wide Web. 4. Experiential learning. I. Aggarwal, Anil, 1949-

 LB1044.87.W42 2003
 371.33'4678--dc21

                                        2002156243

British Cataloguing in Publication Data
A Cataloguing in Publication record for this book is available from the British Library.

NEW Titles
from Information Science Publishing

- **Web-Based Education: Learning from Experience**
  Anil Aggarwal
  ISBN: 1-59140-102-X: eISBN 1-59140-110-0, © 2003
- **The Knowledge Medium: Designing Effective Computer-Based Learning Environments**
  Gary A. Berg
  ISBN: 1-59140-103-8; eISBN 1-59140-111-9, © 2003
- **Socio-Technical and Human Cognition Elements of Information Systems**
  Steve Clarke, Elayne Coakes, M. Gordon Hunter and Andrew Wenn
  ISBN: 1-59140-104-6; eISBN 1-59140-112-7, © 2003
- **Usability Evaluation of Online Learning Programs**
  Claude Ghaoui
  ISBN: 1-59140-105-4; eISBN 1-59140-113-5, © 2003
- **Building a Virtual Library**
  Ardis Hanson & Bruce Lubotsky Levin
  ISBN: 1-59140-106-2; eISBN 1-59140-114-3, © 2003
- **Design and Implementation of Web-Enabled Teaching Tools**
  Mary F. Hricko
  ISBN: 1-59140-107-0; eISBN 1-59140-115-1, © 2003
- **Designing Campus Portals: Opportunities and Challenges**
  Ali Jafari and Mark Sheehan
  ISBN: 1-59140-108-9; eISBN 1-59140-116-X, © 2003
- **Challenges of Teaching with Technology Across the Curriculum: Issues and Solutions**
  Lawrence A. Tomei
  ISBN: 1-59140-109-7; eISBN 1-59140-117-8, © 2003

Dedication

This book is dedicated to my family and friends, especially, my mother, my uncle, Nick, and Milt, who, at some time or another, have helped and inspired me to aim for the best in life.

Web-Based Education: Learning from Experience

Table of Contents

Foreword

This book on Web-Based Education (WBE) invites you to learn from the experiences of a number of faculty members who have been designing, teaching, and managing online courses and degree programs. Although the data or evidence presented are primarily anecdotal, this can be very useful and can prevent "re-inventing the wheel."

The particular strength of this book is its international scope. Among its highlights are chapters that enable the reader to learn about:

- The diffusion of "web-based" education in Australia and Singapore
- Integration of online learning into a "web-enhanced" (hybrid or mixed mode delivery) at an Italian private business university.
- A "Web-enhanced mentoring system" for a diploma in credit union studies at the National U. of Ireland
- Training of specialists in Motor Disability Assessment, also in Ireland
- Experiences of an instructor in health policy and management in Finland
- A "Global Campus" offering a master's degree in Business Information Technology through a partnership between a British and an Egyptian institutions
- A consortium of universities that have created a German "Virtual University of Applied Sciences"
- "Blended" traditional and e-learning for computer science education at the U. of Karlsrue in Germany
- Use of Web-Based technology to support the learning experience of MIS undergraduates in community learning projects at the U. of Alaska, that follows the "relate- create- donate" model for active learning proposed by Ben Shneiderman.

There are three things of special note in the book. One is the proliferation of different terminologies that are currently being used to label forms of learning online. Besides the terms "Web-Based Education" and "e-learning" and the various other terms used above, other terms that occur in the literature include "Asynchronous Learning Networks" (ALN), "computer-mediated" learning, "online learning" and "virtual university," to mention just a few of the plethora of names being used. The second is the treatment of infrastructure support for web-based education. This information can be useful for administrators in the process of institutionalizing web-based education or instructors planning to revamp or to offer web-based courses for the first time.

The third is that the range of course subjects covered is quite broad. Though the most frequent use of "web-based education" is in subjects related to information technology (including information systems, computer science, and business), online courses now span the full range of university and professional education curricula. No matter what subject an instructor teaches, he or she can undoubtedly find useful information in this volume.

Starr Roxanne Hiltz
Distinguished Professor, College of Computing Sciences
New Jersey Institute of Technology
November 2002

Preface

Technological advances in telecommunications combined with Web-enabled technologies have created a new technology known as "Internet Communications Technologies (ICT) & Teaching Technologies." This new technology has changed the concepts of education. Asynchronous Network Learning (ANL), Web-based education (WBE), and eLearning are different names for education on the Web. WBE is becoming so popular that many for-profit colleges and universities are emerging, providing stiff competition to traditional universities. Public and private colleges and universities, from all over the world, are facing the many challenges and opportunities offered by this new technology-based concept. WBE is diffusing across disciplines, curriculums, levels, and even national boundaries. WBE is not limited to the privileged few. Like any emerging technology, "ICT and Teaching Technologies" is not free from problems, controversies, and challenges. There are proponents and opponents of Web-based education, generating anxiety but also some interesting discussions. As many new universities are joining WBE, many old ones are failing. It is important for educators to be aware of the discussions and learn from the successes and failures of the early adopters. The first wave of WBE concentrated on the "what" of WBE, and the next generation is focusing on the "how."

WHY THE BOOK?

Like any new merchandise or service, WBE is going through its own "product" life cycle. In the first stage of WBE, emphasis was focused on the "newness" of the technology, and there were few early adopters. WBE was being pressed into what marketers have called "technology push." However, this is changing. As the number of online students keeps increasing, many for-profit universities are emerging and forcing traditional universities to focus more on the student. Like e-commerce, e-education is becoming "customer" oriented. The customers in this case, of course, are the students. In the second phase of WBE, we are seeing more of a "customer pull." Students are demanding quality education on their terms, often with the desire for online convenience. The education pedagogy is changing from "brick-and-mortar" to "click-and-click." Institutions are taking instruction to the customers, with education becoming time, place, language, distance, and status independent. This pedagogy is creating a completely new and unfamiliar learning environment. Roles, expectations, and interaction among students, faculty, and administration are suddenly different and experimental. Lines of communications are changing. Many early adopters have learned valuable lessons in institutionalizing WBE.

The main objective of this book is to assist the reader in better understanding the practices of the early adopters and to address issues such as, trends, opportunities, and problems facing colleges and universities in effectively utilizing and managing ICT and teaching technologies. The chapters of this book are a compilation of the experiences, knowledge, and research findings of the early adopters of WBE.

BOOK AUDIENCE

This book is intended for anyone interested in developing and institutionalizing WBE. Issues, technology, and how WBE is evolving, both locally and globally, are discussed. And, the factors involved in moving from a synchronous to an asynchronous learning environment are addressed. Greatly beneficial are the authors' descriptions of their experiences, presented with the many questions raised in the first phase of WBE, which provides guidance for individuals and institutions interested in developing, offering, and managing Web programs. This book is also meant for researchers already conducting or looking for new research topics in WBE. With new, challenging ideas presented, further research is encouraged. In many of the chapters, recommendations for further research in specific areas are presented.

BOOK STRUCTURE

Any emerging technology must be defined, the issues must be addressed, and the theories must be tested and validated. I used the same concept in dividing this book into five sections. In the first section, questions around what we have learned from our experiences, where we are, and what can be expected in the future are answered. In the second section, technology and ways it can enhance Web teaching are identified. In the third section, design issues in the development of WBE are discussed. In the fourth section, Web diffusion across disciplines is discussed, and experiences of researchers in various classroom settings are provided. In the final section, diffusion across boundaries is discussed, and insights into ongoing experiments in WBE are provided.

- WBE: An Overview, Current and Future
- WBE: Enhancing Technologies
- WBE: Design Issues
- WBE: Diffusion Across Disciplines and Communities
- WBE: Diffusion Across Boundaries (Case Studies)

These sections are created for the reader's convenience only. The issues discussed are not isolated, and there are overlapping ideas and concepts among each of the sections.

The first section, "WBE: An Overview, Current and Future," consists of five chapters. In these chapters, currency and potential issues based on authors' experiences are discussed. In several chapters, the currency of WBE in the second stage of its life cycle and how WBE needs to be institutionalized to survive and to move into its next stage are discussed. Aggarwal discusses the institutionalization of WBE. He argues that virtual students are opting for a "complete" online education and are demanding virtual convenience from admission to graduation. Aggarwal discusses each of the steps involved in institutionalizing Web education from the perspectives of the three major stakeholders— the faculty, the student, and the technical personnel—and talks about ways of providing online conveniences based on his experiences. Huerta, Ryan, and Igbaria present a theoretical framework for understanding the Web-based learning (WBL) phenomenon, based on disciplines other than education. From the organizational communication field, the authors propose media richness and social influence models to assist in understanding the factors affecting media communication choice in WBL. From the managerial discipline, they propose the theory of knowledge reuse to understand the managerial challenges that instructors face when creating knowledge repositories for WBL. Finally, from the information literature perspective, they offer the information structure framework to assess the adequacy of the information for a particular situation. Klassen and Vogel discuss the sound pillars of ethics for the mass production of e-education. They talk about ethical issues regarding student–student and student–faculty interactions, and discuss assessment of learning, the potential problems and possible solutions. Clulow and Brace-Govan provide perspectives from students and staff who have experienced learning and teaching in a Web-based environment. Based on their experience, they discuss a number of indicators for improving WBL, including development of faculty and preparation of students for an online learning environment and for student-centered Web-based design. Raisinghani discusses the WBE strategy for academia from a global perspective. He presents a transnational model for Web-based education and draws the parallels between industry and academia with respect to virtual organizations. In addition, he takes a closer look at some predictors of teaching and learning issues as extrapolations of current trends.

The second section, "WBE: Enhancing Technologies," consists of four chapters that look at various current technologies and their usage in WBE. In this section, the authors' experiences with Web-enabling hardware and software technologies are discussed, and guidance to their seamless integration in WBE is provided. Klassen discusses design of autonomous language learning courseware based on the constructivist view, where learners only learn how to learn when they are actively involved in the educational process. Her focus is on producing an interactive multimedia package, Virtual Language University, for English-language learning in the context of the general format, coding, and creation of templates, graphics and animation, video specifications, and task interaction. Roldan argues that handheld devices are attractive for educational settings because they are inexpensive, portable, and customizable. He also suggests that the information management and connectivity features of these handheld devices make them ideal for the WBE learning environment. Parikh argues that the Web is only one of many Internet technologies and goes beyond the Web to leverage multiple Internet technologies to support in-class education. She discusses common problems in Web-based education, presents an experiment in developing and implementing a framework that seamlessly integrates various Internet technologies, and describes the increase in learning effectiveness yielded by the new methodology. Sauter reports on an action research project using the Theory of Planned Behavior (TPB) to help manage the process of encouraging faculty to utilize Internet tools in the implementation of their classes. Her research provides an in-depth examination of an innovative experiment to impact the process of faculty website development, faculty training, and faculty support, reflected in terms of the TPB framework.

The third section, "WBE: Design Issues," consists of five chapters. WBE is changing the educational pedagogy, requiring new ways of assessing, mentoring, and facilitating education. Self-centered learning is becoming the norm. Roles are changing, faculty is facilitating instead of delivering lectures, and students are self-learning instead of listening to in-class lectures. Moving from traditional teaching to the WBE requires mapping (not necessarily 1:1) or transformation from one medium to another. Student assessment is probably one of the most important issues in teaching. Traditional exams and classroom monitoring are not feasible or even desirable in WBE. New creative methods need to be developed to assess student learning. In addition, faculty, students, and administrators need support and training for this new WBE environment. Bento and Schuster propose taxonomy for classifying different types of participation in online courses and discuss the pedagogical issues involved. Born examines ways of evaluating students in a Web-based teaching and learning environment. Two techniques, summative and formative, are introduced and discussed, together with related issues including delivery and submission, evaluation and feedback, and dealing with cheating. She also provides guidelines and recommendations for developing and delivering effective Web-based student assessment. Neville, Adam, and McCormack provide an example of a university and an organization collaborating to implement successful training and learning programs. This joint partnership is formed in order to develop employee skills and knowledge in IT and managerial issues, such as knowledge management. The case provides guidance for developing an appropriate platform with which to design an interactive learning environment to mentor distance learners, with the potential to eliminate the barriers imposed by the traditional classroom. Beuschel, Gaiser, and Draheim provide an assessment of the formal and informal aspects of communication in Web-based learning environments. They stress the importance of organizational and technical support of informal communication as an important issue in Web-based education. Baker, Schihl, and Aggarwal propose the development of an integrated educational support system infrastructure to assist WBE students from application to graduation. They argue that such support systems should address the many aspects of the teaching and learning processes.

The fourth section, "WBE: Diffusion Across Disciplines and Communities," consists of four chapters. WBE is moving into its second stage and spreading at an unprecedented pace. It is diffusing across disciplines from business to law, and across educational levels from universities to high schools. The authors' experiences in different course settings are presented. Pareja-Flores and Velázquez-Iturbide discuss WBE diffusion in a programming course. They contend that programming is a demanding task that requires education with the assistance of complex tools, such as programming environments, algorithm animators, problem graders, etc. They provide a comprehensive presentation of the tools for program execution and visualization on the Web. The authors also discuss the technical evolution of these tools, describe educational uses, report on lessons learned, and look at formal evaluations of their educational effectiveness. Benrud discusses WBE diffusion in a finance course. He explores how characteristics of individual students and each section of students can be determinants of student success in a Web-based finance course. He developed a statistical model that has significant explanatory power for variation in performance on individual grade components, such as quizzes, tests, and projects. His findings suggest that developing online discussion skills prior to the start of the course will enhance student performance in other areas of a Web-based finance course. Speaker and Kleist discuss diffusion in an electronic commerce and MIS class. They cover a technical description of a multilocation, top-of-the-line distance-learning facility, and they introduce research that explores critical success factors for technology-assisted use in learning for MBA students. Their results, from a study of 2898 student responses across 117 classes, indicate that certain aspects of information technology may facilitate and enhance perceptions of student learning, despite the challenges of the location disconnect. In addition, they describe a specific case of a mass customization-style educational IT, deployed in a face-to-face environment for a highly compressed MBA class on electronic commerce and MIS. Drinka and Yi-Miin Yen discuss diffusion in a capstone project-based course. They discuss a variety of Web-based technologies that were used to support students in their project development efforts, thereby realizing the benefits of project-based courses, while ensuring project success. They demonstrate how students in a project-based capstone course used technology to assist them in developing community-based information systems. Tan Wee Hi and Subramaniam discuss diffusion in nonformal educational environments. They reason that the virtual annexes by many science centers have given rise to a new genre of learning in Web-based education. They argue that to enhance the outreach effectiveness of nonformal science education initiatives among students and the public, these virtual science centers fulfill a useful role in promoting the public understanding of science. They use the Singapore Science Center as an example with which to explore the topic in detail.

The fifth section, "WBE: Diffusion Across Boundaries (Case Studies)," consists of six chapters. WBE is not only diffusing in the United States, but it is also gaining popularity worldwide. The case studies provide insights into experiments being conducted in many areas, across disciplines, all over the world. Kamel and Wahba discuss their experience of the Global Campus (GC) project, a collaboration between the Regional IT Institute (Egypt) and Middlesex University (United Kingdom). The project's aim was to deliver postgraduate education to the communities in Egypt, Hong Kong, and the United Kingdom, while capitalizing on cutting-edge information and communication technology. They demonstrate the lessons learned from managing a model for a globally extended enterprise in the education sector, through a partnership agreement between the different parties that capitalizes on the opportunities enabled by the Internet. Wong, Gerber, and Toh examine and compare the diffusion of WBE in Singapore and Australia. Their analysis reveals that although Singapore and Australia are different in their approaches and policies to education and technology, they share similar trends and achievements in the development of WBE. Tertiary institutions in both countries have generally achieved all the characteristics of Generations 4 and 5 of the development model of Distance Education as described by Taylor's model. Valenti, Panti, and Leo discuss how Web-based Instructional Systems (WbIS) models could be used to implement "real-life" examples of instructional systems. They discuss each phase of the Instructional Systems Design (ISD) with respect to the implementation of a WbIS for training specialists in Motor Disability Assessment (MODASPECTRA). Klein, Sommer, and Stucky argue for an integration of Web-based and classical education, and present WeBCEIS—our blended learning scenario for integrating Web-based education into classical education—looking at the organizational and the technological aspects of teaching and learning, and our strategy for the implementation of WeBCEIS. Klobas and Renzi discuss a project at Bocconi University. The project is presented as organizational innovation and provides comparison with the stages of the Rogers' model of diffusion of innovations. They argue that the key conditions for success are top management commitment and involvement. In addition, they suggest other important requirements, such as an environment that supports innovation and change, an appropriate ICT infrastructure, and appropriate use of innovation, flexibility, and teacher preparedness. Lammintakanen and Rissanen discuss an evaluation of the experiences of two student partners and their teachers with Web-based education at a university in Finland. Finnish national education policy and some crucial issues concerning Web-based education were used in the framework for the evaluation. Their results indicate that the students' and teachers' experiences were largely positive and correlated with the results of other international research in this field.

Acknowledgments

A book of this nature requires assistance from many individuals. The chapters went through several screenings. The initial proposal and then the first draft were reviewed by at least two experts in the area. Conditionally accepted papers were revised and re-reviewed by the original reviewers. Some papers went through three evaluations before being accepted or rejected. Twenty-five out of 40 papers were accepted. I would like to acknowledge all of the reviewers who gave their time and effort to help make this a quality publication.

I would like to thank Professor Starr Roxanne Hiltz, New Jersey Institute of Technology, who agreed to forward this book and provided suggestions for improving the content. A book like this cannot be completed without sacrifice and dedication of other individuals. My sincere thanks go to Mr. Nicholas St. Angelo for helping with editing, logistics, and streamlining of the content, many times with little notice. This book could not have been finished in time without his help and support. In addition, I would also like to thank M. Alper Yildirim and Mr. Gurpreet Singh for helping with the day-to-day monitoring and correspondence. I appreciate all the support and guidance provided by Idea Group Publishing. My special thanks go to Ms. Michele Rossi, Ms. Amanda Appicello, and Ms. Jan Travers, Senior Managing Editor at Idea Group Publishing for their understanding and patience. I would also like to thank the staff at Idea Group Publishing for their hard work in editing and making this book a reality. Last but not least, I would like to thank Professor Mehdi Khosrow-Pour for giving me this wonderful opportunity to edit this timely book.

Anil K. Aggarwal
University of Baltimore, USA

Part I

WBE:
An Overview,
Current and
Future

Chapter I

A Guide to eCourse Management: The Stakeholders' Perspectives

Anil K. Aggarwal
University of Baltimore, USA

ABSTRACT

Web-based education (WBE) and training is growing by leaps and bounds, and the market is expected to reach almost 28.6 billion by the year 2006 (IDC, 2001). Technological advancements and student demands have necessitated a shift from a "brick and mortar" synchronous environment to a "click and learn" asynchronous environment. Students are demanding anytime, anyplace accessibility, and universities are obliging by bringing education to students. The instructor's role is changing from "lecturing" to "facilitating," and the student's role is changing from "recipient" to "participant." These virtual students require virtual convenience and are opting for a "complete" online education, from admission to graduation. In this chapter, the steps involved in Web education, from three major stakeholders' perspectives—the faculty, the student, and the technical personnel— are discussed, and ways of providing online conveniences are discussed, based on the author's experience.

INTRODUCTION

Anytime, anyplace access is the essence of Web-based education (WBE). Universities are providing education on the students' terms, whether at the student's home, workplace, or other convenient location (Benbunan-Fich, 2002; Ducker, 2001). Students are becoming much like the customers, and universities are becoming much like the businesses competing for these customers. Many for-profit and traditional universities are trying to be among the first to provide Web-based teaching. It is estimated that by the end of this year, almost 200 universities will be offering online courses in some form or another (IDC, 2001, 2002). WBE is diffusing across disciplines, educational levels, and global boundaries. It is expanding into many traditional disciplines of business education, including finance, accounting, management, and marketing, and also into nonbusiness disciplines, like the political sciences, history, arts, and engineering. WBE is not confined to western countries. Many third-world countries are recognizing WBE as an economical alternative to reach the masses and are jumping on the WBE bandwagon. Open universities of Sri Lanka, Bangladesh, India, and Pakistan are examples of this. These universities are trying to reach all classes of people, particularly those living in villages and remote areas. Even the United Nations, in its report (October, 2002) on disarmament and nonproliferation education and training, recommended using such techniques as distance learning, the Internet, and videoconferencing, as well as cost-efficient and cost-effective media such as CD-ROMs for educating the masses.

Like any new product, WBE is going through its own product life cycle (Day, 1981). In the late 1990s when WBE was emerging, there were few adopters, and WBE was in the first stage of the product life cycle. This was an experimental phase, where emphasis was on "defining" the product and making it technically "feasible." Only a few universities, such as the University of Phoenix, University of Maryland at University Park (UMUP), and the University of Baltimore (UB) were experimenting with WBE. In this initial phase, the WBE product was more technology driven. As students saw the benefits of WBE and started moving from traditional face-to-face learning to WBE, many entrepreneurs also started venturing into it. Many for-profit universities began to emerge, forcing traditional universities to come on board (*San Jose Mercury News*, 1999). The University of Phoenix, with virtually no physical presence, captured a large online education market. The momentum continued, and more and more players surfaced, moving WBE into the second phase of its life cycle.

In the second phase, WBE is becoming more demand driven. As competition is growing, universities are streamlining operations, consolidating offerings, and creating strategic partnerships. Efficiency is becoming key, and universities are looking at the cost, value, and (above all) the quality of such offerings. However, all is not rosy for for-profit universities in this phase. Education requires recognition, value, and accreditation from appropriate world bodies, and many for-profits are folding due to the lack of quality, name recognition, and, ultimately, lack of capital. In the second phase, universities are following an organizational strategy to approach "customers," which means paying closer attention to the students. Consolidation is taking place, and eventually, "few" will survive to the third phase of WBE.

Because students are like customers, their satisfaction is important, and they are demanding online education with online convenience. Universities are recognizing this and differentiating their product by revamping curriculums, offering 24/7 online support services and streamlining operations. Effectiveness and efficiency are becoming key to survival, creating challenges for administrators, faculty, and support personnel to provide seamless operations. Based on the author's experiences and discussions with other Web faculty, we provide guidelines for managing Web courses from the stakeholders' (student, faculty, and technical personnel) perspectives.

WEB-BASED EDUCATION

WBE is available anytime, anyplace, to anyone—irrespective of time and distance. Many researchers (www.alnresearch.org) have called this asynchronous learning. Typically, two dimensions are used to describe Web-based teaching: time and place. The scenarios for WBE extend from same-time, same-place (synchronous) to anytime, anyplace (asynchronous) environments. As WBE grows in size and diffuses worldwide, many different experiments, interpretations, and models are emerging. Aggarwal and Bento (2000) suggested three models of "Internetalizing" courses at a traditional university: (a) Web support for information storage, dissemination, and retrieval; (b) Web support for two-way teaching; and (c) Web-based teaching. The nature of Web support and usage increases from Model (a) to Model (c), in that Model (a) requires Web usage mostly for "information" purposes, while Model (c) requires a complete Web-based environment. The Web is included as part of the education in the first teaching mode, whereas it is the only medium of instruction in the third mode. It is this third approach that provides time and place independence and is of interest here. Irrespective of definition, administrators and educators need guidelines on what should and should not be done in order to provide a seamless online Web operation.

Though there are many players, three stakeholders (students, faculty, and technical personnel) play a major role in WBE (Aggarwal, 2001). These stakeholders are directly involved in the day-to-day operations and progression of the course. From the stakeholders' perspectives, WBE activities should support the complete process, from inquiry to student graduation. The difference between WBE and face-to-face education is not the process, but the mode, nature, and management of the delivery process. The mode implies the online nature of education, while the delivery involves the nature of content preparation, delivery and management, and student assessment.

Typical steps in a complete WBE are as follows:

- eInquiry
- eAdmission
- eEnrollment
- eCourse
- eGraduation

Though all steps are essential, none is more important than the eCourse, where the actual delivery, learning, and assessment take place. In the following sections, we will discuss each of these steps in more detail. The WBE process starts with the student online inquiry, or eInquiry.

eINQUIRY

The eInquiry stage consists of activities that prospective students perform before deciding on the actual college for their education. Because prospective students are outside the domain of the academic world, the best that a university can do is to provide an informative and attractive website that includes its mission, academic programs, support services, and general information. It should have a robust local search engine and, above all, email and voicemail contact information. In addition, the university's website should display testimonials from its alumni and examples of national coverage, articles, and publications—all in an effort to assist the prospective student in learning more about the university and its offerings. Universities should look into the possibility of linking their websites to alumni's business or personal sites.

Given a university's advertising budget and commitment to WBE, it may be wise to advertise on some popular online education websites of book publishers and booksellers, in newspapers, as well as in popular magazines like *Business Week* and *U.S. News and World Report*. It may also be possible to link to browsers that will give preferential display to the website (Halford, 2002). One word of caution—a university should not try to be a "jack of all trades," or all things to all people. This could create confusion and disappointment for likely students.

Once students decide on a university, the next step is applying for online admission, or eAdmission.

eADMISSION

The eAdmission step consists of all activities that are necessary for a student to get admitted or let in to a specific program. This includes an application with supporting documentation such as transcripts, standardized test scores, letters of recommendation, statement of purpose, bank and financial statements, and other documents, as needed. Because this is the first contact a Web student has with the university bureaucracy, it should be a pleasant and stress free encounter. This experience may be perceived as a measure of the university's commitment to its Web program.

The admission process should be "modular" or "mentor" oriented. A modular approach implies single entry and exit for a student from the admission module (process). The main admission module consists of many submodules, such as financial aid, transfer credit, and loan. Students, however, are responsible for going through the needed submodules. A "mentor" approach requires the appointment of a single person as adviser or mentor to a student, with responsibility for the student's admission process. Too many individuals or associations can be confusing and counterproductive. Figure 1(a,b) shows the two approaches. Note that in the modular approach, the applicant may be interacting with different people, whereas, in the mentor approach, there is a single point of contact. The mentor may ask for additional documents as needed, but from the applicant's perspective, the admission process is a black box.

For eAdmission to be successful, a university must adhere to the following guidelines:

- Provide appropriate *contact* information, preferably one person. There is nothing more daunting than going from one person to another without much success.
- Make sure that admissions staff are *knowledgeable* and *prompt* in responding to a student's needs, be it via email, in person, or through Web forms. It is likely many prospective students would not have read all the admission requirements and would

Figure 1a: Mentor eAdmission Approach

Application → **BLACK BOX** Application Outcome →

Figure 1b: Modular eAdmission Approach

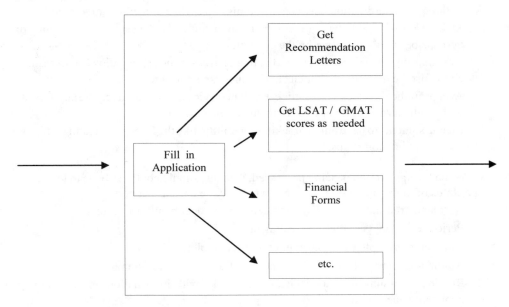

require support in completing the admission process. It is discouraging if the staff is not familiar with rules, requirements, and admission procedures. Staff training that develops computer, communications (specifically, online communications), and people skills are of the utmost importance. We must always remember that students are only a "click" away from going to another website.

- Provide important information with uncomplicated navigation. Directions with lots of twists and turns can be frustrating. Complete online information about the university should be available that includes its programs, procedures, faculty and their expertise, and the names of contacts with their various functions, email addresses, and telephone numbers. This requires a website with manageable frames and hyperlinks to appropriate sites. An added convenience could be 24/7 "real time" online help, where a student could go online and communicate with the "help" desk or persons-in-charge to make inquiries and to get assistance with questions and concerns.
- Assist students who may be interested in grants and financial assistance from outside sources by providing links on the website to those sites and, perhaps, suggestions for other sources of assistantships.
- Make sure that in the case of transfer students, admissions personnel have appropriate credit transfer information or have access to knowledgeable staff within each division and department to help in transfer credit assessment.
- Provide an online application with a possibility for snail-mail application.
- Arrange agreements with major test-scoring agencies to send online, student test scores on standardized exams, like the GMAT, LAST, etc., directly to the admissions office. The admissions office must coordinate this activity with the agencies and applicant to reduce time and fraud.

- Make an agreement to receive a student's transcripts from previous studies. Again, this will require coordination between the admissions office and other universities.
- Make it known that letters of recommendation could also be sent directly online, or perhaps be filled out online by the evaluators.
- Note that any other documents, like the financial assistance application and its results, could also be directly communicated by the respective agencies.
- Accept application fees using online payment services. This would require agreements with credit card or other online payment companies.
- Enable students to have online tracking capability, like the UPS, USPS, and FedEx, to follow application status.

When the application is being processed, students should continually be made aware of the status of their application. The following may be used as triggers:

- Automatic reminders (emails) to students as the documents are received
- Periodic reminders of missing documents
- Automatic prompts when the application is complete
- Automatic communications about the time frame of the decision
- Routine communication as decisions are made, with information on next steps if applicant is accepted

A university has to decide whether to outsource or develop eAdmission capabilities in-house. Before making any decisions, universities must recognize that the face-to-face admission process is very different from eAdmission, and any attempt to mesh the two would shortchange both. Once a student is admitted, the next step is seamless enrollment, or eEnrollment.

eENROLLMENT

The eEnrollment process consists of all steps related to a semester's enrollment practices. This includes activities such as meeting the advisor, course selection, fee payment, course site access, getting familiar with the Web course software, and any other activity needed before the start of the class. For eEnrollment to be successful, a university must adhere to the following guidelines:

- Provide online consultations with advisors regarding course offerings, suggestions, and their approval of the course selected. An automatic check of prerequisites, student standings (FR, JR, or GR) and total semester load must be accessible as the semester schedule is developed. For elective courses, students must have online access to course syllabi, prerequisites, objectives, and requirements for each elective course. It would be counterproductive for students to enroll in courses and realize that they do not have the appropriate prerequisites or that the course was not what they intended to take.
- Provide online availability of semester course offerings, with instructors' names and contact information. In addition, a hyperlink to the complete course description should

be available through the department, school, or university catalog system. This is similar to a "drill-down" approach, where each level can be exploded into the next level for more details.

- Offer online registration capabilities with instant confirmation. If courses are full or not available, a wait list choice and an alternate course list with prerequisites must be shown. However, registration for alternate courses may not proceed without an advisor's approval.
- Make online fee payments available in a secure environment. If grants or scholarships are received, then the account must be automatically credited.
- Automatically generate and communicate triggers or reminders (email) about fee payment, class schedule, and any changes and special requirements.

The next activity is the actual learning process through the online course, or eCourse. The next section describes the eCourse process in complete detail.

eCOURSE

The ultimate goals of education are critical thinking and lifelong learning. These are achieved through courses and programs offered by the university. An eCourse consists of activities related to the course before, during, and after its Web offering. However, before we discuss actual activities, we will talk about the logistics of this process. It involves three major stakeholders—students, faculty, and technical support personnel—and three major stages—pre-, during-, and post-course delivery. The Web creates a cooperative and collaborative learning environment (Kemery, 2000) that encourages interaction between stakeholders. Figure 2 shows the general nature of communication (one- or two-way) between stakeholders.

Figure 2: Nature of Communication between Stakeholders

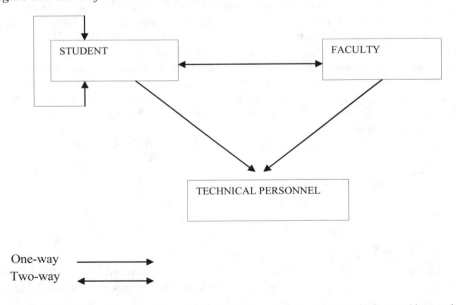

One-way ⟶
Two-way ⟷

As shown in Figure 2, the majority of two-way communication takes place between student and faculty and among students. Technical personnel typically react to communication initiated by other stakeholders. We describe these communications in more detail.

Student-to-Student

This two-way interaction, also known as peer-to-peer communication, is similar to collaborative learning (group interaction) in the traditional classroom. The majority of interaction takes place during the actual course offering stage. It allows for exchange of ideas and group interaction. In the online environment, students communicate with each other through a forum/blackboard/chalkboard,[1] email, and maybe voicemail. Asynchronous forum discussion in the online class takes the place of synchronous group discussions of the traditional classroom. In the traditional classroom, students typically meet before or after class, on weekends, or on other holidays to discuss a group project. Often, this involves a physical commute to the campus. In WBE, group forums are used for group discussions, eliminating the need for the physical commute. Based on the authors' experience, we noted that the technically savvy online groups establish instant messaging that also allows for synchronous communication. In summary, interaction among students is required in the following:

- Forum discussions
- Group projects
- Social communication

Student-to-Faculty

This two-way interaction simulates, to some extent, the in-class (during class hours) and in-office (during office hours) communication between student and faculty, without the limitations of time and place. It is similar to the faculty asking questions in class, guiding students through the responses, and posing follow-up, challenging questions. This stimulates learning and thinking and encourages students to ask questions and seek guidance and clarification. This effect is achieved by WBE through the forum and email. Instead of in-class interaction, faculty participates in the forum to assess and stimulate problem solving through cooperative mentoring. In many cases, faculty may need to constantly monitor and guide students by posting questions to steer thinking in the right direction. One-on-one interaction (similar to office hours) between faculty and student is simulated through email or in the private student–faculty forum area. The difference is the asynchronous nature of the interaction. This interaction is low during the pre-course and after-course stages and highest during the actual course offering.

In summary, faculty–student interaction is required in the following:

- Forum
- Assignment/exam/exercises
- Projects
- Personal situations

Student-to-Technical Personnel

This interaction, mostly one-way, is initiated by students for troubleshooting. It may be to facilitate class access; to minimize system slow downs, failures, and file losses; to provide software access; or for general online account problems. Typically, it is one of two types, general or specific. General communication is required when students need help with general online problems like course access, forum postings, attachments, file posting, and breakdowns. Specific communication is desired when a course requires particular hardware and software, utilities, or file formats. The problems may include an inability to access specific software, problems with a company's firewalls, file downloading and uploading, telneting, and accessing specific utilities. Based on our experience, firewalls have created the maximum problems and should be resolved during the pre-course stage. Interaction between student and technical personnel may be direct or through the instructor. It is low in all three stages except when specific software is needed in a course.

In summary, technical personnel–student interaction is required in the following situations:

- General troubleshooting
- Mobile access
- Firewall access
- Course access
- Software access
- Account issues
- Downed systems and other blackouts

Faculty-to-Technical Personnel

This one-way interaction is needed to facilitate the course and is usually initiated by faculty for hardware and software training, course preparation, management, and delivery. There is no equivalent of this in traditional learning, because lectures are face to face, and there is no specific content preparation (maybe creating slides for lecture presentation). Online, this is important in the pre-course stage, when faculty is preparing and testing lecture contents. It is high during the pre-course stage and low in later stages.

In summary, faculty–technical personnel interaction is required in the following situations:

- Troubleshooting
- Course management
- Training
- Ad-hoc requests
- ISP and ASP infrastructure issues
- Platform issues

Given that the course offering is the "core" of education, we divided eCourse into four (not necessarily distinct) activities:

- ePreparation
- eDelivery
- eManagement
- eAssessment

We will discuss these activities within the context of the three major stakeholders: students, faculty, and technical personnel.

ePreparation

The ePreparation activities involve all interactions and communications required to prepare a course to be delivered on the Web. The ePreparation is performed before the class officially begins. The purpose is to develop content for smooth delivery and management for later stages, similar to a dress rehearsal. The major tasks are getting course "content" and students "ready" for the semester. It is not uncommon for students to ignore directions, emails, and postings before the class starts. To get student attention, it may be necessary to create periodic email triggers. A word of caution: instructors should make certain that students are not overburdened with repeated emails prior to the beginning of class. Students may be too tired from the previous semester, or are traveling and generally not ready for the next school term. As the new semester approaches, however, it may be useful to send a group email that reminds students of the availability of semester postings.

One of the biggest challenges in eCourse is content preparation. Content should not be similar to a regular face-to-face lecture. Based on our experience, one of the biggest mistakes Web instructors make is to use slides from face-to-face lectures. This does not work well, because online lectures should include slide contents *plus* all the explanations, examples, questions and answers, and other supporting materials used in the face-to-face lecture. Instructors need to be creative in order to get the concepts across, as this is the only form of content communication. A rehash of the book material or slides used in traditional lectures will not suffice. Questions and answers, exercises, and examples should be embedded throughout the lecture. Text should be highlighted and linked to other sources for alternate explanations. Tool tip text (i.e., a message box appears when the cursor is placed on the text) should be used for small exercises within the lecture. Figure 3 shows a sample of tool tip text in a database lecture.

Figure 3: A Sample Lecture Explaining Referencing in a Database Lecture Using Tool Tip Text

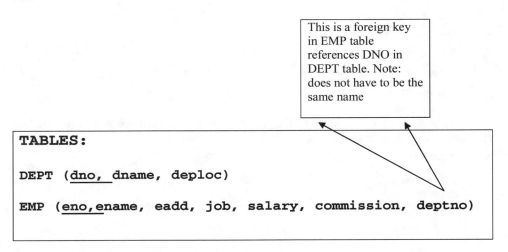

We also suggest making several versions of the lectures, as follows:

- Flash (multimedia)
- HTML with graphics
- HTML with text only

Different lecture versions will accommodate students with varying computer access speeds. In the flash version audio, the video and animation clips may be used to explain or stress a point (Bento, 2000). Based on our experience, we suggest that lectures should not have continuous streaming but should have controlled triggered streaming. Continuous streaming can overburden the system. In controlled streaming, a student would initiate the video, audio, and animation clips as needed. In the future, streaming may become less resource intensive, and the ability may exist to include continuous streaming in lectures at reasonable speed. The graphic version should include frames, hyperlinks, and online exercises but no streaming. The text version, though not advised, may be beneficial to students who do not have fast Internet access. This version of the lecture should be text based with no (or very little) graphics. Figure 4 shows different lecture versions for one of the author's courses. It was noted that the graphic version worked best given the bandwidth limitations for most students.

In addition to the lecture format, lecture currency is important. Websites become obsolete or outdated, and faculty should make sure that all links are current and working. It is quite embarrassing if faculty posts a lecture with a "dead" website.

One of the other challenges in the ePreparation phase is getting the student "ready" for the online course. This involves establishing a forum structure and communication etiquette or "standards," which must be instituted *before* the course starts. Based on our experience, we found the forum works best with several distinct threads (areas):

- General question and answer area
- Assignment and exam area
- Session-related discussion questions
- Group area
- One-on-one area

The general question area is used for *generic* questions. This area is not used for any discussion. Communication is one way, students post questions, and faculty respond to them. Its purpose is to provide general clarification. Students may ask, for example, where to post the homework or where the weekly assignment is placed, etc. The assignment and exams area is for clarification on *specific assignment and exams*. Again, only faculty can respond to these postings. The session area is for discussing, posting, and creating threads related to weekly questions. This is the part of eCourse, where the actual Web learning takes place. This involves two-way communication, where the student can create threads, post responses, and even ask for clarifications, and faculty can discuss, create new threads, or respond to student questions. The group area is used for group filters and group work and should only be accessible to group members and faculty. There will be one such area for each group. If the class size is manageable, a one-on-one group area should also be established. This allows faculty to post additional questions for students needing extra help, on a one-on-one basis. This area obviously should be accessible only to faculty and the student.

Figure 4: Different Sample Lecture Version for Accessing SQL Plus

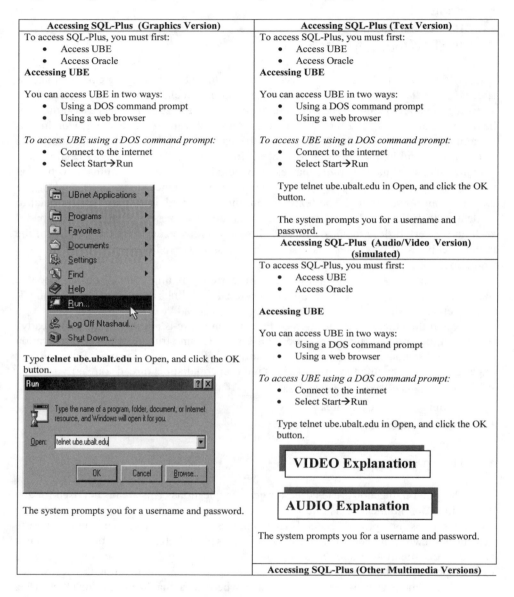

Accessing SQL-Plus (Graphics Version)	Accessing SQL-Plus (Text Version)
To access SQL-Plus, you must first: • Access UBE • Access Oracle **Accessing UBE** You can access UBE in two ways: • Using a DOS command prompt • Using a web browser *To access UBE using a DOS command prompt:* • Connect to the internet • Select Start→Run	To access SQL-Plus, you must first: • Access UBE • Access Oracle **Accessing UBE** You can access UBE in two ways: • Using a DOS command prompt • Using a web browser *To access UBE using a DOS command prompt:* • Connect to the internet • Select Start→Run Type telnet ube.ubalt.edu in Open, and click the OK button. The system prompts you for a username and password.

Irrespective of the number of threads (areas) used, it is recommended that general and specific question areas be separated to make it easier to follow discussion threads.

Forum communication standards must be established and clearly defined beforehand or within the first week of class. It is easy to offend students by posting comments that ignore culture, religion, gender, race, and sexual orientation, or are insensitive to national origin. Because the forum is the major form of communication in WBE, it is necessary to adhere to these standards. Instructors must make sure that students understand these standards, and all comments must follow forum posting policies and guidelines. It may be advisable to provide various samples of acceptable and unacceptable forum postings. Students should be encouraged to post responses and be able to agree or differ in a constructive manner without using offensive language. If a student violates this policy, they should be warned and reminded privately of the violation. If the behavior continues, they should be referred to the appropriate student discipline hearing board for action.

Syllabi must be clear as to objectives, goals, requirements, and schedule. Many online students work, and their travel and activities are planned around the class schedule. Any major deviation from this schedule must be posted well in advance to allow students to accommodate these changes. If forum participation is to be used for grading, the syllabi must make clear what constitutes good participation in terms of number, quality, and length of a posting. For example, does two postings per question per week constitute an "A," "B," "C," or an "F"? It may be necessary to provide examples of what constitutes an "A," in terms of the quality and length of a posting. Students should be made aware that only original postings are considered, and postings such as "I agree" and "good point" are not counted.

The eOffice hours must be specified and typical email response time established. Faculty should avoid 24/7 cyber hours. A certain block of time may be designated as cyber hours when students can ask questions in an online, real-time synchronous mode. Students, however, should be discouraged from coming to faculty offices, as this gives undue advantage to persons living nearby.

All software to be used must be pretested. Software should be tested for accessibility on different platforms, through different modes, from different remote locations. It could be frustrating for students if they are unable to access class-related software from home, work, or other remote locations. From our experience, we have noted that some students wait until the last minute to access course-specific software, only to find compatibility problems. It is important that students resolve this problem *before* the class starts to avoid losing unnecessary time during the semester. Another important aspect of ePreparation involves online accessibility of library readings, articles, and journals. Once a lecture is prepared, a test run should be completed to ensure smooth eCourse delivery.

Following is a summary of the typical precourse activities for each of the three stakeholders:

Faculty Activities
- Content preparation
  - Syllabi
  - Assignments
  - Exams
  - Weekly lecture and discussion questions
- Trial Web posting
- Forum preparations
- Testing software to be used
- Online software documentation
- Formation of student groups, if any
- Student introduction forms

- Forum etiquette
- Library resources availability
- Currency of websites

Student Activities
- Hardware familiarity
  - Compatibility
  - File access and posting
  - Forum access and posting
- Course textbooks
- Digital library access
- Logistics of group workings

Technical Personnel Activities
- Develop and distribute email lists of students
- Account management
- Online technical help
- Trial course run with faculty

Once students have experimented with all the needed software, have compatible hardware, and have bought the appropriate books, the course is ready to go. The next phase is the actual online delivery of course material, or eDelivery.

eDelivery

The eDelivery phase involves the actual delivery of the course over the Internet, and it has two distinct time frames—the first week and subsequent weeks. The first week is different from other times, because housekeeping and initiation take place at this time. Student information is generated, class information is disseminated, and rules and standards are communicated. Frequently asked questions (FAQs) are posted, and students are asked to introduce themselves on the forum to provide a sense of the group. Prerequisite requirements must be specified, and those students who do not have the required prerequisites should be asked to withdraw or provide appropriate waiver documents. If not already provided, faculty should assign email or any other accounts needed for communication or for accessing specific software. Email accounts should be verified, given that this is the medium for private communications between faculty and students. Students should be asked to send a "dummy" email to verify validity of the account. In summary, the following activities should be enforced in the first week:

Summary of First Week Activities
- Student introduction
- Trial software run
- Faculty introduction
- FAQs

- Help forum
- Email validation
- Email policies
- General standards and procedures during the semester
- A bio data form

Once the initiation is over, the course reaches a steady state in terms of eDelivery. The remainder of the semester's activities are fairly repetitive and standardized and are discussed from each of the stakeholder's perspectives:

Summary of Subsequent Weeks Activities

Faculty Perspective
- Discussing and mentoring in the forum
- Appropriate lecture, notes, and readings and any other supporting material postings
- Assignments instructions and posting
- Forum topics postings
- Email responses

Student Perspective
- Access lectures, assignments, exams, and quizzes
- Actively participate in the forum
- Actively participate in group projects
- Communicate with faculty through email
- Maintain current email account

Technical Personnel
- Provide "seamless" access to course contents
- Ad-hoc troubleshooting
- Warn of system down times
- Warn of updates and maintenance

As lectures are delivered over the Internet, the class has to be managed on a daily basis. The next section discusses management of the course, or eManagement.

eManagement
This phase involves course management during the period that the course is offered. It involves forum, assignment and exam, and student and email management.

Forum management is one of the most significant areas, as it requires behavior management. In the forum, faculty becomes a mentor, a facilitator, and a counselor. Students need guidance and monitoring, as the virtual nature of forum communications may provide a false sense of anonymity. Many different forum scenarios are possible, and faculty should be ready to deal with them. We discuss a few based on our experience:

Disruptive behavior: Students may become troublesome if they do not agree with the postings. Based on the author's experience in one online class, one student set off by questioning everything other students posted, to the extent of ridiculing them. Of course, this was offensive to the other students and created a hostile situation, where some students stopped participating altogether in the forum. A timely intervention and private warning to the aggressive student alleviated this situation. It was interesting to note that the offending student did not realize he was upsetting other students and thought he was providing valuable input. Disruptive behavior must be controlled instantly.

Discussion control: Another management issue, as in a face-to-face class, is discussion control. A few aggressive students may take control of the discussion and move it in one direction, inhibiting alternative views. Faculty needs to intervene and challenge students to think from an alternative perspective. For example, the faculty might post questions such as, "who would like to discuss an opposite view," or "who would like to discuss it from a different point of view." In addition, new questions should be posted to move the discussion in the desired direction. The forum should never be static, and, in fact, faculty should continually add new and challenging questions as the discussion progresses.

Knowledge heterogeneity: This occurs when there is a wide range of pre-knowledge of the subject matter. When some students are already well versed, they tend to provide correct answers as soon as questions are posted. In many cases, this leads to conversation monopolization. This does not provide a "fair" chance for other students to respond to the questions. It discourages them from posting and may even make some of them feel inadequate. In such cases, the instructor should encourage experienced students (if a manageable number) to email their postings directly to the instructor for response.

Following is an example of an email sent to alleviate a similar problem in a class of 26:

> *... discussion questions for XXXX week are available. Please ANSWER ONLY TWO questions on the forum to allow everyone a fair chance to try them. You can always email me the remaining ones and I will be glad to look at them. ...I will not respond to questions on the FORUM, to allow everybody to have a fair chance of "first" try...*

Students appreciated this approach, and instead of posting on the forum, emailed their questions.

Another alternative is to post additional questions for students who have not yet participated. If class size is manageable, questions could be posted in a student's one-on-one group area. However, this increases the faculty's workload tremendously because of the individual attention required, the kind of attention that is similar to a face-to-face *independent* study course. Based on the author's experience, it is recommended that one-on-one interactions be kept at a minimum.

Topic focus: Students may veer off topic and lose focus, especially on controversial issues. This is often due to the nonlinear nature of asynchronous discussion. As students create discussion threads, it is possible to go in many different directions. This could happen because of current political, social, or personal situations. In one of the author's introductory management information systems (MIS) class, a discussion on corporate ethics became a trial ground for Enron executives. This particular class had several lawyers, and the discussion became a legal trial that many students did not understand or care about. The instructor had to intervene and mentor by posting new questions to put the focus back to ethics.

Lack of participation: Of the more important forum management issues is the level and quality of forum participation. Students may not participate as expected or may be posting messages such as, "I agree with John." Does that constitute a posting? If a student is not taking the lead in any discussion question and only following with one or two liners ("I agree," "Lily is right," or similar postings) or repeating what others have already posted, they should be made aware of their lack of active contribution and initiative on the forum. It is a good idea to provide periodic assessment of student forum input. It may be necessary to encourage students that lack participatory skills. Students should be reminded periodically of the importance of active participation from the learning and evaluation perspectives.

Discussion overload: Many times, especially for large classes, it may become impossible to keep track of threads and corresponding postings, resulting in discussion overload. It may become confusing for faculty as well as students to follow threads. The authors have taught many classes with different sizes, and based on our experience, we find that a technical class of approximately 18, and a nontechnical class of approximately 15 students provides a manageable balance between quality and size. Many authors (Boettcher, 1998; Nasseh, 1998) have also suggested an optimal class size of eight to 12 students. One way to deal with this is to ask students to identify each posting by their initials, which helps in following each thread and corresponding responses. Following is an email example of discussion overload in a class of 26 students:

> *...I am having difficulties navigating the discussions. Everyone seems to respond using RE: and not explaining what the posting will be about. I am finding that in order to check for new postings, I have to re-read all previous postings. Can we request that people fill in the subject space with the subject of their posting, and perhaps also include their initials in the subject to make it easier to navigate. As it is, the postings all look the same...*

However, this does not work as well in large classes, as discussions tend to clutter and generate voluminous information, which make it difficult to follow individual threads.

We propose two alternatives:

- Group filters
- Multiple forums

In group filters, the class is divided into several groups, and the group rather than each individual does the posting. For each thread, the group discusses topics among themselves before posting them to the forum as a group. Each time, a different individual from the group posts their analysis. This reduces postings by half for a group of two, 75% for a group of four, and 66% for a group of three. Groups should not be made too large or individuals may lose identity, and students needing extra help may feel lost. Based on our experience, we would suggest a group of two for a class of approximately 24 students, creating 12 group postings. Another possibility is to have multiple forums, i.e., divide the class into several large groups and have one forum for each group. However, this creates redundancy for the instructor, who may have to repeat similar postings in each forum. Multiple forum approach is recommended for large classes, where faculty has graduate assistant support.

While managing the forum, faculty plays several key roles—monitor, facilitator, and advisor. Faculty need to be able to stimulate critical thinking in Web-board discussions, give individualized attention to students who need help, provide timely and thorough feedback for assignments, and engage in ad hoc problem solving. Responsible online instructors are finding that their "cyber hours" far exceed the time they normally spend for regular class and office hours.

Email management is another important issue. Because email is another way (similar to office hours in face-to-face) for students to communicate with faculty, it creates tremendous volume. We noticed that email volume increases at least 20-fold (compared to face-to-face), as many students feel more comfortable asking questions one-on-one rather than posting them on the forum. This may be due to a fear of being ridiculed, a lack of understanding of the subject matter, or just a personal preference. Responding to the large amount of email volume creates physical burdens on the faculty. It is suggested that a clear rule be established on what can or cannot be sent through email.

Following is a summary of the stakeholders' perspectives:

Faculty Perspective
- Forum participation, monitoring, and facilitation
- Changing of content as needed by forum progress
- Assignments, weekly lectures, notes, and readings
- Student assessment
- Email responses
- Disciplinary actions, if needed
- Feedback
    - Forum
    - Exams
    - Assignments
    - Group discussions
    - Group projects

Student Perspective
- Active forum participation
- Access assignments and exams
- Assignment file postings
- Interactions with peers and faculty
- Specific questions through emails

Technical Personnel
- Seamless access
- Maintain course infrastructure
- Advance notice of scheduled maintenance

- Ad hoc maintenance notice
- Online technical help

eAssessment

One of the major goals of a course is to assess student learning. This involves all activities that measure student learning, and ultimately results in a grade for the course. This may involve activities like exams, assignments, papers, forum discussions, Web presentations, Web interviews, and Web demonstrations. In face-to-face classes, the typical assessment tools are in-class exams, oral interviews, and laboratory experiments. However, this is not feasible for WBE, at least not in the same format. Faculty need to develop creative methodologies for testing on the Web. Irrespective of the methodology used, students must understand the evaluation process. This includes what percentage of their grade accounts for what, and how their performance will be considered. As already mentioned, students must be clear about forum participation and the criteria for its measurement. Students must be provided with continuous feedback as to their performance and standing in the class.

Based on our experience, we classify exam assessment sites as Web-based, take home, or on-site. The following eAssessment modes can be used at these sites:

- Web-based
  - Tests
  - Presentations
  - Interviews
  - Demonstrations
- Take home
  - Exams
  - Term papers
  - Case analysis
    - Individual
    - Group
- On-site test with supervision

Web-based assessment could include tests, presentations, demonstrations, and interviews. If at all possible, this is the preferred way, because students want online convenience not only for learning but also for performance assessment. There are many standardized tests and quizzes provided by textbook authors. If these tests are not satisfactory, then faculty (with assistance from technical personnel) could develop their own online tests. Once tests are developed and validated, faculty must set time limits and a time frame for students to take exams. Exams could be taken by students within a week, a few days, or on a specified day at a specified time, say two hours, three hours, and so on. This would be similar to an in-class exam in asynchronous mode without supervision. Web-based testing is advisable for introductory courses like an introduction to information systems, management, accounting systems, etc., where breadth is more important than the depth, and multiple choice could be used for assessment. A Web-based, one-on-one synchronous interview could be conducted in the forum, instant messaging area, or the chat room. Students could also use the Web to present their slides in real time. This, of course, requires synchronous communication and may not be feasible for all students.

Another way of testing students is to use the equivalent of a face-to-face take-home exam. In this form, students can use anything they need. Because online students have access to class-related and all other materials, it makes sense to give an exam that can test a student's understanding beyond the contents of the textbook. These exams, typically, place more emphasis on applications, and are analytical and problem-oriented rather than true and false or multiple choice. Over the years, this type of student assessment has worked extremely well for the author, but it increases the workload for faculty who are not accustomed to grading papers online. For such faculty, it requires making hard copies of exams and assignments, grading them, putting comments back on the online exams, and distributing them to students. This form of assessment is advisable for advanced courses that are analytical in nature, like computer science, engineering, and databases that require an in-depth testing of students in specific areas, when multiple choice exams are not desirable.

In many nonanalytical courses, student assessment could also be based on case analysis, papers, and projects. This form of assessment is suitable for the social sciences and management or similar courses, where an understanding of behavioral and managerial implications is of utmost importance. Again, faculty must feel comfortable with online grading.

The first two testing methods, Web-based and take home, do not guarantee a student's identity. Student validation will only be possible when video streaming becomes feasible. Until then, we have to rely on the honesty and integrity of each student. On-site testing, if available, can be used for validation purposes.

On-site testing is closely related to the face-to-face methodology, it requires test monitors or test sites in a student's local area. In this situation, students would have taken the exam in the presence of monitors at a specified time. This is similar to standardized exams given by LSAT, GMAT, etc., where the testing body has a contract or understanding with local sites to host exams. This is the best way to validate a student's identity but may not be economically feasible if students are dispersed geographically. In such cases, students may be asked to provide a credible local monitor. A signed affidavit by the student and the monitor could be submitted, testifying to the authenticity of the exam. This is appropriate when students have limited accessibility to technology and student identity is desirable.

Following is a summary from the stakeholders' perspectives:

Faculty Perspective
- Define method of assessment
- Clearly communicate method of assessment
- Clarify questions
- Post exam, grade, and distribute result
- Provide feedback
- Post solutions
- Assign a grade

Student Perspective
- Find a monitor, if needed

- Take exam as instructed
- Post exam to forum

Technical Personnel Perspective
- Assist faculty in preparing exam (the mode, not the content)
- Assist students with technical problems
- Inform of any downtime

The final step in WBE is graduation and getting a degree, or eGraduation.

eGraduation

Once all requirements are completed, the student is ready to graduate. A Web-based ceremony could be arranged, where students would be given eDiplomas. Actual diplomas could be mailed by snail mail. Web students, however, should be given the option of coming to the regular graduation ceremony.

FUTURE RESEARCH

In this chapter, some of the questions raised in the first book, *Web-Based Learning & Teaching Technologies: Opportunities and Challenges*, have been answered, but many new ones were raised. In the first book, Professor Shneiderman (2000) noted that "…a third generation book would report on extensive surveys, interviews, observations, log data of computer use, and comparative studies to provide a clearer picture of how learning and teaching are changed by Web-based technologies…." Also, commenting on the above book, Professor Alavi noted, "…The next step is to study effective design and application of web-based learning and teaching environments…." This chapter is an attempt in that direction. It has provided a comprehensive view of Web education based on the author's experiences with WBE. In the chapter, the author concentrates on the virtual nature of education from the perspective of three major stakeholders—faculty, student, and the technical personnel—and identifies the complete process from admission to graduation. However, technology is not static, and WBE is constantly evolving, changing expectations and stakeholders' perspective. For example, as technology improves, multimedia lectures will make ePreparation and eManagement much easier; as video streaming improves, student validation will become straightforward, making on-site testing obsolete.

There are no clear-cut rules or simple solutions, as is evident from the increasing number of schools entering and opting out of WBE. This raises serious doubts about the stability and longevity of WBE. Research is needed to study the viability of WBE. As we move from the "brick-and-mortar" to the "click-and-click" environment, researchers must explore the endless, unanswered questions about the effectiveness and diffusion of WBE, the quality of a virtual diploma, factors in institutionalizing WBE, the viability of WBE, etc. Some of these questions are already being studied (Aggarwal & Legon, 2003; www.alnresearch.org/index.jsp; www.aln.org). Many of these questions, however, are unresolved and will be answered over time as WBE moves into the third phase of education. The pursuit will never be completely finished, because WBE is a "moving target"— as some issues are resolved, new challenges appear.

REFERENCES

Aggarwal, A. K. (2001). Web-based education (WBE) and its diffusion—a panel, Proceedings, *ECIS*, Bled, Slovenia.

Aggarwal, A. K., & Bento, R. (2000). Web-based education. In A. K. Aggarwal (Ed.), *Web-based learning and teaching technologies: opportunities and challenges*. Hershey, PA: Idea Group Publishing.

Aggarwal, A. K., & Legon, R. (2003). Institutionalizing Web based education: a case study, Proceedings of the Hawaii International Conference on System Sciences, *HICSS–36*.

Alavi, M. (2000). Meeting today's educational demands: the Web offers a way, From the bookshelf, *Decision Line*.

Benbunan-Fich, R. (2002, June). Improving education and training with IT, *Communications of the ACM*, 45(6).

Bento, A. (2000). Developing a class session using audio and video streaming. In A. K. Aggarwal (Ed.), *Web-based learning and teaching technologies: opportunities and challenges*. Hershey, PA: Idea Group Publishing.

Boettcher, J. (1998), How many students are just right in a Web course? Retrieved August, 2002 from the World Wide Web, CREN: www.cren.net/~jboettch/number.htm.

Day, G. S. (1981). The product life cycle: analysis and applications issues, *Journal of Marketing*, 45.

Ducker, P. (2001). The next society, *The Economist*.

Halford, B. (2002). Tracking Web's "spiders," *The Baltimore Sun*.

International Data Corporation. (2001, April). ETRENDS, eLearning is burgeoning. Retrieved from the World Wide Web: www.idc.com.

International Data Corporation. (2002, September). While corporate training markets will not live up to earlier forecasts, IDC suggests reasons for optimism, particularly eLearning, Press Release. Retrieved from the World Wide Web: www.idc.com.

Kemery, E. (2000). Developing online collaboration. In A. K. Aggarwal (Ed.), *Web-based learning and teaching technologies: opportunities and challenges*. Hershey, PA: Idea Group Publishing.

Kock, N. (2002). Managing with Web-based IT in mind, *Communications of the ACM*, 45(5).

Learning Center Effectiveness Research. Retrieved from the World Wide Web: http://www.alnresearch.org/index.jsp.

Nasseh, B. (1998). Training and support programs, and faculty's new roles in computer-based distance education in higher education institutions. Retrieved from the World Wide Web: www.bsu.edu/classes/nasseh/study/res98.html.

San Jose Mercury News. (1999). Educators are also retooling for the Internet.

Shneiderman, B. (2000). Foreword. In A. K. Aggarwal (Ed.), *Web-based learning and teaching technologies: opportunities and challenges*. Hershey, PA: Idea Group Publishing.

United Nations Study. (2002, October). Using ICT as a tool for disarmament and nonproliferation education. Retrieved from the World Wide Web: http://daccessods.un.org/doc/.

ENDNOTE

[1]   We will use "forum" to imply all.

Chapter II

A Comprehensive Web-Based Learning Framework: Toward Theoretical Diversity

Esperanza Huerta
Claremont Graduate University, USA and
Instituto Tecnológico Autónomo de México, Mexico

Terry Ryan
Claremont Graduate University, USA

Magid Igbaria
Claremont Graduate University, USA

ABSTRACT

This chapter presents a theoretical framework for understanding the Web-based learning (WBL) phenomenon based on disciplines other than education. First, from the organizational communication field, it proposes media richness and social influence models to understand factors affecting media communication choice in WBL. Second, from the managerial field, it proposes the theory of knowledge reuse to understand the managerial challenges that instructors face when creating knowledge repositories for WBL. Finally, from the information literature perspective, it proposes the information structure framework to assess the adequacy of the information for a particular situation. In reviewing these theoretical perspectives, implications of the proposed framework for research and practice are highlighted.

INTRODUCTION

Web-based learning (WBL) refers to the use of Internet technologies for delivering instruction. To some extent, WBL constitutes a new field, because it brings together a number of previously separate domains that underlie practice in education and technology. While the Internet provides the functionality of previous technologies, including audio, video, and videoconferencing, it also affords new technological possibilities that are likely to transform many aspects of education. Among the facets of education likely to change are the forms of content delivery, the level of interaction between students and instructors, and the roles played by students and instructors. To be able to study WBL effectively, researchers will need to be able to apply the theories and findings of diverse disciplines that have been only poorly related until now. With this requirement in mind, the intent in this chapter is to present a framework that supports WBL researchers by connecting the theoretical foundations provided by the reference disciplines of WBL.

Because WBL is a multifaceted phenomenon, different points of view lead to different impressions of it. As an example, from one perspective, the implementation of WBL is its most important aspect. Given this viewpoint, any instance of WBL implementation is a project. Researchers adopting this perspective need to understand the WBL project's resources, its critical success factors, and other issues associated with project management. From another perspective, the learning that students can achieve through WBL, rather than implementation of WBL, is the most important aspect. From this viewpoint, researchers need to understand the determinants of motivation, as well as the influences of students' cognitive characteristics. Still another perspective on WBL focuses on matters of technology acceptance and human–computer interaction, because WBL requires students to use computers.

Recognizing that theory is needed to understand WBL is not new. There have been a number of efforts to create theoretical frameworks for studying WBL. Miller and Miller (2000) discussed theoretical foundations in the design of WBL. Leflore (2000) presented different theories supporting WBL design. Piccoli, Ahmad, and Ives (2001) developed a comprehensive framework to analyze factors affecting WBL effectiveness. In these works, the theoretical foundations have come, largely, from the education field. In this chapter, a framework for the study of WBL is also developed, but it approaches the task of framework development from a different vantage point.

The perspective assumed in this chapter considers that there are disciplines, not specifically focused on educational settings, that can be useful in understanding the WBL phenomenon. For instance, WBL requires that people communicate with each other through the computer. The field of computer-mediated communication has studied, among other things, factors influencing media use, and has developed theoretical frameworks such as media richness theory (Daft & Lengel, 1986) and the social influence model (Fulk, Schmitz, & Steinfield, 1990). These theories, although not originally developed with WBL in mind, provide insights into media capabilities for it.

To summarize, this chapter proposes a framework for the study of WBL based on theoretical foundations from disciplines other than the education field. To accomplish this objective, first, *learning* theories are reviewed, as previous works on WBL do. Then we move on to theoretical foundations from other disciplines. Drawing on the organizational communication field, in the chapter, the literature on media capacity is reviewed. More specifically, the *media richness* model and the *social influence* model are reviewed. Then, drawing on the management field, particularly the knowledge management area, the theory of *knowledge reuse* is reviewed. Following this, we look into the information literacy literature and explore the *information structure* model. In each part in the chapter, it is pointed out how the proposed field can give insights into the WBL phenomenon. Finally, implications of the proposed framework for research and practice are proposed.

LEARNING THEORIES

As a theoretical foundation for WBL, learning theories display a great deal of diversity. To date, there has been less than perfect agreement about the general categories of learning theory or what to call them. Despite this, it may be that some consensus is emerging. Given that different types of learning theories provide different guidelines for WBL, it is worth identifying the major ones. Miller and Miller (2000) suggested that developers of Web-based instruction choose a theoretical approach, with more emphasis placed on being consistent with the chosen theory than on picking the "correct" theory.

Leidner and Jarvenpaa (1995) defined five fundamental categories of learning theory: objectivism, collaborativism, constructivism, cognitive information processing, and socioculturalism. In objectivist terms, learning involves the transfer of objective knowledge from the instructor to the student. From the collaborativism standpoint, learning requires the emergence of shared understanding by multiple learners engaged in a process of communicating personal experiences. Constructivism views learning as the creation of knowledge by the learner. The cognitive information processing perspective defines learning as the processing and transfer of new knowledge into long-term memory. Socioculturalism describes learning as the interpretation of knowledge in a subjective and individualistic manner. Piccoli et al. (2001) simplify the discussion provided in Leidner and Jarvenpaa (1995) by stating that there are two models of learning, objectivist and constructivist, defined as above. The choice of a model of learning is expected to influence the design of the learning environment.

Leflore (2000) presented three categories of learning theory that support the design of Web-based instruction: Gestalt theory, cognitive theory, and constructivist theory. Gestalt theory specifies that individuals automatically use prior experiences to simplify what they perceive. Cognitive theory stipulates that individuals make use of mental schemas, frameworks, etc., to organize experience. Constructivist theory prescribes that learners should interact with other learners to construct shared meanings in contexts that reflect the real world.

In a comprehensive discussion of learning theories, Wilson and Myers (1999) defined four categories of learning theory: behaviorism, information processing, situated action, and situated cognition. Rather than specifying one best learning theory for instructional design, they identified roles for all four categories. Although they indicated that the situated approaches to learning hold the most promise for integration, they clearly expressed that each theory has value for practicing instructional designers.

The behaviorist perspective defines learning in terms of the acquisition and strengthening of responses. Although dismissed by some as a useful basis for instructional design, behaviorism may have value as a theoretical foundation for particular types of learning environments. Designers of learning environments can be guided by behaviorist principles such as the following:

- Learning by doing (i.e., actively engaging students in tasks)
- Behavioral objectives (i.e., linking instructional goals with assessments)

- Task decomposition (i.e., breaking complex tasks into simpler ones)
- Motivation (i.e., applying reinforcement principles when successes occur)
- Response-sensitive feedback (i.e., informing learners about their errors)
- Transfer (i.e., asking learners to apply skills acquired in other settings)

The information processing perspective sees learning as the development of symbolic mental structures to represent the external world and the self. Instructional design based on information processing focuses on developing the mental structures of beginners so that these structures become similar to those of experts. Designers of learning environments can be guided by information processing principles such as the following:

- Stages of information processing (inputs, access of long-term memory, etc.)
- Memory load (limits of working memory, chunking, repetition, elaboration, etc.)
- Selective perception (filtering, expectations, cognitive structures, etc.)
- Kinds of knowledge (declarative, procedural)
- Skill compilation (practice leading to routinization and automaticity)
- Motivation (through incentives, self-efficacy, goals for learning, etc.)

The situated action and situated cognition perspectives see learning as something that occurs in complex social environments. They differ in whether mental processes occur in the individual area of interest. In situated action, such processes are downplayed as factors; in situated cognition, they remain central to explanation. From the situated action/situated cognition standpoint, the designer of a learning environment is guided by principles such as the following:

- Learning in context: Thinking and learning make sense only within particular situations; there is no such thing as nonsituated learning.
- Communities of practice: People act and construct meaning in communities that serve as repositories and conveyors of meaning, legitimating actions, and constructing and defining discourse practices.
- Learning as active participation: People learn by acting.
- Knowledge in action: Development of knowledge involves continued knowledge-using activity in authentic situations.
- Mediation of artifacts: Cognition depends on artifacts, chiefly language and culture.
- Interactionism: Situations and individuals mutually shape each other.

The situated approaches to learning have received a great deal of attention recently. The situated action position developed from work on the cultural construction of meaning and is well expressed in the work of Lave and Wenger (1991) and Suchman (1993). Proponents of this approach to learning often employ the tools and techniques of anthropology, critical theory, and socioculturalism. The situated cognition position developed somewhat differently among researchers interested in cognition for artificial intelligence research. This viewpoint is well represented by Brown et al. (1989), Clancey (1995), and Norman (1993).

COMPUTER-MEDIATED COMMUNICATION— MEDIA CAPACITY

While theories associated with learning have long been salient in design of instruction, the use of Web technologies suggests that other theories might provide guidance to designers. One area in which designers can use guidance is in the choice of media. The media richness model and the social influence model, both from the field of organizational communication, can serve to identify the factors that affect media choice for WBL. Different from traditional face-to-face instruction, WBL offers new communication means that affect the way instructors and students interact. Understanding the factors influencing media communication choice helps in effectively using communication channels provided by the Internet.

The Internet has made possible new means of synchronous and asynchronous communication. These new communication channels have had an impact, not only on individuals but also on society. In education, with the Internet, the communication channels present in traditional learning settings were extended. In addition, the Internet is considered to be the third generation of communications means for distance learning. In the organizational area, with the Internet, the number of options available for organizational communication increased. The organizational communication field studies the impact of technology on communication in organizational settings. Although research in this area focuses on communication within organizations, its findings provide an insight on communication in educational settings.

In media capacity, a subfield of study within organizational communication, attempts to understand the factors affecting how individuals choose a specific medium to communicate are made. Understanding media capacity for educational settings is important, because, in WBL, communication among students and instructors is computer mediated, rather than face-to-face. Therefore, understanding the strengths and weaknesses of different media and the factors affecting their use is important. Media capacity research employs two primary models: media richness and social influence. Currently, both models are seen as complementary explanations of communication media choice (Webster & Trevino, 1995).

The media richness model (Daft & Lengel, 1986) was developed as a rational explanation of media choice. It postulates that people rationally select a specific medium based on the medium's intrinsic richness. Media richness depends on the speed of feedback, the variety of communication channels employed, the personalness of the source, and the richness of language used. An important implication of this theory is that higher levels of task ambiguity require media with a higher degree of richness. Since it was originally developed, the media richness model has been revised, primarily by adding situational constraints on the rational matching process. Factors such as geographical distance, time pressures, and critical mass of communication have been incorporated (Fulk & Boyd, 1991). Empirical results in tests of media richness theory have been contradictory.

The social influence model (Fulk & Boyd, 1991) states that media perceptions, including media richness, are socially constructed. Social influence theory and media richness theory have been considered by many to be competing theories. Some researchers, however, have argued that the two theories are complementary (Fulk & Boyd, 1991; Webster & Trevino, 1995). Webster and Trevino proposed that social factors, as well as rational factors, are important in media choice, but their relative importance depends on the newness of the medium. They speculated that social factors should be more important for new media than for traditional media. Even though their findings do not support their expectations of the importance of newness of the medium, they support the complementarity of the theories. In addition to social and rational explanations of media choice, Fulk and Boyd (1991) proposed that other factors, such as personal media style, should be included when assessing media choice. They suggested including personal media style as a variable affecting media choice, based on Rice and Case's findings. Rice and Case (1983) found that individuals have media styles that favor certain media regardless of the circumstances.

The contributions from the organizational communication field, in particular, from media choice, to educational settings are important. Even though factors affecting media choice remain issues for debate, instructors must be aware of them. Rational factors, such as richness of the media, and social factors have an impact on the media chosen to communicate. Instructors may leave the students to decide which media to use, or they may assign specific tasks to specific media. For instance, chat and videoconference are synchronous communication means. If an instructor has to decide on which medium to use, he or she has to consider rational and social factors. Videoconference is a richer medium than chat, because the former employs more communication channels. However, social factors, such as the formality of means of communication, should also be taken into account. In addition, practical considerations, such as technical expertise and availability, may also play a role in the decision.

In terms of research, media choice models may serve as a theoretical foundation for the study of factors influencing the effectiveness of instructor–student communication using different communication means. Media choice models may also help in assessing the impact of different communication means on the way students interact among themselves.

KNOWLEDGE MANAGEMENT

In addition to making choices regarding the most appropriate media for instruction, many designers of WBL systems will confront situations in which they must be able to store large amounts of knowledge in support of the learning process. The theory of knowledge reuse can provide insights into the challenges associated with creating knowledge repositories. It can help designers to understand the efforts and managerial problems associated with making large volumes of information available to WBL students. Understanding the problems that arise when creating knowledge repositories for student use helps instructors to more efficiently manage the knowledge reuse process.

Knowledge Management (KM) is the managerial process of identifying and leveraging organizational knowledge with the purpose of generating a competitive advantage (Alavi & Leidner, 2001). It arose as a field in management in the 1990s and has its origins in the resource-based theory of the firm (Alavi, 2000; Alavi & Leidner, 2001; Grover & Davenport, 2001). The resource-based theory of the firm states that competitive advantages come from internal resources that are hard to duplicate. Knowledge is an intangible asset hard to duplicate; it is an internal resource that could provide a competitive advantage to a firm. KM research has concentrated on models of organizational design, development of organizational capabilities, and knowledge flows between organizational units and between organizations (Grover & Davenport, 2001). For an exhaustive review of what has been done in the KM area, refer to Grover and Davenport (2001) and Alavi and Leidner (1999, 2001).

Even though KM focus is organizational, KM research gives an insight into the WBL phenomenon. For instance, Alavi and Leidner (2001) developed a framework for analyzing the role of an information system within the organizational knowledge management processes. Based on previous literature, Alavi and Leidner (2001) detailed four knowledge processes: creation, storage and retrieval, transfer, and application. The same processes can be expected to be important in WBL settings. In a similar way, frameworks and taxonomies, such as knowledge market framework (Davenport & Prusak, 2000; Grover & Davenport, 2001), and knowledge management strategies taxonomy (Earl, 2001), originally developed for organizational settings, could be adapted to WBL settings.

This section of the chapter focuses on the theory of knowledge reuse (Markus, 2001), which emphasizes that the ultimate purpose of KM is to reuse the knowledge created within organizations. Certain forms of knowledge can be stored in databases to be accessed and used later. Databases created for this purpose are usually called knowledge repositories. The creation of knowledge repositories is by far the most common KM initiative in organizational settings (Alavi & Leidner, 1999; Grover & Davenport, 2001).

In educational settings, the Internet is also seen as a communication means for learners to access knowledge repositories. Students may access digital libraries, websites (specifically designed for the class by the teacher or publicly available on the WWW), and knowledge repositories created by the students as part of a collaborative work. The theory of knowledge reuse provides insights into the challenges that these repositories pose to the producers and reusers of knowledge.

The theory of knowledge reuse proposes a typology of knowledge reuse situations based on the producer, the reuser, and the purpose. The typology distinguishes producers and reusers of knowledge, because most managerial challenges arise from the differences in knowledge between the producers and the reusers. This difference in knowledge is called knowledge distance. Knowledge distance is measured in terms of the knowledge shared between producers and reusers (Markus, 2001). Therefore, the managerial challenges of a knowledge repository created by researchers to be used by researchers (similar shared knowledge) are different from those of a knowledge repository created by instructors to be used by students (different shared knowledge).

Also, the theory of knowledge reuse makes us aware of the problems on creating knowledge repositories. "Repositories created by one group for one purpose are unlikely to be successfully reused by other groups for different purposes without considerable rework or other kinds of intervention" (Markus, 2001, p. 88). For instance, instructors may upload their notes into a website for students to access them. However, this information may not be useful for students, because knowledge distance might be large. Therefore, for the notes to be useful for the students, the instructors might need to invest a great deal of effort to transform the notes in order to meet students' needs. This could be a big challenge unless the instructors had sufficient motivation and resources to produce high-quality repositories (Markus, 2001).

The great deal of effort required to create knowledge repositories has led to an emphasis on the role of facilitators or intermediaries. Intermediaries modify knowledge content created by knowledge producers and transform it into a form that is useful for knowledge reusers. Activities done by intermediaries are abstracting, indexing, authoring, sanitizing, filtering, and pruning outdated content. This implies that institutions implementing WBL must specify the role of the instructors. Instructors may be knowledge producers only, and intermediaries may be required to transform the content for knowledge repositories. On the other hand, instructors may play both roles, serving as knowledge producers and intermediaries. In this case, issues such as incentives and resources required to create high-quality repositories should be taken into account.

In terms of research, the theory of knowledge reuse can be used as a theoretical foundation to explore knowledge repositories in WBL. It is a question for further research whether the types of knowledge repositories considered in the theory of knowledge reuse apply to WBL settings. Perhaps new types of knowledge repositories will be identified. In a similar way, whether critical success factors for the creation of knowledge repositories found in organizational settings apply to WBL settings is a question for further research.

INFORMATION LITERACY AND INFORMATION OVERLOAD

Along with being prepared to choose the appropriate media and provide access to appropriate bodies of knowledge, instructional designers must know how to minimize the potential for information overload faced by students in WBL situations. The information structure framework (ISF) can serve as an aid to evaluate information and to avoid the information overload problem that students may experience when dealing with a great deal of information. WBL provides students with access to information that needs to be critically evaluated. Understanding the criteria to assess information helps students to deal with large amounts of information, avoiding information overload.

Information literacy is a concept that has been explored in different fields. Mutch (1997) analyzed how information systems, management, and library studies fields define information literacy and called for a redefinition of the term. Bruce (1997) distinguished between information literacy and similar terms, such as information technology literacy and computer literacy. According to the American Library Association, information literacy is the ability "to recognize when information is needed and have the ability to locate, evaluate, and use effectively the needed information" (Mutch, 1997, p. 380). Even though information literacy is not a new concept, it has caught the attention of different fields due to, among other things, its relationship with the information overload phenomenon.

Information overload refers to the point where there is so much information that it is no longer possible to use it effectively (Edmunds & Morris, 2000). Some people argue that information overload has been exacerbated due to technological advances, mainly the Internet, that enable access to a great deal of information (Edmunds & Morris, 2000). The access to unlimited amounts of information, which is seen as one of the greatest strengths of the Internet, is also a great challenge for human information processing. Information overload negatively impacts the decision-making process, leading to low quality in decision making and low complexity of output (Grisé & Gallupe, 1999/2000; Hwang & Lin, 1999). Being information literate reduces the possibility of being overwhelmed by information (Edmunds & Morris, 2000). For a recent and detailed literature review on the problem of information overload in organizations, refer to Edmunds and Morris (2000). For a review on theoretical perspectives and research on information literacy, refer to Bruce (2000).

Königer and Jonowitz (1995) offered a different point of view. They argued that information overload is not due to the amount of information but to the lack of structure in it. That is to say, a person can have a lot of information, but if it cannot be accessed as needed, then the information is useless. Large amounts of information can be used if it is organized; therefore, the value of information depends on its structure. For instance, students using the Internet have access to almost unlimited amounts of information. Using a search engine and a keyword, students can retrieve links to numerous websites. However, for many Web

Table 1: Implications for Practice and Research of Theories from Related Disciplines

	Implications for Practice	Implications for Research
Media Richness and Social Influence	• Higher levels of task ambiguity can benefit from using media with higher richness level. When presenting to students information that may be ambiguous, having video clips to download (one-way communication) or holding a videoconference (two-way communication) may help to solve ambiguities more than written communication. • Individuals have media styles that make them favor a specific media regardless of the circumstances. Instructors should be aware of these preferences and make available, if possible, a great variety of communication media to accommodate all media styles.	• Media choice models can be used to assess the impact that different communication means have on communication effectiveness.
Theory of Knowledge Reuse	• Knowledge distance between students and instructors might be large. Therefore, knowledge repositories for students must be created with students' needs in mind. • Intermediaries or facilitators may be required for creating knowledge repositories. If instructors assume the role of facilitators, then necessary incentives and resources should be allocated.	• The theory of knowledge reuse proposes a typology of knowledge repositories developed from knowledge repositories used in organizational settings. Future research can investigate whether this typology applies to educational settings. • Future research may identify whether critical success factors for the creation of knowledge repositories found in organizational settings apply to WBL settings.
Information Structure Framework	• Students should be taught to deal with large amounts of information. Applying an information profile reduces the complexity and increases the accessibility of the information. • Students should develop skills to critically assess the information they get and not accept it blindly.	• The validity of the Information Structure Framework can be tested for different types of communication means and information.

searches, just reviewing each website would take a lot of time, and the result of the review might be only that the search provided no relevant information. In this context, students may know where to search for information, but they still need to evaluate it. The ISF proposes an explanation of how information is evaluated.

The ISF (Königer & Jonowitz, 1995) proposes four information classification criteria that may serve to explain how students and others evaluate information: selection, time, hierarchy, and sequence. According to Königer and Jonowitz, all information can be described in terms of these criteria. They call such a description an information profile. They state that culturally shared structuring mechanisms for evaluating information exist, and that these are based, to some extent, on the physical sensation of the information. For instance, the quality of the paper and the layout give clues about the information carried. However, digital information disconnects the physical sensation, dissolving and challenging the traditional information structure. All people face this challenge, but it might be more challenging to students who may lack the experience of critically evaluating the information. For instance, Smith-Gratto (2000) described how her students believed there were cows living in trees, because a website displayed that information in what looked like "scientific language."

Originally developed for organizational settings, the ISF might also be useful in educational settings. It could help students to be more aware of the need to assess the information they get and not to accept it blindly. In addition, it provides students with clear elements for creating an information profile. Students could use the ISF to classify incoming information, therefore, reducing its complexity and increasing its accessibility. Being able to classify incoming information supports the evaluation process that is part of the definition of information literacy.

From the research point of view, the ISF suggests that different elements of an information profile can be important. The validity of the ISF can be tested for different types of communication means and information. The ISF can also be used to observe whether literate people are able to identify different elements from those that illiterate people identify. This could be particularly useful for instructors aiming to develop students' skill for assessing the information critically.

The foregoing discussion makes clear how theories such as Media Richness/Social Influence, Knowledge Reuse, and Information Structure Framework can inform research into Web-based learning. In addition to potential contributions to research, these theories have possible value to practitioners. They can provide practitioners with general guidelines for practice. While the best guidelines ultimately would derive from specific findings from better-targeted applied research, general guidelines are likely to be valuable in the interim. In Table 1, the potential contributions of the theories discussed above to the understanding of Web-based learning by practitioners, as well as researchers, are summarized.

CONCLUSION

In this chapter, a framework for the study of WBL from the perspective of three disciplines is proposed. First, from the organizational communication field, media richness and social influence models are proposed to understand factors affecting media communication choice in WBL. Second, from the managerial field, the theory of knowledge reuse is proposed to understand the managerial challenges that instructors face when creating knowledge repositories for WBL. Finally, from the information literature perspective, the information structure framework to assess the adequacy of the information for a particular situation is proposed. The critical evaluation of information is important to avoid information overload; a phenomenon that WBL students might experience due to the large amounts of information available through the Internet.

Even though WBL is mainly an educational phenomenon, it has many facets that can be analyzed from the perspectives of other fields. This broader perspective enriches the theoretical foundations that can be used to do research on WBL. It also takes the advantage of applying to WBL the results found in different fields. However, because these theories were not developed specifically for WBL, the extent to which they can apply is still to be determined.

REFERENCES

Alavi, M. (2000). Managing organizational knowledge. In R. W. Zmud (Ed.), *Framing the domains of IT management* (pp. 15–28). Cincinnati, OH: Pinnaflex Education Resources.

Alavi, M., & Leidner, D. E. (1999). Knowledge management systems: issues, challenges, and benefits. *Communications of the Association for Information Systems, 1*(7), 1–37.

Alavi, M., & Leidner, D. E. (2001). Knowledge management and knowledge management systems: conceptual foundations and research issues. *MIS Quarterly, 25*(1), 107–136.

Brown, J. S., Collins, A., & Duguid, P. (1989). Situated cognition and the culture of learning, *Educational Researcher* (18:1), 32–42.

Bruce, C. (1997). *The seven faces of information literacy*. Adelaide: Auslib Press.

Clancey, W. J. (1995). A tutorial on situated learning. In J. Self (Ed.), *Proceedings of the International Conference on Computers and Education (Taiwan)*, Charlottesville, VA: AACE.

Daft, R. L., & Lengel, R. H. (1986). Organizational information requirements, media richness and structural design. *Management Science, 32*(5), 554–571.

Davenport, T. H., & Prusak, L. (2000). *Working knowledge: how organizations manage what they know*. Boston, MA: Harvard Business School Press.

Earl, M. (2001). Knowledge management strategies: toward a taxonomy. *Journal of Management Information Systems, 18*(1), 215–233.

Edmunds, A., & Morris, A. (2000). The problem of information overload in business organisations: a review of the literature. *International Journal of Information Management, 20*(1), 17–28.

Fulk, J., & Boyd, B. (1991). Emerging theories of communication in organizations. *Journal of Management, 17*(2), 407–446.

Fulk, J., Schmitz, J., & Steinfield, C. W. (1990). A social influence model of technology use. In J. Fulk (Ed.), *Organizations and Communication Technology* (pp. 117–140). Newbury Park, CA: Sage Publications.

Grisé, M.L., & Gallupe, R. B. (1999/2000). Information overload: addressing the productivity paradox in face-to-face electronic meetings. *Journal of Management Information Systems, 16*(3), 157–185.

Grover, V., & Davenport, T. H. (2001). General perspectives on knowledge management: fostering a research agenda. *Journal of Management Information Systems, 18*(1), 5–21.

Hwang, M. I., & Lin, J. W. (1999). Information dimension, information overload and decision quality. *Journal of Information Science, 25*(3), 213–218.

Königer, P., & Janowitz, K. (1995). Drowing in information, but thirsty for knowledge. *International Journal of Information Management, 15*(1), 5–16.

Lave, J., & Wenger, E. (1991). *Situated learning: legitimate peripheral participation*. New York: Cambridge University Press.

Leflore, D. (2000). Theory supporting design guidelines for Web-based instruction. In B. Abbey (Ed.), *Instructional and cognitive impacts of Web-based education*. Hershey, PA: Idea Group Publishing.

Leidner, D. E., & Jarvenpaa, S. L. (1995). The use of information technology to enhance management school education: a theoretical view, *MIS Quarterly* (19:5), 265–291.

Markus, M. L. (2001). Toward a theory of knowledge reuse: types of knowledge reuse situations and factors in reuse success. *Journal of Management Information Systems, 18*(1), 57–93.

Miller, S. M., & Miller, K. L. (2000). Theoretical and practical considerations in the design of Web-based instruction. In B. Abbey (Ed.), *Instructional and cognitive impacts of Web-based education*. Hershey, PA: Idea Group Publishing.

Mutch, A. (1997). Information literacy: an exploration. *International Journal of Information Management, 17*(5), 377–386.

Norman, D. A. (1993). Cognition in the head and in the world: an introduction to the special issue on situated action, *Cognitive Science* (17:1), 1–6.

Piccoli, G., Ahmad, R., & Ives, B. (2001). Web-based learning environments: a research framework and a preliminary assessment of effectiveness in basic IT skills training, *MIS Quarterly* (25:4), 401–426.

Rice, R. E., & Case, D. (1983). Electronic message systems in the university: a brief description of use and utility. *Journal of Communication, 33*, 131–152.

Suchman, L. S. (1993). Response to Vera and Simon's situated action: a symbolic interpretation, *Cognitive Science*, (17:1), 71–75.

Webster, J., & Trevino, L. K. (1995). Rational and social theories as complementary explanations of communication media choices: two policy-capturing studies. *Academy of Management Journal, 38*(6), 1544–1572.

Wilson, B. G., & Myers, K. M. (1999). Situated cognition in theoretical and practical context. In D. H. Jonassen & S. M. Land (Eds.), *Theoretical foundations of learning environments*, Mahwah, NJ: Lawrence Erlbaum Associates, Inc.

Chapter III

New Issues Arising from E-Education

Johanna Klassen
City University of Hong Kong, Hong Kong

Doug Vogel
City University of Hong Kong, Hong Kong

ABSTRACT

The Internet provides access to an unlimited wealth of resources, such as virtual libraries, databases, and electronic communities. In e-education, the World Wide Web and the Internet are the vehicles for information dissemination and retrieval, and also for networking and collaboration. Computer technology is thus broadening choices for the mode of delivery, content, and access, because information can be stored anywhere and transmitted anywhere. There is the danger that the tools of technology are used because they are the latest phenomenon. In this chapter, the focus is on sound pillars of ethics for the mass production of education. We deal first with knowledge processing and the implications for various changes that have arisen in e-education. We discuss ethical issues regarding student–student and student–faculty interaction. We then discuss assessment of learning and the potential problems and possible solutions. Finally, we address institutional management of e-education.

BACKGROUND

The Internet is a worldwide computer network that enables communication among millions of users from around the world. It also provides access to an unlimited wealth of resources such as virtual libraries, databases, and electronic communities. Additionally, it enables electronic communication and collaboration among individuals and organizations to enable e-commerce. In e-education, the World Wide Web and the Internet are the vehicles for information dissemination and retrieval, and also for networking and collaboration (Horvath & Teles, 1999). Whatever term is used—networked learning or e-education or virtual learning or computer-mediated education—this new approach to teaching and learning is challenging the traditional mode of operation for universities. In online learning environments, information no longer emanates from the "throne" of respected academics, in a one-to-one mode of transmitting knowledge, but in this mode, there is a rapid move to a one-to-many mode, where faculty become facilitators of learning (Watts, 1998). Computer technology is thus broadening choices for the mode of delivery, content, and access, because information can be stored anywhere and transmitted anywhere.

Because of the vast amount of information (volume of traffic) available and high-capacity communication links (high speed), the Internet is often referred to as the Information Superhighway. However, this highway still has few guidelines, let alone rules. Gilbert (1996), in comparing the Internet to a library, said: "It's something like a library already overflowing with books, with more arriving all the time, but there's nothing like an Internet Dewey decimal system yet to help you find what you need. It's becoming a librarian's nightmare—or paradise, depending on how you look at it." There is the danger that the tools of technology are used because they are the latest phenomenon. Although these tools of technology can be extremely valuable, Watts (1998) warned that "tools are tools, and just that." Without sound pedagogical principles guiding the use of these tools, we will "fail miserably in our mission to educate." What is needed is a sound pillar of ethics for the mass production of education.

Collins dictionary defined ethics as "moral beliefs and rules about right and wrong that influences the behavior attitudes and philosophy of life of a group of people." There are no universal ethical principles that can apply to every culture, and least of all, to education in all cultures. In general, there have been few guidelines for ethical decision making in education. In fact, ethical issues arising from educational networked learning are a phenomenon only of the last 10 years. We have been catapulted into this revolutionary fast-track of integrating technology into teaching, often without taking a critical look at the ethics surrounding it. An example of traditional ethical beliefs about education is that information is transferred from a specialist to a learner. Seen from specialists' point of view, they have control over the curriculum, the depth of understanding delved into, and the mode of presentation. Similarly, learners believe they have the right to expect a lecture in a one-way format. Learning is thus transferred from one to another. E-education challenges these ethical positions and poses new issues for discussion. It poses questions as to how knowledge should be processed, the demands of the new delivery system, how outcomes are assessed, the right of what is learned, and who has the right to such knowledge.

In this chapter, we look at ethical issues related to networked learning. We deal first with knowledge processing and the implications for various changes that have arisen in e-education. We discuss issues regarding student–student interaction, as well as student–faculty interaction. We then discuss matters related to assessment of learning and the potential problems and possible solutions for assessing such learning without face-to-face contact. Finally, we address institutional management of e-education.

KNOWLEDGE PROCESSING

Inherent in our traditional view of education, there is the belief that information is delivered by face-to-face human contact. This certainly was true until the printing press, television, and video came along. Until recently, it was felt that texts could be read and video/

film could be listened to, but these forms were considered second best without face-to-face contact. A drastic change has come with e-education. There are a number of ethical issues that arise from the context of virtual learning that affect students and faculty.

Faculty: Change of Faculty Role

New Skill of Facilitation

In e-education, there is a distinct role change from lecturer to facilitator. Do we have the right to ask faculty to make such a change? Many faculty members feel there is inadequate research to show that e-learning works. Until there is conclusive evidence showing statistical significance, why should they be coerced into using a new approach? They prefer to remain with what has been done for centuries. They are afraid of the "loss of performance" in the lecture theater, afraid that the video screen will not allow for the same level of inspiration that is felt in a live performance.

Facilitation requires a new set of skills. Instead of a one-way transfer of information, there is a focus on collaboration. Faculty can now create an environment with the use of technology, sometimes referred to as electronic or learning communities (Watts, 1998). This may involve using Groupware tools that allow participants to contribute text asynchronously or synchronously; chatrooms that allow for video or audio transmission, live or delayed, which can be used in the form of a debate or forum; and bulletin boards that allow faculty or students to introduce topics. These new modes of communication drastically change the role of faculty. Not only are they still required to have an understanding of the content of their specialty, but the interpersonal skills of faculty become much more important, because faculty are no longer the only source of information. As participants are respected for their contributions, faculty need to hone their facilitating or communication skills, including active listening, asking questions, adding comments for clarification, and summarizing (Sanders, 2000).

Development and Delivery of Materials

Few academics have any conceptual framework for decision making in the use of technology. If technology tools are embraced without a sound pedagogical basis for use, there is the lack of an overarching sense of support for technology. Faculty need to have assistance from an instructional designer to gain understanding of the pedagogical principles of effective course design and implementation; they need to have training in the tools that will maximize the potential of technology so they can integrate it into their courses. For example, faculty need hands-on training in various tools to encourage collaboration among students and faculty; they need pedagogical assistance from an instructional designer to gain an understanding of the benefits of specific tools, they need training in selecting the appropriate technology based on student needs and syllabi; and they need help in integrating it into the curriculum. This type of training requires support by specialists who understand pedagogy and technology, and it should become an institutional administrative responsibility.

Course design also needs to cater to diverse populations. There is a need for sensitivity to multiple ethical systems or to be ethically neutral. It is no longer appropriate to cater only to a single ethical system. This has ramifications for the delivery of material. It takes longer to prepare materials that are relevant to various cultures. In videoconferencing and audioconferencing, cultural differences become apparent. These differences need to be respected and addressed. Groupware tools, such as Lotus Notes or E-Room or GroupSystems, allow for anonymous comments to be entered. Some cultures have different tolerance levels for what is acceptable for public consumption. Faculty need to be sensitive to the needs of participants from around the world to intervene at appropriate times.

Converting materials to a multimedia format is time consuming. For example, if hypertexts are used, time will be spent searching through the material to highlight the appropriate places to insert the links. And, care must be taken to include the appropriate number of links. Too many hyperlinks can lead to confusion and uncertainty in navigation (Allen, 1997).

Delivery of the materials is even more time consuming, as networked learning requires substantial technical skills. For example, for two classes hooked up to videoconferencing, the faculty member or assistant needs to be familiar with setting up this process or have technical support to do so. Additionally, the planning and preparation time required is substantial. It is not as easy to ad lib when things go wrong. So, refined time management skills are essential.

Technology needs to be driven by appropriate educational and design considerations, not vice versa. Just converting text to html format is not enough. There is the need for a sound educational pedagogical base for integrating technology into the curriculum. For example, choosing when to incorporate student interaction or student collaboration on projects needs to be carefully planned. If e-education is not grounded in sound educational pedagogy, faculty will fail to meet the challenge of encouraging lifelong learning skills.

Students: New Challenges

New Delivery Systems

For students, an e-education makes it possible to manage a job and studies at the same time. Participants can access programs asynchronously; they are no longer required to come to a specific location at the same time. Although location-based classes have advantages, the freedom from place- and time-bound classes opens new vistas for students. With the networked learning approach, students are exposed to multiple systems and perspectives, as opposed to the one-system-fits-all paradigm. Their learning horizons are expanded, as they are introduced to new systems and then learn to integrate them. Direct, convenient access to primary materials allows students to pursue topics at a much deeper level than before (Eisenberg, 1998). Instead of waiting for books that are on loan, access to information is almost instantaneous. This allows for greater development of ideas.

Ease of Plagiarism

The Web offers students strong temptations to cheat in writing papers. There is "Help" available for students who are too lazy or fear writing papers. Term paper auction sites help students to financially sell their best papers. Students need to understand and withstand the temptations that the Web enables. Online text can easily be copied and pasted to an assignment paper. Dragging and dropping from sources already on the Web is easy and appears to be anonymous, that is, no one need know. This can result in students gaining no experience in writing papers. Their skills deteriorate, and little new skills are learned. Although some electronic journals are minimizing plagiarism through the use of Acrobat pdf files, it is still much easier for students to plagiarize. One solution is for faculty to send student papers to a website (http//:www.plagiarism.org) that will indicate the amount of plagiarism from the Web.

Loss and Gain of Study Skills

Although there are new skills learned, especially when students are working with Internet technology, there is also a loss of some skills. As mentioned, writing skills are affected. And, how does online learning affect research and reading skills? Computers have drastically changed today's students' approaches to studying. Table 1 shows the competencies and skills that students need today.

When students are using the Web as a source of information, there are entirely new skills in which they need to be competent. Not only do they need to be familiar with the advantages of various Web browsers (such as altavista, infoseek, webcrawler, metafind, and hotbot), but they also need to develop strategies for navigating the Web and for evaluating the validity of information acquired from sites. An excellent website for guiding students in evaluating websites and information is http://www.sosig.ac.uk/desire/Internet-detective.html.

Students also need to prioritize information that is relevant to their topic. With the vast amount of information available, this is a much needed but often neglected skill to learn. It is easy to become sidetracked by all the seemingly important links to further information.

Although students have always needed to evaluate sources of information from libraries, evaluating the trustworthiness of sources is more complicated. There is more need today for students to "determine content integrity" (Wertheimer & Zinga, 1998). As the authors conclude, assignments of students today look "professional and well crafted," but appearance does not ensure quality of content. Students may also read papers on the Web that have no sources. They often do not know what is a quote and what is a paraphrase. Students also find difficulty in citing Web sources. For example, although a journal that an article is taken from may be given, the page numbers are often left out.

Further, students need to synthesize the collection of information into a coherent and meaningful whole. Knowledge is synthesized through a network of ideas, data sources, information, and interpretation that is interconnected through sustainable exchange (Hawkins, 1993). If students are able to work through and collect related data, providing examples for their main ideas, and give credit where credit is due, the experience can be meaningful.

A timesaving device for students is e-referencing, which provides a writer with a database of all references used in a paper. For example, if all references have been typed into

Table 1: Tools and Skills Required for Virtual Learning

Previous Tools and Skills	Tools Available Today	Skills Required Today
Card catalog and Encyclopedia index	WWW browser, online and CD-ROM databases	Key word searching, evaluating sources, navigating
Books and journal articles	Full-text e-journals	Prioritizing information for relevance, evaluating accuracy, evaluating sources
Handwriting or typewriter	Word-processing packages	Keyboarding, cutting, pasting, and synthesizing information
Dictionary	e-Spell checker, e-dictionary	Setting American/British spellings
Thesaurus	e-Thesaurus	Selecting most appropriate words
Grammar books	e-Grammar checker	Agreeing/disagreeing with checker
Style manuals	e-Referencing, bibliographic software; e.g., Endnote, Procite, e-style indexing	Keeping a database of references, formatting bibliographies, adding key words, reformatting in different styles (e.g., MLA, APA), creating an auto index

the package "End Notes," it allows for automatic formatting of references quoted in a paper. It also has many features, such as adding key words and searching for fields that have been entered. Although it may be time consuming to enter references into the database, it can be used for future papers, with additional references simply added to the base. It is also possible to link to e-libraries around the world and incorporate these into a student's database. This can save many hours searching and typing.

Students are definitely reading fewer books today. If the reading of books or journal articles is reduced, but reading in a virtual library is increased, is this an advantage or disadvantage? The present researchers believe that it is not the type of text or the type of navigation that inhibits or enhances learning; rather, it is the quality of the text content that makes a difference.

If reading is no longer sequential but linked from one hyperlink to another, does that reduce the overall learning? What are the consequences of using hyperlinks? Working in cyberspace is a complex affair. With the possibility of many hyperlinks, it requires maturity and technological prowess to keep from getting lost in cyberspace. Without sequential learning, will students miss important chunks of information? By surfing the net, will they lose by no longer following a disciplined linear syllabus? It is possible to see both sides of the argument. Navigation between hyperlinked nodes of information may slow learning if there is a lack of learning objectives; however, the experience of surfing the Web, of gaining vast amounts of information, and of learning to navigate effectively can be a rich experience. Horvath and Teles (1999) believed that although the possibility of "getting lost in cyberspace" is high, the overall impact of the technology is positive. Woolley (1993) summarized the dilemma: "Interaction with a computer can be characterized as a great learning opportunity, a process that encourages self-exploration and self-expression, and as a tool that forges new links between differently defined communities. And it can also be characterized as an isolating experience, a bewildering brush with unstructured and unregulated information, and as an exercise in solipsistic self-absorption."

Optional Class Attendance

When all class notes are on the Web, accessible even before classes are held, there is less compulsion for students to attend lectures. Additionally, students are often able to buy or otherwise obtain lecture notes from classmates. The class notes may have been sent to a professional site that provides notes organized in a better fashion, and in an enhanced format, such as using Mind Manager to provide a summary of the class. The Mind Manager package uses colors and arrows and visuals to depict main points and subpoints. If students can purchase superior quality notes, it may appear superfluous to them to attend classes. On the other hand, mere lecture attendance accompanied by mostly daydreaming does not guarantee learning either.

INTERACTION
Teacher–Student Contact, Student–Student Contact, and Motivation for Learning

From the constructivist perspective, learning occurs by the individual learner interacting with knowledge rather than from processing information received from an external source

(Forcier, 1996; Roblyer, Edwards, & Havriluk, 1997). So, the process comes about through individual involvement in the construction of meaning. Does this mean that the teacher is no longer required to be the fountain of knowledge? Are students able to learn effectively without face-to-face contact?

Chickering and Ehrmann (1994) proposed that with new technologies, "learning is enhanced when it is more like a team effort than a solo race. Good learning, like good work is collaborative and social, not competitive and isolated." A number of studies have shown that if students are working in pairs or collaboratively using information technology, they are less likely to be distracted and more likely to stay engaged in a task, and as a result, spend a longer time on task and to become more effective (Brush, 1997; Chen, 1997; Novak et al., 1999).

With the interaction capabilities of information technology (IT), students can be even more motivated to learn in the networked learning environment. Shy students, who are afraid to speak in class or visit a professor in his office, feel more confident contributing comments online. They find electronic communication less threatening, because they have time to think before they write, in contrast to the pressure of speaking in class. They feel liberated by the anonymity of working online. They also feel that they are more in control when they can browse a topic. They are learning about topics that interest them or finding information about areas in which they lack information. Najjar (1996) substantiated this view by suggesting that students can move on to new areas when they are ready and do not get bored because of being presented materials they already know. With the possibility of merely filling in gaps of missing information, students feel more motivated to learn.

Communication technologies can even increase the amount of communication between faculty and students. There are a number of studies substantiating this claim (Oblinger & Rush, 1997; Tuller, 1997). As Chickering and Ehrman (1994) pointed out, traditional communication between faculty and students is through assignments, a "rather impoverished form of communication." This common time delay is no longer necessary. "Now, however, electronic mail, computer conferencing, and the World Wide Web increase opportunities for students and faculty to converse and exchange work much more speedily than before, and more thoughtfully and 'safely' than when confronting each other in a classroom or faculty office."

The Social Dimension in E-Learning

There is the concern that online delivery of courses will lead to an overall "dilution" of the university experience. Socially, students may suffer from lack of interaction with their peers, they may feel isolated, and they may not learn the important skill of working in teams (Furnell et al., 1999). The present researchers agree with Stone (1992, 1993), who saw the advantages of the electronic community as overcoming the potential social limitations. Students can work together in "a computer cluster." We cannot deny that the social aspect of online learning is changing the experience of students, but the advantages may be equally satisfying. For example, connections with people, though virtual, may actually increase, as they discover new communities with shared interests that were previously inaccessible to them. Students also learn to break down cultural barriers when they have contact with students from around the world. Working together in teams means working through difficult communication problems until they arrive at a workable solution (Vogel et al., 2000).

Is networked learning for everyone? Networked learning is clearly different from face-to-face contact. The lack of human contact may affect some students more than others, that is, some may lack the motivation to see through assignments and projects without the human contact to which they are used to responding. Sanders (2000) proposed a combination of networked and traditional learning, but believed the "requisite amount of face-to-face contact" for an Internet-delivered program needs to be addressed individually.

Many researchers believe that Internet and networked learning is more suitable for graduate students, especially the more mature students who have jobs and would like to continue studies part-time. They have had the experience of traditional lectures and traditional communication with faculty and students, and are motivated enough to continue without constant face-to-face contact.

Privacy Issues

The anonymity of the Web offers new opportunities for students to assume virtual identities, quite distinct from real identities. Most people tend to be more responsible when the consequences to actions are clearly attached to them. On the Web, especially on Chat programs, students can distance themselves from their deeds: old personalities and limitations can be left behind, and a new sense of identity can be developed. Shy students can become outgoing, and the ugly are described as beautiful.

There are pros and cons as to what may be seen by some as lack of integrity in sharing true thoughts and experiences. The present researchers believe that these online communication skills probably reflect behavior in a real setting. There are fake relationships fostered at every social gathering. Through various experiences, most people learn to develop their real personality.

KNOWLEDGE ASSESSMENT

At the same time that the shift to e-education has been taking place, there has also been a shift resulting in students taking control of and taking responsibility for their own learning. Many universities have made great strides toward such student-centered learning. But what is lacking in this transformative shift is research devoted to the area of assessment. While the teaching and learning paradigm has shifted from teacher dependency to learner independence, from traditional learning to distributed learning, little has been done to evaluate alternative forms of assessment, assessment appropriate for networked learning.

While the traditional mode of assessment by pen and paper has been carried out in a strict time- and place-bound environment, in virtual learning universities, it is no longer possible for students from around the world to come to the same place. The concern of academics is whether in a distance program the registered person is sitting the exam. A possible solution is fingerprint registration, but not all learning environments will be set up with this capability. Ultimately, we need to address the issue of whether knowledge can be assessed without face-to-face contact.

The Use of Tools of Technology to Assess Learning

There are several new approaches using technology that academics can employ in their assessment operation, only three of which will be mentioned: Computer Adapted Testing (CAT), Open Resource Exams, and portfolio assessment.

Computer Adapted Testing

CAT has been especially useful in testing language learning. In a nutshell, CAT uses a calibrated database of questions for testing. Using a process similar to an oral tester, CAT attempts to adjust to the user's level of proficiency. As Wainer (1990) suggested, "...if an examiner asked a question that turned out to be too difficult for the examinee, the next question asked would be considerably easier." The testing program adapts to an individual's ability, finding the difficulty level that is appropriate for the learner within a short time. This means that questions that are too difficult for a learner and may lead to frustration are not repeated. Conversely, those questions that are too easy for a learner and may result in boredom are skipped.

An example of such a procedure is the following. The computer first chooses an average level of difficulty for the learner. If the learner answers the first question correctly, the computer chooses a more difficult question from the item bank. If the learner answers four questions correctly, for example, at the same difficulty level (Meunier, 1994), the learner is brought to the next level. Depending on the item calibration, this is repeated until the questions become too difficult and a "specified stopping rule" is satisfied (Sands et al., 1997). At this point, the test ends, and a suitable mark is suggested. In the same manner, if the learner incorrectly answers the first question, the item bank chooses a less difficult question, and the cycle continues.

According to Sands et al. (1997), Meunier (1994), Larson and Madsen (1985), and Tung (1986), there are advantages and disadvantages of using CAT; however, the advantages seemingly outweigh the disadvantages. The greatest commonly accepted advantage that these authors cite is the tailored effect for the individual, resulting in a challenging test and direction to an appropriate level. Another advantage is the speed of taking the test. Madsen (1991) reported that over 80% of learners required fewer than 50% of the items normally required in an equivalent pen and paper test; that is, the length and duration of the test were reduced. Further, the immediate feedback for learners instead of waiting sometimes for a week or longer for results from their instructor is a decided advantage. Additionally, test security is enhanced, because the questions are randomly accessed, and no students have the same test. According to Sands et al. (1997), an important administrative advantage is the greater standardization of scoring. There are fewer possibilities of clerical or marker errors than with hand-scoring. The authors' studies also reveal that learners clearly prefer using CAT to being tested in the traditional pen and paper method.

Although this approach is clearly a time-saver for faculty in terms of marking, it is questionable whether a student has adequate opportunity to "sell his wares." The program is limited to a specific number of questions at a level (for example, three or four questions), and if the student does not know this content well, he moves to a lower level. Although each topic is evaluated separately, the student may have answered a few details incorrectly but was not asked about the details the student knew. Contemporary researchers believe it is questionable whether this type of objective-based testing promotes lifelong learning.

Open Resource Exams

There is a trend in all education today, but especially in e-education, toward facilitating lifelong learning skills. Specifically in assessment, we are moving away from objective-based tests. Memorization of facts is seen of lesser importance and brings up the issue of whether exams are even necessary. In the real world, few specialists are required to have all the facts in their working memory; rather, they have access to books, files, online information, etc., for details. It appears realistic then to place students in the same situation: solving problems with resources, both hard and soft copies, available to them.

Electronic Portfolio Assessment

The e-portfolio assessment allows students to display a body of work in a virtual folder. They are able to chart their work throughout a time period and highlight specific achievements. The particular advantage is that it shows the development phases of the learning of the student. It is much more individualized and encourages students to show their best work, because it allows them to work in their preferred learning style and allows them to demonstrate the knowledge that they felt was crucial to their learning.

What is of utmost importance is the assessment criteria for standardization. Without clear specifications, students will not know the basis for assessment. With appropriate criteria, the portfolio assessment gives evidence of the ability of students to analyze and synthesize information. Portfolios are, however, time consuming for faculty to mark. In comparison to a computer-based test, which takes time to develop but takes no time for marking, marking portfolios can take many hours per student.

The process of using more interactive technology-based learning is becoming a reality for the new millennium. Students not only want to learn on their own; they want to be assessed individually. What is urgently needed is much more research to transform assessment to conform to our new paradigm of learning.

EDUCATIONAL MANAGEMENT
Overselling the Effectiveness of E-Education

It is clear that advertising has an impact on the selling of products. E-programs, possibly inferior programs, can be advertised effectively and even oversold. Organizations can cash school fees and provide no support for the students—in other words, take their money and run. This is purposeful misrepresentation of education, providing an incomplete view of the learning environment. What is required is a critical look at details of program descriptions to assess the effectiveness of the program. In third world countries, the eagerness for gaining a university education may influence the critical ability of potential students. When the program is run by an overseas organization, it may encourage immediate credibility. The candidates may not have the experience of critically evaluating the program or comparing it to others. Overselling can be done at students' expense.

Filtering Information

There are countries, Singapore for example, that filter incoming information. Should access to the Internet be a right or a privilege? Should governments have the right to restrict academic freedom? Who has the right to decide on information credibility? Who will make the decision of what is available to students? Will some students be disadvantaged, because they do not have all the information at hand?

Regulating Overseas Organizations Running Programs

In many countries, the criteria for overseas organizations to operate a program is lax. Should the government impose restrictions or bar poor programs? Should it regulate the standards for the education of its young people? If standards are set too high, is there a possibility that fewer students may receive an education? Conversely, if they are too low, students may receive a degree that is worth little.

Equal Student Access to Information

Another issue is the differences in students' ability to access materials, especially additional information. Some countries, especially students in outlying areas, may have poor or unreliable Internet access. Another difference may be the Internet charges that may be too high for surfing for information at will. Additionally, students may also not be as computer literate and feel disadvantaged when they are competing with students from advanced countries. When enrollment for courses in a virtual university comes from many different countries, there will clearly be disparate access to information. While some have the latest computers with many applications, others have outdated, slow-working machines. While some have immediate and fast access via broadband width connections, others have limited or slow access. Most often, this disadvantages students from third world countries.

Providing Training for Students in E-Learning Environments

Many students are not aware that the responsibility for their own learning will be placed on their shoulders in an e-learning environment. If they are not given training in establishing their own learning goals, managing their time, and utilizing group discussion tools, they may not adapt to the new mode of learning. They need to be aware of possibly being graded on the number of times they participate in discussion boards or the length of their virtual discussion. They are often expected to participate in a new mode of learning without adequate preparation for a new model of learning. Do we not have a responsibility to alert students and prepare them for the expectations of such an online delivery system?

CONCLUSION

Graduates today need to be prepared for a work environment that differs greatly from that encountered by faculty who may have been at university 25 years ago. Today's graduates need to be prepared for lifelong learning; they need the skills to be flexible in meeting the demands of the changing business world. They need to have portfolios of competencies that give evidence of marketable skills. By working collaboratively and individually in a networked environment, students appear to be learning these skills. Faculty need to encourage these activities.

Technology needs to be driven by appropriate educational and design considerations, not vice versa. If e-education is not grounded in sound educational pedagogy, faculty will fail to meet the challenge of encouraging lifelong learning skills.

Will students suffer from mass customization of education? Will students who graduate from an online university have the lifelong learning skills needed to cope in the real workforce? These questions remain to be answered.

REFERENCES

Allen, M. (1997). To be or not to be? Questions of computer-mediated learning and distance education. In *Strategies for open, flexible and distance education, Website*. Perth, WA: Teaching Learning Group, Curtin University of Technology. Retrieved from the World Wide Web: http://www.curtin.edu.au/learn/DSM/examples/4.html.

Brush, T. A. (1997). The effects on student achievement and attitudes when using integrated learning systems with cooperative pairs. *Educational Technology Research and Development, 45*(1), 51–64.

Chen, L. L. (1997). Distance delivery systems in terms of pedagogical considerations: a reevaluation. *Educational Technology, July–August*, 34–37.

Chickering, A. W., & Ehrmann, S. C. (1994). Implementing the seven principles: technology as lever. American Association for Higher Education. Retrieved from the World Wide Web: http://www.aahe.org.

Eisenberg, D. (1998). College faculty and distance learning, *Virtual University Journal, 1*, 82–84.

Forcier, R. C. (1996). *Integrating technology for meaningful learning* (2nd ed.). Boston, MA: Houghton Mifflin.

Furnell, S. M. et al. (1999). Online distance learning: expectations, requirements and barriers, *Virtual University Journal, 2*, 34–48.

Gilbert, S. W. (1996). Making the most of a slow revolution. *Change, 28*(2), 10–23.

Hawkins, J. (1993). Technology and the organization of schooling. *Communication of the ACM, 36*(5), 30–35.

Horvath, A., & Teles, L. (1999). Novice users' reactions to a Web-enriched classroom. *Virtual University Journal, 2*, 49–57.

Klein, J. D., & Pridemore, D. R. (1992). Effects of cooperative learning and need for affiliation on performance, time on task, and satisfaction. *Educational Technology Research and Development, 40*(4), 39–47.

Larson, J. W., & Madsen, H. S. (1985). Computerized adaptive language testing: moving beyond computer-assisted testing. *CALICO Journal, 3*(2), 32–35.

Madsen, H. S. (1991). Computer adaptive testing of listening and reading comprehension: the Brigham Young University approach. In Dunkel, P. (Ed.), *Computer assisted language learning and testing: research issues and practice*. New York: Newbury House.

Meunier, L. E. (1994). Computer adaptive language tests (CALT) offer a great potential for functional testing. Yet, why don't they? *CALICO Journal, 11*(4), 23–39.

Najjar, L. J. (1996). Multimedia information and learning, *Journal of Educational Multimedia and Hypermedia, 5*(2), 129–150.

Novak, G. M. et al. (1999). *Just-in-time teaching: blending active learning with Web technology*. Upper Saddle River, NJ: Prentice Hall.

Oblinger, D., & Rush, S. (1997). The learning revolution. In D. Oblinger, & S. Rush (Eds.), *The learning revolution: the challenge of information technology in the academy* (pp. 2–19). Bolton, MA: Anker Publishing.

Roblyer, A. D., Edwards, J., & Havriluk, M. A. (1997). *Integrating educational technology into teaching*. Upper Saddle River, NJ: Prentice Hall.

Sanders, E. (2000). Cyber tutoring and learning: how to facilitate action learning online, *Virtual University Journal, 3*(2), 43–58.

Sands, W., Waters, B., & McBride, J. (Eds.). (1997). *Computerized adaptive testing: from inquiry to operation*. Washington, DC: American Psychological Association.

Simsek, A., & Hooper, S. (1992). The effects of cooperative versus individual videodisc learning on student performance and attitudes. *International Journal of Instructional Media, 19*, 209–218.

Stone, A. R. (1992). Virtual systems. In J. Crary, & S. Kwinter (Eds.). *Incorporations*. New York: Zone; Cambridge MA: MIT Press.

Stone, A. R. (1993). Will the real body please stand up?: boundary stories about Birtual cultures. In M. Benedikt (Ed.), *Cyberspace: first steps*.

Tuller, C. (1997). Another paradigm shift. In D. Oblinger, & S. Rush (Eds.), *The learning revolution: the challenge of information technology in the academy* (pp. 35–53). Bolton, MA: Anker Publishing.

Tung, P. (1986). Computerized adaptive testing: implications for language test developers. In C.W. Stansfield (Ed.), *Technology and language testing* (pp. 13–28). Washington: TESOL Publications Manager.

Vogel, D. et al. (2001). Exploratory research on the role of national and professional cultures in a distributed learning project. *IEEE Transaction on Professional Communication, 44*(2), 114–125.

Wainer, H. (1990). Introduction and history. In H. Wainer (Ed.), *Computerized adaptive testing: a primer*. Hillsdale, NJ: Lawrence Erlbaum Associates.

Watts, M. M. (1998). Taking the distance OUT of education. *Virtual University Journal, 1*, 213–219.

Wertheimer, R., & Zinga, M. (1998). Be careful what you ask for: you might just get it. *Virtual University Journal, 1*, 106–109.

Wolley, B. (1993). *Virtual Worlds*. Harmondsworth: Penguin Books.

Chapter IV

Web-Based Learning: Experience-Based Research

Val Clulow
Swinburne University of Technology, Australia

Jan Brace-Govan
Monash University, Australia

ABSTRACT

In this chapter, a synthesis of work from several evaluative studies that the authors have undertaken on the different experiences professionals and students have had with Web-based education is provided. Provided are perspectives from undergraduate and postgraduate students and from academic staff members who have experienced learning and teaching in a Web-based environment. Reflection on these sources of experience provides a number of indicators for improvements to approaches to staff development for online teachers, for the preparation of students for an online learning environment, and for student-centered Web-based design.

INTRODUCTION

Increasingly, formal education and procedural training and management skill development is being accommodated through Web-based learning. Our recent experience and research on the provision of Web-based learning in the higher education sector has shown that although Web-based[1] technologies are well received, there continue to be issues for teachers, learners, and instructional design. This article draws from several projects, each of which was designed to evaluate and reflect on various aspects of the development of different Web-based learning sites. In one project, a professional journal was kept to assess the similarities and differences between traditional distance learning and Web-based learning. In another project, undergraduate students were asked to keep a reflective diary of their experiences of a unit that was delivered entirely online with no support materials, so that we could better understand how they engaged with, and felt about, the process of learning in this environment. The next project was based around interviews with postgraduate students taken at the end of a semester of Web-based learning. In this unit, the students' Web-based learning was supplemented by printed materials and a CD of resources. The evaluation interviews, conducted by a nonteaching staff member, asked how the students compared the Web-based learning experience with face-to-face classrooms. For the student diary study and the interview study, the original data were reanalyzed and are presented here in an original form for the specific and integrated focus this chapter takes. Another evaluation procedure available to staff is the analysis of bulletin board postings from a class conference. Here, two projects are reported, one analysis of postings utilized a cognitive framework, while another utilized the business-based concept of the "experience economy." Therefore, there are five sources of experiential data,[2] each providing a component part to the picture of Web-based education in a large Australian university, as follows:

- Marketing academic's experience with planning and design of Web-based learning materials
- Undergraduate students' experience with learning via Web-based materials, as reported through electronic diaries
- Postgraduate students' views of their experience with learning online, reported through telephone interviews
- Postgraduate students' learning experience reported through an analysis of their bulletin board discussion, using Henri's (1992) analytical framework
- Application of a business model based on the concept of the "experience economy" (Pine & Gilmore, 1999) to an education-focused bulletin board discussion

The five experiential studies that have contributed to our understanding of current issues and directions for the future are summarized in Figure 1.

Figure 1: Web-Based Education: Learning from Experience

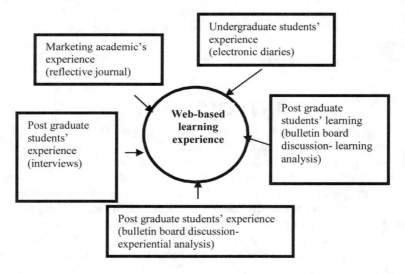

While all of these projects were conducted separately and at different times, there was an underlying interest in coming to grips with the processes of Web-based teaching and learning from the point of view of teachers and learners. A concern for constructivist educational theories consistently underpinned our work and provided a focus for the evaluative material. As the projects accumulated, certain themes emerged, and the data from the student diaries and interviews was revisited and analyzed from this more holistic perspective. Overall, our results indicated the need for closer attention to three important issues:

1. Approaches to just-in-time staff development for online teachers
2. More thorough preparation of students for an online learning environment
3. Greater focus on student-centered Web-based design.

The material presented here has been framed to constitute a case study of the development of teaching experience, which culminates in recommendations for practitioners in the field. However, a valuable source of information is not only the professional experience of a tertiary teacher, but also the insights offered from the evaluation of student experiences of the same educational unit delivered through Web-based technologies. The evaluative inquiry was conducted by a nonteaching member of staff to comply with requirements from the university's Ethics Committee. Therefore, several different perspectives are included in this case study: undergraduate students and postgraduate students; interviews from recent past experience and ongoing diary entries through the semester; diary entries from students and diary entries from a staff member; and comments made on bulletin boards and reflections on classroom work. The diverse nature of the material requires that it be presented in a somewhat segmented manner, in order that each piece information be clearly attached to its source. For this reason, the various studies will be presented in a sequence that builds the story of this case. The reflections will then be drawn together to form some conclusions about the kind of staff development required and the administrative context that could be utilized. The intention is to support staff learning about a new field and to encourage understanding of the similarities and differences with current practices and, ultimately, to give an indication about how effective professional development could be organized.

BACKGROUND

Arguments in favor of Web-based learning rely quite heavily on constructivist principles of learning that focus on, not only the delivery of information to learners, but also, importantly, the ways in which learners make sense of that information in order to fully assimilate it (Jonassen, 1991). Becoming a self-directed learner (Knowles, 1975) can be part of this experience of learning, but centrally, it is about learners communicating with others to establish links between what they know already and what they are engaged in learning (Laurillard, 1993). How they perceive and understand the knowledge that they have and the way they construct links to the new content of the course is a significant process in the assimilation of this new material (Garrison, 1992). Web-based technologies can offer exciting new ways of communicating between students or between students and teachers that readily support and enhance the learning experience: email, discussion forums, passing on useful sources of information through computer files, or sharing URLs.

The initial stages of Web-based learning were marked with a great deal of enthusiasm (Harasim, 1994; Hiltz, 1990; Hiltz & Turoff, 1993). While there are similarities between Web-based education and distance education (Evans & Nation, 1996), there are also opportunities to explore new, innovative delivery options (Mason, 1998). However, it is taking some time for the implementation of this innovative milieu for teaching and learning to diffuse through education in general. There are a variety of means by which to evaluate student learning, such as participatory action research and summative approaches to ascertain how students deal with changes to teaching practice (Kemmis & McTaggart, 1988). The value of continuous monitoring of innovations early in their life cycle is the ability to respond quickly and effectively to positive and negative evaluations. In today's rapidly changing business environment, the importance of education, skills, and training at all levels cannot be overlooked. The fast and effective diffusion of information, codified and tacit, depends on high-quality education and training at managerial and procedural levels. Ongoing training is a vital plank in the creation and maintenance of a knowledge-based innovation-intensive economy (Stenmark, 2001).

The descriptors of innovation Rogers (1995) created some 30 years ago, innovators, early adopters, laggards, change agents, and opinion leaders, have migrated into the common language routinely used to describe events, individuals, and organizational behavior. We suggest that Web-based learning has moved from the enthusiasm of the innovators toward the later stages of the early adopters phase and has brought with it a concurrent growth in the need to train students and staff for IT in education. The study of diffusion of interactive technologies has been one underlying focus of a number of studies by the authors (Clulow & Brace-Govan, 2000, 2001a, 2001b; Brace-Govan & Clulow, 2000, 2001). Principally, our concern has been with how learners experience and engage with Web-based learning technologies in order that the learning experience and the teaching experience can be enhanced. We made an effort to find what was specific to the kind of student who chose to learn through Web-based technologies. What are the students' needs here in terms of communication and support, and how can we best address these needs? What were the issues that students faced in coming to terms with learning in this innovative environment? Although each project was designed separately, taken together from an holistic view, they build a picture of useful recommendations and point to some interesting future trends. The first project discussed here provides a reflection on the transition from planning and design of distance education to considerations for planning and design in a Web-based environment.

MARKETING ACADEMIC'S EXPERIENCE— REFLECTIVE JOURNAL

Studies by pioneers of the adoption of Web-based teaching and learning practices (Gunawardena, 1998; Harasim, 1990; Hiltz, 1988; Lambert & Walker, 1995; Laurillard, 1990; Mason, 1991) provide a valuable point of reference for the "early adopters," which in Roger's (1995) diffusion curve might represent our point of adoption of the innovation of Web-based teaching and learning activity in Australian universities at the end of the year 2001. Focusing on the academic's experience in the online learning environment, Clulow and Brace Govan (2000) provided a personal account of professional practice using journal entries (Kerka, 1996; Janesick, 1998) as the record of the experience of course planning and design. Using

Figure 2:   A (component of) Distance Education Development Model (Note: From University of South Australia, 1991)

Planning and design
- Approaches
- Context
- Support/constrains
- Pre-planning
- Participants
- Detail of proposals
  -purposes
  -content
  -learning
   activity
  -evaluation
- Organizational issues

the known model of the subject planning and design stage (Figure 2) from a familiar distance education model (Appendix 2), the applicability of the steps, and the relevance of the activity that accompanied each step, were reflected upon in terms of relevance to the online environment.

In addition to establishing the relevance of the planning and design stage to Web-based subject planning and design, reflection on the activities and issues pertinent to each step in the distance education model provided valuable enhancement. So, for example, in distance education, "Approaches" meant that the academic should consider matters relevant to a print-based package, such as the inclusion of diagrams, audiotapes, suggested weekly activities, or weekend tutorials. For Web-based subject planning and design, "Approaches" was still a relevant step, but new technologies were reflected at this step in the extension of resources to include electronic innovations, such as online libraries, list servers, and websites, along with issues such as the instructional design for a screen-based delivery.

The complete analysis of each step in the planning and design stage and its relevance to online material development indicated that building on previous experience to provide a framework for handling unfamiliar tasks is a valuable approach. However, where prior experience is limited and the pace of change is rapid, there is more likelihood of confusion, uncertainty, and resistance to change. So for staff already familiar with working with print-based distance education materials, the move to a Web-based learning environment was not as uncomfortable as it was for others moving directly from a lecture-based classroom. Some of this discomfort could potentially be overcome by detailed, close, and critical reflection at this stage of the planning. Its value was noted by Peruniak: "The main reason for looking at the initial stage (planning) is because the ways in which the problem of creating a new programme are conceptualised help to determine the kinds of issues to be faced during the lifetime of the programme" (1986, p. 178).

Of concern in the virtual teaching and learning environment is that the "lifetime of the programme" is ever decreasing. Apart from the subject content, fundamental components of Web-based delivery, such as the version of the communications platform or, even more difficult, a change to a new communications platform, can cause many hours of work for faculty staff. This can create a seemingly constant need for training and updating skills to familiarize staff with new developments, functions, and applications of the technology.

While, as the professional reflective diary demonstrated, there are sometimes previous skills on which new skills can be scaffolded, the need for access to technical support staff and the development of new skills was a constant challenge. Drawing staff into the new teaching environment is accompanied by steep learning curves during the transition into a sophisticated, technical environment. The reflection on "Support and constraints" centered on the need for responsive backup support and quick response to staff "emergencies" as they learned to navigate the technology. In addition, it was obvious that the best time to "learn" was at the time the problem arose. The preparatory training sessions, while essential, were not the times that staff confronted a whole range of situations. Camaraderie between team members enabled sharing of new-found advice, but the key reflection was that when you need to know how to do something in an online environment, that is the best time to learn it. The implications of this reflection for professional development are critical and comprehensive.

Twenty years ago, Meacham's (1982) key tenet was that staff development needs did not necessarily follow neat, linear progression, and a seminar format would not be the most appropriate way of dealing with individual concerns of staff. No more so than in an online learning environment. The reflective diary on the "Planning and design" stage for materials for online delivery provided a window into new demands on staff development, while recognizing the value of using frameworks from prior experience on which to scaffold. In summary, then, this earlier model of staff development could be adapted for academic staff members working online, who would then be able to benefit from exploring the relevance of their prior training and the relevance of their institution's resources in the context of their own specific, immediate needs. However, there was virtually no literature on the student experience of Web-based learning in 1998, and although resources could be put in place to support staff, at this stage, it was not clear what kinds of support students would require. This led us to investigate, concurrently, a further aspect of Web-based delivery of tertiary education: the experience of the learner.

UNDERGRADUATE EXPERIENCE— ELECTRONIC DIARIES

Education delivered through Web-based communication is often presented as having much to offer students (Evans & Nation, 1996; Mason & Kaye, 1990; Turoff, 1999), but there is little material that discusses the issues from the perspective of the learner. While there are clear differences between learning in a face-to-face classroom and learning through computer-mediated communication, how is this actually experienced by the learner, and does Web-based learning offer a viable alternative from the students' perspective? Several educational theorists assert that learners need to communicate with each other (Garrison, 1992; Jonassen, 1991; Laurillard, 1993), and so, we were interested in finding out about their needs for communication with each other, as well as with teaching staff or with technical experts. Another aspect of the student experience that interested us was how they would manage their learning through this relatively new medium. At the time, only a couple of studies discussed the skills that students required to engage with this learning environment (Burge, 1994; Smith, 1999). While there are many methods available to evaluate students' experiences using participatory or action research processes, we were especially interested in monitoring the separate, individual experience of students and the way that this evolved over the course of the semester.

A method that would allow us to investigate the day-to-day individual experiences of students was the personal reflective diary. The disciplines of Education and Nursing make extensive use of this tool during the process of acquiring professional skills (Arrendondo & Rucinski, 1994; Beveridge, 1997; Carroll, 1994; Durgahee, 1998; Thorpe, 1995; Topper, 1997). Using an electronic version seemed especially appropriate for the context and was expected to fit into the student's study routine more easily than a paper version. By using pseudonyms and reply-paid envelopes for 3½-inch discs, instead of email, the students were assured of a high level of confidentiality.

The undergraduate students were studying an introductory marketing unit, where all learning materials and interactions were accessed entirely online. The students were invited to keep an electronic, personal diary of the experiences of their Web-based learning for the duration of one 13-week semester. This particular unit was well placed for exploratory research, because it drew students from two separate locations. The identical marketing unit was offered to students by a leading Australian university through competitive entry, usually for conventional campus teaching, as well as to students who had open access through an organization called Open Learning Australia and who usually studied by distance education. In addition, the marketing unit was delivered to both sources of students entirely online with the support of an asynchronous discussion forum and the usual kind of contact maintained between faculty and learners, i.e., fax, phone, and email. In other words, each group of students could have chosen another more conventional mode of delivery for their type of enrollment: the competitive access students could have attended face-to-face campus lectures and tutorials and the open access students could have taken the conventional distance education version. Therefore, all the students had alternative access to the same subject content, albeit through different avenues.[3]

The diary format for this research focused around three areas, one that gave a base to work from and two areas of interest:
1.   Expectations about Web-based learning
2.   Communication with teaching faculty and other students and technical support
3.   Preferred patterns of working

This format was to be a guide only, and students were invited to make any other comments that they felt were pertinent. The format was transferred onto four discs for each student. The first disc set up a student-selected pseudonym for the project. It also requested demographic information and initial reflective thoughts on the student's expectations about the process of learning online prior to the unit starting. After returning the initial disc, the students had three further discs to return, one for each 4-week period. The study was conducted by a researcher separate to the teaching process and not by teaching staff, in order to encourage the students to be as frank and open as possible.

The response from the students was good, and out of a potential 35 students, 40% (14 students) agreed to take part. There was an even distribution of gender, with seven men and seven women, and a comparable distribution of age, with seven under 26 and seven over 26. There were eight open access students (57%) and six competitive access students (43%). The majority of these students also undertook paid work (10, 71%) and half the sample lived with a partner or a partner and children. In other words, only four of these students (29%) were able to study full-time. The position that is becoming more and more prevalent of juggling education with full time work and family commitments is well-represented in this sample, and as such, their views are a valuable foretaste of the future "student experience."

In general, these students thoroughly enjoyed their experience of learning online and felt that this was a useful extension to their previous learning experiences. Nearly all the students (13) had recent study experience that was print- or face-to-face-based; none had experienced Web-based learning. Most of them expected that Web based study would be more convenient, although there were some concerns, even before the semester had commenced, about the lack of personal contact and whether communication would be as rich. In response to one of the questions on the first diary disc, one student expressed these concerns:

Diary Question: What do you Expect Online Studying to be Like?

Able to go more at my own pace and over the areas I do not have a clear understanding of, but I will also miss out on the student tutor interaction in general conversation and other student queries that I may not have thought of myself (Online Diary 9, p. 3). [4]

In addition to some wariness about "missing out" on interaction, the following two excerpts express two further expectations. The first student expects to be able to learn about marketing while concurrently learning more about information technology:

I am a bit worried about the technical side of it as I am very new to computers but otherwise it should be a double learning experience (Online Diary 7, p. 3).

This is not unusual but could well be misguided, as the potential for cognitive overload in this scenario is quite high, especially if there are technical difficulties to face, such as overcoming firewalls or getting software to run in different Web environments. There are also two implied warnings here for teaching faculty: not all students are experienced in computer technology, and faculty may well be their first point of contact and so be expected to deal with a range of technical issues in addition to the subject content.

The other excerpt draws out two further issues that are contradictory but common:

Hopefully a lot easier than conventional study. The endless supply of libraries, universities and study sites should be sufficient to guide and assist me—and unlike most students who hit the net, I have no intention of pulling someone else' essay on line and passing it off as my own—where's the pride in that? (Online Diary 6, p. 3)

First, this student expects that in some way learning through Web-based technology will make the process of learning easier, which of course is a fallacy. But, there is a deeper issue here and that is the fallacy that the vast array of resources on the Internet will sort themselves out in some mysterious way and actively help the learner. Internet resources are extensive, but they are also mixed, and in reality, students, especially in the initial stages of Web-based learning, need guidance on how to sort the wheat from the chaff, themselves. The last comment about the student's refusal to plagiarize is commendable, but it too points to a growing problem that also needs consideration by faculty and possibly some kind of action plan.

Overall then at this initial stage in the investigation, there was an optimistic tone, but there are some serious underlying issues that need a proactive approach. Levels of computer competency that are required by students should be balanced by the amount and quality of technical support an institution can meaningfully provide. Also, expectations about the kinds of skills that are useful could be explained in full, and ways to encourage a conversational tone with a high level of interactivity would support student learning in the online environment.

During the course of the semester, students returned their disc diaries. In describing their actual experience, the students comments were not especially different than those they had made about their expectations at the start of the semester, they were consistent in their praise for the teaching staff, the unit, and its delivery. Investigations showed the preferred pattern of work that students wanted was to study print on paper, particularly when there was a lot of reading, and especially when they needed to read away from the computer, for example, when traveling to work. As this student noted, "One thing that has not changed in traditional study methods is the need to read the textbooks" (Online Diary 8, Stage 1, p. 4).

The communication issue that emerged was the difference in commentary that developed from students whose alternative mode of delivery was conventional face-to-face teaching as compared with the commentary from students whose alternative was distance education by correspondence. Where the distance education students were excited by the increased access to communication with others, the students with the campus as an alternative were looking for more immediate feedback.

Communicating online is a lot less personal which I like—and you can respond in your own time—there is not so much pressure to be available all the time or to stick to rigid lecture timetables (Online Diary 3, Stage 2, p. 2).

Communication is good. I am able to get in touch with tutors or other students if necessary but don't need to if I don't want to. ... Questions are getting answered promptly (Online Diary 3, Stage 3, p. 3).

I found the Q (question) and A (answer) replies a little bit slow as compared to classroom scenarios but its understandable as the tutor sometimes can only reply to emails the following day. ... I was hoping the online tutorial will be like those envisioned for the 21st century as in tutors being actually "online" to chat with student during the day time or night (Online Diary 4, Stage 1, p. 4).

The first two comments are from a student with distance education as an alternative, while the last comment is from an impatient student who could be on campus. The management issue that arises from this investigation is a need here to be clear about communication and establish parameters for expectations, so that students are fully aware of the environment they will join.

The key points to emerge from the diary study are as follows:

- There is a student learning overload potential, if not fully competent with technology required.
- Plagiarism will be pursued.
- Communication speed is different.

- Communication availability needs to be defined.
- There is an enduring need for print materials to support learning.

To build on this research project and to gain further insights into the student experience, it was decided to develop an interview-based study with a postgraduate cohort.

POSTGRADUATE STUDENT EXPERIENCE— INTERVIEWS

Bearing some of the above issues in mind, the postgraduate units were devised with some alterations. For example, reading materials were provided in printed format and on CD-ROM for easy portability, and a study guide gave clear instructions about communication with staff and described the kinds of response times that were to be expected. The Retail Management unit was the postgraduate subject that was the basis of this project. It drew students from all parts of Australia, and therefore, some students were experienced with distance education and some with on-campus teaching. The researchers again wanted to find out how the students were experiencing online learning, only this time, the information would be gathered through a telephone interview. The interview schedule followed the format of the diary and asked about communication with relevant other people, such as teaching staff, other students, and technicians, and it also addressed expectations about online study and preferred work patterns. However, with the telephone interview, there was now an opportunity for following up and having students explain issues in more detail. Again, the research was conducted by a nonteaching researcher to give the students some assurance of levels of confidentiality and privacy.[5] Pseudonyms were established by the researcher at the time of the interview transcription.

All 23 students were invited to take part, and with 16 accepting, there was a response rate of 69%. The sample was fairly typical of a postgraduate cohort: mature aged (all over 26), middle-management job, working around 50 hours per week, and living with partners (62.5%) and sometimes children (25%). Again, it needs to be clear that these students enjoyed their online learning and were positive about the experience, the teaching staff, and the materials available to them. The spirit of the interview was that this was good feedback, but constructive criticism would be more useful for further development.

In general, these students were studying online because of the flexibility of place and pace that this offered them, and considering their hours at their paid work, flexibility had to be a significant factor. Furthermore, at the time, this was the only Retail Management course that could be studied by distance education, so many students needed the flexibility for reasons of geography. Overall then, convenience and relevance were their principle reasons, but what were their expectations?

The expectations of the group were quite mixed: nervous, excited, and curious, and some claimed to have no expectations. Others, like the undergraduate students, expected Web-based learning to be like distance education only with more interaction.

Interview Question: What did you Expect Studying Online to be Like?

Responses to this question included the following:

Similar to physical documents that you get in the post but with a bit more interaction (Dennis 10/Lines 19–20).[6]

An extension of the distance education program. Like paper and offered electronically. This also offers various libraries and a quicker response from tutors which is a better prospect for me if I am travelling around with time differences and so forth (Dorothy 13/Lines 24–26).

Expectations for both of these students were met, and generally, around this group, the mood was fairly positive, which could be explained in part by their experience of distance education by correspondence, which this student described quite bleakly: "I tried distance education in 1988 and felt very isolated. Not really enjoyable" (Bronwyn 2/Lines 21–22).

However, even though the group comprised experienced distance learners who were excited about learning this way, not everyone had an easy time, as this student explained:

I thought it (online study) would work, and from other students I thought I would be actively involved in emailing and using the board. But it didn't happen because I got behind and because I didn't attend, attend and keep up with things, because I was well behind and because I didn't know anyone, I would see they've moved on to that so I was pretty behind everyone. ... I worked really hard in the last couple of weeks ... but I missed not being able to discuss that online (James 14/Lines 22–29).

This student had clearly lost pace with the rest of the group, and because he was so out of step, he was unable to contribute to the group discussion. The underlying warning here is that even though this appears to be a flexible, work-friendly way to study, in reality, the flexibility is not limitless, and, as James found out, being out of step can have social consequences too. James found that not only was he behind in his work, which he managed to catch up on, but he was behind socially. This was ground that he did not manage to regain in this semester. Another student also found the environment's flexibility to be paradoxically quite restricted:

I am not very familiar with online and I found it hard to type. I prepared everything. I wrote it down and then typed it up. So I didn't get involved in the bulletin board because it was very time consuming (Carmel 6/Lines 22–20).

This student was studying in English, her second language, and found that expressing herself in another language was a challenge. However, the effort of typing in addition to this meant that she spent long hours studying. This student's experience indicates that there is a need here for students to have a reliable way of selecting their mode of delivery effectively. Ponzurik, France, and Logar (2000) explored the reasons why students might choose distance education over face-to-face teaching and concluded that it is convenience that drives their interest, especially as these authors found the delivery method to be unsatisfying for students and less effective. However, the suggestion here is that the situation is far more complex than an "either/or" decision and relies on at least three aspects. Certainly, one aspect may be some practical issues that lead students to choose particular modes of delivery, such as convenience of time and place. As well, there may be other factors that should encourage students to select modes of delivery appropriate to their circumstances, such as language. In addition though, there is a third consideration, and that is the student's need to learn how to learn through Web-based technologies and that needs to be tailored to a specific environment and support students in keeping up with the speed of the group. Just as the faculty staff required individualized support to scaffold onto their prior experience, so too do learners. This is exacerbated by the fact that most people currently experience school (K–12) through face-to-face classrooms and become especially adept at learning in this mode of delivery. It is less usual for learners to approach distance education with the same depth of experience.

Here is the crucial conflict of expectations and experience, which in a face-to-face setting are most often congruent but, in a distance education setting, are potentially at odds due to lack of experience. Here James' expectation that he could take 13 weeks of tuition and complete the study entirely at his own pace was met. However, his quality of experience of this learning was lessened due to his exclusion from the group as a result of his being out of step with them. This kind of information needs to be clearly set out for learners, in particular, learners who have less experience in print-based distance education or through Web-based delivery. If these kinds of issues are attended to through clear communication prior to the beginning of learning, then it is reasonable to assume that distance education and face-to-face education could be equally effective. The final part of this synthesis was to explore this dimension by investigating the sharing of knowledge that occurred in a postgraduate cohort through analysis of their online discussion board postings.

POSTGRADUATE STUDENTS' LEARNING— BULLETIN-BOARD ANALYSIS

A number of analytical models have been developed in recent years to assist educational researchers in gaining greater insight into the nature of online interactive discourse. McCreary (1990) took a behaviorist perspective and used previous models to examine their potential as analytical guides for human behavior in online communities, notably, behavior of the "diffusion manager," the "conference moderator," and the "CMC collaborator." Gunawardena (1998) worked on the development of guidelines for the design of collaborative learning environments mediated by computer conferencing, in particular, the role of the conference moderator/facilitator. Gunawardena, Lowe, and Anderson (1998) investigated interaction analysis through transcripts of computer-mediated conference text to test constructivist and social-constructivist learning theories. Henri (1992) applied an analytical framework with five dimensions, three concerned with the "product" of learning (participative, social, and interactive) and two concerned with "learning process" (cognitive and metacognitive). Henri's cognitive dimension provided an appropriate framework for the study by Clulow and Brace-Govan (2001), in which they sought to analyze the learning process embedded within students' online discussion text by applying Henri's indicators of a number of reasoning skills. In this evaluative approach, the teacher works through the students' postings, and using Henri's indicators, can locate examples of each "reasoning skill" (elementary clarification, in-depth clarification, inference, etc.) and the depth to which the student deals with the content. Through this detailed analysis, the discussion of a particular issue or question can be summarized and provides a profile of the cognitive work undertaken by the students during the discussion.

Posting	Reasoning				Skills					
Interactive/ independent	Elementary clarification	Surface/in-depth	In-depth clarification	Surface/in-depth	Inference	Surface/in-depth	Judgement	Surface/in-depth	Strategies	Surface/in-depth
1/Interactive			✓	In-depth			✓	In-depth		
2/Interactive					✓	In-depth	✓	In-depth		
3/Interactive			✓	In-depth			✓	In-depth	✓	In-depth
4/Independent			✓	In-depth			✓	In-depth		
5/Interactive			✓	In-depth			✓	In-depth		
6/Independent	✓	Surface								
7/Independent			✓	In-depth			✓	In-depth		
8/Independent	✓	Surface								
9/Interactive			✓	In-depth					✓	In-depth
10/Interactive	✓	Surface								
11/Interactive	✓	Surface								
Totals	4	4	6	6	1	1	5	5	2	2

Note. Source: Table 4, Discussion Question 4, Cognitive skills/level of processing. Clulow, V., & Brace-Govan, J. (2001). Learning through bulletin board discussion: a preliminary case analysis of the cognitive dimension. In Moving Online, conference proceedings, September

A summary of analysis of the text of a full discussion is shown here and gives an insightful profile of the reasoning skills indicated by the content of students' discourse, whether the contributions were "surface or in depth" in complexity and whether each posting was considered "interactive" (linked to others) or "independent" (not linked).

In this example, the teacher can see that students are somewhat weaker at venturing to make "inferences" and suggested "strategies" but that they were checking to "clarify" information and were prepared to then make "judgements" based on this information. As an example of an evaluative tool, it provides not only a practical option for teachers but also useful feedback for students on how their reasoning skills are being applied.

Of particular further interest in that study, is the observation made that in their online discussions, these postgraduate students brought together a combination of course content linked with their work experience. While this is not perhaps surprising, the richness of the graduate study forum was most evident and clearly documented (Clulow & Brace-Govan, 2000).

POSTGRADUATE STUDENTS' EXPERIENCE OF WEB-BASED LEARNING

The passing observation that students introduced relevant "tacit knowledge" from their prior experience into the text of their discussion postings is perhaps not unexpected from a postgraduate student cohort. While organizations are building their online learning repertoires, there is little evidence of any evaluative analysis of the nature and content of such learning interactions. Extending on the bulletin board analysis using Henri's (1992) learning model, the researchers took that observation and in a later study (Clulow & Brace-Govan, 2001b) applied a business model by Pine and Gilmore (1999), as suggested by McLellan (1999), to the text of the bulletin board material. In their model, the key proposition is that consumers have moved over time from an "agrarian" economy through to an "experiential" economy, where their expectations are based beyond a "customer service" focus into an expectation of engagement and personal experience (Table 1).

They found through closer examination of the transcriptions, that their work undertaken in an educational context had valuable application to the business learning environment, in that the metaphorical elements presented in Pine and Gilmore's model of the "experience economy" were also identifiable in the students' discussion content.

Table 2 summarizes the elements of "experience," as they are applied to the marketplace, in a business context.

By applying the conceptual framework to the online learning environment, the Web-based bulletin board was the "stage," and the teacher was the "stager." In this sense, the creation of the combination of study materials set the stage. Students joined the discussion by respectfully acknowledging the contribution of the "guest" before them and offered information to the discussion from their own experience. The postings and the way they were written were "personal" additions that "revealed over time" a progressive development of the topic. The students revisited the postings of others and noted their value as if they were "memorable," worthy experiences or "sensations."

With the rapid rate of uptake of online learning materials in the workplace, and the need for organizations to manage knowledge and knowledge-sharing processes (KPMG, 2000), these latest steps toward the evaluation of online learning experiences provide a range of indicators for further research. In business environments, the value of intellectual capital

Table 1: Economic Distinctions Between Agrarian, Industrial, Service, and Experience-Based Economic Activities

Economic Offering	Commodities	Goods	Services	Experiences
Economy	Agrarian	Industrial	Service	Experience
Economic Function	Extract	Make	Deliver	Stage
Nature of offer	Fungible	Tangible	Intangible	Memorable
Key attribute	Natural	Standardised	Customised	Personal
Method of Supply	Stored in bulk	Inventoried after production	Delivered on demand	Revealed over a duration
Seller	Trader	Manufacturer	Provider	Stager
Buyer	Market	User	Client	Guest
Demand factors	Characteristics	Features	Benefits	Sensations

Note. Adapted from McLellan, H. (1999). Online education as interactive experience: some guiding models. Educational Technology, *September–October, 36–42*

Table 2: Experience-Based Economic Activities

	Experiences in the marketplace (and online)
Economy type	Experience
Economic function	Stage
Nature of offer	Memorable
Key attribute	Personal
Method of supply	Revealed over a duration
Seller	Stager
Buyer	Guest
Demand factor	Sensations

Note. Adapted from McLellan, H. (1999). Online education as interactive experience: some guiding models. Educational Technology, *September–October, 36–42*

hard-earned by experience is now well recognized. For companies, their "intellectual capital represents the sum of everything that everybody in the company knows and what gives it a competitive advantage" (Belak, Kovacevic, & Kolakovic, 2001). In the evaluation models developed to date, the role of "experience" has not been fully explored. In Gunawardena's "Interaction analysis model," there is mention in Phase IV(C) of the activity of "Testing against personal experience" in the social construction of knowledge. However, there is a perception that the learner's prior experience is somewhat undervalued, and it is proposed here that this experiential element needs to be made more explicit in evaluative models for Web-based learning activity. The integration of the students' experience with the Web-based course curriculum provides a clear indicator of the need for close attention to a student-centered Web-based instructional design.

SOLUTIONS AND RECOMMENDATIONS

The themes that emerged from the Web-based teaching and learning experiences discussed here offer reflections from which a suggested, dynamic, four-step model has been developed and provides a focus for future action in Web-based teaching and learning.

Step 1: Provide Academic Staff Development on a Just-In-Time Basis

A key recommendation that recognizes the pace of change in a Web-based learning environment is a proposed just-in-time (JIT) Web-based staff development matrix (Figure 5).

Figure 3: Four-Step Experiential Model of Web-Based Education

STEP 4	Develop a student centred instructional design which takes account of the elements of the 'experience economy' (personal, memorable, experiential engagement)and build those into the nature of the web-based interaction.
STEP 3	Check for 'learning' using developing evaluative tools and note the enhancement to learning made possible by students sharing their 'experience'.
STEP 2	Establish clear student guidelines and discuss expectations of web-based education before semester.
STEP 1	Provide academic staff development on a just-in-time basis to take account of the rapid pace of change and the urgency of calls for assistance.

The reflective journal study indicated that while staff can use prior experience as a framework on which to build new skills, there is a point of "readiness" when staff members need to learn how to use the technology for a particular purpose. The matrix has been developed as a way of promoting better recognition of the need for a more responsive staff development approach, which can provide advice at the time it is needed. The JIT staff development matrix provides an alternative to lengthy seminar-based programs scheduled well ahead of time, when potential participants are unaware of their future training needs. The matrix reflects the concept of "learner readiness" in a Web-based environment, where the learner has reached a point in their development needs or in relation to their tasks where new skills or information are relevant.

The matrix addresses learner readiness in relation to each individual academic and their concerns about themselves (self), the task, and performance outcomes. Indicators of "readiness" include "expressions of readiness," and a descriptive area of "focus" further identifies a stage of development. Staff development "strategies" are suggested in three stages to illustrate the "strategic focus" of the stage, the utility of short "workshops," and the need for ongoing "staff support." The "key issues to note" provides brief comments from experience, relevant to each stage.

Step 2: Establish Clear Student Guidelines and Discuss Expectations

In particular, it is important to find a mechanism for making the students aware that Web-based learning is just as substantive an option as classroom-based education. Furthermore, the students need clear guidelines about when, and how often, they are expected to be in communication with each other and with the teaching staff. Giving indicators about availability and response times can be a valuable way to manage students' expectations. Students also need to be aware of the valuable diversity of Web resources, while concurrently being wary about the quality of those resources. In addition, there continues to be a place

Figure 5. JIT Web-Based Staff Development Matrix

Learner readiness	Self	Information/skills	Task	Performance	Outcomes
	Personal awareness		Managing Web-based activities	Collaborative work	Evaluation and review
Expression of readiness	*I'm not sure I can do Web-based teaching, or if I want to*	I don't know much yet, but would like to know more	*Getting this Web-based subject ready is taking all of my time*	*How can I team up with others to improve teaching/learning quality*	*I'll try a better way*
Focus	Interested to try it	Gaining skills/understanding	More systematic approach	Sharing ideas	Update/consolidate subject materials
Strategies					
• Strategic focus	Need to change recognized, desire to learn	Availability of descriptive information/costs and benefits	Sighting of examples/exemplars/trials and pilots	Basics of instructional design/building on prior experience working with others	Supportive learning support team/coaching and support for new ideas
• Workshops	Short, relevant descriptive sessions of instruction/demonstration	Discussions with experienced academics using real materials	Problem-solving workshops on "how to do" things/achieve what is wanted/adapt material	Networking with others/writing papers from experience	New skills of "evaluation/assessment" of Web-based teaching/learning
• Staff support	Facilitation of sharing opportunities/reinforcement	Provision of solutions/contact details of success stories	User groups for shortcuts to learning the ropes	Dissemination of ideas/innovative work and staff presentations	Encourage evaluation of "pilot" programs/links between individuals
Key issues to note	*Not all will be early adopters, accept this*	*Shorter deliveries of chunks of information relevant to staff at that moment is better*	*Avoid staff feeling overwhelmed*	*Step back while staff tries out and encourage them to show others*	*Refocusing and review should not be too far from a "mainstream" benchmark*

Note. Adapted from Concerns-Based Staff Development Matrix, Meacham, E. D. (1982). Distance teaching: innovation, individual concerns and staff development, Distance Education, 3, 2, 244–254 for printed material to support learning activities. Finally, students need to be made aware that they are part of a learning cohort and that, although independent study is possible, it is in their best interests to try to stay in step with the group. There are significant benefits to be gained from having other learners with which to discuss the material. Group work is a valuable way to offer students from larger cohorts a smaller, potentially more manageable number of colearners, with whom to be in close contact.

Step 3: Check for "Learning" Using Developing Evaluative Tools

The evaluative models that have been developed for online learning situations during the last decade offer educators a range of approaches to suit their evaluation perspectives. The cognitive dimension applied from the model illustrated (Henri, 1992) proved to be practical and rigorous for the purpose of profiling a postgraduate class online discussion. The methodology takes time but provides a worthy result for those seeking a better understanding of online learning outcomes. Further dimensions within Henri's model and alternative approaches by other authors are considered to provide valuable feedback on learning and other related dynamics of the online learning environment, such as the social, interactive, and participative dimensions.

Step 4: Take Account of the Elements of the "Experience Economy"

It is suggested that the elements of the "experience economy" are relevant to the "student experience," and if used in addition to building a quality learning program through good instructional design, this will address some of the issues of working with students as clients or customers. Online education is regarded by students as an "experience," and the communications platform is the "stage" provided by the institution. The metaphor is also useful as a prompt for instructional designers, in that students are involved in personal, memorable learning experiences, and if they are regarded as "guests," they are likely, over the duration of the semester, to feel positive regard for their involvement.

FUTURE TRENDS

The studies involving three different groups dealing with Web-based teaching and learning highlighted a number of issues. In projecting policy and practice into the future, it is recommended that these should be viewed as parts of an integrated interaction network. The issues can be summarized separately; however, it is considered most profitable that they be regarded as interrelated components, as the studies to date indicate a trend in demand in online education for a seamless, high-quality experience. Technological change and innovation will demand ongoing training and communication of expectations for staff and students in order to maintain a quality staged experience. The culmination of this research is indicated by three key insights for the future of Web-based teaching and learning. First, that the medium is extremely well suited to dissemination and discourse of learning material, and so, exponential growth is expected. Second, other technologies and mixes of media including face-to-face communication in education will also be maintained, and their demise is not indicated from our research. And third, that real success with Web-based education will come from the development of expertise, including appropriate staff development and student orientation, to fully integrate the components that combine to create, deliver, and evaluate the learning activity.

CONCLUSION

The staff and student experiences in higher education change from semester to semester, as familiarity with the use of technology grows and the technology changes. Tapping into the various experiences of those involved, from their different perspectives, has proven incredibly insightful, though exploratory to date. Research needs to maintain a resilient focus on the users of technology in education and how they maneuver within and around it to suit their needs. Web-based education provides daily challenges and a constant demand on teachers and learners to adapt to the technological learning environment, in addition to their participation in the task at hand. The value of their experience has proven enormously beneficial in gaining a better understanding of the dynamics of change. The benefit of testing models and frameworks from related areas of study to Web-based developments has been shown to be a worthy endeavour.

REFERENCES

Arrendondo, D., & Rusinski, T. (1994). Using reflective journal in the workshop approach in university classes to develop students' self-regulated learning, *paper presented at the Annual Meeting of the American Education Research Association.*

Belak, V., Kovacevic, B., & Kolakovic, M. (2001). Intellectual capital as a base for designing a virtual organisation: the case of Croatia. *Business and Economics Society International conference proceedings,* Paris, July 2001.

Beveridge, I. (1997). Teaching your students to think reflectively: the case for reflective journals, *Teaching in Higher Education, 2,* 1, 33–43.

Brace-Govan, J., & Clulow, V. (2000). Varying expectations for online students and the implications for teachers: findings from a journal study. *Distance Education, 21,* 1, 118–135.

Brace-Govan, J., & Clulow, V. (2001). Comparing face-to-face with online: the learner's perspective. *Academic Exchange Quarterly, 5,* 4 (Winter), 112–118.

Burge, E. J. (1994). Learning in computer conferenced contexts: the learners' perspective. *Journal of Distance Education, 9,* 1, 19–43.

Carroll, M. (1994). Journal writing as a learning and research tool in the adult classroom. *TESOL Journal, 4,* 1, 19–22.

Clulow, V., & Brace-Govan, J. (2000). Course planning and design: does a distance education model fit for online course planning and design. *Moving Online, conference proceedings*, Southern Cross University, Australia, August.

Clulow, V., & Brace-Govan, J. (2001a). Learning through bulletin board discussion: a preliminary case analysis of the cognitive dimension. *Moving Online, conference proceedings*, Southern Cross University, Australia, September.

Clulow, V., & Brace-Govan, J. (2001b). The experience economy: a role for interactive online business education, presented at the Business and Economics Society International conference, Paris, July 22–26 (and in press for *Global Business & Economics Review-Anthology 2001*).

Durgahee, T. (1998). Facilitating reflection: from sage on the stage to a guide on the side. *Nurse Education Today, 18*, 2, 158–164.

Evans, T., & Nation, D. (1996). Educational future: globalisation, educational technology and lifelong learning. In T. Evans, & D. Nation (Eds.), *Opening education: policies and practices from open and distance education* (pp. 162-176). New York: Routledge.

Garrison, D. R. (1992). Critical thinking and self-directed in adult education: an analysis of responsibility and control issues. *Adult Education Quarterly, 42*, 3, 136–148.

Gunawardena, C. N. (1998). Designing collaborative learning environments mediated by computer conferencing: issues and challenges in the Asian socio-cultural context, *Indian Journal of Open Learning, 1*, 101–119.

Gunawardena, C. N., Lowe, C. A., & Anderson, T. (1998). Transcript analysis of computer-mediated conferences as a tool for testing constructivist and social-constructivist learning theories, *Distance Learning, '98 proceedings of the Annual Conference on Distance Teaching and Learning* (14th Madison, WI, August 5–7).

Harasim, L. (Ed.). (1990). *Online education: perspectives on a new environment*. New York: Preager.

Harasim, L. (1994). *Global networks*. Cambridge, MA: The MIT Press.

Henri, F. (1992). Computer conferencing and content analysis. In A. R. Kaye (Ed.), *Collaborative learning through computer conferencing—The Najaden Papers* (pp. 117–136), proceedings NATO Advanced Research Workshop on Collaborative Learning and Computer Conferencing, Copenhagen, Denmark, July 29–August 3, 1991.

Hiltz, S. R. (1988). Teaching in a virtual classroom, Vol. 2. of A Virtual Classroom on EIES: Final Evaluation Report. Computerised Conferencing and Communications Center, New Jersey Institute of Technology.

Hiltz, S. R. (1990). Collaborative learning: the virtual classroom, *T.H.E. Journal*, June, 59–65.

Hiltz, S. R., & Turoff, M. (1993). *The network nation: human communication via computer*. Cambridge, MA: The MIT Press.

Janesick, V. J. (1998). Journal writing as a qualitative research technique, *paper presented at the Annual Meeting of the American Educational Research Association*, San Diego, CA.

Jonassen, D. (1991). Objectivism versus constructivism: do we need a new philosophical paradigm? *Educational Technology Research and Development, 39*, 5–14.

Kemmis, S. & McTaggart, R. (1988). *The action research planner* (3rd ed.) Geelong, Victoria, Australia: Deakin University Press.

Kerka, S. (1996). Journal writing and adult learning, research paper, *ERIC digest 174, Office of Educational Research and Improvement*, Washington, DC.

Knowles, M. S. (1975). *Self-directed learning. A guide for learners and teachers*, Chicago, IL: Follett Publishing.

KPMG Consulting. (2000). Knowledge Management Research Report. Retrieved November 26, 2000 from the World Wide Web: http://www.kpmgconsulting.com/kpmgsite/othermedia/kmreportfinal.pdf.

Lambert, P. E., & Walker, R. A. (1995). Designing collaborative www learning environments—the HENRE project, *proceedings AUUGWS & Asia Pacific World Wide Web '95 Conference and Exhibition*: http://www.csu.edu.au/special/con…5/papers95/plambert/plambert.html.

Laurillard, D. (1990). EH232 Computers and Learning, AC1, Side 1, Band B. The Open University, Milton Keynes, UK.

Laurillard, D. (1993). *Rethinking university teaching: a framework for the effective use of educational technology*. London; New York: Routledge.

Mason, R. (1991). Moderating educational computer conferencing. *The Distance Education Online Symposium News, 1*, 19.

Mason, R. (1998). Models of online courses, *ALN Magazine, 2*, 2, October, 9. Retrieved March 8, 1999 from the World Wide Web: http://www.aln.org/alnWeb/magazine/vol2_issue2/Masonfinal.html.

Mason, R., & Kaye, A. (Eds.). (1990). *Mindweave: communication, computers and distance education*. Oxford: Pergamon Press.

McCreary, E. K. (1990). Three behavioural models for computer-mediated communication. In L. Harasim (Ed.), *Online education: perspectives on a new environment* (pp. 133–184). New York: Praeger.

McLellan, H. (1999). Online education as interactive experience: some guiding models, *Educational Technology*, September–October, 36–42.

Meacham, E. D. (1982). Distance teaching: innovation, individual concerns and staff development. *Distance Education, 3*, 2, 244–254.

Peruniak, G. (1986). Some problems of programme initiation at a distance education university, *Distance Education, 7*, 2, 177–190.

Pine, B. J., & Gilmore, J. H. (1999). *The experience economy: work is theatre and every business is a stage*. Cambridge, MA: Harvard Business School Press.

Ponzurik, T. G., France, K. R., & Logar, C. M. (2000). Delivering graduate marketing education: an analysis of face-to-face versus distance education. *Journal of Marketing Education, 22*, 3, 180–187.

Rogers, E. (1995). *Diffusion of innovations*, 4th ed. New York: The Free Press.

Smith, E. (1999). Learning to learn online, *paper presented at ASCILITE '99: Responding to Diversity*, Queensland University of Technology, Brisbane, Australia.

Stenmark, D. (2001). Leveraging tacit organisational knowledge. *Journal of Management Information Systems, 17*, 3, 9–24.

Thorpe, M. (1995). Reflective learning in distance education. *European Journal of Psychology of Education, 10*, 2, 153–167.

Topper, A. (1997). Comparing face-to-face and electronic discourse: issues and questions raised in a research study, *paper presented at the Annual Meeting of the American Educational Research Association*, Chicago, IL.

Turoff, M. (1999). Education, commerce, communications: the era of competitions, *WebNet Journal*, January/March, 22–31. Retrieved October 1, 1999 from the World Wide Web: http://eies.njit.edu/~turoff/Papers/Webnettalk/Webnettalk.htm.

ENDNOTES

[1]   The terms Web-based learning and online learning have been used interchangeably.

[2]   For a more detailed examination of these data, in conjunction with the specific research objectives of each study, please refer to the appropriate articles: Brace-Govan and Clulow (2000, 2001) and Clulow and Brace-Govan (2000, 2001).

[3] Each group could have enrolled to take the unit in a different mode of delivery. This is not only a point of difference between the two groups, but it is important in driving the expectations that the students have of the Web-based learning environment. See Brace-Govan and Clulow (2000) for elaboration on this point and some suggestions for the management of these expectations.

[4] Coding assigned during research used here.

[5] Without a nonteaching member of staff, it would have been difficult to have these interview schedules comply with the requirements of the Ethics Committee. Perhaps this is one further piece of advice, that funding a nonteaching member of staff to pursue evaluative research is a valuable investment.

[6] Coding used pseudonyms.

APPENDIX 1

Figure 1: A Distance Education Development Model

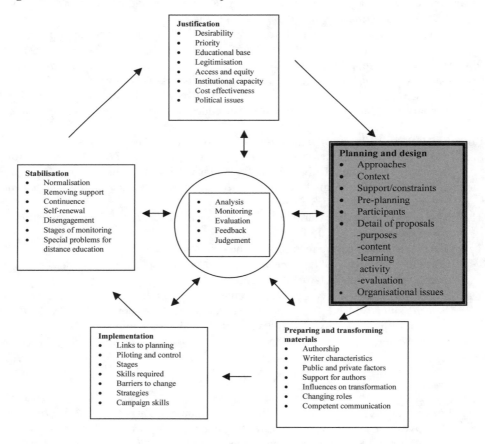

Note. Source: University of South Australia 1991

Chapter V

Web-Based Education in the 21st Century: A Transnational Perspective

Mahesh S. Raisinghani
University of Dallas, USA

"The art of teaching is the art of assisting discovery."
Mark van Doren

ABSTRACT

As with any emerging educational endeavor, the quality of instruction and content varies widely, as do the goals and motivations of the students. In this chapter, we look at the Web-based distance education strategy for academia from a transnational perspective. The key philosophies and principal characteristics of a transnational organization are discussed, and their lessons for Web-based education are extracted for a transnational model for Web-based education. The parallels between industry and academia are drawn with respect to virtual organizations. The implementation strategies of transnational firms provide some valuable lessons for academia involved with Web-based education, as they strive to achieve higher degrees of coordination with low control dispersed throughout the organization. The five dimensions of a transnational strategy taxonomy are applied to transnational Web-based distance education initiatives. Finally, we take a closer look at some predictions for teaching and learning using Web-based education in higher education as extrapolations of current trends. However, we know that we will also be surprised by new developments, just as the growth of the Internet surprised us all. Commencement ceremonies are the starting point to lifetime learning in the digital/knowledge economy.

INTRODUCTION

Globalization is changing the contours of business education. An organization in academia or industry can outperform rivals only if it can establish a difference that it can preserve. The essential problem in organizations today is a failure to distinguish planning, which is about programming, not discovering; from strategizing, which is choosing to perform activities differently than rivals do (Hamel, 1996; Porter, 1996). The significance of a distance learning strategy cannot be overstressed, because the number of people taking undergraduate and graduate courses online will increase from 710,000 last year, or approximately, 4.8% of the nation's 14.6 million higher-education students, to 2.23 million in 2002, accounting for 15% of all higher-education students (International Data Corporation, www.idc.com, 1999).

This chapter is structured as follows: We first review the existing literature for key statistics, trends, and predictions in distance education and Web-based learning environment. Next, we look at the transnational model in Web-based education that can be applied using the global infrastructure of the Internet, followed by some key trends in distance education. Then, we look at the guidelines and elements of a well-designed online course and describe the learning orientation model. Finally, we review the seven predictions for Web-based education and discuss their key implications before concluding the chapter.

LITERATURE REVIEW AND SYNTHESIS: KEY STATISTICS, TRENDS, AND PREDICTIONS

It seems like there is a revolution taking place in the educational environment today. There is also a change in the design, delivery, and development of the learning process. Distance learning is an arena for change in higher education. According to the National Center for Education Statistics (NCES), one-third of approximately 5000 two- and four-year postsecondary institutions offered distance education during the 1997–1998 academic year. The NCES also reported that 1.7 million people were enrolled in distance education during the 1997–1998 academic year. Most faculties fear having a distance education facility, because they feel that it is not secure to have class over the Internet. The technology has not really paved the way for distance education learning. The faculties are also not trained well to plug their courses on to new technologies. As we can see in the recent past, there are private firms who design templates and layouts for faculties to use to insert course information and contents. There is a large potential market for Web-based education across the globe, because the Web is accessible by anyone and everyone (Passmore, 2000).

Online, Web-based communication—seen by many as the key technological innovation of the last decade of the twentieth century—has attracted the attention of educators and trainers to the idea of distance education in a way that no earlier technology managed to do. With explosive growth of the technology, knowledge of how to best apply it—in designing and delivering instructional programs and in facilitating learner–instructor and learner–learner interactions—lags far behind. People sometimes think of distance education as technology; however, technology is just the driver. Distance education is a different paradigm of teaching and learning. It is about teacher–learner relationships and learner–learner relationships (Moore, 2000).

NASSCOM estimated that as of March 2002, the number of active Internet subscribers was 1.5 million. However, by 2004–2005, the subscriber base will rise to approximately 8 million, with the user-base growing by the same period to over 30 million. The U.S. Department of Education pegged the growth of distance education in the institutions of higher education at well over 70% between 1997 and 1998 (Lewis, Snow, & Farris, 1999). Nando.net reported in 1997 that 390 U.S. universities told Peterson's they had classes online. In 1999, the number increased to 798 schools, an increase of 408 universities. International Data Corporation reported that corporate distance education and training expenditure ranged between $7 to $60 billion, depending on factors analyzed and reported.

It is predicted that by 2002, 80% of institutions of higher education will offer some form of virtual education, although the extent and scope of these initiatives will vary (Block & Dobell, 1999). Ahmed (2000) found that the students in a virtual environment reported higher self-efficacy than students in a comparable traditional environment, with performance in the two environments being equivalent.

Alavi and Leidner (2001) called for a greater depth of research that considers the psychological learning processes (i.e., cognitive and information processing activities, motivation, interest, and cognitive structures/memory) and a greater breadth of research in technology-mediated learning by considering the program (e.g., MBA program) and organizational levels of analysis. The focus of future research in the Web-based learning environment could be on the following potential research questions that could address the depth and breadth dimensions:

- How do various Web-based virtual learning environments affect student psychological processes and outcomes?
- What are the most effective models of program design, combining virtual and traditional instruction?
- What structures and processes are needed to encourage adoption of Web-based learning environments and to facilitate dissemination at the university level?

Although these research questions form the basis of a research agenda for the next several years, the following key predictions for electronic (e-) learning in 2002 from experts in the field, help us get a better understanding of where we are headed in the near future (http://elearnmag.org/subpage/sub_page.cfm?article_pk=2920&page_number_nb=1&title=COLUMN, 2002):

> What will be e-learning's successes, failures, and innovations in 2002? As IT rebounds late in the year, so will learning management systems purchases. The best news in 2002 will be that budget constraints will force more trainers to adopt an ROI justification, and more thought will go into building the business case for e-learning. Simulation will emerge as the widely recognized gold standard in instructional design for e-learning.—**Brandon Hall, Ph.D., CEO, brandon-hall.com**

> There will be a greater realization that e-learning has limited value, and that people also need to learn through print and people contact. This will lead to a rebalancing of methods in e-universities. There will be a move toward better video communication via the Internet and mobile devices, and this will begin to be seen as having educational uses as well. There will be real progress towards standards and sharing of e-learning tools and platforms. Maybe some of this is just wishful thinking! But whatever changes happen for the better, they will be slow.—

Professor Diana Laurillard, Pro-Vice-Chancellor (Learning Technologies and Teaching), Open University, UK

Workforce development within government will continue to be a challenge, and e-learning will be seen as a less costly approach to address this significant human capital shortcoming. In both government and the private sector, the main challenges will be how to make e-learning relevant and how to engage employees in this new way of learning.—**Dr. Jacob Lozada, Assistant Secretary for Human Resources and Administration, U.S. Department of Veterans Affairs**

Purchasers of Learning Content Management Systems (LCMS) will continue to be disappointed with overpriced, over-hyped, poorly implemented, and poorly documented software that supplies none of the promised benefits. The SCORM specifications will begin to be better understood, although they won't result in substantial breakthroughs in actual products until 2003. Substantial Open Source e-learning platform alternatives will show up on the market for the first time. "Community" will continue to be a hot topic, although failure rates in implementations will remain high.—**Michael Feldstein, Feldstein & Associates Consulting**

We're going to see significant new thinking in e-learning with a programmable Web freeing innovation. Some changes: partnerships among government agencies, software industries, and universities will focus on technologies that enhance activity-based learning, embedded assessment, immersive collaboration, and extended mobile computing with less importance placed on lecturing and test-taking. You'll see new highly collaborative and visual technologies for education such as gaming and simulations. Quality assurance will be the cornerstone for proof of investment and assessment validation. The accreditation boards will take a harder look at how to accredit these environments as they emerge, especially in science, technology, engineering, and math. And most important, learning will start being fun, and, in some cases, enchanting.—**Randy J. Hinrichs, Group Research Manager, Learning Sciences and Technology, Microsoft Research**

E-learning will become part of the fabric of our daily personal and business routine. We will use a blended learning solutions approach, combining advanced technologies with traditional modalities, to craft learning to meet the needs of individual learners when and where they need it. E-learning will expose the vast wealth of knowledge that exists in the minds of individuals, corporate documents and databases, and elsewhere across an extended enterprise. And new technologies will weave e-learning content into the devices we use and the environment we live in. Through e-learning we will connect those who know with those who need to know, breaking down barriers to yield a better-educated world population.—**Leon Navickas, Chairman and Chief Executive Officer, and Amy Finn, Ph.D., Director eLearning, Education and Training, Centra Software, Inc.**

2001 marked the end of the first round of converting content and delivery to "e." What happens next? A new wave of do-it-yourself tools are reaching the market.

However, even the best tools do not deliver quality content. In 2002, consumers will recognize that sound digital instructional design is the underpinning of quality content.—**Bill Hitchcock, Global Director of EDS' Digital Learning Service Line, and SmartExecutive's E-learning Executive for the Year 2001**

The downturn in the economy will refocus corporate educators on the bottom line and on achieving results. Organizations will take more interest in filling the knowledge gap as a means to increase productivity and reduce cost. This means less focus on technology for technology's sake and a greater emphasis on training workers, customers and partners. Irrational exuberance will be replaced with a greater level of sophistication in how success is measured; more attention will be paid to workers' ability to perform. Watch for e-enhanced informal learning using e-mail, threaded discussions, instant messaging, e-meetings, team-rooms, and virtual workspaces.—**Dr. Margaret Driscoll, Director, Strategy & Venture, IBM Mindspan Solutions**

E-learning is both cultural and technological and the cultural will trump the technological every time; in 2002 there will be more focus on the successful adoption of new technology/processes. More memory and processor power will increase the use of handhelds (PDAs and cell phones). Games are too powerful a way to learn to ignore. A primary focus is and should continue to be how e-learning is improving peoples' performance. Long-range prediction: "guilds."— **Mark Oehlert, Deputy Director for Communications, ADL Co-Lab**

This will be the year that the promise of learning objects comes to fruition. With the advent of authoring tools with built-in standards compliance, and with the distribution of desktop and local server learning object repositories, authors will create small and focused nuggets of learning content instead of entire courses. Commercial learning content providers will continue to extend their hold over an increasingly consolidated industry though exclusive content distribution agreements. Watch for some major LMS or LCMS companies to be acquired by a major publisher.—**Stephen Downes, Senior Researcher, National Research Council of Canada**

There will be a revolt against high price and complex e-learning products and a return to easy-to-use, low-cost and rapid content-creation tools that are less demanding of the user's time. Training Departments will be split up and report to specific functional areas, such as sales and customer relationship management.— **Irwin Hipsman, Business Development, Brainshark**

The current distinction between "e-learning" and "contact sessions" will fade, as more and more companies realize the benefits of blends... and see technology as a tool for more efficient and professional learning support for any participant. Benchmark measures for training departments will shift away from input indicators (number of days of attendance, number of sessions completed, number of logins to a website, etc.) toward meaningful and authentic output measures (evidence that concepts from a course and contacts made within a course result in a meaningful impact on workplace practice).—**Prof. Dr. Betty Collis, Shell Professor of Networked Learning, University of Twente, The Netherlands**

As the new year unfolds, practitioners and decision makers will increasingly realize that they have to make a strategic decision: to adopt a model of e-learning that is as close as possible to face-to-face instruction or to unleash the power of distance education and e-learning. Some institutions will continue to use technology to offer a centralized and uniform system of education. Their graduates will fulfill a need in the job market, but one that will decrease as the century unfolds. Organizations that understand the decentralized, self-organized and emergent characteristics of the new market will see an expanding demand for their graduates. They will thrive and prosper.—**Farhad Saba, Ph.D., Professor of Educational Technology, San Diego State University, and CEO, Distance-Educator.com**

Watch out for a launch in 2002 of a major corporate e-learning initiative backed by some of the most prestigious U.S. universities. Wideband applications will rapidly increase, leading to a spurt in learning object/learning resource management initiatives, but they will get bogged down in intellectual property issues. Faculty associations will start playing hardball over ownership of Web courses. A new computer interface based on speech recognition will have a major impact on the design of e-learning courses.—**Dr. Tony Bates, Director, Distance Education and Technology, Continuing Studies, University of British Columbia**

Successful online courses will be those of high quality in terms of content, instruction, and career relevance. Education may not end the threat of terrorism but ignorance is not bliss—particularly ignorance of different cultural norms and values. World-class online educational opportunities will help developing countries, especially those that have not had access to quality education, as well as contributing to cultural understanding between nations.—**Professor Richard Larson, Director, MIT Center for Advanced Educational Services (CAES)**

Most schools will now proclaim that they offer e-learning, when they only have course home pages or slides available on the Internet. But just as a crystal grows around a seed, teachers and students will hear about, try out, and adapt for their own needs Internet-mediated interaction and learning. The crystal will grow, but it will take years for e-learning to become a viable option—and it will never replace face-to-face instruction.—**Prof. Dr. Debora Weber-Wulff, FHTW Berlin and Virtuelle Fachhochschule**

Customers will demand quality, value and convenience. Quality will be synonymous with a desire for courseware that has measurable impact on business performance (good design); value will come from increasing the scale of e-learning deployments enterprise-wide (efficiency through scale); and convenience arises from ease-of-use.—**Robert Todd, Learning Experience Architect, DigitalThink**

Of the top 50 schools ranked by *Financial Times*, an average of 44% of full-time students were not from the home country of the business school (AACSB, 2002). Among the recommendations of the Management Education Task Force to that AACSB Board of Directors are to facilitate alliances among partner schools and expand partnerships with other information resources such as the Corporate University Xchange, and regional management associations. Because AACSB serves as the hub for the industry, it may be able to create marketplaces and promote alliances among schools, possibly by expanding its Affinity Group structure (AACSB, 2002). Given this backdrop, we next look at the transnational strategy model of the business world and assess how it can inform Web-based education.

THE TRANSNATIONAL MODEL IN WEB-BASED EDUCATION

The key philosophy of a transnational organization is adaptation to all environmental situations and achievement of flexibility by capitalizing on knowledge flows (which take the form of decisions and value-added information) and two-way communication throughout the organization. The principal characteristic of a transnational strategy is the differentiated contributions by all its units to integrated worldwide operations. As one of its other characteristics, a joint innovation by headquarters and by some of the overseas units leads to the development of relatively standardized and yet flexible products and services that can capture several local markets. Decision making and knowledge generation are distributed among the units of a transnational organization.

In drawing the parallels between industry and academia, transnational organizations often enter into strategic alliances with their customers/students, suppliers/international adjunct faculty, and other business/academic partners to save time and resources. As long-term partnerships, these alliances may bring to the organization specialized competencies and relatively stable and sophisticated market outlets that help in honing its products and services, or stable and flexible supply sources. This may result in a virtual organization, consisting of several independent firms that collaborate to bring products or services to the market.

A transnational model in industry or academia represents a compromise between local autonomy and centralized decision making. A transnational organization seeks a balance between the pressures for global integration and the pressures for local responsiveness. It achieves this balance by pursuing a distributed strategy that is a hybrid of centralized and decentralized strategies. Under the transnational model, a multinational corporation's (MNC's)/global education alliance's assets and capabilities are dispersed according to the most beneficial location for a specific activity. Simultaneously, overseas operations are interdependent, and knowledge is developed jointly and shared worldwide.

LESSONS FOR ACADEMIA

The lessons for academia from transnational firms are to attain higher degrees of coordination with low control dispersed throughout the organization (Bartlett & Ghosal, 1989, 1990). Proctor & Gamble and Ericsson are examples of transnational organizations. The five implementation tactics used for implementing the transnational model are mass customization (i.e., synergies through global research and development) (e.g., American Express, Time magazine, Frito-Lay, MCI), global sourcing and logistics (e.g., Benetton,

Citicorp), global intelligence and information resources (e.g., Anderson Consulting, McKinsey Consulting), global customer service (e.g., American Express), and global alliances (e.g., British Airways & US Air, KLM & Northwest) (Vitalari & Wetherbe, 1996). Among the critical issues that need to be addressed are scalability, interoperability, consistency, and flexibility. An example of the transnational model applied in the academic world is The Indian School of Business (ISB) in Hyderabad, India. It is a research-oriented international business school that was established in partnership with Northwestern University's Kellogg School of Management, University of Pennsylvania's Wharton School of Management London School of Business, and McKinsey & Company.

A Memorandum of Understanding was signed by Kellogg, Wharton, and the ISB in November 1997, providing for a sharing of expertise and resources and a close partnership over the curriculum, admissions, faculty recruitment, and exchange programs. The certificates issued by the ISB bear the signatures of all three deans. Kellogg and Wharton infused the best and latest in global management techniques and thinking into the ISB's academic programs by helping to design the curriculum and develop course material. Most importantly, faculty and researchers from these and other leading institutions are teaching regularly at the ISB. They will also participate in research at the school.

ISB students will benefit from exchange programs and collaborative projects with students at Wharton and Kellogg. In November 2000, the ISB also forged ties with LBS, one of the top business schools in Europe. LBS is also collaborating closely with the ISB over its distinguished faculty, knowledge, and research pool, and contributed to developing the ISB's Executive Education Programs.

King and Sethi (1999) defined a comprehensive taxonomy of transnational strategy with five important dimensions of transnational strategy, i.e., the configuration of value-chain activities (this refers to the geographic dispersal of a firm's value-chain components), the coordination of value-chain activities, centralization, strategic alliances, and market integration, which refers to the extent to which the parent corporation views the international market as a single competitive arena. This dimensionality can be applied to the transnational distance learning initiatives.

Although the spontaneity and depth of person-to-person interaction in the traditional classroom setting foster far richer interactions; the students, enrolled in the Internet MBA program at the large southwestern U.S. university where the author works, ask interesting and insightful questions and are able to balance their families and careers while pursuing graduate education. The whole online experience does not necessarily replace the traditional classroom experience, it supplements it. Commencement ceremonies provide just the beginning to lifetime learning in the Internet-age society.

Next, we discuss the guidelines and elements of a well-designed online course.

Building a Creative Learning Environment

Online education is a unique feature that helps students to continue their education. Online education has become a new culture in this era of globalization. The potential for the distance education market is much more than the potential for resident instruction. There are some questions that many instructors struggle to answer when doing online classes.

A student receives a syllabus from the instructor. This is the first document a student receives. This document also tells an overview of the course, books to be used, course objectives, instructor policies, course pedagogy and methodology, grading policies, and so forth.

The following are some basic elements that should be implemented in a well-designed online course:

- First needed is contact information for the instructor. In online classes, the instructor cannot be seen in person. So, there should be some way for the students to communicate with the instructor. To make a friendly environment, the instructor can give little bit of his personal information, like his picture, hobbies, phone number, email, etc.

- Second, a course description is necessary. This is the first document a student can look into. This covers the basic elements of the course, like objectives, topics covered, and what topics will tweak a student personal interest.

- Third, a course schedule of assignments is needed. This will allow the online student to plan for upcoming work. A student can have an assignment schedule in order to deliver their assignment on time.

- Fourth, a clear description of policies is necessary. Classroom policies should include grading policies and weighting of assignments; policy for late submissions of assignments; attendance in online discussions; and participation in online learning experiences, such as discussion boards.

- Last, a disclosure of institutions policy is needed. Plagiarism and cheating is not allowed in any academic institution. Clear description of this policy is important (Farrell, 2001). Appendix A illustrates the Web-Based Tutoring Authoring System (i.e., Figure 1) and a schematic of the logic flow of the system (i.e., Figure 2). In the next section, a closer look is taken at the learning orientation model before prescribing some guidelines for personalized learning in a Web-based environment.

LEARNING ORIENTATION MODEL

The learning orientation model helps us understand the fundamental difference between cognitive learning abilities of our students. The Learning Orientation Model encompasses four learning styles. Martinez and Bunderson (2000) used the three construct factors to describe how learners, following beliefs, values, emotions, and intentions, self-motivate themselves to learn:

1. Conative (i.e., desires, intentions)/Affective (i.e., emotions, feelings) factor, contribute efforts
2. Strategic Planning and Committed Effort factor, and self-manage learning
3. Learning Autonomy factor) to varying degrees

The profiles for learning orientations are illustrated in Table 1.

GUIDELINES FOR PERSONALIZED LEARNING IN A WEB-BASED ENVIRONMENT

We should consider some aspects, such as instructor's experience and intuitive ability

Table 1: Learning Orientation Model

Orientation	Conative (i.e., desires, intentions)/Affective (i.e., emotions, feelings) Aspects	Strategic Planning and Committed Learning Effort	Learning Autonomy
Transforming learner (Transformance)	Strong passions and intentions on learning; be an assertive, expert, highly self-motivated learner; exploratory learning to transform using personal standards	Set and accomplish personal short- and long-term challenging goals that may or may not align with goals set by others	Assume learning responsibility and self-manage goals, learning, progress, and outcomes
Performing learner (Performance)	Focus on emotions on learning selectively or situationally; self-motivated, focused learner when the content appeals	Set and achieve short-term, task-oriented goals that meet average-to-high standards; situationally minimize efforts and standards to reach assigned or negotiated standards	Prefer coaching and interaction for achieving goals
Conforming learner (Conformance)	Focus intentions and emotions cautiously and routinely as directed; low-risk, modestly effective, extrinsically motivated learner	Commit careful, measured effort to accept and reproduce knowledge to meet external requirements	Assume little responsibility, manage learning as little as possible, be compliant, want continual guidance, and expect reinforcement for achieving short-term goals
Resistant learner (Resistance)	Focus on not cooperating; be an actively or passively resistant learner	Chronically avoid learning (apathetic, frustrated, discouraged, or disobedient)	Assume responsibility for not meeting goals set by others; set personal goals that avoid meeting formal learning requirements or expectations
	Situational Performance or Resistance: Learners may situationally improve, perform, or resist in reaction to positive or negative learning conditions or situations		

Note. Source: Martinez, M., & Buderson, V. C. (2000). Foundations for personalized Web learning environments. Journal of ALN, *4(2). Retrieved February 12, 2001 from the World Wide Web: http://www.aln.org/alnWeb/magazine/Vol4_issue2/burdenson.htm*

to recognize and respond to the fact that individuals learn differently, while designing the Web learning environment. In Table 2, some guidelines for three learning orientations, i.e., transforming learners, performing learners, and conforming learners, are presented. These are helpful in planning instruction; promoting interactivity; capturing interests; designing interfaces and environments; delivering instruction, practice, feedback, and assessment; helping learners monitor progress; evaluating performance; and making revisions (Martinez & Bunderson, 2000).

Next, we look at seven key predictions for Web-based education in the new millennium and discuss their key implications.

Table 2: Instructional Strategies for Three Learning Orientations

Learning Issues	Transforming Learners	Performing Learners	Conforming Learners
General environment	Prefer to be loosely structured	Prefer semi-complex and semi-structured	Prefer simple, safe, structured
Goal-setting and standards	Set and accomplish short- and long-term goals	Set and achieve short-term, task-oriented goals	Accomplish simple, task-oriented goals
Learner autonomy and responsibility	Self-motivated	Situationally self-motivated	Cautiously motivated to assume little responsibility
Knowledge building	Able to develop new knowledge	Use relevant knowledge and meaning	Reproduce knowledge to meet external requirements
Problem solving	Prefer interactive case studies	Prefer competitive program	Prefer scaffold support
User interface	Open learning environment	Hand-on learning environment	Minimal environment
Presentation	Interaction for achieving goals	Prefer continual coaching	Prefer continual guidance
Feedback	Prefer inferential feedback	Prefer concise feedback	Prefer explicit feedback
Motivational feedback	Discovery	Coached discovery	Guided afforded
Learning module size	Short, concise, big picture with links to more detail	Medium, brief overview with focus on practical application	Longer, detailed guidance, in a step-wise fashion
Examples	One good example and one bad example	A few good and bad examples	Multiple good and bad examples
Information need	Holistic, specific information needed to solve a problem	General interests, practice, short-term focus	Guidance to fill requirements
Content structuring	Prefer freedom to construct own content structure	Prefer a general instruction, limited ability to reorganize	Prefer to let others decide content structure
Sequencing methods	Hypertext, sorting by meta-tags, precise access	Semi-linear, logical branching, access by subtopic	Linear, page-turner representations, general access
Peer interaction	High, belief that everyone can contribute valuable, holistic insights	Moderate, easily frustrated by time required for peer interaction and theory	Minimal, values group consensus and commitment, wants answers from the instructor
Quality of assignments	Usually far exceeds stated requirements	Fulfills requirements but does little more than that	May not meet the minimal requirements
Questioning habits	Asks probing, in-depth questions about content	Asks questions to complete assignments, too busy taking notes	Asks mechanistic questions about assignments

Note. Source: Martinez, M., & Buderson, V. C. (2000). Foundations for personalized Web learning environments. Journal of ALN, *4(2). Retrieved February 12, 2001 from the World Wide Web: http://www.aln.org/alnWeb/magazine/Vol4_issue2/burdenson.htm*

SEVEN PREDICTIONS FOR WEB-BASED EDUCATION

The time period for predictions cannot be too long or short. It has to be at a moderate level for the proposed plan to happen. For example, seven years is close enough for the impact to happen. There is a radical change in the learning environment today through the use of the World Wide Web and the Internet. What should universities and educational institutions do about this? The following are seven predictions by Boettcher (1999), which are extrapolations of current trends on where higher education will be in the year 2007.

Prediction One: A "Career University" Sector will be in Place

Information is growing at an ever-increasing rate. Education has to change into a new outlook. There are new requirements for education. This prediction states that a new career university sector will emerge, focusing on the nontraditional degree, certification, and career professional areas. The design of education with this respect will be customized and flexible according to the needs of the people. If we see the development of education over the past 10 to 15 years, this change has already been taking place in educational areas. There are major universities that have branches. At some point, these branches will become institutions, based on their own expertise. Higher education institutions will focus on career professional programs. If these programs are successful, the universities may spin-off entire portions of the university into nonprofit foundations or for-profit institutions.

Prediction Two: Most Higher Education Institutions, perhaps 60%, will have Teaching and Learning Management Software Systems linked to their Back-Office Administrative Systems

This prediction invokes a dramatic change in the teaching and learning support systems/administrative systems that are currently traditional. There will be tools and systems that will support the teaching and learning process and be tightly integrated with the back-office administrative systems to leverage efficiency and effectiveness found in other service industries. The software will modernize the work associated with the management and delivery of teaching and learning. The software systems will help faculty and transform faculty control. These systems will hold the course content in a more organized manner. Courses will be packaged and "owned" more easily and also be delivered in different ways.

Prediction Three: New Career Universities will focus on Certification, Modular Degrees, and Skill Sets

This prediction focuses on the shift from an academic degree to updating knowledge, certification, and skill sets, for example, Web mastering, international communications, and online MBA. The focus of the career universities will be on service to career professionals. Institutions will modularize their degree programs. The programs will commence with conference-like activities to facilitate networking, followed by asynchronous delivery of content. Another emphasis will on upgrading and updating knowledge in a specific field, such as medicine, business, law, nursing, and education, by using contextual problem solving, case studies, and networking. Institutions will create new ways to have loyalty over their educational institution by using alumni subscription programs that offer continued growth in nonwork-related programs and offerings or subscriptions to an integrated set of learning opportunities that includes large databases of content, special alerts, and networking.

Prediction Four: The Link between Courses and Content Courses will be Broken

This prediction deals with the ability of the World Wide Web and the Internet to package and deliver content resources in varying sizes and depths in unlimited combinations. There will be discipline databases of knowledge clusters focused on developing competencies. Publishers are moving now to build lifelong learning businesses by building large databases of content on the Web, suitable as "adoptable." Normally, a faculty member develops 40 to 60% of the same course every semester. The faculty will have to redevelop only 30 to 40% of the course. The adoptable portion of a course will increase from an average of 30 to 60% or more. Publishers may also spin-off lifelong learning businesses using their rich sources of content. Faculty can become discipline tutors focused on knowledge clusters comprising core concepts and principles linked to knowledge and problems for applying these principles.

Prediction Five: Faculty Work and Roles will make a Dramatic Shift toward Specialization

The current system and process of higher education teaching and learning is analogous to the cottage industry. There is one faculty member who develops the course, designs the course, monitors the course, and so forth, and this process of creating and doing things is the same every semester. With the help of new technologies, there can be a "technology-intensive" part of the course for each faculty member. The demands on the role of the faculty will increase until specialization is acknowledged and supported. Each faculty member does not need to do everything. With the help of the "technology-intensive" education, there can be a set of faculty members who focuses on design and developing. There can be another set of faculty who takes care of the delivery portion or of managing a number of tutors who manage actual interaction with students. The changing roles and responsibilities of the faculty members also mean that they have to develop new policies about who owns what in the area of courses.

Prediction Six: Students will be Savvy Consumers of Educational Services

Over the coming years, students of an education institution will become a strong customer group. There will be high demands from the students in the new career universities. Their expectations will be that these courses provide an effective learning experience with predictable outcomes in less time. The services that students look upon will be on types of services that are offered to career professionals—customization and responsiveness. Universities will have to support the learner with a goal in mind of providing career enhancement courses. These should be combined with networking with other people in the institutions. It has to be an enjoyable learning experience. Students in the future may not prefer to learn in the physical classroom. In education, we must rethink the concept of the virtual classroom with programs that support multiple career goals and networking with other professionals. The students must have the capability to access the class from whereever they are, at any time convenient to them.

Prediction Seven: The Tools for Teaching and Learning will become as Portable and Ubiquitous as Paper and Books are Today

Just like the decade of the 1990s was the decade of the Web, the next decade will be the decade of the mobile, portable, and wireless technologies that support teaching and learning anywhere and anytime. The barriers for online learning such as bandwidth and hardware are coming down. However, there will be a shift in the cost of accessing the education. To access well-structured content that is easily accessible in a digital library, there may be an additional cost. For example, we have subscriptions to many magazines, cable, and newspapers. In the same manner, we may have subscriptions to many varied databases of content. Although we have seen multiple generations of software agents, we may see them integrated with personal robots by the year 2007 in the form of personal digital assistants that can help us by remembering our preference for information type and format and making proactive suggestions; formulating the questions we might have; providing guides, hints, and insights; and navigating various knowledge clusters. Over the long term, we will see "intelligent" interfaces that will learn about the eLearner over time. Learning will be imbedded in equipment, and economies of scale will fund development of "cool" learning using rich media, popular entertainers, and game interfaces.

KEY IMPLICATIONS: HAZARDS OF PREDICTING THE FUTURE AND STUDENTS AS CUSTOMERS

Arthur C. Clarke's First Law stated that "When a distinguished elderly scientist states that something is possible, he is almost certainly right. When he states that something is impossible, he is very probably wrong." Consider the following megatrends in Table 3 that may help us predict the future.

Table 3: Key Megatrends

•20% of world population mobile users—2005
•Personal network of 5000 connected computers—2010
•Productivity: leisure-oriented business dominate world economy, 1/2 of U.S. GNP—2015
•Biotech: biological age 40 for 200 years—2020
•Advanced materials: end of combustion engine—2020
•Critical success factors: prosperity, ecological sustainability, decreasing violence—2020
•50% of U.S. adults over 50 years old: echo-boom generation (1977–1997), 80 million more economic power than parents—2030

The key exatrend that we have been riding since 500 B.C. is the access to information. When we hope to understand the student's engagement in various activities, we also need to understand their goals and their opportunities to learn. The recognition of the importance of student's goals in our assessment and evaluation efforts has far-reaching implications.

We have to take into consideration every aspect of the student when we design the course, and assess their requirements according to each student. We need to remember that our assessments and the teaching must embody Dewey's mandate that education shape as well as reflect society's needs. It is critical to identify "higher-order thinking" and discipline-specific knowledge as the most common goals. It is found that faculty and students disaggregate higher-order thinking from career preparation. So, the focus needs to be on the design of Web-based courses that can help the students by integrating their academic and career goals.

CONCLUSION: TRANSFORMING THE WHOLE

In this chapter, the transnational model for Web-based education and the learning orientation model, in addition to the seven key predictions for Web-based education, were assessed. As educational institutions assess opportunities to learn, they must develop a competitive market in education technology in even broader areas. Various questions need to be asked to transform education and learning into a new era. For example, how can the faculty collaborate on various online courses and integrate their knowledge for a well-rounded and integrated cross-functional learning experience for the students? Do our outcomes assessments and our tests map to our own high-end goals? What opportunities are we providing our on-campus and online students to apply what they are learning in the Web-based courses to other domains? What assessment techniques should be used in the online learning environment that will foster new thinking about curriculum (Brown, 2000)?

Online universities teach knowledge beyond the books, because peer-to-peer knowledge sharing provides value enhancement in this collaborative discussion and team projects model. This is in stark contrast to the vertical or top-down knowledge delivery model in which the professor lectures or "professes," and there is lack of flexibility to accommodate demanding or erratic work schedules and personal responsibilities. Technological forces, such as the convergence of data, voice, and video to a single platform and wider Internet access that makes Web-based training more affordable and convenient than conventional methods; social forces such as the "baby boom echo," where the baby boomers and their kids need education and training; and economic forces, such as intensified global competition, are coming together to drive demand for Web-based education and training.

REFERENCES

AACSB International. (2002). Management education at risk: a report from the Management Education Task Force, April.

Ahmed, R. (2000). Effectiveness of Web-based virtual learning environments in business education: focusing on basic skills training for information technology. Unpublished doctoral dissertation, Louisiana State University, Baton Rouge, LA.

Alavi, M., & Leidner, D. (2001). Research commentary: technology-mediated learning—a call for greater depth and breadth of research. *Information Systems Research, 12*(1), 1–10.

Bell, S. (2001). Web-based utilities for learning and collaboration in the classroom. *Syllabus*, July, pp. 32–35; www.syllabus.com.

Bhartlett, C. A., & Ghosal, S. (1989). Managing across borders. The transnational solution. Boston, MA: Harvard Business School Press.

Bhartlett, C. A., & Ghosal, S. (1990). Managing innovation in the transnational corporation. In C. A. Bartlett, Y. Doz, & G. Hedlund (Eds.), *Managing the global firm*. London: Routledge.

Block, H. B., & Dobell, B. (1999). The e-bang theory, education industry overview. Equity research, Bank of America Securities, Montgomery Division, San Francisco, CA.

Boettcher, J. V. (1999). 21st century teaching and learning patterns: what will we see? *Syllabus*, June, pp. 18–26; www.syllabus.com.

Brown, G. (2000). The Venn of assessment transforming instructional design. *Syllabus*, November, pp. 36–39; www.syllabus.com.

Charp, S. (2001). E-Learning. *The Journal*, April, p. 10; www.thejournal.com.

Farrell, B. (2001). Developing a successful online class: what works to keep the students motivated and interested? *USDLA Journal, 15*(5). Retrieved February 12, 2001 from the World Wide Web: http://www.usdla.org/html/journal/JAN02_Issue/article01.html.

Hamel, G. (1996). Strategy as revolution. *Harvard Business Review*, July–August, pp. 69–82.

King, W. R., & Sethi, V. (1999). An empirical assessment of the organization of transnational information systems. *Journal of Management Information Systems, 15*(4), 7–28.

Lewis, Snow, & Farris. (1999). Distance Education at Postsecondary Education Institutions: 1997-98, National Center for Education Statistics, Statistical Analysis Report 2000-013; http://nces.ed.gov/pubs2000/2000013.pdf, December 17, 1999.

Martinez, M., & Buderson, V. C. (2000). Foundations for personalized Web learning environments. *ALN Magazine, 4*(2). Retrieved February 12, 2001 from the World Wide Web: http://www.aln.org/alnWeb/magazine/Vol4_issue2/burdenson.htm.

Moore. (2000). Web-based communications, the Internet, and distance education, In M. G. Moore, & G. T. Cozine (Eds.), *Readings in Distance Education No. 7*, August.

Passmore, D. L. (2000). Impediments to adoption of Web-based course delivery among university faculty. *ALN Magazine, 4*(2) Retrieved February 12, 2002 from the World Wide Web: http://www.aln.org/alnWeb/magazine/Vol4_issue2/passmore.htm.

Porter, M. (1996). What is strategy. *Harvard Business Review*, November–December, pp. 61–78.

Rheingold, H. (2001). Face-to-face with virtual communities. *Syllabus*, July, pp. 8–12, www.syllabus.com.

Smith, G. G., & Ferguson, D. (2001). Teaching college courses online vs. face-to-face. *The Journal*, pp. 19–26, www.thejournal.com.

Vitalari, N. P., & Wetherbe, J. C. (1996). Emerging best practices in global systems development. In P.C. Palvia, S.C. Palvia, & E. M. Roche (Eds.), *Global information technology and systems development*. Nashua, NH: Ivy League Publishing, Limited.

Zwass, V. (1998). Foundations of information systems (pp. 643–646). New York: Irwin/McGraw-Hill.

APPENDIX A

In Figure 1, the two schools of research (instructional technology and Web design) are merged to illustrate the prototype authoring system named WebTAS (Web-Based Tutorial Authoring System).

The system facilitates a consistent layout of the screens, incorporates help menus, and also administrates the test taking, grading, and feedback links. A schematic of the logic flow of the system is shown in Figure 2.

Figure 1: WebTAS (Web-Based Tutoring Authoring System)

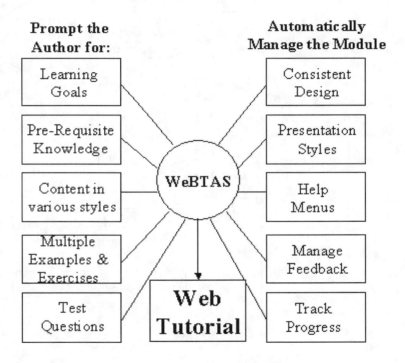

Note. Source: T. Janicki, & J. O. Liegle. (2001). Development and evaluation of a framework for creating Web-based learning modules: a pedagogical and systems perspective, JALN, 5, 1, June

Figure 2: Flow Diagram of WebTAS Authoring System

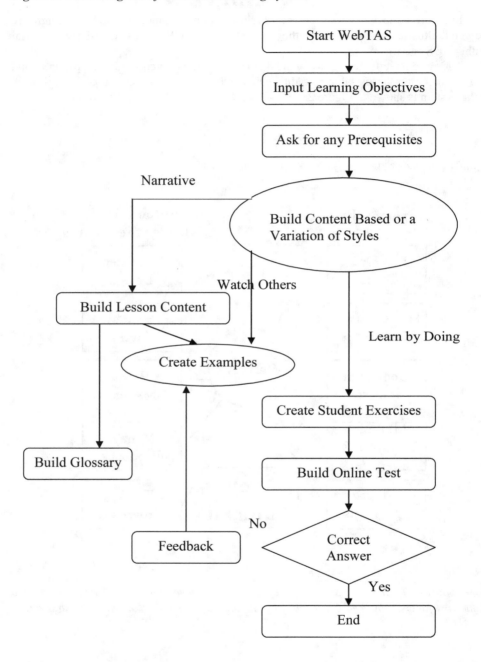

Note. Source: T. Janicki, & J. O. Liegle. (2001). Development and evaluation of a framework for creating Web-based learning modules: a pedagogical and systems perspective, JALN, 5, 1, June

Part II

WBE: Enhancing Technologies

Chapter VI

Preproduction Stages in Multimedia Development: Conceptualization and Scriptwriting

Johanna Klassen
City University of Hong Kong, Hong Kong

ABSTRACT

In this chapter, the focus is on the design of autonomous language learning courseware based on the Constructivist view, where learners only learn how to learn when they are actively involved in the learning process. This calls for programs that are designed to be interactive, encouraging students to select the type and pace of work, and providing feedback for decisions made. The author draws on the experience of producing an interactive multimedia package, Virtual Language University, for English-language learning. The focus is on the decision-making process in front-end design work. The conceptualization stage addresses: (a) specification decisions related to educational needs; (b) interface design with emphasis on metaphor, menu selection, diagnostic testing, and screen design; and (c) navigation. Decisions related to scripting include the general format, coding, and creation of templates, graphics and animation, video specifications, and task interaction. Each phase has examples taken from the Virtual Language University, a CD-ROM package.

INTRODUCTION

The use of technology has been introduced to most areas of teaching for several decades now. In the earliest stages of this transition, researchers considered the prospect of whether the teacher could be replaced altogether. Technology played the teacher's role, and students became accustomed to learning *from* technology (Jonassen et al., 1999). Just as students had learned from teachers before, they now learned from videos, television, computer-assisted instruction frames, or any technology designed to transmit information to the student. Yet, as Jonassen et al. pointed out, understanding cannot be conveyed or transmitted. Understanding takes place only when meaning is constructed by students thinking by themselves. According to this Constructivist approach, learning takes place when students are: "…thinking about what they are doing or what they did, thinking about what they believe, thinking about what others have done and believe, thinking about the thinking processes they use—just thinking. Thinking mediates learning. This requires a shift from traditional "technology-as-teacher" to "technology-as-partner" (Jonassen et al., 1999). Within this learning paradigm, the students are learning *with* the computer, not *from* it. Other researchers confirm that such interactivity is a necessary component for learning to take place (Laurel, 1990). Learners only learn how to learn when they are actively and continually involved in the learning process.

This calls for programs that are designed to be interactive, encouraging students to select the type and pace of work, and providing feedback for decisions made. Interactive Multimedia is a technology that appeals to the sense of sight, sound, and touch by integrating video, audio, graphics, animation, and text applications. Student-centered learning places emphasis on interaction for the learner. Interaction can be between the learner and a tutor (as in a host or animated character), or it can be between the learner and the computer (as in feedback provided in bubbles, online help, etc., based on performance) (Klassen et al., 1999). As this new mode of learning evolves, courseware designers are challenged to produce materials that deepen understanding, promote interactivity, and encourage self-direction (Gatlin-Watts et al., 1999; Hanson-Smith, 1996–1997).

A university professor's task today in preparing for classes is drastically changing. There are, of course, a multitude of stages of using technology in teaching, ranging from replacement of the face-to-face professor to use of technology as an adjunct to teaching. The design and development work involved goes well beyond normal preparation time and certainly beyond the expertise of most academic staff, especially if materials have been produced with tools such as Authorware, Director, Flash, or Dreamweaver. Delivering a script so that a development team can produce an interactive package without constant supervision takes an enormous amount of planning and detailed explanations and instructions.

The author at City University of Hong Kong produced an interactive courseware package *Virtual Language University* (VLU), an interactive multimedia package for language learning that has over 1800 interactive tasks. In the planning stage, it became apparent that there was limited literature available on the front-end decisions to be made before a script can be delivered to a development team, a script that programmers and graphic designers can follow without constant supervision. In this chapter, the author draws on the experience of producing VLU, describes the decisions to be made during the conceptualization stage, and illustrates the method of scriptwriting that was developed.

CONCEPTUALIZATION STAGE
Educational Needs

Educational needs relate to the teaching objectives and to the needs of the learners. There is a dearth of high-quality language learning packages that actually involve students. High quality assumes superior design work with three-dimensional animation, professionally developed video, and challenging interaction for users, including sophisticated feedback. This means that feedback is not generic for all users; rather, it is dependent on the response of the user. Wherever possible, further explanations are also available.

The aim of VLU is to provide a self-directed learning tool for students interested in improving their English communication skills. Although the package was originally designed for CD-ROM format, it is presently being adapted for a website. The four-year project was funded by two Teaching Development Grants of the University Grants Committee of Hong Kong of over HK$5,000,000. Foremost, the package was developed specifically for the Hong Kong context; however, the content is appropriate for any second-language learners interested in developing their English skills autonomously. The package can also be used as an adjunct to teaching.

Such large-scale funding supports a team to carry through the work without changing too many team members. The development team that was responsible for creating VLU consisted of the author as project manager and instructional designer, four computer programmers, a graphic artist, four scriptwriters, and several student helpers. This team worked closely during every stage of production, including the conceptual phase of brainstorming for the interface design, scriptwriting, production of computer programming, video recording, and graphic design, as well as piloting and evaluating.

Table 1: Considerations in the Conceptualization Stages of Developing an Interactive Multimedia Package

Area	Topic	Subtopic	Considerations
Conceptualization	Educational needs	Delivery	Objectives defined
			Type/purpose/availability of host
			Optional features
	Interface design	Metaphor	Match: interest of students and content
		Direction	Movement: sequential or user's choice
			Work in appropriate level
		Diagnostic testing	Appropriate level of difficulty
		Screen design	Type of design: simple, complex
	Navigation	Guidance	Sequential access, guided or self-directed
			Skipping, exiting
			Exiting
	Task design	Types of tasks	M/C, Gap Fill, T/F, Y/N, Dragging, Prioritizing, Click
		Feedback	Immediate or delayed feedback and second tries
		Scoring	Number of tasks completed and scores
		Reporting	Attempts recorded and % for each task
		Help	Type of help

Delivery

The conceptualization stage needs to address the educational needs of the learners. The considerations for each of the stages of conceptualization are shown in Table 1.

The objective of the delivery needs to be defined, for example, whether it is a guided learning package or self-learning package. The former will most often have a host or "information giver," ensuring that the necessary information is available to the user in a predefined sequence. A self-learning package works from the standpoint of "learning by doing," where the user chooses a pathway through the package, gradually processing the information necessary to assimilate the theories needed to develop the attempted skill.

If a host is used, there is the question of the type of host: audio, video, or animated character. Once the main role of the package has been determined, whether for teaching, autonomous learning, or for providing feedback to the user, there is the question of the amount of instruction available. Is the host an optional feature or continuous? Is this teaching element available only upon request, or is it a required aspect specifically linked to a section that must be listened to or read (Klassen & Milton, 1999).

Interface Design

The interface can be described as the face between the user and the program (Klassen et al., 1999). Specifically, it is concerned with functions within the screen layout, for example, navigation buttons, help buttons, icons or descriptions, titles/headings, maps, and styles of menus. Interactive media places users in a one-on-one relationship with a program that can be as intimate, or more intimate than, a face-to-face exchange (Utvich, 1995). It is, therefore, the task of educational multimedia producers to transform this relationship into a successful learning experience.

Metaphor

The design of the package affects the interest level of learners. If the design has a metaphor that appeals to students, it is an instant plus factor. The metaphor will be more effective if there is a match between the presentation of materials and the learner's interest.

The VLU package is based on the metaphor of a university, relevant to most users of the package. Upon entering, users are given a tour of the campus, including four units: the Lecture Theatre for the Listening Unit, the Language Building for Writing, the Library for Vocabulary, and the Gymnasium for Grammar. The units are metaphorically represented as

Figure 1: Campus Map   *Figure 2: VLU Lobby*

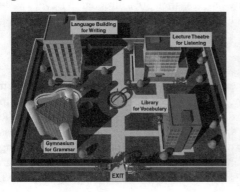
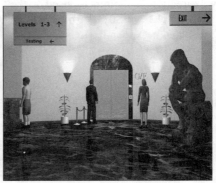

Table 2: Interface Design: Choice of Sequential Movement or Random Selection

Sequential ⇒	Unit selection ⇒	Test ⇒	Results ⇒	Directed to Level 1, 2, or 3 topics
Random ⇒	Unit selection ⇒	No test ⇓		
		Task mode ⇒	Choice of level	
			Choice of tasks ⇒	Topics

four separate buildings in a virtual university campus (Figures 1 and 2). The metaphor continues, with the difficulty levels represented as Floors 1, 2, or 3. The animated host, a friendly Dr. Einstein, provides first-time users with a tour of the campus and explains how the program works.

Menu Selection

If users are given a choice in the level at which they work, they will be working on materials that are challenging to them, at their appropriate level of difficulty. However, this may mean trying different levels until they feel comfortable or using testing features. The learners' interest will be held longer if they are working on a challenging level, resulting in longer time-on-task.

The interface design of VLU is based on two basic choices: sequential work or random selection, as indicated in Table 2. Once the users have selected a building (or unit) to work on, they have two choices: to work through the program based on the computer's direction or to work on areas and levels that are of interest to them.

Diagnostic Testing

If a package has testing capabilities, learners need not try different levels until they reach the one appropriate for them. Through short tests, users can be directed to the correct level for them, thus saving time and interest.

VLU's 15-minute diagnostic tests, with approximately 20 items per test, provide feedback on strengths and weaknesses. For example, in the Grammar Unit, there are 18 grammatical structures tested (e.g., articles, pronouns, gerunds, tenses, etc.), and at the end of the test, a percentage is generated for each structure, as well as an overall mark. The user is then directed to the appropriate level: 1, 2, or 3, with 1 being the easiest. The scoring and level direction in all units is based on the following: less than 50% directed to Level 1, 50–79% to Level 2, and 80% and over to Level 3. A list of the items for which VLU tests are given is presented in Appendix 1.

Screen Design

In a user-controlled environment that enables students to select the sequence of their choice or to turn off the program whenever they want, screen design becomes essential to maintaining learners' interest. Effective screen design allows for maximum learning from the materials, while providing the learner with appropriate control of the learning process (Milheim & Lavix, 1992). An effective screen design sets the stage for meaningful learning to take place and motivates the learner to stay engaged. The importance of the screen design is corroborated by Stemler (Boyle, 1997; Ivers & Barron, 1998; Stemler, 1997; Vaughan, 1998).

Figure 3: Listening Unit Design

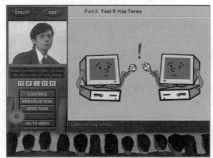

Figure 4: Vocabulary Unit Design

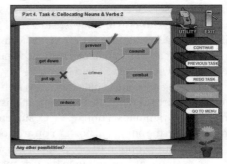

The signs of a poorly designed screen are cluttered displays, complex and tedious procedures, inadequate command languages, inconsistent sequences of action, and insufficient informative feedback (Schneiderman, 1992). Such designs can lead to anxiety, poor performance, and dissatisfaction with the program. Users are most effectively able to concentrate on the multimedia material when the screen is uncluttered and has consistent commands and positioning of buttons (Klassen et al., 2001). The choices for screen design are endless, but the two basic extremes are simple and complex. The primary advantage of keeping the screen "simple and uncluttered" is that it is less likely that users will suffer from immediate sensory overload.

In VLU, the typical screen design is "simple and uncluttered" (see Figures 3 and 4). Wherever possible, graphics and animation are used to replace text.

Navigation

Easy navigation in a package is important for keeping learners on-task. There are several possibilities for how users access materials: sequentially, semi-directed, free choice, or through pathways. Each of these methods can be designed to have extreme linear order or extreme nonlinear order, where users have little or no chance of deviating from a predetermined sequence. Thus, package possibilities can range from strict, prescribed, sequential learning to complete freedom of choice. An alternative is a semi-directed program, allowing for the possibility of choice within certain situations. The ideal is possibly a type of navigation that encourages thinking without losing the purpose of the instruction (Wild & Quinn, 1998). This ensures that the navigation has minimal traveling; that is, that express pathways enable users to arrive at their desired destination as fast as possible with little or no redundancy (Vogel & Klassen, 2001).

In greater detail, movement can be designed so the user progresses in a forward direction only unless a change to a previous menu is made. It is also possible to design a forward and back button, forward taking the user to the next task and back to the previous task. Skipping sections can be important for second-time users, as they may not wish to redo all parts of a task, especially if it involves listening to or reading long passages. Exiting also requires decisions, ranging from being able to exit only when the current task/section/unit is completed to being able to exit at any time.

The delicate balance of giving enough sense of direction to avoid anxiety yet not overdirecting users has been addressed in VLU, so that the learners always know where they are going, but they remain in control. It is important for them to navigate the path of their own learning. Too little freedom may result in students working on tasks that are not relevant to their needs. Users can choose to skip ahead to subtopics at any time, yet are required to select the Main Menu to do so. That is, students have the possibility of moving around to any building or level or topic or task from the Main Menu that is available at all times. However, they automatically enter a linear sequence upon entering the unit but may choose to exit the linear mode by use of the Main Menu.

Choosing the linear pathway may at times be preferable, particularly for work on grammar, where skipping ahead may mean missing important grammatical rules and explanations. In the Grammar section of VLU, students choosing to skip ahead will hear a friendly reminder from the animated host: "You are not advised to go to this task at this stage." Users are then given the option of proceeding anyway, or returning to the previous section.

An example of navigating in the task mode of VLU may be useful. If the user chooses to work in Level 2 of the Listening Unit, one of four multimedia lectures given by university professors can be selected (each of the three levels has four lectures, totaling 12 lectures). The design of the Listening Unit, which incorporates video, graphics, sound, and about 50 interactive tasks per lecture, uses the graphic of a video player with buttons for easy navigation (see Figure 4). Users can control the forward, back, and replay icons of the video, and in this way, monitor their own pace. Using the buttons, users can also work through the tasks in various ways: (a) skipping the video clip and moving to the task, the button *Continue*; (b) repeating the previous task, *Previous Task*; (c) repeating the current task, *Repeat Task*; (d) seeing the Results on their performance, *Results*; or (e) using the Menu selection for random selection, *Go To Menu*.

Task Design of VLU

Types of Tasks

There are seven main types of tasks: Multiple Choice, Gap Fill, True/False, Yes/No, Drag to gap, Drag to prioritize, Click and Write on Notepad. Although multiple choice and click are the easiest to construct, both for the scriptwriter and programmer, there is a balance of other task types in VLU to ensure maximum interactivity. Each task is designed according to the learning objective of the unit; for example, in the Listening Unit, tasks diagnose for skills such as vocabulary, main ideas, key words, note-taking, summary, predictions, and inferences.

Feedback

Each task is programmed to give immediate or delayed feedback and a percentage score after each task. The user soon recognizes the positive beep and tick for correct answers and the low, negative beep for incorrect answers. Immediate feedback allows users only one opportunity to provide correct information or make a decision, while delayed feedback allows for completion of several steps and also allows for a second try. It will also prompt for "Any more possibilities?" if there is more than one answer that is correct.

Scoring

Users can repeat tasks to improve their score as often as they wish; however, they can access the scores only of the last two working sessions, as this information is automatically stored in the computer. As evident from Appendix 2, users can see immediately which tasks have been attempted or not attempted from the ticks in the menu; they can also see their scores for the current attempt as well as scores for the last attempt.

Help

Help is provided for specific tasks in the form of pop-up bubbles or special buttons. The Utilities button allows users to change the sound level.

SCRIPTWRITING

The decision-making stages for scriptwriting are shown in Table 3.

Templates

A prerequisite for efficient development of interactive multimedia packages is a clear and effective script. During the scriptwriting stage, decisions concerning the number and type of tasks, the style of feedback, the sequence of questions, the different levels of tasks, and the type of scoring are made. The decisions should first be organized into an outline form to give a broader perspective and to ensure there is an appropriate distribution among all the categories.

Templates are useful for providing consistency and thoroughness. It is easier for scriptwriters to maintain consistency throughout the scripts with the use of identical terminology, predictable sequences, and the same command language (Vogel & Klassen, 2001). The template is also a reminder to the scriptwriter not to overlook important areas.

Format

Excerpts of the VLU script taken from the lecture "Cultural Connections" in Level 1 of the Listening Unit are provided in Appendix 4. The tasks indicated in the appendix are not sequential but are taken from various parts of the lecture to illustrate points to be made here (for example, Part 1, Task 1, then Part 3, Task 6). The coding system is explained later. Although the details of the script may appear complex and too complicated for the average educator,

Table 3: Considerations in the Scriptwriting Stages of Developing an Interactive Multimedia Package

Area	Topic	Subtopic	Considerations
Script writing	**Use of templates**	**Format**	Columns for (a) graphics/animation, (b) video, and (c) task interaction
		Graphics and animation	Description of animation with codes
			Indication of sequence—numbering
		Video	Codes for capturing and exact placement
		Coding system	Template
			Coding—repetitive items
			Correct answers indicated in bold
			Type of feedback for correct and incorrect answers

a system comprehensible to programmers and graphic designers is essential. The script is divided into three columns: graphics and animation, transcription of lecture, and interactive tasks.

Graphics and Animation

The graphics column provides not only a description of the type of graphic or animation required but also the specific point where the graphic is to be inserted. Graphics related to the lecture have a numbering system starting with LG for lecture graphics and TG for task graphics. The number refers to the parts and tasks that the lectures have been divided into. For example, LG1.1d refers to Part 1, Task 1 and is the fourth of seven graphics (a to g) to be inserted at points indicated in the transcription of the lecture. In the interest of saving space, a series of abbreviations or codes are used as seen at the top of the left column of Appendix 3.

Video

The middle column, the lecture script column, has the transcription of the video. The lecture is divided into manageably sized segments. Each segment is numbered to facilitate work for the graphic designer when capturing the video for digitization, for the programmer for inserting the correct portion of the video, as well as for the camera production team to indicate appropriate zooming in and zooming out for sections. The physical placement of the code (for example, LG1.1a) tells the programmer to insert the graphic at the point of the video indicated, that is, Part 1, Task 1, and "a" is the first of a series. The asterisk symbol (*) after the code indicates that the graphic should be in synch with the word that immediately follows. The X after the code indicates when the graphic should be removed. Sometimes, multiple graphics appear on the screen at once (for example, LG1.1 a, b, c, d, e, f, g X). More often, however, one graphic is replaced by another, so only one graphic is on the screen at one time. For example, the graphic appears at the point in the lecture where LG3.6c is written. Then at the point of LG3.6cX, it is replaced by LG3.6d.

Task Interaction

The task column (see Appendix 3), the column on the right, is much more complex than the other two. A template is used to assist in writing the tasks, with abbreviations detailed at the top right-hand corner of Appendix 4. In Figure 8, details of the template are provided. The bolded column on the left shows the codes that are used for describing each task in a manner comprehensible to the programmer and graphic designer, that is, each task will provide information on the title of the task, the online help (instructing the user on whether to click, drag, etc.), the type of feedback (delayed or immediate), the type of task (multiple-choice, drag and drop, notebook, etc.), the diagnosis (of the skill that is tested), the points per task for scoring, and specific storyboarding instructions for the programmer or graphic designer.

Coding System

Codes are used for saving space for items that are repeated and are necessary for each task. This format conveniently and precisely transmits the desired information to the programmer.

Table 4: Template of Coding System

P1T1: Lecture topic for Part 1, Task 1
OLH: Online help
FDBK: Type and order of feedback to user (CA refers to correct answer)
TYPE: Type of task
DIAG: Diagnosis or item the task addresses
PT: The points per task for scoring
STBD: Storyboard or specific instructions for the programmer

Specifically, the **OLH** (online help) is the text that appears at the bottom of every task, directing users through the task. Minimal text is used, preferably just one line of text but enough to ensure understanding. If a second online help is used later, it is used for tasks that have a delayed feedback mechanism. It also serves as the prompt for the second try (Try again). The **FDBK** (feedback) line is used to instruct the programmer on the sequence of online help and the nature of the feedback to be given, as well as when the correct answer should appear. An example of immediate feedback (IF) is given in P1 Task1 (see Appendix 4). Here, the FDBK is: OLH1 + IF + OLH2 + AOP + CA. This is an example of a task with three correct answers with immediate feedback after each click on an answer; that is, as soon as the user selects an answer, appropriate feedback is given. If the answer is incorrect, a second chance for the first answer (of the three correct answers) is given (OLH2: Try again), until the answer is correct. Then, the AOP (Any other possibilities?) prompt follows, flashing to prompt for a second correct answer. This cycle repeats until all answers are correct.

An example of delayed feedback is in Part 3, Task 6 (P3 T6), where the FDBK reads: OHL1 + DF + OLH2 + CA. The order understood by the programmer is: (a) the first online should say "Drag the correct meaning to each symbol & press RESULTS"; (b) the feedback is delayed until the user has made a first attempt at the task and has had a chance to change before pressing RESULTS; (c) if the answer was incorrect, a second chance is given; and (d) the correct answer is confirmed or if the answer is still incorrect, the correct answer appears.

For each task, **TYPE** refers to the type of task—in this case, a dragging task (DRAG). **DIAG** refers to the skill that is being diagnosed—in this case, comprehension (COMP). **PT** indicates the number of points for the task. And, **STBD** (storyboard) refers to the special instructions to the programmer relating to the task. For example, in P3 T6, instructions are given to ensure that the "user drags the correct 'meaning' (in text format) to the correct symbol."

Directly beneath the uniform coding of the template (see Appendix 3) is a visual presentation of all the written elements to be included in the task. It is designed as a visual mockup of the task to give the programmer a better understanding. Correct answers are bolded. If the lecture segment is in smaller font, it indicates to the programmer that the video does not come on automatically when the task is selected. For example, for a prelistening task, the video obviously should not be heard first; therefore, the video text is in smaller font. Using a smaller font can also show the programmer that it is a repeated lecture segment. The video is available to the user but does not come on automatically.

By separating the graphics, lecture script, and the tasks into three columns, we created a template for the description of graphics and animation, video, and tasks, and thus, a guideline for multimedia development.

CONCLUSION

In this chapter, some of the features of the preproduction stages of developing interactive multimedia materials were discussed. Particular emphasis was placed on the conceptualization and scriptwriting stages. As the field of interactive learning evolves from one of discovery and exploration to an established domain with set standards and practices, greater demands are placed on educational designers and the products they produce. It is now widely accepted that the educational capabilities of multimedia are directly related to the effective use of layers and multiple pathways of learning. The ability to successfully create a product reflecting such multifaceted interaction begins at the conceptual and scriptwriting stage. The challenges of planning the concept design and developing effective interactive multimedia scripts should not be underestimated, as they require a whole new approach to instructional design. The lessons gained from developing VLU have been invaluable. It is hoped that the guidelines outlined in this chapter will help others on the path of interactive learning production.

REFERENCES

Boyle, T. (1997). *Design for multimedia learning.* London: Prentice Hall.

Gatlin-Watts, R., Arn, J., & Kordsmeier, W. (1999). Multimedia as an instructional tool: perceptions of college department chairs. *Education Chula Vista, 120*(1), 190–196.

Hanson-Smith, E. (1996–1997). Why multimedia? *CAELL Journal, 7*(3), 35–36.

Ivers, K., & Barron, A. (1998). *Multimedia projects in education: designing, producing, and assessing.* Englewood Cliffs, NJ: Libraries Unlimited.

Jonassen, D., Peck, K., & Wilson, B. (1999). *Learning with technology: a Constructivist perspective.* Upper Saddle River, NJ: Prentice Hall.

Klassen, J., & Milton, P. (1999). Enhancing English language skills using multimedia: tried and tested. *Computer Assisted Language Learning, 12*(4), 281–294.

Klassen, J., Stone, D., & Vogel, D. (1999, June). *Design issues for development of interactive multimedia: electronic commerce & business simulation application.* Paper presented at the Twelfth International Bled Electronic Commerce Conference, Bled, Slovenia.

Klassen, J., Vogel, D., & Moody, E. (2001). *Interactive learning: design and evaluation.* Paper presented at the HICCS Conference, Maui, Hawaii.

Laurel, B. (1990). *The art of human–computer interface design.* Reading, MA: Addison-Wesley.

Milheim, C. L., & Lavix, C. (1992). Screen design for computer-based training and interactive video: practical suggestions and overall guidelines. *Performance and Instruction, 31*(5), 13–21.

Schneiderman, B. (1992). *Designing the user interface: strategies for effective human–computer interaction.* Reading, MA: Addison-Wesley.

Stemler, L. (1997). Educational characteristics of multimedia: a literature review. *Journal of Educational Multimedia and Hypermedia, 6*(3/4), 339–359.

Utvich, M. (1995). Instructional design: people and the art of interactive. *Multimedia Producer, 1*(9), 1–5; www.kipinet.com.

Vaughan, T. (1998). *Multimedia: making it work*. Berkeley: Osborne McGraw-Hill.

Vogel, D., & Klassen, J. (2001). Technology supported instruction: a perspective on status, issues and trends in delivery. *Journal of Computer Assisted Learning, 17*(1), 104–111.

Wild, M., & Quinn, C. (1998). Implications of educational theory for the design of instructional multimedia. *British Journal of Educational Technology, 29*(1), 73–82.

APPENDIX 1: DIAGNOSIS OF SKILLS TESTED IN FOUR UNITS

Vocabulary:	**Writing:**
Word Choice	Subject
Word Form	Verb
Word Order	Clauses
Compound Nouns	Coordinating Sentences
Synonyms	Subordination with Conjunctions
Antonyms	Pronouns
Adverbs	Participles
Word Building	Appositives
Collocation	Combining Sentences
Homonyms	Appropriateness
Homophones	
Phrasal Verbs	
Idioms	
Connotation	
Grammar:	**Listening:**
Articles	*Topics of Lectures*
Pronouns	**Level 1**
	All about the Internet
Adjectives	
	Poet of the City
Relative Pronouns	
	Shopping in Cyberspace
Gerunds/Infinitives	
	Cultural Connections

APPENDIX 1: DIAGNOSIS OF SKILLS TESTED IN FOUR UNITS (CONTINUED)

Tenses	Introduction to Orgar
Modals	The Rights of the Ch
Adverbs/Adjectives	Software Piracy
Active/Passive	Anna Akhmatova's F
Prepositions	**Level 3**
Connectives	Global Team Suppor
Participles	Global Team Suppor
Relative Clauses	Investigating Crime
Adverbial Clauses	Cultural Differences
Agreement	
Question Tags	**Diagnosis for:**
Conditionals	Note Taking
Questions	Comprehension
Word Order	Key Words
	Vocabulary
	Main Ideas
	Making Inferences
	Predicting Meaning

APPENDIX 2: FEEDBACK ON PERFORMANCE

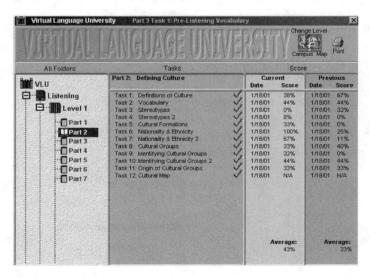

APPENDIX 3: SCRIPTWRITING FOR INTERACTIVE TASKS

Level 1 **Cultural Connections**

Graphic Animation	Audio/Video	Interaction

Part One: Introduction

Graphic Animation

Abbreviations Used:
PHO = Photo
TX = Text
GR = Graphic
LS = Long Shot
BG = Background
MS = Medium Shot
CU = Close Up
LF = Left
CNT = Center
RG = Right

[LGL14] TX (CNT): "CULTURE": with arrows out to subjects covered ...[LGL1b] TX "Cultural Studies & Communications"
[LGL1c] TX "Definitions"
[LGL1d] TX "Cultural formations"
[LGL1e] TX "Characteristics"
[LGL1f] TX "Intercultural Communications"
[LGL1g] TX "Globalization"

[LGL2a] TX (TOP): "SYMBOLS" GR (BG): Pattern with many small symbols (i.e., % @ & ¿¡) [LGL2b] arrow pointing to TX: "MEANING"
[LGL2c] PHO/GR of two hand gestures—hands up as if saying "I don't know" and finger pointing
[LGL2d] PHO/GR—hand making OK sign

[TGL3] GRs of symbols in two or three columns on screen, with room for TX underneath
(1) Person waving
(2) CU hand with thumbs up
(3) Circle with red X inside
(4) ↑ inside rectangle (green)
(5) Green traffic light
(6) CU hand—OK sign with U.S. flag in BG
(7) CU hand—OK sign with Japanese flag in BG

Audio/Video

* indicates when graphic should come in

If the * is to the left of the GR, that means it should come at the same time of the previous word. If it comes to the right, it should come at the same time as the next word. For example, in LG1 1a, this means the GR would come as Culture is spoken. If there is no *, that means it comes in during a natural pause.

[Lecture Segment 1]

[Large Screen] Hello, my name is Pauline Burton and I am a Senior Lecturer in the Language Studies department at the college of City University of Hong Kong. Today, I will be discussing a subject that deeply affects us all, something that is present in just about all aspects of society, and influences the way we speak, look, dress, and eat... can you guess what I am talking about? ... I'm talking about [LGL1a*] culture. In this discussion, I will introduce some key concepts within the fields of [LGL1b*] cultural studies and communications that will enable you to view culture from a range of interesting and new perspectives. In this lecture, we will look at [LGL1c*] definitions of culture, how [LGL1d*]cultures are formed, [LGL1e*] characteristics of culture, [LGL1f*] intercultural communications, and, finally, the impact of [LGL1g*] globalization on culture. So, are you ready? [LGL1 a,b,c,d,e,f,g N]

[Lecture Segment ?]

[LGL2a*] While symbols are significant, what really makes them important is the [LGL2b*] meaning they convey. Meaning refers to the way in which all symbols of a particular culture are interpreted and understood. [LGL2c&2N], [LGL2e*] The same hand gesture may be used in several cultures, but the meaning could be completely different from one to the next. For example, one of the most common hand symbols—[LGL2c&N], [LGL2d*] the OK sign. In North America, and now many places elsewhere in the world, this carries a meaning of approval or agreement. Yet, in Japan, this same gesture represents money. [LGL2d N]

Interaction

Abbreviations Used:
PT = Points per task
OLH = Online help
CA = Correct Answers
IF = Immediate feedback
TON = Task On
DF = Delayed feedback
MID = Main Ideas
AOP = Any other Possibilities?
SUD = Sub Ideas
STBD = Storyboard
DIAG = Diagnosis
FDBK = Feedback
CA = Correct Answer
COMP = Comprehension
PRED = Prediction

P1 T1: Lecture Topics

OLH1: Click on three correct answers.
OLH2: Try again.
FDBK: OLH + IF + OLH2 + AOP + CA (etc.)
TYPE: CLICK
DIAG: PRED
PT: 3
STBD: Three CAs scattered with distracters.

Which lecture topics do you think will be covered?

CAs: globalization, cross-cultural communications, cultural definitions

distracters: Chinese culture, cultivating speech, Victorian culture

Part Three: Characteristics of Culture

P3 T6: Symbols and Meanings

OLH1: Drag the correct meaning to each symbol and press RESULTS.
OLH2: Try again.
FDBK: OLH + IF + OLH2 + CA
TYPE: DRAG
DIAG: COMP
PT: 8

STBD: User drags correct meaning (TX) to each symbol. Symbols appear in two or three rows on screen with spaces for TX underneath. CAs are scattered at screen bottom.

Symbols (GR):	Meaning (TX):
person waving	hello
thumbs up	good job
cross sign	no entry
arrow	straight ahead
green traffic light	GO!

APPENDIX 3: SCRIPT WRITING FOR INTERACTIVE TASKS (CONTINUED)

[LG3.6e] PHO/GR of two hand gestures—hands up as if saying "I don't know" and finger pointing

[LG3.6d] PHO/GR—hand making OK sign

[TG3.6] GRs of symbols in two or three columns on screen, with room for TX underneath

(1) Person waving

(2) CU hand with thumbs up

(3) Circle with red X inside

(4) ↑ inside rectangle (green)

(5) Green traffic light

(6) CU hand—OK sign with U.S. flag in BG

(7) CU hand—OK sign with Japanese flag in BG

(8) Knuckles knocking table (while tea is poured—China)

understood. [LG3.6a,bX] [LG3.6e] The same hand gesture may be used in several cultures, but the meaning could be completely different from one to the next. For example, one of the most common hand symbols—[LG3.6cX] [LG3.6d*] the OK sign. In North America, and now many places elsewhere in the world, this carries a meaning of approval or agreement. Yet, in Japan, this same gesture represents money. [LG3.6dX]

FDBK: OLH1 + DF + OLH2 + CA

TYPE: DRAG

DIAG: COMP

PT: 8

STBD: User drags correct meaning (TX) to each symbol. Symbols appear in two or three rows on screen with spaces for TX underneath. CAs are scattered at screen bottom.

Symbols (GR):	Meaning (TX):
person waving	hello
thumbs up	good job
cross sign	no entry
arrow	straight ahead
green traffic light	GO!
OK sign	approval
OK sign	$
knuckles knocking table	thank you

Chapter VII

Peer-to-Peer Networks as Extensions of Web-Based Education—Handhelds in Support of Coordination and Autonomy

Malu Roldan
San Jose State University, USA

ABSTRACT

In recent years, we have witnessed the rapid evolution of handheld computing devices from leading manufacturers, somewhat fueled by a battle being waged between Palm Computing and Microsoft Corporation. Handheld devices are attractive for educational settings, because they are inexpensive, portable, and customizable. Furthermore, most handheld devices come "out of the box" with infrared ports, enabling them to automatically form a peer-to-peer network with other handhelds. In this chapter, how such peer-to-peer networks could support the interplay of autonomy and coordination underlying current and emerging learning models will be discussed. Findings from a pilot study suggest that the information management and connectivity features of the machines make them ideal devices for such learning environments. The entertainment capabilities of the devices motivate students to learn how to use them. However, students found the machines and add-ons expensive, limited in capability, and difficult to use.

INTRODUCTION

Fueled by the widespread implementation of local area networks in the 1980s and the emergence of the World Wide Web in the 1990s, network computing has become an essential piece of technology-assisted education. Indeed, universities and other educational institutions are even seen as key to "pushing innovations in software and networking into the mainstream" (Hamm, 2000). Web-based education is a viable and thriving model for knowledge delivery in this context. In this chapter, it is proposed that the notion of Web-based education be extended to incorporate peer-to-peer (P2P) networks. Specifically, it will present a model for Web-based education that incorporates P2P via the deployment of handheld computing. Aside from being portable, handheld devices have the capability to communicate with other devices, because most of them include an infrared port. The ports allow devices to communicate with each other without having to route messages through a centralized network, such as the campus backbone or a departmental LAN, thereby creating a P2P network (Gonsalves, 2001; Werbach, 2000; Werbach, 2002). A summary of the various components of P2P networks is provided in the Appendix.

The flexibility and user-driven features of P2P networks of handhelds make them suitable for the fluid, emergent learning environments envisioned by education futurists. Learning models based on coordinated autonomy (Davis, 2001), constructivist philosophy (Abbott & Ryan, 1999), distributed education (Hawkins, 2000), ubiquitous computing (Brown, Burg, & Dominick, 1998; Thompson, 2002), and community service learning (Papamarcos, 2002) suggest an undercurrent of balanced interplay between autonomy and coordination. P2P networks of handhelds hold the promise and a first glimpse of possible technology platforms that can enable and inspire this interplay. In this chapter, the first phase of a study to determine how P2P networks will mesh with Web-based education is reported. It reports on a pilot study that explored how students might use handhelds to support their activities. The study findings are used to develop propositions to guide future deployments of P2P networks to support Web-based education.

P2P networks are emerging as viable adjuncts, even alternative networks, to the more centralized World Wide Web. In P2P networks, users are able to share files with little to no involvement or control from centralized servers. Its most visible application to date is Napster's MP3 distribution network, with success that unfortunately led to its demise. While it is probably responsible for much of the fame and notoriety of the P2P model, Napster, ironically, did not provide a pure P2P network. Napster still required centralized servers to keep track of the locations of files on client machines. True P2P networks, such as those based on the Gnutella protocol (Limewire, BearShare), do not require such centralized directories to find files on computers connected to the P2P network (Fry, 2002). From its roots as an alternative and controversial distribution method for music distribution, the P2P concept has been used to support collaboration, decentralize delivery of large media files, allow complex calculations to be parceled out among clusters of inexpensive computers, and extend the reach of wireless broadband networks (Werbach, 2000, 2002).

A P2P network makes it possible to share information within the localized area of a classroom or a small group discussion, without involvement of the central campus backbone or a local area network. The P2P model allows individual instructors to quickly incorporate networked computing support into their classroom activities, because it reduces the cost and setup effort associated with the establishment of a connection to the campus' central network or department LAN. Although it is also possible to connect the P2P network to the campus backbone through a single machine with networking capability, such connections are expected to occur only once-a-day or even less frequently. Generally, participants in P2P networks do the majority of their sharing directly with peers in the network, rather than with or through servers accessible via the Internet or campus backbone.

This autonomy at the edges of the network affords P2P platforms with the flexibility to reconfigure as computing demands change. Instead of requiring setup assistance, coordination, and approval from a central authority, adjustments to the network can be made by the participants at the grassroots level. Furthermore, every new addition to the network not only extends its reach but also has the potential to enrich the set of data and procedures available to the entire network. In a university environment, this means that a P2P network functioning within a classroom can be reconfigured on the fly, as class demands change. A typical class could start with a lecture, and then the students could spend the rest of the class meeting collecting data using handheld computers. The data can then be shared among these handhelds using infrared ports. Because of this connectivity, every new piece of information stored on each handheld augments the data available for access among the handhelds in the P2P network. If at least one of the handhelds is connected to a backbone network or LAN, the data are also potentially available and enriching to the larger network. This capability for flexible, independent, yet connected computing is an ideal platform for supporting emerging educational models, particularly those that parallel the principle of coordinated autonomy.

P2P IN SUPPORT OF COORDINATED AUTONOMY

Current trends in educational philosophy cluster around the principle of coordinated autonomy (Davis, 2001), particularly those cited in discussions of technology in support of education. Coordinated autonomy involves the juxtaposition of seemingly contradictory principles, a "marriage of autonomy and connectedness." Universities of the future are seen as emerging from the energy and creativity generated by such contradictions. To illustrate this creative tension, Davis (2001) lists eight principles identified by Frank Rhodes, former president of Cornell University. Examples of principles included in the list are as follows:

- Campus-rooted but internationally oriented
- Knowledge-based but student oriented; research driven but learner-focused
- Technologically sophisticated but community dependent

This theory of coordinated autonomy underlies many of the current educational theories in practice, among them constructivist philosophy (Abbott & Ryan, 1999), distributed education (Hawkins, 2000), ubiquitous computing (Brown, Burg, & Dominick, 1998; Thompson, 2002), and community service learning (Papamarcos, 2002).

Constructivist philosophy is one of the most often-cited principles used in current discussions of the design of technology to support education. While there are difficulties in its application to technology (Cates, 1993; Rodrigues, 2000), studies have found it to be an effective mode of instruction and learning (Alavi, Wheeler, & Valacich, 1995; Liaw, 2001; Churach & Fisher, 2001). A constructivist learning approach emphasizes the ability of an individual student to build knowledge and understanding of a given topic. Motivation is intrinsic, and there is a strong emphasis on reflection to build an understanding of the process by which a given answer is found, rather than purely an emphasis on getting the right answer. Exposure to real-life applications of concepts being taught is of paramount importance in the constructivist model of learning. The independence emphasized in the constructivist model is supported by the portability of devices in a P2P network of handhelds. Students can take the computing devices with them wherever and whenever they find the settings from which they can learn the best, including real-life situations, where the handhelds' diminutiveness make them relatively unobtrusive. At the same time, the connectivity afforded by the P2P network allows the students to collaborate in the construction of knowledge and then demonstrate and share this knowledge with their teachers.

Distributed education is perhaps one of the most discussed trends in education these days, as universities wrestle with the limitations of their physical campuses and the emergence of new competitors (Hawkins, 2000). P2P networks of handhelds could potentially serve as another delivery mechanism for distributed education. Handhelds can provide an additional convenience for students on the go, as homework assignments and readings can be downloaded onto the devices for portable access—on the plane, at home, or on a hike. As handhelds gain in their processing power and multimedia capabilities, they may also be used to deliver full lectures and, if connected to wide area networks or the Internet, ongoing class discussions. Teams of students who are co-located can collaborate by forming a satellite P2P network, using their infrared ports for sharing files and other communications.

Ubiquitous computing is often cited as the governing principle for large-scale deployments of computing capabilities (e.g., laptop programs) across campuses (Brown, Burg, & Dominick, 1998; Thompson, 2002). As handhelds become more powerful and start becoming viable laptop alternatives, campuses should start considering P2P networks of handhelds as lower cost, more portable platforms on which to achieve the goals of universal access to computing. Furthermore, as envisioned by its creator Mark Weiser (1991, 1996), ubiquitous computing goes beyond universal access. Weiser saw computing as eventually becoming so integrated and taken for granted in our lives that it becomes invisible. In his vision, computing capability would be embedded in the objects of our everyday life—clothes, books, walls—and by their connectivity, provide the intelligence that delivers the appropriate support for our daily activities. Clearly, laptops and handhelds are only an intermediate step in achieving this vision. But as greater computing power gets concentrated in smaller devices, and these machines become connected through a variety of channels, including P2P, one can sense that Weiser's vision is getting closer to reality. Again, as in the other principles reviewed here, ubiquitous computing involves the balance of autonomy and connectedness that is a core capability of P2P networks of handhelds.

In line with the constructivist philosophy, among many universities today, there is a trend toward pedagogies that increase engagement with local communities. One such pedagogy is community service learning (CSL). CSL points to the community and students' involvement in it as a setting for teaching and applying material for courses in all areas of study. An example would be teaching social justice by having students research death penalty cases, with the aim of gaining the release of a death row inmate. CSL is an ideal model for information systems courses. By working on information systems issues at community organizations, students gain valuable insight into the practicalities of their training in computing technology and management theory. Community organizations, on the other hand, benefit greatly from the knowledgeable help they get from students, in an area that is generally understaffed and underfunded. Because CSL is inherently a distributed learning environment, it benefits from the portability of handhelds. At the same time, the connectivity afforded by a P2P network provides support for the huge amount of effort required to coordinate all parties involved—students, community partners, and instructors.

The discussion of emerging educational models underscores the natural fit between P2P networks and educational environments that require simultaneous support for autonomous learning and connectivity. As will be shown in the next section, there have been successful deployments of handhelds that incorporate P2P networks, although they have not been identified as such.

HANDHELDS IN EDUCATION: CURRENT DEPLOYMENTS

There has been immense interest in the use of handhelds in education, although most of these deployments have not been primarily intended as P2P applications. Leading manufacturers of multifunction handheld devices, Microsoft (PocketPC) and Palm Computing (PalmOS), have been aggressively supporting experiments with the use of these devices in educational settings. Palm Computing has provided grants amounting to a total of $2.3 million, impacting over 175 classrooms, through its Palm Education Pioneer Grant Program (PEP) ("Palm Awards," 2001). More than 800 schools and 125,000 students have participated in the Anytime Anywhere Learning program started by Microsoft and Toshiba in 1996 (Guernsey, 2001). As a result of these efforts, there have been numerous applications of handheld devices in educational settings at all levels—from elementary school to medical school. A partial listing of these efforts is provided in Tables 1 through 4 (based on "Medicine," 2001; "Handspring," 2001; Guzman & Fillo, 2001; Kellner, 2001; Kukec, 2001; Ojeda-Zapata, 2001; "Palm Awards," 2001; "Classroom Connect," 2001; Pulley, 2001; Rosenberg, 2001; Theil, 2001; Walker, 2000).

From the examples in Tables 1 through 4, we can conclude that handhelds have found application in a wide range of activities related to education in all levels. These activities include experiential learning (Table 1), document distribution (Table 2), classroom and campus management (Table 3), and personal information management (Table 4). While not explicitly identified as P2P, many of the deployments incorporate usage of the P2P networking

Table 1: Handhelds in Support of Experiential Learning

Vendors/ Devices	Use	School Level
Palm	Class research project to investigate the lives of U.S. presidents	K–12
Palm	Create and monitor fitness portfolios of students	K–12
Palm	Investigate changes to the territory 200 years after the Lewis and Clark expedition mapped it out	K–12
Palm	Use Palm handhelds in the field to determine the effects of development, human resource consumption, and consumer purchasing decisions	K–12 Environmental science students
Palm	Train lead writers and editors in the use of Palm handhelds for newsgathering, sharing resources and contacts, and fact checking as part of a project to create the Jacket News Service (JNS), a daily online newspaper	K–12
PalmOS (handspring and Palms)	Extend museum activities related to segregation	K–12
Handheld with GPS	Map city area problems (potholes, etc.) to help with affordable housing decisions	High school and university students
Handspring	Take notes during field research	University
Palm	Supplements to Professional Development Courses	K–12 educators

Table 2: Handhelds Used for Document Distribution in Educational Settings

Vendors/ Devices	Use	School Level
Motorola Timeport	Homework distribution and submission	Third grade students and their parents
PalmOS (handspring and Palms)	Note taking, concept mapping	Sixth grade
WinCE devices	Word processing—resulted in improved writing skills for students in Georgia and Iowa	K–12
PocketPC Ebook reader	Distribute textbooks, etc.	
Palm with Mindsurf SW	Wireless school data network	High school

Table 3: Handhelds Used for Classroom and Campus Management

Vendors/ Devices	Use	School Level
Symbol with PalmOS	Scanners used to assess attendance	High school
Symbol with PalmOS	Wireless Parking System	High school
Symbol with PalmOS	Security System	High school

Table 4: Handhelds Used for Personal Information Management in Education

Vendors/ Devices	Use	School Level
PDAs	Information management for students	University
PalmVx w/ Epocrates SW	Real-time clinical information on prescribed drugs	Preclinical medical school students
Palm or PPC	Lecture notes, patient notes, schedules	Medical school

capabilities of the handhelds. The infrared ports have been used for document distribution, sharing of personal information, and collaboration among teammates during experiential learning activities. These successful deployments suggest great promise for the integration of P2P networks with current models of Web-based education. In the next section, we will discuss the initial findings from our study on the use of P2P networks of handhelds in higher education. In this first phase, a pilot study was conducted to determine how students perceive the suitability of the technology for supporting their activities related to an undergraduate class requiring a high level of independent work and coordination.

PILOT STUDY

In Spring 2002, we conducted a pilot study to determine the usefulness of the P2P model in supporting the activities of students in a capstone class on MIS strategy, offered at a large, metropolitan state university serving a diverse population of students. The course required teams of students to collaborate in researching and writing an analysis of how an emerging technology could transform an industry and a company in that industry. The course also included a CSL component, where students were asked to provide information technology support to a local nonprofit agency. The CSL experience was used as a basis for exploring issues related to the Digital Divide.

The purpose of the pilot study was to assess how useful the devices were from the users' points of view. We were also interested in determining how much difficulty would be encountered in the setup and use of the systems. Thus, participants were given limited instructions on how they were to use the system beyond general descriptions of the capabilities of the systems (productivity software, infrared connectivity) and a few suggestions for their use (sharing files, keeping track of schedules). Participants were asked to keep a journal documenting how they used the devices.

Two teams were provided with handhelds for use in coordinating activities related to the course. Each student team was composed of three members. On the day designated for distribution of the PDAs, the first team to arrive at the instructor's office was given the option of choosing the platform that the team would use—PalmOS or PocketPC. The team chose PalmOS, and so the members were given three handhelds running PalmOS from different manufacturers (Palm M100, M125, and Handspring Visor Edge) to use for one semester. The other team was provided with three Cassiopeia E-125s running the first version of the PocketPC operating system. The handhelds were provided to the students with only the software that was packed with the hardware. Students were given the freedom to install software and use the devices in any way for the course of the semester. The journals they kept of their activities are summarized in Tables 5 through 8 on pages 115 through 116.

The students using the PocketPC devices showed more engagement with the devices than the PalmOS students. While some of this is likely due to differences among the teams' enthusiasm for technology, it is also likely that the PalmOS devices were perceived as being somewhat limited in capacity or capability, as shown in this quote from one of the PalmOS users:

> *It is a great device, which can be used to organize personal information and keep track of important appointments. It provides many functions and the ability to extend its capabilities; nevertheless the setback of the storage capacity limits its capability and functions.*

The PalmOS team consistently talked about the limitations of their devices, while the PocketPC team was impressed with many features of their devices (color screen, sound). Interestingly, a member of the PocketPC team started off preferring the PalmOS machines that he had used before, stating: "[PocketPC] is not as [user-friendly] as the OS on the Palm. [Compared] with the Palm, [PocketPC] is much more [complicated] to use." But by the end of the semester, he was a, somewhat qualified, convert to the PocketPC: "Overall, this is a pretty good PDA, I would definitely recommend it to anyone who is interested in getting a PDA. Although the performance was rather slow...it sure beats the Palm...."

Both teams had trouble setting up their devices, and none of the team members was willing to pay for software to augment system capabilities, not even for packages that cost less than $20. The PocketPC team thought that software and peripherals for their devices were quite expensive and difficult to locate, particularly because their devices were running a previous version of the operating system. Still, the PocketPC team showed more enthusiasm than the PalmOS team by making more attempts to download software, despite these difficulties, as illustrated by the following quote:

I am having trouble in trying to download programs from the Internet. I thought that I could just plug in the USB cradle and the Cassiopeia would be ready to receive any downloads from the Web, but it isn't that easy. I am also having trouble searching for downloads that are compatible for the Cassiopeia E-125. Oh my goodness this is driving me crazy, all of the programs have to be purchased.

All six students provided a summary assessment of the usefulness of the PDAs to support the activities of students. Two of the three users of PocketPC devices would recommend the use of the PDAs for students, while only one of the three users of PalmOS devices would make the same recommendation. Furthermore, while the PocketPC users seemed more engaged, the following quote suggests that much of that engagement might be traced to factors beyond the use of the systems to support schoolwork:

I have noticed that people consider the PDA to be a cool toy to have, cause it always seems to [distract] them when I mess around with it, but for the most part, I only have been using it as a day runner and to play games. I have to admit I will miss passing the time by playing Solitaire or Diamond Mine.

The PalmOS users, on the other hand, did not find their devices to be worthwhile replacements for traditional information management tools—pen and paper, plus a cell phone.

...[from] my experience as a student, without my Palm I can always jot down my [things-to-do] on paper manually. I don't know how reliable the Palm can be, but I can trust my paper notepad. It's also light and inexpensive...I think PDAs, especially the Palm M100, [are] not a true necessity for student life. In addition, most of us today have [cellular phones]. [They] can be used to store address [books] or enter [appointments] for certain dates. And if we have a hotmail account, we can also use a free service from MSN to receive our email with our cellular [phones].

Based on their journals, the stronger engagement by the PocketPC team members is also evident in the greater integration of the devices into their schoolwork, even though, admittedly, most of the time they were using the devices for entertainment. This suggests that the entertainment value may have the benefit of motivating the students to incorporate the devices into their activities. If nothing else, finding games on the Internet and learning to play the games helped them become more familiar with the capabilities of the machines. They were then able to apply this knowledge to use the devices to support their schoolwork.

Thus, the PocketPC team came up with ways of using the devices beyond the basic information management functions, e.g., recording a lecture or downloading study aids like a thesaurus and dictionary. In contrast, the PalmOS group members only used the information management capabilities of the devices and did not explore the possibility of downloading software to enhance their machines. Granted, the PalmOS machines had limited storage capacity, but none of the PalmOS team members wrote journal descriptions of any attempts to download or even browse for software. If they had attempted to do so, they may have found that PalmOS software applications are quite small, and that they would have been able to augment the capabilities of their machines, despite the limited storage capacity.

The student journals also list more limitations than positive qualities of the devices. Even the PocketPC team, despite its enthusiasm and general satisfaction with the machines, found much to criticize about the machines. Most of the limitations related to the perceived limited capabilities of the machines and the cost of purchasing the devices and add-ons, like software and peripherals. This suggests that the devices are not quite as simple to learn, despite their reduced complexity, when compared with laptops and desktops. All the students in the pilot study are MIS majors with intermediate to advanced familiarity with computer operations. The difficulties they had with setting up and operating the devices suggest that handheld computing deployments will not be as simple as the scaled down devices—and their associated marketing hype—would suggest. Support for system setup and orientation to the capabilities of the machines is greatly advised, even for the PocketPCs that have GUIs that follow the Windows standard.

The students' perceptions regarding the devices reflect the fact that handhelds are still in the early stages of their development as a technology. The final function and form that handhelds will take—desktop or laptop replacements, adjuncts to current devices, Walkman replacements—are still unclear, and user perceptions reflect this. The lack of clarity also creates ambiguity regarding the fair price to pay for the devices and software. All of the students found the devices and add-ons too expensive for what they were getting. This may be a reflection of their unrealistic expectations regarding the capabilities of the machines and the typical college students' mind-set of trying to get everything, especially software, for free.

With regard to P2P applications, only the PocketPC team described activities that could qualify as P2P. The team members used their infrared ports to share class files among themselves. The teammates also attempted several times to share downloaded applications (games) with each other via the infrared port. They were successful with the latter only once, as it seems most of the software applications they were trying to share were designed so that they had to be installed (along with registry writes) rather than merely copied from one device to another. The team also found the infrared ports to be too slow for sharing the larger files of these applications.

The troubles of the PocketPC team identify two caveats regarding the use of current handheld devices as P2P nodes. First, the infrared ports provide slow connection speeds for the transfer of large files. The team members did not have much trouble sharing their schoolwork files with each other using the infrared ports. Thus, for most P2P applications that involve the communication of class documents, the infrared port should be suitable. However, the slow speed of infrared ports in addition to the fact that infrared ports require line of sight between communicating devices, opens the door for the use of other more powerful network technologies, such as Bluetooth and the family of wireless LAN technologies built around the 802.11 standard. Although they may be more expensive and, in the case of wireless LANs entail more setup effort, these emerging networks will be particularly useful for communications involving large files and nodes distributed throughout a large area, such as the classroom. The more powerful networks will also become necessary as course files start to incorporate multimedia capabilities and, consequently, grow in size. Second, current software design principles limit the applicability of handheld devices for P2P distribution of software. While this may generally be a deterrent to software piracy, some software vendors may benefit more from facilitating the widespread distribution of their software, particularly when revenues accrue more from support and upgrades rather than initial licensing. Given the latter situation, software vendors may choose to design their applications to be self-contained and portable to other devices without requiring an installation process—a capability currently provided by Microsoft.Net. This can also facilitate deployment of software across a classroom network. Once a site license is obtained, it would be possible for students to share the files among each other without having to access the school's central server. Thus, an instructor can provide the files to a few students, who can then transmit the files from their devices to the devices of other students. With powerful P2P networks, the time necessary for deployment is reduced, as several devices are able to transmit the files to other devices simultaneously. Students who missed the class can also obtain the software from classmates who have it stored on their handhelds.

PROPOSITIONS FOR FURTHER STUDY

As expected from a pilot study of such limited scope, the findings reported here are quite idiosyncratic to the groups of students and situation involved. Nevertheless, they have been used here as a springboard for identifying issues for further study with regard to the use of handhelds to support higher education, particularly using the P2P model. These issues can be summarized into four propositions regarding the use of handhelds to support the P2P model:

- The handhelds' information management capabilities will be key to coordinating the various activities that involve students and instructors in the distributed, autonomous nature of future education.
- For current, text-based communications, infrared ports will be sufficient as the main artery for connecting devices into a P2P network. However, as handheld files start to grow with increasing multimedia and computational capabilities, more robust, faster networks, such as those based on the Bluetooth or 802.11 standards, will be required to run effective P2P networks.
- Rather than being a detriment, the entertainment capabilities of handhelds can be a motivating factor in getting students to learn to use the handhelds and in presenting course material in a more engaging manner.
- Handhelds are deceptively simple devices. Any deployment will likely require support for initial setup, as users learn to adjust their computing skills and expectations to bring them in line with the capabilities and limitations of handhelds and P2P networks.

The next phase of this study will test these propositions by following a second and larger set of students and their use of P2P networks of handhelds. Students will be given training on the use of the handhelds and explicit instructions for their use in support of coordination activities and course assignments. To augment the capabilities of the handhelds, students will also be given keyboards and storage cards for use with the handhelds over the semester. The instructor will be provided with a handheld, and students in the study will be asked to use the devices to submit class assignments to the instructor. Aside from being required to keep a journal of their handheld use, students will be asked to fill out a survey to assess their satisfaction with the technology and its support of their class activities. For contrast, teams of students who will not be assigned handhelds will also be asked about procedures they use to support their class activities and their satisfaction with the conduct of their class activities and teamwork.

While the optimal form of the handheld computer will remain undetermined and evolving for some time, there are signs that the concerns of students regarding the technology's use in higher education are going to be addressed very soon. As of mid-2002, 400 Mhz PDAs (by Compaq and Toshiba) entered the market. At the same time, an Indian company introduced a sub-$200 handheld (the Simputer). Handspring introduced a well-received device (Treo) that merged the cell phone with the PDA, T-mobile offered a PocketPC phone that connects with its GPRS network, and Microsoft introduced hybrid cell phone/personal information management devices built around its smart phone platform. Results from the deployment of these and related devices should provide the material for the design of the inexpensive, highly capable, user-friendly, and connected devices that the students (and most everyone else) are searching for.

With a little imagination, such devices will form the core of the P2P networks that will facilitate and coordinate the flexible, distributed learning environments of the future. File sharing among any individuals carrying a connected handheld device could happen seamlessly, particularly as wireless networks become more ubiquitous. Communities of handheld users could fluidly form and just as quickly disperse within the range of an access point or Bluetooth radios. Ideas could have the chance to percolate among these communities, allowing the grassroots to bypass central networks until they are ready for primetime and synching with the centralized backbone. Teams of teachers could share their confidential files somewhat selectively without fear of eavesdropping, if proper encryption protocols are applied. Classes are enriched as students and professors could collect and share pertinent information contained in files beamed to them by individuals they encounter from various disciplines, in reference communities, and the general public. Campus civic engagement gains currency when connected individuals, sharing messages with their nearest neighbors on the

Table 5: Applications Used by Students

PocketPC	PalmOS
• Information management—Calendar, Address Book, DockWare, Notes, Pocket Internet Explorer with AvantGo • Productivity—Pocket Word • Study aids—thesaurus, dictionary • Voice recorder • Entertainment—games [Solitaire, Diamond Mine, Chess, Windows Media Player (to play MP3s)] • Utilities—Pocket Facelift (updates the PocketPC GUI), Handy Zip compression software, SmallTweak registry editor, ACDSee image viewer, Card Backup	• Information management—NotePad, MemoPad, ToDo lists

Table 6: School Settings Where the PDAs Were Used

PocketPC	PalmOS
• Keeping track of finals week schedules for classes taken from two different institutions • Playing games during downtime—waiting for next class, waiting for turn to use desktops at computer center • Recorded a lecture using the Voice Recorder • Class note-taking using handwriting recognition capability • Sharing files among group members	• Keeping track of school schedule

Table 7: Positive Features of the Devices

PocketPC	PalmOS
• Color screen • Great battery life • Handwriting recognition software accepts normal handwriting • Feels solid, does not feel "flimsy"	• Good security option

Table 8: Limitations of the Devices

PocketPC	PalmOS
• Difficult to set up software—incompatibilities between older operating system and current applications • Expensive software (for students' budgets) • Slow data entry with no keyboard • Slow network connections—infrared, serial port • Applications could not be shared by merely sending files to other devices; user has to install applications via connection with a desktop machine • Limited software available for older operating system • Too bulky to carry in pocket but OK in schoolbag • Limited built-in capacity for storing MP3 files	• Limited functionality • Limited storage • No wireless connectivity to the Internet • Poor documentation

network, quickly build a significant physical or virtual statement of protest or support (Schwartz, 2002). It will turn the last-mile of Web-based learning into a Web in and of itself, enabling the collaboration that effectively results in the enrichment and empowerment of the entire network.

REFERENCES

Abbott, J., & Ryan, T. (1999, November). Constructing knowledge, reconstructing schooling. *Educational Leadership, 57,* 66–69.

Alavi, M., Wheeler, B., & Valacich, J. (1995). Using IT to reengineer business education: an exploratory investigation of collaborative telelearning. *MIS Quarterly, 19*, 293–312.

Brown, D., Burg, J., & Dominick, J. (1998). A strategic plan for ubiquitous laptop computing. *Communications of the ACM, 41,* 26–34.

Cates, W. M. (1993). Instructional technology: the design debate. *The Clearing House, 66,* 133–134.

Churach, D., & Fisher, D. (2001). Science students surf the Web: effects on constructivist classroom environments. *Journal of Computers in Mathematics and Science Teaching, 20,* 22–247.

Classroom connect first to offer a K–12 professional development course for the Palm. (2001, January 12). *PR Newswire,* p. 1.

Davis, J. (2001, November/December). Coordinated autonomy. *Educause Review,* 86–87.

Fry, J. (2002, September 16). E-commerce (A special report): selling strategies—Music: the Music Man—What comes after Napster? Vincent Falco may have the answer. *Wall Street Journal,* p. R8.

Gonsalves, A. (2001, December 10). Collaboration software with a familiar look and feel—Peer-to-peer architecture lets people use the interface they prefer. *Informationweek,* 77.

Guernsey, L. (2001, August 23). Take home test: adding PCs to bookbags. *The New York Times,* p. G1.

Guzman, K., & Fillo, M. (2001, December 1). New map speaks volumes: students team up for high-tech look at neighborhood. *Hartford Courant,* p. B1.

Hamm, S. (2000, December 11). The wired campus: how CMU is aggressively adopting net technology to pioneer e-education. *Business Week, 11,* 102.

Handspring brings visor to education channel; company to bring popular handheld computers to universities through partnership with D&H. (2001, February). *Business Wire, 5,* 1.

Hawkins, B. L. (2000, November/December). Technology, higher education, and a very foggy crystal ball. *Educause Review,* 65–73.

Kellner, M. (2001, March 1). Hand-helds; Microsoft reader converts a PocketPC into an e-book. *The Los Angeles Times,* p. T6.

Kukec, A. M. (2001, April 2). Third graders issued handheld computers. *Daily Herald,* p. 1.

Liaw, S.-S. (2001). Designing the hypermedia-based learning environment. *International Journal of Instructional Media, 28,* 43–56.

Medicine in the palm of their hand. (2001, March). *Trustee,* p. 5.

Ojeda-Zapata, J. (2001, February 26). College campuses getting digi with IT digital gadgetry the norm at today's dorms. *The Record,* p. H7.

Palm awards $2.3 million in technology grants to U.S. K–12 schools and colleges. (2001, June 25). *PR Newswire,* p. 1.

Papamarcos, S. (2002). The "next wave" in service-learning: integrative, team-based engagements with structural objectives. *Review of Business,* 31–38.

Pulley, R. (2001, July 6). Program to help pupils research Negro leagues. *Kansas City Star,* p. B3.

Rodrigues, S. (2000). The interpretive zone between software designers and a science educator: grounding instructional multimedia design in learning theory. *Journal of Research on Computing in Education, 33,* 1–15.

Rosenberg, R. (2001, May 7). Handhelds to be Harvard Medical student's first assist. *Boston Globe,* p. C2.

Schwartz, J. (2002, July 22). In the tech meccas, masses of people, or "smart mobs," are keeping in touch through wireless devices. *New York Times*, p. 4.

Theil, L. (2001, February 19). Classroom tech upgraded: Hartland students learn to use handheld computers software. *Detroit News*, p. CL5.

Thompson, A. (2002). Ubiquitous computing: futures for preservice teachers and teacher educators? *Journal of Computing in Teacher Education, 18,* 74, 106.

Walker, L. (2000, November 5). Classrooms, unplugged; can a wireless device like a Palm Pilot or a Pocket PC be a practical teaching aid? Schools across the country are starting to find out. *The Washington Post*, p. W17

Weiser, M. (1991, September). The computer for the 21st century. *Scientific American.* Retrieved May 5, 2002 from: http://www.ubiq.com/hypertext/weiser/SciAmDraft3.html.

Weiser, M. (1996, March). Open house. *ITP Review.* Retrieved July 15, 2002 from: http://www.ubiq.com/hypertext/weiser/wholehouse.doc.

Werbach, K. (2000, November 27). Wireless peer to peer. *TheFeature*. Retrieved January 24, 2002 from: http://www.thefeature.com/index.jsp?url=view.jsp?pageid=7971.

Werbach, K. (2002, January 21). Monster mesh: decentralized wireless broadband. *TheFeature*. Retrieved January 23, 2002 from: http://www.thefeature.com/index.jsp?url=view.jsp?pageid=13890.

APPENDIX: COMPONENTS OF A P2P LEARNING ENVIRONMENT

In recent years, there has been rapid evolution of handheld devices. This has been fueled by several conditions, including the late entry of Microsoft into the market. With its marketing and financial muscle, Microsoft has been making slow but steady progress in chipping away at Palm Computing's market share. Another condition fueling the proliferation of handheld devices is the trend toward convergence among different types of devices—from cellular phones, to portable music devices, to personal digital assistants, global positioning devices, and watches. Everything and anything that fits in a hand has been seen as a possible platform for portable computing. Thus, most manufacturers of such devices are busily trying to develop the one product that merges all handheld technologies, resulting in a dizzying schedule of product introductions. In 2002, Nokia, a cellular handset maker, introduced a hybrid personal digital assistant and phone device (Nokia 9290), while Handspring, a PalmOS personal digital assistant maker, introduced the Treo, a personal digital assistant connected to the cellular network.

Many of the devices introduced in 2002 will probably go the way of the Betamax in a few years, as the market settles into a standard device configuration. Nevertheless, the current proliferation of devices provides a situation in which one can be creative about how handheld computing can be used to support a learning environment. At any rate, given the minimal cost of purchasing and setting up the devices, it may be possible to reap returns on your investment—monetary and otherwise—before the devices reach the end of their useful life.

This discussion of components of a P2P learning environment is organized around five categories: clients, networks, software, peripherals, and server support. Clients are the devices that users carry around with them to various learning environments. These include multifunctional devices like Palm Computing's PalmOS or Microsoft's PocketPC personal digital assistants and laptops. The category also includes single-function devices such as digital slide projectors, digital cameras, text and barcode scanners, and memory card readers. Networks connect clients to each other and to the backbone networks of the Web. In this chapter, the former is emphasized, with the focus on applications that operate primarily on localized P2P connections using standards such as infrared, Bluetooth, 802.11, or radio frequency (RF). Connectivity to a network backbone or the Internet can be achieved via wireless or wired local area network connections, modems, or synching with a connected desktop or laptop. Software primarily involves a choice between the PalmOS and PocketPC platforms. While PalmOS provides a wider range of third-party software choices, PocketPCs come preloaded with scaled-down versions of familiar Windows and Office programs, easing transition to the new devices, though at a price premium. Peripherals provide a range of input and output options. Input devices can take several forms, most popular of which are handwriting recognition, soft keyboard, voice recognition, thumb typing, and touch-typing. Output devices primarily take the form of storage cards in a variety of formats, including PC Card, Flash, Multimedia, Secure Digital, and Sony's proprietary Memory Stick.

Chapter VIII

Beyond the Web: Leveraging Multiple Internet Technologies

Mihir A. Parikh
Polytechnic University, USA

ABSTRACT

Internet technologies are changing the way we provide education and training at all levels. However, we have not yet fully utilized the power of these technologies. The focus has only been on the Web, which is only one of many Internet technologies. In this chapter, we go beyond the Web to leverage multiple Internet technologies to support in-class education. In this chapter, common problems in Web-based education are discussed, an experiment in developing and implementing a framework that seamlessly integrate various Internet technologies is presented, and the increase in learning effectiveness yielded by the new methodology is described.

INTRODUCTION

The Internet has a symbiotic relationship with academia. Academic research incubated the Internet during its first two decades of existence. After the Internet's commercialization in the past decade, academic research continues to contribute to its further development. The Internet, in return, fosters academic research activities by providing easy access to research data and a ubiquitous and around-the-clock forum for researchers with similar interests to discuss research ideas and issues. While the Internet has evolved into a worldwide channel for communication and information exchange, academia is reinventing its use to support instruction. The Internet is viewed as a preferred technology to improve instruction, increase access, and raise productivity in university education (MacArthur & Lewis, 1996).

Most educational institutions now use the World Wide Web in some way to support classroom instruction. Many instructors post lecture notes, course information, class schedule, and assignments on their course websites. Several universities have even started utilizing commercial or in-house software to support instructors in creating and maintaining course websites. However, the experience has been somewhat unenthusiastic. We need to go beyond the Web and integrate multiple Internet technologies in education. We need to deploy the right combination of multiple Internet technologies with appropriate teaching methods and instructional material to improve education (Huang, 2001; Mahoney, 1998; Spooner et al., 1998; Sumner & Hostetler, 1999). In this chapter, a case study of such an effort made by deploying a special Internet-based education support system for traditional classroom setup at a large, urban university in the Southeast United States is presented. The primary objective is to illustrate how multiple Internet technologies can be integrated under one, unifying framework to make classroom-based education more efficient and effective. Provided is a new path that academic institutions can follow in their efforts to improve the learning process by leveraging emerging and yet-to-emerge Internet technologies. This experiment supports the notion that these technologies can revolutionize the way we learn and the way learning is supported in classrooms.

EARLY ADOPTION OF THE WEB

Wilson (1996) classified learning environments in three major categories: computer microworld, classroom-based learning environment, and virtual learning environment. Computer microworld is a self-contained computer-based learning environment, such as computer-based training and intelligent tutoring systems, in which students learn at their own pace using a computerized learning system. A classroom-based learning environment is the most widely used, traditional educational setup, in which students periodically meet face-to-face with their instructors. A virtual learning environment is a telecommunications-based learning environment (e.g., distance learning), in which the students, dispersed over a large geographic area, learn through a communication medium.

The Internet can provide valuable contributions to all three learning environments. In the computer microworld environment, it can help distribute, maintain, and update training software and educational modules. In the classroom-based learning environment, it can help distribute course material, such as lecture notes and assignments, via course websites, and provide email-based communication between the instructor and students. In the virtual learning environment, it can replace the traditional telecommunications-based videoconferencing network with a ubiquitous, multimedia network. To take advantage of these opportunities, many Internet-based, virtual universities, such as Western Governors University (WGU), Jones International University (JIU), California Virtual University, and Concord University School of Law, have emerged recently.

Fascinated by the Internet and its potential use in education, several instructors, including the author, started using the Web on an ad hoc basis to support classroom instruction in the College of Business Administration at Georgia State University (GSU) in 1996, in graduate and undergraduate and core and noncore classes. GSU is a large urban university in Atlanta, Georgia. The number of students in a typical class ranged from 25 to 35, which presented ideal conditions for using the emerging Web technology to support instruction. These individual efforts gradually improved with the availability of better Web technologies, the increased penetration of the Web at homes and offices of students, and upward progress on the learning curve. However, several problems, discussed below, started surfacing immediately after the initial adoption.

Untimely Review of Material

Lecture notes and assignments were regularly updated on course websites but were not reviewed by all students. Students had to continually check course websites for the new or revised course material. Updated or additional course material for an upcoming class was made available on the course website, but often, many students had not reviewed the material before coming to the class. It required conscious effort on the part of the students to make sure that they visited the course website and reviewed the material.

No Confirmation Loop

The instructor did not always know who had reviewed the material and who had not, unless a technically complex and cumbersome log-in process was developed and implemented on the course website. Students often complained of not seeing the material when they went on the course website.

Waste of Classroom Time

In every class, a significant portion of the classroom time went to discussing and resolving technical problems. Like most universities, GSU did not have a special technical support group to support the use of the Web in education.

Waste of Instructor Time

While space on the Web servers was made available and maintained by the university, it was up to the instructors to develop and maintain the course website and provide technical support to their students. This also took up a significant amount of instructor time outside the classroom and often created course management problems.

Lack of Interactivity

Many learning activities and methods, such as group discussion, case study analysis, and real-time questions and answers, require interactivity. A good educational support system has to be active (Schank, 1993). However, websites, by design, are passive. They can simply distribute course material, not inherently support interactive course activities. Bringing interactivity required using advanced programming languages, but the differences in browser technologies and versions made the task difficult.

High Cost, No Reward

Developing Internet-compatible course material involves substantial costs, specifically in terms of faculty time and efforts, but it brings little monetary or professional rewards (Baer, 1998). Often, instructors do not have advanced technical skills or software necessary for the design and development of course websites (Sumner & Hostetler, 1999). Sometimes, instructors are reluctant to put their intellectual property in the public domain. Therefore, not all course material was made available on the course website.

Varied Behavioral Response

Some students embraced the use of new support technologies, as it provided more convenience and quick information, while other students resisted it, as it created new problems and brought technical difficulties. Several instructors were disappointed, and some even retreated to limit the use of the course websites in education.

We reviewed several off-the-shelf software products, like WebCT, TopClass, and BlackBoard, to find solutions to these problems. But at that time, these software products did not have all the capabilities that we thought were necessary. They had server-based content management, which required high bandwidth to transfer class notes and slides every time a student wanted to review them. They required effort on the part of the student to check the website regularly, rather than automatically transferring new information to students. They did not support offline browsing. They required reformatting of the content created using commonly used software like Word and PowerPoint. They could help the technologically challenged instructors to easily develop and maintain course websites, but they could do little to annihilate the above problems. We had to find an alternate solution.

LEVERAGING MULTIPLE INTERNET TECHNOLOGIES

Traditional classroom-based education has benefited little from the information technology revolution (Alavi, 1994; Alavi, Wheeler, & Valacich, 1995; Soloway, 1993). In educational institutions, technological innovations have penetrated only up to the level of the replacement of the library catalog by computer terminals, the use of PCs as sophisticated typewriters, and the explosion of campus email (Brown & Duguid, 1996). The experience discussed in the previous section suggests that the argument also extends, unfortunately, to the Internet revolution, a powerful force with which information technologies converge with communications technologies. Modern academic institutions have high-powered computational infrastructures, but they continue to follow highly conventional educational practice (Brown & Duguid, 1996). They have supercomputers and huge Internet bandwidth but are still operating technology-deprived classrooms and employing minimal technology in the learning process. The problems discussed in the previous section were not specific to the institution or the instructors. Others have experienced that despite the increasing use of the Internet in teaching, the current practice of using the Internet has not met expectations and, in some cases, it even leads to substandard education (Huang, 2001; Mendels, 1999; Neumann, 1998; Nobel, 1998a,b,c; Young, 1998).

Those problems can be attributed primarily to the inherent limitations of the Web and the insufficient utilization of other Internet technologies. It is easy to put documents on course websites, but leveraging the full potential of the Internet requires integrating visual, aural, and textual material and providing nonlinear access to the material (Baer, 1998). Most institutions and instructors put up course websites on an ad hoc basis, whereby they do not utilize all major Internet technologies in their efforts to support learning or utilize them at suboptimum levels. Few course websites use discussion bulletin boards, and even fewer use real-time, interactive question and answer sessions using Internet messaging technology.

This prompted us to develop and utilize a novel technology integration model to support education (Figure 1; adapted from Parikh & Verma, 2002). This model goes beyond the Web to provide a unifying framework that can integrate and leverage various Internet technologies, such as the Web, FTP, chat, security, and Internet-based database, in supporting education in the classroom-based learning environment.

Figure 1: Integrating Multiple Internet Technologies

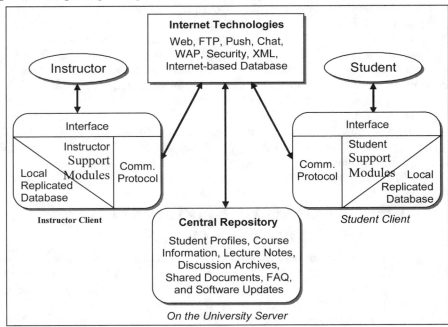

The model has three main modules—the central repository, instructor client, and student client—connected by multiple Internet technologies. The central repository maintains several databases on student information (name, SSN, email address, user ID, password, assignment grades, which files the student has already reviewed, etc.), lecture notes (files, availability date, etc.), course schedule, assignments, archives of threaded discussions, and frequently asked questions. In addition, it also stores the latest version of the software. The relevant parts of these data are automatically replicated on the instructor client and student clients whenever the instructor and students are online.

Instructor client, available only to the instructor, assists the instructor in managing course information and related activities. It uploads files (such as lecture notes and assignments) to the central repository and helps set file preferences, such as availability date, expiry date, and software application to open the file. For example, lecture notes are to be released one week before the class or student grades in assignments are to be given only to the intended students. The instructor can prepare the files and set preferences using the client, even when the instructor is offline. The software automatically uploads the files and preferences in the background when the instructor connects to the Internet. This module helps the instructor maintain class schedule, message board information, and emails to the whole class, different groups, or specific students. It also helps the instructor moderate and participate in group discussions. Built-in email and chat modules also help the instructor communicate with a group of students or individual students, asynchronously and synchronously.

Student client, used by all students, provides the student with access to course information, such as course schedule, information about upcoming classes, lecture notes, assignments, sample tests, and frequently asked questions. Because the relevant parts of the central repository are replicated on the student client, the course information is also available offline. This module uploads completed assignments or work-in-project group project files for group-only use to the central repository. It also helps the student communicate with the instructor, study group, or other students via internal email or chat modules. All of these features are accessible from one screen.

Various Internet technologies connect these three modules and help perform the information exchange task required for effective education.

- Push technology monitors student activities to update student profiles. It also uses these profiles to identify student needs for specific files. For example, if a student has already completed a basic sample test, the profile is updated, and an advanced sample test will be made available the next time the student wants to take a sample test; if the student has not completed a review of lecture notes by a specific date, it will alert the student through a pop-up window, which can be set to be activated even when the student is not using the software.

- A remote file server combined with FTP and file compression technology transfers and manages necessary files between clients and the central repository. This enables access to course information when the student is offline. It also enables the sharing of group project files within student groups. It only does the incremental downloads based on the student profile and, thus, saves time and bandwidth otherwise wasted in redundant file transfers. This feature is extremely useful to working students who have to travel on work assignment during the semester while continuing study and communication with other group members.

- Database servers and integrated database modules on the clients maintain and query the FAQ database, threaded group discussion database, and student activity profiles.

- Email servers enable group and individual email, facilitating student–instructor and student–student communication.

- A telnet-based chat utility provides the real-time chat feature. This helps students interactively communicate with other students in the class, fellow group members, and the instructor.

- The Web provides access to additional course-related information and articles available on external websites, such as Web-based news magazines and information sources. Through arrangements with external content providers, this access can be masked and automatically password-protected to the intended recipients only.

NEW EDUCATION SUPPORT SYSTEM

Based on this model, we developed a new easy-to-use education support system and utilized it in eight sections of various types of courses in three semesters. We found that the new system was more effective in supporting all three types of learning activities (pre-, in-, and postclass activities).

Collaborative Environment

It provided a collaborative environment, in which students could interact more freely and easily with each other. This reduced the problem of lack of interactivity generally associated with Web-based support systems. Having the access to such a social system that fosters reliable relationships and teaches students to deal with complex social structure is an important part of education (Brown & Duguid, 1996). Such a collaborative environment also improves written communication skills, which are increasingly important in today's global, networked business world. However, this is difficult to achieve in pure Web-based education.

Instructor Visibility

The new system increased the visibility of instructors among students. Through synchronous and asynchronous communication with students, instructors were available when students needed them during pre- and postclass activities. This generated continuous presence of instructors outside the bounds of classroom time and space.

Confirmation Loop and Timely Feedback

The new system enabled instructors to track whether a student reviewed the material or not and to provide timely feedback to the needy students. In addition, the built-in software modules provided system-generated positive and negative reinforcements, specifically, on the sample tests. Regular feedback, implicit and explicit, can play an important role in the learning process and has been found to strongly influence learning performance (Kulik & Kulik, 1988; Gagne, 1977).

Increase in Efficiency

While improving the interface between students and instructors, the new system reduced the overall time spent by instructors in managing the course. It increased the efficiency and productivity of instructors.

Reduced Unnecessary Meetings

Information stored in FAQ and discussion group databases also reduced the needs of the students to contact the instructors for the information. This eliminated many unnecessary face-to-face meetings between students and instructors and reduced the frustration involved in coordinating such meetings.

Utilization of Preferred Technology

In addition, the system enabled the instructors to upload lecture notes and other course information in the original format. The instructors were not required to convert the files into Web-friendly PDF or HTML formats. This reduced the time involved in reformatting course material.

Secure Delivery

The new system also enabled secured delivery of course information, a significant part of which was the intellectual property of instructors. This assured the instructors that their work was available only to the registered students of their classes. This also reduced the risk of leakage of sensitive information, such as assignment grades and instructor feedback to a specific student. Such leakage can happen more easily if the system is purely Web-based.

Mass Customization

Combined with a content customization feature utilizing student profiles, the system helped directly target the needs of individual students. Because course information was pushed to the student client in the background whenever the student connected to the Internet without going to the course website, time-sensitive information, such as changes in the schedule or flash news, was readily available to the student. This improved timely review of the updated material by students.

Ease of Use

On the operational side, the system modules were simple to install and easy to use. It took only half an hour during the first lecture to introduce and explain the system to the students. The user-friendly instructor client also helped the instructors manage the course material and administer the course more efficiently and effectively without having them learn a complex software application or a programming language. This significantly reduced the waste of the classroom's and instructors' time.

Ease of Maintenance

Whenever an upgrade of the software or a software patch was available, push technology automatically transferred and installed it on all clients, without the instructors or students knowing it. This significantly reduced the hassles of system administration and maintenance and saved a lot of the instructor's time in providing technical support. It also ensured that all students were using the same and latest version of the software.

Empirical Findings

An extensive empirical evaluation of the effectiveness of the system was also conducted. One hundred and eighty-one undergraduate students used this system in eight classes across three semesters. Their experience with the system was captured through a questionnaire consisting of 25 questions, which articulated eight measures on four underlying dimensions of the system: content, technology, interface, and functionality. The evaluation found that the system was user friendly (85.6% of respondents agreed) and increased convenience (75.7%) for the students and instructor; it provided accurate information (79.6%) in a timely manner (72.9%); it conformed to their needs (70.2%) and was useful (63.5%); and overall, the students were satisfied with it (80.7%). The evaluation also found that the system provided better support in the courses that required a high degree of interactivity and extensive file transfers between the students and instructor and among the students within a project group. Refer to Parikh and Verma (2002) for additional information on the empirical evaluation.

FUTURE TRENDS

This case study relates to the traditional classroom-based learning environment. However, fueled by technological advances, two other learning environments have been growing exponentially in the past decade or so. Technology is an integral part of these learning environments: computing hardware and software technology in computer microworld and communications technology in the virtual learning environment. The model discussed in this chapter can easily be adapted into these learning environments. In the computer microworld environment, a system like this can automatically download and install concept modules in the computer-based training system, depending on the topic chosen by the student. It can help the student communicate with or develop a study group with other students with similar interests. It can also help the student pose questions to experts or to other students who are at the advanced level. In the virtual learning environment, a system like this can simulate an interactive learning platform through synchronous and asynchronous interactivity. It can integrate the video feed surrounded by framed boxes, which flash links to related articles, assignments, concept explanation, the translation module, the tutor that can bookmark or reply, etc.

On the technology front, two types of technologies are expected to have significant growth and influence in the upcoming years: peer-to-peer (P2P) technologies and wireless combined with handheld technologies. We have already tasted the power of primitive P2P technologies in the case of Napster and Gnutella. P2P technologies are changing industry structures and are transforming social behavior. Wireless plus handheld technologies, on the other side, are creating the next front of electronic commerce dubbed as *m-commerce* or mobile commerce. These emerging technologies can also be utilized in the context of education under the same model discussed here, as these technologies become omnipresent in the student community. Such technologies will involve multiple types of student client modules for various hardware types. However, all of these modules will synchronize with the single student profile stored on the central repository and replicated to all clients of the student. These technologies will further increase interactivity, facilitating the creation and sustenance of virtual communities that foster social relationships among the learners. These communities will further blur the boundaries of space and time within which education has been taking place.

Learning is not limited to the confines of academic institutions. Studies have shown that learning continues even in adulthood, as individuals adapt and learn through experiences (McCall et al., 1988; O'Connor & Wolfe, 1991). While academic institutions are not yet at the stage of abandoning traditional degrees and adopting "learning contracts," they are preparing for "lifelong learning," as Alvin Toffler predicted. In close collaboration with corporations, they are embracing eLearning as a form of continuing education. Charles Handy (1989), a famous management guru, has foreseen that corporations would increasingly resemble universities or colleges in the years to come. We are already witnessing the beginning of this effect. U.S. corporations are spending over $60 billion annually on education, with an average growth of 5% over the past decade (Prewitt, 1997). To benefit most from these efforts, going beyond the Web and leveraging all available technologies is necessary. The model discussed in this chapter can be the first right step in that direction.

CONCLUSION

As the Internet is increasingly integrated in education, it is imperative that we understand the limitations of using only one Internet technology, the Web. The Web is a powerful medium for delivering content or transferring knowledge. However, the core competency of educational institutions is developing knowledge, which can be done through intricate and robust networks and communities of students that last beyond the formal degree (Brown & Duguid, 1996). The Web falls short in this respect, probably because it is too broad and too open.

To provide a more effective platform to support learning, we have to look beyond the Web. Many new Internet-based technologies have emerged recently, and new ones continue to surface. These technologies can provide complementary support to various educational activities that are not effectively supported by the Web. In this chapter, a case study of a system that integrated multiple Internet technologies, including the Web, to support learning was presented. The system was indigenously developed with built-in flexibility to adapt to various types of courses. Further development and deployment of systems like this will provide the next frontier and drive the educational effort in the coming decades. References

REFERENCES

Alavi, M. (1994). Computer-mediated collaborative learning: an empirical evaluation. *MIS Quarterly, 18*(2), 159–174.

Alavi, M., Wheeler, B. C., & Valacich, J. S. (1995). Using IT to reengineer business education: an exploratory investigation to collaborative telelearning. *MIS Quarterly, 19*(3), 293–312.

Baer, W. S. (1998). Will the Internet transform higher education? *The emerging Internet: annual review of the Institute for Information Studies.* Aspen, CO: The Aspen Institute; http://www.aspeninst.org/dir/polpro/CSP/IIS/98/98.html.

Brown, J. S., & Duguid, P. (1996). Universities in the digital age. *Change, 28*(4), 11–19.

Choren, R. et al. (1999). Orchestrating technology for Web-based education. *Proceedings of the Fifth Americas Conference on Information Systems* (pp. 130–132).

Gagne, R. M. (1977). *The conditions of learning* (3rd ed.). New York: Holt, Rinehart and Winston.

Handy, C. (1989). *The age of unreason.* Boston: Harvard Business School Press.

Huang, A. H. (2001). Problems associated with using information technology in teaching: a research proposal. *Proceedings of the Seventh Americas Conference on Information Systems,* 39–40.

Ives, B., & Jarvenpaa, S. L. (1996). Will the Internet revolutionize business education and research? *Sloan Management Review, 37*(Spring), 33–41.

Kulik, J. A., & Kulik, C. C. (1988). Timing of feedback and verbal learning. *Review of Educational Research, 58*(1), 79–97.

Leidner, D. E., & Jarvenpaa, S. L. (1995). The use of information technology to enhance management school education: a theoretical view. *MIS Quarterly, 19*(3), 265–291.

MacArthur, D., & Lewis, M. (1996, June). Untangling the Web: applications of the Internet and other information technologies to higher education (DRU-1401-IET). Santa Monica, CA: RAND.

Mahoney, J. (1998). Higher education in a dangerous time: will technology really improve the university? *Journal of College Admission, 24*(3), 161.

McCall, M. W., Jr., Lombardo, M. M., & Morrison, A. M. (1988). *The lessons of experience.* Lexington, MA: D.C. Heath.

Mendels, P. (1999, March 13). Online education gets a credibility boost. *New York Times.* Online.

Neumann, P. G. (1998). Risks of e-education. *Communications of the ACM, 40*(10), 136.

Nobel, D. F. (1998a). Digital diploma mills: the automation of higher education. *First Monday, 3*(1); http://firstmonday.dk/issues/issue3_1/noble/.

Nobel, D. F. (1998b). *Digital diploma mills, Part II: the coming battle over online instruction.* Unpublished manuscript. http://communication.ucsd.edu/dl/ddm2.html.

Nobel, D. F. (1998c). *Digital diploma mills, Part III: the bloom is off the rose.* Unpublished manuscript. http://communication.ucsd.edu/dl/ddm3.html.

O'Connor, D., & Wolfe, D. M. (1991). From crisis to growth at midlife: changes in personal paradigm. *Journal of Organizational Behavior, 12,* 323–340.

Parikh, M. A., & Verma, S. A. (2002). Utilizing Internet technologies to support learning: an empirical analysis. *International Journal of Information Management, 22*(1), 27–46.

Prewitt, E. (1997). What managers should know about how adults learn? *Management Update, 2*(January), 5.

Schank, R. C. (1993). Learning via multimedia computers. *Communications of the ACM, 36*(5), 54–56.

Soloway, E. (1993). Technology in education. *Communications of the ACM, 36*(5), 28–29.

Spooner, F. et al. (1998). Distance education and special education: promises, practices, and potential pitfalls. *Teacher Education and Special Education, 21*(2), 121–131.

Sumner, M., & Hostetler, D. (1999). Factors influencing the adoption of technology in teaching. *Proceedings of the Fifth Americas Conference on Information Systems* (pp. 951–953).

Wilson, B. G. (1996). *Constructivist learning environments: case studies in instructional design.* Englewood Cliffs, NJ: Educational Technology Publication.

Young, J. R. (1998). A year of Web pages for every course: UCLA debates their value. *The Chronicle of Higher Education, 44*(36).

Chapter IX

Web Design Studio: A Preliminary Experiment in Facilitating Faculty Use of the Web

Vicki L. Sauter
University of Missouri, USA

ABSTRACT

Reported in this chapter is an action research project using Theory of Planned Behavior (TPB) to help manage the process of encouraging faculty to utilize Internet tools in the implementation of their classes. The research provides an in-depth examination of an innovative experiment to impact the process of faculty website development, faculty training, and faculty support, reflected in terms of the TPB framework. These results will be of interest to managers in need of encouraging autonomous decision makers, such as faculty, who need to structure, reengineer, and innovate their business processes in terms of an Internet component. Recommendations about incentives and support are provided.

INTRODUCTION

There is no question that the Internet has presented all professors with a range of opportunities with which to support and enhance their curricula. While distance learning has become unleashed through the availability of technology, even traditional format classes have been enhanced by electronic discussions and the rich resources with varied formats that can be used because of the technology. Benefits not withstanding, not all colleagues have rushed forward to avail themselves of the opportunity. Many faculty members do not believe the benefits of creating and maintaining an electronic presence are worth the cost to them. However, many consumers (students and prospective faculty) depend on such a Web presence in the decision of which product (university, major, or course) to select. As the expectations of such consumers become more sophisticated, the need for not only some Web presence, but also increased functionality, will magnify the importance to the institution.

In fact, it is already true that the level of Internet technologies in use at an institution can impact its prestige and the quality and quantity of students it attracts. Thus, if the utility that the university (including the broadly defined university community) receives is greater when faculty provide an Internet presence, it is necessary to develop a strategy that encourages such behavior, by reducing the costs incurred by the faculty or by increasing the benefits to the faculty to compensate for real or perceived losses.

So, the question is how to manage the process so that the university and the students get value from Web-based instruction, given that faculty members need to embrace the technology to make some of it happen. The literature provides some insight regarding faculty attitudes about technology as predictors of their usage of technology. (Davis, 1989, 1993; Davis et al., 1989; Dillon & Morris, 1996; Kottemann & Davis, 1991). Said simply, the greater professors accept the technology, the more likely they are to integrate that technology into their work activities.

One well-accepted framework is the Technology Acceptance Model (TAM) proposed by Davis (1989, 1993). This model posits two factors, ease of use and perceived usefulness, as providing the greatest explanation of technology adoption and integration. In particular, it suggests that the lower the effort for an individual to use the technology and the greater the enhancement of that individual's job performance, the more likely the technology will be adopted and used. While this theory has had wide acceptance among researchers because of its explanatory power (see, for example, Davis, 1989, 1993; Davis et al., 1989; Kottemann & Davis, 1991) , it is not a good framework for consideration of the scenario in this chapter for two reasons. First, the framework does not provide a list of factors that a manager or administrator could affect to bring change in the use and adoption of the technology (Taylor & Todd, 1995). Second, research by Succi and Walter (2001) and Hu et al. (1999) shows that it does not provide good explanatory power for utilization by professionals, such as faculty members.

Instead, reported is an action research project using a framework called the Theory of Planned Behavior (TPB), because it is more likely to provide some guidance to administrators trying to impact the behavior of faculty members. The theory of planned behavior was first extended from the social psychology literature by Ajzen and Fishbein (see Ajzen & Fishbein, 1980; Fishbein & Ajzen, 1975) to explain technology utilization using subjective norms and perceived behavioral control. The model was later enhanced by Taylor and Todd (1995), with extensions from the diffusion of innovations literature (Rogers, 1983) to include various aspects of the user's attitude toward technology. The combined model, shown in Figure 1, has been shown to be appropriate when one examines the behavioral intentions of users (Matheieson, 1991).

In particular, the framework looks at utilization as being influenced by three distinct facts: subjective norms, perceived behavioral control, and attitude.

"Subjective norms" refers to the user's perceptions that influential people (those important to them) believe that they should (or should not) use the technology (Fishbein & Ajzen, 1975). Taylor and Todd (1995) showed that these subjective norms are critical in the early stages of developing attitudes about using the technology. However, because subjective norms are not easily affected by administrators trying to impact technology use, they will be acknowledged as important but will not be included in the study.

Figure 1: TPB Framework

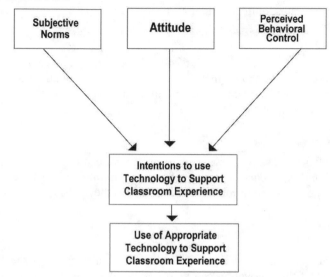

"Perceived behavioral control" measures the comfort level of the individuals in using the technology (Fishbein & Ajzen, 1975). Bandura (1982) defined this as users' self-confidence in their ability to use the technology. Triandis (1977) operationalized this component as a measurement of the users' belief that sufficient resources and other "facilitating conditions" are present for them to be able to use the technology. As a result, training and more usable products are typically called upon to influence usage, but there is some evidence to suggest that conventional training may not be appropriate. Hence, the issue of how to provide training to the faculty is the research intervention being described in this chapter. It is believed that this innovation in training and support is one factor that administrators can adjust to help facilitate the development of faculty usage. Specific details on the intervention are provided in later sections.

While technology-based capabilities often explain professors' reticence to use Internet technologies, it seems appropriate to determine whether other factors negatively influence the adoption of Internet technologies. Taylor and Todd (1995b) adopted attributes from the diffusion of innovations literature (Rogers, 1983) and identified five dimensions of attitude important to user adoption: relative advantage, compatibility, complexity, trialability, and observability.

Relative Advantage

This factor measures professors' perceptions of expected benefits to the learning process (or course delivery process) of using the technology. Rogers suggested that the higher the relative advantage, the greater the likelihood of adoption (Rogers, 1983).

Compatibility

Research has shown that people are more likely to adopt technology if it is well-situated or compatible with their normal professional responsibilities, value system, and working style. This issue has been shown to be particularly important for those whose work is "professional" and, thus, quite autonomous (Teo & Tan, 2000).

Complexity

This factor measures the perception of difficulty a user expects to have in using the technology. Research has shown that as the number of technical skills needed, or even perceived to be needed, to implement the technology increases, the less likely the implementation (Cooper & Zmud, 1990).

Trialability

Some studies have shown that adopters are convinced to use the technology if they can work with it and experience its impact before a commitment to its use has been made. This is a critical component of adoption for those for whom the decision is optional (McMaster et al., 1997).

Observability

Last, research has shown that potential adopters are influenced by the degree to which the use or result of the innovation can be observed by those valued. This tends to have relatively low influence on the decision to adopt among autonomous professionals.

This research provides an in-depth examination of the process of faculty website development, faculty training, and faculty support, reflected in terms of the TPB framework. Ultimately, the goal is to provide direction for managers in need of helping autonomous decision makers (such as faculty) who need to structure, reengineer, and innovate their business practices in terms of an Internet component. Specifically, in this chapter, an attempt will be made to provide greater clarity regarding the range of concerns and the range of benefits perceived by faculty facing the decision of how to use technology in their classes. In addition, the results will help us understand the adoption decision, with a particular focus on the technological support component. We will report the results of an innovative experiment in encouraging faculty to increase their use of Internet technologies in their teaching. Recommendations about incentives and support will be provided.

THE INTERVENTION

In Summer 2001, UM–St. Louis offered a class entitled "Business Web Studio Design" (the "Web Studio"). The Web Studio focused on technical issues associated with design and implementation and maintenance of Web-based systems. This included technical topics (such as advanced HTML, JavaScript, cascading style sheets, metatags and searches), design issues (including issues to improve the look and navigation of the site), and usability issues (including issues of making the pages accessible for disabled users).Students practiced and mastered technical and design tasks through multiple assignments. The most significant of efforts was the group design effort, which was the intervention discussed in this research. Groups of students were assigned to particular faculty members and given the task of (a) converting faculty class materials for Web use for the Fall 2001 semester and (b) training the "client" faculty member so materials could be maintained in the future. In fact, students could not get credit until the client faculty member expressed satisfaction with the materials *and* was adequately trained in its maintenance.

The Students

Fourteen students participated in this class. It was open to undergraduates and graduate students with the prerequisite of having completed the systems analysis or electronic commerce course. Of these, six were undergraduates pursuing a B.S. in MIS, six were graduate students pursuing an M.S. in MIS, and two were graduate students pursuing an MBA. This included five female students and nine male students. All of the students had some previous exposure to HTML, and to programming, but the types and amounts of exposure were varied. All of the undergraduates had taken classes in C++ and had seen basic Web development in their introductory class. All of the students in the M.S. in MIS program had taken classes in Visual Basic, and half of them had also taken other programming languages. The two MBA students had only the introductory IS class, in which they did some Web page development and a small amount of Visual Basic programming. The undergraduate degrees of the graduate students included political science, economics, general business, finance, marketing, and music. Finally, five of the students were from cities and towns outside North America. This distribution of gender, background, and programming experience is not statistically different from the norm of IS-oriented students at this university.

The Faculty

The students worked with a reasonable cross-section of faculty from the college with varied abilities, needs, and goals. Faculty "clients" for this class were all volunteers who responded to a Call for Participants on the College listserv. All 15 individuals who expressed interest in working with the students were accepted for inclusion. This included four faculty members from the Management/Strategy Area, one faculty member from the Marketing Area, five faculty members from the Accounting Area, three faculty members from the Finance/Law

Table 1: Distribution of Faculty Participation

	Participating in Class	Proportion of Study (%)	Total in the College	Proportion of College (%)
Accounting	5	33.33	12	22.64
Proportion of Possible			41.67%	
Finance/Business Law	3	20.00	9	15.09
Proportion of Possible			37.50%	
LOM/IS	2	13.00	15	26.42
Proportion of Possible			14.29%	
Management/Strategy	4	26.67	11	20.75
Proportion of Possible			36.36%	
Marketing	1	6.67	8	15.09
Proportion of Possible			12.50%	
Total	15		54	
Proportion of Possible			28.30%	

Table 2: Distribution of Faculty Participation by Gender

	Participating in Class	Proportion of Study (%)	Total in the College	Proportion of College (%)
Women	4	26.7	10	18.51
Men	11	73.3	44	81.5

Area, and two faculty members from LOM/MIS. Of these, 11 were male faculty, and four were female faculty. Comparisons of the distributions of total faculty with participant faculty are shown in Tables 1 and 2.

While the distribution of faculty discipline does not correspond exactly to that of the College, it is similar. In fact, assuming most of the faculty in IS could create and manage their own course sites because of the technical nature of their field, the distribution of participants is not statistically different from the College as a whole. However, the study included a somewhat higher percentage of women faculty than that represented in the College as a whole. This is not believed to diminish the generalizability of the results.

The faculty were at varying stages in use of technology. Two primary measures were taken: (a) the existence of any Web presence (generally just a home page), and (b) the existence of class materials using Internet technologies. Tables 3 and 4 report these two conditions.

Table 3: Existence of a "Home" Page or other Web Presence

No Home Page	Home Page Existed, but Someone Else Maintained It	Home Page Existed, Maintained by Self
8 (53%)	5 (33%)	2 (13%)

Table 4: Existence of Class Materials Using Internet Technology

None	Used "Blackboard" for Some Materials	Used Class Materials Developed by Someone Else
8 (53%)	3 (20%)	4 (26%)

Notice that over half of the faculty had no Web presence —either a home page or materials they had developed for classes. Only two of the faculty had invested the time and effort to design any kind of Web presence, and neither of those individuals developed pages for classroom use. About 20% of these faculty used the campus-provided tool, Blackboard, to create some class materials; none of these individuals used the product extensively. Some people had found friends to develop materials for them: a third of the group had a home page developed by someone else for them, and somewhat more than a quarter used class materials developed by a colleague (with their permission).[1]

All of these faculty members were adept at using email for communications, although the amount and sophistication of their usage varied. In addition, all faculty members had some experience in "surfing" the Web for materials. However, most faculty had relatively superficial knowledge of the range of opportunities for Web pages, and some had only sought specific hobby-oriented materials or news sources on the Web. Finally, all faculty members were word processor users. However, as in the previous two areas, there was variability on how they used the tools. Most used a relatively recent version of Word or WordPerfect for standard activities; one person still used WordStar for DOS as his preferred word-processing option, and only used limited functionality within that product.

As with the students, these faculty members were not atypical for College of Business Administration faculty. So, examination of the results could provide insights for colleagues at other institutions.

The Assignment

Students were not given specific items they had to produce for the clients, but instead, they were given instructions to identify the client's needs and provide a solution that meets their client's needs and constraints and to transform appropriate class materials for the Fall onto the Web. Further, they were instructed that the issue of what was appropriate should be evaluated (and defended) in terms of (a) usefulness to the specific kind of course; (b) long-term manageability of the technology by the client; (c) agreement of the pedagogy and other philosophical principles of the instructor; and (d) the norm within the discipline. In addition, the group was required to train the faculty member on how to update pages in the future.

The first step of the project was for the students to meet with the faculty to inventory the Internet technologies currently in use to support the faculty's teaching efforts, the pedagogical goals for each class, and the extent of Web development skill mastered and that which the faculty member would like to master. Other, and perhaps more important, parts of the inventory were to identify the concerns regarding and constraints experienced by the faculty member in pursuing Web work and the aspects of Web support the faculty member wished to avoid. Initially, student teams used structured, open-ended interviews to obtain this information. Later in the semester, students validated their understanding of the site needs through the evaluation of prototypes and further interviews.

Students, therefore, helped faculty understand the added value that could be provided with Internet technologies, and worked with them to decide what kinds of functionality would best meet the needs of individual classes. In addition, the student groups decided which technologies best met the functionality requirements, and then, specifically, how to implement those technologies. Students could use the wide range of opportunities available for Web pages developed by coding or by use of a development tool. Alternatively, student teams could elect to provide the course support using "Blackboard," a campus-supported product that, according to its website,[2] "offers a complete suite of enterprise software products and services that powers e-Education infrastructure for schools, colleges, universities and other education providers around the world." Blackboard allows posting of materials, discussion forums, electronic grade books, and electronic testing. Finally, students were allowed to use any of the listserv/majordomo and email functions in meeting the needs of the faculty.

The intellectual content of the Web studio class addressed various Internet-based tools and capabilities, design issues associated with those tools and capabilities, and means for implementing the tools and capabilities. After presentation of foundation materials, students critiqued academic and nonacademic websites in light of the business processes they were supporting.

In an effort to focus students on the needs for their specific projects, they examined the Web presences available in support of a wide variety of courses. Project teams selected three class sites in the same academic area (but not at this university) and prepared presentations critiquing the sites and, where possible, the procedures for developing the sites. These critiques were intended to evaluate the pedagogical process being supported, the image of the university presented, and the technical merit of the design. Among the specific issues each team rated and critiqued were the following:

- What is the purpose of the professor in developing the site?
- Does the site convey a positive or useful message for the university?
- Who is the intended audience?
- What information content is provided?
- What functions are provided?
- Does the student conduct business at the site? How?
- Is the site well designed from the point-of-view of clarity, ease of use, speed of access?
- How well does the site use design and layout features?
- Is the site aesthetically pleasing?
- What are the benefits of the structure provided by the professor?
- What does the university do to provide a competitive advantage?
- What features (security, transaction management, information collection, navigation, search engine, site map, index, help, easily available policies) does the site support?
- How broad is the coverage of the content?

The goal of this exercise was for students to reflect on what functionality provided added value to the *student,* and what actually detracted from the value to the student, while being sensitive to the issues of image and professional characterization of the university. In oral presentations, teams summarized the sites, analyzed the design and content, and speculated on the associated strategies. Teams considered how a variety of stakeholders might respond to the sites, including the faculty member and current students, of course, but also prospective students and faculty, deans, funding sources, community representatives, people who hire the students, tenure review committees, and others.

Support for Focused Training

As stated previously, one factor that impacts technology acceptance is perceived behavioral control. This measure reflects users' self-confidence in their ability to use the

Table 5: Reasons for Current Stage of Web Presence

Privacy	2
Cannot depend on having technology in classroom	3
Question the usefulness of it	4
Do not know how to do it	7
Design concerns	7
Never got around to it	8
Previous training was inadequate	9

technology, because they believe they have sufficient knowledge, resources, and support to use the technology.

Prior to working with the students, the faculty were asked what factors impacted their current use of Internet-based technologies. Faculty members were asked to select as many as applied to them (so the responses sum greater than the number of subjects). These results are summarized in Table 5.

Two things were interesting to note in these statistics. First, of those who answered that they "did not know how to create Web pages," none of them were aware of recent developments in tools that can be used to simplify the development process. Today's Web development tools often provide templates for design use and could help those people who expressed concern that the design of pages was too difficult. In fact, this university provides such a tool[3] and training each semester for it. While many faculty members outside the College of Business have taken significant advantage of this tool for class materials, Business Faculty have not, as a general rule, adopted its use. Second, and more surprisingly, more than 60% of the participants had taken campus training programs on the use of Internet technologies for curriculum and had found them to be inadequate.

In other words, as the "perceived behavioral control" dimension of TPB predicts, faculty in this study, none of whom had adopted the technology for their classes, had been disappointed with current levels of support for technology adoption, and said disappointment was a major inhibitor to the faculty member's further use of Internet technologies in the classroom. This suggests that the current, standard approaches to providing technology support are inadequate for faculty in the College. Among this cross section of faculty, there had neither been diffusion of information nor diffusion of skills to support technology usage. Said differently, the training did not empower the faculty, did not facilitate the development of compatible Internet usage, and did not illustrate to the faculty the added value to their specific classes of using the technology.

To gain perspective on how the training might be improved, the researcher again turned to the literature for possibilities. Several studies identified training as a critical component to achieve sufficient levels of perceived behavioral control to ensure the success of end-user computing (see, for example, Dickson et al., 1984; Harrison & Rainer, 1992; Simon et al., 1996). Other studies have also linked adequate training to the level of satisfaction of end-users of computing (Cheney et al., 1986) However, research indicates that not all training is useful or adequate to support end-users of computing. Decker (1980) and Simon et al. (1996) showed that individualized, focused training provides the greatest efficacy, as well as high levels of efficiency, and thereby would provide the most significant impact upon adoption of technology and satisfaction with its use. Similarly, research conducted at the IBM Watson Research Center (Carroll, 1984) showed that users tend to be overwhelmed with the enormity of a wide range of possibilities of the technology in conventional training procedures and tend to find the effort frustrating, tedious, and inefficient. However, when training included individual's "real work" that was important to them, people learned the technology better and were more likely to adapt it further in their work.

Hence, the literature suggests that training is more likely to be positively accepted (and impact perceived behavioral control, and thereby impact technology acceptance) if it is individualized, focused on specific issues of interest, and includes some kind of example–experiment relationship between the trainer and the end-user. To test these ideas, an action research plan was developed for implementing a focused, work-related training Internet technologies program for faculty, and for studying the implementation of the program. In particular, the intervention used students to provide individualized, focused consulting and instruction to volunteer faculty members. The goal was to develop a course-related Web presence and to train faculty how to maintain it autonomously in the future. Groups of students were assigned to particular faculty members and given the task of converting faculty class materials for Web use for the Fall 2001 semester and training the "client" faculty member to be able to maintain the materials in the future. In fact, students could not get credit until the client faculty member expressed satisfaction with the materials *and* was adequately trained in its maintenance. Fourteen students working in five groups created a Web presence for 15 faculty members in the College of Business Administration.

These students served in the role of what Rogers (1983) called "communications channels" in this diffusion process. That is, they provided focused information about using technology (the innovation) to the faculty user (the end user). This information included some perspectives about how other faculty used Internet technologies, and what uses of Internet technologies are possible, as well as and in terms of what is seen as appropriate usage from a technology perspective. In this chapter, the process the students followed, the obstacles they tackled, and the solutions they found will be reported. As discussed later, the students were required to identify costs and benefits of a Web presence from the perspective of their individual clients. These data will be examined in light of a growing literature regarding Web design principles, and an established literature on training to create a typology of factors discouraging participation by faculty; goals for the use of the technology; and tasks to avoid.

Although only a small sample, the experiment is based upon a good cross section of faculty from the College, and we believe the insights are generalizable. Similarly, the interests of and capabilities of the students are also typical of those found in Colleges of Business. The next two sections will provide an overview of the demographics of the students and faculty to demonstrate their typical nature.

RESULTS

Reviewing Perspectives

Fifteen faculty sites from across the United States were examined by the student groups. The coverage of disciplines included three finance class sites, three accounting class sites, three quantitative methods sites, and six information systems sites. Unfortunately, this does not parallel the proportion of classes generally taught in Colleges of Business, and it does not parallel the proportion of disciplines to be covered in the task assignment. The sites varied substantially in terms of style and functionality. At the "simplistic" end of the scale were pages that appeared to be no more than a standard brief biography of a faculty member that appeared to be created by "publishing" a word-processed document. At the "high end" of the spectrum was the well-known e-commerce site created and maintained by Michael Rappa at North Carolina State University, which includes a wide range of resources for teaching about e-business topics (Rappa, 2002).

This variety of approaches and functionality provided good substance for a class discussion about using Internet resources for class support. Students dissected the sites, considered their usefulness and costs to a wide range of stakeholders, and considered the technical merits of each. As a result of that discussion, the class identified 15 features and characteristics to guide in the design of class websites. While the class did not vote on accepting or rejecting a suggestion, each was discussed until a consensus was achieved. These "guidelines" were also evaluated against good Web design practices found in a number of prescriptive sources (see, for example, Conger & Mason, 1998; Geissler et al., 2001; Horton, 2002; Lynch, 2002; Siegel, 1997; Tomsen, 2000) to ensure that they were consistent with what we know about technology design.

In Table 6, a summary of this design principle distillation exercise is presented. In addition to a short explanation, a citation from the Web design literature is given that provides further explanation of and rationale for the principle. There were no principles proposed by student teams that were not adopted by the class as a whole. Further, there were no principles that were inconsistent with the Web design literature. The only surprising result was that there were no discipline-specific recommendations that were made (other than the concept that there should be links to discipline-relevant materials).Nothing in the derived list is particularly new or shocking to people who regularly design websites or who are educated in the issues of design (especially human–computer interface design). However, in the words of Voltaire, "Le sens commun n'est pas si commun (Common sense is not so common)." Said differently, students derived these "principles" because a number of the sites reviewed or sites supporting classes taken by these students did *not* adhere to rules of good design.

Upon reflection, of course, it is not surprising that not all class-supporting websites were designed well. Faculty members not trained in design and who may or may not have sensitivity to aesthetics would be unlikely to discover principles of Web page design, while *also* learning to use the technology and adapting it to their specific classroom use. However, design mistakes can influence people who view the page, and skew their evaluation of the page, and ultimately perhaps, their evaluation of the university. Said differently, these design issues can impact how the page is received and the potential benefits it can have as a pedagogical tool and as other uses. This importance causes us to highlight them in this chapter as a form of documentation. We suggest that they be provided to faculty in training at other institutions. The Web Studio class used them as the foundation for the preparation of sites for their faculty clients.

These principles may help university administrators in encouraging faculty to develop a Web presence for their classes. Clearly, they need to be supplemented by institution-specific requirements. They provided the guiding principles for the student design projects.

Table 6: Fundamental Design Principles

This is a list of design principles derived by the students as a result of the class experience. In addition, the authors have provided a citation from the Web design literature that provides further explanation for and rationale for the principle.

- Pages should be "attractive" to encourage viewers to explore them and to provide a positive image of the University. Boring pages, or pages with too much activity or unpleasant color combinations, discouraged users. This result has been explored more scientifically by others and found to be a good rule. Unfortunately, the class could not agree on what was meant by an "attractive" page and what was a prohibitively "unattractive" site (Geissler, Zinkhan, & Watson, 2001). They agreed that superfluous graphics, animation, format, and color changes tended to move a page toward being "unattractive." On the other hand, low formatting, no graphics, and plain black on white also was deemed "unattractive." Research has suggested that pages should have two graphics but no more than four graphics to capture the attention of users (Conger & Mason, 1998; Geissler, Zinkhan, & Watson, 2001).
- While the "look and feel" of pages were important, students (including potential, current, and former) look to a site for information. The students emphasized that content should not be sacrificed for form. In fact, pages that did not provide access "ancillary materials" were generally not useful and would not attract students to return to those pages (Barker, 2001; Horton, 2002; Lynch, 2002).
- Pages that were not well designed conveyed a bad impression of the University. A previous meeting with the Dean to discuss this project convinced students of the benefit of class websites to creating and maintaining a particular image of the University in the community. Students agreed that unattractive and low content pages were more likely to provide a negative image than no site at all. An interesting observation, however, was that the University should not "dictate" the form of such pages, because that would appear inauthentic and not reflect the color of most universities (Conger & Mason, 1998; Lynch, 2002).
- Each page needs to stand "on its own." While the professor may move back and forth among pages, other users might not come upon them in order, and hence, other users need to be able to make sense out of them (Horton, 2001; Lynch, 2002; Siegel, 1997).
- Navigation—from the perspective of a variety of stakeholders—among the pages is critical (Conger & Mason, 1998; Horton, 2001; Lynch, 2002; Siegel, 1997).
- Pages that conveyed at least some nonstandard information (not available in university catalogs and phone books) about the faculty member provided a more appealing incentive to enroll in the class. The students indicated that such information was particularly important on commuter campuses, where students were less likely to share impressions of classes and professors prior to registration (Tomsen, 2002; Siegel, 1997).
- Static pages conveyed a sense of not being "up to date" in the material. Some updating of pages is critical for credibility. The more often pages are updated, the more often individuals are likely to view them. Students realized that more dynamic content required a higher commitment (and, hence, cost to) the faculty member (Tomsen, 2002; Siegel, 1997).
- While class jargon might make the pages useful for students, it reduced the usefulness of the pages for attracting outside students (Siegel, 1997).
- Links to external sources were quite appealing and would enrich the value of the website to the student. However, significant amounts of outside links would require an enormous and ongoing investment to keep the links current. Further, links (or information) that were out of date were worse than nonexisting links (Tomsen, 2002; Siegel, 1997).
- An "anonymous comment" feature was desirable on each class page to allow students to share their concerns without fear of retribution.
- Documentation is critical. This should include the name of the page owner, his or her affiliation and location, an email address to contact for questions or comments (or to correct mistakes), and the date the page was last updated. Without appropriate documentation, viewers do not know the source or reliability of the information. Furthermore, the documentation makes it easier to seek further materials if desired or to correct errors if found (Lynch, 2002; Siegel, 1997; Barker, 2001).
- Pages should not just be a replication of the printed page. In order to be useful, pages must allow users to see new presentation formats or new capabilities—hyperlinking, simulations, demonstrations, etc. (Lynch, 2002; Siegel, 1997; Tomasen, 2000).
- Pages need to be proofread just like any other document. Bad grammar and spelling provide an awful image of a class and a university (Conger & Mason, 1998; Barker, 2001; Lynch, 2002; Siegel, 1997).
- Pages need to accommodate "older" browsers and those who elect to turn off the graphical image capability. Students or members of the community who must upgrade browsers via a phone line might not be as likely to update a browser as an on-campus user. However, they are stakeholders whose views must be accommodated (Conger & Mason, 1998; Lynch, 2002).
- Web pages need to convey the same message regardless of the operating system, browser, or resolution. This also makes the question of what is attractive more complex. Furthermore, it requires a text alternative of all graphics and a variety of forms of navigation (Conger & Mason, 1998; Lynch, 2002).

Faculty Feedback

At the beginning of the projects, participating faculty were interviewed by teams regarding their individual perceptions of the disadvantages and advantages associated with the use of Internet technologies in the classroom. Summarized in Table 7 are the disadvantages identified by these faculty members.

We have summarized the issues into five pedagogical groupings. The first of these, labeled, "general," provides the kind of response generally believed to be the primary deterrents to the use of Internet technology: the faculty member does not know how to create the pages and does not want to invest the time to do it. Furthermore, because the production and updating of the pages is not part of a professor's regular process of preparing for class, even updating an existing website was viewed as another time-consuming task. It was in response to the belief that this was the only factor that kept faculty from having such pages that sprung the idea for the class.

However, we were surprised with some of the other factors identified as costs. Privacy of an individual faculty member came across as a primary inhibitor of webpage development. Some faculty wanted to be sure that personal information, such as location of their homes, and especially information about their children, were not included in the pages. While that is a well-known and reasonable expectation (and certainly honored by the student teams), two faculty members believed that the concept of a webpage implied that you advertised such information. Hence, concern about releasing some information had been an inhibitor to webpage preparation in the past. Once assured that they could provide only professionally relevant information on the website, they were more willing to progress with the project. Other faculty members clearly wanted to keep *all* information about themselves to themselves. Some faculty did not even want to publish "professional" information that students might

Table 7: Identified Costs of Web Usage

	Cost Identified
General	• There is a large cost of learning • It takes too much time • This is another task…it is not part of the regular production process (of the class)
Ability to "Express Themselves"	• It takes away from the privacy of the faculty member (who does not want to share values or other issues outside of class) • There is no good reason to share the information
Communications	• With this, we run the risk of cheating • Students will believe faculty members are *always* available • Faculty spend more time supporting students outside of class • "Not my job" to provide marketing materials for the University • Students may not listen in class
Handouts and Other Materials	• People are unlikely to attend class if materials are available outside of class • Expense: students will run off copies of the materials in the labs, and the university will bear the cost anyway; in fact, because they are a "free good," students are likely to run off multiple copies rather than remember where things were put • Students need to learn how to find materials on their own—it is part of the learning process; if we provide too much online, they will not learn how to look for things • Students will learn to over-rely on Web sources that sometimes have dubious credibility • Intellectual property issues are at risk • Maintenance is necessary and can be time consuming

not have other mechanisms to obtain (like editorships, citations of published papers, national offices held, or even committees on which they sat at the university). This was accepted as a design requirement for those faculty members.

A second set of issues was labeled "Communications." Interestingly, several of the faculty members believed that if they provided materials on the Web, students would be more inclined to "cheat" on papers, exams, and assignments. When asked, these faculty members indicated that they thought encouraging students to discuss too much outside of class was dangerous, because it would encourage them to communicate even when it was inappropriate. The other primary cost in the communications category was that faculty believed any serious use of Internet technologies opened the door to spending countless hours supporting students, answering questions, and generally being available outside of class. In fact, one faculty member noted that he "would never be able to check my email again because all those students would be sending me questions…this would be a problem, especially as I work on my research."

The last category of concerns involved handouts and the impact of providing them on the Web. Faculty members were seriously concerned that if materials generally distributed in class were available outside the class, that students would not attend class. Even if they attended class, some faculty believed that students might not listen and participate in discussions. Other faculty members believed that providing materials over the Web would be expensive for the University, because students would "just print them out in the labs anyway" and would be more likely to print out multiple copies rather than keeping track of the copy they already had.

Other faculty members objected to providing too much on the Web—including too many links to related materials—because this robbed students of the valuable learning experience of finding materials "on their own." These faculty members believed it would cause students to become too passive about their learning, which would stand in the way of their long-term intellectual development. Related to this was a concern that students would become too reliant upon materials available elsewhere on the Web, which often have dubious credibility. Finally, faculty members were concerned about intellectual property, copyright, and other guidelines. They felt it was too significant a risk to provide materials on the Web.

This clearly was a summary of specific concerns felt by faculty members about use of Internet technology. It is not meant to enumerate all reasons faculty shy away from using the Web, but rather to illustrate that there are a wide range of concerns beyond those of "I don't know how" or it "takes too much time" that need to be addressed before faculty as a group will use Internet technologies to support their classroom experiences.

As with the previous list, none of these issues is startling. However, few of the issues are addressed explicitly in conventional training programs, documentation, or even university policies. This list is provided here to help begin the dialogue for technology trainers and consultants to discuss how to accommodate these issues in their individual efforts.

These issues can also be evaluated in light of the theoretical framework underlying this analysis. Provided in Table 8 is a mapping of these issues into the TPB framework. Note that this summary shows that for faculty, issues of relative (pedagogical) advantage and compatibility were most mentioned, and thus, as scales, seem most important. Trialability was not mentioned as an issue, and the two items noted under observability might also be considered under compatibility. Hence, while there may be multiple factors under attitude that may impact the acceptance of Internet technologies for course support, this research suggests that two of the factors are more important to professors.

Table 8: Costs of Web Page Design mapped to TPB Framework

Relative Advantage	• Takes too much time to support my classes • There is no benefit to sharing information about myself (even professional information) • Students will believe I am always available for assistance • I will spend too much time on my classes and not enough time on my research • Students will just print off materials in the lab; it will be too expensive
Compatibility	• This is just another task outside of my regular duties • It is not my job to provide marketing materials for the University • If students have materials before class, they may not listen in class • If students have materials before class, they may not come to class • Students will begin to rely too much on Web materials • Students will not learn how to find materials on their own
Complexity	• Too hard to learn • Learning cost is too high
Trialability	
Observability	• Just another task for which I will not get credit • Maintenance is time consuming and not rewarded

Thus, if there is a mechanism for minimizing the complexity issue (such as using student volunteers or easy-to-use software), then two issues remain: (a) I do not want to do anything that will not result in better learning by my students, and (b) I do not want to change my teaching style. Issue one is appropriate, and administrators should not try to influence it. However, the second issue suggests that the faculty might easily get accustomed to teaching using the manner in which they were taught. This may or may not be a good outcome. If it is perceived to be negative, then the administrators will need to provide training and incentives for changing the delivery mechanism for classes. In other words, the benefit to the administration of Internet course presences may not be worth the cost of changing the fundamental practice of some faculty delivery. In those cases, the administration should consider how much it could provide about the class and supporting the class without relying upon the faculty member to do the work.

Each of these faculty members had serious concerns about using the Web in class, and yet volunteered to participate in this experiment. At that same initial interview when the costs of using Internet technologies were revealed, students queried faculty members about their views of the advantages of a Web presence. As with the previous section, these statements were also categorized in four pedagogical groups, "general," "ability to express themselves," "alternative forms of communications," and "handouts and other materials," and a summary of them can be found in Table 9.

As one can see from Table 9, some faculty just wanted a Web presence because it was expected of them; it was the "in thing" to do. They did not really know what they wanted the Web presence to accomplish at the outset. Other faculty members believed that a Web presence was important for helping potential students understand what happened in their classes in order to attract more students to the University, more students to a particular major,

Table 9: Expectations of the Benefits of Web Usage

	Benefit Identified
General	• It is the "in thing" to do • Helps to advertise University and majors
Ability to "Express Themselves"	• Gives a mechanism for explaining one's philosophy without "preaching" • Can provide additional help, such as pronunciation of a difficult name • Allows one to share important values with the students
Alternative Form of Communications	• It is a way to have students share information among themselves • It is a way to allow shy or disabled students to participate more fully in class • Helps keep classes together • Allows timely assignments to be made in between class meetings (especially for once/week classes that rely heavily on current events) • Encourages communication as a form of lifelong learning • Allows the faculty member to be more available
Handouts and Other Materials	• Can provide ancillary materials (especially those from publisher) for extra student support • Can enrich the class with ideas from other colleagues • Can enrich the class with multimedia presentations • Can reduce the cost of providing materials to students, because one does not need to provide paper copies • Easier to handle materials because student is responsible for finding them on his/her own • Can make last-minute changes to materials before class • Encourages building-block learning by allowing class material usage of resources in later classes

and more students to their classes. This was a fascinating contrast with those faculty members who strongly believed it was not "their job" to attract students, and that had kept them from having a Web presence in the past.

Some faculty wanted the Web presence to give them an opportunity to share their values and philosophy with students in a subtle form. They believed students misunderstood the purposes of some of their rules and assignments and wanted an opportunity to "explain" the reasons. Some faculty members provided quotes and links to materials they believed students should read, as a passive way of making statements about values. An interesting example of this is one faculty member who enforces traditional "etiquette" in his classes as a way of preparing students for the workforce. He wanted materials on his website to demonstrate how these lessons would help students obtain better employment opportunities.

Other faculty members believed this was an opportunity to provide support that could not otherwise be provided. One example was a faculty member whose last name was difficult to pronounce—this faculty member elected to have a recording of his name being said correctly on the website. Hence, students who felt uncomfortable because they could not pronounce his name could go to the site to learn how to say it correctly. Other faculty provided links to materials about careers, communication skills, and professional opportunities.

The third category of goals was communications. UM–St. Louis is a commuter campus. As with most such campuses, students come to class and then leave campus and do not form strong relationships with other students. Group projects can sometimes be difficult, because students do not have the knowledge or skills to understand how to work in a job-like group experience. Some of the faculty involved in the project wanted to use Internet technologies to build stronger group cohesiveness and provide a mechanism for communication about ideas, even when students were not on campus. These same mechanisms would facilitate the inclusion of students who might not otherwise participate—especially shy students who fear speaking in crowds or disabled students who have difficulty doing so. Finally, some faculty thought using Internet technologies could make them more available outside of class, giving them flexibility in the times they were available and the amount of time they were available.

The final category of benefits was in terms of handouts. Some faculty members wanted to provide ancillary materials that the publisher provides (such as PowerPoint slides or other tools) that are not used in class. Posting such things on the Web helped them accomplish that. Other colleagues wanted to enrich the class with materials posted by other colleagues, by companies, and professional organizations, especially if they were multimedia in form.

This category also included faculty preferences of no longer needing to worry about handouts, either getting them to the bookstore to be sold or remembering to bring them to class for those absent in previous sessions. The availability of the materials on the Web changed the responsibility from that of the faculty to that of the student. In addition, faculty could make last-minute changes to materials if they were posted on the Web—a phenomenon that could not happen if materials needed to be duplicated in the University copy center.

Again, this list is not meant to be exhaustive but merely illustrative of the issues that encouraged faculty to consider a Web presence. We present it here as a set of possible issues administrators might want to suggest to faculty who are reticent about the value of Web support as a pedagogical tool. Such issues might be included as ideas in a training program or as mechanisms for getting faculty interested.

In Table 10, a mapping of these issues to the TPB framework is provided. As with the cost table, in Table 10, no issues of importance to the faculty on the dimension of trialability are illustrated. Furthermore, the first issue of observability (it is the "in thing" to do) might really be aligned with the compatibility of the style of the faculty member with the autonomous delivery of service.

Table 10: Expectations of the Benefits mapped to TPB Framework

Relative Advantage	• I can give students access to ancillary materials that I do not want to use in the class • I can use a wider range of materials (including multimedia) that may help get my point across better • This will better accommodate students with various disabilities • This will help keep multiple sections working together • If students do not need to write the notes, they can focus more on synthesis and working together
Compatibility	• Students can be reminded of my pedagogical philosophy • I can share my values with students (and perhaps influence them) • I can share important information that is hard to get • I can make assignments between classes • I can extend my influence if students use materials in other classes • I can help to integrate curriculum if students use materials in other classes • This makes me more available to students—on my own terms • Allows me to make last-minute additions and changes
Complexity	
Trialability	
Observability	• It is the "in thing" to do • The Dean will like that I am helping to attract more students

Note that the benefits of relative advantage and compatibility are almost all experienced by the students. This suggests that in order for the administration to rely upon faculty to see the Internet technologies as positive, the faculty must have adopted student growth as an important intrinsic value, or there must be explicit rewards provided for the faculty to try new pedagogical tools.

Resulting Web Presence

In every case except one,[4] students provided an Internet technology solution that met the goals of the assigned faculty member. All faculty members were given home pages in addition to class Web presences. Students obtained accounts for faculty; designed, coded, created, and posted the pages; documented their efforts; and trained their faculty clients in tools necessary for maintenance. About half of the students used the campus tool, "Blackboard," to supplement website presences for the classes because of the ease with which the tool allows one to post materials on calendars (such as daily readings from the *Wall Street Journal* or other assignments) or class discussions (chat rooms). This was particularly true for faculty members who had limited capability for, or interest in, maintenance of websites—this made maintenance more viable.

University Perspective

The College of Business Administration obtained 14 new uses of Internet technology across the curriculum that facilitated the "high tech" image that the campus wants to promote. These pages not only had significant content, but they were also technically well developed. That means that they, unlike many faculty pages, had the following characteristics:

- The pages had a professional appearance with consistent use of colors, fonts, and themes that adhered to good design principles.[5]
- The development was sensitive to browser compatibility differences, color issues, and screen size issues, and hence, the page was easily viewed across a variety of platforms, browsers, and operating systems that students, potential students, and community friends might use (and hence, was more likely to be seen as positive by a wider range of users).
- All pages adhered to good usability guidelines and, hence, were accessible to students with a variety of disabilities.
- All pages are maintainable by the faculty member to whom they belong.
- All pages are documented.
- All pages provide good internal documentation, such as metatag use, so they can be easily found by search engines.

All of these factors contributed to the benefit of the experience to the University. Not only did it obtain new uses of Internet technology to enhance the Business curriculum, but it also obtained a set of Web presences that can, in fact, be used to attract students and faculty as well as to make a positive impact on the community.

The bottom line, though, is whether the experiment was "worth it." This is a difficult question to measure objectively, because many of the benefits are fuzzy, futuristic, and difficult to separate from other interventions. What we know is that the College got 15 new faculty websites, and people are now aware of at least some of the technology and how to use it to support pedagogical goals. This translates into a "higher tech" image for the campus, and for the College, which relates to their respective goal statements. In terms of cost, there is the cost of the faculty member teaching the course, and the opportunity cost of not offering something else, and that faculty member not focusing on some other project. The evaluation of the relative costs and benefits—from the perspective of generalizing this to another institution—is for an administrator in light of his or her own agenda to decide.

Student Perspective

Students completed group cohesion and satisfaction surveys at three times during the class—once early in the development process, once mid-development, and once after the development process—to evaluate the benefits they took away from the experience. Three groups of questions, all using five-point Likert scales, asked students to reflect on their experiences in three areas: (a) with their groups, (b) with their faculty clients, and (c) in terms of meeting their own goals of taking the class.

The group cohesiveness survey was adapted from a validated psychological scale of group cohesion (Malkin & Stake, 2001), with four basic scales to measure the level of congruence among students with regard to the project goals, specific project tasks, bond among members, and satisfaction with the process. Using this instrument, group cohesion scores on all four scales were uniformly high across all groups, with only a small, regular decay in the satisfaction level as deadlines approached. Statistically, there was no difference among groups or over time during the semester. This is remarkable, because it is rare to have a class in which all groups function well, and which function well with a set of clients. This is believed to reflect the students' intrinsic involvement in the process of creating these sites.

Satisfaction with faculty clients was measured with one scale that addressed objective measures of cooperation (such as the number of times the team had met with the faculty member), their understanding of the needs of the faculty, and the student's perceptions of the faculty member's thoughtfulness in responding to questionnaires, requests, and evaluations. In addition, students were required to write a short description of their interactions with the faculty.

As one might expect, students were often frustrated with their faculty clients. The one factor on which they all agreed was that "content is king," and the content needs to originate with the faculty member. Because the page development was "off schedule" for most faculty, students often had difficulty getting materials from them. For this reason, the students recommended procedures for the faculty that incorporated updating of the Web pages with their regular efforts in preparing for class. In the last questionnaire, students indicated that such concurrent scheduling would be a key to success in long-term maintenance of the pages.

Finally, students were questioned in regard to their goals for the class, their satisfaction in meeting those goals, and how important the class was to their long-term professional goals. In each case, the questions were asked in open-ended questionnaires and included no objective measures. Their answers are summarized below.

This assignment presented a fascinating juncture for the students. Virtually all of the students enrolled in the class to learn how to create highly technically sophisticated websites, using the most sophisticated tools available to them. A common goal among the students was to learn the newest technologies to provide the best special effects, such as the use of Flash technologies. This is not terribly surprising, because that is what MIS people do. In that sense, the students were disappointed, because most of the sites needed to be significantly more ōmundane to achieve client goals and maintenance standards. They found, instead, satisfaction in the hands-on experience of working with a client and experiencing the trade-offs of design, the need for various kinds of support that was not entirely obvious to the page viewer (such as documentation). Students were also pleased to have the challenge to figure out how to reflect user differences in personalities, goals, and maintenance capabilities in the pages they developed.[6]

Faculty Perspective

Faculty clients also were pleased with the experience. Faculty perceptions were evaluated using objective and open-ended measures. Each faculty member was provided a short questionnaire using five-point Likert scales regarding the success of the site in meeting his or her needs; satisfaction with the process; and the extent to which he or she felt capable of maintaining the site in the future. In addition, each faculty member was asked to comment on the site and on the process for developing the site. Finally, each faculty member was evaluated in terms of his or her use of the site during the Fall 2001 semester.

Every faculty member expressed great enthusiasm about the solution that had been provided. Satisfaction with the site was uniformly high, and each faculty person stated that he or she could maintain the site in the future. Some specific comments included that they were grateful for a website that reflected their own personalities; they were pleased to have a basic structure provided for them; they were glad they did not need to create the design; and they were impressed by the quality of attention they received and skill of the students. Further, they expressed a positive response to having the one-on-one support of the groups, and the infrastructure on which to build.

From the faculty perspective, three aspects of the project were crucial. The first was that the students provided an infrastructure on which to build. After the project, most clients admitted that they felt overwhelmed at the thought of beginning a Web presence and so had never started one. Now that the foundation had been laid, faculty clients felt comfortable adding materials as they became available.

The second critical aspect was that they now understood how specific technological functions related to specific pedagogical goals. Said differently, they were pleased to have a site developed for which they had a *reason*, rather than just getting on the "bandwagon" of developing a site for no apparent purpose. In addition, they were pleased at having options provided to them of *how* to implement the technology so that they could reasonably select the one that most closely fit their own styles and pedagogical goals. Individualized consulting meant that they could provide the students with a list of goals and let them relate those goals to specific technology functions. Furthermore, this consulting allowed them to express their specific needs without concern about evaluation from colleagues who might not share their goals. There was no pressure to provide specific functionality (for everyone to use the same thing). In fact, the 15 sites differ substantially in terms of what technology was used and how it was used.

This should not be surprising, because faculty members fall in the psychological category of "professionals," or "members of occupations with special power and prestige…special competence in esoteric bodies of knowledge" and to whom are given great autonomy in the practice of their profession (Sharma, 1997). Studies in psychology show that most professionals resist technology when it encroaches on their autonomy (Jackson, 1970). Hence, the provision of support in a manner that supports rather than encroaches on professional autonomy should be more easily accepted by faculty.

The third crucial aspect of the project was the training. As discussed earlier, many of these faculty members attended campus training classes that they found inadequate. However, for this class, the faculty received individualized documentation and training for the maintenance and development of their sites. Faculty members felt this training was more effective than the classroom training, and considerably more efficient, because it focused only on their needs. Faculty expressed that they were also more likely to ask questions and seek other kinds of clarification about technical issues than in a classroom setting.

The same professional attribute discussed above is associated with the phenomenon of faculty not wanting to receive training in a conventional manner. These individuals believe their time is best spent focusing on issues that are of particular importance to them, and ignoring others. Hence, they only want training that is focused on their needs. Furthermore, because these individuals prefer not to show their ignorance about any number of issues in a group, they are more integrated in their training when not participating as part of a group.

Finally, since delivery of the pages, 75% of the faculty clients have spent some time adjusting their Web presences by adding new materials. Most faculty members expressed enthusiasm for being able to build upon the foundation students provided them. Many faculty members also commented that they had never realized how easy it was to make the changes and provide materials for the students, and hence, they were more likely to supplement classroom experiences with Internet technology in the future.

DISCUSSION

This experiment was undertaken to provide an incentive for faculty to use more Internet technologies in their classes. From an objective viewpoint, it is too early to determine if the experiment was a success. At this early stage, it appears to have been a success in getting a number of faculty using Internet technologies to provide a value-added component to their class *and* to provide an Internet presence that might attract new students to the University. In addition, it provided a wonderful laboratory for working with students interested in building better skills in Internet technologies for the future. Said differently, this approach seems to be an interesting way to nudge faculty into using the new technologies, when a university has a small budget to expend upon training, development, and maintenance.

The literature suggests that experiments such as these are only successful if there is a long-term procedure for maintaining the partnership (Leidner, 1999). Therefore, it is appropriate to address the long-term partnership between IS students (with Web expertise) and College Faculty (who need the Web expertise). For this question, there are two answers. First, the specific faculty who participated in the experiment received individualized training on those aspects of the technology used on their sites. Theoretically, then, they should be in a good position to continue in their work autonomously. In fact, each of the faculty members who participated in the experiment indicated on his or her survey that belief in autonomous maintenance of the sites.

However, technologies change, and even the most proficient among these faculty clients will likely need support in the future. Furthermore, if the experiment is to have long-term benefit to the college, additional faculty need to be brought on board to develop and maintain websites. Given budget reductions at the university (which are not uncommon among universities in the 21st century), repeating the course regularly was not a viable option. Hence, the instructor turned to a student-run organization called the "Web Development

Corps" (WDC) to continue the work started by the studio students. These students perform similar (albeit less structured) exercises for faculty members, regular maintenance on their sites, and training for the benefit of the experience. Although the WDC existed before the intervention, it was not popular among faculty. After the experiment, when the benefit of working with the students was apparent, even among nonparticipants, increasing numbers of faculty availed themselves of the benefit of the students' expertise. Students develop an impressive resume starting on small maintenance projects and eventually moving up to more sophisticated, full-site projects. It has, in fact, received such positive, if informal, praise, that projects from off-campus organizations have been brought to the attention of the students and completed successfully.

This approach to providing focused consulting, development, and training has a good theoretical grounding, and, in this experiment, a positive practical experience. It provides a practical, financially acceptable approach to helping faculty adopt pedagogically appropriate technology that is consistent with the concerns and the philosophy of individual faculty members. The key is the individualized and responsive development and training experience.

REFERENCES

Abbott, A. (1988). *The system of professions: an essay on the division of expert labor.* Chicago, IL: University of Chicago Press.

Ajzen, I., & Fishbein, M. (1980). *Understanding attitudes and predicting social behaviour.* Englewood Cliffs, NJ: Prentice Hall.

Bandura, A. (1982). Self-efficacy mechanism in human agency. *American Psychologist, 37*(2), 122–147.

Barker, J. (2001). Evaluating Web pages: experience why it's important. UC Berkeley—Teaching Library Internet Workshops; http://www.lib.berkeley.edu/TeachingLib/Guides/Internet/Evaluate.html (last update November 27, 2001).

Carroll, J. M. (1984). Minimalist training. *Datamation.* 125–133.

Cheney, R. H., Mann, R. I., & Amoroso, D. L. (1986). Organizational factors affecting the success of end user computing. *Journal of Management Information Systems, 3*(1), 65–80.

Conger, S. A., & Mason, R. O. (1998). *Planning and designing effective websites.* Cambridge, MA: Course Technology.

Davis, F. D. (1989). Perceived usefulness, perceived ease of use and user acceptance of information technology. *MIS Quarterly, 13*(3), 319–340.

Davis, F. D. (1993). User acceptance of information technology: system characteristics, user perceptions and behavioral impacts. *International Journal of Man-Machine Studies, 38,* 475–487.

Davis, F. S., Bagozzi, R. P., & Warshaw, P. R. (1989). User acceptance of computer technology: a comparison of two theoretical models. *Management Science, 35*(8), 982–1003.

Decker, P. J. (1980). Effects of symbolic coding and rehearsal in behavior-modeling training. *Journal of Applied Psychology, 64*(6), 627–634.

Dickson, G. W. et al. (1984). Key information systems issues for the 1980s. *Management Information Systems Quarterly, 8*(2), 135–159.

Dillon, A., & Morris, M. G. (1996). User acceptance of information technology: theories and models. *Journal of the American Society for Information Science, 31,* 3–32.

Fishbein, M., & Ajzen, I. (1975). *Believe, intention and behaviour: an introduction to theory and research*. Reading, MA: Addison-Wesley.

Freidson, E. A. (1988). Profession of medicine: a study of the sociology of applied knowledge. Chicago, IL: University of Chicago Press.

Geissler, G., Zinkhan, G., & Watson, R. T. (2001). Web home page complexity and communication effectiveness. *Journal of the Association for Information Systems, 2*(2).

Harrison, A. W., & Rainer, R. L. Jr. (1992). The influence of individual differences on skill in end-user computing. *Journal of Management Information Systems, 9*(1), 93–111.

Horton, S. (2002). Web teaching. Academic computing. Hanover, NH: Dartmouth College; http://www.dartmouth.edu/~Web teach/misc/about.html (last updated January 3, 2002).

Hu, P. J. et al. (1999). Examining the technology acceptance model using physician acceptance of telemedicine technology. *Journal of Management Information Systems, 16*(2), 91–112.

Jackson, J. (Ed.). (1970). *Professions and professionalism*. Cambridge: Cambridge University Press.

Kottemann, J. E., & Davis, F. D. (1991). Decision conflict and user acceptance of multicriteria decisionmaking aids. *Decision Sciences, 22*(4), 918–926.

Larson, M. S. (1977). *The rise of professionalism: a sociological analysis*. Berkeley, CA: University of California Press.

Lee, S. M., Kim, Y. R., & Lee, J. (1995). An empirical study of the relationships among end-user information systems acceptance. Training and effectiveness. *Journal of Management Information Systems, 12*(2), 189–202.

Leidner, D. E. (1999). Virtual partnerships in support of electronic commerce: the case of TCIS. *The Journal of Strategic Information Systems, 8*(1), 105–117.

Lynch, P. J., & Horton, S. (2002). *Web style guide: basic design principles for creating Web sites* (2nd ed.). New Haven, CT: Yale University Press.

Malkin, C., & Stake, J. E. (2001). Changes in social attitudes and self-confidence in the gender studies classroom: the role of teacher alliance and student cohesion. UM–St. Louis Department of Psychology Working Paper.

Matheieson, K. (1991). Predicting user intentions: comparing the technology acceptance model with the theory of planned behavior. *Information Systems Research, 2*(3), 173–191.

McMaster, T., Vidgen, R. T., & Wastell, D. G. (1997). Technology transfer: diffusion or translation? In T. McMaster et al. (Eds.), *Facilitating technology transfer through partnership: learning from practice and research* (pp. 64–75). London: Chapman & Hall.

Moore, G., & Benbasat, I. (1991). Development of an instrument to measure the perceptions of adopting an information technology innovation. *Information Systems Research, 2*(3), 192–222.

Rappa, M. (2002). Managing the digital enterprise: an open courseware project. Retrieved January 5, 2002 from the World Wide Web: http://digitalenterprise.org/index.html.

Rogers, E. M. (1983). *Diffusions of innovations* (3rd ed.). New York: The Free Press.

Schainblatt, A. H. (1982). How companies measure productivity of engineers and scientists. *Research Management*, 10–18.

Sharma, A. (1997). Professionals as agent: knowledge asymmetry in agency exchanges. *Academy of Management Review, 22*(30), 758–798.

Siegel, D. (1997). *Secrets of successful Web sites*. Indianapolis, IN: Hayden Books.

Simon, S. J. et al. (1996). The relationship of information system training methods and cognitive ability to end-user satisfaction, comprehension and skill transfer: a longitudinal study. *Information Systems Research, 7*(4), 466–490.

Succi, M. J., & Walter. Z. D. (2001). Theory of user acceptance of information technologies: an examination of physicians. University of Connecticut working paper.

Tan, M., & Thompson, S. H. Teo. (2000). Factors influencing the adoption of Internet banking. *Journal of the Association of Information Systems, 1*(5).

Taylor, S., & Todd, P. A. (1995). Assessing IT usage: the role of prior experiences. *MIS Quarterly, 19*(3), 561–570.

Taylor, S., & Todd, P. A. (1995b). Understanding information technology usage: a test of competing models. *Information Systems Research, 6*(2), 144–176.

Tomsen, M. (2000). *Killer content: strategies for Web content and eCommerce*. Reading, MA: Addison Wesley.

Triandis, H. C. (1977). *Interpersonal behavior*. Pacific Grove, CA: Brooks-Cole Publishing.

Zmud, R. W. (1982). Diffusion of modern software practices: influence of centralization and formalization. *Management Science, 28*(12), 1421–1431.

ENDNOTES

[1] In all but one of those cases, the colleague also taught the class in question. In the other case, the colleague had built the page for the other faculty member's exclusive use.

[2] See http://www.blackboard.com/ (viewed September 1, 2001).

[3] The campus-provided tool is called Blackboard. More information about this tool can be found at http://www.blackboard.com/ (viewed September 1, 2001).

[4] One student fell ill at the end of the semester and has yet to complete his project. He and the faculty member are currently working on the project, and it is believed the last site will be "live" shortly.

[5] The pages have a professional appearance, although they varied substantially in content and style to reflect the goals and personalities of the faculty clients.

[6] For example, in one team assignment, student groups were required to pursue some aspect of page design in depth and to practice their documentation skills. The class decided on the topics needing attention, and surprisingly, the topics were not limited to the "bells and whistles" of Web design. Topics varied from something so basic (and essential) as "how do I get an account" to "how can I create simulations for topics covered in class?" Some groups focused on the basic layout and creation of pages. Other groups focused more on the proprietary software used at UM–St. Louis for class delivery. Still other groups focused on greater use of technology for additional functionality, such as providing searches, animation, swapping images (or text) on a random (or defined) basis, or forms for communication between students and the faculty member. While groups originally selected more "exotic" features to complete, many changed to less technologically exciting issues, because they realized they would not be able to document them at the level necessary for the faculty clients they were serving.

Part III

WBE: Design Issues

Chapter X

Participation: The Online Challenge

Regina Bento
University of Baltimore, USA

Cindy Schuster
University of Baltimore, USA

ABSTRACT

One of the main challenges in Web-based education is to encourage student participation. Although many instructors would like to increase participation in their online courses, there is no established body of knowledge on the various forms such participation may take, or how it should be measured. In this chapter, a taxonomy for classifying different types of participation in online courses will be proposed, and the pedagogical issues involved will be discussed.

INTRODUCTION

With the increasing popularity of student-centered and constructivist approaches to education, student participation in class discussions is being considered not just something "nice to have," but an essential part of the teaching and learning process. As we move from traditional to virtual classrooms, the challenge of understanding and nurturing such participation becomes even greater. In this chapter, a taxonomy of student participation in online class discussions is proposed, in the context of Web-based courses.

For the purposes of our discussion, Web-based education will be seen as a special case of distance education (DE). DE is "planned learning that normally occurs in a different place from teaching and as a result requires special techniques of course design, special instructional techniques, special methods of communication by electronic and other technology, as well as special organizational and administrative arrangements" (Moore & Kearsley, 1996, p. 2).

Distance education is here to stay. Between 1998 and 2001, the number of universities offering distance education increased by 33% (Alavi & Leidner, 2001). Currently, over 50% of U.S. colleges and universities are offering DE courses, and over 2 million students are taking them. By 2004, it is estimated that almost 90% of U.S. colleges and universities will be offering DE courses, and by 2006, almost 5 million students are projected to be taking them (Fornaciari, 2002; Symonds, 2001).

This growth in distance education, however, has not been accompanied by a proportional growth in the understanding of its pedagogical implications (Gallini, 2001; Shedletsky & Aitken, 2001). This gap is particularly glaring in terms of fully exploring the interactive potential of one special form of DE—Web-based education.

One of the main challenges in Web-based education is to understand and encourage student participation. Although many online instructors profess to value, and industriously attempt to grade online participation, there is no established body of knowledge on the various forms such participation may take, or how it should be measured.

In this chapter, the educational paradigms that explain why participation plays such an important role in the teaching and learning process are examined, the types of interactivity involved in distance education are reviewed, a taxonomy for classifying different types of participation in online courses is proposed, and the pedagogical issues involved are discussed.

"Know your learner" is good advice for all professors, but it is even more so for those of us teaching courses with little or no face-to-face interaction. The proposed taxonomy will help us move in that direction, by contributing to a deeper understanding of the nature and dynamics of student participation in Web-based education.

THE RELEVANCE OF PARTICIPATION AND INTERACTION IN DISTANCE EDUCATION

Distance training and education can be approached from two main paradigms: transmission and transformation (Berge, 1999, 2001). In the *transmission* paradigm, "content and knowledge determined by someone else is *transmitted* to the learner" (Berge, 1999, p. 19). In the *transformation* paradigm, "a learner *transforms* information, generates hypotheses, and makes decisions about the knowledge he or she is constructing or socially constructing through interpersonal communication with others" (Berge, 1999, p. 19). The basic assumption of the transmission paradigm is that there is a body of fixed information that can be passed on to students. In this instructor-centered approach, the instructor selects the content and the teaching methods that will best "push" such preconceived knowledge to the passive students, from whom a specific outcome is expected.

In the transmission paradigm, the main value of student participation is to provide evidence of whether the student has correctly "absorbed" the content that the expert instructor has attempted to transmit.

The intellectual roots of the transmission paradigm can be found in positivism (transmission of knowledge from an expert to a novice) and behaviorism (new behavioral patterns are introduced and repeated until they become automatic).

The assumptions of the transmission model have been questioned by authors such as Paulo Freire (1970), who criticized it as a "banking model" of education, where an instructor deposits information into students. Recent research on education and cognition has been increasingly critical of the transmission paradigm (Kemery, 2000), supporting instead the other major paradigm, transformation.

The *transformation* paradigm focuses on the activities of the learners and how they actively participate in the construction of knowledge. In this learner-centered approach, multiple perspectives and flexible methods make it possible for students to adapt, process, and filter content into their own logical frameworks, resulting in outcomes that may not be thoroughly predictable. Instead of "learning" a discipline exactly as it is known by others, students develop personal ways of framing problems within the broader framework of the language and concepts of that discipline.

The transformation paradigm has its intellectual roots in constructivism and social constructivism. From a constructivist perspective, "what is thought to be critical is the active participation and reflection by the learner, while recognizing the flexible and dynamic nature of knowledge" (Berge, 1999, p. 21).

This emphasis on the dynamic nature of knowledge is also present in social constructivism, where it is combined with an interactionist perspective. Understanding is not a predetermined outcome but a process of co-creation, where students must explain, elaborate, and defend their positions to each other. Interactions involve not only information sharing but also interpretation, evaluation, and criticism of each other's comments and ideas.

Not surprisingly, in the transformation paradigm, student participation is at the center of the individual and collective learning process, as proposed in the constructivism and social constructivism traditions. In this context, student participation is not just a form of testing whether knowledge was transmitted. Rather, social interaction is an intrinsic part of learning. Individual learning does not occur in isolation, but in interaction, contributing to and benefiting from the synergy of a community of learners.

TYPES OF INTERACTION IN DISTANCE EDUCATION

Distance education has been profoundly influenced by the transformation paradigm and its emphasis on interaction. As a matter of fact, "it seems that everybody in distance education talks about interaction" (Moore, 1996, p. 127). Talking about it, however, is not enough. Moore argued that in order for us to better understand and practice the concept of interaction, we should distinguish three basic types of interaction that must take place in distance education: learner–content, learner–instructor, and learner–learner interaction (Moore, 1989, 1996).

Learner-content interaction has long been the touchstone of education. Knowledge construction happens when the learner interacts with the instructional content in order to accommodate new information into preexisting cognitive structures, which then results in changes in understanding (Moore, 1996, pp. 128–129).

In distance education, content may be offered to the learner in a variety of ways, such as textual materials in print or electronic formats, radio or TV broadcasts, audio or videotape, computer software, and interactive multimedia. But, regardless of the level of sophistication in the presentation of content, it is only when the student interacts with that content and incorporates it into a personal cognitive structure that learning actually takes place.

This learning is further reinforced through Moore's second type of interaction, learner-instructor, which involves activities such as seeking and offering explanations, analogies, and examples, and elaborating, discussing, and applying content. Those interactions are meant to accomplish multiple objectives: stimulate student interest and engagement in the learning process; foster the application of content through skill practice and manipulation of information and ideas; organize formal and informal ways to test and evaluate the extent to which learning is taking place and, if necessary, develop alternative pedagogical strategies; and provide support and encouragement to each learner (Moore, 1996, p. 130).

According to Moore, distance educators often content themselves with helping students achieve those two classic types of interaction, learner-content and learner-instructor. But for distance education to move beyond the transmission paradigm and be truly transformative, a third type of interaction is essential: learner-learner.

This interaction among learners can take place with students relating directly with each other or in-group settings, with or without the instructor being present in real-time. Learner-learner interaction is an extremely powerful way of "helping students to think out the content that has been presented and to test it in exchanges with their peers" (Moore, 1996, pp. 131–132).

Berge highlighted the importance of interpersonal interaction in distance education by collapsing Moore's three types of interaction into just two types: interaction with content and interpersonal interaction. When discussing "Interaction with Content," Berge agreed with Moore: for learning to take place, the student must actively interact and cognitively process the content of the course, not just passively be exposed to it (Berge, 1998, p. 27).

Berge departed from Moore, however, in combining "learner–instructor" and "learner–learner" interaction under the single umbrella of "interpersonal interaction": For learning to occur, students must interact with each other and the instructor in order to arrive at shared meaning and to make sense of what they are learning. This social context of learning is crucial for motivation, critical judgement, and problem solving (Berge, 1998, p. 28). Interpersonal interaction provides the social context for the mutual construction of understanding and has been demonstrated to play a major role in the learning process (Fulford & Zhang, 1993).

A TAXONOMY OF PARTICIPATION IN ONLINE COURSES

Designers and instructors of online courses often place a high value on these various types of interaction but rarely seem to be able to achieve as much student participation as they would like. This seems to particularly be an issue in the case of asynchronous interactions that rely on online threaded discussion boards or forums.

In spite of the potential convenience of asynchronous communication, in terms of allowing students to interact with each other and with the instructor when and where they want, and even to control the pacing of instruction (Berge, 1998), asynchronicity is sometimes a double-edged sword (Kemery, 2000). Without the direct stimulation of real-time interaction, some students may decrease the frequency and quality of their participation. Online instructors often react to this by increasing the percentage of the grade that is tied to participation in the discussion boards. The problem, however, is that even those types of reward and punishment approaches may not work, if they do not reflect a real understanding of what constitutes "good" or "bad" participation and the factors that contribute to either. For example, not all "lurkers" are goofing off, and not all hyperparticipants are learning.

Figure 1: Taxonomy of Participation in Online Courses

	QUADRANT III "Social Participants"	QUADRANT IV "Active Learners"
Interaction — Interpersonal HIGH		
Interpersonal Interaction LOW	QUADRANT I "Missing in Action"	QUADRANT II "Witness Learners"
	Interaction with Content LOW	Interaction with Content HIGH

In order to gain a deeper understanding of participation, its causes, and its consequences, we need a taxonomy of the types of behavior involved. The taxonomy we propose here is based on Moore's (1989, 1996) discussion of types of interaction in distance education, as summarized by Berge (1998).

As represented in Figure 1, our taxonomy plots different types of participation into four quadrants, determined by a horizontal axis that corresponds to Berge's "Interaction with Content" (and Moore's learner–content interaction), and a vertical axis that corresponds to Berge's "Interpersonal Interaction" (a combination of Moore's "learner–instructor" and "learner–learner" interactions).

The two bottom quadrants (I, II) share the characteristic of low interpersonal interaction. These are the "invisible" students, the "lurkers" who do not actively participate in the online discussions. Instructors often perceive them as a single category of "nonparticipants," from which it is inferred that they are not learning, and which often leads to lower grades. What Figure 1 reveals, however, is that there can be two different dynamics going on behind the same mantle of "invisibility."

The lurkers in Quadrant I represent the kind of nonparticipation that we call "Missing in Action," low in interpersonal and content interactions, as vividly portrayed in this vignette:

Hsu (1992) reports that the "CEO" of one of the online simulated organizations in his Virtual Management Laboratory simply disappeared. The other group members posted a "missing persons report" and conducted a humorous "detective game" to find him. The peer pressure, delivered in a humorous rather than insulting manner, eventually induced the missing leader to return to his online "company," and it subsequently performed very well (Harasim et al., 1995, p. 209).

This type of lack of participation is not often dealt with in this humorous way, and it does not often have such a happy ending. More frequently, it leads to all sorts of negative feelings toward those students who are "missing" and apparently do not care about the course content or their peers. It ultimately results in no learning, a disastrous grade, or the student quitting the course.

Although the lurkers in Quadrant II may seem equally "invisible," their dynamic is entirely different. These are the "witness learners," who are actively engaged with the course materials and discussions (high content interaction), log in frequently and do all the readings, but do not actively contribute to the online discourse (low interpersonal interaction).

Helmut Fritsch, director of the Center for Research in Distance Education at FernUniversitaet (Germany), proposed the term "witness learners" to characterize students who, while not contributing written entries, are still engaged in the learning process by observing (witnessing) the written exchanges of their peers as an online seminar progresses. Fritsch argued that learning is still taking place, albeit in a more passive and less visible way (1997).

A study of "invisible" students in an online graduate course (Beaudoin, 2002) highlights the importance of not lumping together "witness learners" with their more infamous companions in invisibility, the "missing in action" lurkers. Beaudoin found out that "witness learners" are indeed learning and can perform even better in graded assignments than students with average visibility, although not as well as those with high visibility. Beaudoin compared their learning strategies to an iceberg: there is much more than meets the eye. But, Beaudoin offered an important caution about witness learners: while it is important to understand the causes behind low visibility participation at certain points along the way of an online course, and to determine if learning-related activities are still taking place "behind the scenes," this should not be interpreted as a blanket endorsement of all forms of low visibility:

> *If these students had been noticeably disengaged in their online activity from the very beginning of the course, we would be looking at an entirely different phenomenon, and would not likely be as sanguine about the overall learning taking place, as there would be little to "show" for whatever efforts they were making (Beaudoin, 2002).*

Just as all low visible participation is not equally bad (Quadrants I, II), not all highly visible participation is equally good (Quadrants III, IV).

Quadrants III and IV share the characteristic of high interpersonal interaction. These are highly visible students, who often participate in the online discussions. But, an analysis of the kind of contributions they bring to the discussion reveals that they differ fundamentally in terms of their content interaction.

Students in Quadrant III (high interpersonal interaction, low content interaction) thrive in the social aspect of the online discussions. We call them "social participants": they are great conversationalists, with high communication and interpersonal skills. The problem with them is that their interest in the purely social aspect of the online interactions may actually happen at the expense of reflection and thoughtful consideration of course content.

We emphasize the importance of differentiating high and low content interaction in the case of students with high interpersonal interaction, so that instructors can detect, explain, and help the "social participants" correct the limitations in their style of participation. If the online instructor does not carefully measure "participation," and just goes by surrogate measures, such as number of entries or average number of words per entry, the lack of learning on the part of social participants may go undetected and may even end up being overrewarded with overly high grades. If undetected, the social participant loses because of inadequate learning. If detected but not sufficiently well explained (in terms of high interpersonal interaction, but low content interaction), the social participant may feel the victim of a gross inequity: "I participated so much, how come you gave me a bad grade?"

Students in Quadrant IV ("active learners") represent what online instructors truly mean when we talk about "good participation." They are high on content interaction and interpersonal interaction. Their contributions to online discussions are substantive and frequent. As discussed in the literature on teams (Kemery, 2000; McShane & Von Glinow, 2000; Whetten & Cameron, 1998), they contribute not only to the task but also to building and sustaining relationships in the learning community.

The literature on behaviors conducive to the effectiveness of face-to-face teams can be applied to our understanding of Quadrant IV interactions. Whetten and Cameron (1998, pp. 433, 434) provide an excellent description of the behaviors necessary for task facilitating (direction giving, information seeking, information giving, elaborating, coordinating, monitoring, process analyzing, reality testing, enforcing, summarizing) and for relationship building (supporting, harmonizing, tension relieving, confronting, energizing, developing, facilitating, processing). Some active learners may specialize in some of these roles or may take them on as necessary. The critical point is "to ensure that these roles are fulfilled, so that the team can function effectively" (McShane & Von Glinow, 2000, p. 284). Another important implication is that for students to be effective in their online contributions, they have to be truly prepared, not only in terms of technological but also in terms of behavioral skills (Kemery, 2000, pp. 230–231).

Just as online instructors have to watch out for witness learners not sliding into Quadrant I, and ending up missing in action, they must also monitor active learners so that they do not become victims of their own success. For example, if active learners overemphasize the relationship-building aspect of their roles, they might lack the time and energy to keep up their high content interaction, thus sliding into Quadrant III and becoming "social participants." If, on the other hand, active learners overemphasize the task-related aspects of their roles, they might end up as hyperparticipants, know-it-alls who so dominate the online discussion that they discourage others from participating. If they overemphasize task and relationship roles, they might end up so overextended that they run out of time and energy, sliding into Quadrant II (becoming witness learners who still keep up with content but no longer contribute visibly to the discussions). If the burnout is serious enough, they might even regress to Quadrant I and end up missing in action toward the end of the course.

CONCLUDING THOUGHTS

The taxonomy proposed here has direct implications for practice and research in distance education.

It is crucially important, for pedagogical and fairness reasons, that online instructors take active measures to differentiate "witness students" from those "missing in action." By contacting early and often the low visibility students, an instructor can often help a student move from Quadrant I (missing in action) to Quadrant II (witness learner), and from there to the most desirable Quadrant IV (active learner).

The awareness that high interpersonal interaction does not equate good participation unless it is accompanied by high content interaction should also help online instructors to differentiate between social participants and active learners. Such differentiation is essential for instructors to identify social participants, to avoid over-rewarding into a false sense of complacency, and to help them improve their content interaction. Moving from Quadrant III to Quadrant IV allows the social participants to more fully benefit from, and contribute to, the online community they enjoy.

There is growing evidence that increased participation (in quality and quantity) can increase learning, and that instructors can control a series of elements in course design and delivery that may result in increased participation (Harasim et al., 1995; Kemery, 2000). If instructors are able to move more students into Quadrant IV and keep those who are there from sliding back into other quadrants, the practical benefits for individual and collective learning can be significant.

Our measures of performance in online courses need to be refined and extended beyond the course boundaries to assess the degree to which students are able to apply what they learn in class to their own work environments. We also need to deepen our understanding of how the participation of individual learners can impact the learning process for themselves and for the other learners as well.

The implications for future research are numerous. For example, the taxonomy opens multiple areas of investigation in terms of the antecedents of the various types of participation. How do variables such as course design, technology, characteristics, and behaviors of instructors and students (gender, age, personality, cognitive style, cultural and professional backgrounds, etc.) affect the relative frequency of students in Quadrants I, II, III, and IV? What factors affect the intensity, direction, and speed of movement between different combinations of quadrants?

Another intriguing set of questions involves the consequences of the various types of participation. What are the effects of permanence in a certain quadrant or movement between quadrants on dependent variables, such as learning, grades, satisfaction with course, teacher evaluations, self-efficacy, self-esteem, type of participation in future courses (with the same peers and instructor or with different ones), graduation rates, and loyalty toward the institution?

The answers to those questions can directly affect the level of learning that students achieve in online courses and may even spill over into their ability to improve participation in other types of distance education and traditional face-to-face classes. Learning how to improve course participation may, in turn, influence, in the longer run, their ability to effectively participate in virtual and face-to-face teams in the workplace.

REFERENCES

Alavi, M., & Leidner, D. E. (2001). Research commentary: technology-mediated learning— a call for greater depth and breadth of research. *Information Systems Research, 12*(1), 1–10.

Beaudoin, M. F. (2002). Learning or lurking? Tracking the "invisible" online student. Draft shared by author in advance of publication.

Benne, K. D., & Sheats, P. (1948). Functional roles of group members. *Journal of Social Issues, 4*, 41–49.

Bentley, M. L. (1993). *Constructivist pedagogy*. Retrieved January 15, 2002 from the World Wide Web: http://www.chias.org/www/edu/crcd/crcdcon.html.

Berge, Z. L. (1999). Conceptual frameworks in distance training and education. In D. Schreiber & Z. L. Berge (Eds.), *Distance training: how innovative organizations are using technology to maximize learning and meet business objectives* (pp. 19–36). San Francisco: Jossey-Bass.

Berge, Z. L. (2001). The context of distance training. In Z. L. Berge (Ed.), *Sustaining distance training: integrating learning technologies into the fabric of the enterprise* (pp. 3–12). San Francisco: Jossey Bass.

Bruner, J. S. (1971). *The relevance of education*. Cambridge, MA: Harvard University Press.

Fornaciari, C. (2002). Student personality types and enrollments in distance education: a longitudinal study. Academy of Management Meeting. Denver, CO.

Freire, P. (1970). *Pedagogy of the oppressed*. New York: Herder and Herder.

Fritsch, H. (1997). Host contacted, waiting for reply. (Evaluation report of virtual seminar held January–March, 1997).

Fulford, C. P., & Zhang, S. (1993). Perceptions of interaction: the critical predictor in distance education. *The American Journal of Distance Education, 7*(3), 8–21.

Gallini, J. K. (2001). A framework for the design of research in technology-mediated learning environments: a sociocultural perspective. *Educational Technology, 41*(2), 15–21.

Harasim, L. et al. (1995). *Learning networks: a field guide to teaching and learning online*. Cambridge, MA: MIT Press.

Hsu, E. (1992). *Management games for management education: a case study*. Unpublished doctoral dissertation, Rutgers University, NJ.

Joyce, B., & Weil, M. (1996). *Models of teaching* (5th ed.). Boston: Allyn and Bacon.

Kemery, E. (2000). Developing online collaboration. In A. Aggarwal (Ed.), *Web-based learning and teaching technologies: opportunities and challenges* (pp. 227–245). Hershey, PA: Idea Group Publishing.

Lipnak, J., & Stamps, J. (1997). *Virtual teams: reaching across space, time, and organizations with technology*. New York: Wiley.

McShane, S. L., & Von Glinow, M. A. (2000). *Organizational behavior: emerging realities for the workplace revolution*. New York: Irwin-McGraw-Hill.

Moore, M. G. (1989). Three types of interaction. *The American Journal of Distance Education, 3*(2), 1–6.

Moore, M. G., & Kearsley, G. (1996). *Distance education: a systems view*. Belmont, CA: Wadsworth.

Shedletsky, L. J., & Aitken, J. E. (2001). The paradoxes of online academic work. *Communication Education, 50*, 206–217.

Symonds, W. (2001). Giving it the old online try. *Business Week*, December 3, 2001, 76–80.

Whetten, D. A., & Cameron, K. S. (1998). *Developing managerial skills* (4th ed.). Reading, MA: Addison-Wesley.

Chapter XI

Web-Based Student Assessment

Apiwan D. Born
University of Illinois at Springfield, USA

ABSTRACT

In this chapter, a means of evaluating students in a Web-based teaching and learning environment is examined. Two techniques, summative and formative, are introduced and discussed together with their related issues including delivery and submission, evaluation and feedback, and dealing with cheating. While a summative or traditional technique has been criticized for being too rigid and outdated, a formative or performance assessment technique promises its authenticity, as it requires students to solve real-world problems. It is argued in this chapter, that both techniques serve as essential measures of student learning and should be used in combination. At the end, instructors are provided with guidelines and recommendations for developing and delivering effective Web-based student assessment. The author hopes that understanding the concept and significance of student assessment in a Web-based educational setting will promote the use of proper techniques and render a positive effect on student learning, which we, as educators, value the most.

INTRODUCTION

The opening vignette on the next page describes the real-world experience of an instructor who has taught a Web-based course and demonstrates that student assessment is a continuous and incremental process. Throughout the process, the relationship between students and teacher as a mentor has been strengthened. For example, professor Zenzola has continually provided comments and suggestions and engaged her students in interactive discussions and group activities. A discussion board allows everyone to access from anywhere and to post messages anytime, hence, enriching communication and enhancing socialization among participants. This, in turn, enables students to share experience and improve learning through collaboration.

Achieving Learning Outcomes

Professor Zenzola taught a graduate Web-based course titled, "Introduction to Information Systems." One of the primary learning objectives was to make students aware of the importance of information systems (IS). During the first week, she posed a question on a discussion board, "Why do you choose this course?" Many students responded that it was part of the program requirements; while, only a few pointed out the significance of IS in today's business and economy. From those responses, the professor realized that the objective had not yet been met; therefore, she rephrased the question to "Why do you think IS is an important field of study?" Everyone provided positive responses and identified several benefits of IS. Professor Zenzola was pleased that her students finally achieved the learning objective.

A week later, the professor assigned an exercise for students to find a particular piece of information on the Internet. After the search was complete, they were required to write a short essay to reflect what they discovered. The learning objective of this exercise was two-fold. Students had to demonstrate their ability to use the Internet to extract information, as well as to exercise their critical-thinking skills. Using an assessment rubric, professor Zenzola communicated clearly to students her expectations.

Throughout the semester, Professor Zenzola deployed different types of assessments, such as multiple-choice tests, short papers, and group assignments. She provided her students with timely and constructive feedback. As she interacted with them individually using the course's discussion board, she felt connected to each student. On the same token, the students felt the same way through personal attention given to them, even though they had never met the professor in person. The campus administrators became aware of how professor Zenzola instructed her class and recognized her efforts as excellence in teaching.

Student assessment is one of the most important elements in an education system. Using appropriate assessment strategies can have far-reaching implications for faculty development and student learning. The purpose of assessment is to provide a measure of student performance and a context for improving a course or an academic program. The use of assessment accomplishes three outcomes. First, instructors are able to articulate their expectations and learning outcomes they anticipate students to accomplish. Second, students receive meaningful feedback on their progress toward reaching their learning goals. Third, faculty members report the outcomes of assessment activities in their teaching portfolio, where administrators can review and monitor the faculty's professional development.

Timely assessment is strongly related to student retention. Clearly stated learning outcomes and assessment activities enhance student learning and motivate students to commit to their education (Perrin et al., 1992). When they understand what an instructor expects and continue to receive feedback from the instructor, they are likely to remain in class throughout the program. Implementing an effective assessment strategy, in turn, promotes a positive and lifelong learning experience.

In this chapter, student assessment in an online learning environment, or so called Web-based student assessment, is examined. The terms "online" and "Web-based" will be used interchangeably in the chapter. It should be noted that classroom-based and Web-based courses have the same assessment goal of improving student learning, but the means to achieve that goal can be different. The chapter is organized into five sections. First, the chapter provides broad definitions of Web-based assessment and discusses why it needs to be done. Next, the chapter presents issues, problems, and controversies that relate to Web-based assessment. Current practices are identified along with the discussion to provide better understanding of the topic. The chapter then discusses solutions that are recommended for dealing with the problems stated in the preceding section, and in the fourth section, future and emerging trends are presented. Finally, the chapter is concluded in section five.

BACKGROUND

One of the topics in the Web-based teaching area that has not received much attention is Web-based student assessment. As the number of Web-based course offerings is dramatically increasing, many studies focus a great deal on technologies, strategies, and techniques used in developing and delivering Web-based courses. Web-based student assessment, on the other hand, has not yet been closely examined, and it is incorrectly assumed that it is the same as what is performed in a traditional classroom. Lack of understanding of Web-based student assessment can pose an obstacle to the learning process.

What is Web-Based Student Assessment?

Student assessment is defined as "the systematic collection, review, and use of information about educational programs undertaken for the purpose of improving student learning and development" (Palombra & Banta, 1999) Assessment is an ongoing process (Angelo, 1995) and a means, not an end in itself (Angelo, 1999). There are two major types of assessment: summative and formative. Summative assessment is given after a course or a program has been completed to evaluate its quality or value compared to predefined sets of standards (Palombra & Banta, 1999). On the other hand, formative assessment is conducted during a course or a program with the intent of providing feedback that can be used to improve student learning (Palombra & Banta, 1999). More detail regarding these two techniques will be discussed in the section, "Issues and Concerns."

A student assessment framework in a Web-based teaching and learning environment can be as depicted in Figure 1. An instructor creates, assembles, and delivers the class'

Figure 1: Student Assessment in a Web-Based Teaching and Learning Environment

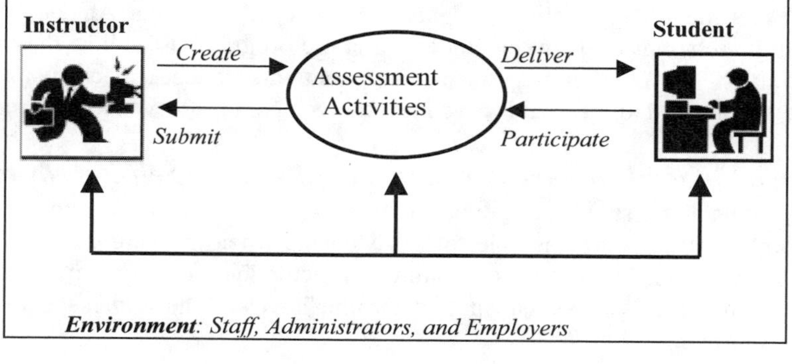

assessment activities (formative or summative) to a student via the Internet. The student participates in those activities and submits answers to the instructor for further evaluation and grading. After the student's submission is evaluated, the instructor sends timely and constructive feedback to the student. Furthermore, student evaluation can be used for revising the existing activities or creating new activities. For example, an instructor experiences a situation where half of students in the class cannot answer one of the quiz questions. This signals the instructor that perhaps words in the question are vague or ambiguous. As a remedy, the question is revised, and everyone is allowed to resubmit the answer.

Why Assessment?

Offering a Web-based course without student assessment is not different from posting a static website on the Internet. An instructor can display the course's materials on the site, but without an assessment or feedback mechanism, it will be difficult to verify that students receive, read, and understand the materials. Assessment enables instructors to evaluate student learning, encourage progress, and give constructive feedback to individual students (Student Assessment in Online Courses, 2001). Several reasons why assessment is necessary are described below.

To Determine Whether the Teaching Goal is Achieved

Bloom (1956) categorizes teaching goals in three domains: cognitive, affective, and psychomotor, all of which provide outcomes that must be observed and measured. The cognitive domain focuses on thinking; the affective domain emphasizes attitudes and feelings; the psychomotor domain requires skills demonstration (Waller, 2001). To achieve these goals requires different class activities, which must be evaluated, and then the results must be discussed with students.

To Identify and Eliminate Bottlenecks in a Learning Process

Bottlenecks prevent or delay students from achieving learning objectives. Many potential causes of these bottlenecks include diversity in student background, poor presentation of course materials, and differences in learning and teaching styles. Student assessment enables an instructor to identify problems and find ways to solve them.

To Motivate and Retain Students

Establishing different assessment tools (e.g., assignments, quizzes, discussion questions, and examinations) motivates students to study and participate in class activities. In addition, assessment helps promote "higher" and "deeper" learning (Angelo, 1999) and strengthen the relationship between students and the program, as well as the institution (Perrin et al., 1992). With an assessment instrument and feedback mechanism in place, students are motivated to study and strive for improvement to achieve their learning goals.

To Learn an Individual's Weaknesses and Encourage Self-Improvement

Assessment gives students the opportunity to discover their own weaknesses. Unlike a classroom's instructor who is able to spot students when they are confused or have questions by watching their gestures, an online instructor does not have that advantage and has to rely on the results of assessment to determine how well the students learn and how much they improve.

To Strengthen Faculty Development Opportunities

Perrin et al. (1992) stated, "Assessment also provides documentation for increases in faculty productivity, efficiency, and effectiveness." Student assessment is viewed as a means for faculty to document their scholarship of teaching (e.g., strategies and techniques used for improving student learning) that contributes significantly to their professional growth.

To Provide a Means of Communication among Faculty, Students, and Administrators

Assessment provides an avenue for stakeholders in an educational system, including faculty, students, and administrators, to identify how teaching, learning, and educational goals can be achieved. With assessment, faculty members gain useful feedback that can be used to improve their course and teaching; students receive constructive comments on their performance; and administrators obtain valuable feedback on program quality and faculty productivity. Consequently, assessment enhances communications among these three parties.

Valuing student learning as the factor that matters the most attributes to effective student assessment. Assessment has vast potential for rendering a positive effect on student learning. Assessment also provides a means to enhance teaching and professional development. Yet, there are still several issues and concerns regarding Web-based student assessment that need to be discussed.

ISSUES AND CONCERNS

As the number of Web-based courses offered are increasing, Web-based student assessment is relatively new and has not been widely discussed in the literature. Many instructors are still skeptical about the effectiveness of Web-based assessment because of an uneasy feeling caused by lack of face-to-face interaction. Some criticize that Web-based assessment makes it easier for students to perpetrate cheating. This section raises several issues and concerns regarding Web-based student assessment and discusses them in further detail. The intent is to provide a better understanding of Web-based assessment and guidelines as to how it can be used effectively. Those issues include Web-based assessment techniques, delivery and submission, evaluation and feedback, and dealing with cheating.

Web-Based Assessment Techniques

As mentioned earlier, assessment techniques are classified into two major types: summative and formative. A summative technique is a traditional way of evaluating learning outcomes by gathering feedback only after instruction has been completed, and a formative technique continuously collects reflection and feedback from students and monitors their progress throughout the period of assessment. Traditional assessment is summative in nature; while, performance assessment is formative. Both techniques are necessary to provide for effective student assessment and learning within the online environment.

Traditional Assessment

Traditional assessment is one of the most widely used assessment techniques. Traditional assessment tools can be seen in many forms, such as tests, quizzes, and examinations. The Internet and its technologies provide an inexpensive way to evaluate student knowledge, skills, and attitudes. Bicanich et al. (1997) conducted a state-wide pilot project including nearly 400 students from Pennsylvania vocational technical institutions, using a test–retest design with control groups. Approximately 360 students received tests in paper-based and Web-based formats. Although the results indicated that Web-based tests provided the same outcomes as those on paper, 75% of students preferred taking the tests via the Web.

The major drawback of traditional assessment is that it rarely requires students to use what they are instructed to solve a real problem (Bond, 1995). A standardized test, for example, has been criticized as not being aligned with the emerging content standards; therefore, over-reliance on this type of assessment often leads to instruction that focuses solely on basic knowledge and skills (Corbett & Wilson, 1991; Smith & Cohen, 1991). Although traditional assessment has been criticized for being too rigid and not measuring currently needed skills, it is still an essential tool for measuring student mastery of knowledge.

Web technologies provide an alternative, yet inexpensive way to evaluate student learning. In today's Web-based teaching and learning environment, traditional assessment tools are widely used. For example, exams or quizzes can be easily made available on the Internet. Feedback is provided after a student completes a question or an entire test. The test results can be recorded or sent automatically to a designated database or email address. More details about advantages and disadvantages of Web-based tests are discussed below.

Advantages and Disadvantages of Web-Based Tests

The article titled "Quizzing, Testing, and Homework on the Internet" (2000) identified several advantages of a Web-based test. First, taking a test becomes flexible in terms of time and place, because students can access it anytime from anywhere. Second, feedback is instantaneously provided with an explanation. Third, immediate feedback saves an instructor time and energy to administer and grade the test, as well as record the score. Fourth, Web-based tests reduce costs of printing, copying, and proctoring. Fifth, unlike a paper-and-pencil test that provides the same set of questions to everyone, a Web-based test can randomly select questions to appear every time an individual participates in a test taking. Administering tests on the Web is considered a convenient way for the students to assess their knowledge as frequently as they need.

Despite many advantages, Web-based tests have a few disadvantages. First, preparing the test is time consuming. Unlike a paper-based test of which questions can be selected from a prepackaged test bank available in paper or electronic formats (.doc, .rtf, .txt, or .wpd), a Web-based test requires a transformation of those questions into an HTML format that is readable by Web browsers (e.g., Netscape and Explorer). Although some course management systems provide a wizard that assists in the test creation process, questions still need to be manually keyed or copied into the systems. Second, technology investment including hardware, software, and training could be costly to an educational institution. These first two disadvantages, however, can be eliminated as technology becomes more advance and less expensive. Third, an instructor does not have control of the testing environment where students are allowed to take a test anytime and anywhere. Fourth, technology used to build and deliver a Web-based test is not totally dependable. Technical difficulty could be an obstacle during a testing period. A student can be disconnected from the Internet while taking a test and is unable to access it again if only one attempt is allowed. The instructor may let the student retake the test, but fairness would become a concern.

Faculty commitment and involvement is key for a successful Web-based test. Due to the fact that it is still difficult to verify who is taking the test at the other end, test scores should not be used as a major part of the total grade. Taking a middle ground, an online instructor should use a combination of various assessment techniques to measure the desired learning outcomes. Before an alternative technique is examined, the next subsection will explain how to create a Web-based test.

Create a Web-Based Test

In this section, how a Web-based test can be created using course management software called Blackboard is presented. Most course management software tools provide an easy to-use wizard.

For example, an assessment manager wizard in Blackboard allows an instructor to create different types of test questions such as multiple-choice, true/false, and fill-in-the-blank (see Figure 2). Once all questions are entered, the instructor can make the test accessible for students at a certain time and date. Blackboard provides many options, including how feedback will be provided, how many times a student can take the test, and how long the test will be available (see Figure 3).

Test design is critical in assessment. A well-designed test enhances education; whereas, a poorly designed test can interrupt and prevent students from achieving their learning goals. For example, a student may not gain any knowledge from feedback that

Figure 2: True/False, Multiple-Choice, and Fill-in-the-Blank Questions

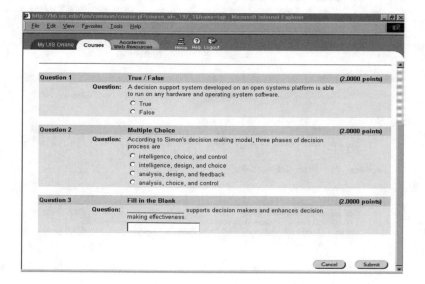

Note. Source: © Courtesy of Blackboard Inc. Used with permission

Figure 3: Assessment Options

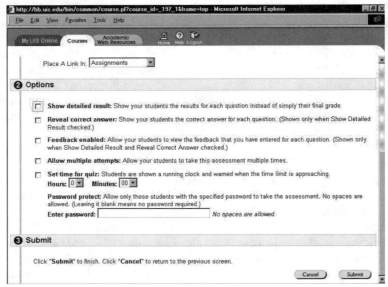

Note. Source: © Courtesy of Blackboard Inc. Used with permission

Figure 4: Providing Constructive Feedback

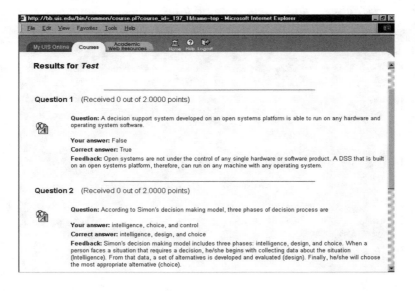

Note. Source: © Courtesy of Blackboard Inc. Used with permission

displays only a one-word response such as "correct" or "incorrect" without further explanation. When a student submits a wrong answer, the correct answer coupled with an explanation must be provided (see Figure 4). A compliment to a student who answers a question correctly is encouraged. On the contrary, an unconstructive or sarcastic comment will not only discourage students but also be counterproductive.

In the next subsection, an alternative assessment technique called *performance assessment* will be presented.

Performance Assessment

Performance assessment is an ongoing process examining student learning and progress. The term performance assessment encompasses two concepts: alternative and authentication (Wangsatorntanakhun, 1999). In the early 1990s, increasing criticism of traditional assessment raised concerns among educators who called for alternative assessment (Madaus & Raczek, 1996). As an alternative assessment, performance assessment distinguishes itself from traditional tests and quizzes. Rather than selecting from a list of possible responses, students must document and demonstrate what they know and convey their knowledge into practice. In addition, performance assessment is authentic, because it requires students to perform tasks that are similar to real-world problems.

Performance assessment contains two major components: tasks and criteria (Rudner & Boston, n.d.). Assessment tasks begin with identifying learning objectives and audiences, matching the assessment technique to the learning objectives, and specifying illustrative tasks that require students to demonstrate a certain set of skills and mastery of the desired outcomes (Herman et al., 1992). Assessment criteria, or "the standards of achievement," need to be described to students before the tasks are assigned (Wangsatorntanakhun, 1999). One of the most popular tools used to organize and present these criteria is known as a rubric.

Rubric Technique

A rubric serves as an assessment instrument as well as a communication instrument between students and instructor. In a rubric, there is a clear list of assessment criteria that the instructor intends to measure and a numerical score associated with each criterion. A student's performance is compared directly to these predefined criteria and indirectly to other students (Elliott, 1995). A well-written rubric can also serve as a means to convey an instructor's expectations to students and act as a common tool to assist with the evaluation process and to monitor student progress.

When designing a rubric, an instructor must focus on assessment criteria that are observable and measurable. A rubric is usually presented in a matrix or checklist format. These criteria can be grouped in two different ways: analytical and holistic (Betts, 1997). An analytical rubric contains several dimensions, each of which is divided into multiple levels of competency. For example, an instructor may assign students to write a short paper reflecting on selected key items learned in the first half of the course. An analytical rubric for the short paper can be designed as shown in Figure 5. The rubric contains three dimensions: Using background knowledge, Presenting new ideas, and Writing. Each of these dimensions is divided into three to four levels of competency. The expectation of each level is explained clearly using a numerical scale. The total score of this analytical rubric is based on a summative scale of all criteria.

A holistic rubric, on the other hand, provides a summary of all assessment criteria on one scale. This scale is also divided into different levels of competency, and a letter grade

Figure 5: Analytical Rubric

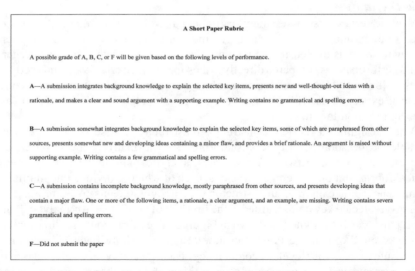

> **A Short Paper Rubric**
>
> A possible point from 0–7 will be received based on a summation of scores from the following three criteria.
>
> *Using Background Knowledge*
> ___ 2 Integrated background knowledge to explain the selected key items
> ___ 1 Provided incomplete background knowledge mostly paraphrased from other sources
> ___ 0 Did not submit the paper
>
> *Presenting New Ideas*
> ___ 3 Presented new and well-thought-out ideas with a rationale and example supporting those ideas
> ___ 2 Presented developing ideas that were not fully thought through and contained flaws; provided a brief rationale without an example
> ___ 1 Presented opinions with personal bias that did not add value to the paper; Did not provide a rationale or example
> ___ 0 Did not submit the paper
>
> *Writing*
> ___ 2 Very few to no grammatical and spelling errors
> ___ 1 Many grammatical and spelling errors
> ___ 0 Did not submit the paper

Note. Source: Adapted from Born, A. D., & Jessup, C. (2002). An exploration of rubric use in online course assessment. The Forthcoming Proceedings of Information Resources Management Association (IRMA)

Figure 6: Holistic Rubric

> **A Short Paper Rubric**
>
> A possible grade of A, B, C, or F will be given based on the following levels of performance.
>
> A—A submission integrates background knowledge to explain the selected key items, presents new and well-thought-out ideas with a rationale, and makes a clear and sound argument with a supporting example. Writing contains no grammatical and spelling errors.
>
> B—A submission somewhat integrates background knowledge to explain the selected key items, some of which are paraphrased from other sources, presents somewhat new and developing ideas containing a minor flaw, and provides a brief rationale. An argument is raised without supporting example. Writing contains a few grammatical and spelling errors.
>
> C—A submission contains incomplete background knowledge, mostly paraphrased from other sources, and presents developing ideas that contain a major flaw. One or more of the following items, a rationale, a clear argument, and an example, are missing. Writing contains severa grammatical and spelling errors.
>
> F—Did not submit the paper

Note. Source: Adapted from Born, A. D., & Jessup, C. (2002). An exploration of rubric use in online course assessment. The Forthcoming Proceedings of Information Resources Management Association (IRMA)

or a point base is assigned to each level. An example of a holistic rubric for the same assignment is shown in Figure 6.

Each rubric emphasizes desired criteria that are considered standards of excellence. As those criteria are stated clearly, the rubric is found to be useful in helping students identify and apply best practices. An instructor can use the rubric to communicate expectations with the entire class. In the meantime, students are not left guessing what is required within each activity. The rubric also makes it easier for the instructor to evaluate a student's work, because it provides a checklist and a rating scale associated with each criterion (see Figures 5 and 6). The students are not compelled to compete against each other but rather compete with themselves to meet those criteria.

Within the higher educational system, assessment rubrics have been used increasingly in the past few years. Many examples of rubrics are available on the Web. Keep in mind that rubric design is not a one-time effort but rather evolves over time. It should also be noted that different course settings, such as teaching and learning styles, subject matters, and types of assignments, could affect the way rubrics are designed and used. In other words, a rubric that is deployed successfully in one class may not work well in another class. Often, rubrics are created and refined to suit an individual class' requirements; therefore, the development process is time consuming and requires patience from instructor and students.

Portfolio Technique

A portfolio is "a systematic, well organized, collection of evidence, used to monitor the growth of a student's knowledge, process skills, and attitudes" (Bonnstetter, 1991). The collection must demonstrate the student's efforts, lessons learned, and accomplishments in one or more areas (Paulson et al., 1991). Portfolio assessment is authentic, because the nature of the task and context in which the assessment takes place represents and relates to real-world situations.

Throughout the period of assessment, students are asked to keep a portfolio or a journal of their work, which includes selected pieces of work, rewards, and accomplishments. The students must document, over time, what they did, how they did it, and what they learned throughout the entire process. In this sense, they assess their learning and reflect on it. The portfolio approach is believed to contribute significantly to student learning and progress (Perrin et al., 1992).

Kemp and Toperoff (1998) pointed out five characteristics of portfolio assessment:

- *Joint effort*: Portfolio assessment is a process that requires a joint effort between students and their teacher(s). To succeed, both parties must be involved in the creation and evaluation of a portfolio throughout the entire assessment process.

- *Selection of work*: A portfolio is not simply a "collection" but a "selection" of student work. A student chooses what piece of work to be included in the portfolio and provides a justification. This not only prevents the student from adding everything into the portfolio without thinking why it should be there but also promotes logical thinking and reasoning ability.

- *Reflection of growth*: A portfolio reflects the growth of student learning over time. Selected items included in the portfolio demonstrate the series of progress made throughout the period that a student has been evaluated. Strengths and weaknesses derived from those items must be identified. The strengths are considered as achievement of the teaching goals, while the weaknesses become the improvement goals that need to be achieved.

- *Clear criteria*: Criteria or standards for evaluating a portfolio must be clear to instructor and students. The question here is not what items in the portfolio need to be graded, but how they will be graded. Bonnstetter (1991) suggested that standards reflecting learning outcomes must be established in a form of different levels of achievement. To succeed, each level must display samples of learning products or artifacts that reflect student achievement of a certain outcome (Bonnstetter, 1991).

- *Single or multiple measure*: The contents of a portfolio demonstrate learning and growth of student learning in an entire field of study or a specific area. Depending on learning objectives, portfolio assessment can be used for measuring one or more skills. For example, a student can create a portfolio that contains personal essays to demonstrate writing skill or research manuscripts to demonstrate reading, writing, and critical thinking skills.

Web-Based Portfolio Assessment

In the previous section, the concept of portfolio assessment is introduced, in general. In this section, how portfolio assessment can be conducted online is discussed.

Using a portfolio technique creates a collaborative learning environment. Unlike a paper-based portfolio for which feedback is usually given at the completion of the portfolio, a Web-based portfolio provides easy and convenient access for students and their instructor during the portfolio development process, without time and place boundaries. Building a Web-based portfolio requires collaboration between instructors and students, and possibly peers. Allowing students to evaluate each other's portfolios provides different perspectives and promotes exchange of ideas and experience. Moreover, to foster student motivation and self-improvement, an instructor can share a few examples of excellent portfolios with the entire class. This technique of learning from the best examples would further empower students as independent learners and is illustrative of the formative nature of portfolio assessment.

The Internet and its technologies facilitate the use of Web-based portfolio assessment. Instructors and students are able to communicate interactively and review a Web-based portfolio together, without a face-to-face meeting. The instructor conveys the goals of what needs to be evaluated to the students. A guideline for portfolio assessment must be clearly presented to the students and periodically reviewed. Without clear instruction and understanding, many students who are not familiar with portfolio assessment are likely to be confused and lose interest in participating in the process.

Bergman (n.d.) suggested several key factors for an effective Web-based portfolio. First, a Web-based portfolio is centered on learners who are responsible for constructing their portfolios or journals to demonstrate and communicate what they learn. Second, a Web-based portfolio must be secure and accessible by only authorized personnel at anytime and from anywhere. Third, technology used to create the portfolio should be easy to use, executable across different platforms, and easy to maintain. Finally, the Web-based portfolio should accommodate a wide variety of document formats (e.g., graphics, text, audio, and video) so that materials can be stored, integrated, and transferred to and from different platforms (e.g., Microsoft's Word and Word Perfect).

Preparing a portfolio involves considerable research, analysis, critical thinking, and writing. A student's time and effort must be spent significantly on observing, collecting evidence, interpreting, and justifying. It is useful and important to have a student's portfolio online 24 hours a day, seven days a week. The student who owns a portfolio can review, update, and reflect on what was learned whenever needed. The student's portfolio reflects interest, knowledge, and skill on a certain subject, which enables an instructor to chart the student's learning progress. It is obvious that using the Web-based portfolio technique successfully requires active participation and responsibility from students under teacher supervision.

Portfolio Contents

Items to be included in a Web-based portfolio must be carefully selected based on well-defined guidelines. The portfolio's content is incrementally and selectively added with a well-justified reason provided by a student who owns it. The portfolio allows students to demonstrate progress on a continuous basis and to become actively involved in the process of self-learning and evaluating.

Items in a Web-based portfolio must be stored in an electronic format. Examples of those items include static documents (e.g., essays, notes, letters, reports, spreadsheets, certificates, and quizzes), audio collections (e.g., speech, interviews, and songs), video collections (e.g., role play, presentation, and live performance), and working prototypes (e.g., database applications, simulation models, and Web pages and sites). A student may create a website to display those items or post them on a discussion board provided by an instructor. It is important for the student to provide an explanation of how those items are selected and what learning objectives are achieved.

Two assessment techniques are presented above. The next two issues that need to be addressed are delivery and submission and evaluation and feedback. Those issues, together with other design aspects such as the number of attempts and the length and time allowed for an assessment activity, will be discussed in the next two sections.

Delivery and Submission

In a Web-based class, an assessment instruction must be delivered to students clearly and on time. Web-based assessment delivery and submission can be done in three different proctoring modes: face-to-face, online, and zero:

- *Face-to-face proctoring*: One of the oldest modes used in on-campus courses and online courses is face-to-face proctoring. A student is required to take tests, examinations, or quizzes under the supervision of a proctor. If the online student populations are scattered across the country or the world, the university needs to appoint a designated proctor center close to where those students are located. A proctored test can be created in a paper format or an electronic format stored on a diskette or CD-ROM or available on the Web. To verify an identity, a student is required to show photo identification. Face-to-face proctoring occurs in a controlled environment, where the proctor can monitor the process of test taking closely and control the start and end times of the test. Once the test is completed, it can be submitted in the same format as it was delivered.

- *Online proctoring*: Another option for delivering and submitting a test is proctoring a test from a remote distance. An instructor or a teaching assistant must control time and monitor test takers. The test can be sent via email or made available on the Internet. A communication channel must be kept open between a test administrator and test takers by previously agreed means, such as email, chat, instant message, phone, and audio or videoconferencing. Two advantages of online proctoring are that a proctor can respond to a question or problem immediately during the test, and costs of printing and duplicating are eliminated. However, a few disadvantages of using online proctoring are high monitoring cost and inconvenience. Expenses of online proctoring include human proctors and additional equipment (e.g., a video camera). Scheduling every student to take a test at the same time could be inconvenient, especially for those with a restricted schedule.

- *Zero proctoring*: Allowing students to take an online test at their convenience eliminates the need for a human proctor. The test is made available at a secured website. Instruction to access the site is sent to students several days ahead to inform them that the test will be made available only for a certain period of time (e.g., a day, a few days, or a week). There are two types of tests that can be delivered through the zero proctoring mode. One is an interactive test, with which a student responds to questions and submits answers immediately. The second type is a take-home test, which a student has more time to complete. Time allowed for this take-home test could vary from hours to days or weeks. In order to ensure timely delivery, every student is required to send an acknowledgement to an instructor once the test is received. On the same token, the instructor should acknowledge a student's submission soon after it is received. While the issue of student identity in an unmonitored testing environment is still questionable, zero proctoring incurs low cost and less time spent on administering and test taking.

Evaluation and Feedback

Effective Web-based teaching and learning requires active participation and feedback. Student work must be frequently evaluated and provided with timely and constructive feedback. Students are motivated to remain in and complete the course if they are regularly kept informed about their grade (Moore & Kearsley, 1996). Due to absence of face-to-face communication, online students become anxious about their performance. Providing feedback and encouraging them to participate in class activities helps lessen the psychological distance between students and their teacher (Comeaux, 1995). The important issue that needs to be addressed is not "whether" but "when" students should be evaluated and receive feedback.

Timing is a critical issue when delivering feedback. Different means of conducing Web-based assessment determine when feedback will be given. For example, technology such as the Internet and an interactive CD-ROM can provide feedback instantly, while delay is expected when a human performs the evaluation. The rule of thumb is that feedback should be sent to students no later than a week after their submission. The longer they wait, the less enthusiastic they become, and they may hesitate to participate in future activities.

Using an automated feedback function in course management systems such as Blackboard and WebCT provides immediate feedback to students. However, this function has some limitations. Although an automated feedback function can evaluate and provide correct answers to different types of questions, including multiple-choice, true/false, and fill-in-the-blank, it cannot evaluate short answer and essay questions. With a fill-in-the-blank question, the function still limits, because a student's answer needs to match a predefined

Figure 7: Essay Questions

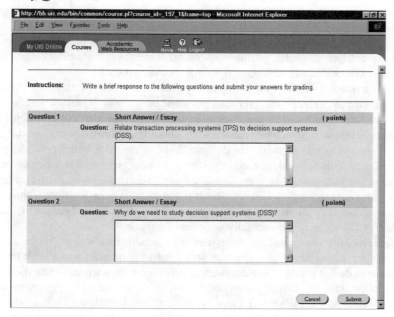

Note. Source: © Courtesy of Blackboard Inc. Used with permission

Figure 8: Feedback for an Essay Question

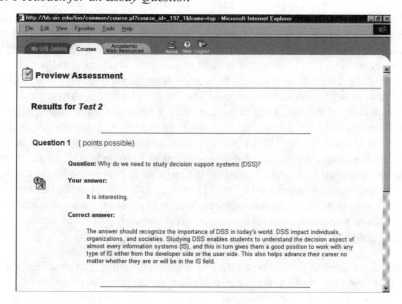

Note. Source: © Courtesy of Blackboard Inc. Used with permission

answer in order to receive credit. For an essay question (see the example displayed in Figure 7), Blackboard simply provides a correct answer without grading (see Figure 8). The response can be forwarded to the instructor for further grading and comments.

Conducting Web-based student assessment can be done in many ways. Horton (2000) suggests five different means of how to perform student evaluation and when to provide feedback in a Web-based teaching and learning environment:

1. ***By a personal desktop or laptop***: A student can work on class activities such as assignments, quizzes, or tests on a personal desktop or laptop. Those activities are prepackaged and sent to the student in a CD-ROM format. An instructor may give specific instruction on when each activity should be taken or let students take it at their own pace. The CD-ROM can be designed to be interactive, which provides immediate feedback. This helps reduce anxiety, because students determine when and where they are ready for a test. However, letting all activities run on a student's computer may alienate the teacher–student relationship and cause procrastination. If those activities are graded, they should not be used as a major portion of the total point, because it is difficult to identify who actually performs the work.

2. ***By a remote computer***: Class activities are available on a website or through a course management system. This requires an Internet connection and a Web browser, and students do not need to have course management software running on their machines. All class activities can be submitted online. Many course management products such as Blackboard and WebCT have an assessment function that provides feedback immediately after a student clicks the submit button. The test result can be sent to an instructor for recording and progress monitoring purposes.

3. ***By an instructor or teaching assistant***: A class activity is submitted via electronic mail or the Internet to an instructor or a teaching assistant for further evaluation. Unlike a machine, a human can provide detailed feedback tailored to each individual student. Two drawbacks of this alternative are a long waiting time and grading that is time consuming. Students have to wait to receive feedback, and an instructor needs to read and post feedback to each student, which is time consuming (Horton, 2000).

4. ***By peers***: With this Web-based student assessment, students are allowed to evaluate each other. The different experiences and expertise each student brings to class can be shared with peers. This process requires a clear and unambiguous appraisal instruction; otherwise, it can create some frustration among students. A peer review is effective only when students have background on the subject of discussion. If an activity is graded, peer evaluation should not be used as a large portion of the total point value, because students may have bias or not be knowledgeable in a certain area.

5. ***By students***: "Having the learner find the answers in the preceding material provides a second learning opportunity," said Horton (2000). By allowing students to review their own assignment, they have the opportunity to review the same material over again. Similar to a peer review, a self-evaluation technique should not be counted toward the final grade because of potential self-bias.

The above alternatives can be used alone or in combination. The benefit of using a wide variety of means to conduct Web-based student assessment is to diversify the risk of depending solely on only one technique. Using various means allows a teacher to measure student learning on different aspects and minimize measurement bias.

Handling Cheating

Known as academic dishonesty through the means of plagiarism is cheating. It is a serious problem that educators face in traditional and online courses. Plagiarism is "an act of using or passing off (the ideas or words of another) as one's own without crediting the source" (Merriam Webster Dictionary, 2001). A report shows an increase in the number of plagiarism activities from the academic year of 2000 to 2001 (Decamp, 2001). The advent of the World Wide Web (WWW), which contains a large number of published documents and enables easy "cut and paste" activity, is the number one factor blamed for the rise in academic cheating. While there is no simple solution to this problem, an instructor should focus on "how to prevent and discourage cheating activities" rather than "why students cheat and how they did it." Spending hours or days trying to figure out where the paper in question was copied does not help reduce or discourage cheating. A proactive approach rather than a reactive approach needs to be used to prevent academic misconduct. Guidelines for online instructors on how to deal with cheating derived from several sources, including Strategies to Minimizing Cheating Online (2000), Van Belle (n.d.), and Preventing Plagiarism and Cheating in Online Courses (1999) are presented below.

Offering Tests, Quizzes, or Assignments More Frequently

A student may receive help from another individual who is not enrolling in a course. If tests are given frequently, that person may not be available for every test and may hesitate to spend too much time and energy on something that he or she cannot take credit for.

Design Questions that Require Discussion rather than Memorization

To answer a discussion question, a student needs to have a good understanding of the material and an ability to apply it to a real-world problem. Asking students to relate the lesson learned to their own experiences and describe them in their own words would be difficult to duplicate from friends or other sources.

Assign Different Questions to Different Individuals

Questions can be randomly selected from a large pool, where every access by a test taker will return a different set of questions. Students will not be able to copy answers from each other, because they do not receive the same questions.

Limit Test-Taking Time

Besides randomized questions, making a test available online for a limited period of time (e.g., a few hours) and requiring everyone to take the test at the same time helps discourage a cheating attempt. This is because each individual worries about finishing the test on time and does not have time to help others.

Proctored Tests

Using a proctored test is another way to discourage cheating. Students are required to come to campus or go to the nearest testing center to take a test. They must show a picture ID to verify their identity. A proctored test is in paper format or in electronic format. For the latter, immediate feedback can be given for true/false and multiple-choice questions, and the result can be automatically sent to the instructor.

Curriculum Rotation

Instructors, especially those in a fast-changing discipline (e.g., information systems/ information technology), should frequently update their materials. Rotating course materials regularly helps an instructor prepare and makes the course interesting, and in turn, students cannot use the old materials such as test questions passed down from those who took the course before.

Treat a Term Paper as a Process not a Product

Asking students to submit a term paper without monitoring their work-in-progress opens the door for cheaters. Instructors need to view a student's paper as a process, not a product that is submitted on the last day of the class. How each student generates ideas, research, and writes a paper must be monitored and recorded to ensure that learning is taking place.

Assign a Group Assignment

Working in a group with members selected by an instructor has a "deterrent" effect on cheaters. It would be difficult to cheat in a group while peers are watching. Students are more likely to report dishonest behavior when they experience it.

In the above section, several issues and concerns regarding Web-based assessment are presented. Most problems in an online course occur not because of technology per se but because of people who are a critical element of the learning process. Old teaching habits, such as a spoon-feeding teaching style or a course schedule with one final test, will not be effective in an online environment. To succeed, an instructor must assume the role of a coach and a facilitator who provides guidelines and facilitates discussions to help students achieve their desired goal. While technology becomes increasingly advanced, the human factor will continue to play a significant role in determining the success of online education. Based on the issues and concerns addressed earlier, provided in the next are solutions and recommendations for successful Web-based student assessment.

SOLUTIONS AND RECOMMENDATIONS

Phipps and Merisotis (1999) indicated that it is important for higher education institutions to realize the potential impact of Web-based teaching and learning on student recruitment and retention; however, it is still inconclusive whether institutions that offer Web-based courses have definitely experienced increased enrollment and retention or decreased operating costs. For example, at the University of Illinois at Springfield, the online enrollment number grew steadily from 1999 to 2002, and the average retention rate throughout those four years is above 90%, which is exceptional (UIS Online Enrollment, 2002).

Assessment has played a significant role in student retention. Although one of the reasons that students drop out of a Web-based course is because of their unfamiliarity with technology, other reasons seem to rest upon instruction and assessment given in the course. Carr (2000) pointed out that inexperienced online instructors together with differences in the instruction mode can affect the retention rate. Using an inappropriate type of assessment or lack thereof can contribute to an increase in student dropouts.

Among online educators, we tend to agree that the rate of student dropout in an online course is higher than a classroom-based course, especially in the beginning courses that are meant to be gatekeepers for a program. In other words, students who take an online course the first time may have difficulty dealing with not only a new subject matter but also new technology. Most universities provide orientations or workshops on online instructional technology for students. Once they overcome a steep learning curve in their first online course, they tend to remain in the subsequent courses.

An online course provides the opportunity to identify what subject an individual student does not understand. Introverted students who more often are too shy to ask questions in a classroom feel more comfortable expressing their thoughts via electronic mail or a discussion board. In a regular classroom, a teacher may not be able to answer all questions or pay attention to a specific student due to time limitation and class size. In particular, for a large class with over 50 students, spending too much time responding to one particular student could interrupt the pace of the class. The instructor may not be able to cover materials as intended, if class time is mostly spent on answering trivial questions. In addition, the instructor cannot tell whether or not a student who sits silently in class understands the subject. In an online environment, on the contrary, a communication channel between participants always open, providing students with one-on-one assistance when needed.

The shift from traditional assessment to performance assessment is driven by the demand of employees who need graduates with an ability to perform tasks assigned. In today's collaborative work environments, not only are the graduates expected to possess a certain level of knowledge and skills, but also they must be able to communicate and express their ideas to others. Unlike traditional assessment, performance assessment is authentic, because it involves real-world problems and requires students to use their knowledge and skills to solve them. Performance assessment could be a more valid indicator of students' knowledge and abilities, because it requires them to actively demonstrate what they know (Sweet, 1993).

Two types of performance assessments presented in this chapter are rubric and portfolio. Rubrics provide impetus for increasing students' understanding of class requirements and expectations. Using rubrics, an instructor can identify strengths and weaknesses of each student and assist them in the area in which they need improvement. Integrating the Internet and its technology to authentic assessment, Web-based portfolios provide 24/7 access to an individual's journal or portfolio and promote a collaborative learning environment. The portfolio technique empowers students to reflect their work and encourages self-learning and self-improving behavior. When designed and implemented properly, a rubric is found to be an effective tool in assessing and improving student learning.

To conclude, recommendations for effective Web-based student assessment are presented below:

- **Require mandatory participation**: Students need to be active participants in an assessment process. Participation is particularly essential to performance assessment techniques, including rubrics and portfolios. Participation fosters two-way communication between instructors, students, and their peers.

- **Write clear instructions**: Regardless of what type of assessment used, an instructor must provide students with clear instructions. Unlike a classroom-based course where face-to-face communication takes place, a Web-based course lacks that privilege. Vague instruction not only causes students to be confused and withdrawn but also creates additional work for an instructor (e.g., responding to emails and answering phone calls from students).

- **Create a collaborative learning environment:** Exchanging ideas and experiences with colleagues who teach online is beneficial. Instead of starting from scratch, novices can learn from their experienced colleagues as mentors who share teaching tips and assessment techniques. A Listserv (an email distribution list) of online instructors can be set up to encourage participants to share stories (e.g., best practices) and collaborate their activities.

- **Continue improving:** Developing and evaluating assessment instruments is an ongoing, incremental process that requires attention and persistence. In addition, feedback from students provides an input for improving the current practice. Instructors continue to refine those instruments as they use them.

- **Keep an inventory:** Assessment tools can be reused over time. An inventory needs to be set up to keep track of what tools were used in what course of which semester, then they must be organized in different files and labeled properly. Making these files handy provides a benefit in a long run when they are needed. For future use, it will be useful to provide a comment such as "dos and don'ts" attached to each of these tools.

- **Plan ahead:** Successful student assessment requires a clear plan. Assessment activities should be incorporated into an instruction plan and should be consistent with the learning goals. Poor planning or lack thereof could lead to chaos or possibly poor course evaluation. Most online students expect an organized and well-prepared learning environment where they know how, when, and by whom their work will be evaluated. If instructors decide to not provide timely feedback, students would be unhappy and could become disappointed with online learning. To succeed, an assessment plan needs to be created and communicated to all students.

- **Enjoy:** Last but not least, conducting assessment should be a joyful and challenging experience for instructors and students. An advocate of Web-based teaching believes that Web-based assessment helps bring an instructor close to students on a one-on-one basis and open continuous two-way communications between them, which is unlikely to occur in a large on-campus classroom. Although many activities involved in online teaching are time consuming, it is rewarding when we see students progressing through their academic program and excelling in their careers.

FUTURE TRENDS

Traditional assessment tools such as multiple-choice, true/false, fill-in-the-blank, and matching are criticized, as they measure what students are able to recall or reproduce, rather than what they integrate and produce (Huerta-Macias, 1995). Traditional assessment such as a standardized tests tends to be summative in nature and does not provide feedback to students until they complete a program or degree. Assessment of student progress is changing, mainly because today's organizations require workers who possess not only knowledge but also abilities to think critically and solve problems quickly (Bond, 1995). Angelo (1999) called for research-based guidelines for effective assessment practice that will increase the chances of achieving better teaching and learning. Therefore, the trend seems to go toward activities that address applications of knowledge and critical thinking rather than memorization and recollection alone. In the rest of this section, the emerging trends of three assessment-related issues—course management software, infrastructure, and implementation—will be discussed.

Current course management technology is still evolving. Many institutions that offer Web-based courses choose to use off-the-shelf courseware products, while many have created their own systems. Course management software packages such as WebCT, Blackboard, and Webboard are relatively easy to use but certainly do not provide all the functionality needed. For example, although Webboard offers easy-to-use discussion board and chat functions, it does not have a test-building function. Blackboard and WebCT have a prebuilt list of categories (e.g., syllabus, course document, assignments, discussion, chat, etc.) that help organize course materials, but their discussion board is difficult to navigate. Unlike Webboard, Blackboard and WebCT provide a grade book and a calendar, in which students can check their grade and look up assignment due dates. Both course management systems allow instructors to create different types of tests, such as multiple choice, true/false, and fill-in-the-blank, and surveys. Moreover, the results of those tests and the survey questionnaires are recorded automatically in the grade book.

Each course management product has strengths and weaknesses. An instructor may create "best of breed" courseware systems by utilizing different products. However, the downside of this is confusion, especially among students who are new to these products. Despite promises made by software vendors, instructors need to use their judgment to decide what product would be the most appropriate for their course. More often, faculty may not have input to the decision to purchase a course management product. In that case, they have to make the best of what is available.

Beyond course management systems, infrastructure is another major concern. As the number of Web-based course offerings rises, infrastructure must be in place to handle the increasing usage. To have a stable assessment environment, infrastructure and its support services must be made available. Technical difficulties not only interrupt the process of learning but also can impact retention and course evaluation. For example, a student's thought is interrupted while taking a test when he or she is suddenly logged out of the system because of network congestion. Take another example—when it takes too long for messages on a discussion board to appear, a student may lose interest in participating in discussions and eventually drop out of the course. Student frustration with technology could have a negative impact on course evaluation. It is suggested that an orientation be given to all students before the class starts to familiarize them with technology and where to seek help when technical problems occur.

Last but not least, success of Web-based assessment depends on implementation. Instructors teaching a Web-based course the first time should begin with a simple technique and slowly advance into more complex ones. Starting simple provides an indication of whether the technique works and is worth pursuing. Web-based assessment implementation is an ongoing process that requires patience and persistence from participants, including course developers, instructors, and students. To succeed, these stakeholders must understand what they are assessing and why it needs to be done.

CONCLUSION

The issue of student assessment in a Web-based course is relatively new and has not been discussed widely. According to Hazari (1998), testing and assessment that remains an integral part of educational systems can be used in a classroom-based course as well as a Web-based course. As the area of Web-based teaching and learning grows rapidly, course developers and instructors have spent a great deal of their time on choosing and learning new tools; creating online lectures, assignments, tests, and other materials; and delivering them in synchronous mode (e.g., chat and videoconference) and asynchronous mode (e.g., electronic discussion board and electronic mail).

More often, student assessment created for a Web-based course is simply a reproduction of tools used in a regular classroom. For example, a paper-and-pencil test can be easily transformed into an electronic form stored on a diskette or CD-ROM, or run on a Web browser. Simply automating an assessment process, however, does not utilize technology at its highest capability. The Internet and its technology can be used to leverage student assessment by enabling students and instructors to communicate anytime, from anywhere, thus creating a richer learning environment.

Two assessment techniques were explored in this chapter—traditional and performance—in an attempt to provide instructors with ideas and suggestions to assist them in conducing student assessment more effectively in a Web-based course. "Effective teachers use a variety of means, some formal and others informal, to determine how much and how well their students are learning," said Angelo and Cross (1993). Formal techniques, including tests, quizzes, assignments, and papers, are summative in nature, and their activities are normally graded, while informal techniques, such as a background knowledge quiz and a minute paper, are formative and not usually graded (Angelo & Cross, 1993). Note that it is not suggested that one technique is better than the other. On the contrary, the author encourages the use of multiple techniques in a Web-based course to ensure all desired learning objectives are achieved.

REFERENCES

Angelo, T. A. (1995). Improving classroom assessment to improve learning. *Assessment Update, 7*(6), 1–2, 13–14.

Angelo, T. A. (1999). Doing assessment as if learning matters most. *AAHE Bulletin*. Retrieved September 23, 2001 from the World Wide Web: http://www.aahe.org/Bulletin/angelomay99.htm.

Angelo, T. A., & Cross, K. P. (1993). *Classroom assessment techniques: a handbook for college teachers* (2nd ed.). San Francisco: CA, Jossey-Bass, Inc.

Bergman, T. (n.d.). *Feasible electronic portfolios: global networking for the self-directed learner in the digital age*. Retrieved December 5, 2001 from the World Wide Web: http://www.mehs.educ.state.ak.us/portfolios/why_digital_portfolios.html.

Betts, B. (1997, August 11). Assessing student learning. Presentation at Ruamrudee International School, Bangkok, Thailand.

Bicanich, E. et al. (1997). Internet-based testing: a vision or reality. *T.H.E. Journal*. Retrieved November 7, 2001 from the World Wide Web: http://www.thejournal.com/magazine/vault/A1918.cfm.

Bloom, B. S. (Ed.). (1956). *Taxonomy of education objectives: Handbook I: cognitive domain*. New York: David McKay Company, Inc.

Bond, L. A. (1995). Critical issue: rethinking assessment and its role in supporting educational reform. *North Central Regional Educational Laboratory*. Retrieved from the World Wide Web: http://www.ncrel.org/sdrs/areas/issues/methods/assment/as700.htm.

Bonnstetter, R. J. (1991). Adding value to evaluation through portfolios. *On Research Column of SCIENCE SCOPE*. Retrieved from the World Wide Web: http://education.calumet.purdue.edu/edci346/pdf/PORTFOLIO%20VALUE.pdf.

Born, A. D., & Jessup, C. (2002). An exploration of rubric use in online course assessment. *The Forthcoming Proceedings of Information Resources Management Association (IRMA)*.

Carr, S. (2000, February 11). As distance education comes of age, the challenge is keeping the students. *Chronicle of Higher Education*. Retrieved from the World Wide Web: http://chronicle.com/free/v46/i23/23900101.htm.

Comeaux, P. (1995). The impact of an interactive distance learning network on classroom communication. *Communication Education, 44*, 355–361.

Corbett, H. D., & Wilson, B. L. (1991). *Testing, reform and rebellion*. Norwood, NJ: Ablex Publishing Corporation.

Decamp, M. (2001, June 29). Academic misconduct numbers show increase at Georgia Tech. *Technique*. Retrieved October 12, 2001 from the World Wide Web: http://cyberbuzz.gatech.edu/nique/issues/summer2001/2001-06-29/2.html.

Elliott, S. N. (1995). Creating meaningful performance assessments. *ERIC Clearinghouse on Disabilities and Gifted Education*, Reston, VA, ERIC Id ED 381985.

Hazari, S. (1998, June 21). Evaluation and selection of Web course management tools. Retrieved November 27, 2001 from the World Wide Web: http://sunil.umd.edu/Webct.

Herman, J. L., Aschbacher, P. R., & Winters, L. (1992). A practical guide to alternative assessment. Alexandria, VA: Association for Supervision and Curriculum Development.

Horton, W. K. (2000). *Designing Web-based training*. New York: John Wiley & Sons.

Huerta-Macias, A. (1995). Alternative assessment: responses to commonly asked Questions. *TESOL Journal, 5*, 8–10.

Kemp, J., & Toperoff, D. (1998). Guidelines for portfolio assessment in teaching English. English Inspectorate, Ministry of Education. Retrieved from the World Wide Web: http://www.etni.org.il/ministry/portfolio/default.html.

Madaus, G. F., & Raczek, A. E. (1996). A turning point for assessment: reform movements in the United States. In A. Little, & A. Wolf (Eds.), *Assessment in transition: learning, monitoring and selection in international perspective*. Oxford: Pergamon.

Merriam Webster's Collegiate Dictionary (10th ed.). (2001). Merriam Webster, Inc.

Moore, M., & Kearsley, G. (1996). *Distance education: a systems view*. Belmont, CA: Wadsworth Publishing Company.

Palombra, C., & Banta, T. (1999). *Assessment essentials: planning, implementing, and improving assessment in higher education*. San Francisco, CA: Jossey Bass.

Paulson, F. L., Paulson, P. R., & Meyer, C. A. (1991). What makes a portfolio a portfolio? *Educational Leadership, 48*(5), 60–63.

Perrin, N. et al. (1992). Program assessment, Where do we start? Retrieved October 9, 2001 from the World Wide Web: http://www.clas.pdx.edu/assessment/program_assessment.html.

Phipps, R., & Merisotis, J. (1999). What's the difference? A review of contemporary research on the effectiveness of distance learning in higher education. Washington, D.C.:

Institute for Higher Education Policy. Retrieved from the World Wide Web: http://www.ihep.com/PUB.htm#diff.

Preventing Plagiarism and Cheating in Online Courses. (1999). *Pointers & clickers: technology tip of the month*. Retrieved December 7, 2001 from the World Wide Web: http://illinois.online.uillinois.edu/ionpointers/ionpointers1299.html.

Quizzing, Testing, and Homework on the Internet. (2000). Illinois Online Network Resource. Retrieved October 6, 2001 from the World Wide Web: http://illinois.online.uillinois.edu/resources/assessment/quizing.html.

Rudner, L., & Boston, C. (n.d.). A long overview on alternative assessment. Retrieved August 28, 2001 from the World Wide Web: gopher://vmsgopher.cua.edu/00gopher_root_eric_ae%3A[_alt]_overv.txt.

Smith, M., & Cohen, M. (1991). A national curriculum in the United States? *Educational Leadership, 49*(1), 74–81.

Strategies to Minimize Cheating Online. (2000). Illinois Online Network Resource. Retrieved November 18, 2001 from the World Wide Web: http://illinois.online.uillinois.edu/IONresources/assessment/cheating.html.

Student Assessment in Online Courses. (2001). Illinois Online Network Resource. Retrieved from the World Wide Web: http://www.ion.illinois.edu/IONresources/assessment/cheating.html.

Sweet, D. (1993). Performance assessment. *Education Research Consumer Guide 2*. Retrieved from the World Wide Web: http://www.ed.gove/pubs/OR/consumerguides/perasse.html.

UIS Online Enrollment, Retrieved September 20, 2002 from the World Wide Web: http://people.uis.edu/rschr1/onlinegrowth.jpg.

Van Belle, G. (n.d.). How cheating helps drive better instruction. *Plagiarized.com: the instructors guide to Internet plagiarism*. Retrieved December 12, 2001 from thee World Wide Web: http://www.plagiarized.com/vanb.shtml.

Waller, K. V. (2001). Writing instructional objectives. National Accrediting Agency for Clinical Laboratory Sciences. Retrieved from the World Wide Web: http://www.naacls.org/docs/announcement/writing-objectives.pdf.

Wangsatorntanakhun, J. A. (1999, September 25). Designing performance assessments: challenges for the three-story intellect. Retrieved from the World Wide Web: http://www.geocities.com/Athens/Parthenon/8658.

Chapter XII

A Web-Based Platform to Mentor Distance Learners

Karen Neville
University College Cork, Ireland

Frederic Adam
University College Cork, Ireland

Colin McCormack
University College Cork, Ireland

ABSTRACT

Highlighted in this chapter is the fact that the majority of organizations face the enormous challenge of supporting their employees' thirst for expanding their skill base. Provided is an example of a university and an organization collaborating to implement successful training and learning programs in order to develop employee skills and knowledge in IT and managerial issues such as knowledge management. The authors hope that the case discussed will inform researchers of an appropriate model in designing an interactive learning environment to mentor distance learners and, additionally, of the potential to eliminate the barriers imposed by the traditional classroom.

INTRODUCTION

The majority of organizations face the enormous challenge of supporting their employees' thirst for expanding their skill base. As a result, universities and organizations are currently collaborating to implement successful training and learning program in order to develop employee skills and knowledge in IT and managerial issues such as knowledge management (KM). For this reason, as early as 1993, the National University of Ireland, Cork, introduced a Diploma in Credit Union studies to provide professional training for a range of Credit Union personnel, including full-time staff, directors, and volunteers. The course is designed on a distance-learning model and has been supported, to date, by a tutorial system in regional centers. However, students identified a need for more support, the type that only a virtual learning environment can provide. The focus in this chapter is on the development of an interactive learning environment to mentor distance learners. Indicated in the case study is a strong requirement for the utilization of such an environment to increase support for and collaboration between the distance learners. We conclude that a structured communication system has the potential to eliminate the barriers imposed by the traditional classroom.

BACKGROUND

Weiser (1991) argued that, "the most profound technologies are those that disappear. They weave themselves into the fabric of everyday life." Technology can and does aid groups, be they educators or students (Hiltz & Turoff, 1985), but it is not as profound as the textbook (Caroll, 1968). Videoconferencing, multimedia, learning systems, and Internet-based training (IBT) are examples of technologies that are having a profound impact on training, however, they cannot be labeled as "profound." At the same time, computers are seen as a merger of hardware, software, and networks through the Internet to form learning communities (Dede, 1996). This alternative is becoming a profound medium for instructional delivery (Harasim et al., 1995). Human interaction through networks facilitates the breakdown of communication barriers and inhibitions that often stifle the open exchange of ideas in traditional classroom groups (Cuban, 1993; Damarin, 1993; Eisenberg & Ely, 1993).

Groups

Groups are defined as people who are aware of one another and have the opportunity to communicate (McGrath, 1984). The study of people as individuals and in groups started as early as the 19th century. For example, Gustave Lebon (1896) investigated the absorption of individuals into a crowd, losing their personality and adopting the collective mind of the group, be it a departmental group (Huczynski & Buchanan, 1985) or a group of students. The role that groups come to play in their organization or university cannot easily be tied to simple models (Adam, 1999). Organizations and the functional areas within evolve over time, and the result is rarely a neat arrangement of groups and procedures (Brown & Magill, 1994; Strassman, 1995). The word group seems to suggest cooperation and collaboration in any environment, be it organizational or educational. However, research is full of as many examples of conflicts as cooperation (Putnam & Poole, 1987; Easterbrook, 1991). Easterbrook (1991) argued that chaos and anarchy are more reliable models for human interaction than any other to provide a basis for the design of computer-supported communications systems. Communication does not necessarily encourage collaboration, for example, discussion forums can, if not properly structured, result in information overload and, therefore, structural chaos; 10 threaded replies can result in 10,000 unstructured responses and queries.

Group Decision Support Systems (GDSS)

GDSS can be seen as outside the frame of this chapter, which is not concerned directly with decision making but with the development of a distance-learning environment (DLE). However, it needs to be addressed as a technological means to enhancing communication between learners. DeSanctis and Gallupe wrote a milestone article on GDSS in 1987, where they defined them as combining "communication, computing and decision support technologies to facilitate formulation and solution of unstructured problems by a group of people" (DeSanctis, 1987). In this context, the GDSS aimed at improving the process of decision making within the group by "removing common communication barriers, providing techniques for structuring decision analysis, and systematically directing the pattern, timing or content or discussion" as would a DLE. To date, researchers have identified several benefits. First, GDSS seem to be able to reduce the inhibitory behavior of participants, especially thanks to the possibility to contribute anonymously to a forum. Second, GDSS seem to solve the issue of dominance and inequality of participation by imposing an equal weight on all the propositions (DeSanctis, 1987). Siegel et al. also found that GDSS improve the overall communication efficiency, thanks to the speed and flexibility it allows: "instantaneous and simultaneous transmission of messages, participants do not have to take turns to speak..." (Siegel et al., 1986). DeSanctis and Gallupe expected that the lack of social cues inherent in the electronic communication could "encourage open input of creative ideas, discovery of optimal solutions, and selection of an alternative based on its merit rather than on compromise" (1987). The effectiveness of GDSS or any other communication network (human or technologically based) remains largely to be proved except in special cases (Huseman & Miles, 1998) of spatially separated participants (distance learners), where the alliance of GDSS and telecommunications can make it easier and faster to reach consensus.

Benefits of Structured Communication

The benefit of online communication emanates from its potential to provide structure to the human communication process within groups (Hiltz & Turoff, 1985). A learning environment, using, for example, discussion forums, where a communication structure is not specifically designed and imposed on the learners will, to be successful, need to result in an emergent structure. Increases in student or employee numbers necessitates structuring in the virtual and the traditional classroom. Structured communication provides the educator and the learner with the following advantages: access to expertise without conforming to the opinion of the group; anonymity of the participants through the medium of distance (Hardy, 1957; Allen, 1965); opportunity to participate in a large group; feedback mechanisms between the teacher and the student; a mediator to assure the flow and value of the discussion; rules to govern the communication process; and some type of motivation, either academic or for promotion purposes. If these are incorporated into any learning or communications network, the system will succeed in supporting the learner.

Distance Learning

Distance learning has been defined as "any type of learning outside the more traditional learning environment"; it is education that connects the participants through technology (Harasim et al., 1995; Dede, 1996). Traditional learning is characterized by the classroom effect, with the instructor at the top of the classroom explaining the topic, while the students listen (Cuban, 1993). By contrast, distance learning involves anything from watching a video, to loading a tutorial from a CD-ROM, to enrolling in a virtual classroom (Harassim, 1990; Harris, 1994). However, each type of distance learning has three factors in common: distance between the instructor and the student, opportunities offered by technology for different delivery techniques, and expectations on the student to work largely independently (Harasim, 1990; Teles & Duxbury, 1992). The goal of a learning environment is to create a community of learners (Davie & Wells, 1991; Harasim et al., 1995) cooperating to achieve a common objective (Johnson & Johnson, 1990). The traditional classroom environment emphasizes the interaction between the educator and the learner (James, 1958; Laurillard, 1993), however, collaboration is not as emphasized as it is in distance learning (Kaye, 1991; Dede, 1996).

Mentorship is a traditional method of teaching that strengthens the concept and objectives of distance learning (Benton et al., 1995). The Oxford dictionary defines the word "mentor" as a "wise counselor, who tutors the learner in intellectual subjects." When this model is applied to a learning network, the student is called a teleapprentice, who studies using appropriate methods (Levin, 1990). The teleapprentice reads messages, answers questions, participates in discussions, and conducts research online to master his or her subject. Mentorship is a method of teaching that has been used for hundreds of years; this design is incorporated into learning networks to develop more effective learning practices (Eisenstadt & Vincent, 1998) and to provide additional support and mediation to the learners (Alexander, 1995). "Access to experts" is one of the many advantages provided through learning networks (Harasim, 1995). Networks are, in fact, modeled on this method (Harasim et al., 1995). Therefore, distance learning environments (DLEs) allow students to communicate with experts in a field and collaborate with their peers (Dick & Reiser, 1989; Crossman, 1997).

Another component intertwined in the distance learning methodology is group collaboration (Wells, 1992). The collaborative model assigns specific roles in the learning environment, and each participant communicates through the network (Luetkehans et al., 1996; Driscoll, 1998). The roles of educators and students are changing (Jonassen et al., 1996; Driscoll, 1998). Learning networks enable the student and the educator to expand the time, place, and pace of education (Harasim et al., 1995). This method is more individualized when compared to the traditional classroom (Teles & Duxbury, 1992), while peer interaction and collaboration are also emphasized (Wells, 1992), resulting in a learning paradox. The distance learning system is designed to provide greater support to the individual learner, allowing everyone the opportunity to speak without conforming to the pressures of "face-to-face" communication and conflict. But, it also allows the learners to anonymously share ideas and pose queries to one another (McCormack & Jones, 1997).

Web-Based Mentoring Systems (WBMS)

Web-based mentoring systems (WBMS) can be described as learning delivery environments in which the WWW is its medium of delivery (Crossman, 1992; Driscoll, 1998). The possibilities of WBMS are limited only by constraints imposed by the university or organization in question, such as technological or managerial support (Neville, 2000). Innovative companies and universities are using this implementation for a number of reasons, specifically to keep employees or students abreast of emerging technologies in their fields and to provide effective training to staff and customers on new products and skills (Khan, 1997). Designing a WBMS requires a thorough investigation into the use of the Web as a medium for delivery (Ritchie & Hoffman, 1996; McCormack et al., 1997; Driscoll, 1998). The designer must be aware of the attributes of the WWW and the principles of instructional design to create a meaningful learning environment (Gagne et al., 1988; Driscoll, 1997). The Web-based classroom is viewed, as already stated, as an innovative approach to teaching (Relan & Gillani, 1997). The virtual classroom, like the traditional method, requires careful planning to be effective and beneficial (Dick & Reiser, 1989). As stated by McCormack et al., (1997) a Web-based classroom must do more than just distribute information—it should include resources such as discussion forums to support collaboration between learners, and ultimately, it should also support the needs of the novice and advanced learner (Willis, 1995; Sherry, 1996). A WBMS is composed of a number of components that are integral to the effective operation of the environment (Banathy, 1992), for example, the development of content, the use of multimedia, Internet tools, hardware, and software (Reeves, 1993a). A developer must understand the capabilities of these components (search engines, feedback pages, and movie clips), as their use will determine the success or the failure of the learning environment (Driscoll, 1998).

Effective Dimensions in WBMS Design

Distance learning is regarded as the "silver bullet" solution to training issues faced by organizations, despite little quantitative evidence to support claims of its effectiveness (Huseman & Miles, 1988). Therefore, it is essential to define the characteristics of interactive education that can be achieved through the WWW (Shotsberger, 1996), and expand the distance learning concept to promote mentoring. The identification of these characteristics is necessary to implement such a concept. Thus, 10 dimensions proposed by Reeves and Reeves (1993) for interactive training and collaboration are reviewed in this section: educational philosophy, learning theory, goal orientation, task orientation, source of motivation, role of the teacher, metacognitive support, collaborative learning, cultural sensitivity, and structural flexibility. The dimensions are proposed to describe the characteristics of a WBMS. Each of the dimensions identified are outlined in the next section:

1. *Educational philosophy* ranges from strict instructivist to a radical constructivist structure, in the approach to training (Kafai & Resnick, 1996). Instructivists debate the importance of identifying objectives that exist apart from the learner. Once the developer has identified the objectives, they are ordered into a type of learning hierarchical structure, addressed through direct instruction. The learners are viewed as passive recipients of the devised instruction. Instructivists believe that learning consists of acquiring knowledge, and that knowledge can be measured through testing (Phillips, 1993). However, the constructivist structure is a direct contrast to this philosophy. The learner is regarded as the focus of the learning, and the learner's intentions, experiences, and cognitive strategies must be considered (McCormack et al., 1997; Driscoll, 1998). This philosophy also emphasizes the belief that learners build their cognitive strategies on previous knowledge and on the learning environment. Therefore, a rich and stimulating environment is required to train the different adult learners. Thus, direct instruction is also replaced with challenging tasks. The constructivists' belief is that the learners have their own objectives and must be motivated to use the environment (Sano, 1996; Driscoll, 1998). However, the majority of WBMS are based on the instructivist structure of direct learning, but there are online resources that enable learners to build their own knowledge base, for example, discussion forums.

2. The design of the environment should be based on researched *learning theories* (McCormack et al., 1997). The two dominant theories identified in the design of training environments are behavioral and cognitive psychology. Behaviorists believe that the most important factors that should be taken into consideration are the arrangement of stimuli, responses, feedback, and reinforcement to shape the desirable behavior of the learners. Inaccurate responses will result in the repetition of content. By contrast, cognitive psychologists place more emphasis on internal mental states than on

behavior (Kyllonen & Shute, 1989). As a result, the WBMS design, using cognitive theory, will be based on direct instruction and practice exercises (Dede, 1996).

3.   The *goals* for a WBMS can vary from sharply focused, where a specific environment is required, to a more general approach (Driscoll, 1998). Cole (1992) stated that knowledge "has undergone extensive social negotiation of meaning and which might most efficiently be presented more directly to the learner," in this instance, direct instruction will suffice. WBMS can also avail of direct instruction and other training facilities, such as a cognitive tool (Joassen & Reeves, 1996; Brandau & Chi, 1996).

4.   The orientation of *tasks* can range from academic to authentic. The majority of WBMS emphasize the importance of context (Brown, Collins, & Duguid, 1989); thus, the majority of the environment's tasks are academic, but they can be developed to focus on the needs of the learners (authentic). An academic-oriented environment will be designed to provide exercises based on the material taught (explicit knowledge). By contrast, an authentic design, for adult education, would require the learners to tackle job-related exercises or cases (tacit knowledge). The design orientation of a WBMS should support the transfer of skills to the learners.

5.   *Motivation* is the main factor for the success of any learning environment. The source of motivation ranges from two extremes, from extrinsic (outside the learning environment) to intrinsic (a part of the learning environment). The motivation of the learner to use the environment can be difficult to identify, but it must be considered in the design of the WBMS (Sano, 1996; Driscoll, 1998). Proponents of distance learning and, therefore, mentorship, argue that components such as content and multimedia will motivate the users, but studies have indicated that learners become bored with flashy elements (Reeves, 1993). Therefore, learners must be provided with a reason to use the environment, such as extra academic credit or as an aid to promotion.

6.   Lecturers and tutors fulfil different *roles* from the traditional role of instructor (didactic) to the facilitative role. Caroll (1968) stated that, "by far the largest amount of teaching activity in educational settings involves telling things to students," to describe the role that lecturers play in the learning environment. However, the role of the lecturer has not changed. Despite an increase in the use of technology to deliver information, they fulfil the traditional role as well as the role of a facilitator. Therefore, the role of the instructor has not changed but has acquired more responsibility. Advances in technology are enabling the instructor to provide the learners with tools to add material to the environment and to evaluate themselves. Discussion forums can be used to allow learners to add material in a logical sequence, and online assessment can be used to provide the student with the option of testing their knowledge.

7.   Flavell (1979) described *metacognition* as the learner's ability to identify objectives, plan, and understand learning strategies. Therefore, metacognitive skills are the skills possessed by the learner in learning to learn. This type of support ranges from the unsupported, which is common practice, to the integrated. Thus, WBMS can be designed to challenge the learner to solve course-related problems (Driscoll, 1998).

8.   The *collaborative* learning dimension for WBMS development can also range from lack of support to the inclusion of facilities to support it. In the traditional environment, students usually work individually; however, a collaborative environment would enable students to work and share ideas with one another, while still supporting the needs of the individual learner (Harassim, 1995). The WWW provides a medium for promoting collaborative learning and therefore mentoring.

9. Reeves et al. (1993) argued that all training environments have *cultural implications*. However, the development of a WBMS cannot be designed to adjust to every rule. Therefore, WBMS should be designed to be as culturally aware as possible.

10. *Structural flexibility* describes a WBMS as asynchronous or synchronous (Driscoll, 1998). Open or asynchronous environments refer to the use of such an environment at any particular time or from any location. However, synchronous refers to fixed environments that can only be used in the training room of an organization. The WWW provides educators and students with the opportunity to avail of resources from more open environments through which students are supported or mentored in the acquisition of tacit and explicit knowledge.

The dimensions were used as an effective guide to the implementation of the Web-based mentoring system (WBMS) illustrated in Figures 1 and 2. The study of the different dimensions and the factors necessary for the collaboration and structure of learning provide valuable information and steps for the analysis and, therefore, the development of such an environment in supporting group and individual learning.

RESEARCH OBJECTIVE

The traditional approach to training and education has always incurred criticism (Banathy, 1994; Reigeluth, 1994). It is viewed as a technique that encourages passive learning. It does not develop problem-solving skills and ignores the individual needs of the learners (Hannum & Briggs, 1982); therefore, it ignores the requirements of its end users. It could be argued that advances in technology, such as multimedia and virtual simulations (Nisbet & Entwistle, 1973), have left the traditional classroom trailing behind, with learners expecting more and more (Driscoll, 1998; Davie & Wells, 1991). The intensity of competition in the business market advances in technology (Crossman, 1997), and a strong shift toward a knowledge-based economy have contributed to the demand for virtual learning environments. "There is no knowledge that is not power" (Emerson, 1843), and the organization (public or private) that can utilize its knowledge resources more effectively than its competitor will persevere (Laudon et al., 1998). An effective training support system can provide an organization or a university with a strategic advantage in the market (Benjamin & Blunt, 1993). Learning environments can help create and maintain skills and, therefore, the corporate knowledge base (Garvin, 1993). They both alleviate the strain on corporate resources and facilitate employees' changing training needs (Driscoll, 1998).

In this chapter, the focus is on the design of a suitable environment to support distance learners and encourage collaboration. The research outlines the factors necessary for the successful implementation and use of the system, through the investigation of current research and the analysis of the case environment. It also highlights the potential of the system to overcome the physical barriers of the traditional classroom. Distance learning environments (DLEs) can, when properly mediated and structured, facilitate cooperation (Entwistle, 1997), reduce conflict, and avail of all of the benefits that technology can provide (Johnson & Johnson, 1990). The authors also identified an interesting paradox; learning environments are customized for the needs of the individual learner, yet are built to promote collaboration. The study concludes that learning environments or Web-based mentoring systems (WBMS) have the potential, when properly designed, to foster learning. Outlined in this chapter are the development and implementation of interactive Web-based mentoring systems (WBMS) to support the educational needs of distance learners. The authors propose to expand the design of the case's original tutorial system to provide a more innovative, virtual classroom that is more akin to the true essence of distance learning. The system will effectively enable tutors and lecturers to mentor the learners. Figures 1 and 2 illustrate the WBMS that has been created to support the learners' requirements, as determined through ongoing discussions and postal surveys. It is also the objective of this chapter to examine the factors necessary for successful implementation and learning. This will be achieved through the removal of the physical barriers imposed by the traditional classroom, allowing the students and the educators to expand the time, place, and pace of learning.

THE PROBLEM CASE

Education is central to the operation of Credit Unions, and it was with this in mind that The National University of Ireland, Cork, introduced a distance-learning Diploma in Credit Union Studies in 1993. The diploma provides professional training to a range of Credit Union personnel, including full-time staff, directors, and volunteers. It is designed to develop a critical awareness of the distinctive nature of Credit Union organizations and their role in promoting socioeconomic development at the community level. It also aims to further develop the knowledge and abilities of Credit Union personnel so that they can more efficiently organize and manage Credit Unions. The course is designed on a distance-learning basis and is supported by a tutorial system in regional centers. The main purpose of the tutorials is to facilitate the learning process, assist in the completion of assignments, and encourage team playing within the group. Students are presented with written modules, which act as "the lecture," and the tutor plays the role of the facilitator, enabling the students to combine the written materials with their own Credit Union experience. Feedback from the students identified the need to provide additional learning support through an online environment. The WBMS would enhance the learning process and enable students from throughout the country to collaborate in supporting each other through the Diploma. Focused on in this chapter is the development of these requirements through an interactive learning environment for students on this Diploma.

Findings of Initial Analysis

Presented here are the findings gathered during ongoing interactions between the organizers and students during the years. A recent postal questionnaire was designed and posted to each of the participants of the target group (past graduates) to determine their reaction to the possibility of an online environment to support future students, one devised to their specification. The information collected and analyzed by the authors is presented in Table 1. The objective of this analysis stage was to determine the requirements of the participants in the study. The obvious finding of this questionnaire, as can be seen in Table 1, is that the participants require an online support system or environment that can only be facilitated by the Web. Participants were required to scale their agreement or disagreement between 1 and 5. The maximum score on the construct is 1, indicating a strong agreement. Therefore, the closer the rating is to 1, the stronger the agreement, and a score of 5 would reflect the participant's strongest disagreement. The instructors were also questioned regarding

Table 1: WBMS Requirements (Postal Survey)

WBMS Requirements	1	2	3	4	5
A Web-based mentoring system	6	5			
Online discussion forum	4	5	2		
Online quizzes and sample questions	6	5			
A "Relevant Links" page that allows you to search for links	5	6			
A links page that allows you to add relevant links	2	8	1		
Lecturer/tutor pages with notes, etc.	8	2	1		
Further information about the course	6	3	1		
Online notice board	6	3	2		
Submission capabilities for assignments	8	2	1		

Note. 1 = mostly agree through 5 = mostly disagree

their requirements, and therefore, the distance learning environment (WBMS) designed to support their classes. The instructors were as optimistic as the participants regarding the predicted success of the environment and the affect of the learning environment on the success of the courses offered to future adult learners.

THE SOLUTION: A WEB-BASED MENTORING SYSTEM (WBMS)

The WBMS (Figure 1) was constructed to support and implement Third Level courses for Credit Union personnel seeking to acquire knowledge management (KM) skills. Course material is available online, but in addition, a discussion forum will enable instructors and students to exchange ideas and add to the environment. This will allow adult learners to provide feedback (anonymously, if desired) to the instructors. It will also enable them to pose queries, which other participants or the instructors can answer. All participants will be able to see the initial queries and the discussion stream of answers from other participants and the instructors. This will further extend the reach of the course, as students can log on to the WBMS at home or at their work and pose questions for which answers will be available when they next log on. The facility will also allow the adult learners to voice their satisfaction regarding the different elements of the environment. This will provide the participants with the opportunity to take part in the ongoing design of the WBMS, and therefore, increase the likelihood of user acceptance.

In Figure 1, the opportunities available to the participants of the case are illustrated. WBMS are designed or customized for the requirements of the individual learner. The learning abilities of students vary, and the traditional classroom is restricted to rules to facilitate the group. The educator instructs a class, but the level of collaboration and the development of problem-solving skills can be directly correlated to class sizes. The greater the size of the group, the less attention individual learners gain or the more intimidated a student is to participate in discussions, thus reducing collaboration. The WBMS, when adequately designed, can reduce the limitations of the classroom and allow the student to work at their

Figure 1: The Web-Based Mentoring System (WBMS)

Mentoring System (WBMS)

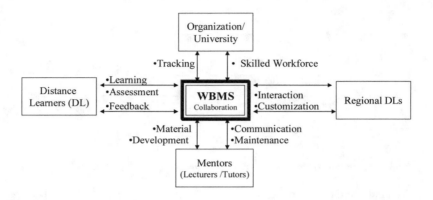

Figure 2: The Web-Based Mentoring System (WBMS)

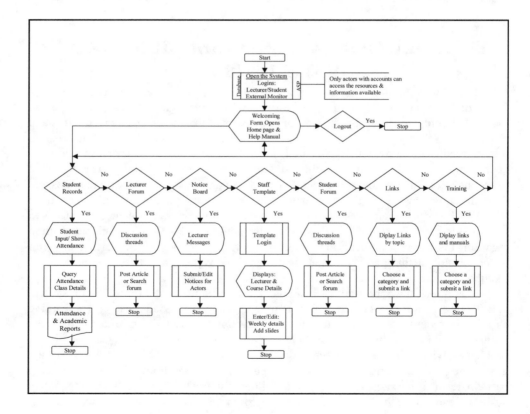

own pace with structured support from the educators and the other learners. In Figure 2, the numerous resources that are provided through the online environment are described.

CONCLUSION

Over the years, students past and present have praised the hands-on approach provided through the instructor-driven system. The organizers of the course have always requested feedback from the instructors and the students. However, through raised concerns regarding increased student numbers and research into strengthening the instructor–student association (mentorship), a current investigation identified a Web-based mentoring system (WBMS) as a solution. The environment provides an extra communication channel, as the number of students applying for the course is constantly increasing. It also enables the tutors and students to collaborate, therefore, providing 24-hour online support. A number of important conclusions can be drawn from this research, which depicts a clear guideline (Figure 2), for the development of a WBMS. The development of a WBMS presents enormous challenges to academics and management in determining distance learners support requirements and eventually benefiting from the support environment. This case is a prime example of a successful course that can and will be availing of technology to ensure ongoing success. After an in-depth analysis, it was apparent that the learners lacked an efficient online support system, which would complement the traditional tutorial system currently in place. An effective training support system can provide an organization or a university with a strategic advantage in the market. Learning environments can help create and maintain skills and, therefore, the corporate knowledge base. They alleviate the strain on corporate resources and facilitate employees changing training needs. In this chapter, focus was on the design of a suitable environment to support distance learners and encourage collaboration. The research outlines the factors necessary for the successful implementation and use of the system. It also highlights the potential of the system to overcome the physical barriers of the traditional classroom. Distance learning environments can, when properly mediated and structured, facilitate cooperation, reduce conflict, and avail of all of the benefits that technology can provide.

Previous research into communication systems, such as Group Decision Support Systems (GDSS), has identified the advantages and disadvantages associated with their use. However, the use of communication or learning systems has never been justified by proving that they can remove the barriers associated with the traditional classroom, increase group collaboration without face-to-face communication, and eliminate conflict from the learning process.

REFERENCES

Adam, F. (1999). An empirical investigation of the information and decision networks of organisations and their implications for IS research. Unpublished PhD Dissertation, National University of Ireland, September.

Alexander, S. (1995). Teaching and learning on the World Wide Web. Retrieved from the World Wide Web: http://www.scu.edu.au/ausWeb95/chapters/education2/alexnder/

Argyle, M. (1994). *The psychology of interpersonal behaviour* (5th ed.). Harmondsworth: Penguin.

Banathy, B. H. (1992). *A systems view of education: a journey to create the future.* Englewood Cliffs, NJ: Educational Technology Publications.

Banathy, B. (1994). Designing educational systems: creating our future in a changing world. In C. M. Reigeluth, & R. J. Garfinkle (Eds.), *Systemic change in education* (pp. 27–34). Englewood Cliffs, NJ: Educational Technology Publications.

Baron, R. A., & Byrne, A. (1977). *Social psychology: understanding human interaction* (2nd ed.). Boston, MA: Allyn and Bacon Inc.

Benjamin, R. I., & Blunt, J. (1992). Critical IT issues: the next ten years, Sloan Management Review.

Benton, V., Elder, M., & Thornbury, H. (1995). Early experiences of mentoring: design and use of multimedia material for teaching. OR/MS' working chapter 95/5, Department of Management Science, University of Strathcycle.

Brown, J. S., Collins, A., & Duguid, P. (1989). Situated cognition and the culture of learning. *Educational Researcher, 18*(1), 32–41.

Caroll, J. B. (1968). On learning from being told. *Educational Psychologist, 5*, 4–10.

Clarke, R. E. (1994). Media will never influence learning. *Educational Technology Research and Development, 42*(2), 21–29.

Cole, P. (1992). Constructivism revisited: a search for common ground. *Educational Technology, 32*(2), 27–34.

Crossman, D. (1997). *The evolution of the World Wide Web as an emerging instructional technology tool.* Englewood Cliffs, NJ: Educational Technology Publications.

Cuban, L. (1993). *How teachers taught* (2nd ed.). New York: Teachers College Press.

Damarin, S. (1993). Schooling and situated knowledge: travel or tourism? *Educational Technology, 33*(10), 27–32.

Davie, L., & Wells, R. (1991). Empowering the learner through computer-mediated communication. *American Journal of Distance Education, 5*(1), 15–23.

Dede, C. (1996). The transformation of distance education to distributed learning. *InTRO*; http://129.7.160.78/InTRO.html.

DeSanctis, G., & Gallupe, B. (1987). A foundation for the study of group decision support. *Management Science, 33*(5).

Dick, W., & Reiser, R. (1989). *Planning effective instruction.* Englewood Cliffs, NJ: Prentice Hall.

Driscoll, M. (1998). Web-based training: using technology to design adult learning experiences.

Easterbrook. (1991). *CSCW: co-operation or conflict.* New York: Spring Verlag.

The Economist Intelligent Unit. (1991). Executive Information Systems, Special Report S123, July 1991.

Eisenberg, M. B., & Ely, D. P. (1993). Plugging into the Net.

Eisenstadt, M., & Vincent, T. (1998). The knowledge Web, learning and collaborating on the Net.

Entwistle, N. (1988). Styles of learning and teaching: an integrated outline of educational psychology for students, teachers and lecturers.

Flavell, J. H. (1979). Metacognition and cognitive monitoring: a new area of psychological inquiry. *American Psychologist, 34*, 906–911.

Gagne, R. M., Briggs, L. J., & Wagner, W. W. (1988). *Principles of instructional design* (3rd ed.). New York: Holt Reinhart Winston.

Garvin, D. A. (1993). Building a learning organisation. Harvard Business Review.

Hannum, W., & Briggs, L. (1982). How does instructional system design differ from traditional instruction? *Educational Technology, 22*(1), 9–14.

Harasim, L. (1990). Computer learning networks: educational applications of computer conferencing. *Journal of Distance Education*, 1(1), 59–70.

Harasim, L. et al. (1995). *Learning networks: a field guide to teaching and learning online*. Boston, MA: The MIT Press.

Harris, J. (1994). Telecommunications training by immersion: university courses online. *Machine-Mediated Learning, 4*(2&3), 177–185.

Hiltz, S. R., & Turoff, M. (1985). Structuring computer-mediated communications systems to avoid information overload. *Communication of the ACM*, July.

Huczynski, A., & Buchanan, D. (1985). *Organisational behaviour* (2nd ed.). Kidlington, Oxon: Prentice Hall International.

Huseman, R. C., & Miles, E. W. (1988). Organisational communication in the information age: implications of computer-based systems. *Journal of Management, 14*(2).

James, W. (1889). *Talk to teachers* (1958 Reissue). New York: W.W. Norton.

Johnson, D., & Johnson, R. (1990). Cooperative learning and achievement. In S. Sharon (Ed.), *Cooperative learning theory and research* (pp. 22–37). New York: Praeger.

Jonassen, D. H., & Reeves, T. C. (in press). Learning with technology: using computers as cognitive tools. In D. Jonassen (Ed.). *Handbook of research on educational technology*. New York: Macmillan.

Kafai, Y., & Resnick, M. (1996). *Constructivism in practice: designing, thinking and learning in a digital world*. Mahwah, NJ: Lawrence Erlbaum Associates.

Kaye, A. (1991). Computer networking in distance education: multiple uses many models. In A. Fjuk, & A. E. Jenssen (Eds.), *Proceedings of the Nordic Electronic Networking Conference* (pp. 43–51). Oslo, Norway: NKS.

Khan, B. (1997). *Web-based instruction*. Englewood Cliffs, NJ: Educational Technology Publications.

Kyllonen, P. C., & Shute, V. J. (1989). A taxonomy of learning skills. In P. L. Ackerman, R. J. Sternberg, & R. Glaser (Eds.), *Learning and individual differences: advances in theory and research* (pp. 117–163). New York: W.H Freeman and Company.

Laudon, K. C., & Laudon, J. P. (1998). *Management information systems, organization and technology in the networked enterprise* (6th ed.). New York: Prentice Hall International Editors.

Laurillard, D. (1993). *Rethinking university teaching*. London: Routledge.

Lebon, G. (1986). *The crowd—a study of the popular mind*. London: Fisher Unwin.

Levin, J. (1990). Teleapprenticeships on globally distributed electronic networks. Chapter presented at the meeting of American Educational Research Association.

McCormack, C., & Jones, D. (1997). *Building a Web-based education system*. New York: Wiley.

McGrath, J. E. (1984). *Groups: interaction and performance*, Englewood Cliffs, NJ: Prentice Hall.

Neville, K. (2000). A Web-based training (WBT) system development framework: a case study. Business Information Technology Management (BIT) 2000, 10th Annual Conference, Manchester, UK.

Nisbet, J. D., & Entwistle, N. J. (1973). The psychologist's contribution to educational research. In W. Taylor (Ed.), *Research perspectives in education*. London: Routledge and Kegan Paul.

Phillips, J. J. (1993). Handbook of training evaluation and measurement methods.

Putnam, L. L., & Poole, S. (1987). Conflict and negotiation. In F.M. Jablin et al. (Eds.), *Handbook of organisatonal communication: an interdisciplinary perspective* (pp. 549–599). London: Sage Publications.

Reeves, T. C. (1993a). Research support for interactive multimedia: existing foundations and future directions. In C. Latchem, J. Williamson, & L. Henderson-Lancett (Eds.), *Interactive multimedia: practice and promise* (pp. 79–96). London: Kogan Page.

Reeves, T. C. (1993b). Pseudoscience in computer-based instruction: the case of learner control research. *Journal of Computer-Based Instruction, 20*(2), 39–46.

Reigeluth, C. M. (1994). Introduction: an imperative for system change. In C. M. Reigeluth, & R. J. Garfinkle (Eds.), *Systemic change in education*. Englewood Cliffs, NJ: Educational Technology Publications.

Relan, A., & Gillani, B. (1997). Web-based information and the traditional classroom. In C. M. Reigeluth, & R. J. Garfinkle (Eds.), *Systemic change in education*. Englewood Cliffs, NJ: Educational Technology Publications.

Ritchie, D. C., & Hoffman. (1996). Incorporating instructional design principles with the World Wide Web. In C. M. Reigeluth, & R. J. Garfinkle (Eds.), *Systemic change in education*. Englewood Cliffs, NJ: Educational Technology Publications.

Sano, D. (1996). *Designing large-scale websites, a visual design methodology*. New York: Wiley Computer Publishing.

Sherry, L. (1996). Raising the prestige of online articles. *Intercom, 43*(7), 25–43.

Shotsberger, P. G. (1996). Instructional uses of the World Wide Web: exemplars and precautions. *Educational Technology*, 36(2), 47–50.

Siegel, J. D., Vitaly Kiesler, S., & McGuire, A. W. (1986). Group processes in computer-mediated communication, organisational behaviour and human decision processes, Volume 37.

Teles, L., & Duxbury, N. (1992). The networked classroom: creating an online environment for K–12 education. Burnaby, BC: Facility of Education, Simon Fraser University (ERIC ED348988).

Weiser, M. (1991). The computer for the 21st century. *Scientific American, 265*, 3, 94–104.

Wells, R. A. (1992). Computer-mediated communication for distance education: an international review of research. Monographs 6. State College, PA: American Center for the Study of Distance Education, Pennsylvania State University.

Willis, J. (1995). A recursive, reflective, instructional design model based on constructivist-interpretivist theory. *Educational Technology, 35*(6), 5–23.

Wriston, W. B. (1992). *The twilight of sovereignty: how the information revolution is transmitting our world*. New York: Charles Scibners & Sons.

Chapter XIII

Communication Needs of Online Students

Werner Beuschel
University of Applied Sciences Brandenburg, Germany

Birgit Gaiser
University of Applied Sciences Brandenburg, Germany

Susanne Draheim
University of Applied Sciences Brandenburg, Germany

ABSTRACT

All learning requires a mix of formal and informal communication. As learning shifts from face-to-face to computer-supported environments, explicit support of informal communication is crucial. An assessment of the formal and informal aspects of communication in Web-based learning environments is provided. The current focus on supporting the formal aspects of communication is questioned. The authors hope that this information will further the recognition of organizational and technical support of informal communication in Web-based education as an issue of prime importance.

INTRODUCTION

Students as well as faculty members, tutors, mentors, or administrators, need to communicate to be able to cooperate well. This holds for face-to-face as well as computer-supported learning environments. Web-based learning environments, where computer support is an ubiquitous element allowing access to learning material around the world, the element of computer-mediated communication (CMC) becomes more important, as face-to-face contacts are reduced or absent. While this argument seems obvious, one important aspect is often neglected. As anyone can state from their own experience, learning usually encompasses a mix of formal and informal communication. Beyond the ever-growing exchange of formal content, like task-related files or data on schedules, the opportunity of informal communication appears increasingly essential for the successful pursuit of online studies.

The value of informal communication seems to be manifold, though not always obvious. It may help students to get a quicker grasp of nonformal requirements during studies, provide opportunities to find fellow students or friends, and, beyond the framework of serious learning, enable contacts to potential partners in pastimes like sports or games. In Web-based learning environments, students and their teachers are usually separated in time and space. Thus, what is lacking is the easy everyday exchange of social cues known from brick-and-mortar institutions and present in traditional environments.

Furthermore, additional technical requirements coming along with Web-based education (WBE) may create frustration if no quick exchange is fostered (cf. Hara & Kling, 1999). Isolation instead of motivation may thus become a hallmark of online classes, impeding successful learning. All these potential deficits are apt to diminish the motivation of online students, thereby endangering online learning success. As a consequence, we plead to put emphasis on support and integration of informal communication in Web-based learning environments.

Though support of communication is a frequent topic in the discussion of learning environments, the focus is generally on their technical aspects (e.g., Communications of the ACM, 1996; Kock et al., 2001; Malaga, 2002). Research on group processes in general, though, provides interesting hints as to our topic. In a recent paper, Cummings et al. investigated the value of online relationships from a social viewpoint (2002). Their findings "... suggest that computer-mediated communication, and in particular email, is less valuable for building and sustaining close social relationships than face-to-face contact and telephone conversations..." (Cummings et al., 2002, p.103). In a similar note, Mortensen and Hinds stated that conflict in groups may increase with physical distance (2001). "Proximity also allows for informal, spontaneous interactions which are either no longer feasible or occur more slowly when teammates are accessible only by email, phone, or videoconference..." (Mortensen & Hinds, 2001, p. 3). They agree with other investigations "...that informal interactions serve to strengthen social ties" (Mortensen & Hinds, 2001, p. 3).

Taken together, the findings in the literature as well as our own experience suggest that communication aspects are generally undervalued in computer-supported learning environments. Thus, to find out more about potential needs for communication support in WBE, we propose to start by questioning the underlying theories and assumptions in order to assess experiences from learning situations. To start with, we provide a short overview of our research background and describe the structure of this chapter.

Research and Project Background

Our research group, named "New Forms of Teaching and Learning," has been exploring organizational, methodological, and technical issues related to computer-supported teaching and learning since 1994, when the group was established. We drew insights from a number of projects, design studies, as well as evaluations and analyses (Beuschel, 1998). Much of the empirical background for the experience presented in this chapter is provided by the German Federal Project "Virtual University of Applied Sciences" (VFH), with which the authors have been involved since its beginning. Within this project, we represent one of a number of research and development groups at 12 German universities. We are trusted with one of the primary tasks in the project, the coordination of efforts on new forms of Web-based teaching and learning (see the homepage: www.vfh.fh-brandenburg.de/).

Running from 1999 to 2003, the project's main goal is to fully implement various online curricula, which are to be self-sustainable after the project funding ends. The curricula are labeled Media Informatics and Industrial Business Engineering. The three-year bachelor course of Media Informatics started in October 2001, to be followed by a consecutive two-year master course. About 70 online modules containing the learning material in German are being developed. Almost all students currently enrolled are professionals working full- or part-time, most of them in Germany, some also abroad. A consortium, built from a subset of the project consortium's universities, is marketing the Web-based learning modules developed by the project (cf. www.oncampus.de).

Structure of the Chapter

Subsequent to the introduction, in "Current Assumptions," we explore learning theories as to their implications for computer-mediated communication in WBE. The first goal is to show that a gap exists between theoretical constructs and practical demands, with regard to communication needs. We investigate cognitive and social aspects of communication and name deficits in online learning support. We borrow the notion of "awareness" from the field of Computer-Supported Cooperative Work (CSCW) in order to expand the scope of the analysis. "From Face-to-Face to Virtual Space," emphasizes the innovative and challenging aspects of online communication from a practical and a theoretical perspective. We provide examples of how current scenarios try to cope with the needs and criticize shortcomings. The chapter also describes a number of "Experiences with Communication Support." We distinguish three scenarios: synchronous, mixed synchronous, and asynchronous (labeled hybrid), and multilevel. A fourth subsection summarizes the experiences. The fifth and last section concludes with a general summary and suggestions for future research.

CURRENT ASSUMPTIONS OF COMPUTER-MEDIATED COMMUNICATION IN ONLINE LEARNING

With the development and introduction of new media into education during the 1980s and 1990s, issues of computer support of teaching and learning situations were reintroduced into the academic discussion. Increased degrees of freedom were seen with regard to the structuring of spatially and temporally independent teaching and learning situations. The development of a new theoretical basis—the constructivist understanding of learning—also revived academic interest. Because constructivism is cited in almost every approach to WBE, we start out with a short critique of its basic assumptions and supplement it with the concept of self-organized learning.

Constructivism in Learning

Constructivism takes as its starting point the issue of "inert knowledge." This term designates the lack of practical applicability of traditionally acquired knowledge. It was observed that students often acquire knowledge they cannot apply to the solution of practical problems (Gräsel et al., 1997, p. 5).

By contrast, constructivist approaches conceive learning not as the mere internalization of content. The constructivist comprehension of learning includes an understanding, by means of the individual's active construction processes within mental models, of the involved interrelations as well as the relevant context of the learning matter. "Learners construct meaning from the material studied by processing it through existing mental structures and then retaining it in long-term memory where it remains available for further processing and possible reconstruction" (Alavi, 1994, p. 161). The construction and transformation of mental models result in a deeper understanding of the issues involved and guarantee, via the transfer of the acquired contents, the applicability of knowledge to practical or analogous situations. The specific character of transfer finds expression in the reconstruction under different conditions. Learning in the sense of construction does not refer solely to knowledge, but also refers to the context and situation-bound relevance. The consequence resulting from these assumptions is generally seen in the posing of application-oriented problems similar to those encountered in real life.

In addition, proponents of constructivist approaches conceive knowledge as the result of construction processes performed by individuals. The concept of knowledge generally covers the sum of information on a certain field that is fixed in human memory. Knowledge is regarded as being tied to the individual and inseparable from the act of learning and "[...] is principally bound to situations" (Gruber et al., 1995, p. 170).

Due to their linkage to specific situations or persons—as postulated by constructivist theory—active and, in particular, individual processes of model formation elude generalizing reflection. Constructivists decline to formulate laws that govern learning processes, claiming that learners can only be provided with adequate conditions that allow stimulation or support active and constructive learning processes.

Initially, hypermedia technologies were regarded as the perfect means for implementing constructivist ideals. Today, the Internet and its various services are favored as the ideal working and learning environment. While this extension of the approach demands support of communication processes, the use of media isolates learners in any case, in particular, when structuring spatially and temporally independent learning situations. From the constructivist point of view, it remains largely an open question how social and cooperative learning arrangements should be methodically supported. The mere provision of a technical environment will not result in the emergence of cooperative processes. Learners should be provided with a comprehensible reason for cooperation.

Many design proposals for online learning environments claim that their goals are based on constructivist assumptions. When such projects are implemented, however, the requirements that result from a strictly constructivist approach are frequently of no consequence. Thus, we cannot fail to observe that in many projects, explicit claims and concepts are worlds apart from their actual implementations. This suggests that in today's academic discussion on computer-supported learning, constructivist ideals in a way constitute a dogma, while traditional concepts of teaching and learning still govern the imagination of the architects of learning systems.

Apart from that gap between claims and achievement, the constructivist learning concept is criticized for being deficient in several ways. As constructivism takes as its sole starting point the present market situation and the demands being made on labor, it also confines the range and validity of learning situations. In addition, under the constructivist perspective, the learning situation is mostly disregarded. "There is (almost) always a gap between computer-based learning environments and reality and therefore a lack of authenticity" (Gruber et al., 1996, p. 181).

The constructivist learning concept does not appear to be sufficient as the sole basis of a concept of computer-supported learning. Therefore, we will widen the scope of our investigation to include the notion of self-organized learning.

Self-Organized Learning and Cooperation/Collaboration

The concept of self-organized learning refers to various basic values and assumptions in formulating its objectives. The concept's central hypothesis consists of the belief in responsibility and autonomy of human beings who, by pursuing autonomous learning activities on their own responsibility, develop independence of thought and action. Accordingly, the learner's competence of self-determined study should be developed. In addition, what is crucially important for problem solving are social competencies, which should also be developed with the help of the concept of self-organized learning. First, communicative skills and insights into the nature of conflict and criticism as well as the ability to deal with these issues play a decisive part. Other objectives are the reinforcement of the self-confidence and self-awareness of the learners, who through self-organized learning should be prepared for lifelong learning.

According to Knoll, self-organized learning takes place when the learners exercise decisive control over the learning situation, i.e., when they formulate and structure the objectives, the contents, the methods, the environment, or the organizational forms and processes of their learning activities (1999, p. 71). It is the learners who independently determine, define, and apply the elements to be employed in this self-organized process. Moreover, the learners identify their needs as to the implementation of the learning process and any obstacles hindering their gratification, and they organize the means for surmounting the latter. The parties involved become aware of themselves as learners and explore to what extent the self-imposed objective has been attained. Thus, a reflection on and an assessment of one's self-organized learning processes take place (Knoll, 1999). The learners determine the basic conditions and the determining factors of the learning situation. It is the learners who control their internal and external learning activities according to the concept of conscious, planned, and intentional learning.

Consequently, the idea of self-organized learning brings about a definite shift of the dominant role from the teacher to the learner, as the learners take all decisions pertinent to the learning process. Thus, any reduction of heteronomy by the same token means an increase in autonomy and emancipation and, as such, owns a sociopolitical dimension. In this context, the idea of self-controlled learning is to be understood as an ideal involving increased self-determination as to learning goals, time, place, study contents, learning methods, and learning partners, as well as increased self-assessment of learning success.

The concept of self-organized learning constitutes a more comprehensive approach than that of constructivist learning. However, both approaches overlap to a great degree and are descendants of the same academic tradition. This becomes particularly evident when one focuses on the concept of learning as an active process and on the action-oriented character of the two approaches. In addition, the concept of self-organized learning puts greater emphasis on humanistic values. It supports the self-determination of the human being, viewed as a personality with thought and conscience, within a pluralist world of ever-increasing opportunities for choice. While constructivism is based on the vision of a "knowledge society," self-organized learning is committed to a "learning society," proposing a culture of participation as the constructive response to rising complexity and increasing demands on labor in today's society (Sembill, 2000, p. 60).

Within the academic discourse, a general agreement there prevails that cooperative learning has positive repercussions on learning success. The fact of a collective agreement on the goals to be reached by a learner's group is considered to be advantageous. At the same time, the individual ability of each learner regarding cooperative work should be maintained (Slavin, 1992, p. 97; Slavin, 1994). The essential advantage of cooperative learning is seen in the collective construction of knowledge. This results in the inclusion of additional knowledge elements and of different perspectives. The articulation and disputation of different points of view are supposed to trigger deeper-reaching assimilation processes essential for cognitive learning (Gräsel et al., 1997, p. 5).

In order to implement computer-supported cooperative learning, technological foundations have to be laid, content-related starting points for collective work have to be provided, and a viable solution for the assessment of individual success has to be found. This means that technologies should be provided that support the cooperation and communication between academic teachers and students as well as among learners. On first glimpse, computer-aided learning environments provide more degrees of freedom than traditional learning arrangements. Ironically, the gain in flexibility in time and space is accompanied by novel rigidities, namely, new coordination requirements for organizing learning. Learners suddenly face an increased demand of self-organized action in order to get together in virtual space.

On the other hand, all of these activities leave data traces in the learning environment. So, in Web-based learning environments, it is easy to collect data on student activities without letting students know. Learning could be subject to even stricter control than in traditional settings. As a consequence, for our aim of supporting self-organization, attention has to be paid to the aspect of how control is exerted in communication channels provided to the students. In addition, content-related starting points for cooperation among the students have to be created and supported by appropriate structuring. This constitutes an argument in favor of group work among students.

As a last point with regard to self-organized learning, it should be mentioned that project methodology, training companies, simulation games, or role play should be utilized, as they are the classical tools of teaching and learning methods in action-oriented teaching. Moreover, students should be assigned appropriate tasks as a basis for cooperative learning activities.

The Importance of Formal and Informal Communication in Learning

The support of cooperative student activities presupposes the analysis of each party's communication needs. We ponder various aspects of communication, considering if they could act as parts of a frame of reference for Web-based teaching and learning.

Following the distinction made by Kraut et al. (1990, p. 145ff), we designate formal communication as planned and intentional, and informal communication as opportunistic and spontaneous. Bismarck et al. (1999, p. 6) identify further characteristics: factual and relational levels, informal language, and missing documentation.

As for the consequences of informal communication processes, Kraut et al. (1990, p. 145ff) list three possibilities. They distinguish between the task-related communicative function that supports problem solving, the social function that gratifies the demand for human contact at the workplace, and the dysfunctional function that may degenerate into a "gossip factory."

Communication covers cognitive and social aspects. We will discuss both sides, though social aspects appear more important in our view, due to their proximity to the concepts of self-organization and informal exchange.

Cognitive aspects subsume the task-related function of informal communication. In contrast to formal communication, this variety of informal communication establishes itself outside of the company's formal channels of communication. Well-known examples are conversations at the office's photocopier or during sports events. Here, hierarchical levels may be disregarded and departmental boundaries crossed when, so to speak, a shortcut is taken for discussing work-related issues.

Interests related to social needs lend themselves to such interpretations as "familiarity with and appreciation of the work of co-workers, the conveying of the organization culture etc., basis for the assessment of other members of the organization, clarified relations within the team" (Kraut et al., 1990, p. 156).

Recent research on work environments in the areas of human-computer interaction (HCI) and computer supported cooperative work (CSCW) focuses on the importance of informal communication for groups and project teams. It has emerged that a major part of informal communication takes place in the immediate working environment. The study of working groups has also revealed that the task-related and the social functions of informal communication are closely intertwined. Of fundamental importance is the observation that, in virtual space as well, informal communication gratifies not only social needs, but above all, may create motivation for collectively performing distributed work, thus constituting a major pillar of "learning as a social process." Social processes only make sense if embedded in groups: "We need to support processes involved in the formation and maintenance of groups: finding others, establishing channels for formal and informal communication, and developing trust and group identity" (Mark, 1999, p. 3).

For the domain of media-bound or Web-based communication, at present, it can be maintained that, in most cases, informal communication is severely hindered. To compound matters, current approaches to computer-aided learning mostly continue to focus on purely formal objectives, while by and large disregarding the social components of learning processes.

In order to grasp the importance and the possibilities of informal communication in Web-based environments, one may start by concentrating on its general conditions and characteristics. The first issue that comes to mind is the quest for situation-related features characterizing informal communication situations.

A first answer could state the emergence of intimacy and privacy or, thus, a dissociation of informal groups from the exterior, the "perceived" public, as it were. The opposite is found for chatrooms and newsgroups with unrestricted access, an observation that might explain the limited utilization of these subspaces. Next, the question arises how to structure these communication situations socially so as to provide maximum motivation for cooperation. Of crucial importance is the attempt to transfer into virtual space the conditions that characterize the face-to-face situation, i.e., the effort to achieve a straightforward, direct, transparent, and, if possible, synchronous exchange. However, notwithstanding its inherently ephemeral and dynamic nature, this exchange will be subject to recording and, in part, to textual fixation. We have discussed this fact above as having severe negative implications for self-organization in learning.

Deficits of Communication Support in Online Learning

In summary, we can state that early approaches to computer-supported forms of teaching and learning were frequently insufficient, insofar as the focus was laid upon formal and content-related aspects much more than on social demands of student learning. Obviously, the social aspects do not add to the formal learning activities as easily when the transition takes place from face-to-face to virtual learning. But, the support of social aspects in learning, and of informal communication as part thereof, is acknowledged as an important ingredient of computer-supported learning, thus motivating students in the process.

If we acknowledge the definition of informal communication as given by Fish et al. (1990, p. 2ff), it seems problematic to get an accurate notion of the peripheral, unplanned elements of formal activities. Informal communication does not lend itself per se to planning, which characterizes the inherent contradiction. This poses the challenge of the postulated necessity to provide means for informal exchanges. Nevertheless, informal activities should be enabled under all circumstances, as learning comprises formal as well as informal components. Mere access to communication tools, though, is no warranty for productive cooperation and ongoing informal communication.

What would an appropriate technology for the support of informal communication look like? There is no straight answer to this question, as there is always an inherent contradiction between the unplanned and informal aspects and the explicit necessities of technical support. To warrant the required intimacy of informal student exchange, the tools have to be controlled by the users, the students. This presupposes a separation of control functions from the learning management system. Control, maintenance, and supervision of the informal platforms should be left to the students. Thus, communication processes can develop that are private and distinctly sheltered from access by third parties. Another requirement is that the tools should be designed so as to be adaptable to variant access rights and provide their users with the opportunity to act as hosts to communication sessions. To indicate an example and counterexample, newsgroups do not exhibit these characteristics, while an instant messaging system like ICQ (an acronym for "I seek you") allows much more elaborate self-organization of communicative situations.

In addition to informal exchanges, spontaneous activities should be enabled. But, nonplanned cooperative actions in virtual space are possible only when the system can provide some reconstitution of what is known as "awareness." Awareness, in a common sense, the conscious knowledge about a situation including the other person(s) involved, is defined in the research areas of HCI and CSCW as the ability "to maintain and constantly update a sense of our social and physical context" (Pedersen & Sokoler, 1997, p. 51). To cite an example, the awareness feature would tell us who is online at any moment and who could be approached: awareness is "knowing what is going on" (Endsley, 1995, p. 36). It allows the individual to comprehend the current situation within an environment and to adapt her or his behavior accordingly. This presupposes that the events occurring in the environment are perceptible. At the same time, the individual needs to have the ability to perceive and discern the environment.

Information on awareness can be represented in different ways. Instant messaging systems like ICQ or Microsoft Messenger use a "contact list," while other systems employ spatial metaphors, figures (cf. Teamwave), or avatars (cf. KICK). Without this support for identifying a situation, informal communication is severely restricted, as without the knowledge that other parties are around, spontaneous contact is impossible.

FROM FACE-TO-FACE TO VIRTUAL SPACE: THE EVOLUTION OF NEW COMMUNICATION NEEDS

In order to specify "new" communication needs, such as those arising within Web-based learning environments, we must distinguish between a number of conceptually different models. On the one hand, there are spatially and temporally uncoupled scenarios favoring individualized learning. In these cases, communication support plays only a minor role. On the other hand, there are concepts that claim to provide computer-mediated support for face-to-face situations.

Between the poles of these didactic concepts, various hybrids exist. In order to provide a more tangible idea, we will present and discuss some scenarios below.

Examples of Communication Needs in Learning Situations

Many conventional universities provide their students with such informal spaces as cafeterias or open lawn spaces, and periodically stage various informal events. Pertinent examples are university sports events and welcoming parties for first-year students. However, occasions for informal exchange arise also at the fringes of formal activities, such as in tutoring groups or even during formal activities, for instance, the chatter students sometimes engage in during lectures.

The mapping of informal spaces within the framework of space- and, possibly, time-independent scenarios seems to pose problems and is, for the most part, disregarded. Examples for its realization and implementation within the framework of online education are sparse. The majority of present approaches to a large extent simply ignore the social needs of virtual learners. In some cases, students are provided with virtual spaces for social interaction, such as chatrooms or even a "virtual cafeteria," while, however, the focus is on imparting knowledge. Taking into account the varying online behavior and different user habits of virtual students, to this end, mostly asynchronous concepts have been developed and implemented as newsgroups. Thus, for instance, on the home page of a virtual university, newsgroups on various subjects are bundled to form a virtual cafeteria. Some chatrooms are provided, as well (cf. http://virtuelle-uni.fernuni-hagen.de).

Also, in learning space management systems such as Web CT (see www.Webct.com) and Blackboard (see www.blackboard.com), attempts to provide support for informal needs can be encountered. Such systems often provide students with the option to create their own home pages, where they can present themselves. In addition, the Blackboard system includes a chatroom. However, the use of chatrooms is technically tied to formal aspects and not to self-organization, as chats are bound to individual courses and executable only while a course is being held.

Formal and Informal Communication in Transition

Formal communication in computer-aided settings is mostly implemented through hypertexts, video recordings of lectures delivered by professors, email for counseling and exams, or videoconferences. Conspicuous within virtual environments are the heavily reduced proportion of spoken language and the preponderance of textual content. What continues to pose problems is the existence of drastic limitations as to the transport and exchange of socially relevant information.

As in media-supported environments, situations for the informal exchange between individuals do not arise automatically—the construct of awareness is of crucial importance (see also the section on "Deficits of Communication Support"). Cooperation presupposes the faculty to act in a given situation as well as the reciprocal perception of individuals, the discernment of their field of action as well as that of objects to be observed or processed, and the perception of the actions that are being performed.

When applied to cooperative computer-aided work, the concept of awareness conjures up the idea that in an electronic setting, too, changes in the environment and their causes should be perceptible. These changes resulting from actions and their consequences have to be perceived to be emanating from and ascribable to a specific actor (Pankoke-Babatz, 1998, p. 5).

In a setting incorporating an awareness feature, communication can be more effective and oriented toward understanding, because the common context—the "grounding" (cf. Clark & Brennan, 1991)—is more transparent, authentic, and appears to be "closer" in a subjective way.

When the involved parties are not simultaneously present at a given location, those who visit this place at a later point in time should be able to discern what has happened in the meantime, while persons that cooperate at different real locations need a shared virtual working environment displaying awareness information. For group work, awareness means that the preconditions for situation-oriented action should be assured, that an understanding of the activities of the other group members and of the general conditions governing those actions will be created, and that the context for one's own actions will be constituted. CSCW authors discriminate between these various ideas of awareness and subsume under the concept of "social orientation" the problem of attaining information, crucial in cooperative learning processes, on the other members of the learning group. This includes knowledge of the parties presently involved in the learning process (social awareness), on the functions or roles assigned to each participant (role identity), as well as on the overall structure of the learning group (group structure). Thus, awareness, as an informational basis, makes it easier for groups to organize their cooperative processes and, consequently, should form the foundation for their collective work (Dourish & Bellotti, 1992, p. 107ff).

There arises the question of how this goal can be attained in virtual space. In shared editing systems, awareness can be provided, e.g., through audio or video systems (Dourish & Bellotti, 1992), while instant messaging systems such as ICQ signal the event of a party listed as a personal contact going online. There are several options for setting the user status, which also can be defined so as to select only certain contacts. This extra information provides clues as to the present situation, in particular, as to each contact's readiness to communicate. For instance, the status messages "free for chat," "occupied," or "away" signal whether and to what extent the user is ready to engage in cooperative activities, so that undesired attempts to establish communication can be avoided.

EXPERIENCES WITH COMMUNICATION SUPPORT IN WEB-BASED EDUCATION

Scenarios used in distance learning are frequently transferred directly from traditional learning. In some cases, only the distribution mode is changed. Distance teachers usually focus on organizational and cognitive issues, the formal aspects in our dichotomy, as they are used to doing while teaching face-to-face. So, it comes as no surprise that in most current projects and activities, only little space is left for informal communication.

Over the last years, our research team conducted several studies involving computer-supported environments. In particular, we investigated the utilization of videoconference systems, the adoption of an instant messaging system by large numbers of students, and the integration of online teaching modules into Web-based environments. These three areas form the background for the following analysis.

A Synchronous Scenario: Videoconferencing

Videoconferencing within learning scenarios has been mainly described within the framework of classroom projects. In a videoconference, the lecture is transmitted between usually two or, in rare cases, several locations. The main thrust of these projects is economic rationalization. No space is provided for informal exchange between the two locations, but, compared to other forms of media support, remote students can form a much more immediate impression of the lecturer.

From our point of view, these projects are not suitable to support informal communication. But, some projects with videoconferencing within cooperative learning scenarios were carried out. These projects can fulfill the assumptions connected with the technology, namely, "[...] that the ability of two people to see as well as to hear one another in conversations is valuable" (Sellen, 1995, p. 403).

Videoconferencing gives rise to a major proportion of informal communication. Making jokes and sharing laughter form a substantial part of activities of student work groups supported by audiovisual means. What seems to be of crucial importance for the emergence of informal communication situations is the simultaneousness of communication support, the ephemeral character of audio-supported communication as opposed to textual forms, and the perceived public character of a communication situation.

Through videoconferencing, students gain the impression of better knowing their remote fellow students, while the actual information they get on their counterparts is just minimal. In interviews, the students declared that audiovisual transmission helped them assess their partners more easily. The use of videoconferencing systems and the transmission of the opposite number's voice and image obviously helps to trigger identification and group-formation processes and to motivate the students for common work. This has positive repercussions on the students' group work. Identical results on videoconferencing were found in the field of CSCW. Fish et al. stated that "[...] the technology can provide, to a degree, an increased sense of shared space between remote coworkers" (Fish et al., 1990, p. 9). However, the spontaneous establishment of communication via videoconferencing is hampered by high expenditures for technical equipment and the required infrastructure.

Formal content elements, too, play a major role in videoconferencing scenarios. In this context especially, the function of application sharing and the whiteboard are suitable for visualizing the common knowledge within the student work groups and for supporting discussions. In addition, this helped the students to orient themselves on the cognitive level. Utilization of the videoconferencing system results in an increased binding force of arrangements. Face to face, the students commit themselves to tackle a certain workload, and partly, this commitment is reinforced by the subsequent emailing of the session's minutes. But also, conflicts such as sloppy emailing discipline are addressed during videoconferences.

However, videoconferencing is less suitable for imparting educational content. As the initial pilot trials in this field demonstrated, it makes little sense to use videoconferencing for the regular transmission of conventional lectures. For the students, the technology forms an extra barrier preventing them from active participation and from making substantial contributions to a lecture. The deficiencies inherent in frontal lecturing are considerably amplified by the technology involved. Therefore, such didactic approaches do not make much sense.

Apart from group cooperation processes and the support of formal communication situations, videoconferencing systems can be meaningfully employed for counseling situations. Virtual office hours, where students can consult the professor in real time, are an example in point.

A Hybrid Scenario: Instant Messaging Systems

Some years ago, we accidentally became aware of the phenomenon of the "mass adoption" of instant messaging systems by students at some European and American universities. In our case, the ICQ system was the subject of student activities (cf. Beuschel & Gaiser, 2002). While the usage of instant messaging systems nowadays appears quite ordinary, especially with users of the big commercial portals, at the time, we became interested in the issue of their suitability for learning environments. Our account departs from the hybrid characteristics: instant messaging systems can be used in synchronous as well as in asynchronous modes. Thus, their utilization can be easily adapted to the user's immediate learning situation, as sometimes one wishes to remain undisturbed, while at other times, one prefers to have company. It should be noted, however, that instant messaging systems are usually but one element of the overall architecture of computer-supported learning environments. They seem to play the role of an intermediary component. Nevertheless, designers of learning environments should be called upon to incorporate their advantageous features into a learning space management system. We will discuss below some of these features and their relevance for informal communication.

When Instant Messaging Systems are employed in learning scenarios, a clear preponderance of informal communication content is observed (Beuschel & Gaiser, 2002). When questioned, the students maintain that this form of exchange is essential for a positive social work atmosphere within each group. The formal or content-oriented exchange within the student work groups consists essentially of the reading of texts authored by the remote group members and mostly exchanged via electronic mail or a Web-based file server.

An analysis of the conversation records reveals some instances of formal explanatory processes. The students explain to each other the functioning and the handling of the media employed for cooperation support as well as the theoretical concepts underlying their collective work.

From the analysis of cooperation between various student groups at two German universities during the 2001/2002 winter term, where the instant messaging system ICQ was used, five clusters of topics could be identified (cf. Draheim et al., 2001):

- Appointments, e.g., for discussions or video
- Feedback, e.g., on organizational agreements

- Subject matters, e.g., brainstorming for structuring task solutions
- Informal matters, e.g., individual exchanges on the learning situation
- Technical problems, e.g., systems failure

Comparing the weight of the individual issues, it became obvious that the focus of the topics was on informal communication, with the topics "appointments" and "feedback" playing a major role. Relatively unimportant seemed the item of "subject matters." Mention should also be made of the overall architecture of the learning situation, because apart from the instant messaging system, a variety of cooperative tools was used, such as Teamwave, BSCW, MS-Netmeeting, or Mindmap (see URLs in the references).

As a result of the analysis, we emphasize the importance of the informal processes for cooperative learning. This shows up independently of all differentiation of subject matters. Here, conflict resolution and identity finding within virtual groups are pertinent indicators. The analysis showed that besides the task-related informal communication, which was utilized to structure and organize learning situations, there existed a second tier of informal exchange, the peer-to-peer contact, which even could be called "communication among friends." This level enabled group feeling to develop as well as provided an opportunity to communicate about personal conditions during the course. With instant messaging, so students claimed, it was much easier to relate situations than with videoconferences, where usually several participants are present. Videoconferences were also perceived as forcing people into a technology-centered behavior, whereas instant messaging was labeled as "intimate."

In general, the analysis shows that students perceive instant messaging as being an easily exploitable opportunity for establishing contacts and exchanging information about the current state of classwork. The key labels describing the advantages were "intimate," "spontaneous," and "uncomplicated."

When an instant messaging system is employed, content elements related to planning and organizing the group's work process are important items to be communicated. Obviously, those students who are susceptible to use computer-supported communication more readily than others make attempts to also use the instant messaging systems for exchanges about organizational and subject-related questions.

A considerable advantage of chat programs results in limited expenditure for technical equipment, ease of handling, and the system's wide dissemination. In contrast with videoconferencing, these systems can be used for the spontaneous establishment of virtual contacts.

A Multilevel Scenario: Online Modules

This section is based on an analysis of online modules developed within the framework of the German Federal project "Virtual University of Applied Sciences." The study accompanied the first semester of an online university course in "Media Informatics," initially tested with students during the winter semester 2001/2002. Test versions of the modules are accessible at http://www.oncampus.de/.

The investigation focused mainly on the didactical and conceptual support of communication and cooperation between students and teachers or tutors, i.e., less on the subject-oriented assessment of the modules. This approach was hampered, however, by the current practice of the institution that entrusts the structuring of terms and the counseling of students to an association of several (presently seven) universities. This means that students enroll at one of the consortia's "brick-and-mortar" universities, where they are listed as ordinary students. They study online along the offered course of Web-based lectures and exercises. On three or four weekends, they attend counseling office hours, write their test papers, and take exams. All of the involved universities use the same learning space management system, namely, Blackboard (http://www.bb.vfh.de).

General and university-specific modules differ slightly in that the general modules provide the basic concept and the didactic adaptation of the subject field (aspects: imparting of knowledge, presentation of exercises, provision of help features), which subsequently are adapted by each university to the needs of their counseling modalities (aspects here are compulsory classes, care for students, consultation hours, exams, group formation).

Within the modules "Introduction to Informatics" and "Mathematics I/II," the "text-book-translated-to-hypertext" model prevails. As their general versions are limited to suggesting the formation of working groups and to providing a number of mandatory group tasks, the organizing of all cooperation processes is once more delegated to teachers and tutors or to the students. More revealing as to the issue of cooperation than the modules, was a visit to the teaching space's Discussion Board. Here, the general forum is held, where questions are asked asynchronously, appointments are made, and propositions for improvement are posted. It is to be suspected, however, that students also use informal, university-specific channels of communication, which we could not easily trace, as the students are dispersed over a wide geographic area.

Some of the modules stand out as integrating communicative and cooperative aspects. They are discussed here in greater detail.

Online Module "Info Physics"

This module's most prominent feature is that it provides the student with comprehensive means for orientation in the form of a sophisticated navigation toolbar, comprising, apart from the Table of Contents, an interactive course map. The map allows students to customize the module to a large extent. Additionally, the module is conspicuous for its didactic presentation that is committed to the principle of self-organization (as an invitation to take the initiative on one's own). Among other things, this comprises an introductory explanation of the module concept. Not only the handling of the module is treated, but also the basic teaching and learning concept is extensively treated. For instance, the "hints" for the course of studies expressly invite communication and work in teams. They refer the student to the navigation tools that enable learners to access, from any page, the communication zone of the Blackboard learning management system. Thus, the concepts of self-organization and teamwork are supported, underlining the assumption that isolated study will not yield optimal learning success.

Online Module "Virtual Preparatory Course"

This module's learning goal consists of imparting the skills that are crucial for virtual studies. This comprises a comprehensive introduction to the Internet, instructions for the use of various tools such as email, FTP, Telnet, newsgroups, HTML, Internet search, and synchronous communication. In addition, learners are instructed how to interact with virtual communities and to conjointly study with them.

The module has been conceived as a synchronous, location-independent lesson for learning groups of approximately 20 persons. Exercises are in part organized as group tasks. While individual study is possible, it is not encouraged, as it is regarded as less than optimal. However, the module may be studied online or offline, an awareness bar providing orientation as course number and designation, log-in date, study term, and status.

Online Module "Information Management"

This module aims at combining the issues of dealing with complex tasks and elaborating solutions in the context of virtual groups. The material is arranged in two distinct sections, the first of which provides hypertext units for self-organized learning covering basic concepts and elements of the substance matter. In the second section, a selection of complex tasks in the form of case studies is offered. By their structure, requirements, and volume, they are to be tackled by two to five students who are to form a virtual group.

Comparison of the Online Modules and Performance Issues

A comparison of these modules clearly shows that they are based on two widely differing didactic concepts that try to transpose into virtual space the ideas of communication and cooperation. The Info Physics module mainly seeks to initiate learning processes and to create the necessary general conditions and a stable informational foundation, coupled with an explicit invitation to self-organization. In contrast, the Virtual Preparatory Course departs from a traditional face-to-face situation characterized by direct interaction of students and teachers.

From our viewpoint, the concept of guidance to self-organization is more appropriate. It seems to more fully comply with the demand for increased flexibility of learning, while also catering to the needs for social and informal communication.

According to preliminary reports on the starting phase in Winter 2001/2002, the authors developed a structure for facilitating and supporting models for the online modules (Arnold et al., 2002). What stands out in the first findings of how the modules performed was the high appreciation expressed as to continuous guidance of online students (Arnold et al., 2002). The acceptance turned out to be much higher than initially expected at the start of the course. As a response, additional learning space management systems were introduced at individual universities. At Brandenburg, for instance, we used, in addition to Blackboard, the Netucate system (see http://www.netucate.de) with good success. Netucate provides only office hours and online seminars, which evolved from the demand during the semester. During these hours, task-related and general questions remaining unsolved from self-organized learning sessions are dealt with. The system represents audio communication and application sharing using a whiteboard and supports presentation areas on the monitor. These are usually run in synchronous mode.

The learning space management system Blackboard (BB), for instance, used throughout the Virtual University project to display the online modules, does not include an awareness supporting function. According to our initial findings during the 2001/2002 pilot semester of the online curriculum, computer-mediated communication works primarily via mail and newsgroups in the so-called Communication Board of Blackboard. Not astonishingly, this is not helpful for the initiation of group processes. As a remedy, the project architects presently discuss the implementation of further support. Several systems are being investigated, which could possibly support virtual communities: Teamwave, Teamspace, and Groove (see reference list for URLs). Any of these can be used in a complementary manner for cooperation, coordination, and communication, thus enabling synchronous awareness.

Lessons Learned

There does not seem to exist any single online teaching and learning model that would be ideally suited to all conceivable situations. So, each scenario should be analyzed with regard to its specific needs for communication and cooperation and should be supported accordingly. Different teaching and learning situations require different forms of support. It is necessary to take into account the specific features of a student group, the knowledge to be imparted, the attained phase in the teaching process, and the communicative situation. In addition, what is of paramount importance is a technical infrastructure providing options for the integration of various technical media.

From a critical point of view, it might be suggested that the much-acclaimed independence of time and space, which is at the basis of every concept and proposal in online learning, is successively taken back with the increasing use of synchronizing systems as mentioned above. Without prematurely claiming general validity, we consider the current phenomenon as an indicator for our hypothesis that social context and opportunities for communication are decisive for orientation, motivation, and, thereby, the learning success of online students. All the amenities, combined with the temporal and spatial flexibility, may not make us forget that social and cooperative processes *must* also be enabled in Web-based learning environments. In this way, we support the claim of putting technology into its place, which means under the primacy of pedagogy and teaching methodology.

The overriding social importance of informal communication as an invigorating element of media-based or "virtual" exchange has been strongly emphasized and justified in great detail. On the other hand, its technical support gives rise to some contradictions that hamper compliance with a comprehensive claim for didactic and strategic integration into concepts of virtual teaching and learning.

On one hand, informal communication thrives on its spontaneity and absence of planning; on the other, it is characterized by lack of documentation—two characteristics that in a computer-based approach can only be implemented to a limited extent. Rather, technical support always is the first step toward standardization, a process that transforms informal communication situations into formalized procedures. A pertinent example is the recording of all transmitted data, even in informally structured programs such as ICQ, a fact that clearly contradicts the definition of the concept of informal communication we initially introduced.

In addition, the sphere of the informal, such as that encountered in student work groups, should remain a protected space unable to be entered by any nonmember without the group members being aware. Thus, the informal action space should evade the control by teachers and, consequently, the teachers' assessment criteria. Within the framework of a didactic concept committed to the paradigm of self-organization, this claim may need to be investigated more intensively. For as a consequence, at this place, important insights for cooperation in work groups may escape the faculty's assessment of group work.

How can we find a productive solution to this apparent paradox between desirable technical support and those characteristics of informal communication that are irreconcilable with that very same technical support? To begin with, it is necessary to perceive the technical platforms provided for informal purposes, such as chatrooms, newsgroups, or virtual cafeterias, as facilities that the students can structure to their own gusto. The spaces should be adaptable to their individual needs, thereby rescuing these spaces from the fate of falling into disuse. A fate, however, that may also be brought about by the lack of session chairing functions or of instruction for use. Again, further research is needed to distinguish the fine line between self-organization and control meant to be supportive.

As a conceivable solution of this dilemma, from the beginning, it might be postulated that the hosting of these forums and their integration within the framework of academic courses is eventually to be managed by the students. The final step in a development-application cycle with regard to the specific informal spaces would then be the withdrawal of all teaching staff, so as to assure the protection and privacy of these spaces.

For any constructive approach, we suggest the integration of future users into the conception and design of the learning environments. While user participation in systems design is a widely acknowledged feature now, at least in theory, it seems that with regard to learning environments, it is still wanting.

CONCLUSION

In Web-based education, a gap exists between didactic aspirations and the implementation of teaching scenarios with regard to providing support for formal and informal communication. In particular, there are barely any explicit approaches to integrating informal aspects. Because in many educational institutions the shift to integrating Web-based learning components is strong or still growing, this deficit gets even bigger.

As we have shown by analyzing various teaching and learning scenarios, which combine asynchronous, synchronous, and hybrid communications, there is a substantial demand for communication support. Crucial preconditions for the success of online university courses are the motivation of students and their ability to organize the flexible exchange of ideas and information. The creation of adequate means of communication is also of pivotal importance for the acquisition of social competence, which is to be regarded as an indispensable part of online education. In this respect, there is a lack of both didactic concepts and technical implementations within the framework of the different scenarios. It is not by mere coincidence that the notion of "blended models" is presently attracting attention. The mix of virtual and face-to-face components is hailed in popular journals as a return to more sound principles for building computer-supported learning environments. But, this cannot be a general recipe for automatically resolving communication support needs.

As far as development is concerned, but also with regard to the assessment and evaluation of learning scenarios, there exists a considerable research gap. Due to differences in settings, the speed of technological change, and the frequent lack of comparative scenarios, quantitative results are often hard to translate into constructive approaches. Therefore, researchers in this field should also fall back on qualitative and reconstructive methods such as document analysis, as e.g., chat and interview transcripts may provide deeper insights into group processes.

As a conclusion, substantial demand for research and development can be stated in the field of communication support in general, specifically, as to the inclusion and more extensive support of informal aspects.

REFERENCES

Alavi, M. (1994). Computer mediated collaborative learning: an empirical evaluation. *MIS Quarterly*, June, 159–174.

Arnold, P. (2002). Training of online-facilitators as a key issue in implementing telematic learning. In *Natural and artificial intelligence systems organizations* (NAISO) (Ed.), Proceedings of the International NAISO Congress, "Networked learning in a global environment—challenges and solutions for virtual education," May 1–4, Berlin, ICSC-NAISO Academic Press, Canada/The Netherlands.

Beuschel, W. (1998). Virtual campus: scenarios, obstacles and experiences. In *Proceedings of the thirty-first Hawaii international conference on systems sciences (HICSS'31), Vol. I: Collaboration Systems and Technology Track* (pp. 284–293). Los Alamitos, CA: IEEE Computer Society.

Beuschel, W., & Gaiser, B. (2002). Usage of an instant messaging system in a university learning environment. In *Natural and artificial intelligence systems organizations* (NAISO) (Ed.), Proceedings of the International NAISO Congress, "Networked learning in a global environment—challenges and solutions for virtual education," May 1–4, Berlin, ICSC-NAISO Academic Press, Canada/The Netherlands.

Bismarck, W.-B.v., Bungard, W., & Held, M. (1999). Is informal communication needed, wanted and supported? Lecture at 8th International Conference on Human-Computer-Interaction, Munich.

Clark, H. H., & Brennan, S. E. (1991). Grounding in communication. In L. B. Resnick, J. M. Levine, & S. D. Teasley (Eds.). Perspectives on socially shared cognition. Washington, DC: American Psychological Association.

Communications of the ACM. (1996). Special issue on learner-centered design. *Communications of the ACM, 39*.

Cummings, J. N., Butler, B., & Kraut, R. (2002). The quality of online social relationships. *Communications of the ACM, 45*(7), 103–108.

Dourish, P., & Belotti, V. (1992). Awareness and coordination in shared workspaces. In CSCW '92—Sharing perspectives (pp. 107–114), Toronto, Canada. New York: ACM Press.

Draheim, S., Gaiser, B., & Beuschel, W. (2001). Chat with a friend—zur unterstützenden Wirkung des Kommunikationsprogramms ICQ in studentischer Gruppenarbeit—eine qualitative Fallstudie. In E. Wagner & M. Kindt (Eds.), *Virtueller Campus: Szenarien – Strategien – Studium*, pp. 56-65. Waxmann, Berlin.

Endsley, M. (1995). Towards a theory of situation awareness in dynamic systems. *Human Factors, 37*(1), 32–64.

Fish, R. S., Kraut, R. E., & Chalfonte, B. L. (1990). The video window system in informal communication. *Proceedings of the Conference on Computer Supported Cooperative Work* (pp. 1–11). New York: ACM.

Galegher, J., & Kraut, R. (1990). Computer-mediated communication for intellectual teamwork: a field experiment in group writing. In *Proceedings of the conference of Computer-Supported Cooperative Work*, Los Angeles, CA. New York: ACM.

Gräsel, C. et al. (1997). Lernen mit Computernetzwerken aus konstruktivistischer Perspektive. Unterrichtswissenschaft. *Zeitschrift für Lernforschung, 1*(97), 4–18.

Gruber, H. et al. (1995). Situated learning and transfer. In P. Reimann, & H. Spada (Eds.), *Learning in humans and machines: towards an interdisciplinary learning science* (pp. 168–188). Germany: Universität Freiburg-Psychologisches Institut.

Hara, N., & Kling, R. (1999). Student's frustrations with a Web-based distance education course: a taboo topic in the discourse. Working paper. The Center for Social Informatics, Indiana University, Bloomington, IN; http://www.slis.indiana.edu/CSI/Wp/wp99_01B.html (last accessed June 4, 2002).

Held, M., & von Bismarck, W. -B. (1999). The acceptance and support of informal communications in organizations. In *9th European Congress on Work and Organizational Psychology: Innovations for Work, Organization and Well-Being*, Helsinki.

Knoll, J. (1999). Eigen-Sinn und Selbstorganisation. In *Arbeitsgemeinschaft Qualifikations-Entwicklungs-Management (Hrsg.): Kompetenzentwicklung '99—Argumente einer neuen Lernkultur* (pp. 61–79). Waxmann, Münster.

Kock, N. et al. (2001). E-collaboration: a look at past research and future challenges. *Journal of Systems and Information Technology, 5*(1), 1–9.

Kraut, R. et al. (1990). Informal communication in organisations: form, function and technology. In S. Oskamp, & S. Spacapan (Eds.), *People's reactions to technology in factories, offices and aerospace* (pp. 145–199). Newbury Park.

Malaga, R. A. (2002). Additional methods when using email for teaching. *Communications of the ACM, 45*(8), 25–27.

Mark, G. (1999). Social foundations for collaboration in virtual environments. In T. F. Tschang & T. Della Senta (Eds.), *Access to Knowledge: New Information Technologies and the Emergence of the Virtual University*, pp. 241-263, Amsterdam: Elsevier.

Mortensen, M., & Hinds, P. J. (2001). Conflict and shared identity in geographically distributed teams. *International Journal of Conflict Management, 12*(3), 212–238.

Pankoke-Babatz, U. (1998). Awareness—Spannungsfeld zwischen Beobachter und Beobachteten. D-CSCW 1998, Workshop: Von Groupware zu Groupaware, (pp. 5–12); http://orgwis.gmd.de/dcscw98-groupaware/ (last accessed July 05, 2001).

Pedersen, E. R., & Sokoler, T. (1997). AROMA: abtract representation of presence supporting mutual awareness. In *Human factors in computing system*, Atlanta, GA.

Sellen, A. (1995). Remote conversations: the effects of mediating talk with technology. *Human Computer Interaction, 10*(4), 401–444.

Sembill, D. (2000). Selbstorganisiertes und Lebenslanges Lernen. In F. Achtenhagen, & W. Lempert (Eds.), *Lebenslanges Lernen im Beruf. Seine Grundlegung im Kindes- und Jugendalter (IV). Formen und Inhalte* (pp. 60–90). Opladen: Leske und Budrich.

Slavin, R. E. (1992). Research on cooperative learning: consensus and controversy. In *Collaborative learning: a sourcebook for higher education*, Vol. II (pp. 97–104). The National Center on Postsecondary Teaching, Learning, and Assessment (NCTLA).

Slavin, R. E. (1994). *Cooperative learning: theory, research, and practice*. New York.

URL LIST

http://bscw.gmd.de, document management system "BSCW" (Basic Support for Cooperative Work) (last accessed June 6, 2002).

http://virtuelle-uni.fernuni-hagen.de, Open University Hagen/FRG (last accessed June 6, 2002).

http://www.bb.vfh.de, Blackboard learning space management system, version of the Virtual University Project, VFH (last accessed June 6, 2002).

http://www.blackboard.com, learning space management system "Blackboard" (last accessed June 6, 2002).

http://www.groove.net, learning space management system "Groove" (last accessed June 6, 2002).

http://www.inm.de/projects/kick.html, platform for informal computer-supported communication "KICK" (last accessed June 6, 2002).

http://www.mindjet.de, brainstorming support software "Mindmanager" (last accessed June 6, 2002).

http://www.netucate.de, learning space management system "Netucate" (last accessed June 6, 2002).

http://www.oncampus.de, Virtual University of Applied Sciences (VFH) (last accessed June 06, 2002).

http://www.teamspace.de, learning space management system "Teamspace" (last accessed June 6, 2002).

http://www.teamwave.com, hyperspace browsing system "Teamwave" (last accessed June 6, 2002).

http://www.vfh.fh-brandenburg.de, project Virtual University of Applied Sciences at Brandenburg (last accessed June 06, 2002).

http://www.Webct.com, learning space management system "Web CT" (last accessed June 6, 2002).

ACKNOWLEDGMENTS

Kai Skrabe, University of Applied Sciences Brandenburg, contributed to the investigation described in "Online Modules." Suzanne K. Schaefer from the University of California, Irvine, Information and Computer Science Deptartment, provided insightful comments on a draft of this chapter. Klaus Rupprecht, Berlin, helped by professionally translating the chapter, though all remaining errors are the responsibility of the authors. The background for the investigation was partially provided by the Federal Project "Virtual University of Applied Sciences (VFH)," funded by the German Ministry of Research and Technology (BMBF), funding No. 21B8184.

Chapter XIV

eLearning Support Systems

Jason D. Baker
Regent University, USA

Robert J. Schihl
Regent University, USA

Anil K. Aggarwal
University of Baltimore, USA

ABSTRACT

Students who choose Web-based education (WBE) declare their preference for time- and place-independent learning. They reject relocating or commuting to university campuses and instead seek courses that they can take from the comfort of their homes or offices. Such students are seeking education that is accessible, practical, and convenient, while still providing a quality learning experience. In the WBE market, students view themselves as customers, and universities and other educational providers must consider how they plan to attract, serve, and retain students throughout the educational experience. The authors propose the development of an integrated educational support system infrastructure to help shepherd WBE students from application to graduation. Such support systems should address many aspects of the teaching and learning process, including administrative support, faculty and instructional design support, technical support, library and reference services, and student and program support services.

INTRODUCTION

Web-based education (WBE) has closed the distance between students and institutions. No longer do students need to travel to North Carolina, Maryland, or New York to attend institutions such as Duke, the University of Maryland, or NYU. Such traditional nonprofit universities compete with for-profit ventures such as the University of Phoenix and Jones International University, offering online programs for distance learners. WBE diffusion is not limited to Western countries; universities in developing countries including India, Nepal, and Africa also offer online courses (Irin, 2002; Dawn, 2002).

The rapid growth of online courses is due in no small part to their low production costs. Unlike earlier distance education approaches, such as print-based correspondence courses and full-motion videoconferencing, WBE does not require significant equipment or publishing costs. A motivated instructor can create and publish components of a Web-based course on a personal computer and then upload the materials to a free Web-hosting service for global access. The relative ease of creating Web-based materials, however, can mask challenges that face WBE providers. Palloff and Pratt (2001) noted that institutions that fail to develop an adequate faculty and student support infrastructure will eventually encounter significant problems. In a recent survey of online students at one university, support services were ranked in the top five issues (Aggarwal, 2001; Legon, 2002).

Legon (2002) and Aggarwal (2001) proposed that organizations should view Web-based education as a form of e-business, because universities are competing with for-profit organizations in the marketplace. They argue that universities should develop WBE using the same process that e-businesses use when developing new products, including project planning, cost–benefit analysis, and market research (Alter, 2002). While universities regularly spend millions of dollars erecting new buildings to support campus-based instruction, comparably little consideration is usually given to the structural support and service needs of Web-based programs. Whether this is a deliberate budgetary decision to keep WBE expenses down or an oversight prompted by the relative ease in which Web-based courses can be created, institutions would be wise to consider the need for quality support services. A comprehensive educational support system infrastructure should be developed to help shepherd WBE students from application to graduation. Such support systems would address many aspects of the teaching and learning process, including administrative support, faculty and instructional design support, technical support, library and reference services, and student and program support services. Based on the authors' experiences with online degree programs, this chapter highlights such support issues and offers recommendations to ensure that the necessary infrastructure is in place to support quality online education.

BACKGROUND

While there has been a significant amount of literature addressing pedagogical aspects of WBE, comparably little has specifically addressed student support issues. In Berge and Mrozowski's (2001) review of distance education research from 1990 to 1999, they found that the quantity of literature addressing learner support, operational issues, and policy and management issues lagged behind more frequently addressed topics such as design issues, learner characteristics, and strategies to increase interactivity and active learning. Similarly, in a panel discussion at the 18th Annual Conference of Distance Teaching and Learning, Michael Moore noted that policy and organizational issues are the major challenges facing distance learning providers, but the research has been largely dominated by pedagogical and technological topics.

Several authors have studied the impact of technology on traditional education and developed various educational analytical models. Agre (2000) defined a university in terms of a commodity and community model and argued that a university infrastructure must combine these two models to reduce what he called "tension" between the two approaches generated by technology. Carolan (2001) developed a cultural model of change and demonstrated how the introduction of a new technology can impact social interactions in a classroom setting. Moore and Kearsley (1996) proposed a systems model that considered all of the component processes that make up education, with the recognition that the different processes interact and influence one another. They noted that the addition of technology into education represented a significant change, and the educational system must be adjusted accordingly. "It is not possible," they declared, "to improve quality, provide for more students, and lower costs without reorganizing education according to a systems model" (p. 7).

The rapid growth of WBE has prompted questions concerning the effectiveness of online learning. Some researchers (e.g., Carnevale, 2002; Nasseh, 1998; Salisbury et al., 2002; Trinkle, 1999; Winner, 1998) questioned WBE's effectiveness and expressed concern that online education is a substandard educational approach. Others (e.g., Aggarwal, 2001; Legon, 2002) argued that WBE is at least as good, and possibly better, than traditional education. Although not strictly limited to WBE, Russell (1999) documented 355 research reports, summaries, and papers that found no significant difference between student learning in traditional, face-to-face classes and their distance counterparts.

In concert with the growth of WBE, a renewed emphasis on student-centered, learning-oriented instruction has been advocated by many authors. Often writing from the constructivist perspective, they question the assumptions of conventional face-to-face learning and argue that traditional models may not fully satisfy the needs of the learner (Bonk & Cummings, 1998; Church, 1999; Fishman, Honebein, & Duffy, 1991; Henze & Nejdl, 1997; Laurillard, 1993; Merrill, 2000; Schlager, Fusco, & Schank, 1998). WBE has benefited from and contributed to this philosophy, as online learning extends the classroom far beyond the geographic and methodological constraints of the traditional classroom.

Preliminary models of WBE have been developed to identify the variety of approaches used in online education. For example, Baker (in press) developed a taxonomy focused on the content delivery method, class size, and use of classroom discussion. Aggarwal and Bento (2000) discussed three models of WBE: Web support for information storage, dissemination, and retrieval; Web support for two-way teaching; and Web-based teaching. The support system requirements vary depending on the type of WBE program. For example, the use of largely textual Web pages for information publication and retrieval purposes requires less support-related infrastructure than using the Web to deliver rich-media asynchronous online graduate courses.

ADMINISTRATIVE SUPPORT

A critical step in developing a WBE program is to consider the administrative support needs for planning and operations. Administrative functions require continuous and systematic support to generate plans to "sell" WBE to potential students. Many universities do not recognize this and attempt to embed online administrative support as part of traditional educational support. This could lead to tepid support for traditional and distance students, resulting in frustration and eventual loss of students. The authors experienced this when designing a new online master's degree program in computer-mediated communication. After the program received university approval, it was left to a pair of professors to handle almost all marketing, recruitment, and admissions tasks for the embryonic program. The result was predictable—the initial cohort of students was limited to those that the faculty personally recruited.

Although individual courses can be effectively taught online by a few motivated faculty, successful online programs require the proper planning, commitment, and support of key administrators. One author recalls speaking at a leading university where the university president sat in the audience and listened to his distance education presentation. The university president weighed the arguments for putting time, personnel, and money into distance education. The statement that convinced the president to adopt WBE was that the Game Boy Generation is at the threshold of the university, and they are legion. Nintendo's Game Boy is the most popular video game system ever, with sales over 100 million units, roughly 25,000 every day since the product was introduced in 1988. Students in the Game Boy Generation have had a radically different educational history than their parents. These were the students that used Texas Instruments' Speak and Spell when they were preschoolers and grew up with computers being as common as televisions.

Can education compete with those electronic gadgets and meet their needs today? Perhaps, but we should consider engaging the students with the same electronic technology that they used growing up. Online education can reach such students, because it uses a familiar environment for instruction—the Web. The university president was convinced that the traditional "sage on the stage" model was not a necessary and sufficient criterion to good education; after all, the most important education he personally facilitated was to his own children as a "guide by the side." Needless to say, that school is on the way to becoming fully engaged in distance learning with the active advocacy of the top administrator.

The administrators of an educational institution should assert leadership beyond simply blessing the initiative and moving on. For example, wise administrators consider personnel issues when planning an eLearning initiative. The decisions to outsource distance course and degree development tasks, hiring content experts during course creation, deciding between a full-time Webmaster and using Application Service Providers, and even considering faculty stipends are significant budget issues that require administrative input. Administrators are also advised to weigh in on standardizing content development and management platforms. Often, administrative declarations are the easiest way to promote standards regarding computer platforms (e.g., Windows versus Mac), software tools (e.g., RealMedia versus Windows Media), uniform Web course management software and support (e.g., Blackboard versus WebCT), and multimedia involvement (e.g., online only, direct broadcast satellite, full-motion videoconferencing, etc.). This does not mean that the leadership should make such decisions apart from the input of faculty, staff, and students, but once the standards have been decided, the administration needs to back them with vocal support, financial resources, and support policies.

Administrators tasked with managing academic affairs (e.g., provost, academic vice president, dean) are also key players in the development of effective WBE programs. Academic concerns are paramount in initiating distance education and range from faculty workload issues to pedagogical concerns, including faculty development, distance course and degree development, and institutional accreditation. If these administrators do not get in front of the online learning initiative, they will find out quickly that what is being done in one school or department differs significantly from what is happening in another. This can lead to wasted resources, student confusion, and even accreditation concerns. Some institutions have responded to such concerns by creating a separate department tasked with overall management of WBE initiatives, while others have created interdepartmental advisory committees to support a distributed administrative model.

The authors have experienced a positive model of administrative support through a combination of centralized and department-specific services. At Regent University, the university maintains a central Information Technology department that makes decisions concerning technology standards. In addition, the university's Instructional Support and Technology Center works with faculty and administration to recommend policies to support effective WBE and offers training and assistance to those instructors involved with online learning. In addition to these central departments, each school within the university has a distance education support specialist to provide personalized assistance to faculty, staff, and students within the department.

It is also important for the administration to recognize that the development of WBE programs generally requires higher up-front personnel costs but lower recurring costs than face-to-face counterparts (Hartley, 2000). Some schools have used course reductions, planning sabbaticals, or additional compensation to address this issue, others have contracted with corporate learning providers to develop and deliver the content the university would provide, and still others created for-profit spin-off companies to support the nonprofit institutions. Regardless of how it is addressed, if new distance programs are developed with administrative support, the burden falls on a few pioneering instructors to carry the load. Although such instructors may be effective online educators, ultimately, the administrative demands will likely exceed their capabilities. As a result, the students will suffer, and the whole WBE effort could be set back significantly.

FACULTY AND CONTENT (INSTRUCTIONAL) DESIGN SUPPORT

Often, the first reaction of faculty committed to online teaching is to devise ways to recreate the face-to-face classroom experience via computer. When one of the author's colleagues first learned of a proposed new online program, he wanted to put a camera in front of himself and lecture to the online students. Other colleagues also envisioned themselves as seated in front of their computer screen with small square images of each of their students dutifully looking back at them. We were reminded of McLuhan's rear-view mirror syndrome (McLuhan & Fiore, 1967). He noted that we tend to live one medium behind and offered the example of filming plays as the first mainstream use of film cameras. Such cameras were usually set up in the center aisle of a theater house and filmed what appeared on the stage; how far removed that is from the film experience of today.

As major stakeholders in WBE, faculty and students must be trained and supported as they venture into the distance realm. Faculty members require assistance in discovering new teaching methods that would be more suitable to effective Web-based instruction. Students need to be understood in the context of the unique learning environment in which they are working, which includes the virtual classroom and the extended off-campus context in which they are learning. While there are numerous books, conferences, and consultants available to assist faculty and students in making the transition to WBE, we have found that a more personal approach is more beneficial. For example, an internal "champion" can often influence and assist more faculty and students than an external consultant. One author has observed this in two university settings where, in both cases, skeptical professors were more likely to respond to an enthusiastic colleague than someone from outside the faculty. This may be done informally, as we have experienced, or in a more formal mentoring process, where experienced online instructors and students offer one-on-one assistance to new Web-based participants. We have also found that online modules, where faculty can experience the online environment before teaching their first course, can be particularly effective.

In traditional education, instructors handle all aspects of course design and development by themselves. After all, they are the content experts and are best equipped to design a quality learning experience for their students. But, does this necessarily hold in WBE? Now that teacher–student communication is mediated online through a computer, the medium affects the learning experience. Furthermore, the typical faculty member is trained in his or her particular field, not in instructional design. It is simply unrealistic, and a poor use of resources, to expect a faculty member to be content expert, Web developer, multimedia designer, and systems administrator all rolled into one.

Just as businesses have learned the value of work teams, so too should WBE instructors team up with instructional designers and other support staff to develop a quality course. In a team approach, the faculty member is partnered with one or more instructional designers, multimedia developers, or student assistants. These individuals should be well-trained in their field and bring a customer-focused attitude toward their work. Instructional designers bring insight into how to design the contents to maximize student learning. They will have the most insight on the media selection, layout of Web pages, and overall instructional approach, and can help the faculty member translate content into a quality course to be delivered at a distance. Multimedia developers not only can convert much of the content into an online format (e.g., creating a streaming audio or video segment based on a classroom lecture), but they can also offer a sense of style to the course design. Finally, to accommodate laborious work involved in developing a distance course (e.g., Web page coding, scanning pictures, etc.), there should be student assistants who can assist the development team in accomplishing such tasks. This is no small undertaking, as it requires a commitment not only from the instructor to collaborate on the course design (which is likely a new, and somewhat unsettling, experience) but also from the institution, which needs to commit the resources necessary for instructional design support.

Staff should ideally be part of a technical support facility and must be familiar with the management of technological infrastructure. A creative way of developing a team is to develop a hybrid academic and support facility, such as a Center for Distance Education, Center for Instructional Development, or New Media Center, which hosts the instructional designers, multimedia developers, and other support staff. This is similar to an information center that assists users with technical problems. Such centers could serve a number of functions, like assisting with the development of new distance courses, promoting the WBE efforts throughout the institution, performing research in WBE, and mentoring students interested in learning about distance education. At one author's university, for example, the Instructional Support and Technology Center recently developed an online media database containing text, pictures, audio, and video clips that can be incorporated into online courses. This effort serves the entire university and provides a means for instructors to share media resources across disciplines and reuse the content in their courses. Although the media database is relatively new, students and faculty have responded favorably and believe that it will help improve the WBE experience.

TECHNICAL SUPPORT

In the WBE environment, technology enables communication between stakeholders. In the early days of distance education, technical support was largely limited to the mass duplication of audiotapes and workbooks. In the current approach to distance education, technology plays a central role in the development, maintenance, delivery, and even day-to-day experience of distance learning. It is essential that an institution provide up-to-date computer, telecommunications, and media services to faculty and students to ensure a quality learning experience.

Quality WBE programs require a robust telecommunications infrastructure. In addition to the network backbone, such infrastructure includes the necessary application servers, system administration, account management, and faculty computer systems. The presence of fault-tolerant application servers is crucial to running online distance education programs. Machines such as Web servers, courseware servers, email servers, and specialty servers (such as database applications, chat servers, and document management servers) may all be used in the WBE program. To ensure that the systems are stable for the distance programs, they require regular maintenance, upgrades, backups, reliable and uninterruptible power supplies, and other services. Such an information technology infrastructure should be managed by dedicated computer support staff with additional support personnel tasked to WBE efforts as appropriate. It is not necessary that this function be handled in-house. There are a growing number of Web-hosting, Internet Service Providers, and Application Service Providers—companies that enable you to outsource technology hosting, Internet access, and support services for a specific product—that support WBE. Leading courseware vendors such as Blackboard and WebCT offer universities the chance to host their courses on the vendors' Web servers, thus eliminating the need for in-house 24/7 technical support. Of course, licensing fees for this service will be increased, but in the long run, it may prove cheaper than the hardware and personnel costs to manage the systems internally.

The authors observed this as the number of online degree programs multiplied at their university. Originally, the university adopted Blackboard CourseInfo as the WBE platform and maintained the server in-house. As the number of online courses grew, the server became increasingly slow and prone to unexpected outages, which resulted in unacceptable amounts of downtime during the semester. Finally, after upgrading the systems, the university decided to outsource the hosting to Blackboard and has seen a noticeable improvement in performance and uptime. As a result, the faculty and students were able to teach and learn online with minimal technical difficulties, and based on recent surveys, student and faculty satisfaction increased accordingly.

While account management issues are fairly mundane, the reality is that if students cannot log onto the system to participate in distance education, the effect is the same as locking them out of a traditional classroom. When committing to a WBE endeavor, it is important to develop account management procedures. Such faculty and student accounts must be created and maintained in a timely manner. This may necessitate creating dedicated email accounts, electronic mailing lists, or user names and passwords to provide 24/7 access to course websites.

Standardization is also an important consideration for effective technical support systems. The myriad of available software programs, from course management systems to photo-editing suites, raise the possibility that students or faculty may choose products the support staff are not familiar with. Organizational and program technology standards increase the likelihood that faculty and students will receive knowledgeable high-quality support when they need assistance.

Finally, all stakeholders of WBE should have dedicated current computers with high-speed Internet connections. Just as it would be considered unreasonable to expect employees to function productively without a telephone, desk, or writing instruments, a professor without an adequate computer system and reliable Internet access is just as crippled in the distance realm. In addition to providing the actual machines, wise administrators would develop a replacement plan (e.g., providing new computer systems every two or three years) to ensure that the stakeholders' systems are capable of supporting current WBE software. Furthermore, there needs to be continuous training opportunities (online and offline) to assist faculty and students as they learn new and upgraded software. Without such training, organizations will find that WBE participants are spending more time with computer problems than educational content issues.

LIBRARY AND REFERENCE SERVICES

The traditional library was built on the assumption that a student would always go to the physical library to access its full range of academic support. That is not the case in distance education. The case that designers of WBE programs must face is the learner at an extreme distance. A university library in the United States needs to be fully prepared to support a distance learner in Russia if the university is to offer quality Web-based learning. While most distance students probably will not be on another continent, many of the challenges are the same.

Effective reference support for WBE participants is the shared responsibility of the student, library, and bookstore. Although the major support systems are managed by the organization, the WBE student needs to bear some responsibility as well. Despite the potential of electronic reserves and overnight mailing of books, a distance learner will find that a local university library will greatly enhance the research opportunities. At one author's university, the library's introduction to distance education reminds prospective students that "Careful assessment must be made, prior to undertaking distance learning, of the information environment available to the distance applicant in one's geographic area."

In addition to local library support, the institutional library is a central support center for WBE students. For many libraries, an online card catalog was probably available to students before the rise in interest in distance education. Online card catalogs not only displayed the desired book but also the number of copies in the collection and how many were on the shelf or already withdrawn. This same service is now a chief component in servicing the distance learner. At a minimum, a library must offer online students the ability to search book and periodical collections through a Web-based online catalog. Ideally, the distance student could search the catalog, reserve individual books, and have them rapidly shipped for borrowing. In addition to electronic catalogs, effective WBE programs will have the support of dedicated librarians to offer personal assistance comparable to what walk-in students receive.

Once a student knows what books he or she wants, the question becomes how to get them to the student. The two primary options are withdrawal (i.e., traditional library loan) or interlibrary loan. Libraries supporting WBE should make book withdrawal available to the student by postal mail, shipping books that the distance learner checks out. A recommended approach would be to mail the books to the distance learner and provide a prepaid postage label for return shipment. Interlibrary loan is another means of getting books to distance students. If the university library makes arrangements with the student's geographically local library, then books acquired through interlibrary loan could be delivered to the local library for pick-up rather than adding the additional delays and overhead of book shipment. In a sense, the student's local library becomes an extension branch of their university library. Ultimately, as distance education grows in popularity, interlibrary efforts will become an increasingly significant way of serving students, regardless of geographic location.

Periodicals, particularly academic and professional journals, are another essential library resource. Given their unique nature, libraries have a number of options available concerning periodical support for distance students. One approach to periodical support is to treat it exactly like book support. When a student requests a particular article, the library could mail, fax, or even email a copy of the article. Electronic databases also offer a method of providing self-service periodical support to WBE students. By providing access to collections such as Lexis-Nexis, PsychInfo, ProQuest, Dow Jones, Dissertation Abstracts, MedLine, JSTOR, and Books in Print, distance students can search through the contents of numerous periodicals and sometimes retrieve the full texts of the articles. As increasing numbers of journals make their articles available in electronic format, this will become a preferred method for distance periodical delivery.

Electronic reserves and online "coursepacks" are becoming an increasingly common aspect of library support. Using this approach, faculty members submit required reading lists (e.g., journal articles, websites, even personal documents), and the materials are gathered, digitized, and made available for secure student access. Libraries can scan the materials using the Adobe Acrobat document delivery system, post them to a password-protected website, and then make them available to the students. This provides the students with immediate access to course-specific materials and can be used to develop an electronic reserve for use in future WBE courses. For those faculty and libraries not interested in doing these tasks in-house, companies such as Xanedu.com will happily do them for you. Typically, these services are free to professors, while the students pay for their course materials. Some textbook providers will also perform similar services, such as offering periodical articles or book chapters in printed and bound format for purchase by distance learners.

Such on-demand publishing blurs the traditional lines between libraries and book-stores. Many students prefer to simply contact a bookstore with their course information and purchase all of their books (including some that may be hard to find elsewhere) in a single effort rather than bargain hunting with companies like Amazon.com or Abebooks.com. Some campus bookstores prefer to handle distance efforts in-house, while others have contracted with a dedicated service provider such as Specialty Books. Such companies provide customer access through Web pages, email addresses, 800 numbers, voicemail, U.S. mail, and fax, but they also make used texts available to distance students and offer to buy back texts after the academic term is over. On the other hand, a dedicated bookstore can handle special requests, such as last-minute readings, software, and other unique requests that may be beyond the scope of typical online bookstores.

When considering a bookstore, one should remember that the role of the bookstore in WBE is more than merely a provider of academic resources. A critical component to WBE, at least in higher education, is the building of student loyalty to the institution. Experienced WBE providers recognize the need to make identity-producing items available to the distance learners, such as coffee mugs, tee shirts, and the like. We are not entirely sensitive to the needs and wants of distance learners if we expect them to get to campus in order to purchase those things every other academic institution parades as loyalty and symbols of belonging. Such products and services not only help the student identify with the institution but also serve as a means of passive marketing long after the student completes a WBE course.

OTHER SUPPORT SERVICES

After all the pieces are in place, and the course begins, inevitably, someone encounters a problem. Whether the instructor needs to add someone to the email distribution list, a student forgets a password, or the streaming audio feed stops broadcasting, a quality program needs helpdesk support. Whether you choose to place the responsibility with the existing helpdesk support staff or create a new one for distance students is not as critical as ensuring that whoever does the task is familiar with dealing with off-campus students and will be sympathetic to their needs. For many campus helpdesk workers, the fall-back position with a particularly difficult problem is to either ask the person to bring their computer to the helpdesk or send a technician to examine the machine. However, neither is possible when dealing with WBE students who might be anywhere in the world, and so, new policies should be developed to deal with such situations.

As with many other administrative issues, the more a helpdesk can use the Internet to educate, inform, and support the WBE instructors and students, the more satisfied the stakeholders will be. Instructions about how to use the appropriate software, frequently asked question (FAQ) lists, status messages about system maintenance, and instructions for reporting a problem should be automated and available online. Students should be promptly informed of glitches and any maintenance work that may affect their studies. (It is frustrating to attempt to submit an assignment just before the deadline, only to find that the computer folks have taken the system down for maintenance.) Finally, administrators should consider implementing an online automated trouble-tracking system for students to use to report problems, check on their status, and receive timely responses to their questions.

Effective support services should also consider the tasks of staff personnel. Whether enrolling students, processing tuition payments, or preparing graduation paperwork, staff personnel are actively engaged in the educational process and require quality support. Specifically, they need technical assistance to reinvent their processes to support WBE without requiring that students travel to campus every time there is a problem. A simple, yet remarkably helpful, way to assist distance students is to publish all the necessary policies, procedures, schedules, and forms online. After making the procedures available online, the next step is to implement real-time online services, such as course registration, drop/add, and transcript requests. Secure online payment systems, permitting students to review charges and pay bills over the Internet, is another means to effectively support WBE students. The more that you can provide online self-service stations, the more satisfied WBE students will be with their educational experience. One of the authors spent over six months dealing with one university registrar concerning some distance course grades and finally had to resort to a trip to the campus in order to resolve the problems. Needless to say, this reflected poorly on the institution's commitment to distance education.

CONCLUSION

For 21st century universities, the question is not when but how to use the Internet effectively for educational purposes. Is it possible to provide quality education to people on the Web? Can WBE conquer time and distance and provide course-related information on demand? Can universities designed for residential campus experiences adjust to the demands of eLearning? The authors believe that the answer to all of these questions is yes, but such progress requires leadership. If WBE is a type of e-business, then institutions offering online instruction would be wise to consider the service and support functions that mark successful e-business ventures. While much attention has rightly been given to leadership in Web-based pedagogy, sufficient support systems must be put in place to ensure that the faculty will be able to focus on teaching, students will be able to focus on learning, and the online educational experience will flourish.

REFERENCES

Aggarwal, A. K. (2001, June). *Web-based education (WBE) and diffusion*. Panel presented at the 9th European Conference on Information Systems, Bled, Slovenia.

Aggarwal, A. K., & Bento, R. (2000). Web-based education. In A. K. Aggarwal (Ed.), *Web-based learning and teaching technologies: opportunities and challenges*. Hershey, PA: Idea Group Publishing.

Agre, P. E. (2000). Commodity and community: institutional design for the networked university. *Planning for Higher Education, 29*(2), 5–14.

Alter, S. (2002) *Information systems: the foundation of e-business*. Upper Saddle River, NJ: Prentice Hall.

Baker, J. D. (in press). A taxonomy of online courses. In K. W. White, & J. D. Baker (Eds.), *The new online learning guide*. Needham Heights, MA: Allyn and Bacon.

Berge, Z. L., & Mrozowski, S. (2001). Review of research in distance education, 1990 to 1999. *The American Journal of Distance Education, 15*(3), 5–19.

Bonk, C. J., & Cummings, J. A. (1998). A dozen recommendations for placing the student at the center of Web-based learning. *Educational Media International, 35*(2), 82–89.

Carnevale, D. (2002). On-line students don't fare as well as classroom counterparts, study finds. *The Chronicle of Higher Education*. Retrieved February 25, 2002 from the World Wide Web: http://chronicle.com/free/2002/02/2002022501u.htm.

Carolan, B. (2001). Technology, schools and the decentralization of cultures. *First Monday, 6*(8). Retrieved from the World Wide Web: http://www.firstmonday.dk/issues/issue6_8/carolan/index.html.

Church, G. (1999, October 4). The economy of the future? *TIME E-Commerce Special*, 113–116.

DAWN. (2002, March 23). *Virtual varsity to provide world class education*. Retrieved April 25, 2002 from the World Wide Web: http://www.dawn.com/2002/03/24/nat22.htm.

Fishman, B. J., Honebein, P. C., & Duffy T. M. (1991). *Constructivism and the design of learning environment: context and activities for learning.* Presented at the NATO Advanced Workshop on the Design of Constructivist Learning Environments.

Hartley, D. E. (2000). *On-demand learning: training in the new millennium.* Amherst, MA: HRD Press.

Henze, N., & Nejdl, W. (1997). *A Web-based learning environment: applying constructivist teaching concepts in virtual learning environment.* Retrieved May 1999 from the World Wide Web: http://www.kbs.uni-hannover.de/paper/97/ifip97/paper15.html.

IRIN. (2002, March 10). *Pakistan: virtual university launched.* Retrieved April 2, 2002 from the World Wide Web: http://www.irinnews.org/report.asp?ReportID=24279&SelectRegion=Central_Asia&SelectCountry=PAKISTAN.

Laurillard, D. (1993). *Rethinking university teaching: a framework for the effective use of educational technology.* London: Routledge.

Legon, R. (2002, May). *The next phase of Web-based education.* Panel presented at the 13th Information Resources Management Association International Conference, Seattle, WA.

McLuhan, M., & Fiore, Q. (1967). *The medium is the massage: an inventory of effects.* San Francisco, CA: Hardwired.

Mendez, R. (1996). *The world lecture hall.* Retrieved July 10, 2002 from the World Wide Web: http://www.utexas.edu/world/lecture/index.html.

Merrill, D. (2000). Learning-oriented instructional development tools. Retrieved September 25, 2002 from the World Wide Web: http://www.id2.usu.edu/Papers/LO_Tools2_final.PDF.

Moore, M. G., & Kearsley, G. (1996). *Distance education: a systems view.* Belmont, CA: Wadsworth.

Nasseh, B. (1998). *Training and support programs, and faculty's new roles in computer-based distance education in higher education institutions.* Retrieved July 10, 2002 from the World Wide Web: http://www.bsu.edu/classes/nasseh/study/res98.html.

Palloff, R. M., & Pratt, K. (2001). *Lessons learned from the cyberspace classroom: the realities of online teaching.* San Francisco, CA: Jossey-Bass.

Russell, T. L. (1999). *The no significant difference phenomenon.* Raleigh, NC: North Carolina State University.

Salisbury, D. et al. (2002). The limits of information: a cautionary tale about one course delivery experience in the distance education environment. *eService Journal, 1*(2), 65–79.

Schlager, M., Fusco. J., & Schank, P. (1998). Cornerstones for an on-line community of educational professionals. *IEEE Technology and Society, 17*(4), 15–21, 40.

Talbott, S. (1998). NETFUTURE: Technology and human responsibility. *Conference Report,* June 2, 1998; http://www.oreilly.com/people/staff/stevet/netfuture/.

Trinkle, D. (1999). Distance education: a means to an end, no more, no less. *The Chronicle of Higher Education.*

Trinkle, D. (1999, April). History and the computer revolutions: a survey of current practices. *Journal of the Association of History and Computing, 2*(1). Retrieved from the World Wide Web: http://www.mcel.pacificu.edu/JAHC/JAHCII1/ArticlesII1/Trinkle/Trinkleindex.html.

Winner, L. (1998, June 2). Report from the digital diploma mills conference. *Netfuture, 72.* Retrieved from the World Wide Web: http://www.oreilly.com/people/staff/stevet/netfuture/1998/Jun0298_72.html#3.

Part IV

WBE: Diffusion Across Disciplines and Communities

Chapter XV

Program Execution and Visualization on the Web

C. Pareja-Flores
Universidad Complutense de Madrid, Spain

J. Á. Velázquez-Iturbide
Universidad Rey Juan Carlos, Spain

ABSTRACT

Programming is a demanding task with an education program that requires the assistance of complex tools such as programming environments, algorithm animators, problem graders, etc. In this chapter, we give a comprehensive presentation of tools for program execution and visualization on the Web. We summarize the technical evolution of these tools, describe educational uses, report lessons learned, and look at formal evaluations of their educational effectiveness. We also deal with a closely related matter, namely, collections of Web documents containing programming exercises. Finally, we outline our view of future trends in the use of the Web for programming education, and we give our personal conclusions. This chapter is of interest to educators and researchers, because it gives a comprehensive presentation of the main issues and results of a field where most of the contributions are sparse in the literature.

INTRODUCTION

Programming is a central theme in the discipline of computer science and, consequently, is the focus of many efforts in computer science education. The teaching and learning of programming is an extremely difficult task, because it is an exceedingly abstract and experimental activity. As a result, logical reasoning and experimentation play a central role.

Traditionally, programming environments have been the main tools used for solving programming problems (Jiménez-Peris et al., 2000). However, a number of complementary tools have been developed in the last decade, for instance, algorithm animators, program visualizers, problem generators, problem graders, etc. Many of these tools have been or are being ported to the Web. Some of the advantages gained from this are platform independence and universal accessibility, which were serious obstacles to widespread adoption of previous systems.

In this chapter, we describe technologies and experiences of using several classes of Web-based tools as a key element in programming courses, especially for problem solving. The tools we refer to support program execution and visualization (including animation). It should be noted that we do not make a comprehensive study of all kinds of Web-based tools that can be used for these courses, because this would require a whole book in itself. For instance, we exclude those uses of the Web that are independent of the subject matter, such as delivering course information or providing a collaborative medium. Such matters have been described elsewhere (Burd, 2000; Cucciarelli, Panti, & Valenti, 2000).

In our exposition, we want to highlight two difficulties. First, some tools are recent, and their educational success has not been formally measured. Thus, the lessons that have been learned come from the experiences of teachers, from questionnaires completed by students, and from informal chats with students. Formal experiments have only been conducted with respect to algorithm animation, e.g., read Stasko and Lawrence (1998). We will report on both kinds of assessments.

A second difficulty is that there is not always a neat separation between traditional tools and Web-based tools. In some cases, such as collections of exercises, we can hardly find experiences other than based on the Web. In other cases, most notably algorithm animations, there is a continuum from graphical or multimedia applications in personal computers to Web applications. We emphasize here Web-based cases and experiences, but we refer to other related systems when their lessons can also be applied to the Web.

The chapter is organized as follows. The next two sections are devoted to two different classes of Web-based tools for programming courses, namely, support for program execution and program visualization (with emphasis on algorithm animation). In each section, a brief overview of the main technical achievements is given, educational uses are described, and lessons learned are reported, and in the case of algorithm animations, the results of controlled experiments on their educational effectiveness are presented. A product related to the algorithm animation activity is presented in the fourth section, namely, the management of collections of Web documents on programming exercises. Finally, we outline our view of future trends in the use of the Web for programming education and our personal conclusions.

PROGRAM EXECUTION

Program construction and execution are the main means of testing whether a computer solution to a problem (i.e., an algorithm) is correct. It is the main laboratory component of any programming course. One important problem involved in using computer environments is that the faculty and the students must have the same version, and it must often be run on specific computers and operating systems. The Web provides the possibility of universal remote access to resources with a common interface (browsers). Consequently, being able to compile and run programs from a distance is a valuable option for programming instructors.

There are few experiences of running programs through the Web. In this section, we report some initial experiences and outline several uses of the Web for these tasks.

Definitions

Problem solving in programming courses typically focuses on algorithmic topics. Problems (or, more technically, specifications) are usually stated in input–output terms, requiring the design of a computational method to transform input data into its corresponding output data. For instance, the task of sorting a sequence of numbers may be expressed in the following way: given a sequence of arbitrary numbers, rearrange them in ascending order. In such problems, input and output data must be unambiguously identified, and some input data will probably be forbidden. In the example given above, there is no restriction on the input sequence.

A computational method that solves a problem is called an algorithm. Ideally, an algorithm must be correct (i.e., it must correctly solve the problem for any input data) and efficient (i.e., it must use few computer resources, by concluding its work in a short period of time and occupying little memory space).

If an algorithm is described following the conventions of a programming language, we say that it has been implemented as a program. A program can be run on a computer if it has previously been translated into "machine language" via a process called compilation. Compilation can produce an executable program or deliver an error message reporting that something is wrong (for instance, that a sentence has been written without strictly adhering to the syntax of the programming language).

Once a program is executable, it can be run as many times as desired. Controlled tests are carried out using selected input data to run the program, giving a high degree of confidence in the correctness of the program. If erroneous results are obtained, the algorithm or its implementation must be reviewed to identify the sources of the errors and to remedy them. For instance, an error in the sorting program could be due to an error in the algorithm, such as the failure to consider the case of an already sorted sequence. Alternatively, it could be due to a human error made when describing the algorithm according to the conventions of the programming language.

This development process is assisted by a myriad of programming tools. Thus, the writing of a program is carried out with an editor, the compiling is carried out by a compiler, and the correction of programming errors is accomplished with the assistance of a debugger. In order to facilitate the flexible use of these tools, they are often integrated into one program, called a programming environment. A help facility is often included to better document the use of the environment tools and the many programming language details.

Programming tools must give information to the programmer about errors, about the progress of the computation, and so on. These explanations can be given in some type of textual format or with the aid of graphical representations. The use of graphical representations for software is called software visualization and can potentially enhance communication between the programmer and the computer. In the third section, we address visualization issues.

Evolution of Web-Based Program Execution

The use of computer tools for programming is now 50 years old (Jiménez-Peris et al., 2000). The state of the art in hardware is one key aspect that has determined the organization of operating systems and human–machine interface, which in turn, has influenced programming environments and languages. Due to this constraint, there were few opportunities for powerful programming environments during the first decades of computer science. Batch processing in the first operating systems only permitted the offline use of compilers and the use of some low-level debugging facilities. The invention of the interruption concept in the 1960s gave rise to the development of time-sharing operating systems, where several users have the illusion of being the only users of the system. In addition, the development of consoles gave rise to the first full-screen editors. During the 1970s, the rate of new developments increased dramatically. High-level languages were designed and implemented, ranging from imperative ones (mainly Pascal and C) to declarative ones (mainly Prolog and ML). Although limited during the 1970s to research and internal production, there were also a number of important developments, such as window-based user interfaces, the mouse, and object-oriented programming, which laid the foundations for the software developed during the next two decades and up to the present day.

The early 1980s are the reference point for the explosion of programming environments. Integrated programming environments provided a set of tools within a single program to assist in the coding phase of program development. Typically these tools were a full-screen multiwindow editor, a compiler or interpreter, a debugger, and support for other mundane tasks (e.g., file handling). Two landmarks in language-based programming environments were Logo for education and Turbo Pascal for professionals. It is also worthwhile highlighting that improvements in debuggers led to the development of the so-called high-level debuggers. These allowed the programmer to debug programs by thinking in a way closer to his/her mental modes than had been possible with previous tools.

The birth of personal computers that took place in the early 1980s quickly led to them becoming popular because of their low prices. From the point of view of education, it meant that computer resources became available to small institutions, teachers, and students. These inexpensive computers could dedicate more resources to input–output, so the most important part of a program changed from its functionality to its user interface. In perspective, this process produced a change in paradigm from batch processing to interactive processing; in other words, from computing to interaction.

In the 1990s, all of these trends extended in several directions, often as a consequence of the synergy of different technologies. Object-oriented languages became widespread, particularly C++ and, more recently, Java. They permitted automation of certain routine programming tasks by means of visual means, such as programming the user interface. This development had a notable influence on educational programming environments, because visualization provided students with higher-level aids for debugging, and with improved assistance for comprehension.

The Internet and the Web have become a novel communication medium that motivates students. While it may have speed and power limitations, it has certain advantages, such as universal accessibility and platform independence. Despite these advantages, it is unusual to see the running of programs via the Web, as is routinely done in programming environments. It is a more common practice to state given problems and to allow the students to submit programs for these specific problems. Let us review some of the most important contributions.

240 Pareja-Flores & Velázquez-Iturbide

Hiltz and Kögeler (1997) described a website for teaching C++ as a first programming language. It can be considered a Web-based electronic book, which although simple, is well designed with respect to structure and navigation. Each lesson proposes a set of exercises, with each one including a program editor form to send the program via GGI to the server for compilation. User code is usually preceded and followed by code provided by the teacher. If there is a compiling error, a message is included within the form as close as possible to the source of the error. If the compilation is correct, input data is required from the user to execute the program.

WebToTeach (Arnow & Barshay, 1999) is a system to assist in solving programming problems via the Web. It can be used independently or within a course and supports six different programming languages. It is intended to give support via the Web to assignments of a programming course by providing different facilities to students and teachers. Students can trace the state of their assignments, find out whether their assignments were submitted on time, continue working from the same point at which the last session finished, and so on. Teachers can incorporate new assignments and communicate with students. An assignment may require the building of a whole program or simply a piece of it. In the latter case, the teacher must provide the system with the rest of the program (consisting of a prefix or a suffix to concatenate with the user solution). Correctness of the program is tested by comparing the output of the program with that specified by the teacher, although some flexibility is permitted (e.g., ignoring spaces or blank lines or not discriminating between capital and lowercase letters).

In the system by Elenbogen, Maxim, and McDonald (2000), a set of interactive Web exercises on C++ is given. The exercises are delivered by Java applets, and students can experiment in a tightly controlled environment, while the instructor is able to separate specific concepts to be explored individually.

We are only aware of three systems with full programming capabilities on the Web. Ibrahim (1994) developed a system that allowed the programmer to use the Web as a front-end to edit a program, send it to the Web server, and debug it. The system allows students to run a program on the server, to insert breakpoints in the code, to display the contents of variables, and to advance execution line by line or until a breakpoint is reached. The display of the variables is text-only, using HTML forms, and is updated by loading new Web pages.

Domingue and Mulholland (1997) developed a system for Prolog programming. Users can submit and run their programs on the server and receive an execution visualization. The system is enriched with collaborative facilities so that students can consult the teacher about their programming errors by annotating directly on visualizations. The teacher can also annotate answers on the visualization.

The KIEL system (Berghammer & Milanese, 2001) allows the loading or editing of programs and expressions and the evaluation of expressions. It supports a subset of the functional language ML and allows experimentation with different operational semantics. Given an expression, the user can control what parts must be evaluated and how.

Educational Uses of Web-Based Program Execution

Web-based program execution can be used in different ways. Given the Web to drive visualizations and animations (as explained in the next section), explanations of wrong programs can be given graphically. For instance, in the following display (Jiménez-Peris et al., 2000), a typical type of analysis in imperative programming is shown:

```
h  +  r  *  sin  ( pi )  <=  n
____  ____  _____  _____  ___
N  RxR→R  R  RxR→R  R→R    R    RxR→B  N

↓                    _____              ↓
                        R

R          _____      R            R
              R

_____
              R

_____
              B
```

While in the next one, the source of an error is explained:

```
i  >  1  and  ok
___  ___  _____  ____
 =
... ...  N  BxB→B   B
        _____
        Error (type mismatch):
        1 is N and it must be B
```

The limitations of these systems for programming can also be an advantage in certain contexts. A typical complaint of students and teachers about many languages is that even to run a single expression or statement, it is necessary to write a complex protocol consisting of program header, variable declarations, etc. Considering only one aspect (Arnow & Barshay, 1999; Elenbogen et al., 2000; Hitz & Kögeler, 1997) allows novice students to concentrate on program fragments that illustrate certain syntactic or semantic elements. This feature is especially important at the beginning, when novices ignore program structure and other details. Some interesting program fragments are the condition of a conditional statement, the body of a loop, the head of a procedure, the declaration of a data type or a variable, etc.

Considering only one aspect at a time also allows for the possibility of giving detailed clues to novice programmers about this topic. For instance, when a type error is found, a simple message like "type mismatch" is not very useful; it is far more useful to offer an explanation of the operation involved and subexpression types. Thus, the analysis shown in the latter figure (see above) makes the cause of the error evident, i.e., the priorities of the operations have been misunderstood.

Finally, an unexpected use of program execution on the Web is as a testing tool. For instance, the teacher can use the system for student inquiry by proposing that the student predict the behavior expected for a given input, or vice versa, by guessing the input that yields an output desired (Elenbogen et al., 2000).

Lessons Learned from Using Web-Based Program Execution

Experience shows that programming students must focus on partial aspects of a language in turn during their learning process. The availability of tools to explore programming, ranging from pieces of code to whole programs, has proven to be useful, because these tools allow students to practice before being able to develop complete programs (Weber, 1996).

From an educational point of view, Web processing resembles batch processing in that the student–computer interaction it provides is too inflexible. We do not know whether solutions will come from unexpected improvements in the Web or from further research on and experience of complex Web-based systems. Currently, inflexibility is the most serious drawback of using the Web for program execution. Transmission delays and server overload produce long response times, which often discourage students and diminish their initial enthusiasm for using the Web.

The use of visualization for explaining compiling or running errors is potentially valuable, but it is also difficult to implement effectively. In particular, using visualization as a debugging tool for wrong programs requires a finer granularity of displayed events than for correct programs.

One important issue is the amount of work needed to support and adequately integrate all the elements necessary for program execution. First, an infrastructure consisting at least of a compiler must be built. Second, exercises must be carefully designed, in addition to their corresponding programs. A partial solution may come from repositories freely available on the Web. However, there are many unsolved problems that make it impossible to integrate different tools in a single educational Web environment. The diversity of programming languages (and hence tools) makes it difficult to share educational materials directly. In addition, the many exercises offered are managed by independent tools, and they cannot be straightforwardly reused by people other than their own developers.

PROGRAM VISUALIZATION AND ANIMATION

Algorithm animation is a task related to program development, mostly to program execution. Its graphical nature makes it one of the tasks that can potentially benefit the most from the hypermedia features of the Web. In fact, many algorithm animations can be found on the Web, and they currently provide a popular complement to lectures in many programming courses. A fundamental reference book on the topic is by Stasko et al. (1998); a recent monograph is by Pareja-Flores and Velázquez-Iturbide (2001).

Definitions

Broadly speaking, a visualization is a visual representation of a given object. We can find many examples of visualizations in everyday life. For example, the well-known map of the London Underground, first designed by Harry Beck in 1931 (Spence, 2001), is a visualization of the actual underground network. It shows a distorted layout, which is more easily understood by the viewer than the actual one thanks to its regularity, use of colors, etc. Information visualization requires an effort to abstract the target entity to visualize, as well as a good graphical design composed of clear layout, colors, etc. However, there is an expectation that a good visualization helps in better understanding certain concepts or fact; as the old adage says, "a picture is worth a thousand words." Most disciplines use some sort of visualization to explain their domain of study, some of them with a tradition that dates back centuries, e.g., medicine or biology drawings.

Software visualization is the discipline of visualizing software entities. Computer science in general, and programming in particular, have always visualized software. Manual indentation is a simple technique for highlighting and helping to better understand the entities in a program. Flowcharts are visual representations of control flow that have been used since the 1960s. More recently, the emergence of graphic displays and printers has fostered the use of computers to support more advanced graphical visualizations.

This broad definition of software visualization includes many aspects of visual representations: text versus graphics, level of abstraction, static versus dynamic visualizations, one or multiple views, etc. Furthermore, visualizations are not restricted to the structure or behavior of correct programs but may represent other aspects (e.g., performance data) or be used to explain compiling errors. In the previous section, we showed an example of a visual explanation of a type error; this kind of visualization is useful for helping beginners understand type systems (Jun, Michaelson, & Trinder, 1999). As the biggest efforts have been directed at the visualization of the structure and behavior of programs, we will focus on this class of visualizations.

The term program visualization is normally used to refer to straightforward representations of static source code, such as selective highlighting, indenting, or design diagrams for a program. Rudimentary forms of program visualization are automatically provided by editors, pretty-printers, or debuggers. However, the term algorithm animation is normally used to refer to abstract representations of the dynamic behavior of programs (i.e., their algorithmic behavior) and is not always directly related to the particular code used to implement the algorithm. Dynamic behavior can be shown as a sequence of discrete snapshots or by means of smooth transitions. Algorithm animations are technically more difficult to generate (they are hardly ever generated automatically), but they have a large potential for educational use.

For instance, in Figure 1, two program visualizations obtained automatically with the functional programming environment WinHIPE are shown (Velázquez-Iturbide & Presa-Vázquez, 1999). The left part displays a formatted textual representation of an expression derived while sorting the list [5,3,7,1,4] with the *insertsort* algorithm; the right part displays the same expression using a graphical representation for lists. In Figure 2, a visualization (Jiménez-Peris et al., 1998) of the execution of an imperative program to append two linked lists is shown. Different windows at the left contain successive activations of the *append* procedure; another window displays the current state of the list data structure.

The reader interested in a more systematic categorization of software visualization can refer to any of the most widely accepted taxonomies (Brown, 1998; Myers, 1990; Price, Baecker, & Small, 1998).

Figure 1: A Textual Visualization and a Graphical Visualization of a Functional Expression

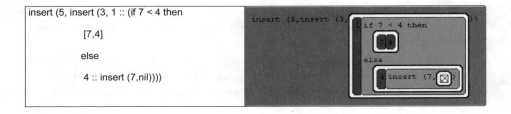

Figure 2: A Program Visualization of an Imperative Program about Linked Lists

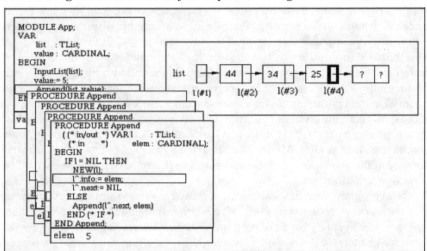

Evolution of Algorithm Animation Systems

Algorithm animation is a research field that is now 20 years old. As a consequence, so many techniques and systems have been developed that it is impossible to give a comprehensive overview in such a short space. In this section, we give a brief outline of some of the important landmarks in the evolution of algorithm animation systems. A large number of animation systems can be found in the literature (Naps et al., 1997, Appendix B).

There is a consensus in considering the videotape *Sorting Out Sorting* presented in 1981 by Baecker (1998) a landmark on animation. It included animations of nine sorting algorithms, it introduced the idea of representing array items by bars and representing the length of a bar as the value of the item, and it used highlighting to indicate elements being compared. At the end, the video showed a race of the algorithms examined, allowing an intuitive comparison of their relative performance.

The Ph.D. dissertation by Brown (1988) on the BALSA system gave the field a good name within the scientific computer science community. Many other works followed that established the main techniques for implementing algorithm animation. The main landmarks were systems that introduced three different approaches to animation specification:

- BALSA (Brown, 1988): This introduced the concept of "interesting event" as an important step in a given algorithm. Algorithms were annotated with calls corresponding to interesting events.

- Tango (Stasko, 1990): Here, animation was also made by annotation, which now corresponded to the paths to be followed by graphical objects in a two-dimensional coordinate system.

- Pavane (Roman et al., 1992): Here, a declarative approach was undertaken, with mappings being defined from program states to graphical objects. Upon program execution, changes in the program state triggered updates to the graphical view of the program.

In the mid-1990s, many of the existing systems were ported to the Web, and many additional systems were specifically designed for the Web. An interesting report about efforts in those years was made by a conference working group (Naps et al., 1997). A representative work from those years is that by Naps (1996), in which he carried out a study of the technical alternatives that could be used to make animations produced by previous systems available on the Web, and in addition, he reported on the extensions he developed. Many other systems were developed in the same spirit, such as CAT and JCAT (Brown & Najork, 1996; Brown & Raisamo, 1997), Mocha (Baker et al., 1995), WebGAIGS, and JAVHÉ (Naps, 1997; Naps, Eagan, & Norton, 2000).

A second group from those years was formed by the systems that were not specifically designed for the Web but were based on stand-alone multimedia and hypermedia. Although they could not be directly used on the Web, their features were similar to Web-based systems, given the hypermedia nature of the Web. A good example is the HalVis system (Hansen, Schrimpsher, & Narayanan, 1999).

From the outset, a common feature of most algorithm animation systems was their use for education. However, they typically included canned animations, where the user could play them but only sometimes introduce input data. In the late 1990s, new systems were developed based around the philosophy of allowing students to create their own animations, mainly by means of scripting languages, which were used interactively. A useful facility consisted of generating scripts from programs and storing them in files, which were later processed to generate animation. This facility provided the animation system with independence from the programming language used to implement the algorithm. Good examples are Samba (Stasko, 1997), JAWAA (Pierson & Rodger, 1998), and ANIMAL (Roessling & Freisleben, 2001).

Finally, some systems were designed in which animations were automatically produced, thus reducing the burden on teachers and students. Strictly speaking, they produced program animations enhanced with graphical representations, rather than algorithm animations. They can be considered as extensions of programming environments with advanced animation capabilities that are usable on the Web. Three examples are ISVL for Prolog (Domingue & Mulholland, 1997), KIEL for ML (Berghammer & Milanese, 2001), and Jeliot for Java programming (Haaajanen et al., 1997).

A related approach consisted of extending a programming environment with capabilities typically found in office applications so that it could be used to develop customized

Figure 3: Three Visualizations of the Same Expression

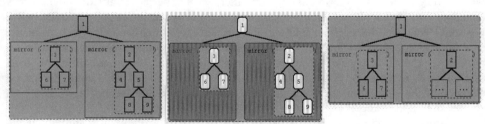

animations, which could then be run on a PC or on Web pages. The use of the office-application metaphor to implement and customize animations greatly facilitates their use by teachers and by students. An example is WinHIPE for functional programming (Naharro-Berrocal, Pareja-Flores, & Velázquez-Iturbide, 2000). Shown in Figure 3 are three different visualizations of an expression computing the mirror of a binary tree that have been customized by simple dialogues, as occurs in office applications. The first two visualizations exhibit different typographic elements, whereas the third is a simplification of the first but with the hidden parts elided.

Educational Uses of Algorithm Animation

From the outset, the main use of algorithm animation was educational. For instance, Mark Brown's BALSA system (Brown, 1988) was intended for use in the following way. A prepared animation with a commentary from the teacher could run on each student's computer. Students could control the speed and direction of the animation, but the contents could not be changed. Most of the systems developed by researchers had an educational use, rather than an industrial one (for instance, as a debugging tool). The best documented experience ran for about 20 years at the Computer Science Department of Brown University (Bazik et al., 1998), but other more modest experiences are also reported in the literature.

Algorithm animation systems have been used in several ways (Rodger, 1996). One possibility consists of using graphical animations as a complement to lectures on algorithms. In addition, their dynamic features give them an advantage over slides or the blackboard because the lecturer does not need to erase or write over previous visualizations. Also, more control is obtained over the direction and speed of the display by including forward and backward advances.

In this approach, the lecturer is the only active agent in the animation. This situation often cannot be avoided; for instance, when the number of students is large. The risk is to make students watch an animation without any other complement, because they will be in the same situation as when watching TV or a movie. This attitude is sometimes described as "hands-on, mind-off."

The passive attitude of students can be partly remedied by interleaving oral explanations and animations, as well as encouraging students to ask questions. An interesting point is that there is some evidence (Roessling & Freisleben, 2000) that most students prefer to see animation immediately after the lecturer's explanation of the corresponding algorithm. Others prefer to interleave explanations and animations or to see animations before the explanation is given. However, leaving all the animations for the end of the class seems to be less preferred.

Algorithm animations can be used more actively by students in an electronic class, where every student has a terminal or a computer. Most experiences at Brown University (Bazik et al., 1998) are based on this infrastructure, for instance, the CAT system (Brown & Najork, 1996) was designed so that the teacher and the students could watch the same animation simultaneously on Web browsers. The teacher had a control panel that allowed him/her to control the pace of the animation, and students were able to see different views (including explanations) of the algorithm. Although they did not have control over the advance of the animation, the students could commute among different views and even change their appearance.

Animations can also be given to students for self-study. Web-based animations are especially useful because of their features of universal access and platform independence. Students can repeat animations used in the classroom by the lecturer at their own pace and as many times as necessary to fully understand them. If animations incorporate certain additional features (explained in the next section), students can use them more satisfactorily.

A dream of software visualization tools is that students will raise their level of abstraction and concentrate on understanding the difficult parts of algorithms. However, the reality does not always resemble that dream, and we find odd uses of animations. For instance, if the animation system asks questions at given moments of the animation, students can use their answers as an additional way of checking whether they understand the algorithm behavior. It seems that this use is especially popular for revision before examinations (Rodger, 1996). It is also common to use automatic visualizations generated by programming environments as a testing tool (Bazik et al., 1998). Although visualization eases understanding, understanding is still more work than guessing, so students find it easier to let the compiler give the verdict about whether their programs are correct.

Another common use of algorithm animation is within laboratories. Naps (1990) reported four uses of the GAIGS animation system in closed laboratories for groups of 10 students:

- Discovery labs: The animation of an algorithm is presented in the lab before it is formally presented in the classroom. By answering questions on the lab sheets distributed with the exercises, the student eventually deduces the algorithm behavior. After the instructor has verified that a student understands the algorithm, the student is allowed to access the algorithm's implementation. The student can also be asked to modify the algorithm and visualize the new version.
- Reinforcement labs: This lab allows a student to reinforce understanding of a particular subtle algorithm presented in a prior lecture period.
- Improvement labs: In these labs, the student is given the implementation of an algorithm that has been previously discussed in a lecture. The student observes that algorithm's performance on a variety of data sets, alters the algorithm to improve its performance, and then views the results of these alterations to verify that the performance of the new implementation is better.
- Comparison labs: In these labs, the student views different implementations of a data structure and uses observations to compare the pros and cons of each implementation. The written lab materials given to the student for the exercise should lead toward deductions about the efficiency of the different implementations.

A more demanding use of animation systems consists of requiring students to build their own animations (Stasko, 1997). Potentially, this is an extremely educationally rewarding task, because students play an active role and, hence, learn more. However, it is a demanding task, where they must typically learn a scripting language and use it correctly to animate programs. To ensure that expectations regarding performance are reasonable, it is important to adapt the task to the level of the students (Rodger, 1996).

Lessons Learned from Using Animation Systems

Visualization and animation are complex fields where many factors converge, including typography, psychology of the user, domain of application, etc. Once again, this makes it difficult to fully summarize lessons learned, although "ten commandments of algorithm animation" can be found in the literature (Gloor, 1998).

Some general recommendations about minor details of animations are valuable. Khuri (2001a) summarized recommendations on display layout, use of color and sound, and interactivity issues. For instance, it is advisable to place the most important view near the top and to the left, because eye-motion studies show that our gaze goes to the upper-left of a rectangular display and then moves clockwise. Another good piece of advice is to restrict the number of colors to a maximum of five, plus or minus two, because studies show that short memory (lasting about 20 seconds) can store five words or shapes, six letters, seven colors, and eight digits.

These general recommendations should be contrasted with the projection equipment and the application used to display the animations (Roessling & Freisleben, 2000). Thus, colors readable on the screen can be less clear at the back of the classroom. Also, different colors or fonts can be supported by some machines and not by others; in particular, Java fully supports only three font families and several font sizes.

Let us review some commonly accepted suggestions for their educational use:

- *Make the meaning of the different graphical representations explicit.* Simply providing icons with graphical representations does not help understanding and, in fact, such use often produces the following paradox. Software visualizations provide concrete representations, which may assist the student, but they do so via the use of graphical abstract representations, which may confuse the student. The meanings of the graphical representations and their relation to the program element should be explained by embedding them in the system, e.g., with a help facility (Stern, Søndergaard, & Naish, 1999), or be reinforced by allocating time to the subject during the course.

- *Adapt to the knowledge level of the user.* Thus, novice students should not be overwhelmed by too many details or windows, and they usually prefer to test the animation with given input data. In contrast, advanced students benefit from additional facilities for controlling complexity and for navigation, or from the capability to enter input data to explore algorithms.

  Novice students can also more easily understand the structure of animations if they are based on well-known metaphors. Most systems rely on the video player metaphor to explain the function of control buttons: rewind, forward, etc. Biermann and Cole (1999) considered that algorithms can be better understood by structuring animations as a sequence of snapshots, conceptually similar to comic strips. The viewer can advance or rewind the animation, but two consecutive snapshots are always shown at a time to illustrate the effect of a given action by means of the state before and after the action.

  Other authors use metaphors to explain the interaction of the user with the system. Jeliot (Haajanen et al., 1997) used a theater metaphor in order to explain the different actors involved in an animation: the animation is a performance, the algorithm to be visualized is the script of a play, etc. Electronic books constitute a common metaphor that helps in understanding the structuring of hypermedia elements that are to form a lesson or a set of lessons on algorithms (Brown & Najork, 1996; Brown & Raisamo, 1997). WinHIPE uses the metaphor of office applications (Naharro-Berrocal et al., in press) to explain how an animation is built or maintained. It involves a process in which different elements are carefully generated, customized, and organized to form animation, in the same way that users build slide presentations or documents in office applications.

Advanced students make extensive use of such facilities as large data sets, multiple views, many visual items in each visualization, and control over the animation progress and over the complexity of the display. A good representative system that supported all of these features was the pioneer BALSA system (Brown, 1988).

• *Be interactive.* A high degree of interactivity is necessary to keep students interested and to improve their understanding of algorithms. In particular, flexible control of the animation should be possible, including movement in a backwards direction. A simple but effective user interface for animation control mirrors a video player, with buttons for the following functions: stop, pause, one step forward, continuous advance, advance to the end, one step backwards, and backtrack to the beginning. Other buttons executing meaningful operations for a given algorithm can also be included.

Interaction can also be fostered by allowing students to customize visualizations. Students should be able to choose the view they wish to watch at any given moment. Customization of layout and typographic elements also helps students feel more comfortable by making them feel that they developed the visualizations themselves (Velázquez-Iturbide & Presa-Vázquez, 1999).

Another way of forcing interaction is to allow the user to enter the input data of an algorithm. This allows the student to explore the animation freely in order to understand the algorithm properly. For instance, the use of extreme cases can be informative, such as the behavior of *quicksort* on a sorted sequence. This facility is naturally provided for any program and data by programming environments with automatic visualization tools, which are probably the most popular visualization systems.

Finally, unexpected short questions requiring a response from the student can be shown on the fly. It is often useful to provide two kinds of questions. Some can pop up in random order but in an appropriate context. They focus the student's attention on specific issues and promote self-evaluation as a means of improving comprehension. Other questions may be placed at critical points beyond which the student cannot proceed until they are correctly answered.

• *Complement animations with explanations.* To avoid a passive attitude of students and to make animations more meaningful, animations must be accompanied by explanations. Such integration can be made in a number of different ways, such as using one or several (coordinated) graphical windows, providing a help facility, or using dynamic Web pages.

It is difficult to give specific recommendations, except in the case of certain uses. For instance, Naharro-Berrocal and colleagues (2001) propose a format for dynamic Web pages describing algorithms. Each page has a header and four sections: the problem specification, the algorithm description, a program coding the algorithm in a functional language, and an animation illustrating the algorithm. The Web page and its elements are semi-automatically generated by the WinHIPE programming environment. Shown in Figure 4 is a generated page for *inorder* traversing a binary tree. Experience has shown that this page structure is roughly adequate, but it could be improved in several ways. The most important lesson is that including only one animation is too restrictive for most algorithms, and therefore, the environment should allow inclusion of several animations that are representative of input cases covering all possible situations.

Some authors are also concerned with the length of explanations. A common suggestion (Roessling & Freisleben, 2000; Stern et al., 1999) is to design the animation and explanations so that the student does not need to use the scrolling bar.

Figure 4: A Web Page Containing an Animation with Explanations

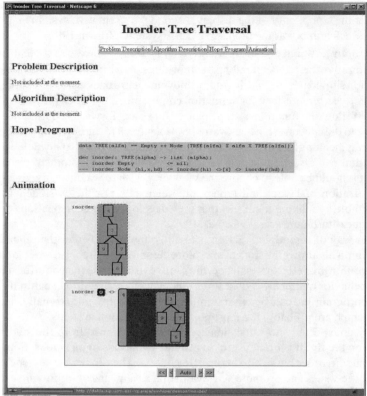

Another approach is a more traditional one, based on paper books. In particular, Bazik et al. (1998), from Brown University, emphasized the need of the tight integration of a textbook and animations, if these are to be integrated naturally into a course. A typical part of this integration is that the book and the animations must be based on the same programming paradigm, and even the same programming language.

- *Provide multiple views.* An algorithm can be watched in many different ways, e.g., control flow in source code, state of data structures, etc. Providing the student with multiple views can facilitate a better understanding of the algorithm. Windows displaying different views should be coordinated to show consistent information. In particular, it is useful to provide a program animation view (where code is shown and highlighted as the program executes) simultaneously with more abstract algorithm animation views. In this way, the student can relate algorithm actions to program code. Another alternative consists of providing pseudo-code instead of raw code. If pseudo-code nodes are enhanced with expand and contract facilities (i.e., simulating stepwise refinement), animations should be coordinated accordingly to ensure the adequate level of granularity. In this way, the student has more control to experiment with the animation. Experience by Stern et al. (1999) suggested that levels of refinement should be restricted to a maximum of three, and that pseudo-code of the highest level should not be a simple statement but should instead outline the main steps of the algorithm. Based on pedagogical considerations, it can sometimes be advantageous to offer different views sequentially. For instance, the HalVis system (Hansen et al., 1999) was designed to show animation in three steps. In the first step, the students were given an algorithm and a familiar metaphor that could help them understand the problem, e.g., bubbling water for the bubble-sorting algorithm. Next, a detailed animation was provided, with synchronous multiple views and explanations. Finally, a large example of an application with fewer details was displayed to enhance understanding of the algorithm performance when applied to large-scale data.

- *Include performance information.* Efficiency analysis is an important part of algorithmic understanding. Thus, including data collected about the algorithm execution can enhance understanding of its efficiency.

  Another way of reinforcing performance information is by animating several algorithms simultaneously, as in the *Sorting Out Sorting* videotape (Baecker, 1998). Different rates for solving the same problem are visually deduced by the user.

- *Include execution history.* After several steps in the algorithm animation, it is common to forget previous steps, to have misunderstood some previous step in the algorithm, or simply to want to have a global view of the history. Including historical information can help overcome these problems. History can be explicitly provided or can be implicitly integrated in some of the algorithm views.

All of the above recommendations should be followed with care, because there is no single animation system that is always the best one for all types of users. In fact, the design of an animation system and its animations should be as carefully planned as any other design activity. Khuri (2000b) presented a user-centered approach, which is a first step in developing methodologies for "animation engineering."

Many of the above recommendations are aimed at an educational use. Anderson and Naps (2001) proposed an "instructional design" scale, which is an attempt to identify levels of support provided by animations to educational use. The fewer elements an animation system has, the lower it is in the proposed scale, and therefore, the less adequate it is for education.

Finally, we want to remark on an important practical issue. Applications used to generate animations are not commercial applications, but they are usually developed in universities or research centers. One advantage is the fact that the system can be carefully designed, so that it can be naturally integrated into their courses. However, an important drawback is the fact that instructors make themselves dependent on such applications for their courses. Evolution in courses must be accompanied with the maintenance of animation tool, which is a labor-intensive and expensive task.

Evaluation of Animation Systems

The lessons that have been described above were extracted from many sources: observations and experiences of teachers, questionnaires completed by students, informal chats with students, and controlled psychological experiments. One fundamental question remains unanswered, however: Do algorithm animations truly assist teaching and learning, and if so, how can they best be utilized?

All the experiences reported in the literature agree that students are highly motivated by algorithm animations. For instance, Roessling and Freisleben (2000) reported that about 85% of students graded the idea of using animations with an "A." Furthermore, more than 90% judged the integration of animations into lectures as "good" or "very good." As students' interest and enthusiasm about a subject are invaluable aids to instruction, algorithm animations have pedagogical value. In some cases, higher motivation caused students to dedicate more time to study algorithms, thus improving their understanding of the algorithms under study (Stasko, 1997).

In general, an increase in motivation is not always equivalent to an improvement in learning effectiveness. Our intuition about the educational value of algorithm animations must be supported by experimental evidence. In order to obtain this evidence, several controlled psychological experiments have been conducted. It is a difficult task, because there is no simple characterization of what it means to learn about an algorithm: to be able to carry out the procedural steps of the algorithm, to code easily the algorithm in a programming language, etc. It is also important to remember that each experiment is based on a particular algorithm animation, which may be problematic. Some initial conclusions can be given from these experiments, but there are no definitive conclusions, and further research is necessary.

We can obtain some initial insight from studies about the effectiveness of other computer-based graphical representations. They agree in that the use of multimedia does not always improve learning. Some studies (Mayer, 1997; Petre, 1995) emphasized the fact that it should not be taken for granted that the meaning of the graphical notation is obvious, and it should be clearly explained. It is also important to have clear goals for the use of graphics (Rieber, Boyce, & Assad, 1990) and to use graphics and text in a coordinated way (Mayer, 1997), typically using text to explain the graphics. With respect to their efficacy for learning, positive results have been obtained in certain cases (Mayer, 1997; Rieber et al., 1990), but results have also been obtained where there is no improvement (Mayer, 1997; Rieber et al., 1990) or where improvement declines after a short period of time (Palmiter & Elkerton, 1990).

The first documented experiments with algorithm animations were carried out in the early 1990s. John Stasko, developer of the Tango and Polka animation systems, carried out an empirical evaluation of these systems (Stasko, Badre, & Lewis, 1993). An algorithm animation was used to teach a complicated algorithm (on *pairing heaps*) to graduate students in computer science, in the hope that the animation would help students understand the dynamic behavior of the algorithm. In a post-test, the results were disappointing, with the group that had used animations performing no better than the control group. Answers by students to a questionnaire allowed the identification of some shortcomings of the system, mainly lack of explanations accompanying the animations and of control over the progress of the algorithm, including a rewind facility.

Several investigators have reported that somewhat better results are achieved by forcing the students to be more active while watching the animation. Thus, Lawrence, Badre, and Stasko (1994) carried out a more complex experiment with students from an introductory computer science course, using the Kruskal algorithm. Here, more encouraging results were obtained. The best results were obtained by students who used animations and also worked interactively in the laboratory. The results also suggested that animations assisted students in forming concepts. Byrne, Catrambone, and Stasko (1996) examined the relation of viewing an animation to making predictions about the behavior of an algorithm. With psychology students, those who made predictions about *depth-first search* scored significantly better in a post-test than others who had merely watched identical visualizations without making such predictions. However, animations were not effective for computer science students to understand *binomial heaps*.

Other experiments have pointed out the importance of designing animations carefully, so that they are suitable for the student level of understanding. Empirical experiments performed by Lattu, Tarhio, and Meisalo (2000) showed that the Jeliot system, with its interface composed of four windows, was well suited for experts but too complex for novices. A new version (Jeliot, 2000) was built, incorporating a simplified interface that was more suitable to novices. It was then used for a long-term evaluation (Levy, Ben-Ari, & Uronen, 2001) of a full-year course in introductory computer science. The students were compared with a control group that received additional instruction without (Jeliot, 2000). The main conclusion was that the vocabulary of terms used in explanations and predictions was found to be considerably better in the animation group than in the control group.

If we seek a global assessment of visualizations, Hansen et al. (1999) suggested that visualization with well-designed hypermedia is as effective as learning from a compilation of the best algorithm descriptions (extracted from textbooks) and then problem solving. They also concluded that hypermedia visualizations can have a significantly higher learning impact than a lecture, and that a combination of both is even better.

In summary, there are different results obtained in different experiences and experiments. One plausible explanation hypothesizes that good results are obtained when the student actively engages in the educational activity using animations (Naps et al., in press).

STRUCTURED COLLECTIONS OF PROGRAMMING EXERCISES

Many animation systems include collections of animation examples, but they are simply lineal collections. We can also find collections of animation on websites, with those by Brummond (2001) probably being the most representative. It should be noted that animations are multimedia documents, because they are usually complemented with textual explanations, multiple graphical views, etc. Although these documents have many elements in common, with the exception of a few cases, they do not generally have an explicit structure. For instance, Naharro-Berrocal et al. (2001) organized a document into problem statement, algorithm description, program, and animation. These documents can form a documental basis for algorithm courses that can be shared on the Web.

As already mentioned, such collections typically have no structure, or, at best, have a lineal structure. Unfortunately, such structure is too limiting for large collections of exercises, where more flexible retrieval is desired. A more advanced form of sharing collections of exercises is by means of repositories containing a large number of exercises classified according to some criteria. In addition, facilities can be provided for mundane tasks (such as searching existing exercises or adding new ones) or for more sophisticated tasks (such as electronic publishing of parts of the collection or the customization of exercises to meet the educational requirements of a particular user). Due to the intensive work that their development requires, there are few working repositories, which we summarize below.

Several initiatives within ACM SIGCSE (Joyce et al., 1997; Knox, 1997) proposed the development of a repository of computer science laboratories containing high-quality laboratory materials to be shared by the community of computer science educators. A first prototype included a database of lab information (including links to full materials) accessed by means of the Web, and it also provided related facilities for lab submission, searching by keyword or topic, and an annotation capability for each lab. Currently, *The Lab Repository* is one of the technical sections of the *SIGCSE Bulletin*. In its current status (Knox, 2002), it contains 66 contributions with different degrees of review.

Another effort by ACM SIGCSE to share teaching resources on the Web is *Computer Science Education Links* (McCauley, 2001). This is a Web page maintained by Renée McCauley, where links to a variety of materials for teaching computer science can be found. It is organized into categories (currently, there are 16 categories with a total of 119 links). There is also a technical section in the *SIGCSE Bulletin* that is being used for the same purpose.

WebToTeach (Arnow & Barshay, 1999) is a website for assisting in programming by means of a collection of programming exercises. WebToTeach provides a good number of exercises in six different programming languages, but the main emphasis is given on the educational features, rather than on the collection.

More advanced repositories are based on structured documents. Documents describing an exercise are marked-up with a language identifying parts such as title, problem statement, hints, etc. A management system allows retrieving, maintaining, and publishing these documents.

A representative example is the eXercita system (Gregorio-Rodríguez et al., 2001, 2002). Exercises are structured documents with structure that is marked-up with the eXercita language, which is an extension of LaTeX. Any retrieved document can be processed with other tools in order to generate a PostScript file (to print the exercise) or a Web page. Other tools are provided for examination and editing purposes, such as searching existing exercises or adding new ones to the collection. The user can also retrieve problems according to different criteria, such as their relationship to a specific topic, or their level of difficulty. Finally, more sophisticated tasks can also be performed, such as electronic publishing of parts of the collection or their customization to the educational requirements of the particular user. Moreover, a paper book containing programming exercises (Gregorio-Rodríguez, in press) is being published. It has been developed by selecting and formatting a good number of the exercises contained in the collection.

A similar system is SAIL (Kovourov et al., 2000). It is also based on LaTeX and a database of exercises, but the emphasis and its main features are quite different. It allows the generation of different instances of the same problem in order to encourage cooperation among students without fear of plagiarism. It also provides support for grading. However, it provides much less comprehensive support and fewer facilities for structuring exercises. Therefore, its searching and publishing capabilities are more restricted, because it simply provides a facility for searching based on text matching.

CONCLUSION AND FUTURE TRENDS

Program execution for programming courses is still a field of application of the Web where few experiences exist. Wider use of the Web will require careful implementation of a whole programming system. These are complex applications, and in this area, they have to deal with the additional complexity of a Web-based architecture and different user interface. It will be some years before a satisfactory level of maturity is achieved in this kind of Web application.

In contrast, software visualization and animation achieved technical maturity in the early 1990s. In the years thereafter, most efforts focused on their educational adequacy. In this respect, some maturity is being achieved, but additional efforts are still necessary. There are several directions in which improvements are expected.

If we are to find the answers to outstanding questions, more research is necessary in the design and use of some of the elements constituting educational animations. What points in an algorithm's execution would be good candidates to be "interesting events"? What examples best illustrate the behavior of an algorithm? The same uncertainty about proper use applies to elements that can enrich animations, such as explanations, questions, etc. More specific recommendations and guidelines for different users must also be developed.

The development of animations is still a time-consuming activity. We believe that we will see more efforts aimed at facilitating the automatic generation of visualizations and animations, as well as efforts to facilitate their easy construction and customization by the user. For example, WinHIPE (Naharro-Berrocal et al., in press) is being enhanced using office applications as the leading metaphor. The facilities typically found in a programming environment (editing, compiling, debugging, etc.) will be made available to the user, and in addition, the user will be able to design and modify animations in a more integrated and user-friendly way than is currently possible. For instance, a generated Web page containing an animation cannot be easily retrieved, modified, and regenerated. Instead, the user must continually generate it again from scratch. This is clearly a problem, and it would be better if the user received assistance from the system at all times when carrying out these tasks, in the same way that the user does when modifying an existing document within an office application.

The integration of theoretical explanations and algorithm animations (each containing explanations, questions, and other hypermedia elements) resembles an electronic book. There are currently several research efforts aimed at designing and developing dynamic electronic books, with dynamic contents and virtual laboratories. We believe that these virtual laboratories for programming will incorporate interfacing with programming tools, such as program compiling and execution, and will include automatic visualization and animation.

The evolution of repositories is still a field of active research, but we think that the next step will lead to the development of digital libraries containing exercises. As mentioned earlier, they have the potential to be dynamic and active digital libraries, where the user will have authentic learning experiences.

REFERENCES

Aggarwal, A. (Ed.). (2000). *Web-based learning and teaching technologies: opportunities and challenges*. Hershey, PA: Idea Group Publishing.

Anderson, J. M., & Naps, T. L. (2001). A context for the assessment of algorithm animation systems as pedagogical tools. In E. Sutinen (Ed.), *Proceedings of the First Program Visualization Workshop* (pp. 121–130). Joensuu, Finland: University of Joensuu.

Arnow, D., & Barshay, O. (1999). WebToTeach: an interactive focused programming exercise system. *Proceedings of the 29th ASEE/IEEE Frontiers in Education Conference* (session 12a9) (pp. 39–44).

Baecker, R. (1998). Sorting out sorting: a case study of software visualization for teaching computer science. In J. T. Stasko et al. (Eds.), *Software visualization* (pp. 369–381). Cambridge, MA: MIT Press.

Baker, J. E. et al. (1995). A model for algorithm animation over the WWW. *ACM Computing Surveys, 27*(4), 568–572.

Bazik, J. et al. (1998). Software visualization in teaching at Brown University. In J. T. Stasko et al. (Eds.), *Software visualization* (pp. 383–398). Cambridge, MA: MIT Press.

Berghammer, R., & Milanese, U. (2001). KIEL—A computer system for visualizing the execution of functional programs. *Functional and (Constraint) Logic Programming*, 365–368.

Biermann, H., & Cole, R. (1999). *Comic strips for algorithm visualization* (Tech. Rep. No. 1999-778). New York: New York University.

Brown, M. H. (1988). *Algorithm animation.* Cambridge, MA: MIT Press.

Brown, M. H. (1998). A taxonomy of algorithm animation displays. In J. T. Stasko et al. (Eds.), *Software visualization* (pp. 35–42). Cambridge, MA: MIT Press.

Brown, M. H., & Najork, M. (1996). Collaborative active textbooks: a Web-based algorithm animation system for an electronic classroom. *Proceedings of the 1996 IEEE Symposium on Visual Languages* (pp. 266–275).

Brown, M. H., & Raisamo, R. (1997). JCAT: collaborative active textbooks using Java. *Computer Networks and ISDN Systems, 29*, 1577–1586.

Brummond, P. (2001). *The complete collection of algorithm animations* [Web page]. http://www.cs.hope.edu/~alganim/ccaa.

Burd, D. D. (2000). Web based support of a programming class. In A. Aggarwal (Ed.), *Web-based learning and teaching technologies: opportunities and challenges* (pp. 175–197). Hershey, PA: Idea Group Publishing.

Byrne, M. D., Catrambone, R., & Stasko, J. T. (1996). *Do algorithm animations aid learning?* (Tech. Rep. No. GIT-GVU-96-18). Atlanta, GA: Georgia Center of Technology, Georgia Tech Graphics, Visualization, and Usability Center.

Cucciarelli, A., Panti, M., & Valenti, S. (2000). Web based assessment in student learning. In A. Aggarwal (Ed.), *Web-based learning and teaching technologies: opportunities and challenges* (pp. 175–197). Hershey, PA: Idea Group Publishing.

Domingue, J., & Mulholland, P. (1997). Staging software visualizations on the Web. *Proceedings of the 1997 IEEE Symposium on Visual Languages.*

Elenbogen, B. S., Maxim, B. R., & McDonald, C. (2000). Yet, more Web-based exercises for learning C++. *Proceedings of the 31st SIGCSE Technical Symposium on Computer Science Education* (pp. 290–294).

Gloor, P. A. (1998). User interface issues for algorithm animation. In J. T. Stasko et al. (Eds.), *Software visualization* (pp. 145–152). Cambridge, MA: MIT Press.

Gregorio-Rodríguez, C. et al. (2001). EXercita: automatic Web publishing of programming exercises. *Proceedings of the 6th SIGCSE/SIGCUE Conference on Innovation and Technology in Computer Science Education* (pp. 161–164).

Gregorio-Rodríguez, C. et al. (2002). *Ejercicios de programación creativos y recreativos en C++* [Creative and Entertaining Programming Exercises in C++]. Madrid, Spain: Prentice Hall.

Gregorio-Rodríguez, C. et al. (2002). *EXercita* [Web page]. http://aljibe.sip.ucm.es.

Haajanen, J. et al. (1997). Animation of user algorithms on the Web. *Proceedings of the 1997 IEEE Symposium on Visual Languages.*

Hansen, S., Schrimpsher, D., & Narayanan, N. H. (1999). From algorithm animations to animation-embedded hypermedia visualizations. *Proceedings of World Conference on Educational Multimedia, Hypermedia and Telecommunications* (pp. 1032–1037).

Hiltz, M., & Kögeler, S. (1997). Teaching C++ on the WWW. *Proceedings of the 2nd SIGCSE/ SIGCUE Conference on Integrating Technology into Computer Science Education* (pp. 11–13).

Ibrahim, B. (1994). World wide algorithm animation. *Proceedings of the 1st World Wide Web Conference* (pp. 305–316).

Jiménez-Peris, R. et al. (1998). Animación de algoritmos en el aula usando presentaciones multimedia [Algorithm animations in the classroom using multimedia presentations]. *VI Congreso Iberoamericano de Educación Superior en Computación - Memoria* (pp. 115–124).

Jiménez-Peris, R. et al. (2000). Towards truly educational programming environments. In T. Greening (Ed.), *Computer science education in the 21st century* (pp. 81–112). New York, NY: Springer-Verlag.

Joyce, D. et al. (1997). Developing laboratories for the SIGCSE Computing Laboratory Repository: guidelines, recommendations, and sample labs. In *ITiCSE '97 Working Group Reports and Supplemental Proceedings* (pp. 1–12), New York: ACM Press.

Jun, Y., Michaelson, G., & Trinder, P. (1999). Explaining polymorphic types through visualization. *7th Annual Conference on the Teaching of Computing*.

Kehoe, C., Stasko, J. T., & Taylor, A. (2001). Rethinking the evaluation of algorithm animations as learning aids: an observational study. *International Journal of Human-Computer Studies*, *54*(2), 265–284.

Khuri, S. (2001a). Designing effective algorithm visualizations. In E. Sutinen (Ed.), *Proceedings of the First Program Visualization Workshop* (pp. 1–12). Joensuu, Finland: University of Joensuu.

Khuri, S. (2001b). A user-centered approach to designing algorithm visualizations. *Informatik/ Informatique*, *2001*(2), 12–16.

Knox, D. L. (1997). Online publication of CS laboratories. *Proceedings of the 28th SIGCSE Technical Symposium on Computer Science Education* (pp. 340–344).

Knox, D. L. (2002). *The computer science teaching center* [Web page]. http://www.cstc.org/

Kovourov, S. et al. (2000). SAIL: a system for generating, archiving and retrieving specialized assignments using LaTeX. *Proceedings of the 31st SIGCSE Technical Symposium* on *Computer Science Education* (pp. 300–304).

Lattu, M., Tarhio, J., & Meisalo, V. (2000). How a visualization tool can be used?: Evaluating a tool in a research and development project. *Proceedings of the 12th Workshop of the Psychology of Programming Interest Group* (pp. 19–32).

Lawrence, A., Badre, A., & Stasko, J. T. (1994). Empirically evaluating the use of animations to teach algorithms. *Proceedings of the 1994 IEEE Symposium on Visual Languages* (pp. 48–54).

Levy, R. B.-B., Ben-Ari, M., & Uronen, P. A. (2001). An extended experiment with Jeliot 2000. In E. Sutinen (Ed.), *Proceedings of the First Program Visualization Workshop* (pp. 131–140). Joensuu, Finland: University of Joensuu.

Mayer, R. E. (1997). Multimedia learning: are we asking the right question? *Educational Psychologist*, *32*(1), 1–19.

McCauley, R. (2001). *Computer science education links* [Web page]. http://www.cacs.usl.edu/ ~mccauley/edlinks/.

Myers, B. (1990). Taxonomies of visual programming and program visualization. *Journal of Visual Languages and Computing, 1*, 97–123.

Naharro-Berrocal, F., Pareja-Flores, C., & Velázquez-Iturbide, J. Á. (2000). Automatic generation of algorithm animations in a programming environment. *Proceedings of the 30th ASEE/IEEE Frontiers in Education Conference* (pp. 6–12) (session S2C).

Naharro-Berrocal, F. et al. (in press). Redesigning the animation capabilities of a functional programming environment under an educational framework. In *Proceedings of the Second Program Visualization Workshop.*

Naharro-Berrocal, F. et al. (2001). Automatic Web publishing of algorithm animations. *Informatik/Informatique, 2001*(2), 41–45.

Naps, T. L. (1990). Algorithm visualization in computer science laboratories. *Proceedings of the 21st SIGCSE Technical Symposium on Computer Science Education* (pp. 105–110).

Naps, T. L. (1996). Algorithm visualization served on the World Wide Web: why and how. *Proceedings of the 1st SIGCSE/SIGCUE Conference on Integrating Technology into Computer Science Education* (pp. 59–61).

Naps, T. L. (1997). Algorithm visualization on the WWW: the difference Java makes. *Proceedings of the 2nd SIGCSE/SIGCUE Conference on Integrating Technology into Computer Science Education* (pp. 59–61).

Naps, T. L. et al. (1997). Using the WWW as the delivery mechanism for interactive, visualization-based instructional modules. In *ITiCSE '97 Working Group Reports and Supplemental Proceedings* (pp. 13–26). New York: ACM Press.

Naps, T. et al. (in press). Exploring the role of visualization and engagement in computer science education. *SIGCSE Bulletin, 34*(4).

Naps, T. L., Eagan, J. R., & Norton, L. L. (2000). JHAVÉ: an environment to actively engage students in Web-based algorithm visualizations. *Proceedings of the 31st SIGCSE Technical Symposium on Computer Science Education* (pp. 109–113).

Palmiter, S., & Elkerton, J. (1991). An evaluation of animated demonstrations for learning computer-based tasks. *Proceedings of the ACM SIGCHI '91 Conference on Human Factors in Computing Systems* (pp. 257–263).

Pareja-Flores, C., & Velázquez-Iturbide, J. Á. (Eds.). (2001). Visualization of software [Special issue]. *Informatik/Informatique, 2001*(2).

Petre, M. (1995). Why looking isn't always seeing: readership skills and graphical programming. *Communications of the ACM, 38*(6), 33–44.

Pierson, W. C., & Rodger, S. H. (1998). Web-based animation of data structures using JAWAA. *Proceedings of the 29th SIGCSE Technical Symposium on Computer Science Education* (pp. 267–271).

Price, B., Baecker, R., & Small, I. (1998). An introduction to software visualization. In J. T. Stasko et al. (Eds.), *Software visualization* (pp. 3–27). Cambridge, MA: MIT Press.

Rieber, L., Boyce, M., & Assad, C. (1990). The effects of computer animation on adult learning and retrieval tasks. *Journal of Computer-Based Instruction, 17*(2), 46–52.

Rodger, S. H. (1996). Integrating animations into courses. *Proceedings of the 1st SIGCSE/SIGCUE Conference on Integrating Technology into Computer Science Education* (pp. 72–74).

Roman, C. -G. et al. (1992). Pavane: a system for declarative visualization of concurrent computations. *Journal of Visual Languages and Systems, 3*, 161–193.

Roessling, G., & Freisleben, B. (2000). Experiences in using animations in introductory computer science courses. *Proceedings of the 31st SIGCSE Technical Symposium on*

Computer Science Education (pp. 134–138).

Roessling, G., & Freisleben, B. (2001). Program visualization using ANIMALSCRIPT. In E. Sutinen (Ed.), *Proceedings of the First Program Visualization Workshop* (pp. 41–52). Joensuu, Finland: University of Joensuu.

Spence, R. (2001). *Information visualization*. New York: ACM Press.

Stasko, J. T. (1990). Tango: a framework and system for algorithm animation. *Computer, 23*(9), 27–39.

Stasko, J. T. (1997). Using student-built algorithm animations as learning aids. *Proceedings of the 28th SIGCSE Technical Symposium on Computer Science Education* (pp. 25–29).

Stasko, J. T., Badre, A., & Lewis, C. (1993). Do algorithm animations assist learning? An experimental study and analysis. *Proceedings of the ACM SIGCHI '93 Conference on Human Factors in Computing Systems* (pp. 61–66).

Stasko, J. T. et al. (Eds.). (1998). *Software visualization*. Cambridge, MA: MIT Press.

Stasko, J. T., & Lawrence, A. (1998). Empirically assessing algorithm animations as learning aids. In J. T. Stasko et al. (Eds.), *Software visualization* (pp. 419–438). Cambridge, MA: MIT Press.

Stern, L., Søndergaard, H., & Naish, L. (1999). A strategy for managing content complexity in algorithm animation. *Proceedings of the 5th Annual Conference on Innovation and Technology in Computer Science Education* (pp. 127–130).

Velázquez-Iturbide, J. Á., & Presa-Vázquez, A. (1999). Customization of visualizations in a functional programming environment. *Proceedings of the 29th ASEE/IEEE Frontiers in Education Conference* (pp. 22–28) (session 12b3).

Webber, A. B. (1996). The Pascal Trainer. *Proceedings of the 27th Technical Symposium on Computer Science Education* (pp. 261–265).

ACKNOWLEDGMENTS

This work was supported by projects TIC2000-1413 of the Spanish Research Agency CICYT and PIGE-02-13 of the Universidad Rey Juan Carlos.

Chapter XVI

Forum Performance in WBE: Causes and Effects

Erik Benrud
University of Baltimore, USA

ABSTRACT

This chapter combines research into student performance in finance courses and student performance in Web-based courses. The chapter explores how a priori characteristics of individual students can serve as predictors of success in a 100% Web-based course in finance. The statistical models developed in the chapter explain up to 31% of the variation in students' final grades. The models have significant explanatory power for variation in performance on individual grade-components such as quizzes, tests, and projects. The models have much less predictive power for student performance in the on-line discussion. Yet, there is a strong relationship between the performance in the on-line discussion and the other grade components. This finding suggests that developing on-line discussion skills prior to the start of the course will enhance student performance in other areas of Web-based courses such as introductory corporate finance.

INTRODUCTION

Over the past 30 years, researchers have generated a lengthy literature on the determinants of students' academic performance, and there has been a commensurate focus on student performance in introductory corporate finance classes (see Borde, Byrd, & Modani, 1998). Such studies examine student background and methods used by professors. With the advent of Web-based learning, this topic has a new dimension to explore. What are the determinants of student performance in an introductory finance class that is taught on the Web? The goal of this chapter is to share some observations that I have made with respect to the interrelationship of the a priori characteristics, the online participation, and the final grade of students in a Web-based introductory corporate finance course.

This chapter was motivated by observations I made in the Spring of 2001 while I taught three sections of a Web-based corporate finance course. I had been teaching 100% Web-based courses for two years up to that point, but in that semester, I observed an interesting phenomena. The section of students that had the lowest average grade for the first quiz was also much more active in the online discussion. That section with the lowest performance on the first quiz but higher online discussion participation began to have the highest average score in most other coursework subsequent to the first quiz. This suggested to me that ability and willingness to participate in the online discussion are important determinants in overall student success in a Web-based course. This chapter provides an analysis of the characteristics, performance, and success of the students I taught in the spring semester and the following fall semester of 2001.

To investigate how participation in the online discussion helps determine student success, first we need to examine the role of the a priori characteristics of the students in determining student success. Many other studies have investigated this topic using grade point average (GPA), gender, age, and other characteristics to predict ex ante student performance. The study here incorporates similar variables and also includes characteristics that directly relate to Web-based learning. Section four includes a complete description of the variables. The second focus of the study builds upon the unique aspect of Web-based learning by exploring the role the online discussion plays in the learning process. Did the online discussions facilitate learning? What is the relationship between student participation in the discussions and student performance elsewhere in the course?

Many of the results are not surprising. Students with a higher Graduate Management Aptitude Test (GMAT) score earned higher grades, for example, and the students who participated more in the discussions earned higher grades. Yet, as Web-based curriculums grow, we must begin to document such observations if we wish to investigate the less salient aspects of Web-based learning. For example, one of the less salient aspects documented here is the strong relationship between online discussion participation and performance on exams. I find the following interesting relationships between certain a priori characteristics and participation in the online discussions and student performance on projects and tests. GMAT score, gender, age, and whether the student is a regular Web-MBA student explains over 31% of the variation of the final course grades in this sample of 76 students. These determinants are poor predictors of online discussion participation, however, but there is a strong relationship between that participation and performance on the exams.

Part of this chapter summarizes student comments regarding how they felt the online discussion aided the learning process. Students in the sample generally appreciated the online discussion. Based on group descriptive measures, the evidence suggests that a class with a generally higher level of experience, comfort, and appreciation for Web-based learning will have a higher level of success, on average. The implications are obvious. Increasing the willingness and ability of students to participate in the online discussions will enhance the learning process. The results suggest that such efforts may have other important implications. As the review of the literature in the next section will note, the gender quality "male" is often a positive and significant determinant for student success in an introductory corporate finance course. The online discussion may prove to be a tool for closing this gender gap.

The chapter goes on to give a more complete discussion of the determinants of success that previous research has documented for finance classes and Web-based classes. The chapter then describes my Web-based finance course and how I used the online discussion.

That section also summarizes assessments made by the students concerning the role of the discussion in the class. Next, the chapter gives summary measures and the results of statistical tests that describe the relationship between student performance, a priori characteristics, and their participation in the discussion. This is followed with a discussion of the results and their implications for designing a Web-based course. A final section is the conclusion.

REVIEW OF THE LITERATURE

As many have said, Web-based learning is here to stay and has become a major force in higher education (see Brooks, 1997; Rahm & Reed, 1997; Phillips-Vicky, 1998). Books such as this one verify that educators want to improve the methods of delivering distance education. Past research has recognized that various student characteristics can serve as predictors for success in certain college courses in a face-to-face (F2F) environment, and educators may be able to enhance some of these characteristics to improve performance. As verified by many researchers, some characteristics serve as predictors of success in Web-based learning environments.

Because the empirical work of this chapter uses data from a corporate finance course, the following discussion first focuses on some of the research into the determinants of student success in F2F courses of this type. One of the earliest studies is by Simpson and Sumrall (1979) that finds the following to be positive predictors of performance in an introductory finance course: age, prior success in other business courses, being a nontransfer student, and having full-time student status. More recently, Borde, Byrd, and Modani (1998) developed an econometric model that explained 33% of the variation in student success, where success was measured by the percentage of total points earned in the course. That model used gender, age, transfer status, grade point average (GPA), whether the student belonged to a student organization, the number of hours the student worked per week, and the average grade in prerequisite accounting courses. That study found that the effects of GPA, the prior grade in accounting classes, and the gender quality "male" were positive and significant. Being a transfer student and being employed had significant negative effects. The influences of age and student organization status were positive and negative, respectively, but they were not significant.

Many previous researchers examined the role of gender in student performance in corporate finance classes. Ferber, Birnbaum, and Green (1983), Heath (1989), and Lumsden and Scott (1987) found that males tended to perform better in the introductory finance course than females. Williams, Waldauer, and Duggal (1992) proposed that this difference may be because males possess greater skills than females in spatial analysis and quantitative abstract reasoning. The findings in this chapter suggest that the verbal dimension added by the online discussion may be a means of making corporate finance more accessible to a wider variety of students.

Some studies investigated the predictive power of personal traits. Filbeck and Smith (1996) found that learning-style preferences of students affect their success in F2F corporate finance courses. They found that testing and teaching styles can influence the performance of various students in different ways. Liesz and Reyes (1989) found that logical thinking ability can be measured and can serve as a significant predictor of student success in a principles of finance course. That study suggests that students planning to study finance should take courses that stimulate logical thought.

With the growth of Web-based learning, researchers have tried to adapt Web-based teaching to the learning-style preferences of students. Personality traits play a role here too. As Noviski (2000), Odom, and Pourjalali (1998) and Chan, Shum, and Lai (1996) noted, personality traits are especially important in distance education. Successful students usually have other motivations for participating in a course other than just wanting a grade. With respect to online discussions, students obviously contribute as part of the required work for the course, but they also use the online discussion as a method of social interaction. Because a Web-based class is a unique environment that can involve people from around the world, when discussing Web-based learning, researchers often use the term "communities." Recent research into Web-based student performance, such as that by Huynh (1999), has drawn upon the work of Habermas (1984, 1987). That literature looks at the role of language in a given culture. Getting students ready for a Web-based class may require training in Web-based etiquette, as suggested by Mandell (1998) and Mohan (1998).

In addition to the need to teach students how to interact online, of course, there is the more basic need for technical training. Nasseh (1998) discussed the results of a survey of students and instructors who had participated in Web-based learning. That survey asked the participants for their opinions on the complex needs of a Web-based learning environment. Communication ranked as a high concern, as did the need to provide adequate technical training to students. There is a growing literature of case studies that share lessons learned on how to prepare students for Web-based learning (Rogers & Laws, 1997; Chalmers, 1999).

Noviski (2000) provided a good summary of technical considerations, student preparation, and instructor preparation for a Web-based curriculum. That work summarized a variety of cases where different software was used in each case. Noviski (2000) concluded the paper with a fairly comprehensive summary of implications for students and instructors. For students, among other things, the author noted that as more students enroll in Web-based curriculum, we can expect a more diverse range of preparation. Students who are less familiar with computers will have to spend time overcoming technical difficulties. Student personalities will play a role in their success. Self-starters will have an advantage. Those students who depend upon cues from fellow students and the instructor to guide them will have more obstacles to overcome.

Instructors who are used to an F2F environment must learn new skills to guide students in a Web-based class. Some authors, such as Novitzki (2001) and Kerka (1996), estimated that the time commitment for a new Web-based course could be twice that of a corresponding F2F course. Once the course has been developed, according to these studies, the Web-based course can take about 50% more time to teach than a corresponding F2F course.

Instructors must find ways to overcome the isolation of many of the students. As Lockett (1998) surmised, distance learning can be a "lonely endeavor." Critics of distance learning point to the lack of interaction as one of its major flaws (Shum & Chan, 2000). To overcome the physical isolation students might feel in a Web-based learning environment, instructors and researchers have generally recognized the importance of online discussion. Educators have long recognized the importance of an active learning environment (Dewey, 1938; Lewin, 1951). It is no surprise, therefore, that later research (Dumant, 1996) recognizes online discussion as one of the strengths of Web-based learning. Some researchers, such as Moore and Kearsley (1995) and Cecez-Kecmanovic and Webb (2000) go on to propose that the online discussion may even challenge the limits of the F2F environment. For those that question often-used methods of assessment in F2F classes, the interaction of the online discussion is an alternative method of assessing what students have learned (Gronlund, 1985; Crabbe, Grainger, & Steward, 1997).

The topic of the online discussion permeates the review of the literature in this section. This review begins with a summary of past research into the determinants of student success in finance courses and then relates that literature to success in Web-based courses. The intuition behind many of the conclusions is obvious, such as students with higher a priori GPAs performed better in a finance course, and students who were "self-starters" performed better in a Web-based class. The discussion of research into Web-based learning points to the importance of the online discussion. One of the goals of this chapter is to show how online discussion can be important even in an introductory and largely quantitative course like corporate finance. Section three outlines the topics and required work for my Web-based corporate finance class. It also explains how I conducted the online discussion and gives some insights into how the students reacted to the discussion in my class. Section four provides some quantitative results from a survey that asked how the students perceived the online discussion. Section four also provides formal statistics that describe the relationships among a priori characteristics, the performance in the discussion, and the other grades. Section five discusses those statistical results, and section six concludes.

A WEB-BASED CORPORATE FINANCE COURSE

As mentioned in the preceding section, an active learning environment serves to stimulate learning. This is an important point in a Web-based learning environment because of the physical remoteness the students generally have to each other and the instructor. Recognizing this, I incorporate into my Web-based corporate finance course several short quizzes, a mid-term exam, a project, a final exam, and an active online discussion for each week.

My Web-based corporate finance course includes all the topics that I have incorporated into my F2F course. The point of a course in corporate finance is to teach students how corporate managers should decide on the type of projects they will pursue and how to finance those projects. To make effective decisions on projects in a corporate setting, the students need to know accounting, time-value of money techniques, methods of measuring risk and return, and methods of raising capital for investing in the projects. These four subjects are the fundamental topics in corporate finance. Shown in Table 1 is an abbreviated syllabus that includes an expanded list of those topics and the weighting scheme of the work the students are expected to perform. In adapting my F2F corporate finance course to the Web, I did not have to change my general approach to teaching the course. When teaching introductory courses, I often rely on using many short assignments to promote an interactive environment. I administer several short quizzes and give one quiz in the first week to make sure that students open the textbook early in the course.

In the classes analyzed in this study, I assigned one project. For that project, each student worked alone to construct a spreadsheet that could automatically generate a multiperiod cash flow for a proposed corporate venture from about 20 initial inputs. The inputs included, for example, the cost of the venture, the needed working capital, and the rate of depreciation. The spreadsheet would be able to compute the appropriate discount rate and determine if the project is acceptable. As with my F2F classes, I gave help to those who asked for it. The amount of help requests for the Web-based classes was about the same as that for my F2F classes. Dealing with the requests for help over the Internet was not new for me,

Table 1: Abbreviated Course Outline

Method of Evaluation			
Grading			
Topic	Number		Total Weight
Project	1	@ 11%	11%
Quizzes	5	@ 3%	15%
Exam 1	1	@ 25%	25%
Exam 2	1	@ 25%	25%
Discussion	8	@ 3%	24%
---------------			----------------
Total			100%
Course Topics			
Topic one	Financial statements review		
Topic two	Financial planning and pro forma statements		
Topic three	Time value of money: present/future value		
Topic four	Time value of money: annuities		
Topic five	Valuing stocks and bonds		
Topic six	Methods of evaluating real projects of a corporation		
Topic seven	Capital markets and deriving measures of risk		
Topic eight	Methods of financing and the cost of capital		
Topic nine	Choosing the optimal capital structure		

because that is how the requests for help often come from students in my F2F classes.

When designing a Web-based course, the new element that I had to learn to use was online discussion. Class time is a precious commodity, and early in my F2F corporate finance course, I have to inform students that we do not have a lot of time for discussion in the class. When appropriate, I mention issues such as environmental concerns and ethics briefly to let the students know that they are important. I quickly move on after briefly mentioning such concerns so that we can focus on the overall theory of how corporate executives choose projects to invest in, and how those executives decide to raise funds to make the investment.

Having taught quantitative courses for the majority of my teaching career, I was not well prepared for conducting regular discussions in a classroom. I had absolutely no experience, furthermore, in conducting discussions in a Web-based learning environment. After investigating various methods, I modeled my discussions after the Socratic dialogue methodology. At the beginning of each week, I would ask an open-ended question. Some of those questions are listed here:

- How is "ease of ownership transfer" an advantage to the corporation and society in general?
- What are the characteristics that we, as humans, have that make us require an interest rate on savings and impose a discount rate on future money to be received?
- Corporations must pay institutions like Moody's and S&P to have their debt rated. What is the advantage to the corporation of having its debt rated?

Occasionally, one student will get the answer right away. More often than not, I have to coax the answer out with a combination of compliments, corrections, and follow-up questions. Table 2 contains a representative series of responses that occurred the first day

Table 2: Excerpts from an Online Discussion

A representative series of initial responses from students and my response to them.	
<u>My initial question:</u>	**What are the characteristics that we, as humans, have that make us require an interest rate on savings and impose a discount rate on future money to be received?**
<u>Student X:</u>	Discounted cash flow is what someone is willing to pay today in order to receive the anticipated cash flow in future years. The discount rate is based on the level of risk of the business and the opportunity cost of capital. Other factors in determining the discount rate include current level of interest rates, anticipated return on the stock, risk associated with the stock, and amount of leverage. One goal of an investor may be to purchase companies at a larger discount to their intrinsic value or what the business would be worth if it were sold tomorrow. Calculating the present value of future cash flows ensures that investors pay the right price now, based on the appreciation in value expected in future years.
<u>Student Y:</u>	The reason people require interest for money they invest is based on the economic concept of **opportunity costs**. When people make choices, they incur opportunity costs because resources are scarce. And I don't know about you but money is a scarce resource. When people look at alternatives and short and long term consequences when making a choice. These choices have varying degrees of risk and people want to be compensated for assuming different degrees of risk.
<u>My response:</u>	Student X mentions some very important points. Her comments relate to how an investor might view stock in a company. She says that: *The discount rate is based on the level of risk of the business and the opportunity cost of capital.* Actually these two points are intertwined. **Who can put them together?** The other points she mentioned like: *current level of interest rates, anticipated return on the stock, risk associated with the stock, and amount of leverage,* do indeed affect the required return, but they are getting too detailed. I am looking for three basic points. Students X and Y mention risk, and that is one of the points. What are the other two? Student Y is correct when he alludes to the fact that resources such as money are scarce. As he correctly states: *people look at alternatives and short and long term consequences when making a choice.* **What is the most basic choice made when a person decides to save and invest?**
Note to reader. Ultimately, I wanted to point out that when a person invests, he/she is making a basic choice between consumption today and consumption in the future. Humans require a reward for waiting. As I went on to bring out in the later discussion, however, the reward for waiting is fairly small. It is about 1.5% per year. Humans must be rewarded for taking risks, and the reward for risk is generally larger. Also, humans must be compensated for inflation.	

that I posted one of these questions in one of the sections. The use of fonts in Table 2 reflects how I use fonts in my online discussions. To call attention to the actual questions, I use a bold font. When I quote a student in my response, I use an italics font.

In those weeks where mandatory discussions occur, a student's participation in the discussion is worth 3% of that student's final grade. To earn credit, the student must add value to the discussion. Students are invited to contribute reasoned guesses, personal anecdotes, and examples from the Web. One well-thought-out and thorough contribution can earn a perfect score for the week. Several small contributions can earn a perfect score as well. They have the entire week to respond. Adding value to the discussion becomes more difficult as the days pass, obviously, as later contributors must work harder to find new ways to add value in that week.

I am active in the discussion and try to react to every message online in a positive way. I grade the first week's contributions liberally and take care to let the students know how they can improve. I provide confidential weekly feedback, via email, early in the course and biweekly feedback later in the course. If a student does not seem to be participating or seems to be way off-track in responses, I react immediately with a confidential email message.

The grades earned from participating in the discussion were generally good. For the 76 students in this study who actually completed the course, the average grade as a percentage of total points is 92.71 with a standard deviation of 8.68. The results are highly skewed, however, and 11 students earned 100% of the online discussion grade. Removing the top 5% and bottom 5% yields an average of 93.96 and standard deviation of 5.58. The corresponding percent of total points earned for the course without the discussion has an average equal to 85.76 and a standard deviation equal to 8.18 for all students. The average and standard deviation of the nondiscussion grades for the middle 90% are 86.20 and 6.25. Section four explores the relationships between these measures.

The students generally reacted favorably to how I conducted and graded the forum. Although it was not my intention when I designed the course, the students said that I was more active in the discussion and generally used the online discussion more when compared to other instructors in Web-based classes. In a poll that I submitted to the students, 60% said that my course used the online discussion *more* than the average Web course they had taken, 76% rated the quality of the discussion *higher* than the average they had experienced in other Web classes, and 55% said that the online discussion significantly aided their understanding of corporate finance. Section four gives a summary of the entire survey.

The survey also made the following request: "Please list any other facts that you feel are pertinent to your level of online discussion participation and your success in the class." About half of the students responded to this question, and positive comments outnumbered negative comments four to one. The following comment was submitted by one of the students. The references to the "forum" in the comment refer to the online discussion:

> *I think that overall, the forum was thought provoking. Towards the end of the semester, I think it became somewhat confusing. I think there was some confusion about what you were asking. Many of us have not taken courses in finance for a while or at all, and what seems clear to an expert in the field is not always clear to those who are not. In spite of this, I learned quite a bit in trying to find an answer. Even when I was wrong, which was most of the time in the last couple of weeks, following it and continuing to attempt to find an answer really gave me a better understanding of whatever we were discussing—particularly this beta thing.*
>
> *I think you do a great job in stimulating thought. Your forum questions appeared to always be focused on an important aspect of the particular chapter, and*

although this was sometimes a hard topic to understand, the process of trying to answer and following the issue really helped me understand things better. I also appreciate your tactfulness when we answered wrong. I think some students are more "uptight" about answering incorrectly, and I think your tactfulness eases this fear—which all students have to some extent.

One advantage I see in this forum is that you must respond. In my three years in law school, I have seen in many classes where certain classmates never say a word unless they are called on, and even then many of them either cannot answer because they have not studied or because they became paralyzed from nerves when their name was called. Although the forum is not the same only in terms of being face to face, I think some people experience the same fears to different extents. This is good I think because it stimulates the student to find the correct answer before responding.

This is probably my own fault because of my course load at the beginning of the semester, but I did not realize you had office hours for us. I probably would have come to see you with math questions. Regardless, I pulled out some old books and brushed up the best I could. This is the first class I have taken in the MBA program, so everything is new.

I am sure you have rolled your eyes on more than one occasion with some forum responses, to include my own—particularly in the last couple of weeks where it is obvious some people are not reading their classmates earlier response before answering.

This survey response is much longer than the majority of other responses, but in being so, it provided insights into how I conducted the online discussion from the perspective of the students. The points this student made are representative of the points of other students. This comment, as with many others, expresses an appreciation for the active question-and-answer discourse that made the students think and find the answers.

In summary, the majority of the students seemed to appreciate the online discussion. The majority felt that it stimulated thought and helped them learn the material. Although I had not set it as a goal, I apparently use the online discussion more than most other instructors. The evidence from the survey suggests the online discussion in my class is a very important tool. This observation will make the statistics in the next section more meaningful.

STATISTICAL ANALYSIS

In this section, I summarize and draw inferences from information gathered from a sample of 76 students in several sections of a Web-based class. The goal is to examine what factors contribute to a student's success in a Web-based learning environment. Those factors include a priori characteristics such as GMAT scores, gender, age, and characteristics that relate to Web-based learning. Also examined is the role of online discussion participation and perceptions of the importance of that discussion. Most of the results are not surprising in that they conform to the results of previous studies or are intuitively appealing; nevertheless, the point of documenting these results for a Web-based corporate finance class can provide an important foundation for future research to build upon.

When I designed my first 100% Web-based course in 1999, my goal was to contribute to the Web-learning initiative at the University of Baltimore. I did not think about where it would lead me, and I did not see myself writing a review of my experiences for a professional book like this. In fact, as mentioned in the introduction, the idea for doing this study did not occur to me until I had the opportunity to teach three separate sections of the course at the same time in the Spring of 2001. Several weeks into the semester, I noticed that one of the sections had a much higher level of aggregate participation when compared to the other two sections. Interestingly enough, the section with the highest level of discussion participation had the lowest average score on the first quiz that was given to each of the three sections. I decided that this needed investigating.

I designed a short survey for the students to take at the end of the course, and that survey directly addressed Web-based learning and the online discussion. A copy of that survey is shown in Table 3. Given in Table 4 are summary measures of the results for each section. In each case, a higher score is assumed to be a positive determinant of success in the course. The number of Web courses taken prior to my course should obviously have a positive effect, for example, as would whether English is the student's first language. Also

Table 3: The Survey Form

End-of-Class Survey for Web Students
1. How many 100% Web courses have you taken prior to this course?
2. Compared to other people, how would you rate your Web skills? Use a 1–5 scale, where 1 = very low, 3 = average, and 5 = among the best.
3. Rate the amount of online discussion work in FIN-504 against other Web courses you have taken. Use a 1–5 scale, where 1 = much lower, 3 = average, and 5 = much more.
4. Rate the quality of the online discussions in FIN-504 against other Web courses you have taken. Use a 1–5 scale, where 1 = totally inferior, 3 = average, and 5 = much better than other courses.
5. How important was the FIN-504 online discussion to your learning Corporate Finance? Use a 1–5 point scale, where 1 = not at all, and 5 = very much.
6. Is English your first language? (Yes/No)
7. How do you perceive your writing skills (in English)? Use a 1–5 scale, where 1 = very low, 3 = average, and 5 = among the best.
8. How do you perceive your math skills? Use a 1–5 scale, where 1 = very low, 3 = average, and 5 = among the best.
9. How do you perceive your public speaking skills? Use a 1–5 scale, where 1 = very low, 3 = average, and 5 = among the best.
10. How many people in the class did you know before the class started?
You do not have to name names, but give a rank, with a number, to each person you knew before class started. Use a 1–5 scale, where 1 = barely acquainted with the person and 5 = very friendly and we interact on matters other than school.
For example, if you knew three people at the start of class, two moderately well and one not very well, your response to Question #10 would be: 3 people: 4, 4, 1. Please list any other facts that you feel are pertinent to your level of participation in the online discussion and your success in the class.

Table 4: Aggregate Results of Survey and Selected Class Grade Averages

Maximum average is in **bold** font.						
Question	Spring 2001			Fall 2001		
Reference moniker ->	**A**	**B**	**C**	**D**	**E**	**F**
Number of all Web courses taken prior to this course	3.07	2.85	**3.79**	2.10	1.80	**2.27**
Self-assessment of Web skills	3.86	3.81	**4.11**	3.60	3.87	**4.04**
Amount of discussion compared to other classes	4.00	3.83	**4.07**	3.60	3.55	**3.80**
Quality of discussions compared to other classes	4.12	3.91	**4.21**	3.70	**4.09**	3.87
Importance of discussion compared to other classes	3.57	3.27	**4.00**	**4.10**	3.42	3.67
English is first language, Yes = 1	**1.00**	0.85	0.93	0.80	0.82	**0.87**
Self-assessment of writing skills in English	3.68	3.69	**3.89**	3.70	**4.09**	3.96
Self-assessment of math skills	3.61	**4.00**	3.86	3.40	3.62	**4.04**
Self-assessment of public speaking skills	3.36	**3.58**	3.57	3.70	3.96	**4.07**
Number of people you knew	0.92	**1.85**	1.64	0.50	0.64	**1.00**
Familiarity factor	1.92	2.16	1.48	**3.71**	1.67	1.67
Class size and grades						
Size of class	14	13	13	10	11	15
Average of quiz one grades	**93.77**	90.92	89.46	83.33	87.88	82.14
Course averages without disc	86.23	87.33	**88.97**	80.75	84.01	**85.82**
Average of discussion grades	88.57	89.23	94.62	**97.21**	93.73	94.18
Average of final grades	86.81	87.81	**90.36**	84.70	86.34	**87.83**

included in the table are the section average for the first quiz, the average course-grade without the discussion, the average discussion grade, and the average final course grade. The first quiz is important, because it gives an assessment of how adept the students were in the topic of finance at the beginning of the class. Including the average discussion grade and average grade without the discussion allows for obvious comparisons.

Given the relatively small size of the individual sections and the objective nature of the data from the survey, we cannot make any statements about statistical significance. There are some interesting patterns, however, and the purpose of this chapter is to report these patterns so that future researchers may use this information to conduct more scientific studies.

The results for the Spring 2001 sections display the pattern that prompted me write this study. In Table 4, the section with the moniker "C" had the lowest average for the first quiz, and it had the highest final average. Section C had the highest amount of Web participation. The students in that section had taken more Web-based courses, furthermore, and they have higher average scores for the questions that addressed Web-based learning issues. That is, on average, the section with the highest final average grade felt their Web skills were higher and felt that the quality and importance of the online discussion was higher in my class than in other Web-based classes they had taken. Although I recognize that the conclusion is not supported by formal statistical tests, the evidence suggests that the one-of-three sections that did not feel superior in math skills and that began with the lowest quiz average was able to overcome these handicaps with a higher level of Web-based skills and a higher appreciation of the role of the online discussion.

This summary conclusion for the Spring 2001 sections is weakly supported by the results for the Fall 2001 sections. Section F had the highest final average, and the students in that section had taken more Web-based classes and felt their Web skills were higher. However, Section F did not give the highest average score to the question concerning the "importance of the online discussion." Also, Section F did not earn the highest average grade for the discussion.

There could be a number of reasons for the differences between the Spring (A, B, and C) and the Fall (D, E, and F) sections. We should notice that Section F is larger than Sections D and E.[1] Because more people were in Section F, individual students had a more difficult time adding value to the discussion each week. Section F had an advantage in that it had the highest number of native English speakers, and the students expressed a higher comfort level with mathematics.

One question that deserves some attention asked, "How many people in the class did you know before the class started?" And, the follow-up question asked the students to give an indication of how well they knew each of the students they "knew." Because the literature on Web-based learning often uses the term "community" and "culture," the effect of a priori familiarity with fellow classmates deserves some attention. We see a seasonality effect in that the Spring sections had a higher average number in response to the first question. This is to be expected, because students in the Fall are more likely to be taking their first classes. Sections B and C have similar numbers for the number of people known before the class started. Section F has a distinctly higher number than D and E. This may suggest that if the people in a section know each other slightly better, then this would enhance the overall performance of the class. Yet, the "familiarity factor" does not support this. The survey asked each student to assign a number between one and five to indicate how well they knew each person in the section, where five represented a higher level of acquaintance. The "familiarity factor" in Table 4 is a simple average of the students' responses. Sections C and F, who have the highest final average, have relatively low familiarity factors. Clearly, this is an imprecise measure, however, because of the subjectivity involved. In addition, the relatively high number for Section D was caused by three people who knew each other very well. Thus, no real conclusion can be drawn from this, but I include the results here in the interest of full reporting. The results may provide ideas for future research.

The next step in the research at hand is to disaggregate the data and explore the relationships of the variables and the predictive power of a priori characteristics. Unfortunately, many of the variables listed in Table 4 were gathered as part of a confidential survey. Thus, they cannot be used as predictors of individual grades. Another important note to make concerns the GMAT score. My introductory corporate finance course is in some sense a preliminary course taken before the regular part of the MBA program. Students can place out of it if they have performed satisfactorily in a comparable undergraduate course recently. Also, students taking the course are often in other degree programs, e.g., law and nursing. A few students are nondegree seeking students. For these reasons, not all students had taken the GMAT prior to enrolling in the course. The entire sample consists of 76 students, of which 55 had taken the GMAT. The reader should keep this in mind when examining the correlations in Table 5. This is also why two sets of regressions are shown in Table 7, one that includes the GMAT as an explanatory variable and one that does not.

The explanatory or a priori variables used here are gender, age, whether a Web-MBA student, and GMAT score. I chose these variables because they represented factors that previous researchers have found significant. As mentioned in the introduction, gender and age have been found to have a significant effect on student performance in finance classes. Including whether a student is a Web-MBA student is similar to whether a student is a full-time student, a factor found significant by Simpson and Sumrall (1979). It may also relate to whether a student is a transfer student, a factor found significant by Borde, Byrd, and Modani (1998). In essence, those that are Web-MBA students will see work on the Internet as their primary means of learning and not a "part-time" endeavor separate from their F2F classes. Similarly, students that are not Web-MBA students are, in a sense, transferring into a new environment. If a student considers him/herself a Web-MBA student, of course, this would probably indicate that the student has a certain level of familiarity with computers. We could argue, therefore, that the level of familiarity generally exceeds that of students who are not choosing to use the Internet as their primary means of learning.

The GMAT score captures an effect similar to the GPA measure used in previous research. The Graduate Management Admission Council offers the following description of the test on their website:

> The Graduate Management Admission Test® (GMAT®) was designed to help business schools assess the qualifications of applicants for advanced study in business and management. It measures basic verbal, quantitative, and writing skills that are developed over a long period of time and is available year-round at test centers throughout the world. Of the several thousand graduate management programs worldwide, nearly 1,700 use the GMAT and more than 1,000 require it. (http://www.gmac.com/GMAT/index.shtml)

In this study, I use the GMAT score instead of the GPA, because students generally take my corporate finance course early in the MBA program. Using undergraduate GPAs would not be appropriate because of the diverse backgrounds of the students.

Table 5 contains the correlations between various components of the grades, discussion participation data, and the four a priori student characteristics. The variables are defined here, and except where noted, they are expressed as a score out of 100 possible points. I applied the Kolmogorov-Smirnov test of normality to the variables. An "N" at the end of a definition below indicates that a null hypothesis of normality could not be rejected for that variable:

Q1:   first quiz grade
Proj: grade for a spreadsheet project
Disc: grade for student participation in the discussion
MT: midterm exam grade, N
FinEx: final exam grade, N
FAvg: final average grade for the course, N
GWD: grade for the course without discussion; to get this, the discussion grade is removed from the final average, and that result is rescaled to represent a score out of 100%, N
DE: number of discussion entries, a simple count of the number of times a student made an entry of any kind in the discussion; the range is five to 43 with a mean of 18, N

WC: word count, the total number of words the student wrote in the discussion; the range is 391 to 5524, and the mean is 2164, N

Gen: gender, this is a dummy variable where Gen = 1 is for male and Gen = 0 for female; the mean is 0.540

Age: the age of the student at the beginning of the class; the range is 21 to 55, with a mean of 31.47, N

WMBA: whether the student considered him/herself a Web-MBA student as opposed to a student who takes most courses in an F2F environment; WMBA = 1 for Web-MBA students, else 0; the mean is 0.684.

GMAT: GMAT score; the range is 380 to 760 with a mean of 527.1, N

Listed in Table 5 are the correlation coefficient and the probability value of that correlation. In those cases where an assumption of normality could not be rejected for both variables, the correlation and p-value in the table are in **bold** font.

Table 5: Correlation Matrix of Grades, Discussion Data and Student Characteristics

Correlation coefficient with p-value underneath, e.g., corr(Disc,Q1) = -0.03 and p-value = 0.796.
Cells in **BOLD** indicate that a null hypothesis of normality cannot be rejected.

	Q1	Disc	MT	FinEx	Proj	FAvg	GWD	DE	WC	Gen	Age	wmba
Disc	-0.03											
	0.80											
MT	0.176	0.126										
	0.127	0.278										
Fin-Ex	0.262	0.31	**0.676**									
	0.022	0.006	**0**									
Proj	0.124	0.171	0.585	0.428								
	0.287	0.139	0	0								
F-Avg	0.216	0.556	**0.809**	**0.864**	0.648							
	0.06	0	**0**	**0**	0							
GWD	0.257	0.294	**0.887**	**0.885**	0.689	**0.958**						
	0.025	0.01	**0**	**0**	0	**0**						
DE	0.038	0.519	**0.341**	**0.337**	0.156	**0.471**	0.362					
	0.747	0	**0.003**	**0.003**	0.178	**0**	0.001					
WC	0.012	0.522	**0.4**	**0.451**	0.262	**0.584**	0.49	0.759				
	0.916	0	**0**	**0**	0.022	**0**	0	0				
Gen	-0.04	0.044	0.36	0.464	0.258	0.383	0.425	0.067	0.156			
	0.734	0.705	0.001	0	0.024	0.001	0	0.564	0.18			
Age	0.132	0.104	**0.019**	**0.103**	0.079	**0.137**	**0.122**	**0.136**	**0.177**	0.041		
	0.257	0.37	**0.873**	**0.374**	0.497	**0.237**	**0.295**	**0.241**	**0.126**	0.726		
W-MBA	0.105	0.236	0.209	0.25	0.026	0.247	0.199	0.28	0.193	0.111	-0.06	
	0.368	0.04	0.071	0.029	0.823	0.032	0.086	0.014	0.095	0.342	0.628	
G-MAT	-0.01	0.195	0.31	0.383	0.34	**0.413**	**0.405**	0.079	0.263	0.517	-0.16	0.262
	0.924	0.158	**0.023**	**0.004**	0.012	**0.002**	**0.002**	0.568	0.055	0	**0.246**	0.056

The results in Table 5 reveal several interesting phenomena. Age is positive but not significant with respect to test performance. The positive relationship between age and the project and discussion participation appears weak also. The GMAT score serves as a good predictor of test scores. It is highly correlated with the project score, but Proj is not normally distributed. The GMAT score is not a good predictor of discussion participation as measured by its relationship with the normally distributed variables DE and WC. Disc appears to have a weak relationship with GMAT.

Although the first quiz grade is not normally distributed, we can note that it has a relatively strong relationship with subsequent test scores. The first quiz grade has a relatively weak relationship with subsequent discussion performance.

The most interesting observations concern the discrete variables Gen and WMBA. The correlations of these variables are included in Table 5 for descriptive purposes. Males performed better in all categories except the first quiz. As mentioned in the review of the literature, this generally higher level of performance by male students has been observed in previous studies. Students who considered themselves Web-students had a superior performance in all categories. To explore the effects of these conditions more formally, I performed an analysis of variance (ANOVA) using the discrete variables as factors. I performed the procedure on the normally distributed performance variables and the nonnormally distributed discussion grade (Disc). As we might expect, WMBA has a positive effect in all categories, and the effect is significant at the 10% level in all cases. The results are shown in Table 6.

The F-statistics are much larger when Gen is the ANOVA factor. The results show that males have significantly higher scores for the final exam, the grades without the discussion grade, and the course grade (FinEx, GWD, FAvg). The reason for the lower level of significance for FAvg is reflected in the fact that there is not a significant difference in the discussion participation for males and females. The discussion area appears to be an area where gender was not a significant factor in my corporate finance class.

To give an idea of the magnitude of the effect of each a priori variable on subsequent performance, I performed ordinary least squares regressions. Using the a priori variables as regressors, I estimated equations for each of the following dependent variables: the final average, the discussion grade, the grade without the discussion, and the word count. I

Table 6: ANOVA Results for Dummy Variables Gen and WMBA

F-statistic and probability value: "F" and "p." Males and WMBA students have higher averages in all categories.							
Factors		**FinEx**	**GWD**	**FAvg**	**DE**	**WC**	**Disc***
Gen	**F=**	20.31	16.27	12.06	0.340	1.84	0.14
	P=	0.000	0.000	0.001	0.564	0.18	0.705
WMBA	**F=**	4.95	3.04	4.80	6.32	2.85	4.35
	P=	0.029	0.086	0.032	0.014	0.095	0.040
*Disc is not normally distributed, so the statistics are descriptive only.							

performed two sets of regressions for each dependent variable. One specification included GMAT, and one did not include GMAT. The reason for this is because of the fact that 22 of the 76 students did not have GMAT scores at the beginning of the course. The results of the regressions are shown in Table 7.

Because this is a preliminary study where the main goal is to provide information for future research, I used a uniform specification for all the regressions. That is, each regression includes all the a priori variables. I regress Disc and Proj on the a priori variables while recognizing that the results for these specifications are suspect given the nonnormality of the dependent variables and the residuals of the regression.

The equations have the highest explanatory power for FAvg and GWD. The F-statistics for both specifications of each equation are significant at the 5% level. For the equations that include GMAT, the F-statistics for Proj and WC are significant at the 10% level but not at the 5% level. When GMAT is removed,[2] the probability value of the F-statistic for the Proj equation increases to 0.147. The explanatory power of each equation for Disc is not significant at the 10% level.

Table 7: Regression of Student Performance Variables on A Priori Characteristics

Results in each cell in the explanatory variables columns are the coefficient, (t-statistic) and probability value. For example, for the first equation for FAvg, the intercept coefficient is 70.940, the t-statistic is 10.1, and the probability value is 0.000.
The t-statistics use White heteroskedasticity-consistent standard errors.

(Dep. Variable)	Const	Gen	Age	W-MBA	GMAT	R^2 adj.R^2	F-stat P-val.
FAvg	70.94 (10.1) 0.000	5.111 (2.76) 0.008	0.137 (0.97) 0.337	2.093 (1.09) 0.279	0.016 (1.72) 0.092	0.317 0.262	5.570 P = 0.00
Disc*	91.16 (9.85) 0.000	3.501 (1.35) 0.182	-0.03 (-.14) 0.892	-0.03 (-.01) 0.992	0.004 (0.50) 0.617	0.0861 0.0115	1.154 P = 0.34
GWD	64.41 (7.55) 0.000	5.600 (2.61) 0.012	0.191 (1.22) 0.229	2.678 (1.13) 0.263	0.021 (1.74) 0.089	0.3037 0.2468	5.342 P = 0.00
Proj*	80.18 (9.24) 0.000	2.837 (1.42) 0.161	0.088 (0.56) 0.579	-1.28 (-.51) 0.610	0.025 (2.22) 0.031	0.149 0.080	2.148 P = 0.09
WC	-257 (-.18) 0.859	238 (0.85) 0.400	31.49 (1.30) 0.199	306 (1.13) 0.265	2.123 (1.04) 0.304	0148 0.079	2.130 P = 0.09
FAvg	78.06 (20.7) 0.000	5.047 (3.23) 0.002	0.140 (1.19) 0.237	3.29 (2.06) 0.043		0.207 0.174	6.282 P = 0.00
Disc*	84.81 (14.9) 0.000	0.221 (0.11) 0.916	0.149 (0.94) 0.353	4.500 (1.78) 0.079		0.070 0.031	1.795 P = 0.16
GWD	75.96 (16.6) 0.000	6.599 (3.64) 0.001	0.137 (1.06) 0.293	2.824 (1.55) 0.125		0.216 0.184	6.631 P = 0.00
Proj*	92.16 (24.0) 0.000	3.72 (2.06) 0.043	0.073 (0.72) 0.477	0.027 (0.02) 0.986		0.071 0.033	1.844 P = 0.15
WC	945 (1.61) 0.112	248 (1.17) 0.244	25.22 (1.42) 0.160	394 (1.77) 0.081		0.088 0.050	2.328 P = 0.08

*Residuals for these regressions do not pass a test of normality.

As we would expect from previous research, Gen has significant coefficients in the equations for FAvg and GWD. GMAT is only marginally significant in the equations for FAvg and GWD, but this could be the result of multicollinearity problems between it and Gen. We see evidence of this when comparing the result for each dependent-variable equation with and without GMAT. In four of the five equations, the coefficients for Gen are more significant when GMAT is not present. Likewise, the coefficient on WMBA is negative in some equations where GMAT is included. The coefficient on WMBA is positive and generally more significant in the equations that exclude GMAT. We should remember in making these comparisons, however, that there might be a selection bias in that the equations without GMAT in the specification include 22 more observations in the analysis.

With respect to removing or including observations, I found that the explanatory power of the equations improves when a few outliers are removed. I did not engage in such editing for the same reason that I did not attempt to correct for the nonnormality of some variables, did not try to transform variables, and did not explore a wide range of specifications. Such extensive measures would be appropriate if we were analyzing a larger data set, where we could scrutinize the appropriateness of data editing and transformation decisions. Given the size of the sample, we must recognize that this is a preliminary study. By presenting uniform results that use all the data, at a minimum, I am providing a solid set of descriptive measures that can provide the foundation for future research. The next section discusses the results and offers suggestions for future work in this area.

DISCUSSION OF EMPIRICAL RESULTS

Despite some problems with respect to the empirical results, many of the statistics are useful. Many of the more reliable results conform to those found in previous studies concerning finance courses. The condition male, a higher GMAT score, and a higher age are positive determinants for overall performance. Although not surprising, one interesting point is that WMBA is positive and significant for most of the grade variables. The most interesting points are that the traditional a priori characteristics do not predict performance in the online discussion, and in this data set, the gender gap closes with respect to this variable.

In-class discussions are generally not a part of introductory corporate finance courses in an F2F setting. The online discussion is an important part of Web-based learning, however, and the results in this chapter that pertain to the online discussion are perhaps the most important contribution of this work. The empirical results here and elsewhere verify that certain a priori student characteristics can forecast success on exams; however, the results here suggest that those a priori characteristics do not predict success for the online discussion.

The coefficient of determination for predicting the final average is 31.7%, and this is similar in magnitude to that found in previous studies (Borde, Byrd, & Modani, 1998). As in that and other studies, age is positive but marginally significant. Males generally have a higher level of success.

Gender displays a weak relationship with respect to the discussion grades. Discussion grades are highly skewed, however, so the results of the statistical tests performed here are descriptive but not conclusive. The word count variable denoted WC is normally distributed. Gen has the lowest level of significance of the independent variables in the equations for WC. The ANOVA results show that the factor Gen is not significant with respect to WC. WC is an unrefined measure, but this is an advantage in that it is a direct measure of effort and it is unaffected by the subjective opinions of the instructor. Also, we observe that it has a significant correlation with all the student class scores except quiz one, denoted by Q1. All those class scores, with the exception of Proj, are also normally distributed.

In summary, Gen, Age, WMBA, and GMAT explain success on exams but not online discussion. These variables do not explain success for online discussion, yet there is a high correlation between performance in the online discussion and exam grades. Are there a priori factors that can predict success in the online discussion? Can promoting these factors through training and prerequisite courses lead to better performance in the online discussion? Will this induced success in the online discussion lead to a higher level of success on the exams?

We should recall how and when the seminal ideas for this study came to me. This study "started" when I noticed significant differences in the online discussion participation between three class sections in the Spring of 2001. One section began with the lowest average for the first quiz, but it had much higher discussion participation and ended with the highest average grade. With respect to a self-assessment of math skills, as revealed in a survey that all the students voluntarily participated in, that section did not have the highest average. The students in that section seemed to have a higher level of Web experience, however, and a higher appreciation for the online discussion.

As previous research mentioned, comfort with and perception of Web-based learning are important factors for student success. This study seems to support that hypothesis. More specifically, the online discussion appears to be a method of allowing students to engage in active learning, which is always positive. Furthermore, the online discussion may make a quantitative course like finance more accessible to students whose verbal skills exceed their math skills. Just as F2F finance classes have prerequisites such as accounting, the results of this study suggest that students in Web-based classes may benefit from prior training in Web-based learning.

CONCLUDING REMARKS

This chapter is one of several works that I hope to write in the near future on my experiences as a Web-based instructor. I have learned a tremendous amount about how the Internet works by being a Web-based instructor, of course, but I have also learned a great deal about the subject I teach and what helps students learn. As some authors have noted, Web-based learning may challenge the limits of the F2F classroom.

Extensive discussions have not been a part of my F2F classes, but discussions are an important element in my Web-based class. The discussions seem to enhance the performance of the students in the Web classes. Furthermore, the class discussions probably enhance the ability of the students to function in future courses as well as in the business world after graduation.

As with any new tool, however, we must learn its costs and benefits. The evidence here suggests that in order for students to get the most out of Web-based learning, we may have to engage in more preparatory training. If Web-based learning becomes a part of high school curricula, however, comfort and familiarity with the Web will be a more common characteristic of college-bound students.

College will become more accessible given that Web-based learning saves time in terms of transportation and information gathering. Yet, even in Web-based learning, time is limited. As has been noted in the literature, Web-based instructors typically work more hours to teach their classes. The online discussion is one of the major elements that can consume the instructor's time. As studies such as this one show the positive results of effective online discussions, educators and software designers will be more motivated to design future products to facilitate the use of this Web-based learning device.

REFERENCES

Borde, S., Byrd, A., & Modani, N. (1998). Determinants of student performance in introductory corporate finance courses. *Journal of Financial Education,* (Fall) 23–30.

Brooks, D. W. (1997). *Web teaching: A Guide to Designing Interactive Teaching for the World Wide Web.* New York: Plenum Press.

Cecez-Kecmanovic, D., & Webb, C. (2000). A critical inquiry into Web-mediated collaborative learning. In A. Aggarwal (Ed.), *Web-based Learning and Teaching Technologies: Opportunities and Challenges.* Hershey, PA: Idea Group Publishing.

Chalmers, R. (1999). Journal of an online student; http://www.att.com/learningetwork/virtualacademy/chapt5.html.

Chan, K., & Shum, C. (2000). The effectiveness of interactive television distance learning in principles of finance. *Financial Practice and Education, 10*(Spring/Summer), 175–183.

Chan, K., Shum, C., & Lai, L. (1996). An empirical study of cooperative instructional environment on student achievement in principles of finance. *Journal of Financial Education, 22*(Fall) 21–28.

Crabbe J., Grainger, J., & Steward, R. (1997). Quality assessment of computer based learning. *Educational Computing, 8*(3), 17–19.

Dewey, J. (1938). *Experience in education.* New York: Macmillan.

Dumant, R. (1996). Teaching and learning in cyberspace. *IEEE Transactions on Professional Communication, 39*(December), 192–204.

Ferber, M., Birnbaum, B., & Green, C. (1983). Gender differences in economic knowledge: A reevaluation of the evidence. *The Journal of Economic Education,* 24–37.

Filbeck, G., & Smith, L. (1996). Learning styles, teaching strategies, and predictors of success for students in corporate finance. *Financial Practice and Education,* 74–85.

Gagne, R. M., & Briggs, L. J. (1979). *Principles of Instructional Design* (2nd ed.). New York: Holt, Rinehart and Winston.

Gronlund, N. (1985). *Measurement and Evaluation in Teaching.* New York: MacMillan.

Habermas, J. (1984). *The Theory of Communicative Action—Reason and the Rationalization of Society* (Vol. 1). Boston, MA: Beacon Press.

Habermas, J. (1987). *The Theory of Communicative Action—The Critique of Functionalist Reason* (Vol. 2). Boston, MA: Beacon Press.

Hall, J. (1997). Evaluating new technologies for teaching and learning in distance education: Current and future developments. *The New Learning Environments, a global perspective,* proceedings from the 18th ICDE World Conference. The Pennsylvania State University.

Heath, J. (1989). Factors affecting student learning—an econometric model of the role of gender in economic education. *Economic Education*, 226–230.\

Huynh, M. (1999). *A Critical Study of Computer-Supported Collaborative Learning.* Unpublished Ph.D., SUNY Binghamton.

Johan, S. (1998). New technology makes communication harder and easier. *InfoWorld, 20*, 114.

Kerka, S. (1996). *Distance Learning, the Internet, and the World-Wide Web.* (Report No. EDO-CE-96-168). ERIC Clearinghouse on Adult, Career, and Vocational Education, Columbus, OH (ERIC Document No. ED 395 214).

Lewin, K. (1951). *Field theory in social sciences.* New York: Harper and Row Publishers.

Liesz, T., & Reyes, M. (1989). The use of Piagetian concepts to enhance student performance in the introductory finance course. *Journal of Financial Education*, 8–14.

Locket, K. (1998). The Loneliness of the Long Distance Learner – Using Online Student Support to Decrease the Isolation Factor and Increase Motivation. Paper presented at WebNet98, Orlando, Florida, USA.

Lumsden, K. & Scott, A. (1987). The Economics Student Reexamined: Male-Female Differences in Comprehension. *Journal of Economic Education*, 365-375.

Mandell, J. (1998). E-mail etiquette. *Software Magazine, 18*, 20.

Moore, M., & Kearsley, G. (1995). *Distance Education: A Systems View.* Belmont, CA: Wadsworth.

Nasseh, B. (1998). Training and support programs, and faculty's new roles in computer-based distance education in higher education institutions; http://www.bsu.edu/classes/nasseh/study/res98.html.

Novitzki, J. (2000). Asynchronous learning tools: what is really needed, wanted and used? In A. Aggarwal (Ed.), *Web-based Learning and Teaching Technologies: Opportunities and Challenges.* Hershey, PA: Idea Group Publishing.

Odom, M., & Pourjalali, H. (1996). Knowledge transfer from expert systems vs. traditional instruction: do personality traits make a difference? *Journal of End User Computing, 8*(2), 14–20.

Phillips-Vicky, A. (1998). Virtual classrooms, real education. *Nation's Business, 86*(5), 41–45.

Rahm, D., & Reed, B. (1997). The use of distance learning, the World Wide Web, and the Internet in graduate programs of public affairs and administration. *Public Productivity and Management Review, 20*(June), 459–474.

Simpson, W. G., & Sumrall, B. P. (1979). The determinants of objective test scores by finance students. *Journal of Financial Education*, 58–62.

Williams, M., Waldauer, C., & Duggal, V. (1992). Gender differences in economic knowledge: An extension of the analysis. *Journal of Economic Education*, 219–231.

ENDNOTES

[1]   Part of the difference in size was caused by several students being called to active military duty at the outbreak of the conflict in Afghanistan. They had to drop out just as the course was starting.

[2]   The reader is reminded that regressions without GMAT have 22 additional observations.

Chapter XVII

Using Information Technology to Meet Electronic Commerce and MIS Education Demands

Paul J. Speaker
West Virginia University, USA

Virginia Franke Kleist
West Virginia University, USA

ABSTRACT

Localized applications of institutional learning obtained from four years of successful use of educational information technology in a distance-learning program suggest that the current electronic commerce educational gap may be mitigated by innovative uses of technology in the management information systems curriculum. Presented in this chapter is a case where an educational information technology intensive approach was found to be useful for improving the management information systems education delivery process, when faced with personnel and curriculum space considerations. Just as encountered in the distance learning data, preliminary results indicate enhanced student learning from the interactive and personalized aspects of the information technology, despite the twin constraints of limited management information systems faculty resources and limited Master of Business Administration curriculum flexibility. Face-to-face applications of the interactive and personalized aspects of information technology that were learned in the distance learning experience suggest that technologically based solutions to management information systems education resource pressures may help to effectively meet new requirements for teaching electronic commerce, without sacrificing the traditional management information systems curriculum.

INTRODUCTION

Localized applications of institutional learning obtained from four years of successful use of educational information technology (IT) in a distance-learning program suggest that the current electronic commerce educational gap may be mitigated by innovative uses of technology in the MIS curriculum. Presented in this chapter is a case where an educational IT intensive approach was found to be useful for improving the MIS education delivery process, when faced with personnel and curriculum space considerations. First, a technical description of a multilocation, top of the line distance learning facility is covered, and research that explores critical success factors for technology-assisted use in learning for MBA students is introduced. Results from a study of 2898 student responses across 117 classes indicate that certain aspects of information technology may facilitate and enhance perceptions of student learning, despite the challenges of the location disconnect. Second, a specific case of a mass customization style educational IT is described, deployed in a face-to-face environment for a highly compressed MBA class on electronic commerce and MIS. Just as encountered in the distance learning data, preliminary results indicate enhanced student learning from the interactive and personalized aspects of the IT, despite the twin constraints of limited MIS faculty resources and limited MBA curriculum flexibility. Thus, face-to-face applications of the interactive and personalized aspects of IT that were learned in the distance learning experience suggest that technologically based solutions to MIS education resource pressures may help to effectively meet new requirements for teaching electronic commerce, without sacrificing the traditional MIS curriculum.

ISSUES, CONTROVERSIES, PROBLEMS

The speed of change of electronic commerce in business and the speed of change in institutions of higher learning involve vastly different scales of measurement. While the growth of the "new" economy has moved at an incredible pace, the question of how to include electronic commerce education in the more slowly moving and resource-constrained university curricula remains unresolved for many institutions. This chapter was motivated by an institutional goal of balancing the MBA student interest and need for new electronic commerce coursework, with the short-term limitations of too few MIS faculty and not enough curriculum space. This increased demand for electronic commerce education by business school students was addressed by offering effective, technology-based solutions based upon the experiences learned to date with distance learning technology and iterative successes in the process of MIS curricular change.

Discussed in this chapter is a semester-long, three credit accelerated MBA-level course that combines electronic commerce and classic MIS topics. The course is unique in that it was delivered via the two parallel streams of heavy applications of information technology and face-to-face classroom instruction. It is an interesting case to review, because we used interactive and customized technology to enhance and exponentially drive more material through the course, thus enabling the coverage of more topics in the space of a one-semester course. By using extensive Web-based teaching combined with the traditional classroom approach, we were able to address the problem of how to teach an electronic commerce offering in addition to the traditional MIS material within the MBA curriculum. Although some students were overly challenged by the additional workload, other students were receptive to this novel format, because they realized the need to understand traditional issues of MIS, along with their desire to learn about the more glamorous aspects of electronic commerce.

There are three instructional aspects to our combined MIS/electronic commerce course at the college. First, we have MBA classrooms that are designed to facilitate the delivery of these courses through the use of unusually sophisticated information technology. Second, use of these facilities has enabled enterprise-wide MBA faculty of many disciplines to acquire a high level of competence with information technology that has pervaded their teaching and business understanding. Useful data about specific aspects of our facilities, when applied in a distance-learning format, indicate positive effects from using educational information technology (IT) for improved learning in general. Finally, the program utilizes a unique course design that interleaves traditional MIS and electronic commerce material into one highly compact course. Described in this chapter is our instructional learning technology design, the data analysis from the program in operation, and the specific topics covered by the combined electronic commerce and MIS course syllabus. These three factors combined to allow West Virginia University's College of Business and Economics to deliver a technologically advanced MBA in a short time frame, and one that incorporates the traditional curriculum, while aggressively integrating current electronic commerce initiatives.

THE DILEMMA

The MBA program at West Virginia University is a 48 credit-hour program packed into a 13½ month time period. While the short time frame permits students to complete their graduate studies in a comparatively short period of time, the 48 credit-hours limits the ability for specialization within the program. Lacking formal areas of concentration within the program, the curriculum has been built around an emphasis on management and technology. That emphasis permits a complementary focus on technological skills within all of the business disciplines in lieu of a menu of specializations, generally offered in the more traditional two-year programs.

Many two-year MBA programs have dealt with the emergence of electronic business issues through the creation of elective courses (AACSB, 2000). While this may be an immediate solution for some programs, it is not a viable solution for all. In our case, the creation of electronic business courses is hampered by the lack of free electives in the program, limited faculty resources within the MIS department, and a lack of widespread expertise in electronic business by MBA program faculty across departments. Our limitations are not unique. The faculty resource issue is prevalent across universities, as all institutions are feeling the market pressure for qualified faculty in MIS. This pressure is exaggerated if the electronic business curriculum solution is centered on courses strictly out of the MIS department.

In a review of several leading MBA programs (AACSB, 2000), a general consensus emerges for the future of programmatic treatment of electronic business issues. In spite of these limitations, there is some promise for electronic commerce business courses in the future in the program. Rather than a trend toward the creation of separate specializations in electronic commerce, we are apt to see intense development of cross-functional curricula in which electronic commerce issues are ingrained within every functional area. Higher education institutions report a variety of similarities with both obstacles and opportunities toward the inclusion of more technology-intensive teaching and learning (Sumner & Hostetler, 1999). In general, more widespread technology implementation in courses was apt to occur when institutions boasted good support facilities (training support and technologically equipped facilities), provided reward systems that encouraged development of innovative courses, and had faculty in all disciplines, not just MIS, to champion development of creative course solutions.

Several factors are in place at West Virginia University to support a multidisciplinary electronic business implementation strategy for graduate business education. College-wide program demands for access to MIS courses, coupled with the knowledge that growth in MIS faculty positions will be stagnant in the near term, require that a general solution for electronic business coursework come from creative use of existing resources. First, the College has made, and continues to make, major investments in general faculty technology expertise through a distance-learning interactive audio and video delivery of the executive MBA (EMBA) program with heavy support from Web-based content and communication. Second, institutional faculty knowledge gained by the faculty using these distance learning technologies has bled into success with IT in teaching in the full-time MBA program. Third, the emergence of the distance-learning program has attracted great corporate and other private support of facilities, and associated technologies, that effectively have transformed all MBA classrooms into Web-connected laboratories. One hundred percent of the MBA technology facilities have been donated by corporate or community groups. Fourth, the classroom laboratory environment extends beyond the traditional classroom, as all traditional MBA students are required to have notebook computers with wireless LAN access. This overall IT use and technological expertise has greatly expanded the capabilities of MIS topical coverage, from positions of breadth and depth.

THE TECHNOLOGY BASE

During the later half of the 1990s, the College developed and initiated the delivery of a distance-learning-based Executive Master of Business Administration (EMBA) program as an addition to the full-time Master of Business Administration (MBA) program. The EMBA program links the host site with one or more similarly equipped remote classrooms via T1 land lines for two-way interactive audio and video. Each classroom includes instructor and student cameras that automatically pan and zoom to the speaker as microphones are activated. The supporting technology encompasses a near virtual classroom with a whiteboard, document camera, laser disk player, multiple VCRs, and 10 Mbps Ethernet wireless notebook computer connections to the College LAN and Internet. Each connected site receives a life-size screen image of companion sites with side monitors to display the accompanying graphics. These distance learning facilities, dedicated for our graduate business school educational use, are located at 10 locations across the state of West Virginia, and they form a ring of technological infrastructure, exceptional in the degree of its virtual sophistication.

Because the EMBA program is offered during weekends and evenings, these facilities were uncommitted during full-time MBA class hours. To take advantage of the opportunity provided by the available facilities and the growing faculty expertise with the technology, the full-time MBA program was modified to include a greater technology emphasis. The momentum, provided by this change atmosphere, has provided some of the keys for the inclusion of electronic business education in the curriculum. These key lessons are centered in the advantages of improved communication between instructor and student, heightened classroom active learning that results from the laboratory environment that technology permits, and timeliness with which relevant information may be accessed from the classroom.

SOLUTIONS AND RECOMMENDATIONS

Lessons from Distance Learning

As a technology-based learning environment with reliance on Web resources, the WVU experience with distance learning technology offered us insights into the introduction of other technology-laden programs. While the literature offers little guidance with respect to electronic commerce courses and their contributions to particular programs, there is a great deal of literature on the "success" of various distance technology mediums. An examination of this literature provides valuable lessons beyond the case history of a single university (e.g., Alavi et al., 1997; Chen & Willits, 1998; LaFollette et al., 1996). These authors demonstrated that many lessons extend beyond an individual application and provide some universal truths.

Distance learning technologies have been adopted as a means to support a variety of strategic objectives. An evaluation of the success of a distance learning strategy is difficult, as the measurement of learning success is a multidimensional issue. Strategic goals may include issues such as the ease of access for students, efficiency from greater economies of scale for the institution, reach into new markets, maintenance or improvement of the quality of teaching and learning, and enhanced customer satisfaction (Smith, 1998). While all of these strategic goals deserve careful review, if a quality learning experience cannot be achieved, the questions regarding the remaining areas may well be moot.

Many researchers have focused on the measurement of the quality issue (e.g., Westbrook, 1997; Moore, 1998). In general, previous examinations of distance learning technologies have found that remote site learners perform at a level equal to, or above, students in a traditional instructor-present setting. The general lesson suggests that the traditional classroom environment is not the only manner in which students may learn. The more specific lesson comes from a demonstration of the value of a technology-rich environment.

Can You Teach an Old Dog New Tricks?

If one route to electronic business inclusion into the curriculum is through a program-wide technology adoption strategy, then an obvious question must be addressed. Does the expertise exist across the business disciplines for the presentation of electronic business? And, if it does not exist, can faculty be trained to include appropriate topics and to coordinate coverage across the program?

Again, our experience with distance learning holds much promise for success in this area. The move to an interactive audio and video delivery was accompanied by a dramatic change in curricular emphasis toward management and technology, where medium and message were intertwined. To accomplish this change, faculty had to be trained with the new technology medium as a support to local and remote learners. Further, the program message was modified to more fully integrate the various business disciplines with technology in management as a unifying theme. This was accompanied by a greater use of Web resources for content and communication.

Formal assessment of the distance-learning program provides some insight into the factors that may enable faculty to successfully use information technology in the curriculum. In an attempt to determine the prime factors that point to successful delivery of courses using information technology in the distance learning EMBA, an assessment of student perceptions was conducted from the onset of the program. Semi-annually, students evaluated faculty and the program (using a five-point scale from 1 = low quality to 5 = high quality) in the areas of emphasis for the program: effective use of technology, remote site involvement, effective use of student teams, speed and quality of feedback, and perceived course workload. These perceptions were combined with the student evaluation of the faculty member directing the course (also on a five-point scale), faculty experience in the distance-learning environment (semesters taught in the environment), and course grade point average.

The semi-annual student assessment included 2898 student course evaluations covering 117 distance-learning courses for the academic years 1995–1996 through 1998–1999. The mean response was compiled for each of the 117 courses, and that mean response was combined with the course grade distribution (4.0 scale) and the aforementioned faculty experience measure.

The following relationship was evaluated using the ordinary least squares method of analysis applied to 117 distance-learning courses, evaluated from the academic years 1995–1996 through 1998–1999:

$$QUALITY = \beta_0 + \beta_1 TECH + \beta_2 REMOTE + \beta_3 TEAM + \beta_4 FEEDBACK + \beta_5 WORKLOAD + \beta_6 EXPERIENCE + \beta_7 GPA$$

Student perception of the learning experience (QUALITY, 1 = among the worst to 5 = among the best) was regressed on perceived expertise with the technology (TECH), remote site involvement (REMOTE), use of student teams (TEAM), quality and speed of feedback (FEEDBACK), comparative course workload (WORKLOAD), as well as faculty experience in the environment as measured by distance learning semesters taught (EXPERIENCE), and course grade distribution (GPA).

The OLS procedure yielded the following estimation (standard deviation in parentheses):

$$QUALITY = -0.75292 + 0.287619\,TECH + 0.603104\,REMOTE - 0.17801\,TEAM$$
$$ (0.71414) \quad (0.115784) \qquad (0.139782) \qquad (0.139782)$$
$$ + 0.331477\,FEEDBACK + 0.06824\,WORKLOAD + 0.055205\,EXPERIENCE$$
$$ (0.07196) \qquad (0.06727) \qquad (0.027039)$$
$$ + 0.029661\,GPA.$$
$$ (0.174707)$$

The OLS estimation yielded an R-Square of 0.76 and an F-statistic of 48.44 (p-value = 1.7503 E-30). These results suggest that the perceived quality of the learning experience is improved as faculty gain experience with the environment (p-value = 0.0436), make better use of the technology (p-value = 0.0145), provide greater interaction (p-value = 0.0004), and provide prompt feedback (p-value = 0.00001). Interestingly, student perceptions of the learning experience are not significantly influenced by workload (p-value = 0.3126) or grades (p-value = 0.8655).

In addition to student evaluation, instructor satisfaction with the technology media is important (Sumner & Hostetler, 1999). Successful use of IT in teaching and learning is bidirectional. Although no formal assessment of faculty satisfaction was undertaken for our distance-learning program, ad hoc experiences suggest that the technology-intensive courses have had the greatest success as courses move away from lecture-based instruction toward a more hands-on discovery by students, as suggested by Chen and Willits (1998) and

Webster and Hackley (1997). It is possible that the new technologies have led to a greater enjoyment of teaching experiences among faculty and have fostered more integration of program material in response to creative solutions. Further, each technology-based class required a new design to adapt teaching material to the new medium, and this may have added an originality to the material that enhanced the experience for faculty and student.

Electronic Business in the Curriculum—Where to Begin?

There are aspects to the distance learning technology that had a stronger effect on perceived educational learning, when compared to other aspects of the technology and the experience. While the move to a greater reliance on the technology was a programmatic move, certain areas demonstrated greater success, both from the mastery of competencies and from student perceptions of the experience. In general, the greater the hands-on experience with technology, the more successful was the student perception of the course. The experience was similar to findings of DeSanctis and Sheppard (1999), namely, that the greater the reliance on the technology for course support (e.g., Web-based resources, instructor contact), the more successful was the perception of the course. Similar indicators of success were found with respect to student performance. As course requirements shifted from traditional classroom interaction toward more electronic means of learning, student performance was heightened in the distance environment.

To see this effect, program performance was evaluated in much the same way as the studies evaluated by Westbrook (1997). Our distance learning delivery of the MBA program provides a classic experimental model, in which each class includes a traditional instructor-present group with the local learners and a group of students at a remote site(s). As Westbrook noted, researchers have generally found that distance learners perform at a level at least as high as students in the classroom with the instructor present. Our examination of remote-site versus local-site performance supports these results. Namely, remote-site students demonstrated higher program grade point averages, but not statistically significant ($\alpha = 5\%$) better performance program-wide. These experiments included evaluation of program performance with a dummy variable for student location (remote site/host site) and student admission qualifications with respect to GPA in prior higher education programs, performance on the GMAT standardized test, and student work experience.

While student achievement program-wide was indistinguishable among host-site and remote-site learners, it appears that differences in performance emerge when there is consideration of technology utilization. In general, it appears that remote-site students outperform their host-site classmates, as courses place a greater reliance on technology-supported discovery above traditional interaction in the classroom. This may be explained by the interactive culture that develops in the program. That is, from the onset, remote-site students communicate with instructors via some distance technology (email, chat, bulletin boards), while host-site students rely more heavily on face-to-face communication. Provided instructors are timely with their feedback, fewer questions go unanswered, and the speed permits students to more quickly progress in their discoveries.

This success apparent in our distance learning facilities was subsequently adapted to our local MBA programming, using the same Internet-based and technology-laden delivery techniques. Specifically, the MBA electronic commerce and MIS class delivery were designed using many of the same distance learning techniques, only modified to fit the scenario of the localized student population. It was apparent that many of these same success factors were also relevant to the face-to-face teaching and learning experience. Where the distance learning courses showed a significant result for the relationship between student perceptions of learning, and the use of the information technologies, faculty experience with technology and levels of faculty interactivity with the students also were variables of interest in the localized MBA classroom.

In the case presented here, the injection of IT into teaching and learning enabled an accelerated electronic commerce curriculum at the MBA level program. The localized MIS and electronic commerce class used the same distance learning facilities as described above, including an interactive Web-based syllabus, slides on the Internet, access to the wireless LAN during lectures, heavy use of feedback through email and document exchange, teaching Web pages with annotated instructor notes, Web-available texts, readings on electronic reserve, links to class-related websites, with all relevant student paperwork distributed via the class Web pages. The class was delivered by a faculty member experienced from several years of using information technology in the classroom.

As was found in the distance learning results for the same facility, the factors of good use of the technology, depth of faculty experience, rapid student feedback, and good student interaction all seemed to be important in the success and quality of the course. Although only anecdotal results are available, it seemed that the most successful aspect of the use of technology in the classroom was related to the level of student and professor interactivity, inside and outside of the classroom, yielding a customized student learning experience. For example, the instructor was rated with a 4.1 out of 5 points on the question "Instructor provided useful feedback regarding performance" ($n = 19$), and a 4.1 for teaching effectiveness, and 4.5 for the syllabus, clarity in answering questions, and organization.

Just as was found to be significant for the distance learning results, preliminary student responses seemed to show that the student-controlled flexibility regarding the syllabus, with its numerous Web-based student selections and options, was the most successful aspect of the class. One anonymously submitted student comment was, "Use of email and quick responses was extremely beneficial." Students could pick among several cases, readings, and question sets for response, and were not held responsible for all of the presented material. Because of the variance in student interests, at least one or more students addressed each topic, and subsequently discussed it in the classroom. Thus, all material was covered, yet was not solely covered by the class instructor. The students had some control over the readings or the topics that were emphasized in the class discussions. The information technology gave the student the option of customizing their own education in MIS and electronic commerce.

Although initial remarks implied a positive response to the level and degree of interactivity, some students were stressed by the amount of material in the course. One anonymous student's comment was a succinct, "Information overload." Student comments indicated appreciation of the availability of the class teaching notes, the prepared questions for the class interactive discussions, and the extent of MIS and electronic commerce material that was covered. Another student wrote, "very real life situations attached to notes." It appears that the use of technology, similar to that experienced in the distance learning program, was instrumental in allowing the course to incorporate more topics than would normally be addressed in the 15-week schedule. Universally required material was marked as such in the syllabus, and the instructor indicated with questions what was basic material that would be necessary to know for the exams. Indeed, similar to the findings reported by Lengnick-Hall and Sanders (1997), the students expressed satisfaction with their role as coproducers in self-determining what topics to study.

THE MIS/ELECTRONIC COMMERCE COURSE

The technology discussed in the previous two sections regarding College facilities and IT success factors enabled the MIS course to be designed in such a way as to "pack" nearly 50% more material into the standard MIS MBA-level course offering. Presented in Table 1 are the specific elements of the MIS/electronic commerce course offering, with the classic MIS topics in the left-hand column and the newer electronic commerce topics in the right-hand column:

Table 1: Combined Electronic Commerce and MIS Course Content

Traditional MIS Topics	Electronic Commerce Topics
1. Strategic Use of Information Technology. Information technology can be applied in business for sustained, strategic competitive advantage. What is IT used for business versus for competitive advantage?	**What is Electronic commerce?** What is electronic commerce, origins of the Internet, Web commerce, electronic commerce growth rates, is electronic commerce a fad or a real phenomenon? How will electronic commerce impact the business world?
2. Ethical and Social Considerations of Information Systems. Technology has had an impact on privacy, our quality of life, and the jobs we do. Not all of these effects are positive, and some may not be ethical.	**Electronic Commerce and the Strategic Use of Information Technology.** Web-based information technology deployments may be a specific use of IT for competitive advantage in the electronic commerce realm.
3. Supply Chain Management and Salesforce Automation Technology. Enterprise resource planning (ERP) tools and other technologies have automated the supply chain to allow improved logistics, scheduling, and customer service.	**Business Models of Electronic Commerce.** The traditional business models of the physical world are not always the same business models that are applicable for success in the electronic commerce environment.
4. Fundamentals of Computer Hardware for MIS. Hardware, vendors, the evolution of IT over time, management issues associated with the speed of hardware change.	**Physical Versus Digital Goods Distribution in Electronic Commerce.** Exploration of the issues associated with physical goods and distance and firm strategy when selling physical products using a digital medium.
5. Fundamentals of Computer Software for MIS. Software types, vendors, use of the Internet, network and middleware software, the nature of code development, management issues of large-scale code development.	**The .com Stock Valuation Puzzle: Justifiable Prices?** Is it reasonable to argue that these firms should use different metrics for stock price valuation? What are the arguments for and against?
6. Database Technology Trends and Management Issues. Traditional databases, principles of database design, database management systems, OLAP, OLTP, new trends in database technology.	**Merger and Acquisition Trends in Information Industry Firms.** An exploration of the patterns of mergers and alliances in the information industry firms in terms of strategy, ownership, and intellectual property acquisition.
7. Telecommunications and Data Communications. New technologies of voice and data communications and the Internet, such as VoIP. How do these technologies work, and what are the managerial issues?	**The Microsoft Case.** A discussion of the issues, merits, and risks of this high-profile government anti-trust lawsuit. As an MIS manager, why would this case be of concern? What is the role of open source code versus proprietary in building systems?
8. Systems Analysis, Systems Development, and Systems Design. Classic coverage of the systems development life cycle, business systems planning, critical success factors methodology, and alternative methods of systems implementation.	**Competitive Web Business Strategies.** Strategic planning for Electronic commerce ventures requires a variation from classic systems planning approaches.
9. Information Systems Security and Control. Reliability, redundancy, and management of risk considerations for information systems. Presentation of the security audit and security business plan approach.	**Trust in Electronic Commerce Infrastructure for Business Exchange.** Electronic commerce will not flourish unless all parties feel secure that the business exchange is safe: firewalls, encryption, digital certificates, digital payment mechanisms, etc.
10. Intellectual Capital and Knowledge Management. A firm's most important asset may be the intellectual capital of its employees. How can information technology help to capture and exploit this intangible, critical asset for gain?	**Web Auctions in Electronic Commerce.** In a traditional business environment, retail prices are fixed. In electronic commerce, information technology allows the reintroduction of the old-fashioned price haggling of the marketplace.
11. Capital Budgeting for Information Technology Systems. The return on investment for an MIS system is often complex to account for, called the Productivity Paradox in the MIS literature. What are the issues, and how are these problems best managed?	**The Unusual Economics of Information Goods Products.** Information goods products may be subject to increasing returns, which implies that firms that market these products may be capable of enormous profits, if they succeed. What are these unique economics?

Material found in nearly every MBA-level MIS class includes some treatment of the elements of hardware and software, systems analysis and design, systems planning, and database management. Other important and related topics that are often touched on are systems security and control, IT enhancement of intellectual capital (the knowledge organization), capital budgeting for IT, and data communications. As can be found in Column 1 of Table 1, these classic elements of MIS are covered in about 11 sessions of 1 hour and 15 minutes in length, leaving adequate room in the 15-week class calendar for a midterm and final, as well as discussion days. Most MIS textbooks support this format, and this approach can easily be adapted from just about any textbook for delivering the classic MIS course.

For the MIS portion of the class meetings, the students were required to read the textbook in advance of the lectures. The accompanying MIS session Web pages included the assigned class readings, slide presentations, detailed instructor lecture notes and interactive discussion questions. During the lectures, the instructor was able to push through complex topics quickly because of each student's advance preparation using the sophisticated instructional technology delivery mechanism. Advance student preparation was encouraged and guaranteed with a few well-timed quizzes, Socratic questioning on the material and impromptu student lectures on mini-topics of the day began. The classic MIS session formats were heavily lecture based, with a 1 hour lecture delivered at high speed and high bandwidth, followed by a 15 minute, intensively prepared, interactive session on the topic.

The second portion of the weekly class meetings was designed to be much more freewheeling, relaxed, and interactive in terms of the nature of the student learning experience. Readings on 11 electronic commerce topics were picked out of current literature, websites, and anywhere *except* in a classic MIS text. Students were given free reign to select from several readings, depending upon their own interest and learning requirements. Effort was made by the instructor to be new, trendy, and on top of the latest stories and issues of electronic commerce. Student input on topics was welcomed early in the semester to keep things lively in the classroom. For instance, topics in the electronic commerce section of the course covered the issues of intellectual property, with the discussion organized around the MP3 technology and the legalities of the Napster music distribution website. Any text material for the electronic commerce portion of the class was strictly Web based, either with a Web text, or Web-based electronic reserves. Electronic reserves are an intranet based, password-protected access to copyrighted material, following all appropriate legal rules for document copying. Popular press articles provided an additional backdrop emphasizing the currency of the readings. Numerous short cases were assigned, sometimes even during the class meeting, to make a point or illustrate an example of an electronic commerce strategy, business model, or technology. Just as with the MIS class meetings, interactive thought questions were posted in advance of the class on the topic in order to provide a framework and direction for the learning. Guest lecturers were invited or accessible, such as electronic commerce .com startup entrepreneurs, LAN networking specialists, or IT executives.

The "hot" topics, or those which seemed to generate the most student enthusiasm, were issues appropriate to the students' personal interactions. Issues such as the underlying legal arguments behind the Microsoft antitrust trial, discussions of .com businesses commonly visited by students, and possible startup opportunities tended to be more stimulating to the students than more remote concepts. Topics such as database development, systems analysis, or the MIS infrastructure for interorganizational systems were less interesting to the MBA students but they were necessary for building fundamentals in the MBA students' education.

The MIS/electronic commerce MBA course also included the requirement of three written cases, two exams, and a 15-page research paper. The cases were a mixed set of traditional MIS and electronic commerce topics. The research paper was permitted to be on any topic of the student's choosing, and more often than not, the students chose an electronic commerce based application. Topics selected by the students included the technologies and long-run potential of day trading as a career, cultural effects of the Internet on international business, the issues of the Microsoft trial, and a demonstration of how to build an effective business website. Other topics were the Air Traffic Control's Information Systems, the use of GPS in business, and the operating systems of various handheld platforms.

CONCLUSION

The dual MIS/electronic commerce curriculum strategy was successful based largely on the technology available to the instructors and the lessons learned from our distance learning program. The availability of the technology and the experience gained by faculty with the distance learning program established a technology adoption framework that enabled WVU to meet the crisis of limited MIS resources in the face of electronic business with an innovative and aggressive MIS curriculum. It has been our experience that some of the problems encountered at the juncture of Internet-speed and University-speed can be resolved with the application of information technology and creativity in course design. The effective use of information technology may help to resolve some of the instructional pressures currently faced by business schools.

REFERENCES

Alavi, M., Yoo, Y., & Vogel, D. R. (1997). Using information technology to add value to management education. *Academy of Management Journal, 40*(6), 1310–1333.

Chen, Y. –J., & Willits, F. K. (1998). A path analysis of the concepts in Moore's theory of transactional distance in a videoconferencing learning environment. *Journal of Distance Education, 13*(2), 51–65.

DeSanctis, G., & Sheppard, B. (1999). Bridging distance, time, and culture in executive MBA education. *Journal of Education for Business, 74*(3), 157–160.

Hurr-E up: B-schools striving to get electronic business courses and resources up to speed. (2000, Winter). *Newsline, AACSB-The International Association for Management Education, 30*(2), 1–11.

LaFollette, W. R., Hoban, J. P., Jr., & Benkato, O. M. (1996). Teaching finance by television. *Journal of Financial Education, 22*, 74–79.

Lengnick-Hall, C. A. & Sanders, M. M. (1997). Designing effective learning systems for management education: student roles, requisite variety, and practicing what we teach. *Academy of Management Journal, 40*, 1334–1368.

Moore, M. G. (1998). Quality in distance education: four cases. *The American Journal of Distance Education, 11*(3), 1–6.

Smith, T. W. (1998). Distance education is a strategy: what is the objective? *The American Journal of Distance Education, 12*(2), 63–72.

Souder, W. E. (1993). The effectiveness of traditional vs. satellite delivery in three management of technology master's degree programs. *The American Journal of Distance
Education, 7*(1), 37–53.

Sumner, M., & Hostetler, D. (1999, Fall). Factors influencing the adoption of technology in
teaching. *Journal of Computer Information Systems*, 81–87.

Webster, J., & Hackley, P. (1997). Teaching effectiveness in technology-mediated distance
learning. *Academy of Management Journal*, 40, 1282–1309.

Westbrook, T. S. (1997). Changes in students' attitudes toward graduate business instruction via interactive television. *The American Journal of Distance Education, 11*(1), 55–
69.

Chapter XVIII

Using Web-Based Technology to Support and Enhance the Learning Experience in a Community-Learning Projects Course

Dennis Drinka
University of Alaska Anchorage, USA

Minnie Yi-Miin Yen
University of Alaska Anchorage, USA

ABSTRACT

Project-based courses present students with unique support and organizational challenges. In these types of courses, students must assume greater responsibility for learning and organizing and must direct their efforts toward satisfying a unique, sometimes ill-structured problem. The enhanced learning potential in these courses is significant; however, so are the risks. Discussed in this chapter are a variety of Web-based technologies that were used to support students in their project development efforts, thereby realizing benefits of project-based courses while ensuring project success. A demonstration of how students in a project-based capstone course used this technology to assist them in developing community-based information systems is presented. More importantly, it also demonstrates how the tools, selected because they contributed to project success, can extend the students' learning environment and enhance their learning experience.

INTRODUCTION

The capstone course for our Management Information System undergraduate degree requires students to design, develop, and implement information systems for community organizations. This course has proven to be successful in developing career-enhancing skills and abilities, and increasing student self-confidence and employability, all while providing useful products for the community. Since its inception, the quality and difficulty of the projects and the satisfaction of the sponsoring organizations have been consistently increasing. One of our area's largest employers has committed to providing our program with multiple projects each year and uses the program as a source of development for projects that might otherwise be too risky or unprofitable to undertake. The contribution of the projects has led to widespread community recognition for our program and students and a broader set of project sponsors (Hoffinger, 2002).

The success of this course can be attributed to two factors. First, its design is based on a long history of widely accepted community-, project-, and technology-based learning theories. Second, its implementation is based on the use of readily available Web-based tools such as those used for email, group collaboration, Web search, and project management. In the background section of this chapter, we will review the theories that describe the benefits that can be realized through this challenging form of course design and that were used to guide its development. The course description section will present the learning objectives of the course and the tasks that must be accomplished by the students for successful project completion. The Web support section will describe the Web-based tools that were implemented in the course to help realize the benefits of the design and will discuss how those tools provided for student success and learning enhancement. Presented in the last section will be lessons learned and conclusions reached.

THEORETICAL BACKGROUND OF THE COURSE DESIGN

Designing a course solely based on technology is not sufficient. Schneider (1994) stated that instruction must be grounded in educational theory and not be solely based on educational content or be based on the technology used to deliver the information. LeJeune and Richardson (1998) believed that while traditional learning theory can be expected to evolve with time as educational technologies become more sophisticated, the majority of traditional learning theories will still serve their original intent, which is to facilitate the transfer of knowledge and promote the construction of new instructional models.

The design of this course is consistent with the engagement theory for technology-based teaching and learning (Kearsley & Shneiderman, 1999). This theory has emerged from Kearsley and Shneiderman's experiences teaching in electronic and distance education environments and has much in common with many of the well-known community- and project-based learning theories. The fundamental idea underlying this theory is that students must be meaningfully engaged in learning activities through interaction with others and with worthwhile tasks. Through engaged learning, all student activities involve active cognitive processes such as creating, problem solving, reasoning, decision making, and evaluating. In addition, students are intrinsically motivated to learn due to the meaningful nature of the learning environment and activities.

A pedagogic model of Relate-Create-Donate proposes that students need to work in teams and work collaboratively to produce ambitious projects that are meaningful for someone outside the classroom. These three components, Relate-Create-Donate, imply that learning activities:

1. Occur in a group context (i.e., collaborative teams)
2. Are project-based
3. Have an outside (authentic) focus

The first principle (the "Relate" component) emphasizes team efforts that involve communication, planning, management, and social skills. The second principle (the "Create" component) makes learning a creative, purposeful activity. Students have to define the project (problem domain) and focus their efforts on application of ideas to a specific context. Project orientation is the essence of Problem-Based Learning approaches that are often used in medical and others types of professional education (Barrows & Tamblyn, 1980). The third principle (the "Donate" component) stresses the value of making a useful contribution while learning. Ideally, each project has an outside "customer" for which the project is being conducted. In many cases, the projects can be work-related, i.e., an activity that fits into a team's occupational or career interests. The authentic learning context of the project increases student motivation and satisfaction. This principle is consistent with the emphasis on school-to-work programs in many school systems and colleges, as well as the "service" philosophy of contemporary corporate training efforts (Jacoby & Associates, 1996).

Community-based learning is a pedagogy that embeds academic study into community service projects. Local community groups are in need of assistance, while students are in need of real-world experiences that relate to their course material so that they might gain a better understanding of real issues and practices by working on actual problems and with nonacademic groups (Lazar & Preece, 1999). While benefiting the community through work performed, this type of learning also increases students' understanding of their academic subjects by putting them directly in touch with what is being studied, as differentiated from learning in the abstract (Keeton & Tate, 1978). The student in an experiential learning situation learns from actually, directly, and actively working with the objects of learning, usually under controlled conditions and under the instructor's supervision (Venkatesh & Small, 2002). John Dewey (1938), Piaget (1970), and Lewin (1951) viewed learning as a continuous, adaptive process driven by experiences where the student is active and engaged with the subject matter at hand. Furthermore, in the technology field, computing is often viewed as a social technology (Iacono & Kling, 1988). Individuals must learn to consider technology not only within the context of work practices but also with that of organizational culture and power. Community-based learning is a productive way to introduce students into the social context of their studies. Learning becomes the product of participation in the actual practice, interactions, and relationships that constitute the community-based project (Lave & Wenger, 1991).

Project-based collaborative learning refocuses learning from short, isolated, teacher-directed activities, to activities that are student-directed, long-term, and interdisciplinary—all within a team-based, collaborative framework. Collaborative learning refers to those methods of instruction where students work together to reach a common goal. Within the context of a community-based course, this collaboration is extended to include the owners and users of the project deliverables. The instructor is included in the collaboration in a supportive role. With collaborative learning, students increase their understanding and knowledge by sharing ideas with their team members and are dependent upon each other for project success. Project team members must work together in learning and knowledge building communities, exploring each other's skills while providing social support and modeling and observing the contribution of each member (Jonassen, 1995). According to Vygotsky's zone of proximal development theory, student learning is extended by the difference between what a student can do alone and what a student can do with supportive collaboration (Vygotsky, 1978). Extending the collaboration pool by including the sharing of ideas, dependencies, and supportive collaboration, and the existing and widely based knowledge of system owners and users extends these benefits well beyond the scope of student-only collaboration, much less, the traditional teacher-centered approach.

Projects provide an ideal organizational structure for supporting collaborative learning, because with projects and collaborative learning, it is necessary that the activity is directed toward solving a problem or creating or discovering something (Schrage, 1991).

Project collaboration also contributes to students' social learning through their observation of behaviors, attitudes, and emotional reactions of teammates, owners, and users (Bandura, 1977), (LeJeune & Richardson, 1998). From the perspective of social constructivism theory, members of the community serve as active agents in the construction of outcomes and activities that produce a development cycle in the social setting. (Shaw & Shaw, 1999). Therefore, combining project-based learning with community-based learning integrates the benefits of both.

Kearsley and Shneiderman's engagement theory also has much in common with other theoretical frameworks. With its focus on experiential and self-directed learning, it is similar in nature to theories of adult learning (i.e., andragogy). In his theory of andragogy, Knowles (Knowles, 1975, 1984) emphasized that adults are self-directed and expect to take responsibility for decisions. Adult learning programs must accommodate this fundamental concept. Andragogy makes the following assumptions about the design of learning:

1.   Adults need to know why they need to learn something
2.   Adults need to learn experientially
3.   Adults approach learning as problem solving
4.   Adults learn best when the topic is of immediate value

With its emphasis on meaningful learning, it is consistent with the constructivist approach that takes the view that learning is constructed. New knowledge is built using what students already know. That is, their prior knowledge influences what they construct. In the constructivist model, learning is active, not passive as in a traditional model. Students confront their understanding in light of what they encounter. They apply understanding and note relevant elements in modifying knowledge (Jonassen, 1994).

Based on the above learning theories, it was determined that the MIS capstone course should be designed around four core principles:

1.   Project-based
2.   Community-based
3.   Team work through collaborative efforts
4.   Utilization of emerging capabilities of Web-based technologies

However, although the potential benefits of this course design based on these principles are, in theory, significant, so are the risks. Projects in this course can be considered successful from the students' perspective only if they truly integrate and enhance their traditional academic experiences; and as a minimum from the community's perspective, they can be considered successful only if they add value to that organization. A project that is not completed up to the expectations of the students or the organization cannot, in actuality, be considered successful. That is, while the learning theories supporting this course design are significant, they are irrelevant if the projects are not successful. In the next section, we will describe the course and its requirements. The section following that will describe how Web-based technology was used in the implementation of the course and how Web-based tools contributed to realizing the potential of the course design.

COURSE DESCRIPTION AND REQUIREMENTS

The Management Information Systems (MIS) degree in our university has developed an integrated sequence of three courses. This three-semester sequence of courses draws upon the technical knowledge and skills acquired through other courses, but it primarily encompasses the traditional set of topics covered in Systems Analysis, Project Management, and Systems Design and Implementation courses.

The last course in this sequence, the Systems Design and Implementation course, is a project-based capstone course that requires students to develop a community-based information system. This course not only completes the sequence but also requires the teams to integrate and apply the knowledge and skills gained from core business courses, from required Management Information System courses, and from upper-division elective MIS courses. The final products of this course, including documentation, are evaluated by a review committee made up of department faculty and information system professionals from the local community and are provided to the sponsoring organization at no cost.

Fortunately, the community provides a large and growing source of projects in the areas of computer and information systems. The changing and growing availability of information technology presents many opportunities for projects that would, without our students' involvement in the projects, go undeveloped. Some examples of projects developed in this course include e-commerce sites, replacement of paper-based processes with electronic processes, implementation of portable devices for tracking contract work or production outputs, guided tour and reservation systems, and data-driven websites for tracking sporting event results. Community organizations sponsoring these projects range from Fortune 100 companies to nonprofit volunteer organizations. Place-of-work of the users of these systems include exotic locations such as Prudhoe Bay on the Arctic Ocean, a base camp of an adventure guide that is accessible only by snow machine or dog sled in the winter, and off-shore oil or gas platforms.

Regardless of the type of project, the size of the organization, or the location of the users, all projects must meet identical minimum requirements in order for students to complete the course successfully. These objectives were selected based on the need to satisfy the expectations of the sponsoring organization (implementable and tested system that meets their requirements) and the learning objectives of students in a capstone course. Potential projects requested by organizations are screened to ensure that these minimum requirements can be achieved. The minimum requirements for students to receive credit for this course are enumerated in Table 1.

An objective of our MIS program in general, and this course in particular, is to prepare students for—and to develop their confidence in—being able to accomplish whatever is necessary to build a successful system and to have students be flexible enough to play any role in a system development project. Given the rate of change in existing technologies and the number of newly emerging technologies, this program is designed to develop students' independence and confidence so as to prepare them to be successful when presented with new challenges.

In order to satisfy the minimum requirements listed in Table 1, students are typically involved in completing a variety of tasks which they set up for themselves as part of their project planning process. Some of the typical tasks that students are involved in are presented in Table 2. In addition to these tasks, maintaining coordination and communication among all parties is the responsibility of the students.

Based on the tasks involved, it was decided that the likelihood of a project's success could be increased by using Web-based technologies to support:

1. Communication between team members, between teams, and sponsors/users, and between instructors and teams
2. Independent research capabilities

Table 1: Minimum Requirements for Course Credit

1. Develop an information system that has been implemented or is in a state that can be implemented
2. Conduct independent research through self-directed learning of technologies not included in the MIS curriculum or by researching and evaluating alternative design or development features
3. Integrate multiple advanced technologies in the system by using technology learned in at least two upper-division MIS required or elective courses
4. Apply systems analysis and project management skills throughout the project
5. Develop user training, user support, documentation, and help files
6. Develop a testing plan, and document test results
7. Prepare a final written report
8. Conduct a final project presentation

Table 2: Typical Project Planning Tasks

• Interviewing users on site
• Holding team meetings
• Reporting project progress and obtaining approvals from the instructor and the project owner
• Investigating problems and identifying solutions to those problems
• Maintaining records of team member work hours
• Coordinating development among team members
• Maintaining quality and consistency of all project deliverables
• Learning new technology
• Researching alternative designs
• Testing the system
• Preparing user manuals and help files
• Documenting all project-related activities
• Presenting results

3.   Requirements analysis
4.   Project planning, scheduling, and management.

Given the above, it was decided that the success of a project could best be supported by implementing the following tools: Project Central, a Web-based tool available with Microsoft Project (renamed Project Server in MS Project 2002); any of a variety of readily available Web-based group collaborative tools such as Yahoo! Groups; and any Web-based search engine the students were familiar with. These tools would increase the productivity of the students and the quality of the project outputs, including documentation and reports. Beyond providing support, it was important to us that any new technology adopted should contribute to our larger objective of enhancing and expanding the learning environment, through expanding the scope of the learning environment or through exposing the students to the use and administration of technology that was new to them.

WEB SUPPORT FOR STUDENT SUCCESS AND LEARNING ENHANCEMENT

Web-based instruction is an increasingly popular method for delivering college courses or as an enhancement to traditionally delivered courses. Most applications of the Web are designed for information delivery; however, some of the more aggressive uses of the Web include its use for collaboration and research. What we have discovered is that Web-based tools originally designed to improve productivity have the added benefit of enhancing the learning environment. In this section, we will discuss some of the enhanced learning opportunities discovered through the use of Web-based technologies that supported students in their project development. The use of these technologies was optional, because students were responsible for their own project design and management; therefore, our objective was to provide the tools while enhancing student learning.

Using Web-Based Tools to Enhance Communication

One of the uses of the Web in this course was for communication. In a traditional classroom-based course, the Web is often used as a method for presenting and sharing information. Its ability to be accessed anytime from anywhere is a significant improvement over previous methods. In a community-based project course, however, communication is nothing short of the key to success. Our projects involve three parties: student teams, in the role of project managers and system designers/developers; course instructors, in the role of advisers, advocates for hardware, software, facilities, and other resource support, and as problem mediators; and community partners, in the role of system owners and users. Coordination between each of these roles is critical for the success of a project; therefore, efficient communication and effective project management is necessary. However, coordination even within just one of these roles, the student teams, has been a difficult challenge in the past, because students have different school, work, and family schedules. Coordinating among all three roles has traditionally been a major problem. Our solution was to encourage students to use Web-based tools to provide an electronic means for communication and project management.

While tools were provided to help students complete their projects, they were also used to enhance the students' learning. An active learning environment involves learning that is interactive, student-centered, exploratory, contextualized, intentional, reflective, and collaborative (Savery & Duffy, 1995). The project-based orientation of this course allows us to implement these learning strategies in various forms through the tools provided for communication support. For instance, learning in this course takes place across a sequence of phases, including understanding, defining, and solving information system problems; each phase presents unique communication requirements that are also opportunities for providing an active learning environment. Opportunities such as working collaboratively, sharing problem solving, locating and interacting with outside experts, interacting with the owners, users, and the instructor all involve interactive, student-centered, and exploratory experiences within the context of real problems, as well as reflection and collaboration.

Additional methods of support that enhance the learning environment include access to informational resources like electronic libraries and search engines and access to the instructor or a facilitator who, through Web capabilities, can guide the discussion, intervene when necessary, and assist students in moving through the project phases until projects are completed.

Similarly, these same tools support conversational learning. For example, according to Gordon Pask's conversation theory, learning is inherently a social, dialogical process in which learners benefit most from being part of knowledge-building communities in class and outside school (Jonassen, 1995). Conversation, communication, and establishment of a community of learners are mediums for a successful teaching and learning process (Pask, 1975). A highly interactive conversation among individuals allows for an exchange of ideas, knowledge construction, critical reflection, and clarification of points of contradiction (Pea, 1994). Pask (1975) also referred to individuals engaging in conversation to share with each other what they know and what they have learned. Additionally, conversation supports the goal of learning that insists that effective learning will only take place if students become involved with communities of practice.

Some of the tools available to students in this course for communication include: email, Web bulletin board postings, newsgroups, Web-based collaboration software such as Yahoo! Groups, and chat facilities. It was decided that Web-based collaborative tools would be the most effective of these, because they combine email, listserv types of features, chat, file sharing, and other capabilities. Teams were encouraged to form a Web collaboration group and to invite their instructor and project owner and users to join that group. Most teams chose to use collaborative groups, although some preferred email.

Some of the benefits that resulted from students using email or Web collaboration groups are included in Table 3. Many of these benefits resulted from automatic documentation inherent in many of the tools. This feature was used by the students to help them prepare their final report and to build references to owner and user requirements.

Whereas previously, projects were restricted to being located within driving distance, with Web-based collaborative tools, project sponsors could be located anywhere. One of the challenges of offering this course is finding qualified projects. Removing the location constraint created a larger pool of potential projects. Web-based collaboration also avoided the problem of having to synchronize student schedules and of commuting to a common location. Students could, if they chose, meet synchronously using chat or asynchronously using email. Almost all teams still held weekly face-to-face meetings rather than relying solely on a Web tool. However, one team held all meetings at a distance, because the members of

Table 3: Some Benefits of Email and Web Collaboration Groups

- Automatic documentation of team correspondence and virtual meetings
- Automatic documentation of team-based system tests, testing progress, and test results
- Automatic documentation of outside tester results
- Support for obtaining access to feedback and guidance from system owners and the instructor
- Support to owners and the instructor for tracking students' contributions, progress, and problems
- Support for geographically distant sponsoring organizations
- Support for geographically distant student collaboration

this team were located in three different states: Alaska, Arizona, and Florida. On another project, the sponsor was physically located in the oil fields on the Arctic Ocean for two-week periods followed by being out of the state (in Texas) for the next two-week period. The only physical contact made with the sponsor was to obtain his signature while he was in the airport transferring between biweekly flights between the Arctic and Texas. In a third project, students never physically met with the owner/user who was located in another state.

The last four of the benefits in Table 3 illustrate some of the practical ways in which the learning environment of the students could be expanded and enhanced. Prior to the use of this communication support, student interaction was limited to initial interviews and sporadic interaction, especially for those projects where owners and users were remotely located. Students gained opportunities for richer interaction with their community sponsors. Student interaction within their teams was also enriched. They were better able to share information and to collaborate on the development and testing of their work without being constrained by time or location. The successful development of a project by students in three separate states is the best example of how well this technology can be used to support student collaboration.

Using Web Tools to Enhance Independent Research

Another use of the Web was to meet the course requirement for conducting independent research. In this course, independent research was broadly defined; it relates more closely to the process of investigation than to the synthesis and reporting of results. It was not evaluated based on a report of findings, but on documentation of efforts made, problems solved, and technologies learned; that is, the objective of this requirement was to develop students' investigational skills, not increase their knowledge in a specific area. Our strategy was to incorporate constructive learning theory into the course through the process of discovery learning on the Web. For example, in relation to the constructivist theory discussed above, students are required to use and apply their existing knowledge acquired in previous courses to help them understand and formulate their information system problem environment, and then are required to develop new knowledge and understandings by extending that existing knowledge toward solving their problem, i.e., designing and developing a new information system. At the same time, the prior knowledge that is brought to use must be constructed rather than retrieved intact from memory, which forces students to develop their own representations and understanding of information rather than having some representation imposed upon them. The final result is students who are majoring in an information-technology-related field, having already acquired fundamental knowledge and skills, learn to explore and investigate the rich and boundary-less Web world that will be a key to their continued learning, while using a constructive learning process to fulfill their project specific requirements.

Within the area of information systems development, the breadth of information and the speed in which it changes are substantial, almost overwhelming. Other than a small core of knowledge, much of what students learn about technology in their classes will change, if not become obsolete, within a few years of graduation. Students will need to be able to learn continuously, and in those cases where they are working with cutting-edge technology, training courses and books will be unavailable; instead they will have to learn through independent research using the Web.

Some of the areas within the Web that are available for this type of research include newsgroups, user groups, search engines, and websites developed for supporting specific software or for sharing information about that software. One research tool that was available to our students was an electronic library that the university subscribes to. This tool can potentially be a major resource for students. Rather than having to physically obtain a book for learning or for reference, students are able to check a book out electronically from any Web-accessible location, including their home or any one of the computer labs. Considering that most development projects use multiple languages, protocols, and technologies, having ready access to reference manuals can be a valuable tool. Unfortunately, most books currently available through our electronic library do not yet satisfy this need, because the selection is neither current enough nor broad enough for our use. Even if access to the most current and comprehensive books were available, most books focus on one technology but do not address problems of integrating different technologies. For information on these and other types of research problems, alternative Web tools such as those discussed below have been found to be more useful by the students. Nevertheless, this may be a potentially powerful Web-based tool in the future.

A new use of the Web for research is to help with code development. Students can now search for and capture code snippets, applets, and other existing code that can be shared and used in their projects. Reuse of existing code is an efficient development strategy and reflects the trend of code development in general, that is, reusability. Students can produce better results more efficiently using code that has already been developed and tested. Many websites are available that are dedicated to providing code snippets related to particular languages or protocols. In other cases, the websites provide detailed examples. Using code snippets or examples, students are able to apply a wide variety of new technologies without having to be experts in them. Students still have had to learn enough on their own to make any captured code work correctly; however, though the comprehensiveness of learning is decreased, its focus and task-orientation is increased. The students develop an ability to determine what they need to know, where to find information about a topic, and how to apply that information to a task in an efficient manner. In many fields, this might be an undesirable learning strategy; however, in the information systems field, this closely reflects what will be expected of them after graduation.

In using the Web for problem solving, students working on the leading edge of technology and those working on especially complex portions of projects or encountering particularly difficult problems have been able to locate developers that had at least some familiarity with the problem issues and have been willing to provide advice to anyone who encountered the same problem. In some cases, in particular, with those projects where many other individuals have encountered the same problem, student research involved locating a posting found on some electronic bulletin board. In other cases, for example, where a particular team needed to combine two technologies in a way that had not been done before, students posted requests for help on multiple electronic bulletin boards. On at least one occasion, replies to their posts indicated that what they were trying to do could not be done. Nevertheless, the students persevered and eventually were able to locate one individual that had solved a similar problem. The students on that project were able to adapt that individual's experience and to solve their own problem. By the time they finished their project, these team members were the experts, and the students were posting their discoveries on the Web to help others. This is a good example of using the Web to extend student research and learning well beyond the classroom or the local community. The students used the discussion groups and bulletin boards to participate in special user groups in order to acquire and exchange knowledge and learning experiences with each other and with experts worldwide; they were responsible for identifying the benefits and disadvantages of their discussion findings. This process of searching, filtering, and choosing, leads the student through a journey of self-learning, where the students were required to have the "ability to diagnose one's own learning needs and to identify the next steps" before proceeding (Scardamalia & Bereiter, 1994).

Regardless of their particular use of the Web for research, the simple fact that students became aware of the resources available on the Web was surely one of the major benefits of requiring them to perform independent research. They increased their knowledge while developing their research capabilities.

Another innovative use of Web-based research was that involved in identifying and evaluating design alternatives. For example, teams often have to evaluate alternate Internet Service Providers based on criteria set by the system owner and on the technology required. This use of the Web is related more toward information collection, processing, and reporting, than to problem solving. It is more similar to traditional research projects than to the types of research described above. Although both forms of research satisfied minimum requirements, the former was evaluated as more difficult than the latter and rewarded accordingly.

A final use of the Web for research involved team members using online training to learn new technologies. Students used free online tutorials for computer languages and applications such as Java, Java applets, Visual Basic, Active Server Pages, and such. These training sites have been particularly useful for new and emerging technologies, because books on these subjects are often still under development.

It is interesting that most students' skills in using the Web for research are advanced, and this is not an area where any in-class training needs to be provided. Nevertheless, through simply using Web browsers and search engines, the students develop their critical thinking skills by navigating through large pools of information and making appropriate and relevant selections on their own.

Using Web Tools to Improve Requirements Analysis

Another way teams used the Web was for assisting them in their requirements analysis task. Requirements analysis is an early task in system development projects. For this task, students must determine what the requirements are for the system they will be developing. It involves gathering information from the users of the systems, from the owner, from records and files, and from any sources appropriate for that system. Traditional methods of acquiring this information include interviewing, onsite walkthroughs, surveys, reviewing databases and reports, and prototyping user interfaces.

In its simplest case, the Web can be used to help with the communications involved in this task. Owners and users are often unavailable for face-to-face meetings because of constraints on time and location. As discussed above, various Web tools are available for assistance in communication.

One of the typical problems encountered by students during this phase is that users often state "I won't know what I want until I can see something displayed on the screen or receive something printed in a report." This leads to a more unique and original use of the Web for this course: prototyping user interfaces on Web development types of projects. Prototyping in this sense involves developing a scaled-down version of a system, or a portion of a system such as the user interfaces, in order to elicit a response from the users. Instead of developing prototypes for the users with a traditional computer-based (but not Web-based) CASE (computer-aided software engineering) tool, students were encouraged to find existing websites that contained features that would be useful on their sites or contained a design that would be similar to their site. Teams would then present these target sites to the users and owners for evaluation and feedback. Various design and style requirements, as well as functionality and dynamic features, could be identified easily and quickly, and the feedback provided would be more reliable. For example, a team that was developing a website for online purchase of wholesale meats directed the owner to various sites that provided similar services. The owner picked a preferred site, and the team targeted their design and development toward the "look and feel" and the functionality of that site. In many other projects, when the owners and users selected sites that have been built using HTML and JavaScript, students were able to capture and modify the captured code from the prototypes and use it as a starting point or supplement for their own development.

This use of tools is another application of the active learning model. In particular, it includes two principle components of learning: experience and dialogue. The benefits of these components are realized by encouraging students to work collaboratively within their teams, with outside experts, and with system owner/users. Research suggests that students enhance their active learning experiences through dialectic interaction (Fink, 2000). Experiences with experts and owners/users, involving a discussion of work accomplishments or project requirements, or simply the observation of the working environment of others, can develop within students a new perspective on their beliefs and values of the real world. Dialogue, either with themselves or with others, has the potential to help students construct meaning from their experience and to gain the insights that come from these experiences (Fink, 2000). During the requirements analysis portion of their projects, students become involved in dialogues in which the students move back and forth between the constrained real-world environment of the owners and users, and the pure, unconstrained concepts of their classroom environment. Having rich interaction between these different environments, being involved with new experiences and engaging in meaningful dialogue about information systems and specific system requirements, increases the likelihood that the students will experience more significant and more meaningful learning.

In our course, Web-based prototyping and Web-enhanced communication tools enable students to gain more information about the systems' requirements. While this interaction facilitated users and owners in articulating their needs, it also enabled students to learn about the real-world environment of the users and their real-world constraints and expectations and to tie these into their existing classroom-gained knowledge, thereby enhancing their learning experience in ways suggested by many authors (see Lazar & Preece, 1999; Keeton & Tate, 1978; Venkatesh & Small, 2002; John Dewey, 1938; Piaget, 1970; Lewin, 1951; and Lave & Wenger, 1991; for example).

Using Web Tools to Enhance Planning, Scheduling, and Management

One of the most useful features of the Web that improved the experience for everyone involved in these projects—owners, instructor, and teams—was Web-based project management. Collaboration among all participants involved in a project was vital to that project's success. The instructor needed to be able to track progress across multiple projects. The owners needed to be able to track progress and provide feedback on their particular project. Student developers were responsible for reporting their hours by task and date. The student serving as project manager was responsible for assigning tasks, monitoring progress, and coordinating the roles of all the participants.

A Web-based project management tool with remote access was provided for supporting the collaborative planning, scheduling, and management needs of the students. This tool could contribute to the success of a project and the quality of the experience by providing, through the Web, access and up-to-date information to all interested parties, while limiting access and permissions to specific information as needed to best satisfy the needs of any individual. For example, the student serving as project manager could remotely assign students to tasks. Students could work on their own schedule and enter their hours worked on a task remotely either by date and hours worked or by percentage of a task completed. The project manager could automatically integrate worked hours into reports, identify if tasks were being completed on schedule, and make adjustments or reassignments as necessary. Summary reports are automatically generated and accessible to interested parties such as the instructor and project owner. These parties can have reports tailored to the information and level of detail they need and can allow them to drilldown for additional information as desired. For example, the instructor could be provided with a Web page that showed which projects were on or not on schedule, while a project owner could have a Web page that showed when a portion of the project was scheduled to be completed, and when it was actually completed.

Through this tool, students were able to enhance their learning through many of the ways already discussed, including through communication, collaboration and group learning, active learning, and social learning.

CONCLUSION

A community-based projects approach was used to enhance and enrich the learning of students in an MIS program capstone course. The underlying strengths of this course were based on the learning improvements that, in theory, could be gained through this type of course design. Discussed in this chapter is how the potential learning enhancements and enriched learning environment could be realized by implementing the course using readily available Web-based technology for support. These Web tools enabled the students to complete their projects successfully—only one project has been delivered after its due date since these tools have been employed. They contributed to the students' success by supporting their communications, independent research, requirements analysis, and project planning, scheduling, and management. They, in themselves, enhanced and expanded the students' learning environment by providing for and supporting client-centered work in natural, place-of-business settings, team work through collaborative efforts, community-based learning through involvement of project owners and users, and through the experience of using emerging technologies. Finally, they contributed to the success of the sponsoring organizations through the delivery of valuable, much needed information system projects. Since these tools have been in place, we have noticed improvements in the quality of the projects delivered, the ability of the students to conduct independent research, their level of real-world knowledge, and their communication abilities. Students' breadth of knowledge has increased by being exposed to these tools, and the depth of their knowledge has increased because of their ability to complete more complex projects. The growth in the number of organizations interested in participating in these projects has grown, and their willingness to entrust students with more complex projects that are important and sometimes critical to their business success has increased.

Through our experience, we have been able to identify key lessons that we learned and the lessons that students have learned. From the perspective of project-based courses, success requires that students be made aware that projects, like internships, are an alternate learning approach that is directed more toward the development of their research, critical thinking, and writing skills than toward knowledge acquisition; that project objectives and user needs must be clearly identified early in the project and agreed to by all interested parties in order to focus team efforts and avoid misunderstanding, and any changes affecting the design of the system must be approved by all participants; and that management and communication skills are important to ensure all parties are contributing when and where they are needed. These conclusions are consistent with the conclusions of the student partici-pants. Students in the course were required to include in their final report a "Lessons Learned: Advice for Future Students" section. Based on these reports, 50% of students listed communication, support from owners and users, and good planning as critical factors affecting success; 36% listed allocating adequate time for research in the project plan; and 29% listed saving information from research, meetings, and testing. Based on these conclu-sions, the Web tools provided for communication, research, and project planning are recognized as valuable to student success. Moreover, these tools exceeded the needs of project success by contributing to enhanced learning—the fundamental goal of the course. As with the tools currently used in this course, new tools will inevitably be developed and will also contribute to enhancing and expanding the learning environment of students. Based on our experience in this course, we expect that further exploration of Web-based tools is likely to continue to produce increased benefits in project success and enhanced learning.

REFERENCES

Bandura, A. (1977). *General theory: social learning theory*. Englewood Cliffs, NJ: Prentice Hall.

Barrows, H., & Tamblyn, R. (1980). *Problem based learning: an approach to medical education*. New York: Springer.

Collis, B. (1997a). Supporting project-based collaborative learning via a World Wide Web environment. In B. H. Khan (Ed.), *Web-based instruction*, Englewood Cliffs, NJ: Educational Technology Publications, Inc.

Dewey, J. (1938) Experience and education. Kappa Delta Pi.

Fink, L. D. (2000) Higher level learning: the first step toward more significant learning. In D. Lieberman (Ed.), *To improve the academy* 2000, for the POD Network in Higher Education. Bolton, MA: Anker.

Hoffinger, T. (2002). UAA student projects save money. *Anchorage Daily News*, February 20, D1.

Iacono, S., & Kling, R. (1988). Computer systems as institutions: social dimensions of computing in organizations. In J. I. Degross, & M. H. Olson (Eds.), *Proceedings of the Ninth International Conference on Information Systems (ICIS)*, Minneapolis, MN.

Jacoby, B. & Associates. (1996). Service-learning in higher education. San Francisco, CA: Jossey-Bass.

Jonassen, D. H. (1995). Supporting communities of learners with technology: a vision for integrating technology with learning in schools. *Educational Technology, 35*(2), 60–63.

Kearsley G., & Shneiderman, B. (1999). *Engagement theory: a framework for technology-based teaching and learning*; home.sprynet.com/~gkearsley/engage.htm.

Keeton, M., & Tate, P. (1978). *Learning by experience—what, why, how*. San Francisco, CA: Jossey-Bass.

Knowles, M. (1975). *Self-directed learning*. Chicago, IL: Follet.

Knowles, M. (1984). *The adult learner: a neglected species* (3rd ed.). Houston, TX: Gulf Publishing.

Koschman, T. (1996). *CSCL: theory and practice of an emerging paradigm*. Mahwan, NJ: Lawrence Erlbaum Associates.

Lave, J. (1988). *Cognition in practice: mind, mathematics, and culture in everyday life*. Cambridge, UK: Cambridge University Press.

Lave, J., & Wenger, E. (1991). *Situated learning: legitimate peripheral participation*. New York: Cambridge University Press.

Lazar, J., & Preece, J. (1999) Implementing service learning in an online communities course. *Proceedings of the International Academy for Information Management Conference* (pp. 22–27).

LeJeune, N., & Richardson, K. (1998). *Learning theories applied to Web-based instruction*. Denver, CO: University of Colorado at Denver.

Lewin, K. (1951). *Field theory in social sciences*. New York: Harper & Row.

Pask, G. (1975). *Conversation, cognition, and learning*. New York: Elsevier.

Pea, R. (1994). Seeing what we build together: distributed multimedia learning environments for transformative communications. *The Journal of Learning Sciences, 3*(3), 285–299.

Piaget, J. (1970). *Genetic epistemology*. New York: Columbia University Press.

Savery, J. R., & Duffy, T. M. (1995). Problem based learning: an instructional model and its constructive framework. *Educational Technology*, Sept.

Scardamalia, M., & Bereiter, C. (1994). Computer support for knowledge-building communities. *The Journal of the Learning Sciences, 3*(3), 265–283.

Schneider, D. (1994). *Teaching and learning with Internet tools*. Geneva: University of Geneva.

Schrage, M. (1991). *Shared minds: the new technologies of collaboration*. New York: Random House.

Shaw, A., & Shaw, M. (1999). Social empowerment through community networks. In D. A. Schon, B. Sanyal, & W. J. Mitchell (Eds.), *High technology in low-income communities: prospects for the positive use of advanced information technology*. Cambridge, MA: The MIT Press.

Toomey, R., & Ketterer, K. (1995). Using multimedia as a cognitive tool. *Journal of Research on Computing in Education, 27*(4), 473–482.

Venkatesh, M., & Small, R. (2002). Active learning in higher education: a model and roadmap. In J. Lazar (Ed.), *Managing IT/community partnerships in the 21st century*. Hershey, PA: Idea Group Publishing.

Vygotsky, L. S. (1978). *Mind in society: the development of higher psychological processes*. Cambridge, MA: Harvard University Press.

Chapter XIX

Virtual Science Centers: Web-Based Environments for Promotion of Nonformal Science Education

Leo Tan Wee Hin
Nanyang Technological University, Singapore

R. Subramaniam
Nanyang Technological University, Singapore

ABSTRACT

The opening of a virtual annex by science centers has given rise to a new genre of learning in Web-based education. Seeking to enhance the outreach effectiveness of nonformal science education initiatives among students and the public, these virtual science centers fulfill a useful role in promoting the public understanding of science. The example of the Singapore Science Center is used as a case study to explore the topic in significant depth. A commentary is also presented on some of the issues, controversies, and problems encountered in this new learning environment. Some possible solutions and recommendations are suggested in light of our experiences.

INTRODUCTION

The advent of the Internet has made a profound impact in the field of education. By promoting a novel setting for the creation of new learning experiences, it is impinging on various aspects of traditional education structures. For example, the Internet has impacted on distance learning (Lupo & Erlich, 2000), student assignments (Collis, de Boer, & Slotman, 2001), online learning (Benigno & Trenton, 2001; Sanders & Morrison-Shetlar, 2001), group learning (Chen et al., 2001), e-experiments (Givens & McShea, 2000), and e-universities (Maes, 2001). Many of these are still evolving, and it is unlikely that any have reached maturation.

The ubiquity of the personal computer, the nature of the client–server architecture on the Internet, the low cost of logging onto the Internet, and the scope for simultaneous access are all factors that have helped to fuel the evolution of various genres of learning on the Internet platform. Most universities and schools, at least in the developed world, have a Web presence, and their portals feature a wealth of information and other resources for learning.

One aspect of Web-based education that has not received much attention in the science literature is that of virtual science centers. It is the cyberspace analogue of traditional science centers, institutions that popularize science and technology to students and the public. Providing distributed learning beyond the confines of their traditional infrastructure, virtual science centers have engendered a unique genre of offerings that opens up another tributary for promoting the public understanding of science.

The popularity of virtual science centers can be gauged from the fact that the website of the Association of Science-Technology Centers (ASTC) has links to over 200 science centers, museums, and other nonformal institutions of learning. Visits to virtual science centers have been increasing over the past few years—for example, The Exploratorium, which is considered to be the pioneer of the science center movement, attracted 132,585,374 visits from 1993 to 1998 (Orfinger, 1998). Among ASTC members, 70% have websites: 34% of these sites are hosted by donors, 23% are hosted by Web-hosting services, and 41% are hosted by the institutions themselves. During 1997, a total of 195.3 million hits were recorded by 77 science centers and museums. Though this figure does not capture the unique number of separate visitors, a point to note is that 38 of these institutions reported that the number of distinct hosts served in December 1997 alone was a staggering 896,362 (Association of Science-Technology Centers, 1998).

Published studies on virtual science centers are rather sparse in the primary science literature. Commentaries on the Web offerings of a few science centers have appeared in newsletters (Orfinger, 1998; Honeyman, 1998) as well as were presented at conferences (Jackson, 1996). Studies of museum portals have, however, been quite extensive (Donovan, 1997; Milekic, 1997; Tinkler & Friedman, 1998; Beauchamp, 1998; Bowen, Bennett, & Johnson, 1998; Gaia, 1999; Keene, 2000; Sumpton, 2001; Crowley, Leinhardt, & Chang, 2001).

The purpose of this chapter is fourfold:

1. To briefly review the science center movement and its migration onto the Internet platform
2. To share the experiences of the virtual science center on the website of the Singapore Science Center; this website is the largest among all science centers in the world
3. To comment on the unique features of science centers on the Web, and the technologies that make their range of offerings possible
4. To comment on the issues, controversies, and problems facing virtual science centers, and suggest possible solutions and recommendations in light of our experiences in the science center movement

Through this, we wish to accord further recognition to an educational genre that has tremendous potential for the nonformal science education of students and the public.

REVIEW OF SCIENCE CENTER MOVEMENT AND ITS MIGRATION ONTO THE INTERNET PLATFORM

Science Centers are nonformal educational institutions of relatively recent origins (Danilov, 1982). They have been established primarily for the purpose of popularizing science and technology to the public and students, thereby contributing to the enhancement of science literacy levels. Initially, the tasks were performed by science museums which were, and generally still continue to be, repositories of scientific artifacts. As the exhibits here represent treasures of historical value, opportunities to appreciate them in an interactive manner were understandably minimal.

Within the framework of a museum environment and as a sequel to their natural evolution, the concept of a science center began to germinate. Science centers were envisaged as vibrant institutions that can popularize science and technology in multidimensional ways among the public. The Exploratorium in San Francisco is to be credited for pioneering the science center movement in 1969 and of making a success of it for others to emulate (Oppenheimer, 1972; Delacote, 1998).

Over the years, the concept gained further recognition, and we have seen the proliferation of numerous science centers across the world. A large number of these science centers are in North America, and a significant number of them are in Europe. Some museums also started to function as science centers or with an interactive science annex, for example, the Launch Pad in the Science Museum of London, and the Xperiment! in the Manchester Museum of Science and Technology. It took some time for science centers to be established in Asia, and in South-East Asia, the Singapore Science Center has been the pioneer (Tan & Subramaniam, 1998). More recently, science centers have been established in Hong Kong, Malaysia, and Indonesia.

Though science centers are sometimes called museums or science museums, they differ significantly from the latter. Museums generally host art collections and other historical artifacts, while science museums display a range of scientific artifacts. Generally, these exhibits are not for hands-on exploration. In science centers, the emphasis is more on interactive exhibitry.

Science centers have now come to be regarded as not only part of a nation's scientific and educational infrastructure but also as important coordinates in the domain of the leisure industry.

With the entrenching of the Internet, science centers have been compelled to colonize the Web in their efforts to stay relevant, address new challenges, and tap new opportunities for growth. In the early years, their offerings were more of a static nature. With advances in technology, a whole new genre of offerings have sprouted on the websites of science centers. These virtual science centers popularize science and technology through virtual science exhibitions and other educational programs. In fact, the Web provides yet another platform for science centers to engage the public as part of their extension education efforts in science literacy. As their principal mission objective is to popularize science and technology, they have considerable leeway, even in the virtual domain, to interpret science education policies within the framework circumscribed by their operational philosophy to present content in interesting ways and in ways that are divorced from the rigors of formal school-based assessment. Being natural nodal points in cyberspace for the public, including students, to seek information about science, the learning potential of offerings in the portals of virtual science centers have increased greatly over the years.

CASE STUDY OF SOME ASPECTS OF THE VIRTUAL SCIENCE CENTER AT THE SINGAPORE SCIENCE CENTER

The website of the Singapore Science Center (http://www.science.edu.sg) is the largest among all science and technology centers in the world. It features static and interactive exhibits as well as a range of other educational resources, characteristic fare for a typical virtual science center.

The core specificity of the website leverages principally around four aspects to meet different learning needs. We have found these aspects to be instrumental in enhancing the dynamism of the website as well as in drawing virtual visitors, not only from Singapore but also from other parts of the world. A discussion of these aspects is thus necessary in the context of the thrust of this chapter.

Virtual Exhibits

Exhibits are the principal means by which science centers communicate their mission objectives on site. This emphasis is also continued in cyberspace, where the exhibits can be static or interactive. In the website of the Singapore Science Center, there are a number of static and interactive exhibits of a virtual nature. By way of example, we focus on one of the virtual exhibits in the virtual science center: ballistic simulator (Figure 1). We believe that this is a good example of what an interactive virtual exhibit should be like.

The ballistic simulator is an exhibit that illustrates how the dynamics of motion of an object along a trajectory can be affected by various factors. It is a good virtual exhibit, because it evokes not only the physicality of a floor exhibit but also harnesses the unique potential of the Web to foster learning experiences. It is not easy to set up this exhibit in the exhibition gallery of a science center because of space constraints, logistics requirements, safety considerations, and operational factors. The Web offers the potential to scale it down to a dimension that offers interactivity while capturing the essence of the physicity.

Figure 1: Version of Ballistic Simulator on Website of Singapore Science Center

More specifically, the online exhibit challenges the visitor to hit a target under a variety of conditions. To enhance the learning potential of the exhibit, a menu of options is available in order to vary the parameter of interest—muzzle angle, muzzle velocity, gravitational field strength, and wind speed. Selection and adjustment of the options can be done through a window on the screen with the use of a mouse. No input from the keyboard is required.

Once the relevant parameters are selected, clicking the start button evokes a mapping of the trajectory of the object under the chosen conditions on the screen. This feedback allows the visitor to see whether he has played the game correctly or, rather, how the chosen parameters have affected the dynamics of the object's motion.

The key features of this exhibit that make it a good example of an online interactive exhibit are as follows:

1. Multiplicity of contexts for the user to connect with the exhibit in a seamless manner
2. Good instructional design
3. Proactive learning contexts
4. Good balance between learning and leisure
5. No text-heavy pages to interfere with the learning experience

Fostering a play element in the learning process makes the exhibit fun to interact with. Even a child who has little knowledge of the dynamics of the requisite physical processes

Table 1: Some Top Documents Accessed at the Virtual Science Center for the Year 2000/2001

	Documents	Views	% of Total Views	Visits	Avg. Time Viewed
1	**Virtual Science Centre Homepage** http://www.sci-ctr.edu.sg/	106,432	4.45%	75,670	00:02:2
2	**Singapore Science Centre Homepage** http://www.sci-ctr.edu.sg/ssc/ssc.html	27,795	1.16%	24,868	00:01:4
3	**VSC WebView Camera** http://www.sci-ctr.edu.sg/Webview/	27,377	1.14%	23,491	00:01:1
4	**ScienceNet : Life Science** http://www.sci-ctr.edu.sg/ScienceNet/cat_life/cat_life.html	25,882	1.08%	22,797	00:02:3
5	**ScienceNet : Physical Science** http://www.sci-ctr.edu.sg/ScienceNet/cat_physical/cat_physical.html	25,032	1.04%	22,202	00:02:2
7	**Welcome To ScienceNet !!** http://www.sci-ctr.edu.sg/ScienceNet/	19,687	0.82%	15,938	00:01:3
8	**School Projects** http://www.sci-ctr.edu.sg/schproj/schproj.html	16,315	0.68%	14,611	00:01:2
9	**Interactive Exhibits** http://www.sci-ctr.edu.sg/interexh/interexh.html	15,910	0.66%	14,481	00:01:4
11	**VSC WebView Camera: Hall of IT Exhibition** http://www.sci-ctr.edu.sg/Webview/viewIT.html	14,503	0.6%	13,008	00:00:5
12	**Educational Resources** http://www.sci-ctr.edu.sg/edures/edures.html	13,918	0.58%	13,001	00:02:3

at work is likely to be drawn by the play elements embedded in the exhibit design, with learning taking place, perhaps, in a subdued or subliminal manner. It is also likely to foster a desire in the child to know more about the workings of the exhibit or the concepts inherent therein.

Of the top 50 documents accessed by the public in the year 2000/2001, about 7.5% of the total views is for virtual exhibits; some entries from the server log file for this section are shown in Table 1. This figure may be considered small, but it has to be noted that because of cost considerations, no virtual science center can afford to place too much emphasis on virtual exhibits. Also, there is a need to feature a diversity of science resources on the website. In the context of the foregoing, the figure of 7.5% is considered to be significant.

Science Net

Science Net is a unique feature of the website of the Singapore Science Center, and it is not found in the portals of other science centers or science museums. It is a Web-based platform for the public to use to obtain answers or explanations for any of their scientific queries. The database of questions and answers is organized according to the following schema:

- Computer Science
- Earth Science
- Engineering
- Life Sciences
- Space and Astronomy
- Others

Since its introduction in 1998, over 19,000 questions have been posted by the public, not only from Singapore but also from other countries, and over 5,000 of these questions have been answered by the organizers! Those not answered are repeat questions, school homework assignments, etc.

It is obviously not possible for a single institution to take on the mammoth task of answering all the questions posed because of the diversity of expertise and the number of personnel that would be required for such an exercise. To address this challenge, the two premier universities in Singapore, the National University of Singapore and the Nanyang Technological University, were inducted as co-organizers of this section. The two universities provide resource personnel who, together with staff of the Singapore Science Center, help to answer questions closest to their field of specialization. Some questions have two answers—this is more a consequence of some interesting or tricky questions being directed simultaneously to two experts. Besides minimizing the response time of getting at least one explanation for the question, the strategy also offers the public the benefit of obtaining alternative perspectives. Often, it may not be that easy to answer a question—such questions are then posted on the website, soliciting for answers. Hyperlinks are sometimes provided in a number of answers; this is not to be viewed as a quick-fix solution for answers that are brief but more as an extension of the textual narrative and also as a recognition that there needs to be a limit on the length of each answer. In particular, the use of hyperlinks encourages visitors to continue their learning experience, an important consideration in their extension education.

To make it easy for the global public to pose questions, user-friendly features are incorporated into the section. They need to key in brief details of their personal particulars before entering the question/s. This helps to capture a profile of the visitors as well as to personalize the question, in that the person who posed the question is acknowledged next to the question in the database. A click-button sends the question to the Science Net coordinator, who then reroutes it to the relevant expert in the resource panel after ascertaining that it is not a repeat question or a school homework assignment.

To ensure that members of the public do not pose questions that have already been answered, a search protocol is available. This allows the public to enter key words describing a concept in order to facilitate checking. Based on analyses of server log files, about 35% of the questions posed by the public have been found to be previously answered. For such cases, an email response is sent, directing them to the relevant section of the Science Net— a time-consuming exercise.

The aesthetics and dynamics of this section have been preserved by the use of a simple layout, presence of a design motif without flamboyant elements on the answers page, minimal use of colors and graphics, and use of simple fonts to present information. All of these help to minimize occular discomfort and make the requisite subset of the website less bandwidth-intensive for access—important considerations in ensuring that the site continues to stay breezy and popular. Explanations are usually kept to about a screen length in order to minimize cognitive overload. Lengthy explanations would require the visitor to connect at different cognitive levels, and have generally been avoided.

An example of a question and answer extracted from the database of the Science Net is presented below:

> *Tue Jul 4 04:57:39 PDT 2000 9233*
> *Dominic Shiells deltadom33@yahoo.com*
> *13 to 20 Engineering Graduate*

> **If a photon travels through a wall of glass, is it the same photon passing in? How does a photon travel?**

> *Answer:*
> *Photon is the elementary particle or "package" (quantum) of energy in which light and other forms of electromagnetic radiation are emitted. The photon has both particle and wave properties. It has no charge, and it is considered massless but possesses momentum and energy. When light shines through a wall of glass, photons of certain frequencies might be absorbed. Electrons in glass have a natural vibration frequency in the ultraviolet (UV) range. When UV light shines on glass, resonance occurs, as waves build up and maintain a large amplitude of vibration between the electron and the atomic nucleus. The energy the atom receives may be passed on to neighboring atoms by collisions, or it may be re-emitted. Resonating atoms in the glass can hold onto the energy of the UV light for a short while (about 100 millionth of a second). During this time, the atom makes about 1 million vibrations. It collides with neighboring atoms and gives up its energy as heat.*
> *At lower frequencies, like those of visible light, electrons in the glass are forced into vibration, but at less amplitude. The atom or molecule holds the energy for less time, with less chance of collision with neighboring atoms and molecules, and less energy transformed to heat. The energy of vibrating electrons is re-*

emitted as light. Hence, glass is said to be transparent to the frequencies of visible light. The frequency of the re-emitted light that is passed from molecule to molecule is identical to the frequency of the light that produced the vibration in the first place. The main difference is a slight time delay between absorption and re-emission. It is this time delay that results in a lower average speed of light through a transparent material. Light travels at different average speeds through different materials.

Access to the Science Net is free and is available globally. The rich repository of information available from the site draws visitors from across the world. It is the public's participation that has helped to generate a vast database of intellectual resources in a public domain. Of the top 50 documents accessed by the public during the year 2000/2001, about 23.5% of the total views are for the Science Net section.

The strategy of the public posing questions for which they seek answers or explanations constitutes an important aspect of furthering the public understanding of science. Often, questions are posed by the public because they have doubts about a topic or a concept which they seek to address in their learning attempts. No institutional mechanisms are currently available to service such learning needs of the public—the Science Net comes closest to this model, and it is a key feature of the Web-based learning environment at the Singapore Science Center. Perusing the various questions and answers on the site is also an educationally enriching experience, and this fulfils a niche in resource-based learning.

Promotion of Gallery Exhibits

A typical science center features a few hundred exhibits. These exhibits represent a significant investment in terms of funds, resources, and expertise. With the advent of the Web, science centers generally publicize these exhibits in the form of a simple listing on their Web pages, with the hope of turning virtual visitors into real visitors.

Currently, technologies are available that help to publicize the unique curatorial aspects of certain gallery exhibits on the Web. For example, the spectacular display of the Waves Machine, created by the British kinetic light sculptor and computer artist, Paul Friedlander, when he was an Artist-in-Residence at the Singapore Science Center, is available either as a video trailer for download on the Real Video platform or as another version that can be clicked and viewed at one's own pace. This has been found to be helpful in encouraging visitors to descend from the cyber realm to the physical domain in order to continue their learning experience.

Not all exhibits, however, permit such effective portrayals. Cost is, of course, another factor to consider.

Another cyberspace initiative to support the gallery-based science exhibitions is the installation of Web view cameras in a few exhibition halls. These allow the public to obtain a live gross view of various exhibitions before deciding to come for the actual exhibitions.

Ancillary Science-Based Educational Resources

To enhance the learning potential of the science portal, substantial text-based resources are also placed on the website. These textual resources encompass various aspects of science and technology, especially those of a contemporary and thought-provoking nature.

Visitors coming to the Webs of science centers are not only looking for opportunities to savor the various core offerings but are also looking for other interesting resources that may appeal to their learning fancy. By presenting a taxonomy of various resources, these initiatives help to extend the educational potential of the Web further. Examples of such resources in the virtual science center include school science projects such as, for example, different ways of taking off a T-shirt; a guide to common vegetables; basic principles of remote sensing; optical litter; and the chemicals we eat and drink. In particular, we have found that the featuring of interesting school science projects is an extremely effective way to incorporate value-added content on the website, because the students do the bulk of the work. In fact, a number of international science projects are now presented on the website.

The principal advantage of hosting textual resources is that these can be digitized easily. Of the top 50 documents accessed by the public in the year 2000/2001, about 15.4% of the total views is for such textual resources.

UNIQUE ISSUES INVOLVED IN THE FABRICATION OF VIRTUAL SCIENCE EXHIBITS

The virtual science center movement, though a relatively new concept in the field of science education, has undergone significant maturing over the past few years. New technologies and tools have greatly facilitated the induction of creative elements in interpreting various concepts in science and technology through cyberspace exhibitry and other means.

In science centers, learning takes place predominantly through interaction with exhibits. A range of scientific concepts can be addressed via interactive exhibitry. When these concepts need to be transplanted into the virtual realm, they should not just be cyberspace equivalents but should aim to exploit the unique features of the Web, which is an entirely new media, in order to foster learning.

Some of the issues that science centers face in the fabrication of online exhibits are explored here.

Choice of Exhibit

The choice of exhibit that can be put up in cyberspace is dictated mainly by curatorial considerations and the emphasis science centers wish to foster. It can develop along two axes: static and interactive, with the former being less bandwidth-intensive and less expensive to set up.

Design Elements in Fabrication of Exhibits

Where curatorial choice leads to consensus in the treatment of an exhibit idea, the design elements that need to be used to present the exhibit idea become important. This is the stage where creative inputs from a variety of sources are harnessed: curators, designers, educationists, and software specialists. The team has to contend not only with a consideration of the traditional elements of conventional exhibitry but also of how to configure it for the digital realm.

Several technological tools are now available to aid in the fabrication and enjoyment of online exhibits. A number of these tools are available as plug-ins to complement the user's browser software, and some can be downloaded for free. Discussion of some of the important tools used for art museum exhibits in cyberspace have been presented by Tinkler & Friedman (1998), Duchastel (1996), and Spadaccini (2001), and these are generally valid for virtual science exhibits. A review of the more important tools is presented here.

Shockwave Flash

This tool allows for the creation of "flash" pieces that are of near theatrical integrity but are less bandwidth-intensive. They thus allow for quicker downloading. It is possible to interface streaming audio with Shockwave Flash and, in conjunction with Java Script, initiate a flash in any section of the Web page.

Shockwave for Director

In the same class as Shockwave Flash, these are larger files that are ideal candidates for fabricating puzzles and independent games.

Both Shockwave Flash and Shockwave for Director are static files. Once they are embedded in an online activity, it is difficult to upgrade the activity without extensive rewriting of the software.

Java Script

This is the most important tool available for the cyber-curator. It integrates the various components of a Web page so that it functions harmoniously, and it also allows other tools to be combined in creative and innovative ways.

Embedded Audio, MIDI, and Beatnik

Sound effects triggered in the background of an online activity in the form of sample loops, MIDI, or Beatnik files allow for the creation of an appropriate mood setting. For narration, Real Audio is good, but for interaction-triggered sound, WAV files are the choice.

Real Media, Windows Media, and Quick Time

These are tools for transmitting streaming video. Streaming feed is possible even on a narrowband platform, because there is no necessity to download entire files in order to appreciate it. Of course, on a broadband platform, the quality of the user experience is distinctly superior on account of the greater throughput of data and picture frames per second.

Dynamic HTML

This tool permits manipulation of any aspect of an HTML document in real time. Other capabilities include creation of layers that appear, disappear, or move upon user interaction.

Java

This is a versatile programming language that allows "dreams to be turned into reality" on the Web. It is only limited by the experience of the programmer.

QuickTime VR and Photovista

These tools allow for an object to be rotated around its axis and be viewed three-dimensionally. It also permits the viewer to be placed in the center of a virtual sphere and be turned in any direction. Thus, these tools are useful for examining small objects or to relish the grandeur of the interior of an object. Being bandwidth-intensive, they have to be used rather judiciously.

Live Picture Viewer
This tool permits a live peep into an institution.

Quick Cam
This permits a streaming video feed, and thus allows the visitor to enjoy live telepresence in an institution.

The foregoing assortment of tools allows for the creation of virtual exhibits that foster innovative learning experiences as well as learning interfaces that are not possible in the physical exhibit. They have to be used judiciously and not as gimmicks. If they are not embedded in context, they may appear invasive and thus detract the user from the learning experience. It is important to bear in mind that there is a difference between real-world manipulation of exhibits and cyberspace manipulation of exhibits. The former fosters experiential learning via a range of senses, while in the latter, there would necessarily be impoverishment of the experiential factor on some counts; for example, the digital realm currently has limitations in the savoring of tactile and aural feedback.

Even trivial issues, such as information overlay, need to be carefully addressed in the design brief so as to minimize cognitive overload and visual fatigue. Judicious use of graphics and eschewing of flamboyant design elements are essential, for otherwise, access can be sluggish, thus detracting the user from the learning experience. High-quality graphics, while embellishing a website, contribute to problems when featured on navigation pages. Also, multimedia files for downloading need to be placed in the lowest hierarchy on the Web page. Generally speaking, images of about 2 Mb or more would cause slow downloads on a narrowband platform (Bowen, Bennet, & Johnson, 1998).

With the proper design elements, cyber-curated exhibits would be able to confer a new dimension in the learning of science through the creation of compelling experiences. This ensures that online exhibits do not degenerate to the extent of being surrogate equivalents of floor exhibits. Indeed, replicating the actual experience of a floor exhibit is not desirable, for then, it affects gate traffic at the institution.

Pedagogical Issues
As interactive virtual exhibits are the anchor attractions on the websites of science centers, we focus in this section on the pedagogical issues associated with their use.

The learning philosophy extant in the interactive exhibits in the galleries of science centers leverages significantly on active learning. This generally means interacting with the exhibit in order to explore the subtleties and nuances inherent in the science concept embedded therein. The cognitive and affective dimensions of learning generated via this approach are perceived to play a useful role in promoting functional understanding of the concept. With virtual exhibits, the foregoing commentary is generally valid, except that there is now a pronounced emphasis in using technology to interpret exhibit ideas and mediate the learning experience. The efficacy of knowledge transmittance is dependent, among other factors, on the richness of the experiential environment, the instructional brief used in the design, and the presence of pro-learning contexts. In particular, the task-oriented approach required for interacting with the exhibit provides a useful focus for generating active learning. Often, the task-oriented approach is facilitated by the layering of game elements in the intelligence embedded in the exhibit idea. This helps in engaging students and capturing their attention, so fostering an environment conducive for promoting experiential learning. The veering off of emphasis from content to process in the instructional philosophy is thus ideal for promoting attributes such as creative thinking and problem-solving skills. Such approaches are congruent with educational initiatives that stress active learning over passive learning (Beauchamp, 1998). As the experiential nature of learning in nonformal learning environments is divorced from the rigors of traditional assessment, such approaches also provide useful ballast to interlace motivational contexts in the learning experience. It is of interest to note that Milekic (1997), in an evaluation of art museum philosophy, stresses that the making of information experientially available to the child leads to more effective knowledge transfer.

In particular, virtual exhibits allow for the presentation of scientific domain knowledge in alternative formats, the only limitation being the creativity of the cyber-curator. This is a plus point in fulfilling cognitive requirements associated with different learning styles. Also, the solitary experience involved in using a PC to access virtual exhibits empowers the user to take control of the learning process, a view resonant with traditional educational theories.

In the context of the foregoing commentary, the pedagogical philosophy involved in the use of virtual exhibits is largely in consonance with Kolb's (1984) theory of experiential learning, which in turn, draws sustenance from Dewey's (1938) theories of learning leveraging on experience, Levin's (1995) philosophy of learning in active contexts, and Piaget's (1984) theories on intelligence arising as a result of interaction between the learner and the environment.

It needs no reiterating that the educational aspects of virtual exhibits have to be pitched at a level that the public can resonate with rather than at a level for those honed in the catechism of a scientific discipline.

User Interface

User-friendliness of an online exhibit is the prime determinant in ensuring the quality of the learning experience. In this respect, exhibits designed from the viewpoint of the user need to meet several criteria.

The focus of the learning experience has to be achieved through the use of instructional contexts that admit guided exploration. Recognizing that the primary mode of interaction is via the mouse and that the spatial dimensions of the clickable areas on the screen are often small, dexterity in visual-motor coordination has to be taken into consideration and be catered for. The navigability of the site must be streamlined to ensure that usability is enhanced, thus, the necessary tools must be made available to the user to get the desired information and so ensure that the learning experience is not distracted by extraneous considerations that would cause him to defocus. A common strategy is menu options, which allow for directedness of the learning experience.

The concatenation of curatorial choice, design elements, pedagogical aspects, and user interfaces will ensure that virtual exhibits, while not engendering the physicality of gallery exhibits, distill the salient aspects of the floor experience.

OTHER ISSUES, CONTROVERSIES, AND PROBLEMS FACING VIRTUAL SCIENCE CENTERS

A discussion of some of the other issues facing virtual science centers is presented in this section.

Educational Potential of Virtual Field Trips

Field trips to science centers are now recognized as constituting valuable out-of-school experiences to students. For the public, it becomes part of their extension education in keeping abreast of contemporary developments in science and technology.

The educational potential of virtual field trips to the portals of science centers, though backed by anecdotal evidence (Honeyman, 1998), has, however, not evolved a consensual framework. In a typical school group visit to a science center, there is enough time to savor a good number and variety of exhibits in an interactive manner; the communal dynamics of the visit is an experience that cannot be replicated in cyberspace. Subject to the availability of a PC with Net connection, a virtual field trip is, in contrast, an individual experience, and the number and type of exhibits that can be relished in the same time frame are far less.

Cost of Virtual Exhibits

The cost of development of digital exhibits is rather high, not surprisingly, because they involve expertise from across disciplines: curators, designers, educationists, and software specialists. In contrast, a gallery exhibit can be developed at rather modest cost using in-house expertise and resources in the workshop.

Generally, science centers face a financial crunch in present times. This means that they have to balance their priorities on whether they need to populate their websites with virtual exhibits that virtual visitors can access free of charge or continue to use the same funds for conventional exhibits, which attract paying visitors. Also, for the cost of a virtual exhibit, substantial textual resources of a scientific and educational nature can be placed on the website.

On the website of the Singapore Science Center, or for that matter, any virtual science center, the number of virtual exhibits compared to other resources is necessarily small, even though such exhibits are considered to be the key offerings in the portal.

Server Architecture

The anatomy of the server architecture is a key determinant in determining the volume of virtual visitors that a science center portal can service simultaneously as well as the amount of resources that it can host. For the website to be touted as a key destination in the virtual realm, the server capacity has to be high. Difficulties in accessing the site or interacting with the Web offerings can sometimes be traced to the inadequacy of the server capacity, though other factors can also be responsible.

Choice of User Connection

The quality of the user experience is dictated by the immediacy of access—that is, the choice of network connection, whether narrowband via 56K modem, or broadband via cable modem, integrated services digital network, or digital subscriber lines.

On a narrowband connection, pages generally take a longer time to load, while plug-ins to complement browser capabilities take an even longer time to download.

The educational potential of virtual science centers can be harnessed to good advantage through the use of a broadband connection, the popularity of which is not yet widespread. In Singapore, the broadband penetration rate is high, so slow access is seldom a problem for local access (Tan & Subramaniam, 2000, 2001).

What is not commonly realized is that broadband is an entirely new platform, which has to be relished using a taxonomy of offerings geared at a higher hierarchial level. As it is, the content in the websites of science centers is seldom designed to tap the unique potential of broadband.

Evaluation of Virtual Exhibits

Assessment tools for the evaluation of exhibits in the galleries of science centers are well established in the literature (Sneider, Eason, & Friedman, 1979). The issue of assessment of virtual exhibits is, however, still fraught with problems, because the field is new and has not attracted much attention from researchers. A consensual framework has yet to emerge. One complication is that a single evaluation tool cannot be applied across a spectrum of exhibits because of the diversity in the range of offerings.

Hit counts are commonly used to tout the popularity of a site. For example, in the year 2000/2001, there were 14,310,069 hit counts registered at the website of the Singapore Science Center. However, these hit counts give only general feedback. Questions such as the effectiveness of online exhibits in conveying the educational message, the quality of the learning experience, the length of the dwell time, and the type of domain from which surfers came (edu, org, com, etc.) are not apparent from hit counts. Also, it makes no distinction between new and repeat visitors.

SOLUTIONS AND RECOMMENDATIONS

In the light of the issues, controversies, and problems facing virtual science centers, we present a commentary on possible solutions and recommendations in light of our experiences in the science center movement.

Educational Potential

On the educational potential of virtual field trips to science centers, there needs to be further research. Virtual trips are a relatively new phenomenon, and time is needed to underline their utility. A survey of current practice obtained from anecdotal evidence suggests that virtual trips can be an educationally enriching experience provided that the offers onsite are tailored more to capitalize on the potential of the Web and are carefully structured for visits by students of the desired level. The potential of virtual visits in overcoming constraints such as distance, time, and cost is a strong factor in their favor. While the focus of field trips to science centers is normally controlled by the teacher, the directedness of virtual trips is often set by students, even though the broad terms of reference are set by the teacher; to what extent this interferes with the learning experience is not clear and has to be addressed by research.

Orfinger (1998) has suggested that virtual field trips may not confer a level of intellectual stimulation comparable to traditional field trips but can whet the curiosity of the child to learn more about the physical world.

Web Cost

To sustain a Web presence is not inexpensive. At the virtual science center, we have found that a full-time Webmaster is indispensable for ensuring that the site remains dynamic and does not get dated. Even more expensive is the cost of fabricating digital exhibits and other online programs.

New models of partnerships will have to be explored in order to support such website initiatives. For example, in supporting the Science Net at the Singapore Science Center, the two premier universities in Singapore were inducted as coorganizers of this section; this allows reliance to also be placed on a large pool of university staff from various disciplines in order to help answer the various questions posed by the public. This has proved to be an useful strategy in obtaining premium grade service at essentially zero cost. For software expertise in developing digital exhibits and other online programs, use of university and polytechnic students majoring in computer science would be a helpful option. Short periods of internships can be traded for credits toward project modules in their course of study. Licensing of content to multimedia developers is another option. Science and technology centers' networks should also not be overlooked, for the pooling of expertise, resources, and funds opens more opportunities for collaboration.

Server Architecture

The dynamics of server architecture is basically a factor under the ambit of the institution. Technological advances and economies of scale are fueling an increase in server capacity with a concomitant decrease in price. Upgrades of server hardware or use of higher-capacity server software programs will have thus to be looked into on a regular basis. Of interest to note is that the educational content in the portals of science centers, being significant investments in terms of time, funds, and resources, are seldom deleted: they are merely archived, thus adding to the volume of content hosted by the server.

The reliability of the website is predominantly a reflection of server capacity to meet virtual traffic demands. At the virtual science center, one of the ways used to monitor server effectiveness and, therefore, reliability of the website (Table 2), is to determine the percentage of successful hits. Of the 14,480,409 hits recorded in the year 2000/2001, about 98.83% were

Table 2: Reliability of Website of Virtual Science Center for the Year 2000/2001

Technical Statistics and Analysis	
Total Hits	14,480,409
Successful Hits	14,310,069
Failed Hits	170,340
Failed Hits as Percent	1.17%
Cached Hits	2,733,175

Table 3: Summary of Activity by Time Increment at the Virtual Science Center on Some Days for the Year 2000/2001

Time Interval	Hits	Page Views	Kbytes	Visits
Sat 04/01/2000–Fri 04/28/2000	1,126,789	196,968	25,473,992 K	67,161
Sat 04/29/2000–Fri 05/26/2000	981,294	166,796	22,592,491 K	60,850
Sat 05/27/2000–Fri 06/23/2000	1,017,619	170,205	24,017,263 K	58,891
Sat 06/24/2000–Fri 07/21/2000	821,835	141,770	22,981,956 K	45,927
Sat 07/22/2000–Fri 08/18/2000	772,558	162,094	19,906,933 K	42,742
Sat 08/19/2000–Fri 09/15/2000	927,139	157,869	19,709,180 K	51,163
Sat 09/16/2000–Fri 10/13/2000	904,822	136,263	18,466,108 K	56,453
Sat 10/14/2000–Fri 11/10/2000	1,287,570	178,302	24,408,553 K	75,466
Sat 11/11/2000–Fri 12/08/2000	1,263,911	183,319	31,153,874 K	77,551
Sat 12/09/2000–Fri 01/05/2001	1,074,333	227,111	18,569,643 K	64,338
Sat 01/06/2001–Fri 02/02/2001	1,480,974	244,241	14,729,031 K	79,284
Sat 02/03/2001–Fri 03/02/2001	1,326,404	251,086	15,114,915 K	73,819
Sat 03/03/2001–Fri 03/30/2001	1,282,029	282,084	19,918,490 K	70,076
Sat 03/31/2001–Fri 04/27/2001	42,792	11,802	481,807 K	2,168
Total	**14,310,069**	**2,509,910**	**277,524,236**	

serviced with a good response time; only 1.17% were failed hits. This is considered to be an acceptable figure.

A summary of activity by time increment is also useful for understanding the bandwidth requirements of the site (Table 3).

Connection

Though a broadband connection would be helpful in savoring bandwidth-intensive fare on the Webs of science centers, quite a number of fare can be relished using a 56K connection. Generally, a broadband connection permits faster access and speedier downloads, and in this respect, enriches the learning experience of surfers. Offerings of science centers are, as indicated earlier, rarely configured to tap the unique potential of the broadband platform, which is a new ball game altogether with its own taxonomy of offerings. Currently, migration of content onto the broadband platform is constrained by the lack of a critical mass of users. Uptake of broadband is, however, on the increase.

Assessment

The problem of assessment can be addressed at a number of levels. Though there are a number of drawbacks involved in the use of hit counts, the point is that they are still important. Hit counts indicate that the site is drawing traffic, an important consideration for administrators and stakeholders. Also, they are politically less sensitive to present than other profiles. This also applies to general statistical information (Table 4).

Rigorous analyses of server log files can, however, reveal more useful information, for example, the number of pages accessed by a visitor, which is an indication of the quality of the visitorship (Table 5); the demographic profile of the visitors, which is an indication of the outreach effectiveness across various segments of the population (Table 6); and the domain from which surfers accessed the Web page, which is an indication of the institutional profile of surfers (Table 7).

Table 4: General Statistical Information on the Virtual Science Center for the Year 2000/ 2001

General Statistics		
Hits	Entire Site (Successful)	14,310,069
	Average per Day	39,205
	Home Page	106,432
Page Views	Page Views (Impressions)	2,509,910
	Average per Day	6,876
	Document Views	2,387,515
Visits	Visits	825,889
	Average per Day	2,262
	Average Visit Length	00:14:27
	Median Visit Length	00:00:01
	International Visits	10.55%
	Visits of Unknown Origin	83.81%
	Visits from Singapore	5.62%
Visitors	Unique Visitors	244,170
	Visitors Who Visited Once	209,663
	Visitors Who Visited More Than Once	34,507

Table 5: Number of Pages Viewed per Visit at the Virtual Science Center for the Year 2000/ 2001

Number of Pages Viewed	Number of Visits	% of Total Visits
0 pages	222,873	26.99%
1 page	362,250	43.86%
2 pages	97,766	11.83%
3 pages	43,338	5.24%
4 pages	24,019	2.9%
5 pages	15,588	1.88%
6 pages	11,906	1.44%
7 pages	8,024	0.97%
8 pages	6,105	0.73%
9 pages	4,789	0.57%
10 pages	3,878	0.46%
11 or more pages	25,221	3.05%
Totals	**825,757**	

Table 6: Activity Level at the Virtual Science Center by Country Access for the Year 2000/2001

	Countries	Visits
1	United States	88,526
2	Singapore	31,908
3	United Kingdom	3,749
4	Canada	1,562
5	Hong Kong	1,386
6	Australia	1,141
7	Japan	960
8	Malaysia	491
9	Great Britain	418
10	New Zealand (Aotearoa)	389
11	Czech Republic	305
12	Saudi Arabia	284
13	Germany	283
14	The Netherlands	226
15	France	154
16	Sweden	153
17	Taiwan	144
18	Austria	140
19	Italy	108
20	Mexico	98
Total		**132,425**

Table 7: Activity Level at the Virtual Science Center by Domain for the Year 2000/2001

	Visitor	Hits	% of Total Hits	Visits
1	203.116.254.180	21,938	0.15%	2,245
2	203.124.2.70	68,508	0.47%	2,057
3	203.124.2.85	69,566	0.48%	1,863
4	203.116.254.183	18,336	0.12%	1,832
5	sbproxy3.mystarhub.com.sg	42,558	0.29%	1,783
6	sbproxy2.mystarhub.com.sg	39,399	0.27%	1,698
7	lunar.zapsurf.com.sg	25,482	0.17%	1,675
8	203.124.2.50	50,304	0.35%	1,564
9	165.21.83.156	53,261	0.37%	1,536
10	203.120.170.113	47,991	0.33%	1,420
11	205.252.144.29	9,611	0.06%	1,419
12	sbproxy1.mystarhub.com.sg	33,794	0.23%	1,409
13	10.207.128.51	77,976	0.54%	1,358
14	216.35.116.108	3,534	0.02%	1,297
15	palo1.pacific.net.sg	18,188	0.12%	1,290
16	palo10.pacific.net.sg	31,349	0.21%	1,233
17	216.35.103.55	2,014	0.01%	1,224
18	203.116.61.132	27,366	0.19%	1,217
19	152.163.188.5	2,031	0.01%	1,213
20	152.163.189.101	1,958	0.01%	1,207
Subtotal for Visitors Above		**645,164**	**4.5%**	**30,540**
Total		**14,310,069**	**100%**	**825,889**

In the case of the Singapore Science Center, extensive use is made of such data in order to obtain valuable feedback, which is then used to enhance website performance. Each of these statistical tools is a potential assessment instrument. It is important to bear in mind that these tools should not be used in isolation, and that cognizance is borne of some of its limitations. For example, it is not possible to obtain the number of separate visitors accessing the virtual science center by an examination of the number of unique Internet Protocol (IP) addresses captured by the server (Table 7). This is because corporate networks and large Internet service providers using a proxy server will always register a single IP address on server log files, even though they service a large number of clients. In the absence of real data on the number of separate visitors to a website, the number of unique IP addresses captured by the server log file is still the nearest indicator of such visitations. Also, surfers accessing the site by dial-up access will be assigned a floating IP address that may not always be the same for subsequent visits; this may show up as separate IP addresses on the log files, thus causing a spurious increase in the number of domains served.

Of interest to note is the fact that of the top 20 nations whose surfers visit the website of the Singapore Science Center, the United States ranks first with 88,526 visits, while Singapore is quite a distance away with 31,908 visits (Table 6). In fact, the website is rather popular with foreign visitors, especially those from the Western world

Another useful assessment tool is the level of activity in each of these content areas; this is presented in Table 1 as percentage views. We have found this to be extremely useful in monitoring the effectiveness of content hosted in the virtual science center as well as in helping to strategize the range of offerings. For example, this indicator shows that of the top 50 documents accessed by the public in the year 2000/2001, the Science Net section constituted nearly 23.5% of the total views.

Table 8: Activity Level by Top Entry Page for Selected Entries for the Year 2000/2001 for the Virtual Science Center

	Page	% of Total	Visits
1	**Virtual Science Centre Homepage** http://www.sci-ctr.edu.sg/	10.83%	65,327
2	**VSC WebView Camera** http://www.sci-ctr.edu.sg/ Webview/	3.52%	21,273
3	**ScienceNet : Physical Science** http://www.sci-ctr.edu.sg/ ScienceNet/cat_physical/ cat_physical.html	2.33%	14,096
4	http://www.sci-ctr.edu.sg/ robots.txt	2.33%	14,069
5	**ScienceNet : Life Science** http://www.sci-ctr.edu.sg/ ScienceNet/cat_life/cat_life.html	2.21%	13,328
6	**Online Publications : A Guide to Common Vegetables** http://www.sci-ctr.edu.sg/ssc/ publication/veg/contents.html	1.56%	9,448
7	**Maths Puzzle : Square Puzzles** http://www.sci-ctr.edu.sg/ssc/ quiz/maths/square.html	1.49%	9,042
8	**Optical Illusions** http://www.sci-ctr.edu.sg/ssc/ quiz/opt_ill1.html	1.23%	7,472
9	**Welcome To ScienceNet !!** http://www.sci-ctr.edu.sg/ ScienceNet/	1.13%	6,822
10	**ScienceNet : Space & Astronomy** http://www.sci-ctr.edu.sg/ ScienceNet/cat_space/ cat_space.html	1.12%	6,779
11	**Singapore Science Centre Homepage** http://www.sci-ctr.edu.sg/ssc/ ssc.html	1.06%	6,423

In Table 8, data is shown according to the top entry pages for the year 2000/2001. The entry page is the first page that a visitor accesses when entering the website. Usually, this is the home page, but it can also be a specific page that has been accessed directly though a URL link from the user's browser. In the case of the latter, it indicates that the user has most likely bookmarked the page, an indication that he has assigned sufficient value to the site for revisits. Statistical analyses show that 23.2% of the direct access is for the Science Net section, 11.1% is for online exhibits, and 10.0% is for the Webview cameras.

While percentage views of virtual exhibits are a useful indicator of their effectiveness, more rigorous assessment tools are necessary. One useful determinant would be to determine to what extent such an exhibit has been configured for the Web. This, however, would require user studies of a structured nature, involving possibly online feedback from surfers as well.

It is of interest to note that the analyses of content hosted in a virtual science center through the use of server log files have not previously been reported in the literature.

FUTURE TRENDS

Predicting the future lies less in looking at a crystal ball and more by looking at an organization through a wide-angled lens (Hamel & Prahlad, 1994). The Internet will become even more pervasive in the years to come, and this will see the migration of more content onto the Webs of science centers. With enabling technologies becoming more powerful, virtual science centers will evolve in size and complexity.

The following are possible scenarios for the future:

- With the ubiquity of the personal computer and increase in content hosted by virtual science centers, field trips to virtual science centers are likely to become more popular among school groups. Such virtual trails will open another dimension in the learning of science. Needless to say, careful planning by the teacher as well as the necessity to ensure greater access to personal computers for students is necessary.

- Virtual science centers will become strategic nodal points for the collection of more science learning resources. There would, thus, be greater migration of content from other science portals to virtual science centers.

- There will be greater collaboration between science centers on the Web, and this will lead to rationalization in their range of offerings. Because a virtual exhibit in one science center can be accessed by people in other countries, there is little justification in "reinventing the wheel," when a hyperlink is all that is needed to host a virtual exhibit.

- The cost of virtual reality, videoconferencing, broadband, and other enabling technologies will come down further, thus offering scope for positioning three-dimensional and other high-end exhibits on the Webs of science centers.

- Credits for the public understanding of science are likely to be obtained from the portals of science centers.

- There will be cooperative endeavors between schools and science centers to create exhibitions and other programs on the Web. The prestige of showcasing school-based endeavors on the website of an important institution such as a science center is a potent factor that science centers can leverage in order to enhance the dynamism of their Web offerings.

CONCLUSION

The virtual science center movement is a new genre in the taxonomy of Web-based learning environments. By providing a novel platform for the promotion of nonformal science education, it offers science centers a unique opportunity to entrench their role as purveyors of scientific knowledge—not capitalizing strategically on this opportunity would mean the risk of being left behind in the technological avalanche fueled by the Internet. It is likely to mature further and become a focus for promoting the public understanding of science, thus opening another tributary for distributed learning.

REFERENCES

Association of Science-Technology Centers. (1998). *Yearbook of science centers statistics* (p. 18). Washington, DC: ASTC.

Benigno, V., & Trenton, G. (2001). The evaluation of online courses, *Journal of Computer Assisted Learning, 16,* 259–270.

Beauchamp, C. (1998). Museums in cyberpace: serving a virtual public on the technocratic frontier. Retrieved July 14, 2001 from the World Wide Web: http://www.du.edu/~cheaucha/cybermuseums.html.

Bowen, J. P., Bennet, J., & Johnson, J. (1998). Virtual visits to virtual museums, *Museums and the Web.*

Chen, G. D. et al. (2001). Intervention and strategy analysis for Web group learning, *Journal of Computer Assisted Learning, 17,* 58–71.

Collis, B., de Boer, W., & Slotman, K. (2001). Feedback for Web-based assignments, *Journal of Computer Assisted Learning, 17,* 306–313.

Crowley, K., Leinhardt, G., & Chang, C. F. (2001). Emerging research communities and the World Wide Web: analysis of a Web-based resource for the field of museum learning, *Computers & Education, 36,* 1–14.

Danilov, V. J. (1982). *Science and technology centers.* Massachusetts: MIT Press.

Delacote, G. (1998). Putting science in the hands of the public. *Science, 280,* 252–253.

Dewey, J. (1938). *Experience and education.* New York: Macmillan.

Donovan, K. (1997). The best of intentions: public access, the Web and the evolution of museum automation. *Conference on Museums and the Web.*

Duchastel, P. (1996). Design for Web-based learning, *Conference on Museums and the Web.*

Gaia, G. (1999). Promoting a museum website on the Net, *Museums and the Web Conference.*

Givens, N., & McShea, J. (2000). Learning though remote practical experiments over the Internet: a case study from teacher education, *Journal of Information Technology for Teacher Education, 9,* 125–135.

Hamel, G., & Prahlad, C. K. (1994). *Competing for the future.* New York: HBS Press.

Honeyman, B. (1998). Real vs. virtual visits: issues for science centers, *Australasian* Science & Technology Exhibitors Network, April.

Jackson, R. (1996). The virtual visit: towards a new concept for the electronic science center. In *Conference on here and how: improving the presentation of contemporary science and technology in museums and science centers,* London.

Keene, S. (2000). Museums in the digital space. *Cultivate Interactive, 2.*

Kolb, D. A. (1984). *Experiential learning: experience as the source of learning an*d *development*. Englewood Cliffs, NJ: Prentice Hall.

Levin, K. (1935). *A dynamic theory of personality: selected papers*. New York: McGraw Hill.

Lupo, D., & Erlich, Z. (2000). Computer literacy and applications via distance learning. *Computers & Education, 36*, 333–345.

Maes, J. T. (2001). Quality in an e-university. *Assessment and Evaluation in Higher Education, 26*, 465–473.

Milekic, S. (1997). Virtual museums: how to make digital information child-friendly, *Conference on Museums and the Web*.

Oppenheimer, F. (1972). The exploratorium: a playful museum combines perception and art in science education. *American Journal of Physics, 40*, 978–984.

Orfinger, B. (1998). Virtual science museums as learning environments: interactions for education. *The Informal Learning Review*, 1–10.

Piaget, J. (1984). *The equilibrium of cognitive structures: the central problem of intellectual development*. Chicago, IL: University of Chicago Press.

Sanders, D. W., & Morrison-Shetlar. (2001). Student attitudes towards a Web-enhanced instruction in an introductory biology course. *Journal of Research on Computing in Education, 33*, 251–262.

Sneider, C., Eason, L., & Friedman, A. (1979). Summative evaluation of a participatory science exhibit. *Science Education, 63*, 25–36.

Spadaccini, J. (2001). Streaming audio and video: new challenges and opportunities for museums. *Museums and the Web Conference*.

Sumpton, K. (2001). Beyond museum walls: a critical analysis of emerging approaches to museum Web-based education. *Museums and the Web Conference*.

Tan, W. H. L., & Subramaniam, R. (1998). Developing nations need to popularize science. *New Scientist, 2139*, 52.

Tan, W. H. L., & Subramaniam, R. (2000). Wiring up the island state. *Science, 288*, 621–623.

Tan, W. H. L., & Subramaniam, R. (2001). ADSL, HFC and ATM technologies for a nationwide broadband network. In N. Barr (Ed.), *Global communications 2001* (pp. 97–102). London: Hanson Cooke Publishers Ltd.

Tinkler, M., & Freedman, M. (1998). Online exhibitions: a philosophy of design and technological implementation. *Museums and the Web Conference*.

ACKNOWLEDGMENT

We'd like to thank Mr. Edwin Teng, Technical Manager at the Singapore Science Center, for his assistance in generating statistical profiles from server log files for this study.

Part V

WBE: Diffusion Across Boundaries (Case Studies)

Chapter XX

The Use of a Hybrid Model in Web-Based Education: "The Global Campus Project"

Sherif Kamel
The American University in Cairo, Egypt

Khaled Wahba
Cairo University, Egypt

ABSTRACT

Education is one of the key sectors that benefited from the continuous developments and innovations in information and communication technology. The changes have affected the concepts of teaching, the methodologies used in class and online and the delivery mechanisms providing multiple opportunities for educators and scholars to engage in an invaluable knowledge-based environment that represents a unique opportunity for educators and scholars around the world to benefit and excel in their disciplines. In that respect, one of the technologies stemming from the innovations in information and communication technology has been Web-based education as a medium for learning and a vehicle for information dissemination and knowledge delivery. However, Web-based education has been implemented using different methodologies to maximize the quality level, where a primary concern has always been whether Web-based education matches traditional teaching mechanisms. Covered in this chapter is the experience of the Global Campus (GC) project whose idea is the delivery of academic programs using a hybrid model of traditional and unconventional methods. The project is a collaboration between the Regional IT Institute (Egypt) and Middlesex University (United Kingdom), aiming at delivering postgraduate education to the community in Egypt, Hong Kong, and the United Kingdom, while capitalizing on cutting-edge information and communication technology.

The focus in this chapter is on demonstrating the lessons learned from managing a model for a globally extended enterprise in the education sector through a partnership agreement between the different parties that capitalizes on the opportunities enabled by the Internet, which is probably the most transformative technology in history, reshaping business, media, entertainment, and society in astonishing ways but also perceived to dramatically transform the learning process.

INTRODUCTION

Egypt is the cradle of an ancient civilization dating back to 3000 BC. Currently, with a population of more than 68 million (www.idsc.gov.eg), there are more than 19 million in the workforce and over 16 million enrolled in education (Kamel, 1999a, 2000). Cairo, the capital of Egypt, like many developing nations, possesses most of the advanced infrastructure and resources. However, since the late 1980s, as part of the comprehensive structural adjustment program carried out by the government of Egypt and strongly supported by the private sector, many investments and infrastructure buildups have been carried out across Egypt's 27 provinces (Kamel, 1999b). Computing was introduced in Egypt in the 1960s, and it was spread due to the presence of a number of multinationals within a number of sectors; however, it was still limited to a number of applications and industries (Kamel, 1999b). In 1985, information technology diffusion and building a comprehensive information base was put on the national agenda as a priority and as a building block of Egypt's business and socioeconomic development process.

During the period 1985–1999, massive developments were introduced in the information and communication technology sector, with thousands of training centers and projects launched to introduce information and communication technology into different sectors and diffuse its various uses and applications (Kamel, 2002). Most of these projects and initiatives were launched and co-initiated by the Cabinet of Egypt, Information and Decision Support Center. IDSC is a government think-tank that was established in 1985 to support top policy and decision makers to introduce information technology in decision-making processes and to help in building the nation's information infrastructure. Moreover, to strengthen the nation's strategic plan to integrate advanced information and communication technology into its developmental plans, in 1999, the ministry of information and communication technology (MCIT) was established to help accelerate the efforts for building an ICT literate society capable of competing on a global scale and keeping pace with the new trends of the digital economy. Parallel to the establishment of the ministry, a national plan was formulated to help build the nation's information infrastructure (NII) and to invest in people to support in the formulation of a knowledge-based society to close the digital divide between the haves and have nots in Egypt and also between Egypt and other developed nations (Kamel, 2002).

The focus in this chapter is on demonstrating the experience of the Global Campus[1] project, a collaboration between the Regional IT Institute (Egypt) and Middlesex University (UK), in managing a successful partnership to deliver postgraduate education through a hybrid model capitalizing on innovative information and communication technology as well as traditional learning techniques, where the promise of widely available high-quality Web-based education is made possible by technological and communications trends that could lead to important educational applications (www.hpcnet.org/Webcommission). Moreover, also stressed in this chapter is the importance of the learning process among partners to be able to formulate and retain competitiveness, productivity, and innovativeness in uncertain technological and market circumstances (Steil, Barcia, & dos Santos, 1999).

EVOLUTION OF VIRTUAL ORGANIZATIONS

The evolution of virtual organizations is the outcome of a number of changes that relate to organizational restructuring and rapid innovations in information and communication technology. Their establishment has led to sharing information, developing standards, reducing costs, and maximizing outcomes (Palmer, 1998). Virtual organizations are defined as networks of geographically distributed institutions that use information and communication technology for communication, collaboration, and cooperation, and help provide a value-added competitive advantage (Strausak, 1998; Ahuja & Carley, 1999). Virtual work is becoming a key process in various organizations. How people work as individuals and as part of work groups is a key issue in the ability to compete effectively (Fritz & Manheim, 1998). The virtual integration of different capacities enables the realization of common objectives and helps organizations become more competitive in local and global marketplaces and supports the achievement of market differentiation and better performance (Appel & Behr, 1997). Virtual organizations are a rapidly emerging organizational form in knowledge-based societies, helping to forge stronger links between individuals, organizations, and nations (Ungson & Trudel, 1998).

They aim at achieving market differentiation by performing better together by improving competitiveness and productivity, enhancing efficiency and responsiveness, and decreasing overheads (Strausak, 1998). However, it is important to note that virtual organization structures are not permanent; on the contrary, its survival and success are based on change and adaptation to market conditions, locally and globally. Virtual organizations depend primarily on information technology, which is the enabler of the communication and the data integration necessary for the successful operation of the virtual organization and virtual models for collaboration (Goodhue, Waybo, & Kirsch, 1982; Stevenson, 1993; Hirschheim & Adams, 1991). Virtual organizations[2] and models for extended organizations are expected to have a vital role in the organization of the 21st century, addressing intensive information and knowledge-based issues, where the critical building block in the organization is people (Kamel, 1998b). In the context of Egypt, faced with so many classical problems of developing nations, there will be a vital need for the development and successful implementation of organizational models that can leverage the existing capacities and deliverables in the educational sector, while capitalizing on the scarce resources available. Based on the advances and innovations in information and communication technology, vertical and horizontal expansion might be costly and time consuming; however, virtual extension of existing educational institutions would probably be effective and rewarding. Moreover, the role of traditional academic institutions will continuously be changing to be able to compete with a growing number of other educational providers or vendors. Such promotion should encourage and promote collaborative work between businesses, industry, and academia to provide high-quality and innovative education (Porter, 1997). In the years to come, countries around the world will focus on developing new methods to absorb the growing learning needs of the society and on managing knowledge, or otherwise, their business and socioeconomic development plans will be difficult to realize, and developing countries will risk losing more ground to the developed world (Kamel, 1998a). The socioeconomic changes currently taking place will continue to change the learning behaviors and expectations of learners; moreover, globalization will lead to the need for continuous learning and access to learning on demand, which will require various educational paradigms (Liegle & Meso, 2000). There is no doubt that there are several elements that will escalate the growth of virtual teams in the 21st century (Platt & Page, 2001).

INVESTING IN PEOPLE—THE CASE OF EGYPT

Education reflects investing in human resources, which represents a vital issue in societal development and growth. Therefore, Egypt has been increasing its focus and investment in its precious resource, "people," in order to build a new generation capable of meeting market and industry challenges, a society that is competitive and equipped with capacities and skills that can compete at the highest levels and capable of adapting to global changes and trends. The 21st century will create a knowledge-based society, where the fundamental sources of wealth will be knowledge and communication rather than natural resources and physical labor (Ungson & Trudel, 1998). Therefore, since 1985, Egypt has invested heavily in human resource development through two dimensions: education and training. Thus, over 1000 training centers were established, addressing management and information and communication technology issues addressing market needs. These centers had an effective impact on the development of human capacities, skills, and knowledge (Kamel, 2002). The achievements include a large number of programs that contributed in leveraging the skills and knowledge for many fresh graduates as well as employees across different organizational levels. However, it is important to note that operating in a remote environment brought many different management challenges and will require an adapted management style that caters to changing market conditions (Staples, 2001).

With an increasing investment in education and a growing population, the challenge in Egypt was to develop modalities to be able to educate and train more people, while optimizing the allocation and use of available resources. The use of advanced information and communication technology was perceived as a solution to increase or leverage the productivity of the education sector. They are seen as a multiplier force leading to productivity increases and cost savings (Neilson, 1997). Therefore, building hybrid virtual learning models represented one of the possible vehicles that could be pursued through the formulation of strategic alliances with learning institutions around the world to deliver degree and nondegree programs for the market in Egypt, using state-of-the-art information and communication technology. This model can help cater to the increasing number of educators and a relatively less-growing volume and capacity of the infrastructure required. The benefits of the virtual model could include greater cost-effectiveness by training and educating more people; increasing impact by realizing real-time updates and just-in-time knowledge and learning at all times; interactive programs with multiple sites networked for group learning; and higher-quality learning by providing different choices of programs, accessing remote experts, and realizing multiple student–teacher interaction opportunities. Covered in this chapter is one of the initiatives managed by the Regional IT Institute[3] (RITI) located in Cairo and working as a base for a satellite of programs in cooperation with a multiplicity of world leading institutions. The criteria for the selection of the partners were based on the following: its feasibility; the market needs in terms of specializations required and scarcity in the local market in Egypt; the willingness of potential partners to deliver their programs through an alliance with the institute, pending the fulfillment of all logistical and infrastructure require-ments; and, more importantly, the ability to manage organizational core competencies, including competence identification, development, leverage, and protection between the institute and its potential partners (Balinet & Kouroukils, 1998). It should be noted that since 1994, there have been seven attempts with different organizations to develop partnerships with academic institutions in Europe and the United States; only three have matured and started operation, and others were deterred due to a number of reasons.

Among the deterring factors were the financial feasibility of the project, lack of adequate technology required, lack of enough demand on specific programs, as well as unwillingness of some organizations to conduct programs through a hybrid model, due to relative costs involved or the marginal profits realized. Some of them preferred the pure online-cyber model, which was not to be successful in Egypt for eReadiness purposes to that mode of education. In a related note, a key lesson identified during the development of the institute's alliances was the focus on value imperatives for both parties. Such values were better determined tangibly and intangibly when both parties were convinced that their partnership was developed based on a win-win formula, where each partner in its selection process attempts to realize three key objectives from the partnership—excellence, utilization, and opportunism. Moreover, once in business, increased dependence among partners is a critical factor, because in the context of virtual organizations, it leads to greater equality and provides a sense of commitment and contribution (Jagers, Jansen, & Steenbakkers, 1998). Respectively, each partner, through this collaborative effort, plays its own role and contributes to the improvement of the end product and service, and leverages the contribution of its partner.

The Regional IT Institute (www.riti.org) was established as a not-for-profit organization supported financially by its various services and programs to support in transforming the society using the latest technologies and methods in education and training. The Institute's motto is "building through learning." The institute pioneered in Egypt in introducing a new mode of operation based on virtual teams. This led, since 1994, to the enrollment of over 1075 students, 500 of whom have already graduated[4] with a master's degree, in addition to training over 14,000 participants from over 1100 organizations in around 90 countries[5] in Africa, Europe, and Asia. The mission of the institute is to contribute to business and socioeconomic growth in Egypt through investing in people of the 21st century, the societal backbone of the future and the nation's most precious resource. The building-up of an information and communication infrastructure has been a deciding factor in the success of the institute. Being connected to its partners through the GC project was the enabling factor for the institute to realize organizational virtualness (Davidow & Malone, 1993; Byrne, 1993; Goldman, Nagel, & Preiss, 1995). The definition of virtualness in this context is the ability of an organization to consistently obtain and coordinate critical competencies through its design of value-added business processes and governance mechanisms involving external and internal constituencies to deliver differential, super value in the marketplace (Strausak, 1998). It was important to study the experience of managing the programs through the GC, because it represented an opportunity to maximize the outcome as a requirement for a developing nation with limited resources. The Regional IT Institute utilized a hybrid of information and communication technologies that encompassed a mix of traditional methods for knowledge delivery with a number of online tools and techniques that capitalized on emerging technolo-gies. Among these were mature technology such as facsimile and electronic mail as well as innovative technology such as the World Wide Web in an attempt to link core competencies and serve its market (Palmer, 1998). Capitalizing on the above-mentioned technologies and other infrastructure used, the institute delivers degree and nondegree professional programs to leverage the capacities of human resources. One of these programs is jointly delivered with one the institute's partners—Middlesex University[6] (UK). The model is used to disseminate knowledge through the use of methods including class sessions and distance learning techniques, and it capitalizes on Web CT technology through the GC project. It is important to note that distance learning technologies revolve not around the technology itself, but how it is used, diffused, managed, and controlled (Rayburn & Ramaprasad, 2000a). Technology and the use of collaborative techniques have been used to assist learning in classroom contexts (Alavi, 1994). It has also been used to link classes, whether they are located within a country or between countries (Alavi et al., 1997; Jarvenpaa & Leidner, 1998).

THE GLOBAL CAMPUS (GC) PROJECT

The Global Campus (GC) is a partnership between Middlesex University and franchised institutions, which offers the Master of Science in business information technology (BIT) by supported distance learning techniques. The lead organization in the GC is Middlesex University, with a number of support centers all over the world. The GC model reflects the virtual model in which a lead organization creates alliances with a set of other groups, internal and external, that possess the best-in-world competencies to build a specific product or service in a short period of time (Greiner & Metes, 1996). Such alliances using distance learning techniques present a number of advantages and opportunities for the higher education environment (Rayburn & Ramaprasad, 2000b). The program is running in a number of countries, including Hong Kong and Shanghai in China, Singapore, and Egypt. The GC Master of Science in business information technology is, therefore, an innovative version of a tried and tested program, which was already being delivered in Egypt since 1998; however, the new version (Web-based) uses a computer-based learning environment and the World Wide Web, in addition to tutorial facilities at local learning support centers (such as the Regional IT Institute). One of the elements that facilitated the migration from the traditional to the Web-based (hybrid) model was the trust built between the different partners during their collaboration; therefore, it is important to note the importance of trust and stability in business relationships to support emerging forms of virtual organizations (Holland, 1998). The learning environment is based on Web technology and is used offline and online with a requirement to connect to the Internet on an occasional basis. The GC learning environment provides the following: access to the materials for each module on CD-ROM and on the Web; some personal management tools such as a calendar for the program; a students' personal profile for grades and assessment; a communication tool to allow students to contact their local and UK-based tutor as well as other students through electronic mail and discussion groups; and online access to libraries, in addition to other tools that will assist the students' learning process. In general, information and communication technology represents a key enabler of remote work for the alliance model undertaken by the GC model (Staples, 2001).

THE ELEARNING MODEL

The joint delivery of the Master of Science in business information technology using the GC project model started in September 1999 with 11 students enrolled, which was followed by a second and third cohort with 14 and four students consecutively (www.gc.mdx.ac.uk).

Table 1: Different Learning Models

	Traditional Model	Web-Based Education	Hybrid Model
Learning Theory Components			
Immersion (hands-on practice)	Very high	Low	High
Teacher–student dialog	Very high	Very low	High
Role of faculty member to assist the students	Very high	N/A	High
Collaborative activities among the students	High	High	Very high
Teaching Environment Dimensions			
Time constraint	Very high	Very low	Moderate
Place, location constraint	Very high	Very low	Moderate
Technology requirement	Very high	Internet only	Moderate + Internet
Staff requirement	Very high	Very Low	Low
Faculty presence	Full time	N/A	Freelance
Exam logistic (seating)	Controllable	Uncontrollable	Controllable
Using multimedia	Limited	Flexible	Flexible
Information richness	Moderate	High	Very high
Cultural acceptance	Very high	Very low	High

The enrollment number reflects the status of distance education in Egypt, which is still not well diffused among the community of students. However, the GC project is a unique initiative and experience in the market that provides local students with the opportunity to study for a Master of Science degree in business information technology[7] from the partnering university—Middlesex University—while being in Egypt. The management of the project revealed the fact that students still desperately need to interact with the tutor, though initially, they had agreed on the GC model by meeting only a few times per course for moderation and consultation. Experience showed otherwise.

In higher education, learning should follow the basic foundations of the learning theory (Mitchell, 2002). Compared in Table 1 are the traditional model and the pure Web-based education model against the hybrid model. The GC implements a hybrid model which, based on the experience documented in the literature and on the experience of the Regional IT Institute since 1994, attempts to capitalize on the benefits the traditional and the Web-based models bring to the learning process. At the same time, it tries to overcome its respective problems and challenges in a blend of technologies and processes that aim at optimally serve the knowledge management and delivery cycle.

The format of the GC is developed based on the fact that in each trimester, two modules are studied: a 20-credit module and a 10-credit module. All modules are split into learning units, with one learning unit per credit. Each learning unit takes nine hours of study. For example, the 10-credit module involves 90 hours of study with a test at the end of each unit and an examination at the end of each module. The delivery mechanism comprised regular tutorial sessions. The duration of each tutorial is three hours, and it runs twice a week for the duration of three weeks, i.e., a total of 18 contact hours per module of 10 credits. Usually, students meet in class to exchange ideas with fellow students as well as to interact with the moderator. Moreover, a local and a UK-based tutor are allocated for each cohort. They are also in continuous contact with students via electronic mail or through the communication tools in the GC learning environment. On average during courses, students communicate with their tutors on a daily basis, where the ratio of tutors-to-students is one to 10. However, during the project module, the ratio of tutors-to-students is one to five to cater to the additional consultation and communication required. Students do not need to be online all the time; however, they need to log in regularly.

The learning environment is built around the students, and it attempts to create awareness among the students' community that they should be interactive and proactive to address different issues related to the program and to the learning experience. It is important to note that such initiatives from students require massive efforts from the program coordinators. The education system in Egypt depends heavily on one-way communication from the lecturers to the students and does not allow, in many occasions, two-way interaction, due to the large number of students in the classes. Therefore, on many occasions, the management of the program had to add more sessions for the students to meet with the tutor or moderator.[8] This was part of the learning curve of the management, which mainly related to the adaptation of the program to fit local needs. Respectively, it is important to note that it took some time and a number of scenarios to reach the optimal schedule to properly run an effective hybrid model combining online and offline mechanisms for delivering knowledge and education.

Regular tutorial sessions were scheduled at the Regional IT Institute that worked as the local learning support center[9] (LSC). These meetings gave the students opportunity to meet and work with their tutor and other students. It provided an opportunity for students to benefit from the traditional methods of education and provided an opportunity for students to interact with their tutors and exchange ideas face-to-face. The role of the tutor[10] was primarily to facilitate the learning process of the course content, rendering it more interactive, as well as to explain to students various issues and learning techniques and mechanisms. Based upon the program requirements, each student should attend at least eight of the twelve scheduled tutorial sessions for each module. However, beyond the sessions, each student was allocated a tutor, who was available via electronic mail and by telephone to answer all queries concerning the academic content of the module. The tutor could also be reached by facsimile; however, the cost element should be looked at carefully. Students received their study materials on CD-ROM and via the World Wide Web in addition to on courseware and in textbooks. All other updates were conveyed through the electronic bulletin boards on the Web-CT. The model of the GC tries to map the global reality that implies that among the currently available media types, the Internet takes center stages as the most popular and useful learning vehicle. Additionally, it is important to note that while electronic learning is increasingly becoming popular, statistics do not show that traditional techniques are losing ground easily; therefore, the GC model builds its delivery mechanism on a hybrid of the two models to attempt to capitalize on the optimal elements in both platforms (www.elearningmag.com).

The GC model for distance education helps students engage and interact with the study materials provided through the Web-CT environment as well as through the use of traditional teaching mechanisms. Moreover, students engage in discussions with fellow students and tutors to help check their understanding and reflect on what they are learning, (using a hybrid model) partially in class sessions and partially online, which caters to students preferences and allows for a large degree of flexibility and adaptation. However, it should be noted that within such an environment, students should be self-disciplined by working through the material with great care, reading the materials, working through exercises and computer-based activities, and more importantly, committing to due dates and submission deadlines. It is a must for students to engage with the materials on the World Wide Web—some of which are only available online for specific periods of time—that are announced to students through emails or the Web-CT bulletin board and are intended to build on the students' experience and apply new concepts and skills.

There are two forms of assessment. Assignments make up what is often called coursework in each module; they enable students and their tutor to ascertain progress and highlight strengths and weaknesses. Moreover, students will be able to keep track of their grades throughout the program via the personal management tools on the Web-CT. It is important to note that the growth of electronic communication has increased the popularity of the GC as a model for distance learning, reflecting a new platform of studying and breaking the time and distance barriers between students and their tutors, the institute, the university, and among students themselves. Moreover, there is the possibility of instant and ongoing feedback on students' progress at the end of each unit and electronic conferencing with all students studying the course. Additionally, the GC provides computers at the Regional IT Institute, which means that students are not required to personally own a PC. However, irrespective of the infrastructure, to succeed in the GC, students need to be well-motivated, organized, and good at time management.[11]

The case of the Regional IT Institute realizes the new working world order, where corner offices, paper memos, and personal secretaries are out, and laptops and teleconferences and periodical meetings are in (Gray, 1995). The cooperation between the Regional IT Institute and Middlesex University could best be described as virtual arrangements with a vital role played by their joint virtual team, which is one of the success factors in this operation, being one of the core components of virtual organizations (Knoll & Javernpaa, 1998). Such a virtual team is represented by the program tutors, administrators, and lecturers in London (UK) and Cairo (Egypt). The basic driving factor behind the collaboration between both teams separated by thousands of miles was the development of a dynamic system that set the responsibilities for each institution and structures the relation between both (Rockart & Short, 1991).

The learning formula is simple to satisfy the needs of both parties by clearly setting the duties and responsibilities of each institution. Therefore, while Middlesex University takes full responsibility and accountability of all academic-related issues, the Regional IT Institute focuses on the marketing, management, and administration of the program. In other words, while the institute undertakes all operations of the program, the university handles all academic elements. Respectively, the duties and responsibilities of each partner could be described as follows: the university is responsible for curricula development, coursework, instruction, examination, and grading in addition to setting the acceptance criteria, the rules and regulations related to academic progression and the sole rights to granting the degree upon completion of all academic requirements. The Institute is responsible for the ICT infrastructure required, such as smart classrooms, computer labs, and the library, as well as promotion and marketing, recruitment of students according to the university regulations, day-to-day administration and follow-up of classes and students, assignment delivery, and commitment to various rules and regulations.

MANAGING ELEARNING PROGRAMS

The management process of the GC, with an average of 28 students enrolled, was a difficult task using the Regional IT Institute-Middlesex University model. The day-to-day follow-up of the operation was something new to the staff of both institutions, which entailed efficient and effective process for operations management. However, their partnership was built around collaborative learning and participation; without it, neither collaboration nor learning occurs (Leidner & Javernpaa, 1995; Alavi, 1994). The partnership was formulated around jointly exerting efforts, allocating capacities, learning from past experiences, and overcoming challenges and turning them into opportunities to set the rule for future growth. It is important to note that based on the early success of the GC Master of Science degree in business information technology, another degree in electronic commerce was launched in February 2001 to further the collaboration between the Regional IT Institute and Middlesex University. Eighteen students enrolled. More programs are expected to be launched in the future. It is believed that the expansion through the virtual model of the GC is the sole solution to address increasing enrollment in Egypt universities[12] per year, which mounts to over 150,000 university graduates per year, excluding postgraduate education (www.mcit.gov.eg).

However, it is important to note that, at the organizational level, the key issue was to optimize the learning curve. Therefore, the team involved in the management and coordination of the degree programs was exposed to continuous training in management of daily operations, communication skills, planning and follow-up, crisis management, time management, and customer relationship management. As for the staff, with the use of electronic mail and other ICT facilities, they were able to communicate and collaborate well (Schrage, 1990). The Regional IT Institute-Middlesex University team meets four times every year, twice in Cairo and twice in London, attending exam and study board meetings. Meetings are usually attended by the link tutors[13] of both organizations as well as the dean of the school of computing and the quality assessment manger from the university, in addition to the technical, operations, and marketing coordinators from the

Institute and the Institute's director. However, the use of electronic mail is intensive between both institutions on a daily basis, reaching up to 50 exchanged emails per day and more than 150 emails between the students and the university, including sending assignments and inquiries. The Regional IT Institute model reflects the concept that the virtual organization can be taken to be one with a relatively small headquarters, operating with different internal units, alliances, and subcontractors, in many countries. However, the most important success factor is the model and how to synchronize in a way to be able to properly manage the value chain leading to a global-scale operation, while being built on a minor volume of resources. The model capitalized on the development of work processes that could maximize the internal supply chain of information and procedures within the Regional IT Institute as well as the external chain with Middlesex University.

LESSONS LEARNED

Based on the experience of the Regional IT Institute with the GC, it is important to address the lessons learned from implementing such an experience in Egypt for around 8 years. Such lessons are important to allow the migration of the experience to other similar environments, in order to capitalize on the available technology and render the outcome more effective and rewarding.

In that respect, the lessons learned from the GC project could be identified as follows. First, virtual integration of the institute–partner capacities enabled the optimization of resources and rendered the alliance more competitive in the marketplace, which led to an increase in enrollment numbers and helped serve a market need in the field of education and training. Second, virtual partnership cooperation depends heavily on the proper formulation of the virtual team involved in the management and operation of the organization—it is important to note that such a team applies also to the staff, faculty, and students. Third, virtual dissemination of knowledge should pass through the adoption, diffusion, and adaptation phases to account for varying cultural differences among societies. Fourth, training, awareness, and using a hybrid model are a must, because the program caters to a wider variety of cultures and attitudes, and it is easier to disseminate and can be liable to less resistance. Fifth, the management of virtual partnership should be built on collaborative learning, and participation among different partners should be based on the fact of having one team with members working together rather than two teams collaborating via information and communication technology. Finally, virtual partnership should be formulated around jointly exerted efforts, allocation of resources, learning from experiences, and overcoming challenges and turning them into opportunities, reflecting the fact that partners should complement each other using a win-win formula.

CONCLUSION

The GC model, with its virtual teams, presented the Regional IT Institute and Middlesex University with a competitive advantage over its 42 competitors delivering similar programs in Egypt, which was only realized through steady growth and the focus on quality output rather than increasing the number of enrollments. Moreover, the GC model was based on a well-studied investment model capitalizing on the use of only the required and relevant infrastructure in terms of people, information, and communication, providing insights into telecommuting in the educational sector in terms of organizational and individual productivity gains. Moreover, the improved delivered service to students in terms of collaboration between both institutions was due to the trust built between the team members (Davidow & Malone, 1992), the adaptation to local conditions, and the improvement of the learning process of the virtual team.

Virtual team in the context of the GC model reflected small groups of people working across boundaries in Egypt and the UK, supported by advanced computing and communication technologies (Lipnack & Stamps, 1997). It is expected to be the peopleware of the 21st century, being able to use traditional and unconventional methods to communicate all the time and everywhere. The coming generations will grow up surrounded by digital media and more accepting of different information and communication technologies in all areas, including education and learning (Tapscott, 1998). However, it is important to note that the success of virtual teams depends largely on building and maintaining trust between team members, which represents the defining feature of a virtual collaboration (Ishaya & Macaulay, 1999).

However, it is important to note that, despite the trust and collaboration between the different partners that is a vital factor, making partnerships, strategic alliances, and networks of organizations successful (Lane & Bachmann, 1998), there were a number of barriers that were faced by the management team to diffuse the GC model among the community, and that included some cultural issues and legal problems (Grimshaw & Kwok, 1998). It was never easy to transfer the programs as is and implement them successfully in the Egyptian market due to diversity in norms and values. Moreover, the earlier versions of the GC model, which mainly relied on Web-based delivery mechanisms, led to a decreasing number of enrollments due to the lack of awareness and appreciation by the students to that model. This led the Institute and the organization to revert to the hybrid model that proved successful in gaining an increasing market share. Students became more accustomed to the hybrid model, because it caters to various needs and requirements.

The Regional IT Institute was established to support the enhancement of human skills and capacities in information and communication technology, aiming at the formulation of a knowledgeable information-based society. The model of the GC relied on a category of learning that is technology-based, and where the instructor and the students are separated geographically. This was reflected in the hybrid model, with face-to-face lecturing and virtual follow-up, study, coaching, and examinations. The model provided access to knowledge for students, regardless of their geographical locations, while being in Egypt, using familiar technology and accommodating different cultural norms and values. The case of the GC as a hybrid model for virtual organizations implemented through a well-built strategic alliance showed that the world is rapidly moving away from the belief that there has to be one theory of organization and one ideal structure. It demonstrates that options are wide open to adapt organizational development and knowledge management to fit local market needs and conditions (Drucker, 1997). It is important to note that in the years to come, for organizations to grow and remain successful and competitive, they need to continuously adapt various information and communication technology in ways that match customer needs, irrespective of their profession or industry, including students in a learning environment. Moreover, technology and groupware in the future will provide a way to bridge distance without physically disrupting people and potentially enable synergy to emerge among different parties (Vogel et al., 2000).

REFERENCES

Ahuja, M., & Carley, K. (1999). Network structure in virtual organizations, *Organization Science, 10*, 6, 741–747.

Alavi, M. (1994) Computer-mediated collaborative learning: an empirical evaluation, *Management Information Systems Quarterly, 18*(2), June, 159–174.

Alavi, M., Yoo, Y., & Vogel, D. (1997). Using information technology to add value to management education, *Academy of Management Journal, 40*, 6, 1310–1333.

Appel, W., & Rainer, B. (1997). Towards the theory of virtual organizations: a description of their formation and figure. *Virtual-Organization Net Newsletter*, 2, 2.

Balint, S., & Kourouklis, A. (1998). The management of organizational core competencies. In P. Sieber, & J. Griese (Eds.). *Organizational virtualness* (pp. 165–172). Bern: Simowa Verlag.

Byrne, J. A., Brandt, R., & Port, O. (1993). The virtual corporation: the company of the future will be the ultimate in adaptability (Cover Story). *International Business Week*, February 8, 36–40.

Chritel, L., & Bachmann, R. (1998). *Trust within and between organizations*. Oxford University Press.

Davidow, W. H., & Malone, M. S. (1993). *The virtual corporation*. New York: Harper Collins.

Drucker, P. F. (1997). Introduction: toward the new organization. In F. Hessekbein, M. Goldsmith, & R. Beckhard (Eds.), *The organization of the future* (pp. 1–5). San Francisco, CA: Jossey-Bass Publishers.

Electronic Learning Magazine. Retrieved May 2002 from the World Wide Web: www.elearningmag.com.

Fritz, M. B., & Manheim, M. L. (1998). Managing virtual work: a framework for managerial action. In P. Sieber, & J. Griese (Eds.), *Organizational virtualness*. Bern: Simowa Verlag.

Global Campus. Retrieved May 2002 from the World Wide Web: www.gc.mdx.ac.uk.

Goldman, S. L., Nagel, R. N., & Preiss, K. (1995). Agile competitors and virtual organizations: strategies for enriching the customer. New York: Van Nostrand Reinhold.

Goodhue, D. E., Waybo, M. D., & Kirsch, L. S. (1992). The impact of data integration on the costs and benefits of information systems. *Management Information Systems Quarterly*, September.

Gray, P. (1995). The virtual wworkplace. *ORMS Today*, A publication of INFORMS, August.

Grenier, R., & Metes, G. (1996). *Going virtual: moving your organization into the 21st century*. Englewood Cliffs, NJ: Prentice Hall.

Grimshaw, D. J., & Kwok, S. F. T. (1998). The business benefits of the virtual organization. In: M. Igbaria, & M. Tan (Eds.), *The virtual workplace*. Hershey, PA: Idea Group Publishing.

Hirschheim, R., & Adams, D. (1991). Organizational connectivity. *Journal of General Management*, Winter, 17, 2.

Holland, C. P. (1998). The importance of trust and business relationships in the formation of virtual organizations. In P. Sieber, & J. Griese (Eds.), Organizational virtualness (pp. 53–64). Bern: Simowa Verlag.

Information and Decision Support Center. Retrieved May 2002 from the World Wide Web: www.idsc.gov.eg.

Ishaya, T., & Macaujlay, L. (1999). The role of trust in virtual teams. In P. Sieber, & J. Griese (Eds.), *Organizational virtualness and electronic commerce*. Bern: Simowa Verlag.

Jagers, H., Jansen, W., & Steenbakkers, W. (1998). Characteristics of virtual organizations. In P. Sieber, & J. Griese (Eds.), Organizational virtualness (pp. 65–76). Bern: Simowa Verlag.

Jarvenpaa, S., & Leidner, D. (1998). Communications and trust in global virtual teams, *Journal of Computer Mediated Communication, 3*, 4.

Kamel, S. (1998a). *Humanware investment in Egypt*. Proceedings of the IFIP-WG9.4 Conference on Implementation and Evaluation of Information Systems in Developing Countries, Asian Institute of Technology, Bangkok, Thailand, 18–20 February.

Kamel, S. (1998b). *IT diffusion through education and training*. Proceedings of the 8th Annual BIT Conference on Business Information Management-Adaptive Futures, Manchester, United Kingdom, 4–5 November.

Kamel, S. (1999a). Delivering an MBA program: a virtual approach. In P. Sieber, & J. Griese (Eds.), *Organizational virtualness and electronic commerce*. Bern: Simowa Verlag.

Kamel, S. (1999b). Web-based interactive learning. *Information Management Journal, 12*, 1-2, 6–19.

Kamel, S. (2000). Virtual learning networks in higher education: the case of Egypt's Regional IT Institute. *Journal of Global Information Management, 8*, 3.

Kamel, S. (2002). The role of virtual organizations in post-graduate education in Egypt: the case of the Regional IT Institute. In F. B. Tan (Ed.), *Cases on global IT applications and management: successes and pitfalls*. Hershey, PA: Idea Group Publishing and Information Science Publishing.

Knoll, K., & Jarbenpaa, L. (1998). Working together in global virtual teams. In M. Igbaria, & M. Tan (Eds.), *The virtual workplace*. Hershey, PA: Idea Group Publishing.

Leidner, D. E., & Jarvenpaa, L. (1995). The use of information technology to enhance management school education: a theoretical view. *MIS Quarterly, 19*(3), September, 265–291.

Lipnack, J., & Stamps, J. (1997). *Virtual teams*. New York: John Wiley and Sons, Inc.

Liegle, J. O., & Meso, P. N. (2000). Web-based instruction systems. In L. Lau (Ed.), Distance learning technologies: issues, trends and opportunities (pp. 186–207). Hershey, PA: Idea Group Publishing.

Ministry of Communications and Information Technology. Retrieved May 2002 from the World Wide Web: www.mcit.gov.eg.

Mitchell, A. C. (2002). Developing a learning environment: applying technology and TQM to distance learning. In M. Khosrowpour (Ed.), *Web-based instructional learning*. Hershey, PA: IRM Press.

Neilson, R. (1997). *Collaborative technologies and organizational learning*. Hershey, PA: Idea Group Publishing.

Palmer, J. W. (1998). The use of information technology in virtual organizations. In M. Igbaria, & M. Tan (Eds.), *The virtual workplace*. Hershey, PA: Idea Group Publishing.

Platt, R. G., & Page, D. (2001). Managing the virtual team: critical skills and knowledge for successful performance. In N. J. Johnson (Ed.), *Telecommuting and virtual offices: issues and opportunities*. Hershey, PA: Idea Group Publishing.

Porter, L. R. (1997). *Creating the virtual classroom—Distance learning with the Internet*. New York: John Wiley and Sons, Inc.

Rayburn, W. E., & Ramaprasad, A. (2000a). Three strategies for the use of distance learning technology in higher education. In L. Lau (Ed.), *Distance learning technologies: issues, trends and opportunities* (pp. 52–68). Hershey, PA: Idea Group Publishing.

Rayburn, W. E., & Ramaprasad, A. (2000b). Distance learning alliances in higher education. In L. Lau (Ed.), Distance learning technologies: issues, trends and opportunities (pp. 69–81). Hershey, PA: Idea Group Publishing.

Regional IT Institute. Retrieved May 2002 from the World Wide Web: www.riti.org.

Rockart, J. F., & Short, J. E. (1991). The networked organization and the management of interdependence. In M. S. Morton (Ed.), *The corporation of the 1990s*. New York.

Schrage, M. (1990). *Shared minds*. New York: Random House.

Staples, D. S. (2001). Making remote workers effective. In N. J. Johnson (Ed.), *Telecommuting and virtual offices: issues and opportunities*. Hershey, PA: Idea Group Publishing.

Steil, A. V., Barcia, R. M., & dos Santos, R. C. (1999). An approach to learning in virtual organizations. In P. Sieber, & J. Griese (Eds.), *Organizational virtualness and electronic commerce*. Bern: Simowa Verlag.

Stevenson, M. (1993). The new consumer revolution: virtual mergers. *Canadian Business*, September.

Strausak, N. (1998). Resumee of VoTalk. In P. Sieber, & J. Griese (Eds.), *Organizational virtualness* (pp. 9–24). Bern: Simowa Verlag.

Tapscott, D. (1998). *Growing digital—The rise of the Net generation*. New York: McGraw-Hill.

Ungson, G. R., & Tundel, J. D. (1998). *Energy of prosperity: templates from the information age*. London: Imperial College Press.

Vogel, D. R. et al. (2000). Sociocultural learning in globally distributed teams. Working Paper 00/03, Department of Information Systems, City University of Hong Kong.

Web-Based Education Commission. Retrieved May 2002 from the World Wide Web: www.hpcnet.org/Webcommission.

ENDNOTES

[1]   The GC has a number of collaborating partners, including the World Bank, the United Nations Development Program, and the Regional Information Technology and Software Engineering Center (RITSEC), which is the parent organization of the Regional IT Institute that was established in 1992 as a not-for-profit center to promote information technology in the Arab region.

[2]   In the context of this chapter, the virtual model referred to is "the development by the Regional IT Institute of strategic alliances with learning institutions from around the world to deliver degree and nondegree programs for the market in Egypt using state-of-the-art information and communication technology with over 90% of all correspondences and administration of operation done remotely.

[3]   The Regional IT Institute was established in 1992 and amongst its different activities and projects is the development of human resources in different information and communication technology.

[4]   It is important to note the impact of the role played by the Institute in introducing change and diversity in the platform for delivering learning, which had positive implications on the quality and magnitude of the market served.

[5]   The Institute specializes in information technology, management, and business-related topics and caters to the needs of individuals as well as organizations, both private and public. It has managed over the last decade to build a strong reputation in the training and education sector, not only in Egypt but also in the Arab region and in the countries and regions it served.

[6]   The rationale behind choosing Middlesex University was the fact that it was already collaborating with the Regional IT Institute in the delivery of a master's degree program in Egypt using traditional methods, and it was only natural to revert to well-established partnerships to launch another delivery mechanism—the Web-enabled model—through the GC.

[7]   It is important to note that according to the agreement between the university and the Institute, students are not required to attend any courses outside the institute's campus in Cairo.

[8]   Change and adaptation in curricula and modality of operations has been always key for the successful partnership as well as the success of the hybrid model.

[9]   The GC model requires the availability of a local support center in each country that delivers academic programs; in Egypt, the Regional IT Institute acts as the local support center.

10   Tutors could be local from the Regional IT Institute or from Middlesex University, and they are teaching and research assistants as well as lecturers.

11   The resources available at the Regional IT Institute, which acts as the GC local support center in Egypt, are available for the students in regular class sessions and 24 hours a day to cater to the different needs of the students and also to complement the environment that is based on the removal of all time and distance barriers.

12   There are 18 different universities and 127 specialized institutes in Egypt, including private and public organizations.

13   The link tutor role is to act as a conduit for information between the university and students at the local support center and is the one contacted for general information about the program.

Chapter XXI

A Comparative Study of Diffusion of Web-Based Education (WBE) in Singapore and Australia

Y. Y. Jessie Wong
Independent Educational Researcher, Canada

R. Gerber
University of New England, Australia

K. A. Toh
Nanyang Technological University, Singapore

ABSTRACT

Examined and compared in this chapter is the diffusion of WBE in Singapore and Australia. These two countries were chosen in this study because of the close educational collaborations and developments between them. A number of Australian universities have offshore bases in Singapore. It would be more cost-effective and profitable to use WBE instead of using the usual corresponding method, or flying professors into the country a few times a year for intensive residential studies. In this chapter, WBE at some selected institutions is reported in detail, because these institutions represent the more advanced developments of WBE in the respective country. Meta-analysis, using a modified Taylor's model (Taylor, 2001), reveals that though Singapore and Australia are different in their approach and policies to education and technology, they share similar trends and achievements in the development of WBE. Tertiary institutions in both countries have generally achieved all the characteristics of Generations 4 and 5 of the development model of Distance Education, as described by Taylor. However, this is not to say that face-to-face teaching has been phased out. This study also indicates that WBE supports the development of distance education and e-universities in Australia. On the other hand, it is hard to say when Singapore will develop its first e-university.

INTRODUCTION

The Internet has transformed the way to deliver education in the 21st century. Web-based education has been developed on the basis of the capability and potential of the Internet. The idea of Web-based education was first developed about 15 years ago from a simple form of online learning, using mainly email as a form of communication, and consisting of mainly text, with no multimedia. Soon after, a variety of new software and services were developed to support WBE. In the late 1990s, the development of new technologies for this purpose accelerated. They gradually transformed the way by which distance education was delivered. Today, it is common for private and public educational institutions to offer Web-based courses. However, only a few virtual universities exist today, with all of their courses and activities Web-based.

Books discussing the different aspects of WBE have also mushroomed. Khan (Ed.) (1997), Tan, Corbett, & Wong (Ed.) (1998), Aggarwal (Ed.) (2000), and Moore & Cozine (Ed.) (2000) provide a good understanding of the major aspects in WBE, such as Web-based instructions, Web-based communications, WBE technology, and WBE education diffusion. Taylor (2001) described distance learning now as having reached the fifth generation, involving Web capabilities. In his report entitled "Fifth Generation Distance Education," he described the fifth generation of distance learning as the intelligent flexible learning model. Here, he provides a comprehensive basis for considering Web-based education as a distinctive form of distance education that possesses a variety of characteristics of delivery technologies. According to Taylor, the key elements of WBE are as follows:

1.   Offering interactive multimedia online
2.   Offering Internet-based access to WWW resources
3.   Providing computer-mediated communication using automated response systems
4.   Having campus portal access to institutional processes and resources

What is distinctive about these elements is that they are delineated according to the following differing characteristics of delivery technologies. Each element offers flexibility in terms of time, place, and the pace at which people can learn using the materials. The materials that are developed for WBE are highly refined and involve advanced interactive delivery. Through this approach, it is possible to reduce the institutional variable costs to a low figure (Taylor, Kemp, & Burgess, 1993), thus making the WBE cost effective. Therefore, when compared to other forms of education delivered by distance, WBE is likely to be less expensive; provide students with better quality learning experiences; be more effective in pedagogic terms; and allow for more efficient administrative services. Such a form of learning allows institutions to become "fast, flexible and fluid" (Taylor, 2001, p. 8). It provides the opportunity for students from any global location to engage in a highly personalized educational experience at a relatively modest cost.

Taylor categorized the five stages of the development of distance education as shown in Table 1 as follows: the Correspondence model that is based on print technology; the Multimedia model that is based on print, audio, and video technologies; the Telelearning model that is based on the applications of telecommunications technologies to promote

Table 1: Models of Distance Education—A Conceptual Framework

Models of Distance Education and Associated Delivery Technologies	Characteristics of Delivery Technologies					
	Flexibility			Highly Refined Materials	Advanced Interactive Delivery	Institutional Variable Costs Approaching Zero
	Time	Place	Pace			
First Generation **The Correspondence Model**						
• Print	Yes	Yes	Yes	Yes	No	No
Second Generation **The Multimedia Model**						
• Print	Yes	Yes	Yes	Yes	No	No
• Audiotape	Yes	Yes	Yes	Yes	No	No
• Videotape	Yes	Yes	Yes	Yes	No	No
• Computer-based learning (e.g., CML/CAL/IMM)	Yes	Yes	Yes	Yes	Yes	No
• Interactive video (disk and tape)	Yes	Yes	Yes	Yes	Yes	No
Third Generation **The Telelearning Model**						
• Audio teleconferencing	No	No	No	No	Yes	No
• Videoconferencing	No	No	No	No	Yes	No
• Audiographic communication	No	No	No	Yes	Yes	No
• Broadcast TV/radio and audio-teleconferencing	No	No	No	Yes	Yes	No
Fourth Generation **The Flexible Learning Model**						
• Interactive multimedia (IMM) online	Yes	Yes	Yes	Yes	Yes	Yes
• Internet-based access to WWW resources	Yes	Yes	Yes	Yes	Yes	Yes
• Computer-mediated communication	Yes	Yes	Yes	Yes	Yes	No
Fifth Generation **The Intelligent Flexible Learning Model**						
• Interactive multimedia (IMM) online	Yes	Yes	Yes	Yes	Yes	Yes
• Internet-based access to WWW resources	Yes	Yes	Yes	Yes	Yes	Yes
• Computer-mediated communication, using automated response systems	Yes	Yes	Yes	Yes	Yes	Yes
• Campus portal access to institutional processes and resources	Yes	Yes	Yes	Yes	Yes	Yes

Note. Source: Taylor, J. (2001). Fifth generation distance education (p. 3). Higher Education Series Report, 40, Canberra: Department of Education, Training and Youth Affairs synchronous communication; the Flexible Learning model that is based on online delivery via the Internet; and the emerging Intelligent Flexible Learning model that extends the fourth model by focusing on selected features of the Internet and the World Wide Web. He declared that for the first four models, variable costs tended to increase or decrease directly with the variations in the volume of the activity. However, the final model is one that can actually decrease costs by providing access to institutional processes and online tuition. The distinctive feature of the fifth-generation model is that it is Web-based, and therefore, cost effective. Perhaps, this is the direction in which education should be moving.

Table 1 shows clearly that there are some applications of WBE in Generation 4, but it increases in Generation 5. Traditional methods of correspondence are generally used in Generations 1 to 3. Taylor does not suggest that WBE is perfect. The power of WBE to transform the educational experience is tremendous, but there are also risks (Web-based Education Commission, 2000). Most countries have realized the need to develop new policies to ensure that WBE will enhance, and not frustrate, learning. However, it needs to be developed and used properly. It is not a means to sell and buy education with increased profits, but it is a means to promote more efficient and effective education for all, irrespective of nationality, age, and gender. In the United States, the Congress has established the Web-based Education Commission to address this important issue. The Commission is aware of the tremendous power of the Internet to empower individual learners and teachers, as well as the barriers that frustrate learning in this new environment. They were given the task of addressing these challenges of a rapidly changing educational landscape. In Singapore and Australia, similar bodies are also established to consider the issues of the development of WBE in their respective countries. These establishments are important to ensure that the benefits of WBE are being harnessed and that the risks are being minimized.

SECTION 1: WBE DEVELOPMENTS IN SINGAPORE

Singapore's first encounter with the Internet occurred in 1991, when the National University of Singapore and the National Science and Technology Board jointly established the Technet Unit, Singapore's first Internet service provider (ISP). Its main purpose was to provide the local R&D community with Internet access so that they could communicate and keep up with their counterparts in other parts of the world. The idea of using WBE for teaching some or all of the modules in a course was not yet conceived. Access to the Internet was strictly limited to organizations with R&D interests. However, the news spread quickly, and the potential of the Internet extended far beyond R&D. By 1993, more and more organizations began requesting access to the Internet; and by 1994, some 50 organizations comprised of R&D institutions, educational institutions, government bodies, and commercial organizations were already connected. In 1994, the Singapore government completed a detailed study on "the Internet" and concluded that it should be made available to all organizations and the general public. Therefore, there was the need for more ISPs. Singapore's three ISPs—Singnet, Pacific Internet, and Cyberway—were launched in 1994, 1995, and 1996, respectively.

Singapore's national website, the Singapore Infomap (http://www.sg), was launched in March 1995; and the Singapore government website (http://www.gov.sg/) was launched in April 1995. Following that, the Internet was made available to the entire civil service via the Government Resources on Internet (GRIN) network. Most institutions of higher learning, especially the universities, and the polytechnics were wired to access the Internet. In 1996, Singapore Polytechnic developed its Virtual College, aiming to experiment with WBE for its "on and off-campus" students. It started with six modules online during the first year. But, the idea was promising. Today, the Virtual College serves as many as 5000 students who regularly access the WBE portion of their courses. In early 1997, Temasek Polytechnic also developed its eLearning environment. Called OLE (Online Learning Environment), it came with the basic features for online learning. By 2002, more than 30 courses were Web-based. Now, Temasek Polytechnic is proud to share its experience on the development of OLE with other interested institutions, and it is ready to help other institutions develop their own eLearning environment. At the university level, the National University of Singapore developed its Integrated Virtual Learning Environment (IVLE) in 1998. WBE was thus introduced to this otherwise traditional university. Its self-developed Open IVLE is now serving 28,000 students, and it has more than 2,400 courses online.

At the school level, RADM Teo Chee Hean, Minister for Education and Second Minister for Defense, launched the Masterplan for IT in Education (MOE, 1997)—a plan to introduce the use of WBE at the school level. It was a blueprint for the integration of information technology (IT) in education as a strategy to meet the challenges of the 21st century. This Masterplan sought to provide a broader base of access to IT among young people so as to achieve equity in learning opportunities. In a new way, every child was given the opportunity to enhance learning through an IT-enriched curriculum and school environment. The plan has four important goals in relation to the introduction of WBE to schools:

1.   To enhance linkages between the school and the world around it, so as to expand and enrich the learning environment. This meant that the Web-based element was added to the conventional learning environment. Teachers and pupils are able to tap into a growing wealth of educational resources outside the school. They will also be able to communicate and collaborate with other educational institutions anywhere in the world.

2.   To encourage creative thinking, lifelong learning, and social responsibility. IT-based curriculum helps pupils develop habits of independent learning. Pupils are able to access Web-based materials and to use them independently.

3.   To generate innovative processes in education. The integration of IT in education will engender several broader innovations. IT-based and Web-based teaching and learning strategies will open possibilities for designing new curricula and new methods of assessment. The Masterplan will, in addition, provide schools with autonomy to use IT resources flexibly to meet the needs of their pupils, including the use of WBE for part of the curriculum.

4.   To promote administrative and management excellence in the education system. IT will be used to promote greater and more efficient communication within the school, among schools, and between the Ministry of Education and schools. It will enhance the effectiveness of educational administration. Ready access to online data and information will also support effective decision making at all levels.

There are four key dimensions in the Masterplan: curriculum and assessment, content and learning resources, physical and technological infrastructure, and human resource development. Stage by stage, all schools will become involved in WBE. This Masterplan has been crucial to WBE diffusion at the school level in Singapore. Without it, the process of introducing WBE in the schools would have been very different.

The story of WBE diffusion in Singapore becomes clearer by examining in detail WBE at key institutions of learning, such as the National University of Singapore, Temasek Polytechnic, and Singapore Polytechnic.

WBE at the National University of Singapore (NUS)

In December 1998, The Integrated Virtual Learning Environment, Version 1.0 (IVLE), a courseware management system, was designed and developed by the Center for Instructional Technology at NUS to support teaching and learning, and to manage courseware over the Internet. It started with modest applications, with features consisting of a frequently-asked-questions builder (Phase I), a course outline template, a discussion forum, a chat room, a quiz management system (Phase I), a class distribution list, and a digital media gallery. This was the beginning of WBE at NUS.

The IVLE development team worked so hard, that by June 1999, Version 2.0 was ready. New features included hard-copy and online user guides, a new workspace interface, a multiple read facility, write access to course outlines, multilingual support, a detailed lecture plan, a new discussion forum and work-bin features, a frequently-asked-questions builder (Phase II), a class roster, and an enhanced course outline module. Improved Phase II features automatically replaced older version Phase I features. Far from being perfect, IVLE 2.0 enabled lessons to be online. A discussion forum was useful for interactions among learners. Some professors made use of this new environment to enhance their teaching. Some did not.

By December 1999, the development team had constructed a course-centric workspace, where all relevant courses could appear together with a course calendar, a quiz management system (Phase II), staff photographs, a student personal email facility, and a discussion forum on improvements that could be made. At this stage, called Version 3.0, NUS launched its eLearning environment, called "Open IVLE." The team continued to evaluate their product to deal with bugs and to improve features and capabilities. In June 2000, Version 4.0 was ready. There were some further improvements and additions on this course management system. Part-customization of workspace was available. There was also a consistent management screen for quizzes, a lecture plan, a work-bin and a frequently-asked-questions builder. Support features included project and peer support for the work-bin and tutorial group support. It came with integration to Oracle software, a course mode time table, improvements to the course calendar and lecture plan interface, an IMS course outline generator, a course website template, an improvement on the site browser for notes publishing, and a link builder. At this stage, users did not need to learn HTML. IVLE enabled lectures to be put on the Web with ease.

A survey of the level of utilization of IT tools by NUS academic staff from the Center of Development in Teaching and Learning (CDTL) was conducted in September–November 1999. The response from the staff was low, only 10.8% of NUS teaching staff responded to the questionnaires. However, there were useful numbers generated. The findings indicated the following:

1.   30% of teaching staff had accessed one NUS online discussion forum
2.   10% of teaching staff had accessed one NUS online chat
3.   52% of teaching staff had accessed one NUS online bulletin board
4.   69% of teaching staff had set up a course website or personal Web page on NUS server, but 36% never update information on their Web pages

The findings also showed that 78% of teaching staff considered that having a course website would improve the teaching and learning processes in their courses. In December 2000, IVLE was given a complete facelift. With its 5.0 version, a more dynamic workspace was incorporated. With it, real-time information links to live lectures were available dynamically. New tools were added, such as a Course Web Builder, a list of Class Groups, Media Channels, and a Question Bank and Glossary. Other existing tools were updated and improved.

June 2001 marked another important date in the establishment of the University's own eLearning environment. IVLE 6.0 was ready. This version maintained the already familiar interface introduced in version 5.0, while expanding what was available.

The biggest improvement in the IVLE platform was the introduction of professionally developed contents from international publishers such as McGraw-Hill and Thomson Learning. Professors were now able to adopt supplementary contents into their course with ease. They could also register students from other institutions as guests to their courses through IVLE 6.0. In this way, they could open their classes to interaction with students from all over the world. In this version, familiar tools like the assessment, Webcast lecture, and multimedia tools were improved. Better graphical assessment reporting enabled professors to develop a good understanding of how students were progressing through the course. Online editing components were also reworked and improved. This meant that professors could include equations and pictures with greater ease. The image bank located at the Multimedia tool helped professors to manage and reuse graphics for their courses.

Other features in this version included interfaces for multilingual support, an integrated whiteboard, a personal to-do list and events organizer, and links to many important NUS resources.

The student workspace included links to the following:
1.   Faculty-specific student services
2.   A complete listing of all offered NUS modules
3.   Past year examination papers
4.   Library Instruction Online (LION)
5.   Library Integrated Catalogue (LINC)
6.   The Digital Library collection
7.   Skills training
8.   Community knowledge resource

These features are discussed, because they are the components of a Web-based course. IVLE now supplements classroom teaching to more than 2400 courses and reaches some 28,000 students. These students are becoming more dependent on the Web-based portion of their courses. There is now no need for them to rush to lectures or tutorials. They are able to access up-to-date course materials while working on campus, at home, or while traveling. With open IVLE, professors are able to expand the range of materials available to students, enhance communications, save time for themselves and their assistants, and help students to prepare better for their classes. IVLE Version 7 is in use in 2002.

WBE at Temasek Polytechnic

Like NUS, Temasek Polytechnic chose to develop its own eLearning environment, instead of purchasing already developed products like WebCT, Blackboard, Topclass, etc. It preferred to start small and think big. The Center for IT in Education and Learning at the polytechnic had developed its online learning environment, called OLE (Online Learning Environment) in early 1997. It was a small project, running on an ordinary desktop PC based on a Windows NT Server 3.51. It relied on a Microsoft Access database and a third-party Internet server. The main purpose was to offer tutorials and other examination preparation materials online. More than 1,000 students visited the Web-based materials on a daily basis at its initial stage, especially during the examination period. OLE was improved by upgrading it to a Windows NT Server 4.0, an Internet Information Server, and a Microsoft SQL Server 6.5. The single desktop PC was later upgraded to seven server-level machines.

In the year 2000, there were already 29 Web-based courses. Approximately 4000 students were using some form of WBE provided by OLE. It received, on average, 8300 hits per day. OLE was cost effective to build and maintain, the tools were easy to install and use, and the site provided students with the functionality and ease of access that they needed. With no intention of keeping all of their students off-campus, OLE's main function was not a total WBE solution. Rather, it provided online materials for student access outside lecture hours.

There are altogether 36 courses online now. Temasek Polytechnic aims to use OLE to deliver 30% of its curriculum online in 2002.

OLE is a Singapore One service. With increasing numbers of subscribers to Singapore One Broadband Cable Service, it is estimated that WBE courses on OLE would be accessed by more than a quarter of the population in 2002.

WBE at Singapore Polytechnic

Singapore Polytechnic developed its Virtual College to provide WBE for on- and off-campus students. In 1996, with less than full online learning features, there were six modules online. Since then, the average increase was 20 modules each year. Virtual College uses Singapore Cable Vision Modems and Singnet Magix ADSL modems. Self-developed, it consists of seven components, merely the basic necessity for WBE:

1.   For your information
2.   Lecture notes
3.   Tutorials
4.   Assignment tasks
5.   Virtual laboratory
6.   Digital resources
7.   Assessment center

In 1998, only 250 students were given access to Virtual College via Singapore One Cable Vision modems. These students were the first to experience the program. Then, 100 students were given the opportunity to use the Virtual College in a fully remote learning way, this time using Magix ADSL modems. After a trial period, it was found that it worked, and only then were the WBE services extended to all students. Today, there are over 300 part-time students on- and off-campus, and approximately 4,000 full-time students who regularly access the Virtual College through the campus-wide SPICE network or remotely via a modem. WBE via the Virtual College environment at Singapore Polytechnic has been successful so far. While the Internet is expanding at a phenomenal rate, the Singapore Polytechnic Virtual College is also expanding to offer more courses to industry and to support on-campus students. However, WBE diffusion is slower than expected for several reasons. The fact that not all students have their own personal computers, and many of the computers that the students possess are not suitable for bandwidth services that the Virtual College delivers, are obvious factors limiting the growth of WBE at Singapore Polytechnic. In addition, the broad bandwidth providers charge monthly fees that some of the students cannot afford. These problems may diminish with time, as broad bandwidth services become cheaper and students upgrade their current computers.

WBE at Primary and Secondary Schools

Web-based education did not become a new method of teaching and learning in Singapore schools in just one day or one year. The training of teachers to use IT to teach, and students to learn, and to harness the great potential of Internet technology at the initial stage of introduction has taken about five years.

Singapore's interests in developing WBE and meeting the new challenges of the information age were well reflected in The IT2000 Report published by the National Computer Board in 1992. Various plans were developed to ensure that Singapore would achieve its vision of becoming an intelligent island within the first decade of the 21st century, with an advanced nationwide information infrastructure. Every home and every school would be connected. In this way, the IT2000 Report initiated the introduction of WBE at all levels of education. Before the IT2000 Report, schools were already implementing the use of computers, as early as 1980, focusing on computer awareness and literacy. However, from 1990 onward, the emphasis changed to using computers for instruction. In 1995, the Internet had become important, and the use of multimedia in education was introduced. Schools had begun creating learning materials on the WWW. Various projects, including "Accelerating the Use of Information Technology in Primary schools," and "Internet in Junior College" were introduced to provide students with opportunity to learn to use IT. The IT2000 Report considered that the provision of the necessary infrastructure for WBE would be possible in primary schools, secondary schools, and junior colleges.

With the launching of the Masterplan of IT in Education in 1997, teachers were being trained to use IT in their lessons, including Web-based materials for actual teaching, as well as using them as supplementary resources. Students were taught to use Web-based materials and access the Internet. In 1998, teachers from 90 schools were trained in using IT for instruction, whether Web-based or nonWeb-based. Teachers from the remaining schools were trained in 1999. By the year 2001, teachers in every school were trained to use IT competently in their classroom teaching and were using some Web-based tools.

The Masterplan established national standards for the use of IT in schools by the year 2002. Schools were given flexibility to determine how quickly they would meet the national standards before 2002, depending on their readiness to use IT meaningfully to meet learning objectives. Initially, all primary schools were provided with the hardware and software required for IT-based learning to take up 10% of total curriculum time. Secondary schools and Junior Colleges (JCs) were given initial provisions, enabling IT to be used for roughly 14% of curriculum time. In 2002, every school should have a pupil–computer ratio of 2:1, and 30% of curriculum time should be IT-based or Web-based. To enable teachers to have ready and frequent access to computers during and after curriculum hours, all schools were equipped with sufficient computer notebooks for use by teachers.

The Masterplan provided for whole-school networking in every school. In this way, access to courseware, Internet, and digitized media resources was provided for every classroom and for all learning areas. Networking for sharing of teaching resources within and between schools, and WBE were technically possible. Finally, all schools would be linked to a Wide Area Network (WAN), connected to the high-speed backbone of Singapore One. At this point of time, all teachers and pupils from Primary 4 and above were provided with email accounts.

WBE DEVELOPMENTS IN AUSTRALIA

The higher education sector in Australia consists of 38 institutions that were basically the amalgamations of former tertiary institutions in the late 1980s. In the past decade, most of these institutions have engaged in a rush to see who can make most use of the Internet to transform flexible forms of learning offered to students around the world from Australian bases. In the rush to embrace the Information Age, varying degrees of consideration were given to maximizing learning using WBE, with varying rates of success. Experimentation has been more the order of the day rather than careful research into Web-based teaching and learning in higher education. There are still some questions of the intentions of some higher education institutions as they rushed to embrace eLearning. Some adopted rather sophisticated approaches to WBE, whereas others were satisfied to place their Distance Education teaching notes on the Internet for students to read.

Anyway, there is certainly strong growth in WBE in the higher education sector. This varies from whole awards through individual modules and subjects. Much of this learning is grounded on established software platforms, e.g., WebCT, Blackboard, and TopClass. These software platforms offer opportunities to bring WBE to reach Generation 4 and 5 in Taylor's model of Distance Learning, increased flexibility, and lower costs (Taylor, 2001). However, there are still costs involved when using these platforms. Most universities pay a one-time cost or an annual charge for unlimited access or usage. Therefore, it is fair to say that it is cost effective, but not yet approaching zero cost. The Technical and Further Education Colleges (TAFE) may be more advanced than the universities in applying new technologies to providing WBE for their students. Projects such as NSW TAFE Online http://www.tafensw.edu.au/ and TAFE Online Queensland are evidence of attainment in WBE in the TAFE sector (see Table 2). The universities in general are more traditional than the TAFE sector.

The situation in the school sector is variable. All schools in Australia have general Internet access, but the extent of actual Web-based learning varies considerably from school to school. Selected private schools have moved a considerable distance along this form of flexible learning, whereas most schools still generally focus on conventional forms of face-to-face learning. The availability of WWW resources and advanced interactive delivery technology means that WBE at the school level is possible if there is the need, the funding, and the desire for any school to decide to use it.

WBE at the Universities

Taylor (2001, p. 2) described WBE in Australian universities as the fifth generation in Distance Education. It is fair to say that in Australian universities, few institutions would have reached the fifth model, even though Taylor indicated otherwise. Most are experimenting in the vicinity of model 4 with the provision of flexible learning models, usually via the use of particular software platforms, including WebCT, Blackboard and Top Class. While some institutions will claim that they have most or all of their teaching units available for WBE, it is common to find no more than one-third of these units being delivered in a fully integrated flexible manner that involves close integration of Web-based materials, chat rooms, bulletin boards, and administrative systems. This is principally because the institutions have not completed adequate research on the best ways to maximize student learning using WBE in Australia.

Further evidence to suggest that Australian academics have experienced moderate success in using WBE may be derived from a 1998 survey of Australian academics' declared use of the Internet. Clayton et al. (1998), in the first nationwide quantitative survey of academic staff use of the Internet, found that while almost all of the Australian academics (95.6%) had access to the Internet, 28% used it daily, 39% used it weekly, and 25.9% used it less than once per week. Only 7.1% reported that they never used the Internet. In addition, the users declared that they were relatively competent Internet users. However, only 55.5% of the academics declared that they belonged to electronic discussion groups or newsgroups. The authors conducted a smaller study in one university in 1995. At that time, only 13% of the respondents used the Internet on a daily basis and another 19% used it weekly. In 1998, these numbers had increased to 33% and 47.6%, respectively. In 2002, we expect that these figures will have increased even further. Finally, the academics were asked to comment on the usefulness of the Internet for teaching. At least 50% of the beginning Internet users, 70% of the component users, and 80% of the experts, believed that there was an important relationship between the usefulness of the Internet for teaching and the perceived skill that was required to do so. However, these results merely point to the possibility that Australian academics see the Internet as a powerful source or support to teaching and learning. It does not indicate that they actually use the Internet for this purpose.

As an example of one of Australia's more advanced universities in WBE, Taylor (2001) described how the University of Southern Queensland developed its eLearning to become the 2000–2001 joint winner of the Good Universities Guide's Australian University of the Year for criteria that focused on developing an e-university. Here, the university's activities were developed around three foci: e-Information repositories, e-Applications, and the e-Interface. Through the Generic Online Offline Delivery (GOOD) Project, students are now able to receive their courseware in a variety of delivery modes, e.g., print, online, CD, DVD, etc., from a single document source. Here, learning is based on providing students with an interactive study chart that details the broad parameters of the teaching unit's subject content and a list of exemplary text or reference books that are hot-linked for ready access. Students are able to surf the Net for other references and helpful assignments on the topic. They are supported by the interactions between students, academic staff, and other experts who act as mentors to their learning. These interactions occur through asynchronous discussion groups and informal social interaction among students. These interactions are stored in relational databases for later use by students and academics. These databases can be searched using predetermined keywords. In addition to these pedagogic activities, the interaction between the university and existing and prospective students is managed using the USQAssist initiative. Using this tool, the university can communicate directly with students from more than 60 countries, 24 hours per day, seven days per week. These initiatives are being extended to the fifth generation model by personalizing the intelligent object databases, developing a customizable e-Interface, and integrating an on-campus wireless network to provide on-campus students with the same flexibility in learning that off-campus students now receive. Shortly, this will enable the university to become a fully flexible learning institution.

WBE at TAFE Colleges

TAFE Colleges in Australia are the equivalent of polytechnics in Singapore. These are the colleges that focus on Vocational Education and Training (VET) in Australian education. They straddle secondary and higher education in Australian education but are primarily focused on the development of people's competencies to take up jobs across the Australian workforce. TAFE Colleges are organized in Australia on a State or Territory basis, and considerable variation is to be found in the way that TAFE Colleges are linked to the other education sectors. For example, in some States and Territories, e.g., Victoria and the Northern Territory, these colleges are linked and integrated in the higher education sector. In the other states, they remain separate institutions. This context helps to explain how there is such variation in the development and implementation of VET across Australia. Harper et al. (2000), in their comprehensive review of online education and training in VET, concluded that there is a mix of implementation models that have been informed by the principles of flexible learning. For example, they illustrate these variations as follows:

1.   In South Australia, TAFE has developed a flexible delivery model as its framework for online delivery. This framework is designed to integrate online and on-campus learning activities. In 2000, TAFE South Australia offered around 200 modules with some online component, with a range of Certificate courses that are available completely online. In some cases, students can choose between online or face-to-face teaching. The content areas that are online focused tend to those that relate to State priorities in VET.

2.   In Victoria, the TAFE Virtual Campus (TAFE VC) has been designed to make online tools available to teachers across the State. The aim of the online learning activities is to improve education for all students, rather than to offer alternatives to some students. Because the idea is to integrate online learning in all campuses, this is likely to change the way that campus-based learning occurs. The subjects chosen for online education are those that relate to the State VET priorities, subjects with high enrollments, and those that are suited to online delivery.

3.   In Queensland, TAFE has developed two delivery options—flexible entry to a completely online program from enrollment to completion, or modules offered through individual institutes, perhaps across a number of sites, involving the usual enrollment procedures and on-campus activities. Online options are available for at least 30 government-funded, fee-for-service modules. They are intended to enable online students to be self-sufficient.

In the TAFE sector, the extent of online delivery depends on the technical, pedagogic, content, and marketing expertise available in these institutes. Sometimes, this expertise is derived from the development of partnerships with commercial, educational, and government providers, for example, TAFE in South Australia markets WebCT training and consultancy services to local and international educational institutions, and the Canberra Institute of Technology developed online training for Qantas airline staff. A fuller indication of these types of projects in Australian TAFE Colleges has been summarized in Table 2. This led Harper et al. (2000, pp. 16–42) to conclude that within the Australian TAFE sector, there is:

1.   Extensive experimentation and exploration in online learning
2.   Not yet a mainstream online delivery system in VET
3.   A variety of adopted implementation models
4.   No one acknowledged way to implement online learning in VET

Table 2: Selected Projects for Australian TAFE Colleges

❖ NSW TAFE Online http://www.tafensw.edu.au/
The NSW TAFE Online project is a major initiative that aims to promote and support online delivery in New South Wales. The purpose of the project is to create an online environment that encompasses information and communication and supports the interaction between teacher and student.

❖ TAFE Virtual Campus http://www.tafevc.com/
TAFE VC is an online platform that supports a complete learning environment for the management and delivery of training. It provides an interface between students at home, the workplace, or within a LAN (local area network) environment, and Victorian TAFE providers, including institutes, adult community education (ACE), and private providers.

❖ ACENET http://www.tafe.net/
ACENET is one of the 10 learning networks established by the Office of Post Compulsory Education, Training and Employment (PETE) in Victoria. Students can study online courses and modules, accessing the Internet at home or in local community centers.

❖ TAFE Online Queensland http://www.tafe.net/
TAFE Queensland offers online programs, such as automative apprentice courseware, business courses, creative writing courses, disability studies engineering courses, IT courses, justice studies, lifestyle courses, mutimedia, recognized prior learning, Telstra site induction courses, and workplace courses.
The programs are supported through the central TAFE Queensland, which is a Queensland Government tertiary education and training system that delivers technical and vocational education and training and adult community education to around 360,000 local and international students per year.

❖ OTEN_DE IT Virtual Campus http://www.oten.edu.au/oten/
The NSW Department of Education and Training is developing policies and models to offer online training through its Distance Education branch OTEN-DE. The IT Virtual Campus is the major NSW initiative in online learning in the VET sector.

❖ Queensland Open Learning Network http://www.qoln.net/
As an experienced user of older Internet technologies such as Audiographics, QOLN is expanding the range of technological tools available to students and is training providers in order to offer Web and email access.

❖ TAFE South Australia Online http://www.tafe.sa.edu.au
The SA TAFE Online project site offers users access to the individual institutes and campuses, course information, award courses and locations, student services, VET access and equity information, committee information, specific data for international students, and details about specific online services.

❖ WestOne http://www.westone.wa.gov.au/
WestOne Online was established by the Western Australian Government, with a mission to enhance vocational education and training in Western Australia through the use of digital technologies.

❖ Toolbox Development Project http://www.anta.gov.au/toolbox/
The Toolbox Development Project is funded by ANTA as one of the National Flexible Delivery Projects. The purpose of the project is to develop multimedia training resources to assist registered organizations to deliver training flexibly against training packages.

❖ VETTWeb http://www.vetWeb.net.au/
VETTWeb has been designed as a global Internet campus to offer a world of new educational opportunities for people involved in training, from students to private companies and training providers. VETTWeb is a Virtual Building consisting of many Floors that contain organizations primarily focused on training.

---

5.   A partnership developed to consolidate technical, pedagogic, content, and marketing expertise in online learning
6.   Evidence that suggests that designers have adapted online technologies to their own needs and circumstances
7.   Acknowledgement that the instructors' roles change with online learning, e.g., greater flexibility in learning and greater cognizance of instructional design approaches
8.   A need for learners to be prepared and supported through the initial stages of using online learning environments
9.   A focus on developing in-house expertise to cater to the increasing demand for online learning modules in VET
10.   Evidence that many TAFE institutions developed policies for online delivery and training, but few have formalized their approach to online delivery
11.   An impression that much of the evaluation of online learning in the TAFE system is informal in nature

These conclusions have been augmented by other research in the Australian TAFE context that concludes that stakeholders in the online learning process experience varying demands. For example, Schofield et al. (2000) found that TAFE teaching staff experienced a general shift in their professional practice from an instructor role to a facilitator role. This role, while including more than online learning, really focused on self-paced and self-directed learning experiences for their students, including through online delivery. Where online learning was involved, it was a positive experience for these educators that increased their sense of professional satisfaction and challenge. Some teachers were concerned about the way that online learning caused the teacher to become a learner again, by being a learning facilitator rather than a "knowledge giver," and developing a feeling of not being in control of the learning situation. These educators became involved in online learning largely through professional curiosity and interest. They declared that they were not pressured by their TAFE colleges or the wider industries to get involved with online learning.

Primary and Secondary Schools

Like the TAFE sector in Australia, school education is the matter of the States and Territories, even though the Commonwealth Government provides some funding. The school system in this country is also segmented into public and private providers, with around 65–70% of the students attending public or government schools. The most important recent initiative in the public school education arena has been the widespread provision of Internet access to most schools throughout the country. The private education sector has literally done the same thing through their different schools. Therefore, we have a situation in which most Australian students have access to the Internet in their schools. Another snapshot of this situation is provided in a recent survey that was conducted in Government, Catholic, and Independent schools across Australia into the use of information technology by teachers (Schoolsnet Australia, 2000). This survey of teachers in metropolitan, rural, and regional schools revealed the following details about teachers' use of information technologies in their work:
1.   Almost all teachers had access to the Internet (98%).
2.   This access was easy for at least 80% of the teachers in all of the educational sectors but was marginally higher in the metropolitan areas.

3. The most common points of access to the Internet were in the school library, the administration area, a laboratory, or in a classroom. However, access via classrooms is a recent phenomenon. Access to the Internet in the library is especially prevalent in Government schools.

4. The Internet is used on a daily to weekly basis by around 65% of the teachers, with a higher frequency in secondary schools as opposed to primary or elementary schools.

5. The main uses of the Internet in Australian schools are for research (86%), accessing the World Wide Web (82%), and for email usage (73%).

6. Approximately 75% of secondary teachers used the Internet in their regular teaching environment, whereas 57% of primary or elementary teachers used the Internet in their teaching environment. This variation was 67% in the Government sector and 67% in the Catholic sector, as opposed to 46% in Independent schools.

These results do not describe the WBE that occurs in Australian schools. However, they indicate that the WWW is being used increasingly in these schools. However, this usage is not even.

Australian schools and teachers receive a considerable amount of advice on how to maximize their use of the Internet. For example, The Victorian Department of Education, Employment and Training (2000) published SafetyNet as its guidelines to schools on using the Internet. Besides advising schools of their responsibilities for using the Internet, considerable emphasis is placed on good practice using it. Unfortunately, these policy documents contain little on the concept of Web-based learning. Australian schoolteachers have been assisted in their approach to WBE by a range of guidebooks that introduce them to WBE and also to methods for introducing WBE in their classrooms. Books such as that by Hixson and Schrock (1999) come across as guides to teachers on how to develop Web-based learning activities and how to implement them in their curricula. Other reference books advise Australian teachers on ways to improve information literacy through using the Internet (e.g., Hancock, 1999). Professional educational journals have taken up the challenge in Australia to provide excellent commentary on good WBE practices and their pedagogic uses. For example, in the science education journal *Investigating*, articles have appeared on the evaluation of Internet-based Primary science packages (e.g., Haq, Longnecker, & Hickey, 1999) and developing Internet science projects (e.g., Fitzpatrick, 2000). In some schools, enthusiastic teachers have promoted the development of WBE through science, English, and mathematics classes by having students prepare data and then share it via the Internet, together with their explanations. Other students then interact with the authors to discuss the results and how they were achieved. These practices are still in the minority of schools, but will expand rapidly over the next decade.

METHOD OF COMPARATIVE STUDY

There are two steps in this study. First, the stages in education are seen as they occur in the schools, the polytechnics (equivalent to TAFE in Australia), and the universities. WBE diffusion in Singapore and Australia are compared at these three levels. Meta-analysis is conducted using a modified Taylor's model, and the results are represented in the achievement table (Table 3). Second, NUS and USQ are compared in their attainment of using WBE for distance education as well as for on-campus programs. They are chosen because they represent more advanced universities in WBE in their respective countries. A detailed comparison is done in this way in order to focus on the differences and similarities as experienced by the particular university in each country (see Table 4).

The Problems in Comparing WBE Diffusion between Singapore and Australia

Singapore is a democratic city-state with a small population and one educational system for the whole nation. It is obvious that there is less difficulty for the diffusion of WBE to occur consistently nationwide in Singapore than in a bigger nation such as Australia. Individual territories and states in Australia have their own educational policies and practices. Therefore, there ought to be varieties instead of consistencies. To arrive at a general picture in WBE for the whole of Australia is difficult or inaccurate. In order to achieve a fair result of comparison between WBE in Singapore and Australia, there is a need to look at not just the generalization but some case studies. While this study is general, an attempt is made to look at developments at some individual institutions.

Meta-Analysis

The result of meta-analysis is shown in Table 3. The x-axis indicates the three levels of education in Singapore and Australia. The y-axis indicates the fourth and fifth generations of Distance Learning, and their respective characteristics. An additional row is added to show the actual level of usage of WBE applications on the y-axis. Each matrix is then marked with "Yes" or "No" or "Var," indicating the attainment of WBE, respectively. Only Generations 4 and 5 are included and applied, because Generations 1–3 in Taylor's model refer to characteristics of distance learning other than the Web-based approach. They are, therefore, not taken into consideration in this study.

A quick perusal of Table 3 would suggest that at the school level, there is consistency in Singapore in the application of WBE. In Australia, there are more variations and differences across the schools. While all schools are guaranteed access to WWW resources, interactive multimedia online and online or computer-mediated communication by the Ministry of Education in Singapore, the situation is different in Australia. Some schools have already been doing good work in WBE, with good use of interactive multimedia delivery in their teaching and learning, flexible access to WWW for all in the school, and use of management systems for all processes in administrative work. This is an exception rather than the norm in the school sector in Australia. Most schools in Singapore and Australia have the basic infrastructure for WBE. However, as shown in Table 3, the situation is different in practice. The proportion of WBE to conventional face-to-face education is still small at the school level. The main reason is that while WBE is considered worth trying, and may enhance teaching and learning, there is no intention for all courses to be Web-based at the school level. In Singapore, the Ministry of Education set the standard of 30% of the curriculum in school to be Web-based by 2002. In Australia, there is no such standard set. Thus, there is a greater variation in terms of WBE at the school level in Australia than in Singapore. In practice, the level of usage of WBE is less than 50% in any case, in Singapore and Australia. One would enter a normal classroom with some forms of Web-based delivery at some time only. Students, however, are involved in a Web-based learning activity once in a while; more often in some schools and less frequently in others.

Table 3: Comparative Attainment Chart: 3 Levels of Education in Singapore and Australia

Models of D.L. involving WBE and their characteristics	Levels of education Singapore			Levels of education Australia		
	School	Poly	University	School	TAFE	University
Generation 4						
Interactive multimedia online	Yes	Yes	Yes	Var	Yes	Yes
Characteristics:						
Flexibility through time, place, and pace	Var	Yes	Yes	Var	Yes	Yes
Evidence of refined materials	Yes	Yes	Yes	Yes	Yes	Yes
Advanced interactive delivery	No	Yes	Yes	Var	Yes	Yes
Institutional costs approaching zero	No	No	No	No	No	Var
Internet-based access to WWW resources	Yes	Yes	Yes	Yes	Yes	Yes
Characteristics:						
Flexibility through time, place, and pace	Var	Yes	Yes	Var	Yes	Yes
Evidence of refined materials	Yes	Yes	Yes	Yes	Yes	Yes
Advanced interactive delivery	No	Yes	Yes	Var	Yes	Yes
Institutional costs approaching zero	No	No	No	No	No	Var
Computer-mediated communication	Yes	Yes	Yes	Var	Yes	Yes
Characteristics:						
Flexibility through time, place, and pace	Yes	Yes	Yes	Yes	Yes	Yes
Evidence of refined materials	Var	Yes	Yes	Yes	Yes	Yes
Advanced interactive delivery	Var	Yes	Yes	Var	Yes	Yes
Generation 5						
Computer-mediated communication using automated response systems	No	Yes	Yes	Var	Yes	Yes
Characteristics:						
Flexibility through time, place, and pace		Yes	Yes	Yes	Yes	Yes
Evidence of refined materials		Yes	Yes	Yes	Yes	Yes
Advanced interactive delivery		Yes	Yes	Yes	Yes	Yes
Institutional costs approaching zero		No	No	No	Var	Var
Computer portal access to institutional processes and resources	No	Yes	Yes	Var	Yes	Yes
Characteristics:						
Flexibility through time, place, and pace		Yes	Yes	Yes	Yes	Yes
Evidence of refined materials		Yes	Yes	Yes	Yes	Yes
Advanced interactive delivery		Yes	Yes	Yes	Yes	Yes
Institutional costs approaching zero		No	No	Var	Var	Var
Level of usage of WBE applications						
100% of D.L. Web-based	N.A.	No	No	N.A.	No	Var
50% or less of D.L. Web-based	N.A.	Yes	Yes	N.A.	Yes	Var
100% of on-campus courses Web-based	No	No	No	No	No	No
50% or less of on-campus courses Web-based	No	Yes	Yes	Var	Yes	Var

Note: "Yes" means the institution has attained the level of WBE indicated; "No" means it has not; "Var" means the variation is too wide to generalize accurately; "Poly" refers to polytechnics in Singapore as equivalent to TAFE in Australia in this study; "D.L." means distance learning; "N.A." means not applicable

Each of the five main characteristics in Generations 4 and 5 are further defined by four ingredients: flexibility through time, place, and pace; evidence of refined materials; advanced interactive delivery; and institutional costs approaching zero. As shown in Table 3, there is no case where the costs approach zero in delivering WBE. In Singapore, the cost for all schools to install WBE infrastructure is high. However, the cost for usage is less so and becoming increasingly less expensive as time passes. There is certainly evidence of refined materials in some schools. However, the schools share these resources through the WWW. Advanced interactive delivery is certainly available in all schools in Singapore. However, the usage by teachers varies considerably. Unlike in higher institutions of learning, there is less flexibility for school students to gain access to WWW resources and WBE materials; some schools in Singapore arrange a schedule for each class for using a computer lab, where the main access to the WWW is organized. After school, the students may access most of these materials through their own computers at home. Not even half of the students have access to the WWW at home. There are other common areas, such as the library, where students can access resource materials through the WWW at all times the library is open. It is not fair to say that such access and sharing of resources through the WWW is not available in Australian schools. It is true that there are different mechanisms open to students for such access in Australia. There is still a reasonable amount of resource materials meant for internal access only in some schools in Singapore. Some are good learning materials but are not being shared.

It is clear that there is little or no sign of any school attaining Generation 5 of WBE as defined in Taylor's model. Generation 5 features are more common at higher institutions of learning, especially those with nearly all or all of their courses off-campus.

WBE diffusion at the polytechnic level in Singapore is compared with the TAFE in Australia. They are not exactly functioning in the same way, but they both sit between the schools and the universities. In Singapore, the polytechnics are modern in their teaching approach. Emphasis is given to learning more about technologies. They are keen on WBE and offer off-campus courses. As shown in Table 3, in some ways, TAFE in Australia and polytechnics in Singapore have achieved all the features of WBE as described by Generations 4 and 5 in Taylor's model. One exception is, however, that the cost for providing WBE in Singapore polytechnics is still high. As there are variations in Australia, a small number of the TAFE colleges may be operating WBE with the cost approaching zero. In general, the cost factor is there, and the institutions are not fully virtual institutions of learning. This is shown as having 50% or less of the courses being taught fully via WBE. As compared to the school level, there is much more flexibility through time, place, and pace in learning. Of course, there are refined materials that are Web-based, both for sharing and for individual use. Interactive online multimedia delivery is possible in all six polytechnics in Singapore, although the degree of use may differ. There is a moderate degree of usage of computer-mediated communication and portal access at the polytechnics and TAFE colleges.

Also shown in Table 3 is that the universities in Singapore and Australia have achieved most of the characteristics defined by Generations 4 and 5 in Taylor's model in WBE, with one exception. This exception is the "operational cost approaching zero." In Singapore, the universities have developed their own course management system or purchased a license from developers of Blackboard or other platforms. Considering the use of manpower in development, and the time taken to develop it, the cost is not negligible. However, it is cost effective if the university developed its own platform, such as IVLE. Right now, the cost is far from approaching zero. Taking the cost factor away, it is fair to say that WBE programs at universities in both countries are actually in Generations 4 and 5 in Taylor's model. However, in actual practice, not even 50% of the courses are totally Web-based. Therefore, Taylor's model is only theoretical, and the actual situation of WBE diffusion cannot be clearly shown. In this study, we go beyond this model and look at the actual practice of WBE.

The second part of this analysis involves a closer look at what NUS and USQ have done to promote eLearning. These two institutions were chosen because of their advanced approach to WBE. Comparing one institution in Singapore with a similar institution in Australia would help to reflect the similarities and differences not included in a general comparison.

As can be seen from Table 4, USQ focuses on developing into an e-university, concentrating on three main areas: e-Information repositories, e-Applications, and the e-Interface. NUS focuses on developing an advanced integrated virtual learning environment, with features increasingly catered to the needs of the learners at the university. Main areas of interest include links with the outside world, library resources, and access to interactive lectures and tutorial materials. There is no plan to give up its on-campus program. However, it aims at providing equivalent quality of WBE for its on-campus students and its off-campus students (mainly local part-time students). There is also no plan to develop into an e-university. On the other hand, USQ has developed its e-university, where students learn and are supported through the innovative and strategic use of educational Web-based technologies that encourage e-world expertise. It has an online education arm, providing a good number of courses in almost all areas of learning, ranging from an award of a Certificate to a Masters degree. Using the USQOnline (which is the Internet-based delivery mode developed by the university as part of its commitment to provide quality flexible education, anywhere, anytime), students from all over the world can register and receive an award from the university at a cost, ranging from AUD3000 to 15,000 (in 2001). USQOnline was developed for students who would like to enhance their career or attain university accredited qualifications by study via the Internet. USQOnline is also a way for people all over the world in many different situations to continue their education and enhance their professional skills.

Table 4: WBE Diffusion at NUS and USQ

	NUS	USQ
WBE platform	IVLE	USQOnline
WBE for internal courses	Yes	Yes
Applying Generations 4 and 5 in WBE—Taylor's Model	Yes	Yes
Cost of WBE approaching zero	No; cost is moderately high	Moderate; gradually decreasing
Separate distance education arm	No	Yes; using WBE instead of correspondence
Developing e-university	No	Yes

There is no flexibility on when to start a course or program. USQOnline offers three periods of study per year. Semester 1 commences in March, Semester 2 commences in July, and Semester 3 commences in November. NUS has not used its IVLE online in the same way as USQOnline. The main objective is to provide WBE experiences for its local students. The main users are the professors and the students, definitely not for enrolling Distance Learning students from all over the world, as USQOnline is doing now. Unlike USQ, which is already operating an e-university within the main university, NUS is still operating on a single arm, emphasizing traditional on-campus courses, using WBE applications and convenience from the benefits of modern technology.

Having compared the main areas in regard to WBE in these two universities, it is clear that in terms of WBE diffusion, they have attained a similar level. They are considered more advanced universities in the application of and approach to WBE. In terms of usage, they are very different. In terms of using WBE in the truest sense of providing distance learning, USQ has achieved that. NUS has not and is unlikely to do so in the near future. IVLE is an added advantage for its local students, both part-time and full-time. Using WBE to enhance learning, teaching, communication, resources, and other administrative work will continue to form the main focus of NUS for the time being.

DISCUSSION

The Singapore situation is unique in the sense that the control and planning of WBE have been from the top down, especially in the case of planning for WBE at the school level. Consistency was an important issue. The Ministry of Education has plans for all schools, and it makes sure that no school is disadvantaged. This approach has proved successful in a small nation with a strong government. An interesting observation suggests that this top-down direction is strong, but it discourages private WBE developments. Australia is not a small nation. Instead of consistency, there is a great deal of variation in WBE experimentation and practices at all levels of education. This is expected. The initiatives were from the institutions or from the individual states or territories. As a small nation, Singapore is alert to world developments. The idea of developing its IT infrastructure for the better of the whole nation came rather early. The concept of introducing WBE at different levels of education was just part of the main concern. Singapore is not behind the bigger nations, such as Australia, in its preparation and implementation of WBE. However, there are sizeable differences in the choices of WBE platform, and development of WBE as a whole. With the National University of Singapore developing its Open IVLE; Singapore Polytechnic, its Virtual College; and Temasek Polytechnic, its OLE; it gives an impression that each institution in Singapore favors the development of its own WBE platform instead of adopting one from somewhere else. And, all of them chose to use Microsoft technology. An obvious advantage of developing one's own platform is that it serves its own purpose. One can choose a cost-effective development method. The experience of developing is challenging and valuable. The product can also be sold to other interested institutions. It is not to say that Australian institutions of higher learning prefer adopting well-developed platforms such as WebCT, TopClass, or Blackboard. However, this study suggests that WebCT, TopClass, or Blackboard have been adopted for use by some universities in Australia. Of course, there is a price to pay for using them as well. It is simpler than developing its own. Perhaps, it is easier and faster to adopt WBE by using developed and already tested platforms than having to develop one's own in each university.

There are also a number of online learning platforms being developed in Australian institutions, such as USQonline, WestOne Online, TAFE South Australia Online, Queensland Open Learning Network, TAFE Online Queensland, and so on. Their purposes range from offering online courses for adult students to just promoting and supporting online delivery for everyone involved in training, including private companies.

A number of Australian universities have their bases in Singapore and other countries. However, Singapore universities do not have bases in other countries. Therefore, WBE platforms in Singapore universities mainly serve their local students. Those Australian universities with bases in other countries are using WBE to revamp their Distance Education arm from a traditional correspondence method to total eLearning environments.

The situation of WBE diffusion at the school level in Australia is unclear. Unlike the Singapore schools, there is no central agency to plan and implement WBE in the schools nationwide. As a result, pockets of schools with well-developed WBE may exist side by side with schools that have little or no usage of WBE at all. Unless a thorough study covering all schools in the entire country is done, there are not many ways we can compare between schools. Which is better, a consistent development of WBE in all schools or to let the schools choose to introduce WBE? This comparative study indicates that even with a central agency to overlook this matter, schools in Singapore are at different levels of using WBE. One thing for sure is that WBE is planned to supplement the school curriculum, not to replace face-to-face learning. All students are required to attend school, and the teachers teach in a classroom environment, whether using Web-based materials or not.

Full technology adoption (the virtual university) has not yet happened in Singapore. Perhaps it will, but not in the near future. Considering the distance learning experiences of some of the universities in Australia, it appears that the virtual university will become common in the future. While the successful top-down approach in Singapore may provide lessons to learn for other nations, the top-down direction is found to be minimal or nonexistent in Australia.

CONCLUSION

This study leads us to conclude that though Singapore has never been known as an advanced country like the United States, Australia, Canada, or the United Kingdom, it has embraced WBE as quickly as these countries. Today, WBE is playing an increasingly important role in all levels of education. The consistency of the development in line with government policies suggests that all students in Singapore have a chance to use Web-based resources in the school and to experience the nature of WBE, with guidance from their teachers. All students at the polytechnics or the universities have the same opportunity to use WBE as a student at a similar level of education in an advanced country. It also leads to the conclusion that because of the size of Australia, and therefore, the greater variation in the development of WBE in Australia, may suggest that not all children at the primary level would have a chance to participate in WBE. The opportunity definitely increases as one advances up the ladder in education. All university students should have opportunities for Web-based learning in one way or another. The broader picture suggests that virtual or e-university is in the making in Australia. It is not in Singapore.

REFERENCES

Aggarwal, A. (2000) *Web-based learning and teaching technologies: opportunities and challenges*. Hershey, PA: Idea Group Publishing.

Center for Development of Teaching and Learning. (2000). NUSCast: instructor perspective. CDTL: Singapore.

Center for Development of Teaching and Learning. (2000). Survey on level of utilization of IT tools by NUS Academic staff. CDTL: Singapore.

Center for Development of Teaching and Learning. (2001). NUSCast: student perspective. CDTL: Singapore.

Clayton, P. et al. (1998). Australian academic use of the Internet, Adelaide '98—Pathways to knowledge (pp. 159–165).

Corbett, P. S., & Wong Y. Y. (1995). Pictures, soundbites and learning: the potentialities and implications of computers in the Singapore school system. Paper presented at the Principals' Conference, Shangri-Lah Hotel, Singapore, 4–6 September.

Corbett, P. S., & Wong, Y. Y. (1999). Seeding the clouds of change: the planned evolution of Singapore into an intelligent island. In F. B. Tan, P. S. Corbett, & Y. Wong (Eds.), Information technology diffusion and development in the Asia Pacific: perspectives on policy, electronic commerce and education (pp. 35–41). Hershey, PA: IDEA Group Publishing.

Department of Education, Employment and Training. (2000). SafetyNet: Internet usage— guidelines for schools. Melbourne: Department of Education, Employment and Training.

Education Statistics Digest. 1987–2000. Singapore: Ministry of Education. Annual.

Fitzpatrick, S. (2000). Interactive Internet science projects. *Investigating, 16*(3), 34–37.

Fries, B., & Monahan, B. (1999). Low cost distance learning strategies for educators. ERIC Report.

Hancock, J. (Ed.). (1999). *Teaching literacy using information technology*. Carlton South: Australian Literacy Educators' Association.

Haq, K., Longnecker, N., & Hickey, R. (1999). Judging the effectiveness of an Internet-based primary science and agriculture educational package. *Investigating, 15*(2), 14–18.

Harper, B. et al. (2000). *The online experience: the state of Australian online education and training practices*. NCVER: Leabrook, South Australia.

Hixson, S., & Schrock, K. (1999). *Developing Web pages for school and classroom*. Cheltanham, Victoria: Hawker Brownlow Education.

Imel, S. (1996). *Distance education: trends and issues alerts*. Columbus, OH: ERIC Clearing-house on Adult, Career and Vocational Education.

Jacob, G., & Rogers, C. (1997). Remote teaching with digital video: a trans-national experience. *British Journal of Educational Technology, 28*(4), 292–304.

Kangas, K., & Puhakainen, J. (2000). Web-based seminar work. In A. Aggarwal (Ed.), *Web-based learning and teaching technologies: opportunities and challenges* (pp. 347–359). Hershey, PA: Idea Group Publishing.

Khan, B. H. (1997). *Web based instruction*. Educational Technology Publication: USA.

Latta, G. F. (1996). The virtual university: creating an emergent reality. ERIC Technical Report.

Lawton, S., & Barnes, R. (1998). Developing distance learning courses in a traditional university. *Quality Assurance in Education, 6*(2), 106–111.

Leidner, D. E., & Jarvenpaa, S. L. (1993). The information age confronts education: case studies on electronic classrooms. *Information Systems Research, 4*(1), 24–54.

Levin, B. (1998). Distance learning: technology and choices. Office Institutional Research, Blue Ridge Community College, Weyerss Cave, VA.

Moore, M. G., & Cozine, G. T. (2000). Web-based xommunications, the Internet and distance education. American Center for the Study of Distance Education.

National Computer Board. (1992). A vision of an intelligent island: the IT2000 report. Singapore National Computer Board.

National University of Singapore. (2000). Annual report. Singapore: The University.

Nayang Polytechnic. (1999–2000). Annual report. Singapore: The Polytechnic.

Nayang Technological University. (1998–2000). Annual report. Singapore: The University.

Ngee Ann Polytechnic. (1999–2000). Annual report. Singapore.

Palvia, S. C., & Tung, L. L. (1999). Internet use and issues in Singapore and USA: a comparative study. In F. Tan, P. S. Corbett, & Y. Y. Wong. *Information technology diffusion in the Asia Pacific: perspectives on policy, electronic commerce and education* (pp. 163–173). Hershey, PA: Idea Group Publishing.

Porter, L. R. (1997). *Creating the virtual classroom: distance learning with the Internet.* New York: John Wiley.

Rice, R. E. (1984). *The new media: communication, research and technology.* Beverly Hills, CA: Sage.

Schofield, K., Walsh, A., & Melville, B. (2000). *Online learning and the new VET practitioner.* Sydney: UTS Centre for Vocational Education and Training.

Schoolsnet Australia. (2000). Teachers and the Internet. North Melbourne, Victoria.

Singapore Department of Statistics. (2000). Census of population 2000. Changing Education Profile. Advanced data release No. 1.

Singapore IT usage survey. (1992–1994). Singapore: National Computer Board.

Singapore Polytechnic. (1999–2000). Annual report. Singapore.

Tan, F., Corbett, P. S., & Wong, Y. Y. (1999). *Information technology diffusion in the Asia Pacific: perspectives on policy, electronic commerce and education.* Hershey, PA: Idea Group Publishing.

Taylor, J. (2001). Fifth generation distance education. Higher Education Series, Report 40. Canberra: Department of Education, Training and Youth Affairs.

Taylor, J., Kemp, J., & Burgess, J. (1993). Mixed-mode approaches to industry training: staff attitudes and cost effectiveness. Report to the Department of Employment, Education and Training's Evaluations and Investigations Program, Canberra.

Web-Based Education Commission. (2000). The power of the Internet for learning: moving from promise to practice. Report of the Web-based Education Commission to the President and Congress of the United States.

Webster, J., & Hackley, P. (1997). Teaching effectiveness in technology-mediated distance learning. *Academy of Management Journal, 40*(5), 1282–1309.

Wong, S. H. (1992). Exploring information technology: a case study of Singapore. *World Development, 20*(12), 18–20.

Wong, Y. Y. (1999). Exploring the Internet for teaching social studies. In M. Waas (Ed.), *Enhancing learning: Vol. 1, Challenge of integrating thinking and information technology into the curriculum* (pp. 162–169). Singapore: Educational Research Association.

Wong, Y. Y., & Hsui, V. (1998). Using email to enhance teaching across the curriculum. Paper presented at the Educational Research Association 1998 Annual Conference, Parkroyal Hotel, Singapore, 23–25 November.

Wong, Y. Y., & Hsui, Y. V. (1999). Using email to enhance teaching across the curriculum. In M. Waas (Ed.), *Enhancing learning: Vol. 1, Challenge of integrating thinking and information technology into the curriculum* (pp. 154–161). Singapore: Educational Research Association.

Wong, Y. Y., & Yan, V. H. (1999). Using the Internet to enhance cross-curriculum learning. *Teaching and Learning (Singapore), 20*(1), 79–88.

WEBSITE REFERENCE

A guide to Singapore Official Statistics. http://www.Singstat.gov.sg.

Ministry of Education. Launch of Masterplan for IT in Education, 28 April 1997, http://www.moe.edu.sg.

Nanyang Technological University. http://www.ntu.edu.sg.

National University of Singapore. http://www. nus.edu.sg.

Singapore Government Directory. http://www.gov.sg.

Singapore Polytechnic. http://www.sp.edu.sg.

Temasek Polytechnic. http://www.tp.edu.sg.

Chapter XXII

Relevant Issues for the Design of a Successful Web-Based Instructional System: MODASPECTRA

Salvatore Valenti
Universitá di Ancona, Italy

Maurizio Panti
Universitá di Ancona, Italy

Tommaso Leo
Universitá di Ancona, Italy

ABSTRACT

Instructional systems are aimed to support and partially automate the instructional process on a subject domain, ranging from a simple lecture to a whole degree. The interest in designing Web-based Instructional Systems (WbIS) needs no more to be outlined. In the last few years, there has been a huge diffusion of such an approach to support and partially automate the instructional process. The term Instructional Systems Design (ISD) refers to the process of instructional program development from start to finish. Many models exist for use by different levels of instructional designers and for different instructional purposes: what is missing in the current literature is to show how these models could be used to implement "real-life" examples of Instructional Systems. This chapter is aimed to fill this gap, by discussing each phase of the ISD with respect to the implementation of a WbIS for training Specialists in Motor Disability Assessment (MODASPECTRA). The project ended in the implementation of a successful WbIS; in fact, the Dublin School of Physiotherapy received approval from the University College Dublin, Ireland, to offer one of the courses belonging to the MODASPECTRA educational package as a distance learning certificate course from the coming academic year. The course has been renamed to "Outcome Assessment in Motor Disability." Directed mainly at physiotherapists throughout Ireland and Europe, the course consists of standardized and validated measures to be used before and after treatment to evaluate the effectiveness of the intervention. It could also be relevant to the practice of other health professionals. Therefore, we strongly believe that this chapter may be of great interest for any Institution willing to start its own effort in building WbIS.

INTRODUCTION

Instructional systems are aimed to support and partially automate the instructional process on a subject domain, ranging from a simple lecture to a whole degree. Nowadays, instructional systems make extensive use of network technologies, mainly the Internet and the World Wide Web, because of their flexibility and reusability. Aggarwal and Bento (2000) classified instructional systems in four categories according to the time and place dimensions of their teaching environments. The focus in this chapter is on the discussion of a Type IV learning environment, where:

> *...education and human contact are available any time from any place. Students can learn from home, office or wherever they are, by accessing Web-based lectures, tutorials, materials, and books, completing and submitting Web-based assignments, exercises and research, interacting in Web-based forums and taking Web-based quizzes and exams (Aggarwal & Bento, 2000, p. 5).*

Usually, such systems are referenced in literature as Web-based instructional systems (WbIS). The interest in designing WbIS needs no more to be outlined. In the last few years, there has been a huge diffusion of such an approach to support and partially automate the instructional process. The claim that more than 2000 institutions in 80 countries have been adopting, over the years, WebCT (http://www.Webct.com/), one of the most widely used Web-based authoring/delivery system, may be interpreted as an indicator of the widespread interest in WbIS.

Instructional Systems Design (ISD) refers to the process of instructional program development from start to finish. ISD may be simply stated as the process providing a means for sound decision making to determine the "who, what, when, where, why and how" of education and training. The concept of a systems approach to education is based on obtaining an overall view of the instructional process (Clark, 2000).

The most widely applied instructional design theory is largely based on the work of Gagné and his associates (1965) at Florida State University. This approach assumes a cumulative organization of learning events based on prerequisite relationships among learner behaviors:

> *Gagné's original work was based on the experimental learning psychology of the time, including paired associated learning, serial learning, operant conditioning, concept learning and gestalt problem solving. Recent versions of his*

work (Gagné, 1985) have incorporated ideas from cognitive psychology (Merril et al., 1991).

Gustafson and Branch (1997) stated that instructional development models are almost as numerous as the practitioners of instructional development. Many are unnamed, and many are created daily. It is not unusual for educators to design models for their own use with their own class material in their own classes. Thus, for instance, the Gagné and Briggs (1992), the Dick and Carey (1990), the Gerlach and Ely (1980), and the Hannafin and Peck (1988) models may be cited among the most renown examples of first-generation ISD models (Merril, 1991). The discussion of those models and a review of their characteristics are outside the purpose of this chapter. The interested reader may consult the works by Andrews and Goodson (1980), Edmonds et al. (1994), and Gustafson and Branch (1997) to obtain conceptual frameworks and procedures for comparing such models. However, first-generation ISD models have been grounded on a set of beliefs that, when implemented, include Analysis, Design, Development, Implementation, and Evaluation, as summarized in Figure 1.

Highlighted in Figure 1 is the importance of evaluation and feedback throughout the entire program. It also stresses the importance of gathering and distributing information in each of the five phases and shows that the instructional design process is not a static (waterfall) model, but an iterative flow of activities (dynamic or spiral). The five phases are ongoing activities that continue throughout the life of an instructional system. The phases listed in Figure 1 do not end once the system is implemented. They are continually repeated on a regular basis to see if further improvements can be made (Clark, 2000).

In this chapter, each phase will be discussed by referring to a case study: the MODASPECTRA (MOtor Disability Assessment SPEcialists' TRAining) system. The project was aimed at developing quality teaching and training of postgraduate specialists in Motor Disability Assessment (MDA). The specialists targeted came from a background of physiatry, bioengineering, or physical therapy. The aim was to offer to the European professionals involved in MDA a means for upgrading their skills in a lifelong learning (LLL) context in the line of good practice in dissemination and standardization. The project's goals included the implementation of a WbIS usable by students, according to suitable tutoring pathways and schedules, and assisted by online evaluation during the learning. The project

Figure 1: Five General Phases of Instructional Systems Design

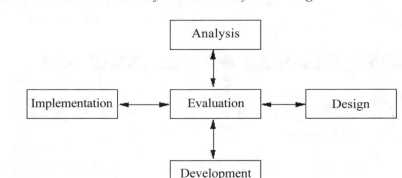

also was aimed to implement databases of context-based experiences provided by recognized practitioners (Valenti et al., 2002).

ANALYSIS

The analysis process represents the foundation for all other phases of ISD. Although designers agree that analysis is the most important phase, many people tend to underestimate its role inside the entire development process. Thus, analysis is often seen as a waste of time and money. As research in software engineering has taught the scientific community, the analysis phase is essential, because any mistakes in it are carried forward and may threaten the whole design process. As an instance of this well-known issue, the relative costs to repair traditional software in relationship to the life cycle stage are listed in Table 1.

The analysis phase may include specific research techniques such as needs, audience, and task analysis.

Therefore, analysis is aimed to determine the need for instruction, what factors led to the instructional need, and what past experiences indicate that the instruction being planned can effectively meet this need. Furthermore, the audience targeted by the instructional system must be analyzed. This requires gaining a better understanding of the distance learners and of their needs, taking into account factors as cultural background, age, past experiences, and educational level. Finally, the analysis phase is aimed at establishing the instructional goals and objectives, based on the results obtained in the earlier steps of this phase (needs for instruction and audience analysis).

In the early stage of the MODASPECTRA project, the need for instruction in the field of Motor Disability Assessment (MODASPECTRA, 1998) and a wide analysis of the user requirements was conducted (MODASPECTRA, 1999a). At the end of these phases, the following functional specifications were devised:
1.   The didactic courses composing the degree
2.   The student evaluation tools and procedures
3.   The authoring tools to be used to design the learning material
4.   The media communication approaches to be adopted
5.   The quality assurance procedures for the degree

Table 1: Relative Effort to Repair Traditional Software in Relationship to the Life Cycle Stage

Stage	Relative Cost of Repair
Analysis	0.1 – 0.2
Design	0.5
Implementation	1
Test	2 – 5
Operation & Maintenance	20

Note. Adapted from Davis, A. M. (1990). Software requirements. Englewood Cliffs, NJ: Prentice Hall

Obviously, it is impossible to present in this context the full range of functional specifications obtained. The interested reader may consult the literature (MODASPECTRA, 1999b). Therefore, in this section, the discussion will be limited to the functional requirements for course content, for the delivery platform and for the authoring tools.

Functional Specifications for Course Content

Movement analysis and its clinical use cover a wide spectrum of methods, techniques, and applications. For a course aimed to provide a postgraduate degree, it was impossible to deal with all relevant aspects of movement analysis. Thus, the consortium had to face the challenge of limiting the scope of course contents in a way that was optimally relevant, complete, and consistent for a student wishing to improve skills in clinical movement analysis.

Over the last decade, the interest for clinical application of movement analysis has grown considerably, and movement analysis instrumentation has gradually found its way from the biomedical research laboratories into the clinics. Nevertheless, it is important to be aware that clinical use of movement analysis is still in an early stage of development. Reliable equipment is available, but methods for applying such equipment in real clinical protocols are still under development. Furthermore, there are many ideas and different opinions about what should be measured, how it should be done, and how data should be interpreted. At the beginning of the project, there was no generally accepted definition of Movement Analysis and Clinical Movement Analysis. After considerable discussion, an agreement was reached on the following definition of Movement Analysis: "The set of methods and techniques for the scientific description of human movement. This scientific description is obtained using instrumentation that provides records of aspects of the movement under study" (MODASPECTRA, 1999b). A simple model of the current clinical treatment approach, which will be used to identify processes and their objectives, where movement analysis can play a material role, is depicted in Figure 2.

A patient with a health problem comes to the clinical institute for treatment. Sometime later, when the treatment is completed and the health problem is alleviated, the patient leaves the institute. It is the task of the clinician to select the most suitable treatment for the patient with his individual pattern of pathology. Thus, a reliable patient assessment is needed. This assessment generally comprises an anamnesis, a clinical investigation, and additional special

Figure 2: A Simple Model to Describe the Role of Movement Analysis in the Clinical Process

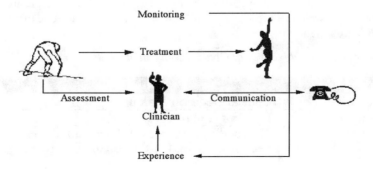

investigations if desired (for instance, x-rays). The clinician interprets the information collected via the assessment based on knowledge and experience and selects a treatment. Movement analysis techniques are potentially useful in such a special investigation, because they may reveal information that is not accessible with the naked eye and may provide information that is more reliable than clinical observation alone. During the treatment, the clinician monitors the patient. He observes and records the response of the patient to the treatment, watches for unwanted side effects, and keeps track of progress. This activity enables the clinician to learn from each individual case. Each patient contributes to enhance the clinician's experience and skills. This monitoring process can be conducted in a rigorous manner as clinical research or it can take place more casually in the form of clinical follow-up. Movement analysis provides objective and quantitative data that are essential in the monitoring process. Only fairly recently was it recognized that movement analysis can play a role in patient treatment where telemedicine techniques apply. Objective movement analysis data unambiguously describes the patient's impaired movement pattern. Because such objective data are independent form the observer, a clinician can describe the movement pattern of patient to a remote party and discuss the problems and solutions, without suffering the limitations of verbal descriptions. In this way, it becomes possible to consult specialist expertise for a given patient. This type of consultation can significantly improve local clinical decision making, mainly in the case of new forms of treatment and of rare disorders. Therefore, movement analysis has an important role in the communication processs and in enabling new teleconsultation and second-opinion services.

According to the above discussion, clinical movement analysis can be defined in terms of processes and objectives, as shown in Table 2.

Movement analysis techniques and methods alone are not sufficient for any application that materially affects patient treatment. Patient data obtained using traditional clinical examination are also required. Clinical measurement is the process of collection and registration of information regarding impairments, disabilities, and participation problems in order to assess, monitor, or communicate (MODASPECTRA, 1999b).

Thus, clinical movement analysis is defined as "the process using movement analysis and clinical measurement that materially affects patient treatment through patient assessment, treatment monitoring and communication." The MODASPECTRA concept of clinical movement analysis is simple: the clinician has a toolkit (Toolkit Paradigm) at his disposal containing tools for movement analysis and clinical measurement. Depending on the problem encountered, the most appropriate tools are chosen to solve the problem. This paradigm applies for students too. MODASPECTRA introduces the toolkit to the students to assist them in the assessment, monitoring, and communication processes for the treatment of human movement disorders. Furthermore, the knowledge and skills needed to productively use the toolkit are taught.

Table 2: Processes and Objectives of Clinical Movement Analysis

Process	Objective
Assessment	Clinical Decision Making
Monitoring	Learning and research
Communication	Telemedicine services, Tele-consultation Second opinion, On-the-job medical training

The toolkit paradigm affects the content design and influences the instructional design, as far as the organization of the courses within the degree. The content design was intended to provide strategic knowledge and skills aimed at enabling physiatrists, physical therapists, and bioengineers to apply movement analysis methods and tools in the clinical processes of patient assessment, treatment monitoring, and communication. This led to classify the courses as homogenization courses and common courses (Table 3).

Homogenization courses are meant to provide basic knowledge to professionals having different backgrounds in order to allow them to attend in a homogeneous manner the common courses.

The common courses extensively discuss movement analysis and clinical measurement. The courses "Instrumented measurement for clinical movement analysis" and "Clinical measurement for clinical movement analysis" belong to the area of "Fundamentals of measurement" and describe state-of-the-art methods and techniques and methodological aspects, such as their validity and reliability. Because not all existing methods and techniques can be addressed in the courses, a limited but practically relevant set of measurement tools are presented to the students. The selection of the techniques discussed is guided by the requirements that appeared in the user needs analysis (MODASPECTRA, 1999a). The users from a clinical background expressed the view that the courses' content should be oriented toward practical application.

The course "Clinical applications of clinical movement analysis" presents practical clinically useful examples of the use of movement analysis and clinical measurement that were introduced in the courses belonging to the area of "Fundamentals of Measurement." The material presented in the above-mentioned courses would enable the student to properly apply the measurement techniques needed for a given clinical problem using the presented protocols. Anyway, the student will not be able to interpret the resulting data. This requires a substantial body of background knowledge that will include knowledge about normal movement patterns, important abnormalities, compensation and adaptation mechanisms, etc. These issues are covered by the course "Fundamentals of normal and pathological movement." Finally, the course "Telematics for clinical movement analysis" addresses the use of telematics for the rehabilitation process.

To attain the degree, a pathway composed of eight courses is drawn: five common courses that should be attended by all the students, and three out of six homogenisation courses that will be selected according to the previous academic career of the learners (Table 3).

Table 3: Didactic Offer of the MODASPECTRA Degree

Category	Name
Common courses	Telematics for Clinical Movement Analysis Fundamentals of normal and pathological movement Instrumented measurement for clinical movement analysis Clinical measurement for clinical movement analysis Clinical applications of clinical movement analysis
Homogenisation courses for Medical Doctors and Physical Therapists	Basic Biomechanics Fundamentals of measurements and signal processing Basic Informatics
Homogenisation courses for Bioengineers	Functional Anatomical Basis of Motor System Basic Physiology Fundamentals of Pathology and Procedures for Interaction with Patients (to be implemented during the final exploitation phase of the project)

Functional Requirements for Delivery Platform and Authoring Tools

The delivery of the material is Web-based, except for the final examination that will be performed face-to-face according to the regulations for accreditation enacted by the interested parties and to the requirements imposed by the National legislations.

The delivery environment is WebCT. This choice was based on the technical and managerial motivations performed by the Centre for Curriculum, Transfer and Technology (http://www.c2t2.ca). In synthesis, the technical arguments supporting the choice of WebCT are that the environment has all the relevant features needed for the delivery of the MODASPECTRA material, it is extensively tested according to its large adoption, it has a good level of reliability, and it is friendly and easy to use. The managerial arguments have been particularly important in such a choice. First, it appeared not appropriate to design and implement a specific delivery environment in the case of MODASPECTRA. In fact, it was a two-year project focused on producing quality learning material in a domain having multidisciplinary requirements with fragmented knowledge. The main scientific objective was to produce "quality teaching" in the domain. The target of not wasting resources could have been nullified by the choice of a commercial delivery environment, should the costs for obtaining the licenses be high. In the case of WebCT, the costs were linked to the number of actually enrolled students; thus, the whole operation of the project has been free of costs.

The architecture adopted is shown in Figure 3.

The WebCT interface is used by the students for the visualization of the learning material and by back-office for managing the student career information.

It is universally agreed that no constraints should be placed on the development environment in order to guarantee a real openness of the learning technology system. This specification has been strictly respected in MODASPECTRA, so that the authors did not have any specification on the authoring tools to use. This had the limiting side effect that

Figure 3: Architecture of the MODASPECTRA System

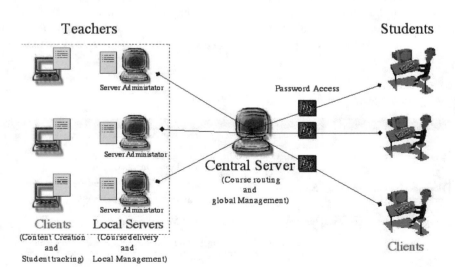

most of the material developed is not particularly sophisticated from the point of view of attractiveness. On the other hand, this solution eliminated any kind of organizational and economic constraint for the authors, as for instance, appointment of multimedia professional developers, purchase of smart authoring tools, etc.

DESIGN

The design phase uses the outputs from the analysis to plan a strategy for developing the instruction. During this phase, it must be outlined how to reach the instructional goals determined by the analysis phase, and the instructional foundation must be expanded.

The design phase involves the following:

1. The identification of the granularity level of the individual chunks of instruction
2. The preparation of their objectives, keeping in account the pedagogical model, the instructional design, and the possibility of indexing the learning material for reuse
3. The development of assessment techniques and tasks
4. The planning of the project evaluation activities

The design phase may include writing a description of the target population, conducting a learning analysis, writing objectives and test items, and sequencing the instruction.

In this section, the approaches adopted for the organization of the learning material, for the selection of the pedagogical model, and of the instructional design approach and for the reuse of content will be discussed.

Organization of Content

According to emerging European standards (CEN/ISSS, 2000) the organization of content within a learning technology system may be described using four levels, as shown in Table 4.

Thus, courses can be decomposed in different ways, depending on the minimum level of granularity adopted. The minimum level of granularity selected for the content of the MODASPECTRA material is content unit. A content unit represents a piece of information not divisible anymore without losing its economic or didactic significance from the user's point of view, e.g., a number of HTML pages treating a specific and self-contained set of information.

Table 4: Organization of Learning Material as Proposed by CEN/ISSS

Level	Content
0 - Atoms	Atoms representing raw media data, e.g. text, video, audio or images.
1 - Content Units	Self contained learning resources not sensibly divisible.
2 - Composite Units	Groupings of content units augmented with uniform navigation aids within the Learning Technology System
3 - Courses	They are the largest level of granularity and represent composite learning experiences with a wider temporal horizon often connected with accreditation.

Composite units represent a way of grouping content units together through an index page. With the help of composite units, it is possible to provide a uniform navigation within the learning technology system on the one side, and to allow the usage of a content unit in more than one arrangement on the other side. Composite units are similar to a table of contents in a book and may be dynamic in terms of adding or removing entries at any time. This allows high reusability and modularity within a learning technology system and gives a clear added value for its users (CEN/ISSS, 2000).

The workload of each course, composed of about 10 composite units, lies between 80–120 hours. Each course is meant to be self-contained from the point of view of the instructional design, even if logically related to the others. A specific entry test for each course is devised to provide the learner with a personalized pathway within the degree. The entry test will explore the existing competence of the learner on the topics addressed by the composite units of the course.

Links to other courses are indicated in an explicit manner, even if no direct access is allowed, according to administrative and economic requirements.

A personal interaction with the tutor or teacher is planned for the final examination of each course.

In the case of learners attending the whole degree, a further workload involving 200–250 hours was considered for the final dissertation needed to obtain the award granted by the degree.

The number of credits for each course has been defined according to the European Credit Transfer System (ECTS, 1998). Thus, the MODASPECTRA degree constitutes a workload and provides a number of credits corresponding to that of a postdegree master course in the context of ECTS.

Pedagogical Model and Instructional Design

Mason (1998) proposed a simple framework for classifying "the very wide range of exiting online courses." According to such a framework, three basic models of online education have been identified:

- Content + Support Model

    Here, a relatively static body of content (e.g., a Web package) provides the core of the course and is supplemented by tutorial support. The level of online interaction is low (typically no more than 20% of the students' time). This model is most akin to traditional teaching and is, currently, the most prevalent in use.

- Wrap-around Model

    Here, the course materials are wrapped by activities, online discussions, etc. Mason refers to this as the 50/50 model, as online interactions and discussions occupy roughly half of the students' time, while the predetermined content occupies the other half. In Mason's words:

    ...this model tends to favour a resource-based approach to learning, giving more freedom and responsibility to the students to interpret the course for themselves. The tutor's or teacher's role is also more extensive than that in the first model, because less of the course is pre-determined and more is created each time the course is delivered, through the discussions and activities (1998, p.).

- Integrated Model

    This is a resource-based model in which the course is defined by collaborative activities, discussions, and joint assignments. The course contents are dynamic and are determined largely by individual needs and group activities. Resources are contributed by participants or tutors as the course develops.

The general pedagogic philosophy followed by MODASPECTRA with respect to the use and development of its electronic learning environment, refers to the Content + Support and to the Wrap-around Models defined in Mason's taxonomy.

According to Norman (1993), learning occurs through the phases of accretion, tuning, and restructuring. In accretion, learning takes place by means of accumulation of new information. Real-world situations are evaluated and matched with some appropriate set of schemata, representations for the current situation are formed, and the newly acquired knowledge is stored into long-term memory. The newly created schema of knowledge is an instantiation of the previously existing one, changed only in the values of the variables that are stored in the schema (the relationships between such variables still holding the same). In tuning, learning occurs when an existing schema is served as the base for the development of new ones by minor changes. This mode of learning is restricted to the cases where the basic relational structure of the schema remains unchanged. Through practice or consistent use of schemata, they are tuned or finely adjusted to meet specific task demands or adapted to particular knowledge domains or contexts. However, if the only learning processes were memory accretion and tuning, one could never increase the number of conceptual categories over those initially given. Thus, it is essential that new schemata be created. In restructuring, learning occurs when existing memory structures (networks of schemata) are not adequate to account for new knowledge, and new structures are created. New structures are created by erecting new schemata specifically designed for the troublesome information or by modifying (tuning) old ones.

The learning objectives that ensure direct matching with each of the learning phases discussed above are static knowledge, skills, and strategic knowledge. Concepts, facts, principles, and relations are usually labeled as static knowledge. Ryle (1949) stated that static knowledge is knowing that something exists. There is little, if any, understanding associated with static knowledge.

Knowing how to apply the static knowledge is generally named "skill." Many researchers use this term as a synonym for procedural knowledge. As opposed to knowing "what," procedural knowledge is knowing "how." Finally, strategic knowledge consists of the knowledge of learning strategies and activities to invoke in order to perform a task. Thus, strategic knowledge is the knowledge needed to apply concepts, facts, principles, relations, and skills and to reason and elaborate on the knowledge involved (Johnasen, 2000).

Accretion allows creating static knowledge that can be accumulated via learning by being told. Tuning allows creating skills and occurs via learning by doing, while restructuring, which fosters the creation of strategic knowledge, can be obtained via learning by communicating.

Learning by being told can be obtained via expository text, graphics, and video material; learning by doing can be obtained through self-assessment, homework assignments, and exercises; and learning by communicating with the tutors and the other students occurs by means of discussion groups, group work, and collaborative assignments.

Traditional university teaching methods have been followed, at first glance, with respect to the information content of the largest part of the courses. Innovation in MODASPECTRA relies mainly in the training part of the courses, where "learning by doing" has been largely substituted by "learning by seeing and remotely doing" under the direction of experienced professionals discussing in a remote site a number of real cases and working situations. The consequences of using telematics tools on the information content and on the way of delivery of the different modules will thus be explored.

In principle, every composite unit refers to all three phases and types of learning products established: static knowledge, skills, and strategic knowledge. This means that the composite units consist of the expository texts (needed for the accretion phase) and of the exercises the students have to perform outside the system environment (required for the tuning phase) as well as the online discussions that are to take place in the restructuring phase.

The level of content of each composite unit has been defined according to Bloom's taxonomy (Bloom, 1956). For the composite units belonging to the common courses, the level of content was deemed to evaluate. On the other hand, the synthesis level was deemed quite universally appropriate for the composite units belonging to the homogenization courses, except for those involving basic skills learning, where the evaluation level was assigned. At the content unit level, not necessarily every phase is addressed; thus, it may solely aim at the transfer of static knowledge. Each composite unit has been designed keeping in mind the following distribution of workload: no less than two hours should be spent online, in activities of accretion and restructuring (half an hour is for accretion). In such a context, the simplicity of the language and the effectiveness in exploiting the multimedia potential is essential. Residual time must be spent on tuning activities. Self-assessment must be accomplished during this slice of time too. Self-assessment and feedback are meant to be done via tests to be answered online, via homework composed by practice, or exercises according to the topics discussed by each composite unit and via communication with the teacher through managed discussion lists. For such a purpose, the teacher will extract from the learning material offered a certain number of key topics organized in "Questions of the week," and the students will be asked to discuss them within a prescribed time interval.

The interaction of the teacher with the students is pursued through personal questions and answers via email, by discussion lists, and via videoconferences at agreed meeting times. Furthermore, a directory of experts that may be consulted by the student with a preset schedule of availability has been defined. This provides the learners with the unique opportunity of exploiting the advice of leading experts "everywhere" resident. It has to be underlined that without a Web-based approach, such experts would be inaccessible or reachable by traveling to their premises at extremely high time and money costs.

It is worth mentioning that according to the particular nature of strategic knowledge and skills to be learned in the degree, practice and exercises have been mostly planned and organized according to a minimum threshold criterion. This is due to the fact that most clinical test as, for instance the "Fugl Mayer" test for stroke assessment, cannot be mastered by learning to apply its individual parts. Therefore, the students must gain ability in administering the whole test at an acceptable level of correctness or fail in the learning process.

Remedial teaching has been planned at the level of content unit. At this point, remedial teaching occurs mainly through repetition of specific parts of the learning material and interaction with the tutor. This is a rather primitive way of providing remedial teaching and will be revised as the experience of the authors in the distance learning field increases, during the operation phase of the project.

For a more in-depth discussion of the instructional design approach, the interested reader may consult Valenti et al. (2002) and MODASPECTRA (2001a).

The Knowledge Pool

Metadata represent the key to resource discovery, to effective use of resources, and to interoperability across protocol domains. According to the IEEE Learning Technology Standards Committee, metadata is information about an object, be it physical or digital. Thus, "digital repositories may hold actual assets or the metadata that describe assets—although, strictly speaking, metadata can be viewed as an asset particularly as new value chains are developed in the information economy" (IMS, 2001). Metadata are useful to:

- Enable learners or instructors to search, evaluate, acquire, and use learning objects
- Enable sharing and exchanging of learning objects across any technology-supported learning system
- Enable developing learning objects in units that can be combined and decomposed in meaningful ways
- Enable computer agents to automatically and dynamically compose personalized lessons for an individual learner
- Complement the direct work on standards that are focused on enabling multiple learning objects to work together within an open, distributed, learning environment
- Enable documenting and recognizing the completion of existing or new learning and performance objectives associated with objects
- Enable a strong and growing economy for learning objects that supports and sustains all forms of distribution: nonprofit, not-for-profit, and for-profit
- Enable education, training, and learning organizations, including government, public, and private, to express educational content and performance standards in a standardized format that is independent of the content
- Provide researchers with standards that support collecting and sharing comparable data concerning the applicability and effectiveness of learning objects
- Define a standard that is simple yet extensible to multiple domains and jurisdictions so as to be most easily and broadly adopted and applied
- Support necessary security and authentication for the distribution and use of learning objects

The structure of metadata inside MODASPECTRA has been chosen coincident with the one proposed by IEEE (IEEE-LOM, 1999). Other standardization initiatives are converging on the same model, as for instance, ARIADNE (http://www.ariadne-eu.org) and PROMETEUS (http://www.prometeus.org/). Metadata contain all the instructional characters of every content unit, composite unit, and course, along with complete information on their physical location.

In our design approach (Valenti et al., 2002a), a content unit augmented with metadata and with the set of related documents as quizzes, remedial teaching, and glossary, constitutes a physical content unit. Thus, physical content units represent the assets of the

MODASPECTRA project and are stored in a repository with a location addressed by the metadata. Because of the chosen level of granularity and of the structure of the content units, the metadata database represents the knowledge pool (KP) of MODASPECTRA. In fact, the description of the content units included in the metadata covers all their instructional characters and provides complete localization information. The metadata database is easily accessible by the different potential users in the way corresponding to the privileges they have. At the moment, the users of the KP are the authors, the editors, the editor-in-chief, and the system administrators.

The shift from the whole degree perspective adopted in the earlier stages of the project to the possibility of delivering single courses in a LLL context added constraints to the problem and suggested reducing the granularity of the contents. This is in line with the specifications of an easy and limited-cost maintenance of the learning resources, with their possible reuse in different learning contexts, and with the possibly rapid evolution of the domain knowledge in specific aspects. In fact, we expect that the domain knowledge evolution in the next few years will affect specific topics, which, being managed as content units, do not require updating of the entire composite unit containing them. This implies the best reuse of the existing material and an easy pipelining of the updated learning resources. The updated composite units will be assembled with the new content units properly positioned among the older ones. This represents a matter of integration via the proper use of the relevant metadata.

DEVELOPMENT

The development phase builds on the results obtained by the analysis and by the design phases. The main purposes of the development phase are the generation of the lesson plans and the construction of the learning material. Thus, the instructional material, along with all the media to be used in the instruction and any supporting documentation, has been developed.

Three main classes of procedures have been defined and followed in the development of the system:

- Authoring procedures, dealing with content creation and learning material construction
- Teaching procedures, to guarantee proper monitoring and support and assistance to the learning process
- Didactic and administrative procedures

Authoring Procedures

The stakeholders of the authoring procedures are the editor-in-chief, the editors, and the authors.

The editors are appointed by the faculty and have the responsibility of organizing courses. Thus, each editor may be in charge of one or more courses and is responsible for defining their instructional design, and for organizing their structure in term of composite units. Each editor appoints one or more authors to produce the composite units. Finally, the editors are in charge of verifying the learning material produced by the authors and of authorizing its storage in the database of contents.

The editor-in-chief manages the validation of the learning material and takes care of the relationships with the faculty in order to decide the acceptance of a course and its activation within the degree.

The authors are in charge of producing the contents of one or more composite units of a course, together with the relative assessment procedures, remedial teaching, glossary, and metadata. They have to respect constraints in the time and in the formats allowed for producing the learning material. They interact with the editor during the verification of the produced material. Authors must define the instructional design of the assigned composite and content units. The instructional design has to be coherent with the learning objectives of the course as defined by the editor and has to be defined according to the principia discussed in the section of this chapter entitled "Pedagogical Model and Instructional Design."

Teaching Procedures

The teaching procedures include discussion management, assessment, and tutoring.

The teacher/tutor activates specific bulletin boards in order to foster discussion with the students on specific topics via "Questions of the week." The discussion lists are open for contributions during limited time slots. The teacher interacts asynchronously with the students by answering their questions and by suggesting some correction on the items under discussion. The schedule of the discussions is communicated to the students by means of the calendar of course events provided by the delivery platform. At the end of the time allotted for the discussion, the teacher summarizes any obtained results and includes the summary in an addendum that will be used for upgrading the learning material at suitable times.

Personal communication between teachers and students is performed using the internal email system of the delivery platform.

The discussion tools are used mainly during the restructuring phase of learning and provide the student with significant feedback on the presented concepts.

The assessment occurs by means of a discussion with the teacher, performed face-to-face or by videoconference. In this latter case, the presence of the tutor at the student site is needed in order to guarantee the transparency of the assessment. The assessment policy requires the verification of the achievement of the learning objectives at the desired level of competence.

A final dissertation has to be produced by the students attending to the whole degree, in order to demonstrate their capability to face specific MDA issues at the evaluation level of Bloom's taxonomy. Students should also be able to demonstrate the awareness of the multidisciplinary character of MDA.

The tutors have the responsibility of enforcing the effectiveness of the learning path of groups of students. They are committed in monitoring such paths and assisting the students in overcoming educational and technical obstacles. The tutors interact with the students face-to-face, by email, and by videoconference.

Didactic/Administrative Procedures

The didactic/administrative procedures involve the activities of student enrollment, faculty operation, and back-office operation.

Students intending to enroll to the whole degree or to one or more courses in a LLL perspective must contact the back office and provide their curriculum vitae. A section

386 Valenti, Panti & Leo

containing explanatory pages, compliant with the administrative office specifications, and a form to be filled online by the applicant learner has been included in the MODASPECTRA server. Once submitted, the form is resent to the applicant for verification, modified if needed, and finally confirmed. At this point, the learner will be inserted in a student database and will be recognized by the administrative office and by the teachers. Once the enrollment is finalized, the learner is allowed to interact with the teachers for performing the placement assessment and for receiving the assignment of the composite units corresponding to his/her entry level.

The faculty define the award policies from the didactic and managerial points of view. They appoint the editor-in-chief and provide him/her with the specifications for the quality of the courses and of the composite units. The faculty appoint the editors, the teachers, and the tutors.

The faculty authorize the activation of the courses, based on the results of the validation provided by the editor-in-chief. The faculty manage the authorization of the learning material via properly defined procedures. The quality of these procedures is guaranteed by the traceability of the decisions taken in this respect by the faculty and communicated to the editor-in-chief. The communication is actually performed by email. The trace mechanism is based on the daily backup of the incoming messages. Possible improvements of the communication traceability depend on the specific implementation enacted by the faculty that will exploit the results of the project.

Among the operations performed by the back office, it is worth mentioning the following:
1. The communication of the appointments to the editors, to the teachers, and to the tutors
2. The processing of the registration requests from the learners and the evaluation of the adequacy of their curriculum for the requested courses
3. The communication of the acceptance to the course(s) and of their plan and scheduling to the learners
4. The verification of the payment of course fees

Furthermore, the back office is in charge of communicating the list of the students attending a course to the teachers/tutors and of managing the storage of the results attained by the students.

IMPLEMENTATION AND EVALUATION

The implementation phase refers to the actual delivery of the instruction, should it be classroom-, lab-, or computer-based. The purpose of this phase is the effective and efficient delivery of instruction. This phase must promote the students' understanding of material, support the students' mastery of objectives, and ensure the students' transfer of knowledge from the instructional setting to the job.

The implementation phase was conducted by identifying a population of learners selected according to the criteria that will be discussed in the part of this section devoted to the evaluation. From the technical point of view, and according to the results of the preliminary verification (MODASPECTRA, 2001b), the following cautions were taken:
• The MODASPECTRA site was duplicated at the premises of the Dutch partner to reduce times and costs of connection.

- A hybrid solution was adopted for the delivery of courses involving heavy multimedia material. According to the primary technical requirement of using exclusively current browsers and free plug-ins, the learners were provided with a CD-ROM that is activated by the Web-based material. Such a solution appears mandatory at the present level of the everywhere-available technology: no broadband connections available at the lowest fares.

The evaluation phase measures the effectiveness and efficiency of the instruction. The evaluation should occur throughout the entire instructional design process—within phases, between phases, and after implementation. Evaluation may be formative or summative. The former is ongoing during and between phases and is aimed to improve the instruction before its final version is implemented. The latter usually occurs after the final version of instruction is implemented and assesses the overall effectiveness of the instructional process. The results gathered from the summative evaluation may be used to support decisions concerning the instruction, as whether to purchase an instructional package or to continue or discontinue an instructional program (Kirkpatrick, 1998).

In the remaining part of this section, the methods and the results of the formative evaluation process of the MODASPECTRA system will be illustrated. The formative evaluation was aimed to evaluate the aspects of the system independent from the learning contents; namely, functionality and usability of the tools. This phase provided useful feedback for the technical improvement of the demonstrator. Furthermore, the formative evaluation was aimed to investigate the effectiveness of the pedagogical approach and of the discussion management system and the user friendliness of the tools and of the materials developed. These objectives fit well within the 4E model developed by Collis and Pals (1998) and aimed at predicting the individual use of telematics-based educational systems. According to the 4E model, the success of an educational system is critically dependent on four clusters of variables that are grouped under the following headers: educational effectiveness, ease of use, personal engagement, and external influences. The tools adopted for the verification (summative evaluation) were designed to extract information from respondents about these critical variables.

Two groups of stakeholders have been involved in the final verification: students acting as lifelong learners and indirect users, i.e., administrators of institutions having already expressed interest in the philosophy of MODASPECTRA system.

Procedures for the Students' Verification

The students were asked to find their own time, environmental conditions, and facilities needed to perform the verification of the learning material. The educational effectiveness of the material has been assessed by testing the self-awareness of the learners about what they have learned and by verifying the time spent in the exercise. This was done on samples of the material due to the limited amount of time that could have been really spent by the learners. Moreover, the subjective evaluation of easiness and pleasantness of learning was investigated. Finally, the usefulness of the managed discussion was subjectively evaluated by each participant in the verification, along with the significance of the self-assessment procedures.

The samples of the learning material have been selected according to coverage of the following:

- Technical and clinical topics
- Tools homogenization and domain-specific topics
- Different instructional goals pursued by different learning objectives in MODASPECTRA
- Different media-dependent modalities of communication

Four composite units, evenly distributed with respect to the above criteria, were submitted for verification: one from a course meant to have a rather high perceptive character and one from a course meant to have a rather high reflective character. Then, one composite unit from a course meant to have a reasonably high perceptive character and one from a course meant to have a reasonably high reflective character. Perceptive and reflective are used in the sense given to these terms by Norman (1993). The composite units were sorted in couples to each student, according to his/her known background and to the technical facilities available.

Questionnaires were designed and constructed according to modularity criteria, to allow the widest possible exploitation. They were composed by five main sections, devoted respectively to the following:

- Collect general information about the respondent and his/her familiarity with the most current software packages enabling individual productivity and allowing Internet navigation (Section 1, General)
- Test the friendliness of the system and the effectiveness of the tools developed to guide the users in the correct usage of the system (Section 2, System use)
- Evaluate the pedagogical effectiveness of the learning material submitted to verification and its ease of use (Section 3, Pedagogic effectiveness)
- Appraise the usefulness of the self-assessment material associated with the learning material under verification (Section 4, Self assessment)
- Evaluate the effectiveness of the tools made available for dialogue and appraise the perceived usefulness of the dialogue phase (Section 5, Discussion)

All the questions had predefined answers with a Likert scale ranging from 1 to 5. An effort was made to phrase the questions in a direct and unambiguous way. The questions were phrased in order to avoid placing the best or the worst judgement in the same position on the scale. Moreover, a limited space was left for suggestions, for explaining the kind of problems encountered, and for describing unforeseen operation modalities. The suggestions and indications provided by Oliver and Conole (1998) and the operative indications provided by the Evaluation Cookbook (1998) were followed. An effort was made to limit the number of questions to be asked; thus, the process ended up in a questionnaire containing 43 questions, each one comprehensive.

The questionnaire started with an extensive introduction aimed at explaining the general concept of the MODASPECTRA package.

Results of the Students' Verification

Twenty students that provided 34 questionnaires composed the population addressed. Shown in Table 5 is a subset of the answers related to Section 1 of the questionnaire.

Table 5: Answers to the General Section of the Questionnaire (Fragment)

Question	Answer	Freq.
Age	Average	29
	Standard Deviation	8
Gender	M	9
	F	11
Type of organisation	University	7
	Hospital	9
	Research centre	3
Use a computer	Once a week – Once a day	2
	Every day	17
Internet connection	Analog phone line	6
	ISDN	3
	LAN	11
Access to MODASPECTRA from	Office	16
	Home	3
	Elsewhere	1

By considering the answers to general questions, it is possible to state that the population of respondents was well balanced, in respect to gender and age, and in respect to the distribution among universities and hospitals. Furthermore, most of the respondents used the computer every day and accessed the MODASPECTRA system from office via a LAN.

Clear indications about the ease of use of the MODASPECTRA environment by the tested population are provided in Table 6. In fact, 50% of the respondents did not use the manual, and five out of eight respondents considered verbal instructions not needed. Among the respondents that used the manual, eight did not receive verbal instructions. Thus, we can argue that an important fraction of the respondents did not need instructions for using the system, and that the manual is rather effective. Finally, we can conclude that the system seems rather friendly, and that verbal instruction is appreciated, even if not needed.

In Table 7, the results obtained with respect to the following issues are summarized: appropriateness of the material for learning, appropriateness of the material for being learned by the target population, ability of learning skills (application in the daily practice), and ability in gaining strategic knowledge.

Table 6: Ease of Use of the System

Issues	Score		1	2	3	4	5	Score
	Low							High
Did you use the manual...?	Yes	10					10	No
Opinion on the manual	Incomplete	0	0	0	2	2		Complete
	Useless	0	0	0	1	4		Needed
Received other instructions?	Yes	11					8	No
Opinion of the instructions	Incomplete	0	0	1	1	7		Complete
	Useless	0	0	1	2	5		Needed
Verbal instructions are needed	Yes	8					5	No

Table 7: Appropriateness of the Learning Material

Issues	Score Low	1	2	3	4	5	Score High	Median
Was it clear what you were going to learn?	Yes	30				3	No	
Was it clear what you were expected to do?	Yes	30				3	No	
Confident in the knowledge of the object of the Composite Unit	Very Unconf.	0	6	11	12	4	Very conf.	3.5
Course Material								
Able to complete the material in the expected time	Yes	28				6	No	
	Minutes (mean; std)	74	54					
Ability to apply what learnt in daily practice	Yes	21				6	No	
Quizzes								
Are the quizzes helpful	Very much helpful	5	6	6	3	0	Not helpful at all	2.5
Was it clear what you were expected to do?	Yes	19				2	No	
Confident in the knowledge of the object of the Composite Unit	Still Very Unconf.	0	4	6	8	2	Much more conf.	3.5
Dialogue Phase								
Was it clear what you were expected to do?	Yes	25				4	No	
Confident in the knowledge of the object of the Composite Unit	Still Very Unconf.	1	4	11	5	5	Much more conf.	3.5
Time spent to feel confident with MODASPECTRA system	Minutes (mean; std)	83	95					
How is the time spent with MODASPECTRA system	Spent well	9	5	9	2	0	Wasted	2.5

Appropriateness of the Material for Learning

The answers to the questions relative to the ability in completing the material in the expected time (28 Yes in face of 6 No, Table 7) represent a relevant indicator with respect to the appropriateness of the material for learning. In fact, one of the main design criteria of the learning material was that composite units should require no more than half an hour to be completed, for the sake of compliance with the current estimation of the attention time of the learner. Taking into consideration the average values of 74 minutes (mean plus 54 minutes of standard deviation) relative to all the composite units submitted to verification, it could be argued that they are too long. Anyway, it must be noted that two of the composite units selected for the verification contained video material showing laboratory sessions and protocols for administering largely used clinical tests and cannot be subdivided without losing their instructional value.

Appropriateness of the Learning Material for Being Learned by the Target Population of Students

Some useful indications about the effectiveness of the adopted pedagogical approach and of value of the content as perceived by the learners was obtained, even if the verification of one single composite unit may not be sufficient to evaluate the learning potential of a course.

From this point of view, the sections of the questionnaire devoted to course material and quizzes have to be considered with particular attention. In particular, the cross consideration of the question dealing with the level of confidence in the knowledge about the object of the composite unit, before studying it and performing the self assessment, and immediately after answering the quizzes, is deemed revealing (Table 7). The initial answers are positive (median at grade 3.5). At the end of the quizzes, there is a shift toward the medium grades, with a mild reduction of the fully confident answers. This seems to indicate that the novelty of the approach and the perceived increase of fun, along with no increase in the difficulty and a decrease in the effort, induced a more optimistic attitude toward the acquired knowledge than the verification made by self-assessment should justify. However, even with the more realistic awareness induced by self-assessment, the confidence in having acquired medium to good knowledge on the object of the content units is maintained. Furthermore, it can be argued that the students found that their initial level of confidence was inappropriate, and that they had more to learn than they previously realized, because of their study.

Speed, Fun, Easiness, Effort, and Attractiveness of the Learning Material

There is a significantly positive evaluation with respect to the ease of learning in comparison with books and lectures (Figure 4). The learners considered attractiveness and fun in a substantially positive way—all the answers are placed in the positive half of the grading scale (Figure 4). This appraisal was confirmed by the results associated with each composite unit, too. This seemed to indicate that the novelty of the approach and the perceived increase of fun, along with no increase in the difficulty and a decrease in the effort, induced an optimistic attitude toward the acquired knowledge.

Appropriateness of the Multimedia Level to the Learning of the Specific Arguments

A first, substantially positive evaluation of the appropriateness of the multimedia level to the learning of MDA can be inferred by crossing the questions relative to fun, speed, easiness, effort, and attractiveness (Figure 4). However, cautions have to be taken before adopting a positive attitude about the multimedia level of the learning material, because the argument can be seriously taken only after a complete evaluation of each course.

Ability of Learning Skills (Application in the Daily Practice)

The ability in developing learning skills is, as expected, a more controversial issue. The lesser number of positive judgements (Table 7) was partly expected by the authors, editors, and editor-in-chief, because learning a single composite unit cannot be completely appropri-

Figure 4: Speed, Fun, Easiness, Effort, and Attractiveness of the Learning Material

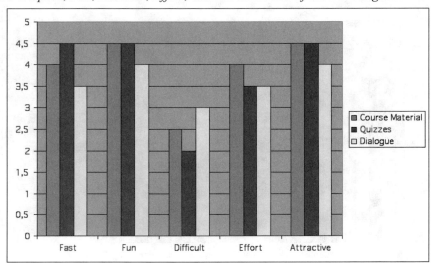

ate for developing learning skills. However, the cross-examination of the answer to this question and of the suggestions for improving the learning material is revealing. In particular, some flaws in the preparation of the learning material for two of the courses under verification were revealed. For instance, in the case of one course, it was put into evidence the lack of description of instrumentation for measuring some physical quantity. The focus of the course was on the principles underlying measurements, and the use of some equipment was deemed obvious, probably due to the engineering background of the authors. The comments allowed examples on the use of the equipment to be added and links to the sites of outstanding manufacturers to be included, where the possibility of going in-depth on some practical measurement subtleties is provided.

Similar remarks hold for the answer relative to the ability in gaining strategic knowledge. In this case, the flaws calling for amendment pertained to a different couple of courses.

Indications about the Effectiveness of the Discussion Tools

By looking at the answers, it can be argued that the contacts among learners have been more effective than those between learners and teachers (Figure 5).

This result can be evaluated from two points of view: one related to the effectiveness of the people acting as teachers in the present verification phase, and the other related to the importance of the discussion among peers as an effective way of learning.

With respect to the effectiveness of the teachers (members of the project team), it must be said that the discussion phase was probably poorly prepared at the time of the final verification, because the people acting as teachers were not used to this kind of tool to exploit it in an effective manner. This was mainly due to the difficulty in adopting a synthetic communication style perceived as inappropriate for discussing complex topics by the teachers. However, the answers by the learners were not negative, even if they could not be defined positive.

On the other hand, the results of the verification seemed to indicate that the students

Figure 5: Effectiveness of the Discussion Tools

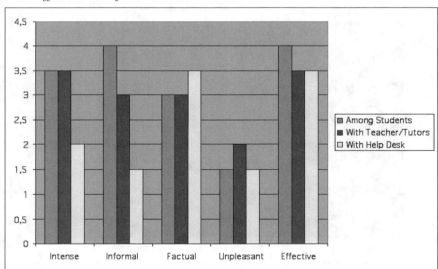

learned from their peers more effectively than from tutors. This could be interpreted as a huge success for the project. In fact, this result probably reflects the way in which these professionals prefer to learn, and therefore, this kind of collaboration should be enhanced. It also suggests that the project might become more cost-effective in the long run—rather than requiring great numbers of tutors, part of the teaching role can be undertaken by peers at no expense for the hosting organization.

It appears that the verified material is suitable for learning and, much more important for us, that it is suitable for the specific learning addressed by MODASPECTRA. It also appears that the time spent for learning is reasonable and substantially corresponding to the intentions of authors and editors.

The main points resulting from the comments collected can be summarized as follows:

- Learning material
  The self-evaluation tools have to be improved, in the language and in the number and phrasing of the predefined answers. The contents of one course have to provide more operative indications. The effectiveness of another course could be improved.
- Dialogue phase
  Due to the limitation in the preparation of a sound management of the dialogue phase, some reflections were done, and the following indications have been produced for the validation phase:
  - The different dialogue tools (namely, calendar of course events, bulletin board, and internal mail) have to be exploited in a synergistic manner by the teacher/tutor in order to focus the attention of the learner on the discussion.
  - Discussion has to be promoted, which means that the questions opening discussion have to be provocative and stimulating, and that the learners have to be motivated to participate by adding their experiences and reflections. Teachers/tutors should be committed to animate discussion, not only launch an argument. This implies that they have to enter the discussion more than once, capturing and putting into evidence every element introduced by the learners that may add value to reflection and foster the discussion.

Verification Procedure for Indirect Users

The indirect users of the contents were selected among the administrators of institutions (educational organizations, potential exploiting parties), having already expressed some preliminary interest in the philosophy of the MODASPECTRA course. It was argued, in fact, that only people already interested in Web-based instruction could appraise the effectiveness of samples of the system. Indirect users not interested in distance learning would provide significant evaluation only at the end of the validation phase, when the learning material would be used in a complete and real-life manner, so that a substantial comparison with the traditional approaches could be established. The indirect users were mainly focused on the overall instructional effectiveness of the courses or of the whole MODASPECTRA package. The indirect users were asked to evaluate the material by comparing it with their expectations. This meant that their expectations had first to be recognized and described, and then, the measure of the perceived matching between the tested samples of the learning material and the expectations could be given. This activity seemed rather complex and unable to be managed by questionnaires, unless the involved users would contribute a preliminary provision of their expectations in a structured form. This appeared to be exposed to the risk of circular operations, cumbersome and time demanding. Therefore, the need to have face-to face meetings with the indirect users, based on a planned interview strategy, went into evidence.

The interview guide was organized in three sections, preceded by a short introduction illustrating its goals to the interviewer. Section 1 provided a synthetic description of the MODASPECTRA package and was meant to guide a demonstration. Section 2 summarized the meeting details and identified the respondent and its position and role. Section 3 considered generic organizational factors aimed at identifying the attitude of the person and of the institution represented with respect to ICT for learning and focused on the practical conditions for the possible adoption of the MODASPECTRA system.

Results of the Indirect Users' Verification

A cautious attitude with respect to the organization and costs of distance learning initiatives, and a responsible position with respect to a radical and complete migration from traditional education to the new paradigms under development by means of the new and evolving ICT tools emerged from the interviews. However, the indirect users expect that this kind of learning will have an important role in the near future, and they all share the opinion that the MODASPECTRA system would be exploitable for such developments. Some of them focused the attention on the potential of learning evidence-based practice. Probably, this sort of perspective is also interesting for the trainees with clinical background coming from the Anglo-Saxon educational system, where some pioneering experiences in the MDA field have been developed at the level of producing examples of good practice.

The above indications are naturally relevant for the exploitation policy of the MODASPECTRA team. In the present context, they put into evidence a substantial appreciation for the demonstration that accompanied the interviews and positive expectations with respect to the results of the validation.

According to the purpose of the interviews, namely to verify whether the MODASPECTRA system could match the expectations of the indirect users, a positive verification seems to have been attained.

The main results obtained from the point of view of verification can be summarized as follows: the education of therapists is still strongly dependent on the country's needs and tradition. Because the learning material has been developed in English, the language may represent a barrier in large measure, especially in the Southern European countries.

However, specific issues of the MODASPECTRA learning material, namely, the exploitation of technology for the sake of rehabilitation, are perceived as being universally interesting.

The use of telematics is deemed useful, even if in different contexts and time horizons, according to the different infrastructures and diffusion of the Internet access at country-level. Someone considered telematics useful for educating the educators of the European therapists; some other considered the medium useful to teach undergraduate students. In every case, the focus was on teaching, instead of on learning, and this can be significant for understanding the importance of the need for an innovative European approach to the education of such professionals.

The demonstration of the MODASPECTRA system was appreciated, and specific interest was indicated:

- On the system
- On the contents of technology-oriented homogenization courses
- On the contents of some courses specifically oriented to the appreciation of motor disorders

The appreciation of the different items was greatly country dependent. It can be deemed significant for the sake of the present verification.

On the contrary, the organizational and cost problems that the particular education area has to face make much more problematic a medium-term horizon (within five years) for a systematic and Europe-wide exploitation of the open and distance learning approach in the specific domain.

With respect to the verification, it appears that the instructional effectiveness of the samples of the MODASPECTRA system demonstrated within the focus group received a substantially positive evaluation.

REFERENCES

Aggarwal, A. K., & Bento, R. (2000). Web-based education. In A. K. Aggarwal (Ed.), *Web-based learning and teaching technologies: opportunities and challenges* (pp. 2–16). Hershey, PA: Idea Group Publishing.

Airasian, P. W., & Madalus, G. J. (1975). Functional types of student evaluation, measurement and evaluation in guidance. In J. M. Polardy (Ed.), *Teaching today* (pp. 412–426). New York: Macmillan Press.

Andriole, S. J. (1997). Requirements-driven ALN course design, development, delivery & evaluation. *JALN, 1*(2), 57–67.

Bloom, B. S. (1956). *Taxonomy of educational objectives: the classification of educational goals: Handbook I, Cognitive domain.* New York, Toronto: Longmans, Green.

Britain, S., & Liber, O. (1999). A framework for pedagogical evaluation of virtual learning environments. University of Wales-Bangor, JSC TAP report 41; http://www.jtap.ac.uk/reports/html/jtap-041.html.

Carswell, L. (2001). Pragmatic methodology for educational courseware development; http://www.ulst.ac.uk/cticomp/papers/carswell.html.

CEN/ISSS/WS-LT Project 1 Draft Report (2000). March 22.

Clark, D. (2000). Introduction to instructional system design. Retrieved from Big Dog's ISD page: http://www.nwlink.com/~donclark/hrd/sat1.html.

Collis, S. B., & Pals, B. (2000). A model for predicting an individual use of a telematics application for a learning-related purpose. International Journal for Educational *Telecommunications, 6*(1), 63–103; http://www.edte.twente.nl/collis/homepage/pub.htm.

Davis, A. M. (1990). *Software requirements.* Englewood Cliffs, NJ: Prentice Hall.

Dick, W., & Carey, L. (1990). *The systematic design of instruction* (3rd ed.). Glenview, IL: Scott, Foresman & Company.

ECTS. (1998). European Credit Transfer System—Users' guide; http://europa.eu.int/comm/education/socrates/guide-en.doc.

Edmonds, C., Branch, R., & Mukherjee, P. (1994). A conceptual framework for comparing instructional design models. *Educational Technology Research and Development, 42*(4), 55–62.

The Evaluation Cookbook. (1998). J. Harvey (Ed.), Learning Technology Dissemination Initiative. Institute for Computer Based Learning. UK: Heriot Watt University.

Gagné, R. M. (1965). *The conditions of learning* (1st ed.). New York: Holt, Rinehart & Winston.

Gagné, R. M. (1985). *The conditions of learning* (4th ed.). New York: Holt, Rinehart & Winston.

Gagné, R. M., & Briggs, L. J. (1992). *Principles of instructional design* (4th ed.). Fort Worth, TX: Harcourt, Brace, Jovanovich College.

Gerlach, V. S., & Ely, D. P. (1980). *Teaching and media: a systematic approach* (2nd ed.). Englewood Cliffs, NJ: Prentice Hall.

Gustafson, K., & Branch, R. (1997). Revisioning models of instructional development. *Educational Technologies Research & Development, 43*(3), 73–89.

Hannafin, M. J., & Peck, K. L. (1988). *The design, development, and evaluation of instructional software*. New York: MacMillan Publishing Company.

IEEE LOM. (1999). IEEE Learning Technology Standards Committee (LTSC) Learning Object Metadata, Working Draft Document 3; http://ltsc.ieee.org/doc/wg12/LOM-WD3.htm.

IMS. (2001). IMS Digital Repositories White Paper. Version 1.6. IMS Global Learning Consortium, Inc. 2001; http://www.imsglobal.com.

Janicky, T., & Liegle, J. O. (2001). Development and evaluation of a framework for creating Web-based learning modules: a pedagogical and systems perspective. *JALN, 5*(1), 58–84.

Johansen, D. (2000). Knowledge is complex: accommodating human ways ok knowing. In *Proceedings of the 11th ASIS&T SIG/CR Classification Research Workshop* (pp. 1–7), Chicago, IL, November 12.

Kirkpatrick, D. L. (1998). *Evaluating training programs—the four levels* (2nd ed.). San Francisco, CA: Berrett-Koehler Publishers.

Lindner, R. (2001). Expertise and role identification for learning environments (ERILE). Draft open to discussion at http://prometeus.org/.

Mason, R. (1998). Models of online courses. *ALN Magazine* 2.

Merril, M. D., Li, Z., & Jones, M. R. (1991). Second generation instructional design (ID2). *Educational Technology, 30*(1), 7–11; *30*(2), 7–14.

MODASPECTRA. (1998). Project programme. Project MM 1041—Joint Call Educational Multimedia; http://www.modaspectra.org.

MODASPECTRA. (1999a). User requirements. Deliverable 2.1. Project MM 1041—Joint Call Educational Multimedia; http://www.modaspectra.org.

MODASPECTRA. (1999b). Functional specifications. Deliverable 3.1. Project MM 1041—Joint Call Educational Multimedia; http://www.modaspectra.org.

MODASPECTRA. (2001a). MODASPECTRA educational system (teaching and training system tools of a specialist training course in MDA, 2nd ed.). Deliverable 3.1. Project MM 1041—Joint Call Educational Multimedia; http://www.modaspectra.org.

MODASPECTRA. (2001b). Final verification. Deliverable 5.2. Project MM 1041—Joint Call Educational Multimedia; http://www.modaspectra.org.

MODASPECTRA. (2001c). Results of the validation of the MODASPECTRA educational system. Deliverable 6.1. Project MM 1041—Joint Call Educational Multimedia; http://www.modaspectra.org.

Norman, D. A. (1993). *Things that make us smart. Defending human attributes in the age of the machine*. Reading, MA: Addison-Wesley.

Oliver, M., & Conole, G. (1998). The ELT toolkit, as communicated to the ALT Workshop, December 14.

Valenti, S. et al. (2002). Teaching motor disability assessment over the Web: MODASPECTRA. *Educational Technology & Society, 5*, 1, 184–192.

Valenti, S. et al. (2002b). Preliminary results from the validation of a specialists' degree in motor disability assessment. In Kinshuk (Ed.), *Proceedings of the International Conference on Computers in Education* (in press). 3–6 December, Auckland, New Zealand. IEEE CS Press.

Valenti, S., Panti, M., & Leo, T. (2002a). Design for reuse in a Web-based degree. *Proceedings of the World Conference on Networked Learning in a Global Environment: Challenges and Solutions for Virtual Education* (NL2002). ICSC-NAISO. Canada/The Nederlands: Academic Press.

* *Note.* Access to the MODASPECTRA deliverables is restricted via a username and password that may be requested by contacting the Web administrator.

Chapter XXIII

WeBCEIS — A Scenario for Integrating Web-Based Education into Classical Education

Müge Klein
University of Karlsruhe, Germany

Daniel Sommer
University of Karlsruhe, Germany

Wolffried Stucky
University of Karlsruhe, Germany

ABSTRACT

Web-based education implies many advantages for teachers and learners, such as independence of time and place, personalization, and interactivity, but an important factor in learning, namely, face-to-face communication in traditional classrooms, cannot be adequately emulated. Students in a classical university education would lose many important social interactions in a purely Web-based education scenario, which would have important repercussions on their university education. The trade-off is a "blended learning" scenario, which is the integration of assorted learning delivery methods to benefit from both education scenarios. We are, therefore, arguing for an integration of Web-based and classical education, and present WebCEIS— our blended learning scenario for integrating Web-based education into classical education—looking at the organizational and the technological aspects of teaching and learning, and present our strategy for the implementation of WebCEIS.

INTRODUCTION

eLearning, especially Web-based education, has developed rapidly in recent years. There has been excessive publicity surrounding the advantages of Web-based education, such as time- and location-independent learning, the easy updating of teaching material, and, as a consequence of these advantages, cost savings in training scenarios, and it seemed that Web-based education would totally supersede traditional education. But, many experiences in the field of virtual universities and virtual learning communities have emphasized that eLearning also has drawbacks, which include social isolation, and that such a substitution would just mean throwing away all the benefits of traditional education. As an alternative, "blended learning" scenarios have arisen. Blended learning combines eLearning compo-nents with traditional classroom components to ensure maximum effectiveness in teaching and learning (Lawhead, 1997; Rosbottom, 2001). The degree of integration of eLearning and the traditional classroom can vary, dependent on the learner type and the current education scenario. For "part-time learners" in professional training scenarios, the degree of substitu-tion by Web-based education could be higher than for "full-time learners" in classical school and university education, because in professional training, the cost savings are more important than the face-to-face communication.

We are offering computer science education to business engineering students at the University of Karlsruhe in Germany. Based on the experience we have gained in different eLearning projects and some products that have been developed in these projects, we have generated a blended learning strategy for our students, in order to obtain the new advantages of Web-based education, while retaining those components of traditional education that are not replaceable. In this study, we will present a scenario whereby Web-based education is integrated into classical education. This has been developed particularly for use at univer-sities, also in subjects other than computer science.

We have used our experience from various projects and activities in which we have been involved for this work: in the ViKar project ("Virtual University Group Karlsruhe") (ViKar, 2001), six universities of different types are cooperating in the field of eLearning, especially in the context of the development and usage of Web-based learning material. Because the cooperating universities have different types of students, but partly the same learning content, they want to develop the material jointly in order to use part of it in all the participating universities. One of the main goals of the project is to find concepts for this development of learning material by several authors and for different groups of learners. For this purpose, special concepts for the modularization of learning content have been developed. Another project in which we are involved is VIROR ("Virtual University in the Upper Rhine Valley") (VIROR, 2001). In the context of this project, four universities are cooperating in order to create a common multimedia education program. These universities want to offer a more multifaceted curriculum to their students, for example, by exchanging special lectures or jointly organized seminars. Both ViKar and VIROR are financed by the state of Baden-Württemberg as part of the "Virtual University of Baden-Württemberg" program (VHBW, 2001). Apart from these projects, experiences from several other activities in the field of eLearning have been used for this work. For example, we have been organizing teleseminars together with several partner universities since 1995.

In this work, we will first compare Web-based and classical education in regard to technologies, roles, and scenarios in order to identify the advantages of both types of education and to find out which will suit different learner groups. In the following, we will introduce WebCEIS, our **Web-b**ased and **C**lassical **E**ducation **I**ntegration **S**cenario. In this context, we will describe the organizational and technical aspects of our scenario in detail. We will then present our strategy for implementing WebCEIS, before we close with a conclusion and outlook.

INTEGRATION OF WEB-BASED EDUCATION AND CLASSICAL EDUCATION

On the one hand, Web-based education is regarded as a total substitute for classical education. But on the other hand, Web-based education is seen as a barrier in education, because it disregards important social aspects of teaching and learning. The whole education process and the new types of teaching and learning have to be regarded in a wider perspective considering the advantages and the disadvantages of both education types. In some situations, the Web-based type of education would be more efficient, and in others, the classical one. There could be education scenarios for which an integration of both types would be useful. In order to determine which education type is more suitable and more effective in which education scenario, we will first compare Web-based with classical education. We will then draw up a classification of learners, in order to determine which type of education would be more beneficial for which learner group.

Web-based Education Versus Classical Education

The classical education scenario is well known—the instructor stands at the front next to the blackboard and the students sit at their desks, and the presentation of learning content can be supported by video projectors and electronic presentation software. Learning happens first by listening and discussing in the classroom and second by reviewing the lecture slides or reading a book. Web-based education can simulate this classical education scenario in different ways: using a synchronous type of Web-based education scenario, students and instructors do not have to be present in the same room; pictures and voices of the students and instructors, who are sitting in different places, can be transmitted by video conferences, as can all the lecture slides. For such conferences with audio and video transmission, a lot of technical equipment is required, e.g., video cameras, microphones, video projectors, and adequate networks. Interpersonal communication is supported by electronic communication. A simple way of achieving synchronous communication is a chatroom; a better and more expensive way is a videoconference. Asynchronous as well as synchronous communication must be supported: paper-based messages used in classical education can be superseded by email and newsgroups, for example. A special groupware system can be used to support the communication and the collaboration of people working in virtual groups. This asynchronous type of Web-based education is based not only on place-independence but also on time-independence—students can view recorded lectures and even learn using interactive Web-based material that accompanies the lecture. Therefore, all the learning material has to exist as electronic documents. In order to manage and provide Web-based material, an eLearning platform is needed. eLearning platforms integrate the communication and groupware technology introduced above to a greater or lesser extent. Some important and widely used eLearning platforms are, for example, Hyperwave eLearning Suite (Hyperwave, 2001), TopClass (WBT, 2002), and WebCT (WebCT, 2002). A detailed comparison of these and other platforms can be found in the literature ("Online educational delivery applications: a Web tool for comparative analysis," 2002). Such systems supporting the entire teaching and learning process do not have any equivalent in classical education.

Web-based education implies new roles in educational settings and new tasks for the existing roles. All the content for Web-based education is created by *authors*, and courses where this content is used are given by *instructors*. In classical education, the author and the instructor are often the same person, but in the context of Web-based education, a distinction should be made between these roles. The development of Web-based learning material is much more expensive than the development of classical content. For this reason, an instructor will not generally be able to perform this task, and the electronic material, including Web pages and interactive exercises, for example, will be developed by special authoring teams. Sometimes, the instructor will tailor this material to his own requirements, but in general, the instructor will focus on the knowledge transfer. In this connection, the instructor is supported by *tutors*. This role is well known from classical education scenarios, but it takes on a greater significance in Web-based education. Typically, an instructor using Web-based education has to look after more students than a classical teacher, and therefore, needs assistance with his supervisory functions. For this reason, some of the standard jobs in Web-based education are taken over by tutors. They can act as the first point of contact for students, mark their homework, and advise them on organizational issues. The preceding explanation has already shown that the role of the *student* will also change in Web-based education. The major task of the student has not changed, because the student simply wants to learn, but the way in which the student does so varies dramatically. If Web-based education is used, the student is able to learn independently of a given location and, depending on the scenario, can learn more or less time-independently, too. Another role not directly concerned with learning and teaching, but which is also important, is the role of the *administrator*. The tasks of the administrator are similar in classical and Web-based education: for example, the administrator is responsible for the enrollment of students, financial affairs in this regard, and certificates, but the way in which these jobs are done is different in each case. In the context of Web-based education, the administrator will use electronic information systems, and may also use all the communication and collaboration tools described above.

Integration Scenario according to Learner Classification

In order to specify the degree of integration of Web-based education into classical education, the characteristics of the learners should be taken into consideration. We regard education scenarios from the universities' point of view. Universities can take part in educating different learner groups. We can identify two main education fields in which universities are active:

- Classical university education: The "classical university education" students are usually between 18–25 years old; after finishing high school, they study a certain academic subject, and their main occupation is studying. They are what we call *"full-time learners."* Depending on where they learn, we can distinguish two types of full-time learners:
  - *Local full-time learner*: Local full-time learners live near the university campus and attend university regularly.

- *Nonlocal full-time learner*: Nonlocal full-time learners live in another city or another country, but they are interested in studying a certain academic subject at a certain university, which is not located in their neighborhood.
- Professional training: An interesting and emerging education area for universities is the area of professional training. More universities want to use their know-how (especially in the field of IT) to gain financial advantages. The professional training learner groups are different from students. This group is typically older than the students, they work in industry, may have studied years ago, and they want to (or have got to) train themselves in order to learn new subjects in their professional domain. They are "*part-time learners.*"

In the context of classical education, the local full-time learners attend lectures, where they can discuss topics with their instructors, they are active in laboratory courses, and they learn in groups with other students. In contrast, the nonlocal full-time learners receive their learning material by post in order to learn at home. They have to take their examinations about twice a year in a college or a university near their home. This is a typical scenario for so-called "open universities." Professional training usually takes place in a training center over a few days, where many people from a company or from many companies come together in order to learn a specific topic.

Web-based education is ideal for supporting the education of nonlocal full-time learners and part-time learners. Web-based education is more efficient than the classical open university, because the learning material is interactive and can be renewed more quickly and cheaply. Professional training can also benefit from Web-based education. It is cheaper and more efficient for companies not to send their employees to a training center for many days, thus enabling them to work while they are learning. But, what about Web-based education for local full-time learners? If their learning was totally Web-based, it would no longer be possible to differentiate them from the nonlocal learners. Like Holmes (1999), we also do not believe that it is better to replace classical education completely and to teach local full-time learners using only a Web-based approach. We believe that a classical university education scenario *not replaced by, but supported by,* all the possibilities of Web-based technology is much more efficient for teaching and learning quality.

AIFB WEB-BASED AND CLASSICAL EDUCATION INTEGRATION SCENARIO: WEBCEIS

The AIFB (Applied Informatics and Formal Description Methods) Institute has been offering informatics education to business engineering students at the University of Karlsruhe in Germany for 30 years. In our university's education system, there are three main training types: first there are lectures, where an instructor gives a presentation on a subject and discusses it with students. Second, in laboratory courses, these topics are addressed by the students with the help of tutors. And the third training type is the seminar, which has two subtypes. In classical, more theoretical seminars, the students have to carry out a small research project on a specific topic and present their results in a seminar. All this can also be done in small student groups, where they can learn while working together. In more

Table 1: WebCEIS Versus Classical and Web-Based Education

	Classical education	Web-based education	WeBCEIS
Organization			
Knowledge Supply	development of presentation material and script	development of Web-based material	development / tailoring of - presentation material - Web-based material
Knowledge Transfer	lecture	Web-based material, video conferencing	lecture + Web-based material, video conferencing
Knowledge Acquisition	seminar, laboratory courses	teleseminar, Web-based tutoring	seminar + teleseminar, laboratory courses + Web-based tutoring
Knowledge Control	classical examination	Web-based examination, Web-based self-assessment	classical examination, Web-based self-assessment
Administrative affairs	paper-based	Web-based	Web-based
Social affairs	face-to-face communication	Web-based communication	face-to-face communication supprted by Web-based communication
Technique	blackboard, chalk, overhead projector	network, teleclassroom, browser, authoring tool	blackboard, chalk, overhead projector, network, teleclassroom, browser, authoring tool

practical seminars, groups of students have to work on a certain project, for example, in the context of software engineering. In this kind of seminar, the practice of teamwork is the main teaching objective.

We have decided to integrate Web-based education elements into those positions of our classical education training types where they fit best, and where we can see additional value for teaching and learning quality. In this section, we will present our integrated WebCEIS scenario (Web-based and Classical Education Integration Scenario). We will consider the organizational and technical aspects of our scenario. The characteristics of WebCEIS, which are specified below, are mapped in Table 1 in order to contrast the characteristics of classical and Web-based education.

Organization

Education scenarios usually consist of several phases. In the first phase, called the *knowledge supply* phase, all the teaching content is developed. This is then transmitted to the students in the *knowledge transfer* phase, so that in the *knowledge acquisition* phase, students can assimilate the content. The students' knowledge is then verified in the *knowledge control* phase. Parallel to these phases, the *administrative* and *social affairs* phases are executed. Administrative affairs include the organizing and managing of education activities (such as registration, information, etc.) and social affairs imply the organizing of social activities such as meeting, talking, playing, and working together (see Figure 1).

Figure 1: Phases of an Education Scenario

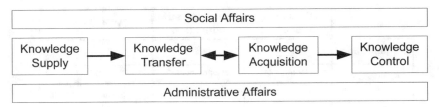

Knowledge Supply

In the context of *knowledge supply* in our WebCEIS integrated education scenario, we have concentrated on the following activities:

- Development of electronic presentation material for the instructor
- Development of interactive and multimedia Web-based material for the lecture
- Tailoring of presentation and Web-based material

The development of Web-based material is taking place in the context of the ViKar project (ViKar, 2001). Because the main goal of the ViKar project is reusing the same lecture material in different types of university, it was important to build the Web-based material pool in a modular fashion, in order to construct different courses using the same material pool. The modular generation of the Web-based material for lecture content and for laboratory course exercise content took place according to a process model for software engineering techniques, which is specified in the literature (Klein & Stucky, 2001). After decomposing the whole teaching subject into smaller items called "modules," their content is developed in HTML and extended with multimedia items according to their specification. The relationship

Figure 2: Web-Based and Presentation Material Reusing the Same Multimedia Element

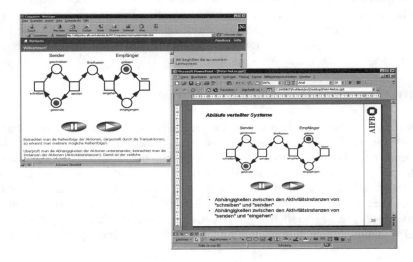

between these modules is also modeled according the learning sequence. Courses can be built by composing the modules according to this so-called relationship model. We then tailored the material for the Web and for the presentation to bring them in line with each other. The tailoring of the presentation and Web-based material also involved reusing the lecture content—we used the same multimedia elements, such as animations, in both material types (see example in Figure 2).

Knowledge Transfer

The main activity of *knowledge transfer* in WebCEIS is still the lecture, where the instructor shows his slides and other presentation material electronically and discusses them with students. The presentation material used during the lecture and also information on external digital resources relating to the lecture's subject are made available on the Web. In addition to this type of classical lecture, Web-based interactive material on the same topics is made available to the students. They may use it in order to understand a lecture better or to assimilate the lecture topic from scratch if they did not attend. This learning material can also be used as a preparation for examinations.

In the last few years, we developed such Web-based interactive learning material for three of our lectures. Our server log files are analyzed after each term, and our students are asked for their opinion regarding the quality of the material in appropriate polls. From such a survey after a lecture on Applied Computer Science in 2001 with 188 registered students, we know that those students who regularly made use of our material used our system for about 80 minutes per week on average. Approximately 85.7% of our students sometimes used our material from home, and 64.3% used it in computer pool rooms at the university (multiple answers were allowed). Some of the results relating to the quality of our material can be found in Tables 2 and 3.

The other innovation in the field of knowledge transfer is that interesting lectures that are not part of our own curriculum are transferred from other universities cooperating with

Table 2: Working with Web-Based Learning Material

Question: How do you feel about working with the learning material?

(Scale from 1 to 5, median)

	1	2	3	4	5	
tiring			●			motivating
troublesome				●		trouble-free
disheartening			●			heartening
unfamiliar				●		familiar
inefficient				●		efficient
unsystematic				●		systematic
uninteresting				●		interesting
undesirable				●		desirable
confusing				●		clarifying

Table 3: Rating of Web-Based Learning Material

Question: How do you rate the learning material?

(Scale from 1 = "predication is false" to 5 = "Predication is true to a great extent", median)

Basically programs like this are not very helpful	1
Such programs should be used more widely	5
I would recommend this program to other students	4
I liked using the learning material	4
Programs like this should be improved further	5
I am interested in using learning methods that support time- and place-independent study	4.5
I would have preferred to use a paper-based text	3
The possibilities of computer-based learning programs have not been exhausted	4

us using videoconferencing technology. Likewise, some of our lectures are transferred to other locations. This means we can offer more lectures to our students, and other universities can use our lectures. However, support for such telelectures (Lienhard, 2001) is carried out locally, as for classical lectures. This means that there are also laboratory courses, online tutoring, and Web presentations for each telelecture that we transfer from another location.

Knowledge Acquisition

In WebCEIS, *knowledge acquisition* takes place in three forms: seminars, laboratory courses with tutoring, and laboratory courses without tutoring.

Some new technology is also used in classical seminars. For example, students are supposed to use a document management system for preparing their seminar papers. As a special form of our classical seminars, we offer so-called teleseminars to our students. The difference between classical seminars and teleseminars is that teleseminars take place by means of cooperation with other universities, supported by videoconferencing and groupware technology. In such teleseminars, about 10 students at each location are familiarized with communication and document management tools, thus enabling them to acquire media competence and virtual teamwork in addition to the academic subject of the seminar. As another positive effect, teleseminars on special topics can be offered by means of cooperation with several universities, even if there are not enough interested students in each of the universities.

Classical laboratory courses are also extended by Web-based support. For example, laboratory courses take place once a week with one tutor and a few students. Each laboratory course has a Web page giving students the possibility of downloading their weekly exercise sheets. We are also increasingly offering Web-based exercises for self-training on our Web pages. It is, of course, also possible to communicate with the tutor via email. Furthermore, we intend to offer newsgroups for all our courses, so that students can discuss exercises among themselves or with the tutor. In addition, the tutors of all laboratory courses should have fixed times when they are online on the learning platform. The students can then chat with them and ask questions, if they have any problems with their weekly exercises. The implementation of this communication technology is in progress for all our courses.

Laboratory courses without tutoring are a type of self-learning, where students come to computer rooms or sit at home in front of their computers and learn interactively. The learning material used for this purpose has to be adjusted to the other material that has been provided for the students in the knowledge transfer phase.

Knowledge Control

In the field of knowledge control, a differentiation has to be made between two essentially different types—official examinations held by the university, and the self-assessment of students. Because the risk of cheating is high when using new technology during examinations, we have not made any changes in this context within WebCEIS yet. There is one test for each lecture in a term, and this is not Web-based. It would be possible to offer programming examinations in computer rooms, for example, and marking them automatically would be conceivable, but the initial effort required is quite significant.

In contrast to the examinations, the self-assessment of students has been improved in many ways. Some of our interactive learning material supports the students in testing their knowledge. For example, there are interactive elements in which a certain problem has to be solved. Moreover, examinations can be simulated using special assessment material. They are evaluated in part automatically, and in part by the students.

Administrative and Social Affairs

There are many *administrative* and *social affairs* in a classical university education scenario. Our integrated WebCEIS scenario is based on supporting them using the Web. For example, in our scenario, all information on the content and scheduling of lectures can be found on the Web. Registration for lectures can also be carried out electronically. Students can also provide information about their examination dates and results on the Web.

In contrast to administrative affairs, social affairs such as meetings in the campus café are difficult to replace, because face-to-face communication is impossible to replicate. We are not, therefore, trying to develop virtual cafés, etc., with avatars. We are just giving students the opportunity to chat with each other wherever they are and whatever they are doing in our system, and also to enter newsgroups with interesting topics. They can use these possibilities to organize their real social activities.

Technique

The following description of the technical infrastructure used in WebCEIS is divided into the specification of our networks and the description of the hardware and software equipment used by the university and students, respectively.

Networks

For the distribution of our eLearning material to students, we use standard Internet connections. The students can therefore access the material from computer rooms on the campus and also at home via any Internet provider.

In addition to these common methods of Internet access, a wireless LAN has been installed on the campus. Using this LAN, it is possible to establish Internet connections with any notebook containing an appropriate PC card. The installation of our wireless network was carried out by the Computing Center of the University of Karlsruhe (Wolf, 2000). Important aspects were the privacy of wireless connections and the linking of the wireless network to existing networks.

In order to hold the videoconferences described, a guaranteed quality of service is absolutely necessary, because even minor malfunctions would seriously disrupt seminars. For this reason, we are using a wideband network providing a reserved bandwidth which was installed between the cooperating universities. It was implemented as a virtual LAN within their ATM network. Using this LAN, it is possible to implement sessions with standard MBone technology (Kumar, 1996) as well as sessions using MPEG2 compression (Orzessek & Sommer, 1998). The necessary network extensions were implemented as part of the VIROR project (VIROR, 2001; Kandzia & Ottmann, 1999).

Hardware and Software: The University

For our videoconferences, we also need quite expensive hardware equipment in the cooperating universities. In each of our so-called teleclassrooms (see Figure 3), we need at least:

- Two video cameras, which film the student giving the talk and the auditorium, respectively
- Three wireless microphones, for example, one for the student giving his talk, one for the moderator of the session, and one for the auditorium
- One, or preferably two, projectors to display screen content and photos of all the participants not present

For high-quality conferences using MPEG2 technology, we also need a special MPEG2 coder and decoder. For other sessions using standard MBone technology, we only need a standard PC with the following appropriate software:

- sdr ("session directory tool") to allow the announcing and joining of conferences on MBone (Kumar, 1996)
- vic ("videoconferencing tool"), responsible for the transmission and reception of video data (Kumar, 1996)
- rat ("robust audio tool"), which is the corresponding software for audio data (Kumar, 1996)
- dlb ("digital lecture board"), which is an enhanced whiteboard developed at the University of Mannheim (Geyer & Effelsberg, 1998; dlb, 2001). dlb can be used for shared slide presentations and is specially adapted for use in synchronous teleteaching scenarios.

Apart from the videoconferencing hardware, no other nonstandard hardware is needed in the university, i.e., we only need standard servers and workstations.

On one of our servers, we installed a Hyperwave eLearning Suite (Hyperwave, 2001) as our eLearning platform. The Hyperwave eLearning Suite includes much of the technology needed for Web-based education that has been described above. More precisely, it provides so-called virtual classrooms, from which learning material can be accessed. Furthermore, it supports the communication and cooperation of all the participants involved, for example,

Figure 3: Teleclassroom

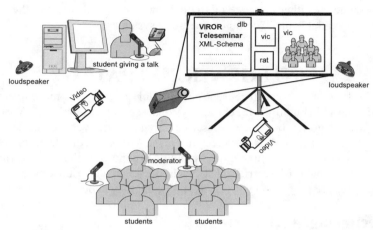

via email, chats, or discussion forums. Our decision to use the Hyperwave eLearning Suite was made following a requirements analysis and detailed comparisons of eLearning platforms such as those in the literature ("Online educational delivery applications: a Web tool for comparative analysis," 2002). The most important arguments in favor of the Hyperwave eLearning Suite were that it offers special support for annotating the learning material and for ensuring the consistency of the learning material, for example, in relation to the linking of learning modules. Furthermore, the Hyperwave eLearning Suite can be used free of charge by academic users who are taking part in the "Hyperwave Academic User Program (HAUP)".

Some more special software is needed by the authors of our eLearning material. We use professional authoring tools to create our material, including interactive animations and simulations:

- For the development of Web pages, we use Macromedia Dreamweaver. This tool is one of the most common Web editors. Besides a broad range of design functionality, it provides support for the collaboration of authoring teams.
- Animations and simulations are created with Macromedia Flash. Flash animations are also popular, and they can be used with many Web browsers on many platforms.
- For the creation of most of our graphics, we use Macromedia Fireworks. It is specially adapted for Web graphics and for animated graphics, in particular.

For some complex simulations, the capabilities of Macromedia Flash are not adequate. In such cases, it is easier to develop Java applets, which can be used on many platforms. For the programming of these Java applets we use Borland JBuilder.

Hardware and Software: The Students

In our scenario, students currently do not attend videoconferences from their home offices. For this reason, they only need the hardware and software to access our eLearning material.

As already described, this material is developed using only standard Web technology. Therefore, the students do not require any nonstandard software, and compatibility problems can be avoided. Our students only need an industry-standard PC with a standard Web browser to access our eLearning material. The plug-in needed for Flash-animations and a Java virtual machine are either integrated into the browsers or, in the case of the most popular browsers, are available on all common operating systems.

INTEGRATION STRATEGY

In the following, we will present one possible strategy for the implementation of WebCEIS. Shown in Figure 4 is the chronology of the appropriate activities. We have divided them into two categories: first, we will describe activities that have to be carried out only once, and after that, we will look at the recurring ones. We have completed the nonrecurring activities as per the following integration strategy. In contrast to the nonrecurring activities, the recurring ones have to be carried out for each course. The corresponding implementations for our lectures are progressing at varying rates, but they should all be completed soon.

Nonrecurring Activities

Here, we will specify the activities that have to be carried out only once in our process of integrating Web-based education into classical education:

• *Analysis of situation*: First, the current situation in the university has to be analyzed. In this connection, a survey of the existing technical infrastructure should be carried out as a basis for further planning. Here, the equipment of the university and its employees should be considered as well as the students' equipment. Important aspects of this analysis are the hardware and software and the networks used by the institutions and persons involved. As well as the technical aspects, the organizational circumstances also have to be considered. This step is important, because the integration of Web-based education should be adapted to existing organizational procedures. Another important part of the analysis is the inspection of the financial scope. Because

Figure 4: Integration Strategy Activities

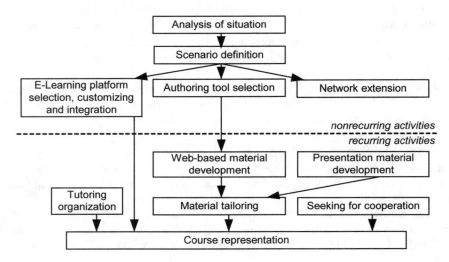

short-term savings cannot be expected, it has to be decided which of the planned expenses can be met with the regular budget and where applications for special project promotions should be made.

- *Scenario definition*: After the analysis of the current situation, the target state of the planned teaching and learning scenario has to be defined. The result of this phase has been presented in detail in the preceding chapter. To reach these results, it is necessary to consider all the requirements of the parties involved and their individual concepts.

- *eLearning platform selection, customizing and integration*: As a basis for eLearning activities, an eLearning platform has to be selected. Therefore, a requirements analysis should be carried out, and different products on the market should be evaluated. Once the decision for a particular platform is made, it has to be customized to meet specific requirements. The next step in the implementation of the eLearning platform is its integration into the infrastructure of existing information systems. For example, the user administration functions of different services on the campus should be merged or at least linked.

- *Authoring tool selection*: For the authoring of Web-based eLearning material, appropriate authoring tools have to be selected. Although the text in such material could be created with any HTML editor, it makes sense to concentrate on only one product. This way, the definition of a uniform layout and the exchange of material between different authors are greatly simplified. In addition to the HTML editor, tools for the authoring of animations and simulations have to be selected. We have decided to use popular and coordinated tools from a single company to avoid incompatibility and to reduce the authors' workload. If, for example, platform-independent Java applets were also used in the material, a suitable programming environment would have to be selected for this purpose.

- *Network extension*: To implement WebCEIS, an extension of the network infrastructure will be necessary in most cases. Basically, two components have to be taken into account: the wireless network and the network between the university and its partner universities. Important aspects in the context of the wireless network are the privacy of wireless connections and the linking of the wireless network to existing networks. For the cooperation of partner universities, wideband networks are needed to achieve a guaranteed quality of service, for example, during videoconferences.

Recurring Activities

Recurring activities that must be repeated for each lecture in our process of integrating Web-based education into classical education can be summarized as follows:

- *Web-based material development*: After selecting the authoring tools, the teaching material can be developed. For typing in the HTML code for the Web-based material, special graphical HTML editors such as Macromedia Dreamweaver can be used in addition to text editors. This also facilitates editing and managing the hyperlinks between different teaching materials. Graphics and animations, which will be integrated into the HTML-based teaching material later, can be developed with authoring tools like Macromedia-Flash or Fireworks, or can be programmed using languages such as Java. The authoring tools have the advantage that nonprogrammers can also develop good animations easily using these tools, but they are restricted to some predetermined functionality, and therefore, in contrast to programming languages, they do not give the authors the ability to develop more complex animations.

- *Presentation material development*: The development of presentation material for the instructor is the other content development activity. Because Web-based material supplements the classical lecture, it is important that the content of the presentation material be developed in line with the Web-based material. Otherwise, the students would have problems deciding which parts of the material in the two types were relevant for their examination. The presentation material can also be developed in HTML or using presentation programs such as Microsoft PowerPoint.
- *Material tailoring*: The Web-based material has to be adapted to the lecture presentation material, and the Web-based exercise material also has to be adapted to the exercise sheets for laboratory courses. This can be achieved best by using the same interactive elements, such as multimedia animations, in the presentation and the Web-based material.
- *Tutoring organization*: The tutoring for real and virtual laboratory courses should be organized by determining the activities and the manpower for them.
- *Seeking cooperation*: Another important activity is identifying cooperation opportunities with other universities in order to exchange lectures and seminars that will be supported by videoconferencing technology. This can open new types of virtual collaboration in a classical education scenario. For example, we benefited from many cooperation opportunities with universities in Germany in order to hold our teleseminars and telelectures.
- *Course representation*: Each lecture, each laboratory course, and each seminar has to be represented by a page on the eLearning platform. These pages can also be extended with material, chats, newsgroups, etc.

CONCLUSION AND OUTLOOK

The comparison of classical with Web-based education in regard to technology, roles, and scenarios helped us to find out which education type will best suit which learner group. We have discovered that for the "*local full-time learner*" group, on which we have concentrated, an integration of classical and Web-based education would be the best solution. As an example of such integration, we presented our WebCEIS scenario (Web-based and Classical Education Integration Scenario), examining organizational and technical aspects. In order to implement WebCEIS, we followed a special integration strategy consisting of nonrecurring and recurring activities.

We plan to continue using our integrated education scenario and, of course, to expand it. We have the following ideas on integrating Web-based education into our classical training types: we plan to widen the classical seminar work in our teleseminars through virtual project work. Our purpose here is to concentrate more on collaborative working. In the short term, we plan to set up rooms with PC workstations for laboratory courses. In the longer term, we are sure that every student will have his own notebook, which he can take to lectures and laboratory courses. In lectures, he can annotate the Web-based material instead of writing notes on paper as he previously did. This means he gets his own personalized Web-based material for each lecture. Students can also use their notebooks for interactive exercises on laboratory courses. Another objective is to extend the local network so that video conferencing is possible anywhere as quickly and easily as chatting is today.

REFERENCES

dlb—digital lecture board. Retrieved December 17, 2001 from the World Wide Web: http://www.informatik.uni-mannheim.de/informatik/pi4/projects/dlb/.

Geyer, W., & Effelsberg, W. (1998). The digital lecture board—a teaching and learning tool for remote instruction in higher education. *Proceedings EDMEDIA '98, World Conference on Educational Multimedia and Hypermedia*, Freiburg.

Lawhead, P. B., Alpert, E., & Bland, C. G. et al. (1997). *The Web and distance learning: what is appropriate and what is not.* Report of the ITiCSE'97 Working Group on the Web and Distance Learning, Working Group Reports and Supplemental Proceedings SIGCSE/SIGCUE ITiCSE'97.

Holmes, W. N. (1999). The myth of the educational computer. *IEEE Computer, September, 99*, 36–42.

Hyperwave AG. Hyperwave eLearning Suite. (2001). Retrieved December 19, 2001 from the World Wide Web: http://www.hyperwave.com/e/products/els.html.

Kandzia, P.-T., & Ottmann, T. (1999). VIROR: the virtual university in the Upper Rhine valley—a new challenge for four prestigious universities in Germany. *Proceedings Role of Universities in the Future Information Society (RUFIS'99)*. Flagstaff.

Klein, M., & Stucky, W. (2001). Ein Vorgehensmodell zur Erstellung virtueller Bildungsinhalte. *WIRTSCHAFTSINFORMATIK, 43*, 35–45.

Kumar, V. (1996). *MBone: interactive multimedia on the Internet.* Indianapolis: New Riders Publishing.

Lienhard, J. (2001). *Problems and solutions while transmitting lectures.* Retrieved December 11, 2001 from the World Wide Web: http://www.viror.de/service/publikationen/dokumente/lienhard-enable99.doc.

Online educational delivery applications: a Web tool for comparative analysis. Retrieved January 9, 2002 from the World Wide Web: http://www.c2t2.ca/landonline/choices.asp.

Orzessek, M., & Sommer, P. (1998). *ATM & MPEG-2: integrating digital video into broadband networks.* Upper Saddle River, NJ: Prentice Hall.

Rosbottom, J. (2001). *Hybrid learning— a safe route into Web-based open and distance learning for the computer science teacher.* Proceedings of the 6th annual conference of Innovation and technology in computer science education, Canterbury, United Kingdom.

VHBW—Virtual university of Baden-Württemberg. Retrieved November 8, 2001, from http://www.virtuelle-hochschule.de.

ViKar—Virtual university group Karlsruhe. Retrieved November 8, 2001 from the World Wide Web: http://www.vikar.de.

VIROR—Virtual university in the Upper Rhine Valley. (2001). Retrieved November 8, 2001 from the World Wide Web: http://www.viror.de.

WBT Systems. TopClass. Retrieved January 9, 2002 from the World Wide Web: http://www.wbtsystems.com/products/server_index.html.

WebCT Inc. WebCT. (2002). Retrieved January 9, 2002 from the World Wide Web: http://www.Webct.com/products.

Wolf, L. (2000). DUKATH—das drahtlose Netz der Universität Karlsruhe. *Praxis der Informationsverarbeitung und Kommunikation, 4/2000*. München: K. G. Saur Verlag.

Chapter XXIV

Integrating Online Educational Activities in Traditional Courses: University-wide Lessons after Three Years

Jane Klobas
University of Western Australia, Australia and Bocconi University, Italy

Stefano Renzi
Bocconi University, Italy

ABSTRACT

This chapter presents a case study of how a university responded to educational and technological change. After an introduction to Bocconi University (an Italian private business university) and the recent changes in the Italian university system, the case describes the initiation and management over three years of a project to integrate Web-enhanced learning (WEL) into classroom-based courses. The case includes identification of profiles of WEL adoption and description of the technology choice, how the teachers adopted the innovation and how students responded. The project is presented as organizational innovation and compared with the stages of the Rogers' model of diffusion of innovations. Two groups of conditions for success were identified. Conditions common to IS innovation included top management commitment, a supportive environment, and appropriate ICT infrastructure. Conditions specific to WEL included teacher preparedness, appropriate use, appropriate scale, and flexibility.

This chapter addresses the issue of integration of online learning into classroom-based learning to achieve effective and manageable Web-enhanced learning (WEL) for on-campus students. The focus is on change across a university system rather than in an individual classroom. While some excellent works are now available on implementing new approaches to learning in individual courses (e.g., Palloff & Pratt, 1999; Palloff & Pratt, 2001), and general texts and models of conditions needed for wider diffusion are emerging (e.g., Bates, 2000; Surry, 2002), the available case studies tend to be about new wholly virtual universities or about the adoption of new technologies for wholly distance learning. Many of these are short vignettes rather than analytical case studies, and with few exceptions (e.g., Friedlander, 2002; López del Puerto, 1999), lessons are not clearly drawn from these cases to wider principles or to applications for other universities. Those principles that are drawn tend to focus on specific lessons for implementing distance learning (DL) rather than for using Web-based technologies to complement or to improve the quality of classroom-based learning (e.g., Friedlander's "Use DL only when other traditional forms do not work," p. 3).

Systematic studies of traditional universities' attempts to introduce large-scale WEL have not identified great success. After a two-year study of the UK context, Pollock and Cornford (2000) concluded "that the universities which we have studied have found the introduction of new technologies, alongside their more traditional methods of providing teaching and learning, extremely difficult ... What we have found is that the Virtual University works in theory but not in practice." Pollock and Cornford place the blame on the approach taken by universities. They criticize the bottom-up approach, in which individual teachers and courses adopt new technologies in the absence of a university-wide vision. They note how implementations have failed to engage all aspects of the university required for success, including academic staff, computer services departments, and partner institutions. Finally, they caution against approaches that call for standardization without vision.

Attempts to identify characteristics of successful diffusion of instructional technology in higher educational institutions have produced several different models. Some focus on aspects of diffusion: Hall & Hord (1987) considered the role played by people in facilitating change; Ely (1999) considered the conditions that facilitate the implementation of an innovation; Stockdill and Morehouse (1992) developed a checklist of the factors that affect adoption; Farquhar and Surry (1994) listed four categories of factors affecting the adoption. Other authors have taken a broader view, incorporating evaluation of teaching technologies among their models of success (Bates, 1995, 2000; Surry, 2002). Despite their apparent differences, most of the cited works have roots in diffusion of innovation theory and, more specifically, the work of Everett Rogers (1995), yet none uses Rogers' complete framework of organizational diffusion of innovation to systematically study technology-based innovation in education.

The case study presented here describes how Bocconi University, a private business university in Milan, Italy, is developing methods for integrating Web-based education into its classroom-based courses. The case identifies the vision that has driven the change, and the ways in which critical actors have been engaged during the first three years of the university's experience. Diffusion of innovations theory (Rogers, 1995) is used as the organizing and analytical framework for the case. Working from this established theory, the case demonstrates how change associated with adoption and diffusion of new educational technology follows stages similar to those of innovation processes in other types of organizations (Holloway, 1996). As Pollock and Cornford's work suggests, the case demonstrates how nontechnical, as well as technical, issues are critical to the success of changes that involve information technology.

BACKGROUND: CHANGES IN ITALY'S UNIVERSITY SYSTEM

In Italy, as in other countries, universities are undergoing great change. During the academic year that began in October 2001, the entire university system moved from a mix of short (three-year) and long (four- to six-year) first degrees to a two-tiered system designed to be more compatible with the systems in other European countries. In this new system, all universities offer a three-year first degree that may be followed by a two-year higher degree.

At the same time, the availability of new educational technologies has fueled debate about the ways in which teaching and learning are conducted. Italian universities have traditionally emphasized theory over work tools, methods, and other techniques. Most lessons consist of lectures, often in large lecture halls, with little student participation and few tutorials or other forms of small group work. University teachers in Italy are not required to have undertaken any formal education in pedagogy or the practice of teaching. Leading educators have suggested that new technologies provide an opportunity to improve the quality of teaching and learning at Italian universities. Proposed advantages include opportunities for self-study at a distance from the classroom and for small group work through online collaborative learning (Calvani & Rotta, 2000).

RESPONDING TO EDUCATIONAL AND TECHNOLOGICAL CHANGE: A CASE STUDY IN WEB-ENHANCED LEARNING AS TECHNOLOGY-ENABLED CHANGE

This case study examines how Bocconi University responded to the challenges and opportunities presented by changes in the university system and technological environment, at the same time as the university was planning significant growth. The case traces the university's introduction of Web-enhanced learning to support new approaches to teaching, from the time that the changes were announced in 1998 to the end of the third year of implementation, in 2001–2002.

Bocconi University and the New Educational System

Bocconi University was founded in 1902, the first Italian University to have a faculty of economics and commerce. Today, it is one of the world's leading business universities (http://specials.ft.com/businesseducation/FT3S5ND9MWC.html), with graduates in senior positions in government and industry throughout Europe. Bocconi is a private (nonprofit) single faculty university that offers seven first-level degree programs in economics and commerce, and several courses at higher levels. (The university also has a semi-autonomous business school, SDA Bocconi, which offers executive programs including an MBA. This case study is concerned with actions taken by the central university rather than by SDA.)

In total, 14,000 students are enrolled to take the formal degrees of the university, 1,000 of them in postgraduate programs, including the new higher-degree courses. More than 300 units are offered within the first level programs.

The university sets high standards for students. It was the first university in Italy to introduce admission exams. Demand for places exceeds availability, student motivation is high, and the university has higher completion rates than other Italian universities. In the period before introduction of the new system, 89% of enrolled Bocconi students completed the four to six year *Laurea*, while the national mean for students enrolled in economics and commerce was 38%. Mean completion time for Bocconi students was 5.9 years, while the national mean for other universities was 7.8 years.

The quality of education provided is also important to the university. Bocconi introduced the new Italian university system for students who commenced their course in the 1999–2000 academic year, thus beginning two years before adoption of the new model was compulsory. This initiative was combined with two others: a plan to substantially increase student numbers, and a push toward further improving the quality of education at the university. The university set several quality goals, including to break with the traditional way of teaching at Italian universities by increasing the active participation of students in their learning.

The first two years of undergraduate study at Bocconi consist primarily of compulsory core courses, while in the final year(s), students take a combination of core and elective courses. Each year, students are assigned to a class of around 150 students for their core courses. Depending on the degree, a first-year core course may have up to 15 classes. Each course has a coordinator, and a team of teachers who teach to a set syllabus. In some courses, all teachers use common material. In others, the teachers have more freedom to choose how to meet the needs of the syllabus. All courses have a classroom component, and at the time the changes were announced, almost all followed the common model for Italian universities, consisting entirely or almost entirely of lessons delivered by the teacher from the front of the room.

Investment in educational services reflects the university's commitment to quality. It has long made a significant commitment to information and communication technology (ICT). By 1999, the university therefore had a well developed ICT infrastructure which was widely used by staff and students for administration. Nearly all teachers and administrative staff had a PC connected to the university network, email was widely used for communication within the offices of the university, and an increasing number of applications was available to cover internal administration needs. Students were able to interact with the university via Internet (e.g., for enrollments) or to obtain updated information, such as timetables and last-minute changes of classroom. Each student was supplied by the university with a personal email address. A network-connected PC was available in each classroom for use by the teacher, but relatively few PCs were provided for student use: 240 computers in general access laboratories and 200 in classrooms. Around 25% of students had their own PCs. These facilities were sufficient to meet demand.

The strategy of the university is to maintain its investment in ICT (continually updating to new technologies) to be able to satisfy a growing number of users for increasingly sophisticated applications. Even before the new educational initiatives were introduced in 1999, Bocconi had an established multimedia committee and had planned to upgrade all network infrastructure to provide sufficient bandwidth to carry streaming video for educational purposes.

Initiating the Web-Enhanced Learning Project

In May 1998, the multimedia committee established a working party to introduce a platform for Web-enhanced learning. The working party began work on what came to be called the B-Learning (Bocconi eLearning) project in June 1998.

The cross-functional working party consisted of all the people needed to implement an initial pilot project, from the pilot teachers, to the people in charge of technological infrastructure design and implementation, to those responsible for computer center operations. This composition was designed to ensure that the working party was able to monitor all aspects of the feasibility of the project from its initiation. In addition, the most senior figures in university administration (the Managing Director) and teaching and learning (the Pro-Rettore for teaching) participated in working party meetings, where key decisions were to be made. In this way, information could be exchanged directly, and decisions could be made quickly. This arrangement ensured that all the people involved in the project were not just personally involved in planning, but also shared responsibility for project success.

One characteristic that set the Bocconi working party apart from those set up in other universities at the time was its focus on a long-term vision. From the beginning, the Bocconi working party saw the aim of the project as effective implementation of Web-enhanced learning to improve the quality of teaching and learning at the university, a long-term vision rather than a one-off pilot or test project. The group's short-term goal was to introduce Web-enhanced learning in a limited number of pilot or exemplar courses, commencing in the first semester of the 1999–2000 academic year.

The first actions of the working party were to identify the critical technical elements in an eLearning project and a model for representing use of the World Wide Web to enhance the learning of on-campus students. Critical technical elements included the availability of PCs, provision of laboratories, network bandwidth, remote connections, and training.

Drawing on Angerhn's (1999) classification of Internet business strategies as creating virtual spaces for information, communication, distribution, and transactions (the ICDT model), the working party defined five profiles of use of the Web to enhance on-campus learning. The profiles are listed in Table 1 by increasing level of complexity. Each of the higher levels includes the features of the lower levels.

All courses at Bocconi have a *Traditional Web* presence. The project was therefore concerned with enabling *Advanced Web* and more complex uses. The university's goal to increase active student involvement in their learning would be achieved partially through use of WEL to support the *Interactive Web* profile, and more fully in implementation of *CSCL* environments.

The working party decided to support the most complex of the operational profiles, the *CSCL* profile. In addition, they decided to include a large number of students in the initial implementation. This approach carried some risk. Nonetheless, it was decided that the best test of an approach that would be suitable for the entire university would be a pilot implementation that incorporated all the components of successful larger-scale implementation: teachers, students, organization, network, hardware, and software.

In August 1998, a report on the working party's considerations was delivered to the Pro-Rettore for teaching and the Managing Director. These senior university decision makers then met with the working party to confirm the strategy and business plan for the project, and to give the go-ahead to commence work. This meeting confirmed the working party's approach.

Table 1: A Hierarchy of WEL Use Profiles

Level[a]	Label	Use
1	Traditional Web	*An environment to inform about the course.* This is the course website structure usually available at universities, containing at least: description of the course, list of suggested textbooks, lesson timetable, teacher name(s) with location and availability for students, exam procedures, and calendar
2	Advanced Web[b]	*An environment to distribute educational material.* In this case, the Web becomes something more dynamic, and the contents are put online from time to time during the life of the course. Some examples of contents: educational material used by teachers in the classroom (slides, case studies, newspaper articles, and site URLs related to the course content), text of past exams, exam solutions, communication from the teacher(s) and the University
3	Interactive Web	*A bidirectional interactive environment.* This profile includes teacher–student and student–student interactions. The interactions are mainly based on the use of course forums, resource contributions, self-evaluation tests, delivery of assignments, and secure online exams
4	CSCL	*A CSCL (Computer Supported Collaborative Learning) environment where the teaching and learning are mainly based on student groups.* This profile is more complex than the interactive Web, in that it supports collaborative group learning and activities that go beyond those possible with simple course forums. Activities supported may include group projects that involve sharing materials or preparation of joint documents.
5	Experimental	*An experimental environment for pilot applications testing new ideas.* The final profile was thought of as an environment available for teachers to experiment with new tools or technological solutions.

a. Use at each level includes the uses at each preceding level.
b. This level was later split into two: (2A) Distribution of standard course material and (2B) Distribution of additional material by individual teachers

Selecting the Software Platform

Once the decision had been made to enable teachers to use WEL for CSCL, and to reach a large number of students from the beginning of the project, the working party studied the approaches taken by similar universities. In the absence of published case studies, most of this analysis rested on use of the contacts of teachers who already had experience in online and computer-supported learning, and on visits to other universities. A template was developed for collecting and reporting data, and four detailed case studies of leading business schools in the United States, UK, and Europe were collected. The most well-known software platforms were examined, taking into account not only system features but also compatibility with the university's current technical environment and the availability of personnel with the skills required to run the system. A key criterion for selection was the availability of support for the proposed innovative and extensive implementation of the learning platform. At the end of this period, Microsoft and IBM were identified as providers in the Italian market with the most potential to meet Bocconi's criteria. A solution from Microsoft would involve development of a custom-made system, while a solution from IBM would involve implementation of IBM-Lotus LearningSpace (an application based on Lotus Notes client and Domino servers).

By the end of November 1998, the working party had received preliminary proposals. During December 1998 and January 1999, members held meetings with Microsoft and IBM-Lotus and evaluated the companies' offerings. By the end of the period, group opinion was split between those who preferred a Microsoft-based solution and those who preferred to adopt IBM-Lotus LearningSpace. The dilemma was referred to the university's senior managers who opted for LearningSpace, but allowed those who wished to do so to experiment with Microsoft-based development.

Despite potential compatibility with the university's desktop environment and earlier success with a small-scale online learning environment developed with Microsoft tools, development of a custom-built Microsoft-based solution as a potential platform for use across the entire university was not considered feasible (at least in the short term) on several grounds. Management considered the Microsoft option too risky in terms of the effort needed for the application design, the time required to have an application running, and the people and skills required for development and maintenance.

A university-wide solution based on IBM-Lotus LearningSpace had several points of particular strength. The solution was based on a software product that had been in the market for several years and was fully supported in Milan by IBM-Lotus. From a user's point of view, it has a simple but powerful structure that permits it to be used as a course management environment. The four components of the system—course schedule, repository for course materials, testing and assignment submission facilities, and a system to support student group activities such as discussion and document sharing—are linked. Furthermore, the system architecture (based on the Lotus Notes concept of replication) is robust and suitable for a multilocation campus and for staff and students working from off-campus locations. The contents of the system (or a subset of it) can be replicated across servers and between a server and a client. All contents are published as Web documents and are, therefore, accessible by Web browser.

Some points of weakness with LearningSpace were also identified. The most critical of these was user definition. Ability to rapidly enroll large numbers of students in the online course environment at the beginning of semester was critical, but in the version available at the start of the project, the system administrator was required to establish each user account individually. This weakness was resolved by assigning a group of temporary administrators to the task of enrolling students during the first weeks of semester.

The Technology and External Support for the Project

The choice of technology was strongly influenced by the technology provider's commitment to the project. On the technological side, there are many layers involved in a Web-enhanced learning platform: the network (including the need for adequate bandwidth and reliable connections inside and outside the university), the server(s), and the application. Configuring the server requires attention to several interrelated factors, including appropriate configuration of the physical machine to react properly to a high volume of transactions, appropriate positioning within the network, the operating system, and tuning the operating system to work in the presence of the applications. The application relies on several layers of underlying software, including a Web application. Diagnosing a problem encountered by a user can therefore be quite complicated, and the solutions may be complicated. A support mechanism was required to enable rapid identification and resolution of problems in such a complex, but time-critical environment.

Senior management decided that the best solution was to make an agreement with a single partner who would have responsibility for all layers of the technology. A special agreement was signed with IBM Italia (whose software group is now responsible for the formerly independent Lotus software). The agreement involved IBM as a partner in all aspects of the project: network capacity planning, identification of the characteristics of the server to be used, its position in the network, installation of the server software and of the LearningSpace system, tuning, and monitoring of the system. In addition, IBM provided specialized personnel on-site and training for the computer center personnel involved in the project. IBM was also charged with organization of training courses for all the teachers, tutors dedicated to system support, and students.

This agreement was challenging for IBM as well as for Bocconi. The complexity, the approach, and goals, and the numbers involved, made the project unique in Europe. The project and the agreement would, if successful, provide a model to be reproduced in other universities.

Internal Organization for Project Support

The risk associated with introducing a technologically complex new system at the beginning of the academic year, with relatively large numbers of students enrolling and placing a heavy and somewhat unpredictable load on the system, was sufficiently high that other aspects of project initiation were designed to be as low risk as possible. The teachers involved in the pilot project were chosen because they already had considerable experience in use of technology in education. Within the university's strategic vision, and with the support of a platform that enabled a variety of uses of WEL, each teacher was free to find their own way to integrate the new technology with their teaching.

The computer center was selected as the most appropriate internal organizational unit to take responsibility for the project. The computer center already had a small subunit dedicated to supporting teachers' use of technology. This subunit acted as project manager, point of reference for the teachers involved in the project, and interface with IBM.

Preparing for Implementation

Preparation for implementation required much effort. Detailed analysis of the technical and human requirements for implementation was conducted between February and April 1999.

Three courses were selected for pilot implementation in the first semester of the 1999–2000 academic year, beginning in September 1999. One course was a core fourth-year unit in Strategic Management; three classes of students in this course participated in the pilot. The other two courses were electives available to students in their third or fourth year. One of the electives was a unit in management consulting, while the other was an advanced course in the Internet and Data Processing. Altogether, around 500 students in five classes were involved in the pilot implementation.

Training for the teachers began in May 1999. The teachers prepared their course materials in parallel with their training. The training, provided by experienced IBM LearningSpace trainers, combined online course design with technical skills for use of the software. This approach provided an opportunity for trainers to advise the teachers on ways in which LearningSpace might be used to meet their educational goals. All of the courses were at least partially redesigned to include group learning activities for students. All these pilot courses, therefore, adopted the approach described as the *CSCL* profile (level 4) in Table 1.

By July (after a delay) the teachers involved were equipped with high-end multimedia capable portable PCs. The system was made available to the teachers through Lotus Notes client software on their portable PCs. Students were able to use the Lotus Notes client installed in student laboratories and specialized classrooms or to access their class LearningSpace via Internet using a standard Web browser.

By August 1999, almost all was ready for implementation. The information technology infrastructure was upgraded, a Lotus Domino server was activated, and the buildings office had fitted out two new classrooms, which were equipped with 60 and 90 PCs dedicated for the semester to project activities. Online courses in use of LearningSpace were developed for the students, and a tutor was assigned to each of the new classroom/labs to help students if they encountered problems. By the first day of the semester, initial course materials were loaded, and the system had been tested and load simulations done.

B-Learning Goes Live!

There was great tension as the courses that used LearningSpace began. Even though system testing and load simulations had been done, all the people participating in the project had enough experience with new system implementations to expect the unexpected. In the spirit of excitement and team work that had accompanied the seven months of preparation, the entire implementation project team (both internal and external) was prepared to manage unexpected problems or failures. The university and IBM were conscious of the size of the project and the extent of innovation it involved, and each group had confidence in the other, creating a strong spirit of collaboration.

The most critical problems appeared during the first weeks following implementation, but the implementation task force was able to deal with them. Perhaps the most significant of these problems was that the system, under peak load, had poor response time. This problem generated a chain of subsequent problems. The tools used to monitor the situation revealed bandwidth saturation at a critical point in the network. In a combined action, the computing center and IBM rapidly installed and configured a second server and reallocated resources within the university network. This solved the problem and provided information with which to review some components of the system architecture and plan additional features to balance the load.

Initial Evaluation

One month after the start of semester, the project team held a planned review meeting. Despite the early problems, all the teachers involved in the project declared their full satisfaction and intention to continue. Students had not raised any significant problems with their teachers or tutors, either in the labs, or in response to specific questions in class; instead, they seem simply to have accepted the LearningSpace, and therefore WEL, as a normal part of their university learning environment.

At the end of semester, a formal evaluation was conducted for the advanced course in Internet and Data Processing. This course retained standard classroom lessons. In addition, the new design used directed online discussions, collaborative online group work, and in-class group presentations to provide opportunities for more active student engagement with the material and with the teachers and one another. Participation in the online and group activities was voluntary, but those who chose to participate received grades for their work during the semester, and the percentage contribution of their final exam was reduced commensurately. Of the 104 students enrolled in the course, 95 chose to participate in the LearningSpace supported activities. While participation in the WEL activities was not expected to result in higher grades, it was expected to result in higher student satisfaction with the course and higher achievement of meta-outcomes (generic competencies and attitudes) believed to be important among university business graduates. Responses to the postcourse evaluation questionnaire returned by 75% of the completing students confirmed that student satisfaction with the course was high for all students except a small group that preferred a more theoretical than active approach to learning. Students who participated in the CSCL activities had higher self-efficacy for learning and a stronger preference for collaborative work at the end of the course than at the beginning, thus confirming that participation in these activities had valuable meta-outcomes over and above subject learning. These effects were greater for those students who participated most actively in the collaborative activities than for those who participated less actively (Klobas & Renzi, 2001).

Semester 2, 1999–2000: Implementation for Simple Uses of WEL–and some Spontaneous Adoption

After the success of the ambitious pilot project, an unexpected problem emerged. The pilot demonstrated that LearningSpace was suitable for CSCL. But, would it be suitable for more simple uses of WEL? Some members of the working party suggested that there may be a need to select another software platform designed specifically to support simple uses. They argued that providing the same platform for both simple and complex uses could be a barrier to adoption for simple uses and, therefore, to initial trials of WEL. Others argued that, while a simpler platform might be easier to learn and use, it could become a barrier to migration to the more complex uses required if the university is to meet its goal for more active student participation in learning.

It was decided to test the performance of LearningSpace for simple WEL use profiles with a full test in a real course. A new course was therefore added to the project. The selected course was a compulsory first-year course in Financial Accounting. This course was taken by 2000 students in 2000–2001. LearningSpace was used to put online, and therefore to make available electronically to all students, educational material that existed elsewhere in electronic form. This was a test of the second-level WEL use profile, *Advanced Web*, in a simple form that involved no additional preparation of material and no change to course structure or teaching methods. LearningSpace was simply a mechanism for distribution of existing material.

This type of use did not require identification of individual students or of the class to which each student was assigned. The LearningSpace system was activated for the course as a whole, rather than class by class, and all students used a generic user-id and password to access materials. Within LearningSpace, only the functions needed to view and download material were activated. Because use of the Notes client provided no substantial advantage for this type of use, student access was limited to access by Web browser. In this way, the PC labs remained dedicated to students in courses that used LearningSpace to support more complex forms of WEL. This implementation proceeded smoothly.

A surprising development occurred during the semester. Teachers who had used LearningSpace in the first semester and who also taught second semester courses asked the computer center to make a LearningSpace environment available for their second semester courses. After the semester began, other teachers who had observed the success of the initial implementations, also asked for LearningSpace environments. In all, eight standard courses used LearningSpace outside the formal pilot project during second semester, 1999-2000.

Overall, the second semester ran smoothly, confirming that the configuration of the system (software, hardware, and network) was able to support WEL for relatively large numbers of students. The decision was made to continue to use LearningSpace.

EVOLUTION OF THE B-LEARNING PROJECT
2000–2001: Spontaneous Adoption

As the university prepared for the 2000–2001 academic year, the computing center received additional requests from teachers not involved in the pilot project to enable them to use LearningSpace in their courses. Access was provided to all teachers who requested it. Two additional courses used LearningSpace during the first semester, bringing the total to five courses and 10 classes. In the second semester, there were 18 (including Financial Accounting). In the full year, 44 classes used LearningSpace for 22 different courses: two compulsory first-year courses, two compulsory second-year courses, and one compulsory third-year course, in addition to 17 elective courses for third- or fourth-year students. This represents around 3,000 enrolled students (the precise number is not available) and 5,910 instances of LearningSpace use (many students used LearningSpace in more than one course).

One of the courses activated for the second semester was a first-year core course in microeconomics. This course had 15 classes, around 2,300 students in total. Each class had a different teacher. While the full LearningSpace environment was activated for the course as a whole, each teacher was free to use it as they wished. The use varied from a simple implementation of *Advanced Web*, which delivered just the base educational material for the course (adopted by two teachers), to an enhanced *Advanced Web*,which included the base educational material and other material selected by the teacher (five teachers), and an *Interactive Web* that enabled student-led discussion forums (eight teachers). The course coordinator reported that the procedure to put material online for the simple Advanced Web was quick and easy.

The wider implementation in 2000–2001 demonstrated that LearningSpace was technically robust, even for large student numbers. It was able to satisfy, in terms of functions and ease of use, the teaching needs of simple WEL use profiles as well as more complex ones, even across different classes in the same course.

Evaluation of Student Response in 2000–2001

Student response to this wider implementation was mostly positive. In his informal evaluation of the microeconomics course, the course coordinator estimated that 80% of the students had no trouble using the system, while 20% encountered some difficulties. More formal evaluation among a larger subset of students who used LearningSpace during 2000–2001 confirmed that the majority, but not all, found the system valuable.

The university's office for educational evaluation conducted an independent evaluation of student satisfaction with participation in the LearningSpace-enabled courses. (The Financial Accounting course was omitted from this evaluation.) A total of 2,869 responses was received. Frequency of use varied considerably: 27% of students used LearningSpace more than once a week, 25% used it weekly, 28% used it every two weeks, and 20% used it only at the end of the course. The low-frequency uses were associated with courses in which LearningSpace was used only to distribute material.

Student opinion about the value of LearningSpace was mostly positive. Sixty percent of the students described it as a useful and effective innovation, but 16% said it was not. More than three quarters of the students (77%) agreed that LearningSpace should be used for more courses.

All four primary system functions were more often rated as useful than not. Provision of access to educational material through LearningSpace was rated positively by 56% of the students, but negatively by 19%; teachers speculate that a substantial proportion of the negative evaluations came from those students who found it less convenient to download material from LearningSpace at the end of the semester than to buy a course package from the bookstore as they could have done in the past. Use of the LearningSpace Courseroom as a forum for discussion with the teachers and other students was evaluated as a way to improve the learning process in 41% of responses, but not considered so by 28% of the students. Of the 27% of responses related to courses where the teacher used LearningSpace to support collaborative learning in student groups, 57% described this as a useful experience with the potential to improve the learning process, while 13% disagreed. Student response to uses of LearningSpace for CSCL was therefore more positive than their response to more passive methods of enabling student interaction through discussion forums.

An additional evaluation study was conducted under a nationally funded research project to study psychological metaresponses (Klobas, Renzi, Francescato, & Renzi, 2002); this study was an extension of the study conducted in one course in 1999–2000. While there were no differences between the learning of students in classes that used Web-enhanced learning and those that did not, students who used Web-enhanced learning were more confident about their ability to use computers and more willing to use them for learning in the future.

Teacher Observations on the First Two Years

In July 2001, the most active LearningSpace teachers held a meeting to reflect on their experiences during the first two years. Until this meeting, there had been little discussion among teachers in different courses about the ways that they had used LearningSpace.

In addition to exchanging experiences, the 14 teachers at the meeting discussed their overall evaluation of their experiences and specific problems they had encountered. As a result of this discussion, the teachers developed a list of 11 suggestions for enhancement of WEL at the university:

1.   Developing a revised framework for description of the ways in which WEL is used, allowing for a distinction between simple use of the *Advanced Web* to distribute shared course material and use by individual class teachers to post additional material
2.   Enabling planned and ad hoc enhancements or additions to the Web platform (such as support for synchronous chat) to meet specific teacher needs and therefore to enable uses more complex than asynchronous *CSCL*

3. Providing a suggested migration path for teachers as they move from traditional classroom-based teaching to online teaching
4. Providing a suggested migration path for teachers who begin with simple uses of the Web, to enable and encourage them to move to more complex uses
5. Ensuring students have the necessary skills to participate in courses that use all levels of WEL, from simple distribution, to CSCL
6. Providing guidelines for preparation of educational material
7. Considering new methods of student assessment, given the potential for continuous individual and group evaluation rather than the single, final oral exam common to most Italian university courses
8. Conducting deeper analysis of the relative roles of teachers, tutors, and other support staff as the modes and methods of teaching and learning change
9. Reducing class size to support more active student participation
10. Providing incentives for teachers
11. Increasing the role of the project support group in production of multimedia material and managing WEL platforms

2001–2002: The Point of No Return?

University planning for 2001–2002 assumed that LearningSpace would be available as a tool for Web-enhanced learning. Regardless of the issues identified by the more experienced LearningSpace teachers, the project had arrived at the point of no return. More teachers adopted LearningSpace for their courses, and students pushed teachers to adopt LearningSpace, at least to put material online.

Nearly 20% of the courses offered by the university during first semester 2000–2001 used LearningSpace (31 courses in all, an increase of 25 over the same period the previous year). Four of these courses used LearningSpace to distribute material to all enrolled students, using the single user-id and password system introduced during 2000–2001 to support simple distribution of material. The remaining 27 courses (plus one course in which both course and individual user-ids are being used) used LearningSpace for distribution of additional material, interaction, and CSCL. A total of 41 classes was involved.

In second semester, 25% of courses (44, an increase of 26 over the same period in 2000–2001) used LearningSpace. The range of uses was similar to that of the first semester: three courses used the single user-id and password system to distribute material to all enrolled students through a simple *Advanced Web*. The remaining 41 courses (plus one course that adopted a mixed solution) used LearningSpace across a total of 85 classes.

June 2002: Formal Review

In response to the issues raised by teachers at their July 2001 meeting, and to further discussion within the university during the 2001–2002 academic year, the Pro-Rettore for teaching initiated an eLearning workshop. The workshop was held at the end of the third year of the project, in June 2002. The goals of the workshop were to share experiences in WEL and its adoption across the university, to collect more detailed information about the ways that WEL is being used across the university, to evaluate the different uses of WEL in different disciplines, to identify actions to improve coordination among the different organizational units involved with eLearning activities, to identify problems or areas for improvement and to propose solutions, and to define future directions for eLearning within Bocconi University.

Prior to the workshop, several issues were raised in informal discussion among teachers. Many of these issues expanded on those raised at the July 2001 meeting, while others were associated with observations that can be drawn from this case study: not all students are satisfied that the system improves their experience at university; some teachers are still reluctant to adopt the system; there has been no test of the assumption that teacher adoption for simple WEL use profiles will lead to adoption for the more complex profiles needed to engage students more actively in their learning; and evaluation of progress toward meeting the university's goal of more active student involvement would benefit from introduction of systems for recording the ways in which WEL is used, accurately monitoring levels of adoption, and obtaining consistent and regular feedback from students and teachers.

New suggestions emerged from the informal discussions and the subsequent workshop. Many of these strike at fundamental aspects of the university's organizational structure and systems for measuring teachers' work and contribution. Among the issues raised at the June 2002 meeting were: the need to reestablish a formal working party to take responsibility for redefinition of goals and for defining the strategy for future directions; the value of establishing a center for innovation in learning to coordinate efforts and support teachers and students; the need to develop proposals to conduct more systematic research and evaluation of educational technology-based innovation in a model similar to that of the Stanford University Learning Laboratory (Friedlander, 2002); the potential for a community of practice among teachers to share experiences gained and to act as a forum for sharing successes and resolving difficulties; and changes in the system for measuring teacher workload and contribution as the relative proportions of hours in the classroom, course preparation, and student interaction change.

Another set of issues concerns ICT infrastructure and support for WEL environments and software other than LearningSpace. Although Bocconi has continued to upgrade its infrastructure, some signs that specific attention to infrastructure for WEL is needed have emerged from student and teacher evaluations. Student demand for computers to access LearningSpace is putting pressure on the computer laboratories. While the university has a scheme to help students buy portable computers, and new buildings are amply equipped with network ports in all student work areas, student take-up of the purchase scheme is low, and satisfaction with access slipped between the second and third years of the project. In addition, as more teachers use computers in the classroom, the demand for portable computers and for upgrade of the classroom demonstration computers is also higher than can be met by the standard university infrastructure upgrade plan.

While the project has successfully introduced a single platform that supports use of WEL up to the level of asynchronous CSCL, a development environment is needed to support the highest level in the WEL use hierarchy, the *Experimental* level. Although IBM-Lotus offers a development environment, members of the multimedia committee who are active in developing alternative WEL environments are more familiar with the Microsoft environment and are proposing that extensions use this environment rather than IBM-Lotus. The advantages and disadvantages of selecting one environment over another, or of formally committing to the dual environment, are yet to be considered.

REVIEWING THE B-LEARNING PROJECT

At the end of its third year, the participants in the B-learning project consider it a success. It has demonstrated that the selected system is technically feasible. The system is able to support active student involvement in learning in ways that are satisfactory to teachers and students, and student use of the system for CSCL can enhance the meta-outcomes of being a university student. The technology has enabled and encouraged improvements in the quality of teaching by enabling and encouraging teachers to adopt more varied approaches to teaching and learning than they have used in the past. Where teachers have incorporated more active learning in their courses, students have expressed high satisfaction with the learning technology and a desire to have it adopted more widely across the university.

The project did not allow for monitoring of the WEL use profile adopted by each teacher, or for each course and class. Nonetheless, it is possible to see that most courses enabled student interaction (fitting the *Interactive Web* or *CSCL* profile) rather than simply using an *Advanced Web* to distribute material. Table 2 distinguishes between those courses that enabled interaction among students who had their own user-id and password, and those that only adopted LearningSpace to distribute material to all students using the same shared user-id and password. Only 5 (6.5%) of the 77 courses that used LearningSpace in 2001–2002 used the system just to distribute common course materials.

WEL Adoption over the First Three Years

The extent of adoption of WEL during the three years since the first pilot implementation in Semester 1, 1999, is summarized in Table 2. Course and class numbers in this table are precise. The exact number of students using the system in courses for which the single user-id and password system was adopted is unknown but could be estimated on the basis of class size and computer center logs. Overall, several thousand students—a significant proportion of the university's student body—were using LearningSpace by the end of the third year of the project.

The rate of adoption of WEL over the period is demonstrated in Figure 1, which plots the percentage of courses that used LearningSpace in each semester. This chart clearly shows the marked growth in adoption over the three years since the initial pilot implementation in first semester 1999. Although the university has never formally invited teachers other than

Table 2: WEL Adoption During the First Three Years

Academic Year	Sem	Individual student user-id and password			Shared course user-id		Total Courses	Total Student instances
		Courses	Classes	Student instances	Courses	Student instances		
1999–2000	1	3	5	500	—	—	3	500
	2	8	8	500	1	2000	9	2500
2000–2001	1	5	10	1150[a]	—	—	5	3150
	2	17	34	3910[a]	1	2000	18	5910
2001–2002	1	28	41	4715[a]	4	4370[a]	31[b]	9085
	2	42	85	9775[a]	3	2530[a]	44[b]	12305

[a]Calculated as number of classes times average class size.
[b]One course adopted a mixed solution.

Figure 1: Percentage of Courses using WEL in Each Period

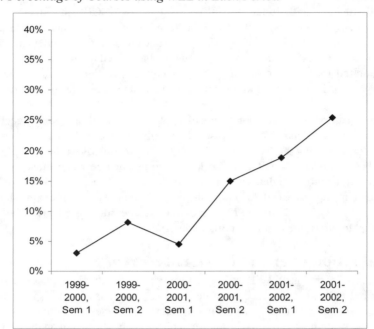

the initial pilot group to adopt WEL, spontaneous adoption has resulted in 25% of its courses using WEL in some form, and almost all of these for uses beyond simple distribution of material to students.

Influences on Adoption

Close inspection of Figure 1 suggests that the greatest growth each year occurred between Semesters 1 and 2 rather than at the beginning of the academic year. This pattern suggests that adoption is influenced by observation and word of mouth among teachers and students, and by the availability of time for teachers to prepare their course LearningSpace environments and revise their courses. The summer holiday between academic years reduces the visibility of WEL implementations and the time available to prepare.

Differences in use were also associated with course coordinators' approaches to use of LearningSpace and WEL. In some courses, such as microeconomics, the full LearningSpace was made available for the course, but individual class teachers were free to adopt WEL in their own way. Students enrolled in these courses were able to compare the different uses made of the system by different teachers. Student pressure encouraged teachers to adopt the *Interactive Web* in these cases, even if the teacher had not initially considered this level of use. The teachers were able to observe students using the Interactive Web informally, even when formal course activities did not require it. In other courses, where the coordinator activated a single LearningSpace solely to act as a repository for teaching materials, and students accessed materials anonymously, there was little incentive for individual teachers to adopt more interactive profiles and to move to more engaging educational models.

Discussion among teachers also played a role. In multiclass courses in particular, the teachers were able to support one another by sharing methods, experiences, resources, and tips in teaching team meetings.

The B-learning Project as Organizational Innovation

The progress of Bocconi University's eLearning project closely mirrored the stages of organizational innovation identified by diffusion of innovation theorist, Everett Rogers. Rogers (1995) described five stages in the process of innovation within an organization. Although there may be overlap between stages and some reiteration of earlier stages later in the process, the five stages can be distinguished as agenda-setting, matching, redefining/restructuring, clarifying, and routinizing. The stages reflect two higher-level activities. The first of these, *initiation*, consists of agenda-setting and matching of an innovation with the organization's agenda. At the end of this period, a decision is made to adopt (or reject) an innovation in a particular form. The remaining stages in the innovation process represent the *implementation* period, when the innovation is redefined or "reinvented" to fit the organization, its role is clarified, and its use finally becomes such a familiar part of the organization's activities that it is no longer recognizable as an innovation. Figure 2 presents these aspects of the innovation process using Rogers' words.

Figure 2: Stages in the Innovation Process in an Organization

I. INITIATION		Decision
1. AGENDA-SETTING	2. MATCHING	
General organizational problems that may create a perceived need for innovation.	Fitting a problem from the organization's agenda with an innovation.	

II. IMPLEMENTATION		
3. REDEFINING/ RESTRUCTURING	4. CLARIFYING	5. ROUTINIZING
The innovation is modified and re-invented to fit the organization, and organizational structures are altered.	The relationship between the organization and the innovation is defined more clearly.	The innovation becomes an ongoing element in the organization's activities, and loses its identity.

Note: From Rogers, E. M. (1995). The diffusion of innovations (4th ed.) (p. 392). New York: Free Press

Table 3 maps the steps of the project against Rogers' stages. *Agenda-setting* occurred when the university established its goal to improve the quality of education through more active student involvement in learning. The working party's initial activities—identification of the different ways in which WEL could be used and development of the profiles described in Table 1; identification of potential technology platforms; and assessment of the platforms against the technical and business criteria established for WEL at the university—consti-

Table 3: The Innovation Process for WEL at Bocconi University

Rogers stage	Time line	Bocconi steps
1. Agenda-Setting	pre-May 1998	Management sets goal to improve quality of education through more active learning
2. Matching	1998 May	Working party established to consider potential for WEL
	1998 June	Working party starts works
	1998 August	Working party final report and top management go-ahead for the B-learning project
	1998 September	Evaluating learning technology solutions available on the market
	1998 November	Microsoft and IBM-Lotus preliminary proposals received
	1998 December 1999 January	Evaluating Microsoft and IBM-Lotus proposals
Decision	*1999 February 5*	*Choice of IBM-Lotus LearningSpace*
3. Redefining/ Restructuring	1999 February 1999 April	Detailed analysis of the technical and human requirements for implementation and selection of teachers and courses for pilot implementation
	1999 May 1999 August	Training for teachers; pilot course preparation, including course redesign; Other preparations for start
	1999 September 1999–2000, Semester 1	Initial pilot courses began
	1999–2000, Semester 2	Pilot of simple *Advanced Web* for large classes; Spontaneous adoption following requests to computer center
	2000–2001, Semester 1	Spontaneous adoption grows
	2000–2001, Semester 2	Spontaneous adoption continues
4. Clarifying	2001 July	Experienced teachers meet to review the first two years
	2002 June	Management-initiated university-wide eLearning workshop
5. Routinizing	Began 1999, Semester 1	For participating students, routinizing may begin with their use of WEL
	Began 1999, Semester 1	For individual teachers, routinizing begins with their first use of WEL
	Began 2000–2001, Semester 1	For the university, providing access to LearningSpace for WEL is routine, but many organizational aspects remain to be routinized

tuted the *matching* stage. Throughout this period, and indeed throughout the project, the innovation was defined as eLearning or Web-enhanced learning for on-campus students, rather than in terms of adoption of specific software. The project was therefore a business project, driven by business goals, and implemented through new ICT. The initiation period ended with the *decision* to adopt IBM-Lotus LearningSpace.

The *implementation* process began with the working party's definition of the technical and human requirements for implementation, and the selection of teachers and courses for pilot implementation. *Redefinition* of the teaching and learning process began for these teachers during their training. As other teachers adopted WEL and LearningSpace, they too redefined their modes of teaching and learning. Redefinition of the innovation occurred at several stages during this initial implementation period, notably when the university adopted a reduced LearningSpace for simple Advanced Web courses, enabling all enrolled students to access material using the same user-id and password. *Clarification* of the relationship between the organization and the innovation began with the teachers' meeting in July 2001 and their subsequent report to the Pro-Rettore. The Pro-Rettore initiated workshop in June 2002 continued this process.

Routinizing is occurring at different rates at different layers of adoption. For individual teachers and students, WEL using LearningSpace becomes routine during the first course in which it is used. Once a teacher has used LearningSpace in one class, it seems natural for them to use it in other courses that they teach. Student pressure on teachers to adopt LearningSpace is an expression of how its use is routine for the students. At the organizational level, routinizing began when the computer center, without questioning, activated LearningSpace for any teacher who requested it. Nonetheless, the issues raised at the teacher's meeting in July 2001, in informal discussions leading to the June 2002 workshop, and at the workshop itself, indicate that implementation is not complete and that each stage will need to be revisited. While the June 2002 workshop was an important step in clarifying the role of WEL at Bocconi University, it showed that several issues, including those related to organizational structure and organizational reward systems, need to be resolved if WEL is to become routine.

LARGE-SCALE INTRODUCTION OF WEL: CONDITIONS FOR SUCCESS

The success to date of this innovation process reflects attention to the several interrelated dimensions of technology-related change: business, human, and technical. Many of these have also been noted by Bates (2000) in his overview of managing technological change in universities. They are summarized in this section in two categories, those associated with successful information systems projects in general, and those associated specifically with successful implementation of WEL.

Information Systems Success and WEL

The need for attention to nontechnical as well as technical factors in successful organizational information systems projects is well known (DeSanctis & Poole, 1994; Markus, 1983; Swanson & Ramiller, 1997). They include an existing environment that is supportive of innovation and change; appropriate ICT infrastructure (Weill & Broadbent, 1998);

management support and involvement in the change project; focus on business goals; strong communication and teamwork among those involved in the change; and good planning with attention to technical detail and process redesign.

An Environment Supportive of Innovation and Change

The B-learning project was initiated in an organization that had a focus on and a reputation for quality in education. There was already a group of teachers who were experienced users of technology in teaching. These teachers had wide networks of contacts among educational technology innovators in universities throughout the world. The computer center already had a group of staff who had considerable experience in implementing educational technologies ranging from computer-based training to support for multimedia case studies. The project was therefore able to build on an already sound basis of technology, knowledge, and skill.

Access to Appropriate ICT Infrastructure

At the initiation of the B-learning project, Bocconi had a robust, fast, and mature university-wide technical infrastructure, a high level of use among teachers and administrators, and experienced and knowledgeable support staff. Attention to ICT infrastructure at the start of an initiative is, however, not enough. The infrastructure must be maintained and modified in order to meet changing demands and growth. Student and teacher demands for more or different computers to access LearningSpace suggest that revision of the university's ICT upgrade plan should be included in the university's steps toward routinization of WEL. This is a business issue, not just a technology issue.

Focus on Business Goals

Rather than being limited to initial pilot implementation of technology, the project was guided by the university's business vision. This was therefore a long-term project with goals that would be achieved only when the university's wider, business goals of higher quality teaching and learning and more active student participation in learning were met.

Top Management Sponsorship and Involvement

Throughout the project, senior management participated, attending working party meetings when requested and making key decisions quickly and firmly. The value of this approach was particularly evident when the working party was divided on the best technology solution to adopt. Senior management, with a clear view of university strategy, decided on a solution to fit that strategy, rather than relying on the more technology-focused arguments developed by the working party. At a critical stage for continuation, during the third year, management again took a critical role by initiating a workshop to review progress and define future directions.

Communication and Teamwork

The project benefited in clear, practical ways from the decisions made about project management. The decisions to establish a cross-functional internal working party with ready access to senior management, to appoint a single external project partner, and to have these two work as a single implementation task force, enabled a 360 degree view of the technical and nontechnical issues associated with implementation, and rapid and effective reaction to problems as they arose. The strong spirit of cooperation among all internal and external participants in the project, along with shared understanding of the business goals, provided incentives for participation in the project.

Specific Dimensions of WEL Success

Ten principles associated with the introduction of educational technology to enable distance learning have been identified by members of the Stanford University Learning Laboratory (Friedlander, 2002). Some of these principles echo those already known for information systems projects: "Let educational values and not technology drive your projects," "Central institutional planning is vital." While other principles are expressed in ways that are specific to distance learning, the description of the principles suggests issues to consider when planning and managing Web-enhanced learning for on-campus students. We have called these issues appropriate use, appropriate scale, and flexibility. In addition, several of the issues raised by the Bocconi teachers at their July 2001 meeting echo those raised elsewhere in the literature of online learning and suggest additional conditions for success of WEL: teacher preparedness and support, educational material design (or redesign), and the economics of new educational models.

Appropriate Use

Based on Stanford University's experience with distance learning in undergraduate courses, Friedlander noted "Undergraduate education is perhaps the most problematic…we have successfully used DL within large lecture courses as a way to promote joint work among students and venues for discussion and experimentation not possible in a large group" (p. 3), and "The most successful programs are combinations of on-site and distant learning" (p. 4). The Bocconi experience echoes that at Stanford: WEL in which educational technology supports interaction among students is an appropriate approach to improving undergraduate students' experience of and growth at university.

Appropriate Scale

Friedlander's principles included "Scale versus quality is the central dilemma" (p. 4). Bocconi's staged approach to WEL has not yet encountered this dilemma. By beginning with pilot studies designed to test the ability of WEL to improve quality in a large-scale implementation, the B-learning project began with a deliberate attempt to maintain quality and scale. Subsequent extensions have demonstrated that WEL can support quality on a larger scale. Nonetheless, important issues of scale are emerging in student demand for more computers and in teachers' requests for smaller class sizes.

Flexibility

The B-learning project permitted more flexibility than most university-wide eLearning projects. Bocconi enabled voluntary adoption of WEL, as well as individual teacher definition and redefinition of how the LearningSpace technology could be used. It also permitted individuals and groups to experiment with other technologies, albeit without the substantial human and financial effort invested in LearningSpace. It is difficult to tell at this stage whether this model of voluntary or "free" adoption will be successful in the long term. The more common model is where a university adopts a single software platform and requires it to be used in a standardized way. One university that has had particular success with this model is Monterrey University in Mexico (López del Puerto, 1999). As Pollock and Cornford (2000) pointed out, however, many universities have had limited success or failed with this approach.

How important, then, is flexibility? While the Bocconi and Monterrey projects differ on this apparently fundamental aspect of the approach to implementing eLearning, they are similar in their attention to all the other dimensions described in this section. It is possible that attention to these elements of implementation is more important for success than the decision to permit voluntary adoption or define compulsory technologies and methods of use. Nonetheless, the free adoption model may have some advantages over standardization, as we note in the next section.

Teacher Preparedness and Support

When teachers are already proficient users of technology, as they are at Bocconi, the most valuable kind of support that can be provided for implementation of educational technology is pedagogical (e.g., for migration from traditional delivery to more active involvement of learners) rather than technical. Such support is best provided just-in-time, i.e., when the teacher is ready to change (Brown, Collins, & Duguid, 1989). Bocconi's flexible, free adoption model may have built into it a method of identifying when educational support is needed. If the university leaves teachers free to use Web-enhanced learning as they choose, but identifies those situations where only the simplest profiles are being used, it will be able to identify those teachers who have begun to adopt the technology but may value assistance in using it in more interactive ways. Concentration of initial efforts on support for teachers who wish to move to more interactive uses of Web-enhanced technology should provide a greater overall increase in quality than concentration of support among those teachers who have already adopted more complex WEL profiles.

Educational Material (Re)Design

A related issue is support for the production of educational material. When slides used by a teacher in a classroom lesson become available to students online, the way the material is used is changed. For fully distance learning, a different approach to development and presentation of material is required. But, is it also necessary (and worthwhile) to redesign material prepared initially for classroom use so that it can be used effectively outside the lesson when accessed from a WEL platform? While use of slides and graphics in class is common, video streaming provides a potential solution for delivery and storage of classroom-based lessons, but do lessons on video really add value to the business model the university is introducing? The university needs to consider the cost of production in relation to the relatively short life of the material and to provide appropriate assistance to teachers (either training to replace existing methods or production staff to prepare new forms) if material of a new kind is needed.

Incentives for Adoption

An additional issue concerns effort and incentive for adoption of WEL. There are no formal incentives at Bocconi for use of WEL. While there is little extra effort involved in adopting WEL for the Traditional Web or simplest forms of Advanced Web profile, more complex uses involve quite considerable effort, particularly during the course redesign phase. The teachers who had implemented more complex uses were in no doubt that an improvement in the quality of the teaching also involves more work for the teacher.

The Economics of New Educational Initiatives

The economics of WEL need close attention from many points of view. Bocconi teachers have recommended an increase in tutoring and a reduction in class size to support more complex uses of WEL. They suggest that classes of 150 be divided into smaller sections to support effective discussion and collaborative learning, but Italian universities do not have a tradition of tutorials and small group work, and the economics of introducing smaller class sizes is daunting. The educational models adopted must therefore be economically manageable, adding to the complexity of each of the issues discussed here.

CONCLUSION

We are often asked "What software platform do you suggest?" This case demonstrates that the choice of software is only one of the many choices to be made in a multidimensional decision, and that the software implementation is just one of many aspects of successful implementation.

High commitment is required to deal with a project of this complexity: a clear vision of the business and educational goals, the need to ensure the software meets teacher and student needs for usability and functionality, sustainable technology choices, capacity planning for the entire university network, and assessment of the organizational impacts of change all need to be understood in themselves and in terms of how they are related to one other. Additional dimensions to be considered include: an environment supportive of innovative and change, appropriate ICT infrastructure, focus on business goals, top management sponsorship and involvement, communication and teamwork, appropriate use of WEL, appropriate scale, flexibility, teacher preparedness and support, educational material design and redesign, incentives for adoption, and the economics of new educational initiatives.

In addition, an understanding of innovation in organizations reminds participants that innovation is a process during which clarification, redefinition, and reinvention occur and recur. Furthermore, because innovation is a process, and implementation a subprocess within it, a project that is considered a success at one point in time may not be a success in the long term. Difficult issues associated with successful innovation, including organizational redesign and redesign of reward systems, need to be reviewed and resolved before an educational innovation such as WEL becomes routine.

ACKNOWLEDGMENTS

Many people provided information and data for this chapter. They include the members of the working party, the project management team, teachers whose courses were formally included in the pilot implementations, the senior management of the university, and the university office of statistics. We acknowledge their contributions with thanks.

REFERENCES

Angerhn, A. (1999). Designing mature Internet business strategies: the ICDT model. *European Management Journal, 15*(4), 361–369.

Bates, A. W. (1995). *Technology, open learning, and distance education.* New York: Routledge.

Bates, A. W. (2000). *Managing technological change.* San Francisco, CA: Jossey-Bass.

Brown, J. S., Collins, A., & Duguid, P. (1989). Situated cognition and the culture of learning. *Educational Researcher, 18*(1), 32–42.

Calvani, A., & Rotta, M. (2000). *Fare formazione in Internet.* Trento, Italy: Erickson.

DeSanctis, G., & Poole, M. S. (1994). Capturing the complexity in advanced technology use: adaptive structuration theory. *Organization Science, 5*, 121–147.

Ely, D. P. (1999). *New perspectives on the implementation of educational technology innovations.* Paper delivered at the Association for Educational Communications and Technology Annual Conference, Houston, TX, February, 1999.

Farquhar, J. D., & Surry, D. W. (1994). Adoption analysis: an additional tool for instructional developers. *Education and Training Technology International, 31*(1), 19–25.

Friedlander, L. (2002). Next generation distant learning. In F. Fluckiger et al. (Eds.), *4th International Conference on New Educational Environments, Lugano, Switzerland, May 8–11* (pp. 3–6). Lugano: University of Applied Sciences Southern Switzerland and University of Southern Switzerland, Berne: net4net.

Hall, G., & Hord, S. (1987). *Change in schools: facilitating the process.* Albany, NY: SUNY Press.

Holloway, R. E. (1996). Diffusion and adoption of educational technology: a critique of research design. In D. H. Jonassen (Ed.), *Handbook of research for educational communications and technology* (pp. 1107–1133). New York: Simon & Schuster Macmillan.

Klobas, J. E., & Renzi, S. (2001). Student psychological response to computer-supported collaborative learning. In T. Hahn (Ed.), *Information in a networked world: harnessing the flow, Proceedings of the ASIST 2001 Annual Meeting, Washington, DC, 3–8 November.* American Society for Information Science and Technology.

Klobas, J. E., Renzi, S., Francescato, D., Renzi, P. (2002). Meta-response to online learning. Meta-risposte all'apprendimento online. *Ricerche di Psicologia, 25*(1), 239-259.

López del Puerto, P. (1999). Monterrey Institute of Technology, Mexico. *European IBM Forum for Education and Learning (EIFFEL)*, April 28–30, Grenoble, France.

Markus, M. L. (1983). Power, politics, and MIS implementation. *Communications of the ACM, 26*(6), 430–444.

Palloff, R. M., & Pratt, K. (1999). *Building learning communities in cyberspace: effective strategies for the online classroom.* San Francisco, CA: Jossey-Bass.

Palloff, R. M., & Pratt, K. (2001). *Lessons from the cyberspace classroom: the realities of online teaching.* San Francisco, CA: Jossey-Bass.

Pollock, N., & Cornford, J. (2000). Theory and practice of the virtual university. *Ariadne, 24*, http://www.ariadne.ac.uk/issue24/virtual-universities.

Rogers, E. M. (1995). *The diffusion of innovations* (4th ed.). New York: Free Press.

Stockdill, S. H., & Morehouse, D. L. (1992). Critical factors in successful adoption of technology: a checklist of TDC findings. *Educational Technology, 1*, 57–58.

Surry, D. W. (2002). A model for integrating instructional technology into higher education. *Annual Meeting of the American Educational Research Association, April 2002, New Orleans, LA*. Online: http://iphase.org/papers/aera021.pdf.

Swanson, E. B., & Ramiller, N. C. (1997). The organizing vision in information-systems innovation. *Organization Science, 8*, 458–474.

Weill, P., & Broadbent, M. (1998). *Leveraging the new infrastructure: how market leaders capitalize on information technology*. Boston, MA: Harvard University Press.

Chapter XXV

An Evaluation of Web-Based Education at a Finnish University

Johanna Lammintakanen
University of Kuopio, Finland

Sari Rissanen
University of Kuopio, Finland

ABSTRACT

In this chapter, an evaluation of two student cohorts' and their teachers' experiences of Web-based education at a university in Finland is presented. Discussion of Finnish national education policy and some crucial issues concerning Web-based education provide the framework for the evaluation. The results indicated that the students' and teachers' experiences were largely positive, and correlated with other international research results in this field. The authors are convinced that sharing these experiences will highlight the strengths and weaknesses of such online learning, as well as the skill requirements and needs for cultural reshaping in Web-based education. Such an exchange of experience should facilitate online education collaboration nationally and internationally. However, the overall consequences of Web-based education still remain unclear and must be carefully considered.

INTRODUCTION

The aim of this chapter is to provide an evaluation of Web-based education from our own perspective, as teachers, and that of two student cohorts from the Department of Health Policy and Management at the University of Kuopio in Finland. Our areas of expertise are social and health management sciences, thus, our interest is concentrated on Web-based education at the macrolevel, as part of Finnish educational policy, and also at the microlevel as a pedagogical issue. The chapter is structured such that the background section offers a discussion of three main factors that have affected educational policy and the implementation of Web-based education in Finland, thereby providing a macrolevel frame for our study. Following this is a focus on some crucial issues in Web-based education based on previous research and literature. The empirical part outlines the results of the evaluation of an online course at the University of Kuopio, and finally, some concluding remarks on the basis of the empirical findings are made, and some future trends are discussed.

BACKGROUND

As in many other countries, the development of Web-based education has been rapid during recent years in Finland. A variety of features related to this development can be identified at different levels, and these are determined by numerous factors. Although these factors can also be identified at other educational levels, we prefer to focus on the information society, lifelong learning, and the quality of teaching and learning at university level as examples.

Finland is a good example of an information society, and many educational projects have been launched to promote this development. The Ministry of Education has published a document entitled "Education, Training and Research in the Information Society. A national strategy for 2000–2004," in which it outlines its vision for Finnish education:

"By the year 2004 Finland will be one of the leading interactive knowledge societies. Success will be based on citizens' equal opportunities to study and develop their own intellectual capacity and extensively utilize information resources and educational services. A high-quality, ethically and economically sustainable mode of operation in network-based teaching and research will have been established" (Education, Training and Research in the Information Society, 1999).

An information society is built largely on the principle of lifelong learning, the adoption of which is a prerequisite in meeting the increasing new skill requirements of working life in such a society. In this context, Web-based education is said to be a flexible way in which work and educational organizations can cooperate, and in which individuals can shift between working life and education (e.g., Pulkkinen, 1997). Concurrently, the supply of education is broadened to different learning organizations, e.g., universities and polytechnics, nationally and internationally (e.g., Rhinesmith, cited in Morss, 1999).

The education provided by Finnish universities has also met the expectations and opportunities raised in the information society. Traditionally, the basic mission of the Finnish universities has been to conduct research and provide education based on research (Higher Education Policy in Finland, 2000). Such a mission places greater emphasis on research than teaching, something that has created conflicting challenges for teachers. Individual careers and academic communities have been evaluated on the basis of the scientific merits of the research undertaken only, with the consequence that all investments in developing teaching have been viewed as detracting time and resources from scientific work (Sinko & Lehtinen, 1999, p. 117).

However, in recent years, the balance at universities has shifted toward more pedagogical issues. Quality of education, university teachers' education, and different methods for learning and evaluation have all been the subject of extensive discussion. The Finnish Higher Education Evaluation Council, the body responsible for evaluating the quality of education, and organizing institutional, program, and thematic evaluations, has been active in these discussions (Higher education policy in Finland, 2000). Students have also taken part. Their expectations of the quality of teaching have risen in recent years, and they expect a more individual, flexible, and humanistic approach in education.

To summarize the macrolevel trends, there have been many different factors that have had an effect on educational policy during recent years. Universities ignore these trends at the risk of becoming excluded from the effects of globalization and technology development. One of the ways to meet these new challenges has been the adoption of Web-based (virtual) learning environments (Volery & Lord, 2000; Katz et al., 1999).

Previous studies and literature highlight some crucial points regarding the implementation of Web-based education from a pedagogical point of view. These have been summarized into four themes: learning theory, concept of knowledge, the changing roles of teachers and students, and new skill requirements.

Usually a new innovation, such as a Web-based learning environment, is compared to the old model, for instance, traditional lecturer-driven teaching. Such comparisons are implicitly value-laden—old is not appreciated, while new is achievable and valuable (see, e.g., Farrington, 1999, p. 78). It therefore follows that critical comparisons are needed in which the pros and cons of each are taken into consideration. It is also important to note that there is no consistent paradigm for Web-based education, rather there are multiple ways of making use of the Web in education, and these will vary depending on the subject being taught and the needs of the learner.

Recently, constructivism has challenged learning theory (e.g., Rathwell et al., 1999). Although the choices made during the planning process of the online course determine whether it is based on constructivism or other learning theories, constructivism is usually closely related to Web-based education (Jefferies & Hussain, 1998).

It is believed that the Web-based learning environment promotes a constructivist approach by allowing all-round interaction, transferring the responsibility of learning to the student, and enhancing the construction of knowledge by interaction. It has been shown, however, that although teachers have adopted the model of constructivist epistemology in principle, they have not always implemented it in the ways they organize the learning situations (Sinko & Lehtinen, 1999; McFadzean, 2001a). One explanation for this may be that constructivism is not always the most suitable learning approach for every student and subject, i.e., not all students may be able or ready to take responsibility for their own learning.

The concept of knowledge is an essential part of constructivism. Knowledge is constructed in social interaction, it changes over time, and contradictory explanations of reality may even exist (e.g., Pulkkinen, 1997). Web-based education provides good opportunities to make use of the many information sources available via the Internet, and this was evident in the students' evaluations (Jefferies & Hussain, 1998). The problem is, however, the quality of knowledge; how to select appropriate information from among the mass, summarize it, and how to appreciate information that does not only strengthen the students' and teachers' existing knowledge but also awakens new inspirations.

At best, Web-based education can be seen as a tool for social interaction and collaborative interactivities (Sinko & Lehtinen, 1999), and this requires changes in the roles of the teacher and the student. Previous research has shown that the role of the teacher is not diminished in Web-based learning, however, traditional teacher duties, such as instructing the learners and information communication, are. The teacher's new role can be described as a learning catalyst and knowledge navigator or as tutor acting as a facilitator for learning and group processes (see Volery & Lord, 2000). Moreover, the tutor's duty is to maintain a safe environment for learning and encourage novel problem-solving processes (McFadzean & McKenzie, 2001; McFadzean, 2001ab).

Web-based education also encourages the student to take control over his or her learning regardless of time and place. At best, this requires a totally new way of thinking from students: from what they hope to acquire from the course, to what they contribute to knowledge creation (McFadzean & McKenzie, 2001.)

In addition, a virtual learning environment enables experimental learning in that it allows students to exchange experiences and learn from each other (Kolb, 1984; Rathwell et al., 1999; McFadzean, 2001b). This reflects the future need for experts who are able to share their expertise in active networks and "learning organizations" (Senge, 1990; Sinko & Lehtinen, 1999).

Such a model, however, raises the critical issue of whether or not everyone is able to be self-directed. It has been shown in andragogy that this is not so: not all students find it easy to learn from each other, and some prefer courses that are lecture-driven (McFadzean, 2001b). Volery and Lord (2000) identified two especially vulnerable groups–those students who are less motivated, and those who are most advanced. This raises the question of how the learning needs of different groups should be taken into consideration when using a Web-based environment.

To briefly summarize, previous studies have shown that the technology affects learning in many ways (e.g., Sinko & Lehtinen, 1999; McFadzean & McKenzie, 2001). One practical but important point is that online education requires skills from the teacher and the student that are different to those of traditional teaching. In Finland, many resources have been allocated to promote ICT education and to establish proper facilities in order to make effective use of Web-based learning.

The evaluation conducted by the Ministry of Education (1999) showed that almost all students and teachers were willing to use new technology. However, only one fifth of the

Table 1: The Main Obstacles to Using ICT in Education in Rank Order

Teachers	Students
Teachers' lack of time	Lack of students' workstations
Lack of pedagogical support	Students' lack of time
Teachers' ICT pedagogical skills	Students' ICT skills
Teachers' ICT skills	Course overlap
Lack of technical support	Insufficient course hours
	Teachers' lack of time

Note. Sinko, M., & Lehtinen, E. (1999). The challenges of ICT in Finnish education (pp. 116–117). Helsinki: Atena. Electronic Publication available via the Internet: http:// www.sitra.fi/eng/index.asp?DirID=297

teachers actually used the new technology to support teaching. According to Sinko and Lehtinen (1999), the lack of students' and teachers' ICT skills, time, and workstations are still the major obstacles in making use of Web-based learning (Table 1). These issues must be resolved before Web-based environments can be used to their full potential.

THE MANAGEMENT AND EVALUATION OF THE WEB-BASED COURSE

Course Description, Student Analysis, and Planning Process

In 1999, the University of Kuopio established a policy for the use of a Web-based (virtual) learning environment. WebCT was the platform chosen (see, e.g., Morss, 1999; Volery & Lord, 2000), and the first online courses using this learning environment were planned during the academic year 1999–2000. The Department of Health Policy and Management was one of the pioneers in this area.[1]

The department offers master's degree programs (160 Finnish credit units; one credit unit equals 40 hours of work) and postgraduate studies in three main subjects: health management sciences, information management in social and health care, and health economics. In 2001, the intake to the master's program was 60 students. Graduates are employed as managers, researchers, teachers, and experts in the field of welfare services at local, regional, and national levels (ECTS guide for foreign students, 2000–2001).

A course entitled "Social and health care services" was chosen for development by the department. The main content of this course includes different welfare state models, social and health care services in Finland and abroad, social and health policy, and legislation. The content-related learning goals were based on these issues. However, this evaluation does not focus on these goals, rather our aim was to evaluate the broader educational goals, which were to familiarize the students with the new learning environment; to strengthen the students' skills in the use of the Internet as an information resource; to strengthen information analysis and summary skills, and critical evaluation of the information retrieved; and to develop students' feedback and evaluation skills within the online learning environment.

This course was chosen for online education, because its content and learning goals permitted the use of different kinds of teaching and learning methods. In addition, the participating student cohort was heterogeneous. Essentially, our students are registered nurses with a great deal of work experience in health care who are studying part time. There are also full-time students with no experience in health care and no previous education in this field.

The students' ages range from 18 to over 50 years. A large number of students are not permanently resident in the Kuopio area, and as many come from the capital, Helsinki, the average distance of their domicile from Kuopio is 250 miles. Fortunately, most have access to a computer at their workplace or at home. However, there is great variation between the computer skills of the younger and older students.

The planning process for the online course took almost a year. In 1999, we participated in a course for teachers called "The planning and utilization of Web-based environments in education" at the University of Kuopio. During this course, we planned the basic structure of the course evaluated here.

To begin with Web-based education, we decided to combine different teaching methods (face-to-face and Web-based), because we felt it would be easier for the students to learn to use the Web-based learning environment gradually. In addition, this was our first experience as teachers of an online course, although we had both been students of such courses.

EVALUATION

Evaluation Tasks and Approaches

The aim of this evaluation was to ascertain whether or not WebCT was a suitable tool for learning in a heterogeneous student group, and systematically to acquire information from students on how to develop the course further. The research tasks were as follows: to describe the students' experiences of Web-based learning according to three dimensions (the student's own learning experience, tutoring and assignments, and the usability of the virtual learning environment); to clarify what measures the students felt should be taken to improve the course; to describe our own experiences as teachers involved in Web-based education; and to evaluate the achievement of the educational goals.

We used goal-orientated, process, and multiple constituency evaluation in this study (Øvretveit, 1998; Clarke, 1999). The evaluation of achievement of the educational goals represented the goal orientation. The teachers' own evaluation during the process is seen as process evaluation. Here, a multiple constituency approach means a combination of teachers' and students' evaluations. As a new learning tool was being discussed, particular emphasis was placed on the importance of combining students' evaluations with those of the teachers (Bingham & Ottewill, 2001).

Evaluation Data and Methods

Evaluation data from two different student cohorts was gathered (in 2000 and 2001) using an evaluation form specially designed for this study. The evaluation form consisted of open questions concerning, for example, the students' own learning experience, tutoring and assignments, and the use of a Web-based learning environment. In addition, students were able to make recommendations on how to improve the course. Open questions were used as a part of the qualitative approach in order not to restrict the evaluations to detailed aspects only. It was our intention that the respondents be able to describe more freely their experiences.

The number of students was limited, and therefore, the possibilities for quantitative analyses were weak. Out of a total of 110 students over the two-year period, 70 replied to the questionnaire. Not all students filled in the evaluation form, as the evaluations were collected during the last optional face-to-face meeting, and responding was voluntary.

A qualitative approach was also used in the data analysis. The student data were processed and analyzed by both authors using qualitative content analysis. The data were read and sorted into dimensions according to the research tasks. The students' evaluations were then classified as positive or negative according to each dimension, and for each dimension, a student comment was selected that encapsulated the general view of the group. It was felt that as we were interested in deviating cases that are important in developing the course further, the data would not be quantified (see, e.g., Silverman, 1993).

"The planning and utilization of Web-based environments in education" course provided us with the guidelines to evaluate ourselves as teachers, and also engaged us in peer review. The evaluation centered on our experiences of course planning and delivery, focusing on the learning process when using a Web-based environment. This evaluation data consisted of discussions, discussion notes, and memos. We found the self-evaluation a natural part of our work, because we have been working together for several years in the fields of education and research, and this has enabled continuous development, reflection, and evaluation, i.e., learning from experience (Kolb, 1984). The evaluation research design is summarized in Table 2.

Table 2: Evaluation Research Design

Dimensions and evaluation tasks and data gathering methods	Year 2000	Year 2001	Years 2000 and 2001
Students' evaluation (Tasks 1,2)	$n = 30$	$n = 40$	**Educational goals (Task 4)**
Own learning process			To familiarize the students with the new learning environment
Tutoring and assignments	How students evaluate		
WebCT as a tool for learning	these dimensions in		To strengthen the students' skills in the use of the Internet as an
Improvements for the course	both years		information resource
			To strengthen information analysis and summary skills, and criti-
Evaluation form			
Teachers' evaluation (Task 3)	$n = 2$	$n = 2$	cal evaluation of the information
How have the students' learning processes advanced?			retrieved
	How teachers evaluate		To develop students' feedback
Own and colleague's role in tutoring processes	these dimensions and processes		and evaluation skills within the Web-based learning environment
WebCT as a tool for teaching			
Discussions, memos, notes			How these educational goals were achieved from the students' and teachers' perspectives

Experiences

The findings will be presented in two parts: the students' evaluations and our own evaluation as teachers. Following the evaluation from the Spring 2000 cohort, the course was remodified for the second cohort (Spring 2001) on the basis of the student evaluations and our own experiences. However, the changes made were minor, and included remodification of the assignments through elucidation of the instructions, and improvement of the discussion structure. For this reason, the student's results are presented mainly as a whole. The students' and teachers' comments are also compared to the educational goals of the course.

Students' Evaluation

The main results of the student evaluation are presented in Table 3. Essentially, the students found the Web-based learning experience positive, and they were motivated to participate in the course (see Morss, 1999). It seems that for many students, the new learning environment was a motivating factor. Furthermore, those students who at first were anxious about using computers also expressed positive attitudes in the evaluation when their computer skills had improved. In addition, the flexible way of working was appreciated (see Tricker et al., 2001).

Some negative comments were also made. Students found the course workload heavy, and held the view that the course should be worth a greater number of academic credits. The requirement of familiarizing themselves with the WebCT course delivery system may well have placed additional learning requirements upon them (see also Morss, 1999; Rathwell et al., 1999). Some of the students also made critical comments about having to pay for online time themselves when using computers at home. A further comment was that too few computers were available for their use on campus.

Students were largely satisfied with the tutoring and assignments related to the course. However, they felt that the relationship between contact teaching and assignments should be closer, and the assignments were considered as being too extensive. Some students liked the discussions related to the assignments (see Tricker et al., 2001), but others found them fruitless and meaningless.

Students also criticized the fact that some fellow students tried to demonstrate active participation by sending trivial messages. Students had been told beforehand that one requirement for passing the course was active participation in WebCT discussion, and this was controlled using WebCT's tools. Otherwise, the students had freedom of choice when and where they wanted to participate in discussions within a certain time period.

All the students learned to use WebCT, and although there were no major technical problems, the students criticized the platform's technical clumsiness (e.g., attachments were difficult to send and open, see also Rathwell et al., 1999). The students found it difficult to follow the discussions in WebCT because of the large number of fellow students and the unclear structure of the discussion area. A clearer structure for discussion and smaller groups were suggested as improvements for the following course.

In summary, the student evaluations were largely positive, and were similar in the two years observed. Some contradictory views among students, however, were found. The 2001 intake had more advanced computer skills and knowledge of the Internet, therefore, this group's evaluation did not emphasize the computer skills and the use of WebCT as the most useful learning issues. In 2000, only a small number of students were familiar with WebCT compared to over half in 2001.

Students evaluated dimensions such as discussions, the balance between WebCT work and contact teaching, both positively and negatively. It appears that the major challenge in improving the course is how to find the balance between the different needs of a heterogeneous student group.

Teachers' Evaluation

We found that using Web-based education did not ease the teacher's work, and from the teachers' point of view, the course required a great deal of effort. McFadzean (2001b), for example, recognized five different teacher roles, which were also apparent in our curriculum development process: topic author, course tutor, the technologist, facilitator, and collaborator. The first three roles were especially demanding and time-consuming in our process.

The planning of the course was challenging (also Volery & Lord, 2000), requiring both pedagogical and content expertise in addition to technical and visual expertise. At that time, there was no technical and pedagogical support unit at the University of Kuopio. Such a unit would have made course delivery much easier and reduced the teachers' workload. The current situation is better, because the Learning Centre (established in 2000) offers pedagogical and technical support services for teachers.

One observation was that the tutor's role is one more of enabling than directly supervising the learning processes. At best, a tutor can inspire and promote the students' learning process. We, however, found this difficult and also contradictory, because we had to reconsider our ways of teaching and working. It also led us to discuss the quality of learning in the Web-based environment and the skill requirements of the students. Students have to be self-directing enough and have developed the necessary meta skills to manage their own learning process. They must be capable of synthesizing the crucial points of information and constructing knowledge in social interaction. Therefore, WebCT as a learning environment enhances the ideology of constructivism and may strengthen the skills required in working life in an information society.

Furthermore, tutoring on the Web requires good written communication skills (also Tricker et al., 2001). In particular, evaluation and feedback in the Web-based environment is demanding, because it emphasizes verbal communication. Students interpret the written feedback differently and give it different meanings. However, teaching in the Web-based environment is an interactive learning process and indeed, also the tutors learned and benefited from the learning experience.

The Evaluation of Educational Goals

After comparing the student evaluations and our own experiences to the educational goals of the course, it seems that the goals were largely achieved. The students became familiar with the new learning environment, and their skills of using the Internet as an information resource were improved. However, the skills of analyzing and summarizing the information could have been improved more. Some of the criticisms regarding the clumsiness of WebCT and its unclear discussion structure were partly due to the students' inability to summarize their messages. It was difficult to read lengthy assignments on the screen, and this was another factor that led to decreased motivation for the students and the teachers.

Table 3: Summary of the Students' Evaluation in 2000 and 2001 (Citations in this Table are Typical of the Evaluations; 2000 Refers to the First Course, 2001 to the Second)

Dimension of evaluation	Positive comments	Negative comments
Learning Experience	*Motivation* My own motivation increased because of the new and different learning environment (2000; 2001) No literature could offer as broad an understanding as the discussions in WebCT (2000; 2001) The Web-based learning keeps the learning process ongoing during the course, not just before the examination (2000) *Flexibility* As a learning experience, the Web-based course was sensible and flexible. For the full-time worker, the course was the optimal choice (2000; 2001) The learning is not constrained to time and place (2000; 2001) *Computer literacy* The most useful thing in the course was that you had to use the computer (2000) The use of the Internet became more familiar. I learned to be critical of the information found on the Internet (2000) You learned to search for information from the Internet (2000; 2001) The assignments required different means to search for information (2000)	*Motivation* Toward the end of the course my motivation decreased a bit. The reason for this was that the discussion in WebCT diminished (2000) The course timing was too long—motivation decreased (2000) *WebCT as a tool for learning* Working in WebCT is time-consuming (2001) Working in WebCT is quite expensive if you are using the Internet at home (2000) Working in WebCT would have been enough, because I do my best when working alone (2001)
Tutoring and Assignments	*Tutoring* Tutoring and feedback were encouraging (2000; 2001) It was nice that teachers participated actively in the discussion and the questions were answered quickly (2000) *Assignments* The learning assignments helped in understanding the wider issues. Con-	*Tutoring* More feedback from the assignments could have been given during the contact teaching (2000) *Assignments* Contact teaching should have a closer relationship to the assignments (2000; 2001)

One of the goals was to learn to critically evaluate information retrieved from the Internet. This was a challenging goal for us as teachers, too. Although students' awareness of the origin and quality of the information increased, we believe that better guidelines for publishing information on the Internet are needed in order to allow the users to evaluate the quality of information. The fourth goal was to improve students' feedback and evaluation skills. These were improved during the course, but the students found it difficult to give feedback using only the computer, as did the teachers.

Table 3: Summary of the Students' Evaluation in 2000 and 2001 (Citations in this Table are Typical of the Evaluations; 2000 Refers to the First Course, 2001 to the Second) (continued)

	teaching provided the basic information on the issue (2000; 2001)	
	The instructions for the assignments were clear (2000; 2001)	The assignments were too wide. It is not good that all students are doing the same assignments. This kind of structure makes it difficult to follow the discussions and the motivation decreases (2000; 2001)
	Discussions in the WebCT Discussions on the assignments were active, if fellow students did not take the comments too personally (2000)	*Discussions in the WebCT* Participation in discussions was not possible all the time because of the lack of access to a computer (2000)
		The different time tables of the students compromised the discussion groups (2000)
		Discussions were interesting, but superficial (2000)
		Discussions were sometimes fruitless and it felt that fellow students just wanted to show their participation by sending ok messages (2001)
WebCT as a technical tool for learning	No technical problems (2000)	The environment was clumsy (2000; 2001)
	The environment was good and worked well (2000; 2001)	Discussion area was unclear. Old stuff should be abolished quicker (2000)
	WebCT is easy to use after you have learned the basics (2001)	It was hard to find the instructions among the discussion (2000)
		The structure of discussion area is unclear (2001)
How to improve the course?	*Means to improve the course* The lectures can be given via videoconferencing (2000)	
	The slides of the lecture should be available in WebCT (2000)	
	Smaller groups for WebCT discussions (2000; 2001)	
	The balance between the WebCT and contact teaching The whole course could be transferred to WebCT (2001)	
	I think that it is not good to transfer the whole course to WebCT. One lecture day could be added to the course (2001)	
	The course has a good balance now (contact teaching + WebCT work) (2001)	

DISCUSSION AND FUTURE TRENDS

The main aim of this study was to evaluate an online learning experience from both the students' and teachers' perspective. When comparing our results to others (e.g., Morss, 1999; Rathwell et al., 1999; Tricker et al., 2001) it appears that despite the cultural differences, the challenges concerning Web-based education are similar from country to country, thus the sharing of experiences between different countries should help universities and other educational institutions to cooperate and utilize Web-based education more effectively. Similarly, online education provides universities and other educational institutions with an excellent opportunity to cooperate at national and international levels (Whittington, 2000).

To evaluate the Web-based course, data was collected from the students and ourselves during two different years. Although not all students completed the evaluation of the course, the student data were diversified and rich. Our impression was that we gained valid information for the development process, because instead of focusing on the quantity of answers, we emphasized the quality and content of the students' evaluations. The approach and level of the data analysis were also suitable for this purpose. We, as teachers, were both actors and evaluators in the process. Our position in the process as well as our subjective expectations and experiences have somewhat affected the interpretation of the results. However, our active role in the evaluation has helped us to use the information in the further development of the course, which was the evaluation's main aim (e.g., Clarke, 1999).

We identified four important lessons learned from the curriculum development process described in this chapter:

1. We noticed that the only way to manage this type of curriculum development process is through learning by doing. Cooperation between students is a crucial part of the process, and a multiple constituency approach is a suitable approach for evaluation. The students' evaluations were important, although we will have some problems in using them to improve the course because of their contradictory nature. For example, some students wanted more face-to-face teaching, while others did not (also Jefferies & Hussain, 1998). One reason for this was the students' heterogeneous expectations and experiences.

2. Many students were satisfied with the course, as it enabled their participation despite the potential barriers of distance and available time. Others were less satisfied, and one reason for this was that they had to pay for use of the Internet if going online at home. This may be compounded by the fact that in Finland, university education is free, and students are not used to paying for it themselves. In addition, the students complained that the computer facilities were not good enough (e.g., number of computers) at the University of Kuopio. As one of the students wrote: "WebCT is the future way of learning. Not everyone has access to the Internet (2000)."

3. Both students and teachers need training in using the virtual learning environment. The range of skills required by teachers and students was different than that required when using traditional approaches to teaching (e.g., Sinko & Lehtinen, 1999). Therefore, teachers and students also need some kind of technical and pedagogical support unit (e.g., Learning Center) to facilitate the Web-based education during the learning process.

4. In addition to the actual teaching, a great deal of time went into the planning and running of the course. This is an increasing challenge for the managers in the academic world, at least in Finland, because most of the resources, including time, have been and still are allocated to research activities.

As described in the background section, Finland has adopted the principles of an information society, and national policy has shown strong support for Web-based education by allocating many resources to ICT. However, this has not automatically meant that Web-based education has been implemented at the microlevel. As we have shown, there are certain problems in resource allocation (e.g., computer facilities, teachers' time, support services) at the microlevel.

Resource allocation is not the only factor that will affect the implementation of Web-based education now and in the future. How long will this new tool continue to fascinate the students and teachers? Are we just implementing a new tool for learning or are we reshaping the learning culture? As Pulkkinen (1997) noted, the implementation of a Web-based learning environment requires a change in educational culture and, especially, in teachers' attitudes. It is not sufficient merely to commence course delivery via the Internet. What is required is a reappraisal of existing course structure and approaches to teaching and learning. Issues that must also be carefully considered include how the tool suits the particular area of teaching, and what is the added value for learning. Basically, it should be remembered that Web-based learning is a teaching aid to facilitate learning, i.e., a means to an end and not an ending itself (see, e.g., Katz et al., 1999).

It seems that a parallel educational system with Web-based and face-to-face learning is needed in the future. Web-based education is not suitable for all students, teachers, and kinds of educational programs. There are certain concerns about increasing inequalities between generations and different subgroups (e.g., well-educated versus less educated) because of their different abilities and opportunities to utilize Web-based learning (e.g., Sinko & Lehtinen, 1999, p. 242). Furthermore, the consequences of Web-based education partly remain unknown. An interesting question is what happens to different cultures if the education is globalized via Web-based learning? How, for example, do different countries maintain their identity, language, and culture in a globalized world (Sinko & Lehtinen, 1999)?

REFERENCES

Bingham, R., & Ottewill, R. (2001). Whatever happened to peer review? Revitalizing the contribution of tutors to course evaluation. *Quality Assurance in Education, 9*(1), 32–39.

Clarke, A. (1999). *Evaluation research: an introduction to principles, methods and practice.* London: Sage Publications.

ECTS Guide for Foreign Students. (2000–2001). Faculty of Social Sciences. University of Kuopio. Retrieved on August 25, 2002 from the Internet at: http://www.uku.fi/intl/YhteiskuntaECTS 2000_2001.pdf.

Education, Training and Research in the Information Society. A National Strategy for 2000-2004. (1999). Ministry of Education. Retrieved on August 25, 2002 from the Internet at: http://www.minedu.fi/julkaisut/information/englishU/index.html.

Farrington, G. C. (1999). The new technologies and the future of residential undergraduate education. In R. N. Katz & Associates. Dancing with the devil. Information technology and the new competition in higher education (pp. 73–94). San Francisco, CA: Jossey-Bass.

Higher Education Policy in Finland. (2000). Ministry of Education. Helsinki. Retrieved on January 24, 2003 from the Internet: http://www.minedu.fi/julkaisut/Hep2001/index.html.

Jefferies, P., & Hussain, F. (1998). Using the Internet as a teaching resource. *Education + Training, 40*(8), 359–365.

Katz, R. N., & Associates (1999). *Dancing with the devil. Information technology and the new competition in higher education.* San Francisco, CA: Jossey-Bass.

Kolb, D. A. (1984). *Experimental learning.* Englewood Cliffs, NJ: Prentice Hall.

McFadzean, E. (2001a). Supporting virtual learning groups. Part 1: pedagogical perspective. *Team Performance Management: An International Journal, 7*(3/4), 53–62.

McFadzean, E. (2001b). Supporting virtual learning groups. Part 2: an integrated approach. *Team Performance Management: An International Journal, 7*(5/6), 77–92.

McFazdzean, E., & McKenzie, J. (2001). Facilitating virtual learning groups. A practical approach. *Journal of Management Development, 20*(6), 470–494.

Morss, D. A. (1999). A study of student perspectives on Web-based learning: WebCT in the classroom. *Internet Research: Electronic Networking Applications and Policy, 9*(5), 393–408.

Pulkkinen, J. (1997). Avoimien oppimisympäristöjen toiminnallisia lähtökohtia [Functional Principles for Web-Based Learning Environments.]. *Aikuiskasvatus, 4,* 275–282.

Rathwell, T. et al. (1999). Looking over the horizon: an Internet-based international course in healthcare management. *The Journal of Health Administration Education, 17*(3), 159–173.

Senge, P. M. (1990). *The fifth discipline: the art and practice of the learning organization.* New York: Currency Doubleday.

Silverman, D. (1993). *Interpreting qualitative data. Methods for analyzing talk, text and interaction.* London: Sage Publications.

Sinko, M., & Lehtinen, E. (1999). The challenges of ICT in Finnish education. Helsinki: Atena. Retrieved on August 25, 2002 from the Internet: http://www.sitra.fi/eng/index.asp?DirID=297.

Tricker, T., Rangecroft, M., & Long, P. (2001). Evaluating distance education courses: the student perception. *Assessment & Evaluation in Higher Education, 26*(2), 165–177.

Volery, T., & Lord, D. (2000). Critical success factors in online education. *The International Journal of Educational Management, 14*(5), 216–223.

Øvretveit, J. (1998). *Evaluating health interventions: an introduction to evaluation of health treatments, services, policies and organizational interventions.* Buckingham: Open University Press.

Whittington, D. (2000). Evaluating three years' use of virtual university. *Quality Assurance in Education, 8*(1), 48–52.

ENDNOTE

[1] Department of Health Policy and Management has used WebCT for an international course in healthcare management since 1998. Dalhausie University offered the learning environment for this course (Rathwell et al., 1999).

About the Authors

Anil K. Aggarwal is the Lockheed Martin Research Professor in the Merrick School of Business at the University of Baltimore, USA. Dr. Aggarwal has published in many journals including, *Computers and Operations Research*; *Decision Sciences*; *Information and Management*; *Production and Operation Management*, *Journal of EUC*, *transactions of DSS*, and in many national and international conferences. He is the Associate Editor of several journals and is also on the editorial boards of many journals. His current research interests include Web-based teaching, digital divide, global IT systems, model-based organizational systems, and educational issues in MIS. He is also the Editor of the book *Web-Based Learning and Teaching Technologies: Opportunities and Challenges* (published by IDEA Group Publishing).

*   *   *   *   *

Frederic Adam is a Senior Lecturer in the department of Accounting, Finance, and Information Systems at University College Cork in Ireland. He holds a Ph.D. from the National University of Ireland and Université Paris VI jointly. His research has been published in a number of international journals including the *Journal of Strategic Information Systems*, *Decision Support Systems*, and *Systèmes d'Information et Management*. He is the Co-Author of the "Manager's Guide to Current Issues in Information Systems" and "Postgraduate Research" (Blackhall Publishing, Dublin, Ireland) and is the Associate Editor of the *Journal of Decision Systems*. He acts as a consultant in the areas of information systems selection and implementation and executive systems on a regular basis.

Jason D. Baker is an Associate Professor of education at Regent University, USA, where he teaches and conducts research about online distance education. Previously, he worked as an educational consultant at Loyola College in Maryland. He has written a number of Internet-related books and articles, most recently serving as co-editor of *The New Online Learning Guide* (Allyn & Bacon). He has advised and trained faculty in the use of educational technology, both in traditional classes and in the design of online classes, and has been an active online instructor and distance learner since 1996.

Erik Benrud, CFA, Ph.D., has been on the finance faculty at the University of Baltimore, Loyola College in Maryland, and at the University of Virginia, USA, where he earned his doctorate. Dr. Benrud developed the first 100% Web-based finance course in the now successful Web-MBA program at UB. He has taught finance in South America, and he has taught review courses for the Chartered Financial Analyst® program and the Certified Financial Planner program. Dr. Benrud's publications include cross-sectional and time-series analysis of financial data, and he has published theoretical game-theory models.

Regina Bento (http://home.ubalt.edu/rbento) is the Hatfield-Merrick Distinguished Professor at the Merrick School of Business, University of Baltimore, Maryland, USA. After graduate studies at UFRJ, the Federal University of Rio de Janeiro (M.D. Psychiatry, 1977; M.S. Administration, 1980), she came to the United States for doctoral studies at Harvard and MIT (Ph.D. MIT, 1990). She taught at UFRJ (1980–1982) and UC Riverside (1988–1991) before joining UB in 1991, where she has been among the pioneers in using the Web for education. Regina has received several teaching and research awards, including the 1999 USM Regents Award, the highest honor in the University System of Maryland.

Werner Beuschel is a Professor of Information Management in the Department of Economics at the University of Applied Sciences in Brandenburg, Germany. He received his Ph.D. from the Technical University Berlin in 1987. His current interests include Web-based applications and their interaction with virtual user groups, eLearning, and cooperative systems in organizations. Since 1999, he has been on the board of directors of the German Federal project "Virtual University of Applied Sciences," where he coordinates the research efforts of seven universities in the realm of "New forms of teaching and learning." As a member of the working group "Multimedia," he is counseling for the State Ministry of Education in Brandenburg. Since 2001, Dr. Beuschel acts also as an expert with a German accreditation agency (see http://www.vfh.fh-brandenburg.de/).

Apiwan D. Born is an Assistant Professor of Management Information Systems (MIS) at the University of Illinois at Springfield, USA. She earned a Ph.D. in MIS from Southern Illinois University at Carbondale (SICU). Her dissertation title, "Exploratory Study of Information Systems Infrastructure and its Link to Performance," received a doctoral dissertation award from SIUC. She holds a B.S. in statistics (honor) from Chulalongkorn University, Bangkok, Thailand. She has a master's degrees in MIS (MSMIS) and in business administration (MBA) from Mississippi State University. Dr. Born recently received the Master Online Teacher Certificate from the Illinois Online Network and the University of Illinois. Since 1999, she has taught online graduate courses including Introduction to MIS, Technology Management, and graduate project seminar. Her primary research interests are effective strategies for Web-based teaching and learning, student assessment in an online learning environment, and impacts of information systems infrastructure on organizations.

Jan Brace-Govan holds a Ph.D. in sociology and qualifications in program evaluation. She is a research fellow in the Department of Marketing, Monash University, Australia, and has published several education-based studies covering curriculum design, internships, and transition to distance education. One of her research interests is in the role of ICTs in interaction and communication. She also maintains her research interests in sociocultural aspects of the body and the links between physical activity and social identity. Currently, she is working on the impact that ICTs have on knowledge sharing among professionals.

Val Clulow is Associate Professor of Marketing at Swinburne University of Technology, Australia. She has research interests and publications in online education, mentoring, peer tutoring, experiential learning, in addition to marketing and business discipline-based studies and publications. She holds a Bachelor of Arts, a Master of Education degree, and a Ph.D. in Education. She supervises several postgraduate research students whose areas of study include business education, improvisation in business, internal service in business organizations, and deregulation of electricity industry. She has recently undertaken research studies to evaluate online interactive exercises developed for students learning business Japanese language.

Susanne Draheim studied Social Education and Applied Cultural Sciences at the University of Lüneburg, Germany. She received her diploma in 1999. Since 2000, she has been a Research Assistant with the German Federal project "Virtual University of Applied Sciences" at the University of Applied Sciences in Brandenburg. Her main interests are aspects of formal and informal communication in computer-mediated enviroments, the evaluation of computer-supported systems, and social dimensions of information technology.

Dennis Drinka is an Assistant Professor of Management Information Systems at the University of Alaska Anchorage, USA. He received his B.S. degree in finance from the University of Illinois Urbana-Champaign and his Ph.D. in management science and information systems from the University of Texas at Austin. Among others, he has published in *Decision Sciences*, *European Journal of Operational Research*, and *Applications of Management Sciences*. His research interests are in the areas of decision support, mathematical modeling, and innovative course design. He currently teaches systems analysis, project management, rapid application development, Web development, and systems design and development courses.

Birgit Gaiser studied Business Administration at the Technical University Berlin, where she received her diploma in 1994. From 1994 to 2000 she worked as a Research Assistant in the Department of Economics at the University of Applied Sciences Brandenburg, Germany. She was involved in a number of pilot studies in distance learning. From 2000 to 2001, she was a research assistant with the German Federal project "Virtual University of Applied Sciences." In 2002, she earned her Ph.D. with the Department of Education at the University of the Armed Forces in Hamburg. Her areas of interest include telematic learning environments, the evaluation of computer-supported systems, organization and didactics for telematic forms of learning, and the use of videoconferences for teaching and learning.

R. Gerber worked as the Executive Dean, Faculty of Education, Health and Professional Studies, UNE (1995–2002), Australia. He has extensive research and a scholarly record in education with people from children to aged people in the area of learning, especially through aspects of technology and graphics. He also holds an extensive professional record, e.g., Chair of IGU Commission on Geographical Education (1996–2000).

Esperanza Huerta is an Associate Professor in the Management and Accounting Department at the Instituto Tecnológico Autónomo de México (ITAM), where she is currently on a leave-of-absence. She is a doctoral candidate in the Management of Information Systems at Claremont Graduate University. She earned a BS from ITAM and an MS in the Management of Information Systems from Claremont Graduate University. Her research focuses on the use of information technology in education and human–computer interaction.

Magid Igbaria died August 3, 2002, after a lengthy illness. Magid earned a Ph.D. from Tel Aviv University. He held the rank of Professor at both Claremont Graduate University, USA, and Tel Aviv University. He was ranked as the most productive researcher in the IS field in a number of studies. He published over 100 articles on topics such as e-commerce, virtual workplace, computer technology acceptance, IS personnel, and the management of IS. Magid was loved by his family, friends, students, and colleagues. His life was one of compassion, intelligence, energy, humility, and dedication. He will be missed.

Sherif Kamel is an Assistant Professor of MIS and Director of the Institute of Management Development at the School of Business, Economics and Communication of The American University in Cairo, Egypt. From 1992 to 2000, he was the director of the Regional IT Institute, and during the period 1987 to 1992, he worked at the Cabinet of Egypt Information and Decision Support Center, where he co-established and managed its training department. Dr. Kamel designs and delivers professional development programs in various information systems management and applications for public and private sector organizations. He has formulated a large number of training alliances and partnerships and has conducted many training programs for organizations in Africa, Asia, the Middle East and Europe. In 1996, he was one of the co-founding members of the Internet Society of Egypt. Dr. Kamel has many publications in IT transfer to developing countries, electronic commerce, human resources development, decision support applications, and knowledge management. He serves on the editorial and review boards of a number of information systems and management journals and is the associate editor of the *Annals of Cases on Information Technology Applications and Management in Organizations*. Dr. Kamel is currently the VP for Communications for the Information Resources Management Association (IRMA). He is a graduate of the London School of Economics and Political Science (UK) and The American University in Cairo (Egypt).

Johanna Klassen received her doctorate in education from Bristol University, U.K. Her primary interests are in pedagogical support for faculty in using technology in teaching. From 1997 to 2001, she worked full-time in developing a large-scale interactive multimedia program, Virtual Language University, at City University of Hong Kong. She has also developed business simulations for autonomous learning. From 1992 to 1997, she was the manager of the Self-Access Language Learning Centre.

Born in Istanbul, Turkey, in 1973, **Müge Klein** graduated from the Technical University of Vienna with a Master of Information Systems (Business Informatics). Since 1998, she has worked as a Research Assistant at the Institute of Applied Informatics and Formal Description Methods at the department of Economics and Business Engineering, University of Karlsruhe, Germany, where she earned her Ph.D. in 2002. Her fields of research comprise eLearning, teleteaching, Web-based training, cooperative learning, and especially courseware engineering for reusable Web-based education resources.

Virginia Franke Kleist (Ph.D. University of Pittsburgh) is an Assistant Professor of Management at West Virginia University and specializes in MIS, data communications, and electronic commerce. In addition to her formal education, Dr. Kleist spent 10 years in telecommunications network management operations for GTE Corporation, Joy Technologies, Inc., PNC Corporation, and the Allegheny Health, Education and Research Foundation (AHERF). Her research interests include the long-term impacts of information technology on organizational structures; the unique economics of the information industries, the Internet, and electronic commerce; the value of information and issues of knowledge transfer; the performance and productivity of information systems investment, with a special focus on the telecommunications technologies; the coalescing of the telecommunications industries; and the use of economics as a reference discipline for MIS research.

Jane Klobas, Ph.D., is an experienced user of online communication for research, teaching, graduate student supervision, and administration. She has published, with international colleagues, several research papers on evaluation of international educational applications of online technologies, as well as other works on information management and educational technology. She is currently a Visiting Professor at Bocconi University in Milan, Italy, and Professorial Fellow at the Graduate School of Management, University of Western Australia. Jane Klobas and Stefano Renzi are the coordinators of Bocconi University's postgraduate course in Online Education and Training. They are also collaborating on Italian nationally funded research on university students' psychological response to online education.

Johanna Lammintakanen works as a Researcher at the Department of Health Policy and Management at the University of Kuopio, Finland. She has a master's degree in Health Management Sciences and is now conducting her Ph.D. in the same field. She has also completed teacher education and has a great deal of experience of teaching at university level. In addition to research on Web-based education, her main areas of research are politics and policy making in health care, and the use of ICT in the professional development of health care managers.

Tommaso Leo has been the Coordinator of the MODASPECTRA project. He is Full Professor in Automatic Controls at the University of Ancona, Italy. He has served as dean of the Faculty of Engineering from 1990 to 1996. He has been chairman of Robotics, Automation and Human Movement Analysis programs at DEA. He is responsible for the eLearning initiatives of Ancona University. He worked in Analysis and Modelling of Human Motor Behaviour, in Measurement Systems and Techniques, in Signal Processing and Optimal Filtering methods, in Adaptive Control and System Identification, in Friendly Interfaces for medical use of the Movement Analysis, in the development of Web-based applications for Learning, and accreditation. He is author and co-author of about 200 scientific contributions, and editor of some scientific books and special issues of scientific journals. He is a member of IEEE, of the International Society of Biomechanics, of the International Society for Postural and Gait Research. Presently, he is the coordinator of the Ph.D. program in "E-Learning: Methods and Techniques for computer assisted education" offered by the University of Ancona.

Colin McCormack is a Lecturer with the Department of Computer Science in University College Cork, Ireland. His M.Sc. and Ph.D. were in the area of Computational Intelligence. His research interests currently include Neural Networks, Data Mining, Education Information Systems, and Intelligent Tutoring. He has designed a number of Web-based education systems and developed software to develop them. He has published a textbook in the area of Web-based education systems as well as a number of related papers.

Karen Neville holds both a Masters of Science in Management Information Systems and a Bachelor of Science in Business Information Systems from University College Cork, Ireland, where she is employed as a College Lecturer. She is currently registered as a Ph.D. student, under the supervision of Professor Philip Powell, at the University of Bath, U.K. Her publications, to date, include papers focusing on ICT initiatives, eLearning, and Educational Systems that have been published in some of the top information systems conferences and journals. However, the focus of her research has now expanded to incorporate the areas of Knowledge Management and Security.

Maurizio Panti is Associated Professor of Computer Science at University of Ancona, Italy. Previously, he was a researcher at University of Urbino and University of Salerno (1971–1974) and assistant professor at University of Ancona (1974–1984). He teaches Data Bases and Fundamentals of Computer at Universities of Ancona. He managed the Computer Centre of University of Ancona and now is member of the Academic Senate of the same university. His research interests concern databases, information systems, and agent technologies for IS integration. He is serving as member of the program committee in international conferences as CAISE, WMC02, SEBD, CoopIS, and served as referee in international journals.

C. Pareja-Flores holds a M.Sc. degree in Mathematics and a Ph.D. in Computer Science from the Universidad Complutense de Madrid. Since 1998, he works as an Associate Professor at the Department of Computer Systems and Programming at the Universidad Complutense de Madrid. His interests include innovation in CS education and research on functional and concurrent programming, and programming environments. He has collaborated and led several research projects. He is an author of three books and over 30 publications in national and international conferences and journals. He is an Editor of the journal *Novática* and is an habitual referee in many scientific conferences on his topics of interest.

Mihir A. Parikh is Assistant Professor of Management at Polytechnic University in New York City, where he leads several research initiatives and teaches executive degree courses in the management of information technology and systems, telecommunications technology management, and digital strategy. He has published over 25 refereed papers in various journals, such as *Decision Sciences, Decision Support Systems, Communications of the AIS, International Journal of Information Management*, and *Engineering Management Journal*, and the proceedings of national and international conferences of leading academic associations and institutes. He has been invited to lecture at various forums and universities in the United States, the United Kingdom, Greece, Denmark, India, Israel, and Taiwan.

Mahesh S. Raisinghani is a Program Director of e-business and a faculty member at the Graduate School of Management, University of Dallas, USA, where he teaches MBA courses in Information Systems and e-business. Dr. Raisinghani was the recipient of the 1999 UD

Presidential Award and the 2001 King Hagar Award for excellence in teaching, research, and service. His previous publications have appeared in *Information and Management*, *Journal of Global IT Management*, *Journal of E-Commerce Research*, *Information Strategy: An Executive's Journal*, *Journal of IT Theory and Applications*, *Enterprise Systems Journal*, *Journal of Computer Information Systems*, and *International Journal of Information Management*, among others. He serves as an Associate Editor and on the editorial review board of leading information systems/e-commerce journals and on the board of directors of Sequoia, Inc. Dr. Raisinghani is included in the millennium edition of *Who's Who in the World*, *Who's Who Among America's Teachers*, and *Who's Who in Information Technology*.

Stefano Renzi has worked on development of infrastructure for online communication in education and research for many years and was involved in several university projects to integrate online educational activities in traditional courses. He is currently a Researcher at Bocconi University in Milan, Italy, where he teaches Internet technologies and related applications. He is co-author of several technical and evaluative papers on use of technology in education. Stefano Renzi and Jane Klobas are the coordinators of Bocconi University's postgraduate course in Online Education and Training. They are also collaborating on Italian nationally funded research on university students' psychological response to online education.

Sari Rissanen is a Senior Lecturer and Vice Director of the Department of Health Policy and Management, at the University of Kuopio, Finland. She has a Licentiate degree in Health Management Sciences as well as a Doctoral degree in Social Policy. She has also completed teacher education, and has been invited to lecture at many educational organizations. In addition to Web-based education, her research interest areas are issues related to the organization, funding, and quality of social and health care, in particular, care of the elderly.

Malu Roldan is a member of the faculty of the Management Information Systems Department at San Jose State University, USA. Her research focuses on electronic commerce, mobile computing, and engaged learning. Her publications have appeared in *Communications of the ACM*, EDI Forum, *Journal of Informatics Education and Research*, and *Internet Marketing Research*. She is co-author of the book, *In Search of Digital Excellence* (McGraw-Hill).

Terry Ryan is Associate Professor of Information Science at Claremont Graduate University, USA. His research interests include Web-based learning, Web-based customer support, IS in the state government sector, applications in support of dialogue, work systems flexibility, discontinuous changes in websites, and a number of other topics having to do with the development and evaluation of information systems. He has published articles in *DATA BASE*, *Interface*, the *Journal of Computer Information Systems*, the *Journal of Database Management*, and the *Journal of Systems Management*, as well as in numerous refereed conference proceedings. Dr. Ryan earned a Ph.D. in MIS from Indiana University.

Vicki L. Sauter is Professor of Management Information Systems in the College of Business Administration at the University of Missouri–St. Louis, USA. She received her Ph.D. in Systems Management Science from Northwestern University. Her articles have appeared in journal such as *Journal of Management Information Systems, Omega: The International Journal of Operations Research, Information and Management, Annals of Mathematics and*

Artificial Intelligence, Socio-Economic Planning Sciences, International Journal of Policy and Information, and *Medical Care.* In addition, she has published a book, *Decision Support Systems: An Applied Managerial Approach.* Dr. Sauter's research interests are in making decision support systems and Internet-based systems more responsive to users' needs.

Robert Schihl is currently Dean of the School of Communication and the Arts at Regent University in Virginia Beach, VA, USA. He completed his doctoral studies at the State University at Buffalo. His area of interest has principally been media studies. He became interested in distance learning in 1994 when he translated a fully-accredited Ph.D. program to computer-mediated distance distribution. He since has done the same for two M.A. programs. He was an early adopter of the Blackboard course delivery system, becoming a trainer to his own faculty. He has taught graduate distance courses since 1995, contributed chapters in edited collections of articles about distance learning, and regularly presents papers at national conferences.

Cindy Schuster works at the University of Baltimore (UB), USA, in Langsdale Library's Instructional Technology Department as an Instuctional Technology Specialist. She provides technical and facilitator support to UB's videoconferencing classrooms using Interactive Video Network (IVN) of the University of Maryland System. She trains and provides support to electronic classrooms and portable media equipment to the University of Baltimore community. Cindy teaches adjunct information systems and computer science. Cindy has an M.A. in publications design from the University of Baltimore (1989) and is working toward a master's in distance education from the University of Maryland University College. Her research interests include motivation of online students and student services in distance education.

Daniel Sommer, born 1973 in Neustadt, Germany, graduated from the University of Hannover with a diploma in mathematics. Since 1999, he has worked as a research assistant at the Institute of Applied Informatics and Formal Description Methods at the Department of Economics and Business Engineering, University of Karlsruhe, Germany. His research focus is in the area of eLearning and teleteaching, especially the quality management and the design of quality information systems for eLearning applications.

Paul J. Speaker (Ph.D. Purdue University) is an Associate Professor of Finance and serves as the Director of the MBA Programs at West Virginia University, USA. Dr. Speaker's research activity is concentrated in economic modeling of regulated industries, the role of not-for-profit institutions, and the impact of technology. His teaching areas include corporate finance and financial institutions. He has been active with curriculum design, integration of course work, and developments in distance learning.

Wolffried Stucky, born 1939 in Bad Kreuznach, Germany, earned his Ph.D. of mathematics in 1970 at the Saarland University. Before he became full professor at the University of Karlsruhe in 1976, he had worked for the pharmaceutical industry in the areas of biometry, statistics, and data processing. His present position is Head of the Institute of Applied Informatics and Formal Description Methods at the department of Economics and Business Engineering, University of Karlsruhe, Germany. The fields of research comprise database and information systems, workflow management systems, strategic IT-planning, and organization, eLearning, teleteaching, and cooperative learning. He will be acting as CEPIS (Council of European Professional Informatics Societies) president until the end of 2003.

R. Subramaniam has a Ph.D. in Physical Chemistry. He is an Assistant Professor at the National Institute of Education in Nanyang Technological University and Honorary Secretary of the Singapore National Academy of Science. Prior to this, he was acting head of Physical Sciences at the Singapore Science Center. His research interests are in the fields of physical chemistry, science education, theoretical cosmophysics, museum science, telecommunications, and transportation He has published several research papers in international refereed journals.

Leo Tan Wee Hin has a Ph.D. degree in Marine Biology. He holds the concurrent appointments of Director of the National Institute of Education, Professor of Biological Sciences in Nanyang Technological University, and President of the Singapore National Academy of Science. Prior to this, he was director of the Singapore Science Center. His research interests are in the fields of marine biology, science education, museum science, telecommunications, and transportation. He has published numerous research papers in international refereed journals.

K. A. Toh heads a team of 34 science educators at the National Institute of Education, Nanyang Technological University, Singapore. He holds postgraduate degrees from Stanford and Oxford, and works actively to improve the education of teachers through meaningful inquiry and innovative change.

Salvatore (Sal) Valenti is Senior Researcher at the University of Ancona, Italy. He has been a member of several research projects funded by the Ministry of Instruction, University and Research (MIUR), by the National Research Council (CNR) and by the European Community. His research activities are in the fields of computer-based assessment and on distance learning. He is member of the WAOE© World Association for Online Education. He is board member of the *Journal of Information Technology Education*. He is serving as reviewer for *Educational Technology & Society* and for *Current Issues in Education*. He has been chair of the track on "Virtual Universities" at the 2002 International Conference of the International Resources Management Association. He is author of more than 60 papers published in books, journals, and proceedings of international conferences. Now, he is a faculty member of the Ph.D. program in "E-Learning: Methods and Techniques for computer assisted education" offered by the University of Ancona.

J. Á. Velázquez-Iturbide holds a M.Sc. degree (1985) and a Ph.D. (1990) in Computer Science from the Universidad Politécnica de Madrid. He is an Associate Professor, previously at the Universidad Politécnica de Madrid, and since 1997, at the Universidad Rey Juan Carlos. He is the coordinator of the Department of Computer Languages and Systems at his university and the Subdirector of Computer Science Studies at his Technical School. His interests include innovation in computer science education and research on programming tools and environments, software visualization, and multimedia and Web applications. He has led several research projects on his topics of interest. He is an author of two books and over 50 publications in national and international conferences and journals. He is an editor of the journal *Novática* and is an habitual referee in many scientific conferences. He is a member of AACE, ACM, and IEEE Computer Society.

Doug Vogel is Professor (Chair) of Information Systems at the City University of Hong Kong and formerly at the University of Arizona. He received his Ph.D. from the University of Minnesota in 1986, where he was also research coordinator for the MIS Research Center. His research interests bridge the business and academic communities in addressing questions of the impact of management information systems on aspects of interpersonal communication, group problem solving, collaborative learning, and multicultural team productivity. He is especially active in introducing group support technology into enterprises and educational systems.

Khaled Wahba is an Assistant Professor at Cairo University, Egypt, Department of Systems and Biomedical Engineering. Dr. Wahba is also the Academic Advisor at the Regional IT Institute (RITI), Cairo, Egypt. He graduated (B.Sc.) from Systems and Biomedical Engineering Department at Cairo University in 1985. He got his M.Sc. from the same department in 1989. Dr. Wahba got his Ph.D. from the Technical University of Aachen (RWTH Aachen), Germany, in 1996. Dr. Wahba's fields of interest are System/Business Dynamics, the Web-Based Applications, Information Systems, Distance Education, eLearning, Simulation and Modeling, Control of Dynamic Systems, Stochastic Processes, Statistics, Decision Making Analysis, Pattern Recognition, Research Methodology, and Knowledge Management. Dr. Wahba has supervised more than 70 theses in Business Administration, Computer Science, and Business Information Technology, as well as more than 17 senior projects in Systems and Biomedical Engineering. He evaluated more than 350 theses and final projects in different fields, including Business and Computer Science. Dr. Wahba has reviewed papers for submission in different international conferences in the field of information systems. Dr. Wahba is a member in the Information Resources Management Association (IRMA), and a member in the International Society for System Dynamics as well as the president of the Egypt Chapter of the System Dynamics Society. Dr. Wahba is teaching Information System, System Dynamics and Stochastic Process and System Control. He is also acting as an adjunct professor at the University of Louisville, USA, and as a link tutor in Cairo for the School of Computing Science at Middlesex University, UK.

Y.Y. Jessie Wong received her Ph.D. in Education from the University of Liverpool, U.K., in 1991. She has taught at Nanyang Technological University in Singapore until 2000. Her research interests include teacher education, IT in education, and Web-based learning as lifelong learning.

Minnie Yi-Miin Yen is an Associate Professor of Management Information Systems in the Department of Computer Information Systems, University of Alaska Anchorage, USA. She received her Ph.D. in Management Information Systems from University of Houston. Dr. Yen's work has appeared in *IEEE Transactions on Software Engineering*, *Journal of Database Management*, *International Journal of Management*, *Human Factors in Information Systems*, and a book chapter of *Managing Business with Electronic Commerce: Issues and Trends*. Her current research interests focus on human–computer interaction, client–server database systems, e-commerce and Web-based learning.

Index

A

academic research 120
account management 229
accretion 381
active learner 162
adequate training 139
administrative and social affairs 407, 408
administrative support 225
adoption 425
AIFB 402
algorithm animation 242, 246
algorithm animator 236
algorithmic topics 238
analysis 373
animation engineering 251
append procedure 243
Association of Science-Technology Centers (ASTC) 309
attitude 132
Australia 347
authoring tools 375
autonomous language learning courseware 90
autonomy 105

B

backbone network 107
BALSA system 246
banking model 157

behavioral response 122
behaviorism 26
binomial heaps 253
bioengineers 377
Blackboard 137
blended learning 398
Bloom's taxonomy 382
Bocconi University 416
bulletin-board analysis 60
business 416
business information technology (BIT) 336

C

Center of Development in Teaching and Learning (CDTL) 352
central repository 124
classical education 400
classroom-based learning 416
classroom-based learning environment 121
clinician 375
CMC collaborator 60
coding system 98
cognitive information processing 26
cognitive theory 26
collaborative environment 125
collaborative learning dimension 194
collaborativism 26
commitment 421
communications 146

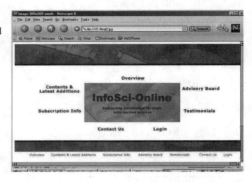

International Journal of Distance Education Technologies (JDET)

NEW!

NEW!

The International Source for Technological Advances in Distance Education

ISSN: 1539-3100
eISSN: 1539-3119

Subscription: Annual fee per volume (4 issues):
Individual US $85
Institutional US $185

Editors: Shi Kuo Chang
University of Pittsburgh, USA

Timothy K. Shih
Tamkang University, Taiwan

Mission

The *International Journal of Distance Education Technologies* (**JDET**) publishes original research articles of distance education four issues per year. **JDET** is a primary forum for researchers and practitioners to disseminate practical solutions to the automation of open and distance learning. The journal is targeted to academic researchers and engineers who work with distance learning programs and software systems, as well as general participants of distance education.

Coverage

Discussions of computational methods, algorithms, implemented prototype systems, and applications of open and distance learning are the focuses of this publication. Practical experiences and surveys of using distance learning systems are also welcome. Distance education technologies published in **JDET** will be divided into three categories, **Communication Technologies, Intelligent Technologies, and Educational Technologies**: new network infrastructures, real-time protocols, broadband and wireless communication tools, quality-of-services issues, multimedia streaming technology, distributed systems, mobile systems, multimedia synchronization controls, intelligent tutoring, individualized distance learning, neural network or statistical approaches to behavior analysis, automatic FAQ reply methods, copyright protection and authentification mechanisms, practical and new learning models, automatic assessment methods, effective and efficient authoring systems, and other issues of distance education.

For subscription information, contact:

Idea Group Publishing
701 E Chocolate Ave., Suite 200
Hershey PA 17033-1240, USA
cust@idea-group.com
URL: www.idea-group.com

For paper submission information:

Dr. Timothy Shih
Tamkang University, Taiwan
tshih@cs.tku.edu.tw